AMERICA'S LOST PLAYS

IX

FIVE PLAYS

X

THE BANKER'S DAUGHTER
and Other Plays

A series in twenty volumes of hitherto unpublished plays collected with the aid of the Rockefeller Foundation, under the auspices of the Dramatists' Guild of the Authors' League of America, edited with historical and bibliographical notes.

BARRETT H. CLARK
GENERAL EDITOR

Advisory Board

Five Plays

BY

CHARLES H. HOYT

EDITED BY DOUGLAS L. HUNT

INDIANA UNIVERSITY PRESS

BLOOMINGTON

Requests for authorization of the use of any of the plays in this volume on the stage, the screen, or for radio or television broadcasting, or for any purpose of reproduction, will be forwarded by Princeton University Press to the proper persons.

CONTENTS

INTRODUCTION

I.

CHARLES HALE HOYT was born in Concord, N.H., on July 26, 1859. There was no theatrical or literary background in his family. He was the son of George W. Hoyt, of Concord, and his wife, Mary Ann Hale Hoyt, originally of Wells River, Vt. At the time of Hoyt's birth his father was operating a hotel in Concord. When the boy was eight years old, his father gave up the hotel and moved the family to the village of Charlestown, N.H., which thereafter remained the legal residence of the playwright.

Hoyt, senior, became a railway mail clerk. Later he served one term in the state legislature. Mrs. Hoyt was a woman of no particular gifts or attainment. There were no other children. She died in 1868, and her one son was thereafter left much alone while the father was away on the rail trips.

Charles Hoyt's formal education was meager. He attended a small private school in Charlestown and the Boston Latin School for a time. Then he was successively a law student in a Boston office, a journalist in St. Albans, Vt., and a worker on a cattle ranch in Colorado, before he became a permanent fixture on the staff of the Boston *Post* at the age of nineteen. He made use of many of his experiences in these fields in his plays.

His first employment on the *Post* was as a reporter; in a few months he took over the conduct of a semi-humorous column on the front page. He wrote daily, under the heading "All Sorts," a combination of small news items, announcements of impending events, humorous comments, and epigrammatic statements. In this column is to be found the genesis of many of the humorous characters in his plays. Just as Dulcy and the Old Soak were born into print in newspaper columns, so were Hoyt's characters of the office-seeking Negro, the dilatory plumber, and the temperance crank brought forth as butts to the author's wit under the "All Sorts" heading.

Soon Hoyt became musical, sporting, and dramatic editor. It is hard to imagine Hoyt as a musical critic; he could not sing and his ear was hopelessly bad. The sporting assignment he could handle in satisfactory manner; evidence of his interest in organized sports is afforded by his play, *A Runaway Colt,* built up around the game of baseball and having for its hero Captain "Pop" Anson of the old Chicago "Cubs." As a dramatic critic Hoyt was conservative, more likely to praise than to condemn; he prided himself on being impersonal in his criticisms and scrupulously kept himself in the background. He was quick to censure vulgarity, a significant point when one remembers how clean he kept his own plays. He realized that, in his own time, offending good taste was bad business. He recommended revision, and in his own plays constantly watched for audience reactions and frequently changed dialogue and stage business during the course of a play's run.

The variety of his experiences, his interest in human nature, and his spontaneous wit are the qualities responsible for his later success as a writer of farce comedies.

When he was twenty-one years old Hoyt attained his first experimental knowledge of dramatic composition. In his rambles about Boston he met, in 1881, William Harris, who controlled the old Howard Athenaeum. During that year Harris once faced the situation of a cancelled booking, and he found himself in dismal possession of a stock company with no play in which to present it. He told young Hoyt of his predicament. Immediately Hoyt's mind began to work in a field wholly new. He proceeded to create a melodrama; he wrote it, rehearsed it, and produced it in a week. It was called *Gifford's Luck*. Although the play has not survived, it was a success. It was played by a company that included Frank Wright, Leonora Bradley, and Ben Gilfoil.

The next year Hoyt wrote a four-act comedy called *Cazalia,* produced in May 1882, at the Globe Theatre, Boston, with W. J. Ferguson, R. J. Dillon, Frank Losee, Emmie Wilmot, and Clara Ellison in the cast. An immediate failure, it was quickly junked.

One of the cleverest comedians of the day, Mr. Willie Edouin, was appearing with his wife, Alice Atherton, in a play by Nathaniel Childs called *Dreams.* The first Boston performance was vigorously panned by the critics, including Hoyt. Childs and Edouin knew Hoyt personally and had heard of his success with *Gifford's Luck*. They came to Hoyt with *Dreams,* appealing for help. Hoyt took the play, revised it, wrote in a couple of new scenes of his own, and made it a success.

One day in 1883 Hoyt remarked to Edouin that he knew a man who had tried to run a hotel without any previous experience in the business. Undoubtedly Hoyt was thinking of his own father. Edouin was highly amused by the recital and said that he would like to produce a play based on the incidents of the tale. Hoyt thereupon wrote what was to be the first of the typically Hoytian farces, entitled *A Bunch of Keys*. Edouin and Frank W. Sanger paid Hoyt five hundred dollars for the manuscript and put the play into rehearsal. It was first produced in Providence, R.I., and went rather badly. Hoyt, having seen it acted, believed he knew what was the matter and felt that he could doctor it up successfully. Charles W. Thomas, a fellow

worker on the *Post* staff, had told him that it was the beginning of a new
type of farce writing, but he insisted that the actors were doing the thing in
an antiquated style. Hoyt attempted to buy the play back from Edouin, but
Miss Atherton, who had urged its purchase in the first instance, still had faith
in it and dissuaded her husband from selling his rights. They, however, hired
Hoyt to rewrite it; he revised carefully in the light of audience reaction,
directing all the rehearsals himself. It was produced again, this time in
Lowell, Mass. Immediately it was a hit. On March 26, 1883, it was produced
in New York in the San Francisco Opera House on the west side of Broadway between 28th and 29th Streets. Thereafter it was a great success;
Edouin played it from one end of the country to the other; it was performed
as late as 1900. It made Edouin rich, but Hoyt received only the sum Edouin
paid for the manuscript and its revision.

At this time Hoyt formed a partnership with Charles W. Thomas, his
friend and newspaper colleague. The two men retired from the staff of the
Post and devoted their time exclusively to the writing and producing of plays.
Thomas handled all the business details, for Hoyt realized that his own
business talents were mediocre. For ten years the two men worked together,
and were very successful, their greatest achievement being the leasing in
1892 of the famous Madison Square Theatre, later known as Hoyt's Theatre.
Before Hoyt was thirty he was a very rich man. In the 'nineties he was a "big
shot" on Broadway, largely because of the financial acumen of his business
associates. The partnership with Thomas continued uninterrupted until the
latter's untimely death in 1893. After that Hoyt's business manager and
partner was Frank McKee, who survived Hoyt and helped to administer his
estate after the playwright's death on November 20, 1900.

Hoyt was twice married. His first wife was an actress, Flora Walsh, whom
he married in July 1887. She died in January 1893. His second wife, also an
actress, was the beautiful Caroline Miskel, whom he married in March 1894.
She also died before her husband did; after her death in October 1898, Hoyt
himself became ill. His complete physical breakdown occurred early in 1899.
In July 1900 he was committed to an insane asylum in Hartford, Conn., from
which, however, he was released in a short time; but soon thereafter, on
November 20, he died in his home in Charlestown, N.H. He was buried in
a mausoleum in the town's cemetery beside his two wives. He had no sur-
viving children.

II.

By one of the oddities that govern the minds of dramatic chroniclers, Hoyt
has been unaccountably neglected. There is a short sketch in *The Dictionary*

of American Biography written by Professor Quinn, who also mentions Hoyt briefly in his *History of the American Drama*. Hornblow refers to him twice; Brown has a few comments to make. But Hoyt is important in the history of American farce comedy. He does not follow entirely the tradition of his predecessors, Harrigan and Hart, for they emphasized types—the Negro and the Irishman—while Hoyt's characters are all individuals, living persons. Hoyt is the forerunner of George M. Cohan and Messrs. Kaufman, Connelly, and Moss Hart. Like their work, his comedy was purely national in tone. He did not make use of unpleasant marital complications in the manner of French farce; he did not suggest the sex motives that appear so frequently in twentieth-century plays; he was seldom vulgar and never nastily offensive. His material came from the everyday experiences of ordinary people; he poked genial fun at the impatient traveller and the harassed railroad officials, the plumber who overcharged his customers, the woman who wanted to vote, the preacher who was "unco' gude," the shyster lawyer, the superstitious clerk, the worthless but wholly lovable drunkard. Hoyt's satire was pleasant, kindly, universal in tone; even he who was hit hardest could find something laughable in the presentation.

In the sixteen years between 1883 and 1899, Hoyt wrote and produced seventeen farce comedies and one comic operetta. One of the plays and the operetta were failures; all the rest may be designated as successful, several of them tremendously so. *A Trip to Chinatown,* here printed for the first time, was performed 657 consecutive times, a record of continuous running that was not broken until Frank Bacon produced *Lightnin'*. Simultaneously, road companies were performing the play in every section of the country, and on one occasion a secondary company entered New York and exhibited at another theatre in the city while the original company was still performing on Broadway.

The list of actors who appeared from time to time in the Hoyt farces comprises the best-known names of the time. Anna Held made her American début in *A Parlor Match,* singing

> "I have such a nice little way wiz me . . .
> I should like to have you play wiz me,
> Play wiz me all the day long."

Maude Adams's first New York appearance was as Dot Bradbury in *A Midnight Bell*. Lillian Russell and Tony Hart teamed in *The Maid and the Moonshiner,* Hoyt's operetta that failed, and, incidentally, the only play Hoyt wrote after *A Bunch of Keys* that did not begin its title with the article "A." James T. Powers, Otis Harlan, Evans and Hoey, Tim Murphy, Harry Conor,

Richard J. Dillon, Frank Keenan, and a host of others, the best in their time, were engaged in various Hoyt pieces. Bessie Clayton danced in *A Black Sheep,* and Loie Fuller did her famous skirt dance in a Hoyt play. Julian Mitchell, Hoyt's producer, later became famous as the stage manager of most of the Ziegfeld musicals.

Hoyt gave the country several of its best-known songs. "Reuben, Reuben, I've Been Thinking" and "The Bowery" became part of the nation's singing habit. Charles K. Harris wrote his melancholy "After the Ball" when he was an impecunious young man in Milwaukee and persuaded the manager of a travelling company of *A Trip to Chinatown* to insert it experimentally, without Hoyt's knowledge, into a matinée performance. It stopped the show and was thereafter part of the regular routine of the play, despite Hoyt's usual feeling against material that he did not contribute himself. Nothing of a musician in his own right, Hoyt was fortunate in having Percy Gaunt associated with him to write the melodies for his lyrics.

III.

The earlier Hoyt plays are farce, purely and simply. There is little connected plot structure in them and the effects are secured almost wholly by fast action and slapstick comedy. *A Bunch of Keys,* here printed, is representative of the type. Later Hoyt became more socially conscious and his plays took on a theme. In *A Contented Woman* he satirized the movement for women's suffrage; in *A Temperance Town* he had his say about local option and the Prohibition movement; in *A Milk White Flag* he poked gorgeous fun at the hypocrisy of the home guard companies. *A Midnight Bell* is simple melodrama, and *A Runaway Colt* deals with baseball and a gambler's attempt to bribe one of its players.

Even, however, in these satires, Hoyt could not overcome the temptation to insert farce elements. When the prohibitionists entered Oakhurst's saloon in *A Temperance Town,* the second act closed with an explosion of a barrel of beer and the resultant discomfiture of the raiders. The most sentimental scene in the play, as well as the most ironic—the one in which the outcast daughter listens to her father, the minister, preach a Thanksgiving sermon while she sits abjectly outside the church in a snowstorm—ends with general turmoil as the emerging congregation tumbles in an undignified heap over the piece of farm machinery that Mink Jones carelessly left on the church steps. Such instances throughout the plays might be multiplied; they are the rule, not the exception. Hoyt knew that such scenes were expected in his plays; they always caused laughter and delighted the audience; so he put them in.

Hoyt's method of workmanship was a combination of sloppiness and careful technique. He made notes at odd times on bits of paper, putting down witty remarks he heard or conceived, remembering strange names or peculiar people. Later he assembled his scrambled notes and made from them a working script of the play. After a piece was put in rehearsal it was constantly being altered. Later, before the New York openings, Hoyt would travel with the company, sitting night after night in the audience and watching the reactions of those about him to the situations and quips; after the performance he made still other changes to suit the needs of an actual production before an audience. Frequently he kept a piece on the road for months, sometimes almost a year, before he let it open in New York. Always through that period he was trying to perfect its gags and business so that it would run smoothly with the maximum effects when he showed it to Broadway.

IV.

Following is a list of the Hoyt plays with dates of their New York openings and the theatres in which they were performed:

1. *A Bunch of Keys,* March 26, 1883, San Francisco Opera House.
2. *A Rag Baby,* August 16, 1884, Haverley's Theatre.
3. *A Parlor Match,* September 22, 1884, Tony Pastor's Theatre.
4. *A Tin Soldier,* May 3, 1885, Standard Theatre.
5. *The Maid and the Moonshiner,* August 16, 1886, Standard Theatre.
6. *A Hole in the Ground,* September 12, 1887, Fourteenth Street Theatre.
7. *A Brass Monkey,* October 15, 1888, Bijou Theatre.
8. *A Midnight Bell,* March 5, 1889, Bijou Theatre.
9. *A Texas Steer,* November 10, 1890, Bijou Theatre.
10. *A Trip to Chinatown,* November 9, 1891, Hoyt's Madison Square Theatre.
11. *A Temperance Town,* September 17, 1893, Hoyt's Madison Square Theatre.
12. *A Milk White Flag,* October 8, 1894, Hoyt's Theatre (formerly Hoyt's Madison Square Theatre).
13. *A Runaway Colt,* November 12, 1895, Hoyt's Theatre.
14. *A Black Sheep,* January 6, 1896, Hoyt's Theatre.
15. *A Contented Woman,* January 4, 1897, Hoyt's Theatre.
16. *A Stranger in New York,* September 13, 1897, Hoyt's Theatre.
17. *A Day and a Night in New York,* August 30, 1898, Garrick Theatre.
18. *A Dog in a Manger.* (Never produced in New York. It played only one week in Washington, D.C., opening on January 30, 1899, and was never revived.)

V.

One of the bequests in Hoyt's will provided for the typing and binding of five sets of his plays to be distributed as follows: one set to the Lambs' Club Library; one set to the New York Public Library, then known as the Tilden Library; one to the Actors' Fund of America; one to the library in Charlestown, N.H.; and one to his partner, Mr. Frank McKee. The first four copies are still in the possession of the libraries to which they were assigned. I do not know where the fifth one is; probably it is owned by the heirs of Mr. McKee. But no one knows what became of the original manuscripts from which these copies were made. I have written to Mr. Daniel Frohman of the Actors' Fund; to Sanger and Jordan, play agents, Times Building, New York; to the law firm that settled the estate; to the trust company that acted as agents for the trustees under the will; to the librarian of the Silsby Free Public Library in Charlestown, N.H.; and to several of Hoyt's friends. None of them could direct me to any autograph manuscripts; it is doubtful in my mind that they are now extant.

Therefore the matter of the texts of the plays is somewhat perplexing. Only one play by Hoyt has ever previously been printed. In 1925 Mr. Montrose Moses included *A Texas Steer* in *Representative American Dramas, National and Local* (Boston: Little, Brown and Company); he used the copy in the New York Public Library and compared it to one which he found in the files of Sanger and Jordan, noting some variant readings. There are a number of prompt copies of the different plays in existence in various places; I have made use of several in preparing this volume.

Had Hoyt himself made the copies that are now in the bound volumes above mentioned we might be sure that they were as he wanted them to be. But the fact remains that they were typed after his death. Furthermore I have been assured by several persons who knew Hoyt, some of them actors who had appeared in the plays, that the copies in the New York Public Library are not, in all respects, as the plays were acted. Nevertheless, they remain, so far as there is such a thing, the authentic copies, made in accordance with the terms of his will, and as such I have used them freely in this edition. *A Bunch of Keys* and *A Milk White Flag* are here printed directly from the bound volumes in the New York Public Library and the Lambs' Club, both of which I have used. They apparently are identical. I have not seen the copies in Charlestown and the Actors' Fund collection, but I assume they are carbons of the two I have examined.

A Temperance Town is here printed from a typed copy of the play in the University of Chicago Library, with a few slight emendations made on the basis of the "official" copy in New York. In that copy appear two characters that are not found in the play as here printed: a litigious widow and her daughter, somewhat in the manner of the Widow Blackacre and her son in Wycherley's *The Plain Dealer*. They are very minor characters and their omission from the prompt copy examined indicates that they were left out of at least one acting version of the play. This bit of evidence is further proof of the fact that the text of the plays was frequently changed from time to time. Different companies performed the plays in different ways; those on the road may not have used at all the same versions that were performed in New York, and many of the plays were acted for years in travelling and stock companies long after the New York performances had been closed.

A Midnight Bell is here printed from a copy of the play supplied me by Mr. Barrett H. Clark, the general editor of this series. It differs in numerous instances from the New York Public Library's copy, but it is undoubtedly a version that was performed, for the stage directions are much fuller than those in the "official" copies.

A Trip to Chinatown is printed as supplied to me in a copy of the play sent me by Mr. George W. Poultney of San Francisco, Calif., a gentleman who appeared in at least one of the Hoyt companies playing on the Pacific coast. He assures me that it is the form of the play in which he acted. It differs radically from the copy in the bound volume in New York, so much so, in fact, that I have printed the entire last act of both versions. The first version is Mr. Poultney's copy; the second is the New York Public Library's copy. The music for the songs from *A Trip to Chinatown* was also supplied me through Mr. Poultney's kindness. The copy of the play which he gave me, however, has some very obvious faults in it. In Acts I and II the character of Flirt is presented as a friend of the Gays; in Act III she appears as Mrs. Guyer's maid. Somewhere in Mr. Poultney's copy was a bad mix-up which the manuscript does not straighten out, nor could Mr. Poultney offer any explanation when I questioned him on the subject. On the other hand, in the Public Library's version, Act III, the character of Slavin is wrongly given as Noah.

Mr. Poultney could not tell me at exactly what point and in what order the songs were to be introduced into the play. I have placed them where they seemed most logically to belong. The fact that the most famous song that Hoyt ever wrote, "The Bowery," appears in the third act of Mr. Poultney's copy and not at all in the New York copy indicates certainly that in one respect at least the former is the more accurate. Furthermore, Mr. Poultney could not supply me with all the songs mentioned in the script; there are, therefore, several omissions of songs that I have not been able to supply. And there is no indication where Mr. Harris's famous "After the Ball" was sung in the play. However, I have already remarked that it was inserted into the piece first in a road company playing in Milwaukee and very likely did not appear in all companies. As a matter of fact, there is ample evidence that the plays differed so vastly as presented that it is not at all certain that even Hoyt's own songs were always sung in the same spots or that the same songs were sung all through the long run and by the many road companies presenting the piece.

It will be noted that the plays printed from prompt copies contain much fuller stage directions than do the ones in the bound volumes. I have faithfully included all the directions for action to indicate how greatly Hoyt depended on fast movement for his effects. In all copies the punctuation is so unbelievably bad that I have repunctuated according to decent standards and modern demand.

A BUNCH OF KEYS;
Or, THE HOTEL

CAST OF CHARACTERS

The cast of *A Bunch of Keys* for its New York opening on March 26, 1883, was as follows:

TEDDY KEYS	ALICE ATHERTON
ROSE KEYS	ANNA GUENTHER
MAY KEYS	ANNA BREVOOR
DOLLY DOBBS	MARIETTA NASH
MATILDA JENKINS	GENIE HOLTMEYER
JONAS GRIMES	JAMES T. POWERS
GILLY SPOONER	JULIAN MITCHELL
TOM HARDING	CHARLES STEVENS
SAM POTTS	WILLIAM SMITH
LITTLETON SNAGGS	WILLIE EDOUIN
BOATMAN	

ACT I: EXTERIOR OF THE HOTEL.

ACT II: OFFICE OF THE GRAND VIEW HOTEL.

ACT III: SAME AS ACT II.

ACT I.

SCENE: *Village landscape in 3. Hotel in R.2.E. Veranda. Steps up to door on second floor. Practical window opening onto balcony from which hangs lamp (practical). Barrel outside hotel door upstage. Wheelbarrow outside hotel door downstage. Signal post, practical, L.C. at back. Cottage, L.2.E. Two rustic chairs by window. As curtain goes up Dolly enters from cottage L. Crosses to C.*

Dol. I'm glad somebody about this place feels like singing. Ever since the hotel has been closed, I've had a most miserable time. There's been no drummers along and I've had nobody to flirt with but brakemen. [*Enter Grimes*] I suppose brakemen are very nice if you think so, but I much prefer drummers. [*Grimes business at a signal. He is singing*] Well, Grimes, how have we offended you?

Gri. Oh, talk United States!

Dol. What have we done to you?

Gri. Nothing as I knows of. If you had somebody'd 'a' got licked. What made you think you had?

Dol. Why, I had supposed we had offended you, somehow, and that you came down here and made that noise to get revenge.

Gri. If you don't like my singing, you ain't obliged to listen to it.

Dol. Yes, we are, unless you send us word you are coming an hour beforehand, so we can take to the woods.

Gri. All right. I'm going to begin singing in just an hour from now. Why don't you take to the woods?

Dol. What do you want down here anyway?

Gri. Well, we're all out of oil up at the station and I didn't know but you'd let me have some for my red lantern.

Dol. Who ever heard of red oil in a private house?

Gri. Well, that tears me all out! Red oil! D'ye think it's red oil that makes the light red?

Dol. You don't mean to say it's the wick! I never knew that before.

Gri. Get onto it! That beats anything for freshness you'd find at a railroad restaurant. Will you let me have the oil? [*Chorus heard outside L.*]

Dol. Yes, if you'll promise not to sing in this vicinity again. [*Exit into cottage L. Enter Tom, May, Rose, and Boatman, singing and laughing*]

Tom. [*C.*] Ship ahoy!

Gilly. [*Outside*] Hello!

Tom. What's your cargo?

Gil. [*Outside*] Fish!

Tom. What kind of fish?

Gil. [*Outside*] Suckers! [*All laugh. Enter Gilly, laughing and singing*]

Tom. Well, we had a jolly row.

May. Yes, if Teddy hadn't been along with her fishing-pole. She's a terror.

Tom. Well, she's only a little rough.

Gil. She wouldn't let me sing, because she said I'd frighten the fish. [*All laugh*]

Tom. I don't blame her for that. We got back in plenty of time for the train.

May. Yes. You must see Grimes and tell him to signal the train to stop.

Gil. I shouldn't think they'd stop the train for one passenger. Stopping is so expensive.

May. Why, Gilly?

Gil. Why, they have to break up the whole train.

Tom. Good, Gilly.

Gil. Yes, isn't it? I thought you'd say so. [*Aside*] I wonder what I said; it must have been funny.

Tom. [*Up C.*] There's Grimes! [*Calls*] Grimes!

May. Oh, don't call him.

Gil. I never could endure that horrid brakeman.

Rose. Don't say anything against the profession. Remember poor, dear uncle was a brakeman. If he hadn't been, he never would have had the money to buy the hotel.

Gil. Now we've been talking about the will all day, who gets the property?

Tom. I know one who gets—

May. Yes, Tom?

Tom. Nothing!

Gil. Well, I expect to get—

Rose. Yes, Gilly?

Gil. Left! [*Laughs. All look disgusted*]

Rose. Perhaps May will get it. Uncle was very fond of her before he died.

Gil. Yes, but hang it, how has she been since he died? That's the question!

Rose. Gilly, you're a fool!

Boat. [*Laughing*] That's the best thing I've heard today.

GIL. [*To Boatman*] Excuse me, the laugh don't come in there.

MAY. You don't know anything. I shouldn't wonder if Teddy got the property. It's just her luck. Uncle thought everything of sister Teddy. I don't know why.

GIL. Why? Why, when he got—hic—When did you buy it? Didn't she used to help him tumble upstairs to his room?

MAY. She ought not to have done so.

TOM. Well, I must go up to the depot. The train will be here in a minute.

MAY. Oh, Tom, I'm so sorry you must go. [*Cries*]

TOM. There, there, don't cry! Let's part in jolly good style. [*Sings*] Good-by, sweetheart, good-by. [*Kisses May. Exits 2.E.L. Boatman goes up C. to go out; knocks Gilly; meets Grimes entering. Business and exit*]

GRI. Things around here are going to him.

ALL. What's the matter with you?

MAY and ROSE. Teddy, I suppose.

GRI. I can't say anything to her, for if I do, she'll begin to sing. I'll join in and that'll settle it.

GIL. What of it?

GRI. [*Rushing at him*] What of it! It's been holding the Express up at the station for ten minutes, making it ten minutes late. They'll blame it on me and I'll get the grand bounce. [*Exits with a rush, R.3.E.*]

GIL. Mr. Snaggs must be on that train.

ROSE. And it's ten minutes late. That'll just give us time to dress. Come, May.

GIL. [*Stopping her*] But you're not going.

ROSE. Yes, we are.

GIL. But haven't you forgotten something?

ROSE. What?

GIL. Haven't you forgotten to kiss something?

ROSE. Don't be silly. May's here.

GIL. Well, she's engaged. She knows how it is.

ROSE. You're a goose. Come, May. [*Exits to cottage*]

MAY. Bye-bye, tootsy-wootsy. [*Exits laughing*]

GIL. [*Solus*] Rose is a delicious girl. So much prettier than her sisters.

SNAG. [*Heard off 2.E.R.*] What d'ye mean, sir? It was your fault.

GRI. Oh, let up!

SNAG. What right had you to start the train? You want action brought against the company? What's your name?

GRI. Grimes.

SNAG. What's your other name?

GRI. Jonas.

SNAG. You're in hard luck.

GRI. What's the matter with my name?

SNAG. Why, if I had it, I'd bring an action against the parties that gave it to me.

GIL. He seems to be in trouble with that horrid Grimes. [*Enter Snaggs followed by Grimes with baggage. Snaggs places coat, umbrella, etc., on barrel by hotel*]

SNAG. Ah, Gilly, how are you? [*To Grimes*] Through your stupidity— [*To Gilly*] I hope I see you well. [*To Grimes*]—I'm ten minutes late. Do you want me to bring action against the road? I brought an action against a road once. [*Dolly is at the window*]

GIL. Did you win it?

SNAG. No, but I came near it. [*Sees Dolly*] Ah, Dolly, come here. [*She leaves window*] Nice girl, Dolly! Going to marry her, aren't you?

GIL. I marry a servant girl!

SNAG. Of course not! I forgot. A servant must marry someone who can work for her and help her to live. [*Enter Dolly*] Ah, Dolly, I will impress a kiss upon that classic brow. [*Kisses her*] Illegal, but pleasant. Dolly, one clothes brush for one gentleman, if you please. [*Dolly going*] Ah, Dolly, come here, come here. Dolly, we will break the law once more. [*Kisses her. Exit Dolly*]

GRI. When I do that, I get my jaw slapped.

SNAG. Ah, young man, it all depends on how you do it. It's assurance— what you call, gall—that does it. You've got the natural qualifications for a master. You'll get there some day. If you have good luck. [*Enter Dolly with a barrel hoop*]

DOL. I couldn't find a clothes brush, but we might scrape the mud off with this barrel hoop.

SNAG. Go gently, Dolly. So this is the hotel in which my friend the brakeman invested his fortune. No one but a member of the B.U.M.S. would do that.

GRI. Look here, you go easy on the Brakeman's United Merciful Society.

SNAG. Well, nobody but a brakeman would have put his money into that old rattrap.

GRI. It's mighty few brakemen have money to put into anything.

SNAG. That's because brakemen are fools. My client was a fool, or he might have been alive today and worth $50,000. Didn't he bring an action against the road, and recover damages? Didn't he get $2,000 when he had two fingers cut off? $3,000 for an ear? $5,000 when he had both legs broken?

$7,000 when he had an eye put out? If he had economized himself, he might have been alive today and worth $50,000 and had enough of himself left to enjoy life with. But what did he do? What did he do? Went and broke his neck like a fool and spoiled the entire business. [*To Grimes*] And you want me to make a fortune the same way.

GIL. What's the trouble between you and Grimes?

SNAG. [*Crosses to Gilly*] Trouble! He tried to kill me. I can recover for it. I'll prove it to you according to law. Sit down. [*Pushes Gilly into chair*]

GRI. I don't like the law.

SNAG. Why? Ever try it?

GRI. Yes.

SNAG. How far did you go?

GRI. As far as the jail. [*Exit Grimes R.2.E.*]

SNAG. Dolly, fair one, for your kindness receive—[*Feels in vest pocket*]

DOL. [*Curtsies and holds out her hand*] Yes, sir.

SNAG. [*Kisses her hand*] Many thanks.

DOL. Well, how Miss Teddy can like him, I don't see. [*Exits into cottage*]

SNAG. [*Aside*] I wonder where my little wildflower Teddy is. I want to cross-examine the witness. [*Aloud*] Well, Gilly, how are you? Pretty well? And how are the ladies?

GIL. Oh, Rose is charming.

SNAG. Yes, of course. And her sister?

GIL. Oh, she's engaged.

SNAG. Engaged? Who to?

GIL. Why, Tom Harding. May's very spoons on Tom.

SNAG. May, and her sister?

GIL. Oh, Rose is charming. Going to marry me.

SNAG. Poor girl, poor girl.

GIL. Sir!

SNAG. Oh, of course. But the brother, so to speak?

GIL. Brother? There is no brother.

SNAG. Of course not; but—er—what is her name?

GIL. Perhaps you mean Teddy.

SNAG. Yes, that's it: Teddy. How is Teddy?

GIL. Just the same: harum-scarum, ne'er-do-well.

SNAG. Too bad, too bad. Prettiest girl of the lot.

GIL. Oh, you're wrong! Rose is far prettier.

SNAG. Nothing of the sort, sir! Rose is pretty, but Teddy is a beauty.

GIL. Well, we won't quarrel about it.

SNAG. Now then, when the ladies are ready, we'll proceed to business. See here, it's pleasant out-of-doors. Better bring a table out, and have the will read outside here.

GIL. I'll see to it. [*Exit Gilly to cottage*]

SNAG. [*Takes chair and sits upstage*] Nice young man, that! Don't know much, but he's not to blame for that. Lots just like him. And he's a frightful bad judge of beauty. Why, Teddy is far prettier than her sister! I can see it. It takes a mighty pretty girl to look handsome to you after she has played a dozen practical jokes on you. But Teddy does, and it's not paid-for good looks, either. She doesn't trouble the dressmaker. I think she'd be happy in a hat of this description. [*Holds up hat. Brick flies over. Snaggs rises and looks around; then sits*] Ha! Somebody trying to get square with the hotel. Probably Grimes. That Grimes is evidently a desperate character. Teddy ought not to associate with him. She should go into refined society. I don't see why an ordinary brush and comb wouldn't make her hair look decent, and there is no good reason why she should wear men's shoes size No. 8, when she has a remarkably small foot; and if every lady in the land chose to ride a horse as Teddy does, sidesaddles would never have been invented. [*Holds up hat and scratches head. Brick flies and strikes hat. He starts up. C.*] Great heavens! That's Grimes! I'll bring action! [*Teddy laughs*] No, it's Teddy! Teddy, where are you? [*Enter Teddy, with pole, which she drops on stage*]

TED. Here I am. I've been trying for ten minutes to hit that.

SNAG. Hit what?

TED. Why, that! [*Knocks hat up. When it falls, Snaggs puts it on hotel steps*] Grimes calls 'em dicers.

SNAG. Pretty, but unlaundered.

TED. Say, why don't you wear a white hat? The bloods all do.

SNAG. Thank the Lord, I'm not a blood. [*Business of shaking hands. Teddy pulls him from R. to L. Snaggs falls on hands and knees. Teddy pulls him up by the collar and then shakes him*] Teddy, this is not the way to treat a friend.

TED. Oh, I believe in a good, hearty greeting. Makes you feel at home.

SNAG. How are you?

TED. Oh, I'm pretty comfortable.

SNAG. Well, that's right. But why don't you ask how I am?

TED. Don't want to know.

SNAG. Don't you care whether I'm well or sick?

TED. Yes, I'd rather you'd be well.

SNAG. Yet you said you didn't care.

TED. Well, I didn't just mean that, but I didn't quite like to ask you how you were.

SNAG. Why not?

TED. I was afraid you'd think I was curious.

SNAG. Why should I?

TED. Oh, you men are always complaining that women are too curious. I don't think they're a bit worse than men. If you knew that Tom and May were in the parlor courting, I'll bet you a pretty you'd be just as apt as I would to have business under the parlor window.

SNAG. I believe I would. [*Teddy brings down chair. When Snaggs approaches to take it, she twirls it on one leg so that it strikes his shins; he tries to take it three times during the succeeding dialogue*] Well, Teddy, are you glad to see me?

TED. Yes, indeed, I am. Mike's been sick for three days, and I've been dreadful lonesome.

SNAG. Hm, yes. Too bad about Mike. Who's Mike?

TED. Why, the donkey.

SNAG. But, Teddy, if the donkey were well, don't you think you'd be glad to see me?

TED. I dunno. Mike's dreadful good company. [*Snaggs now takes chair and sits down*]

SNAG. Well, I'll be hanged if I don't think I'm better company than a donkey.

TED. I dunno. He's so different from you. He's so lively.

SNAG. Thank you. I'm glad I'm different.

TED. Say, would you kick Grimes into the pool and then squeal?

SNAG. I would. [*Teddy, D.C., takes frog from her pocket unseen by Snaggs*]

TED. The donkey did, and when Grimes got out he grabbed a board and made him squeal some more.

SNAG. Good for Grimes. [*Laughs*]

TED. Mr. Snaggs, why don't you wear a larger coat? One that would fit a shorter man. The bloods all do. [*Snaggs rises from chair, looks at coat, back to Teddy*] Mr. Snaggs, do you see May at the parlor window? [*Teddy puts frog down his back*]

SNAG. No, I don't! What's that! Have you put a piece of ice that's alive down my back?

TED. [*Laughs*] Don't be disturbed. It's only a frog.

SNAG. [*Dances furiously*] Take it out, I say! I can't reach it!

TED. You dance beautifully. Now if you could only sing.

SNAG. I'd like to sing like a parrot—all swear-words. Damn!

TED. [*Crosses to him*] You mustn't swear within half a mile of any house in this town.

SNAG. I must remember that. [*Crosses to corner R.*]

TED. Hold on! I'll fish for you.

SNAG. Hold on, Teddy. There's no law to justify you in putting a frog down my back.

TED. [*Gets fishing-pole. Puts line down his back*] Sh! I think I have a nibble. Hi! [*Jerks up pole. Snaggs jumps up and yells*]

SNAG. Oh, you've hooked me! [*Starts upstage*]

TED. Where are you going?

SNAG. Half a mile into the country. [*Rushes out L.*]

TED. He's awful funny. I do wish I could make him sing. [*Enter Grimes and Dolly, R.3.*]

GRI. Maybe you think a man's of no account.

TED. Say, what's the row?

DOL. Mr. Grimes has been very disagreeable. He says woman is inferior to man.

TED. [*Rushes Grimes to corner, R.*] What!

GRI. Hold on, hold on, I say! I merely told her that scientists said so. I read it in a paper.

TED. Don't you take any stock in science, Grimes?

GRI. Well, probably you know.

TED. Of course I do. I know all about science. That's just where I live. Say, are you busy? [*Grimes goes upstage, but watches Teddy*] Are you very busy? [*Dances and breaks over to L.*]

GRI. [*Up R.*] Well, I'm not too busy. [*Grimes puts on Snaggs's hat and coat, takes umbrella. Teddy and Dolly tie handkerchiefs on their heads. Song and dance, after which Grimes exits R., Dolly L. Enter Snaggs with frog in hand from L.*]

SNAG. With such evidence as this, I actually think I could get a verdict.

TED. I did catch him after all! I knew I should. That's the jolliest fishing I ever had. Let's try it again.

SNAG. Well, I should say not! [*Throws frog down. Goes R.*] As I once said to a jury—

TED. What's a jury?

SNAG. A jury, Teddy, is a body of twelve men organized for the purpose of deciding which party to a lawsuit has the smartest lawyer. [*Gets chairs and places them downstage C.*]

TED. I'd like to be on a jury. I'd never decide as the rest did.

SNAG. Teddy, there are plenty of men just like you. Teddy, sit down. Teddy, you are rapidly approaching womanhood.

TED. Yes, I'm getting a big girl now. [*Laughs*]

SNAG. Have you ever experienced a fluttering sensation of the heart?

TED. I dunno. I suppose not. Is it like anything the way you feel after you've eaten too much custard?

SNAG. Something similar. Have you ever loved?

TED. Oh, yes. I love—Mike.

SNAG. I'll murder Mike.

TED. Do you mean get spoony, like Rose and Gilly? Not any in mine, please.

SNAG. But you should. Every woman should have a lawsuit.

TED. What?

SNAG. I mean get married.

TED. It's the same thing.

SNAG. Yes, pretty much the same thing. Every woman should get married. As I remarked to the jury in the celebrated breach of promise case of Johnson v. Anson—which I lost—"Gentlemen of the jury, it is the mission of every woman to marry, to become the guiding star of some man's existence, to make his home a sanctuary of bliss and—"

TED. [*Who has been looking for frog and can't find it*] Say, where did you throw that frog? [*Sees frog, picks it up, and puts it in her pocket*]

SNAG. That remark is irrelevant and should be ruled out. As I once remarked to the jury—set down—[*Teddy sits*]—regarding certain evidence introduced by the other side, "May it please Your Honor, this evidence is as much out of place as a parrot in a Sunday School. It is a deliberate attempt to hound a weak and defenseless woman to the grave. [*Teddy yawns and goes to sleep*] Your Honor, gaze upon this fair and innocent young creature, and see if you can find it in your big, warm heart, beating for humanity, to admit this evidence which these cowardly assassins of character have attempted to foist upon a confiding jury." [*Teddy snores. Snaggs looks at her, disgusted*] The usual results of my arguments. Well, this is encouraging. Teddy, Teddy! Wake up! [*Shakes her*]

TED. [*Wakes up*] Mm. What is it? Why did you wake me up? I was just dreaming. I could hear Mike calling me.

SNAG. I'll kill Mike! [*Sits down*] Teddy, I'm not worth a tinker's damn. [*Rises and bows*] I beg pardon. [*Sits down*] That is, I'm not at all good at love-making, but I'm very fond of you.

TED. Mashed! Clean gone!

SNAG. Precisely! Teddy, will you marry me? I mean me?

TED. Well, I don't know. Think what a funny-looking couple we'd make.

SNAG. We'd make a very handsome couple. You've got good looks enough for two. [*Aside*] No eyewitness, I'll venture. [*Puts arm around her*] Come, Teddy, what do you say?

TED. Say? Does your arm pain you?

SNAG. No. Why?

TED. I see it's out of place.

SNAG. Oh, I'm very comfortable. [*Enter Gilly and Dolly with table*]

TED. [*Aside*] I wish I could find a pin.

DOL. [*To Gilly*] Oh, just look there!

GIL. Oh, I understand. I've been there myself.

DOL. Yes, I guess you're there most of the time.

GIL. When I can get there. Well, having seen all that's to be seen, I suppose it's our duty to let them know that we are here. Ahem! [*Louder*] Ahem! [*Crosses to R.*]

SNAG. [*Jumps up. Aside*] Great heavens, witnesses! I can be sued for breach of promise! [*Aloud*] I was extracting something from Miss Teddy's eye.

GIL. Mr. Snaggs, that's too thin.

TED. [*Backs Gilly to corner, R.*] You think you're very smart to catch us, don't you, Gilly? Well, we should have been on the lookout for you, if we'd known your mammy let you out so early. [*Slaps his face. Teddy crosses to L., takes Dolly around the waist and goes upstage*]

DOL. I never was hugged, Miss Teddy. How does it seem?

TED. It's more than being able to eat and drink at the same time, and you know how I love to eat! [*Dolly moves chairs*]

GIL. Well, Mr. Snaggs, are you ready to proceed to business?

SNAG. I am, sir.

GIL. The ladies will be out at once. Have you the will?

SNAG. I have. Is it proposed to contest it?

GIL. No! It is not.

SNAG. Hm. That makes a short case of it. [*Enter Rose and May*] Ah, here come the ladies. [*Crosses to Rose*] Miss Rose, I am delighted. [*Crosses to May*] Miss May, I am charmed.

TED. What an awful flirt he is! I won't stand it!

ROSE. We are very glad to see you, sir. It is some time since we met.

MAY. Yes, a very melancholy event has taken place since then. The death of our poor, dear uncle!

SNAG. This family has indeed been sorely afflicted. I understand you have had no less than three funerals within a year.

TED. No wonder we're poor!

MAY. This is a very solemn occasion.

SNAG. [*Crosses to Gilly*] It is. It is.

MAY. [*Crosses L. Aside to Rose*] Ought we to cry a little?

ROSE. [*Aside to May*] I think it would be proper.

MAY. Dear Uncle Jotham was so good and kind! [*Cries*]

ROSE. And we thought so much of him! [*Cries*]

TED. [*Comes down C.*] Why, they hated him!

MAY. He was so sweet and gentle! [*Sobs*]

GIL. [*In R. corner*] He was the toughest brakeman on the line!

ROSE. Oh, if he were alive today! [*Sobs. Rose and May sob in each other's arms*]

TED. [*Disgusted*] That makes me tired!

SNAG. Ladies, it is quite unnecessary, rather old-fashioned, in fact. A gentle melancholy is the proper caper. [*They stop crying*]

TED. [*In L. corner*] Well, I don't care for the fashion. Uncle used to get drunk and swear, but he was always good and kind to me, and I'm going to do a weep if I feel like it. [*Cries loudly*]

ROSE. Teddy!

MAY. Don't do so, Teddy! If you're to remain and hear the will read, you must be decorous.

TED. Be who?

MAY. Decorous.

ROSE. [*Crosses to Teddy*] And look at your shoes! They're all unbuttoned and covered with mud. Will you promise to keep still?

SNAG. Can you oblige me with a glass of water?

DOL. Certainly, sir.

SNAG. Dolly, don't put anything in it. [*Exit Dolly. Aside to Gilly*] Now then, there are the girls together; compare them. Rose and May in silks and satins, so to say, and Teddy in rags, but Teddy is the beauty.

GIL. Mr. Snaggs, it's a wonder to me that you haven't got the reputation of being an ass.

SNAG. I have. [*Enter Dolly with a glass of water. She gives it to May, who hands it to Snaggs. Exit Dolly*] Ah, many thanks. It's very kind of you. If you will pardon me for quoting a little original poetry:

> A sweeter draught from fairer hands
> Was never quaffed.

[*Drinks and spurts it over Gilly, looks disgusted, and then smiles*] Very refreshing. [*To ladies*] Ladies, be seated. [*Business of sitting on chairs. Teddy sits in chair intended for Rose. Snaggs hands Rose to chair, not seeing Teddy and seating Rose in Teddy's lap. She turns Teddy out. Same business with May. Teddy pushes Snaggs against table, takes Gilly's chair away; Gilly sits on floor; he then gets up and sits in chair. Teddy goes to F.C., sits on stage, but afterwards gets up, comes behind Gilly, catches fly, and puts it in glass of water on table*]

OMNES. Teddy, sit down!

SNAG. As I said before, this is a very solemn occasion. [*Drinks water and chokes*]

TED. Don't be disturbed. It's only a fly.

SNAG. I thought it was a horsefly. [*Takes it out of the water and throws it in Gilly's eye*]

TED. There it is!

GIL. I've got it.

SNAG. I can't drink that!

TED. I can't please you, fly in or fly out. Shall I catch a spider for you?

OMNES. Teddy! Proceed, Mr. Snaggs.

SNAG. We are assembled to read the last will and testament of our esteemed friend, the late Jotham Keys.

TED. Testament! I didn't know he had a testament! I never saw him read anything but a dime novel.

OMNES. Teddy! Proceed, Mr. Snaggs.

SNAG. He was indeed a man of peculiar tastes. He had strange likes and dislikes.

TED. Yes! He liked whiskey and he didn't like water.

OMNES. Teddy! Proceed, Mr. Snaggs.

SNAG. [*Reads*] "Know all men by these presents, that I, Jotham Keys, of the town of Leominster, state of Massachusetts, being of sound and disposing mind, do hereby declare this to be my last will and testament. Before stating my bequests, I have a few suggestions to offer. A homely woman has a hard time in this world; a pretty one may be a fool, but she will get a husband. Beauty, I am also aware, is a matter of opinion. We are apt to consider the people we like beautiful. Therefore, the only competent judge of beauty is a total stranger to the person judged. For these reasons, I direct that my property consisting of the Grand View Hotel, cottage, and personal property, etc., etc., be disposed of as follows: The hotel shall be opened within one month of the date of my death, and the first drummer who is a total stranger, that shall arrive at the hotel, shall be requested to decide which of my three nieces, otherwise the Bunch of Keys, Rose, May, and Theodosia Keys, is the homeliest—"

OMNES. What!

SNAG. "The homeliest! And to her I bequeath my entire estate."

OMNES. [*Rise and cross*] Mercy on us!

GIL. [*Crosses to Rose*] Rose dear, we shall be very happy. The hotel is just the home we want.

ROSE. What do you mean, sir? I don't get the hotel! [*Walks up and down the stage excitedly, followed by Gilly*]

SNAG. Teddy, you're an heiress.

TED. Indeed, I'm not.

ROSE, MAY, and TED. [*Together*] I think it was a shame for uncle to leave me nothing. [*They cry*]

SNAG. But, Teddy, he has left you the hotel!

GIL. Rose, don't cry. You'll get the hotel!

ROSE. I shan't! I won't have it! It's Teddy's!

SNAG. Of course, it's Teddy's!

MAY. [*Crosses to Snaggs; puts fist in his face*] It isn't mine, anyway, and I'm awful glad. I'd rather never have a cent than be called the homely one of the family. Besides, Tom wouldn't permit it!

SNAG. Don't you strike me! [*Exit May L. hurriedly*]

TED. So would I, but I'm catching it all 'round. I don't dress to kill, but if you were to see me ragged out, you'd find I'm not the homeliest one of the family. [*Walks around stage followed by Snaggs*]

GIL. Rose, dear, the hotel is an elegant piece of property.

ROSE. You wretch! To say I'm homely! I'm not vain, but I know I'm as good-looking as they, and I'd die before I'd take that hotel!

TED. I guess it will stand idle, then.

SNAG. Teddy, the hotel is yours. I can prove it to you by law. [*Snaggs and Gilly meet C.*]

GIL. I tell you, the hotel belongs to Rose!

SNAG. Nothing of the sort, sir! Didn't you quarrel with me half an hour ago because I said that Rose was not the prettiest?

ROSE. [*To Gilly*] You mean, contemptible wretch! [*Exits to cottage; slams door in Gilly's face*]

TED. [*Brings will from table to Snaggs*] Oh, say, here's some more writing in the will.

SNAG. [*Grabs will. Aside*] Yes, another clause, a codicil. "In case my nieces prefer to divide the property equally among themselves, they may do so." Hm! Won't do to let them see that. They'd all refuse it, and the result would be a division of this most magnificent property. They would rather be poor and pretty than homely and rich. [*Aloud*] I shall at once proceed to open the hotel, as the month expires in two days.

GIL. But what right have you to open the hotel?

SNAG. Why, somebody has got to do it, and I am the proper party.

GIL. [*C.*] No such thing! I'm going to marry Rose, and the hotel belongs to her.

TED. [*Pushes Gilly*] Now, Gilly, you had better go and look after that homely sister of mine. [*Pushes him to cottage. Exit Gilly*]

SNAG. [*Walks down F. from L. to R., followed by Teddy. Aside*] I must keep this last article of the will a profound secret. Open the hotel at once, and run it according to law until the first drummer arrives, get a decision in Teddy's favor, get Teddy to marry me, and—

TED. Say, Mr. Snaggs, what did the will say?

SNAG. It's all right, Teddy, my dear. The hotel is yours.

TED. You don't know what you are talking about.

SNAG. Don't say that, Teddy. I've been told that so many times in court, I'm sick of hearing it.

TED. But I'm not homely.

SNAG. Teddy, be reasonable.

TED. [*Screams*] I won't!

SNAG. Of course you won't. I forgot your sex.

TED. Rather than have them stuck-up sisters of mine say I was so homely I couldn't get a husband without the hotel, I'd marry anybody. I'd even marry little old Grimes!

SNAG. I'll assassinate little old Grimes!

TED. I think you're as horrid as you can be to say I'm the homeliest.

SNAG. Well, Teddy, it's not for me, but the first drummer who is a total stranger who stops at this hotel to say who shall have the property. [*Enter Grimes R.3.*] So let's not quarrel about it. Give me a kiss and call it square.

TED. Oh, get out. A kiss ain't square. It's round, like this. [*Makes a mouth, and exits to cottage*]

GRI. I'm on to your little game. You're gone on that girl.

SNAG. Gone, sir! Prove it!

GRI. Not that I blame you. She's right pretty.

SNAG. Pretty? Well, the folks down this way are the worst set of idiots I ever did see. She's plain, absolutely plain! Now, see here. You're acquainted with the sisters. Which of the three is the prettiest?

GRI. I dunno. I guess Miss Rose.

SNAG. Right! Quite right! And the next?

GRI. Miss May.

SNAG. Just so! And Teddy's the homeliest?

GRI. That's about the size of it.

SNAG. Grimesy, my boy! [*Shakes hands and business of getting squeezed, etc.*] You're not such a fool as you look. You've got a big head.

GRI. No, I haven't got the big head.

SNAG. Grimesy, I like you! [*More shaking business*] I see I was mistaken in you at first. Do you know, I wish we were total strangers.

GRI. We can be, if you don't like my society. [*Turns to go*]

SNAG. No, no, Grimesy, my boy. [*Shaking business*] I do like your society. You're a man of sound judgment. [*Enter Teddy and Dolly with keys*]

TED. Say, Mr. Snaggs, if you're going to open the hotel, I'll help you run it. It won't be much work. The guests will only require ice-water, and Dolly and Grimes will help, too.

SNAG. Grimesy, my boy, I'll engage you. [*Aside to him*] Teddy is the homeliest! [*Aloud*] I want you to help run the hotel. Do you know anything about a hotel?

GRI. No.

SNAG. Then you are just the man I want. I'll engage you. I'll give you a big salary.

GRI. But what'll become of the railroad if I leave it?

SNAG. I suppose it'll stop running. Come, Grimesy, my boy, let's go inside and inspect the house.

TED. I'll show you the way to the linen room.

DOL. And I to the pantry.

GRI. Come on, I know the way to the—

SNAG. Where?

GRI. Bar. [*Teddy and Dolly go first. Snaggs and Grimes are last into the hotel. Enter Gilly*]

GIL. Ah, there's Snaggs in the hotel. I wonder what they are up to. I'll go and see. [*Exits into hotel. Enter Rose and May*]

ROSE. You are quite right, May. The hotel belongs to Teddy.

MAY. Of course, the stranger will at once decide that she's the homeliest. You don't feel afraid he'll select you, do you? [*Enter Tom quietly; sits on barrel*]

ROSE. Certainly not! But then, May, accidents will happen.

MAY. Oh, how I wish Tom were here.

TOM. Tom is here, ready to console or advise. What's the bother?

MAY. Tom, dear, uncle's will has been read, and it leaves all his property to the homeliest of his three nieces. [*Cries*]

TOM. Never mind, dear. You're sure to get it.

MAY. What! [*Screams and stamps her foot. Enter Gilly from hotel, all broken up. They go to him and assist him to rise*]

MAY. Are you hurt?

GIL. No. I only saw Teddy.

TOM. Why did you get into a fight with her?

GIL. I couldn't help it. Girls, there is villainy going on here! There's a codicil to your uncle's will!

ROSE and MAY. A codicil? We never heard of it!

GIL. And Snaggs is determined you shan't. He's going to open the hotel, and once he gets possession, goodness knows how we shall get him out!

TOM. The scoundrel! How shall we turn the tables on him?

GIL. Look at me! I'd rather throw the tables at him!

ROSE. I have it! Let us arrange with the visitors to come here and worry the life out of him.

TOM. Visitors! Why, there won't be any for a month.

GIL. Happy thought! We will be the visitors!

OMNES. Good!

GIL. Let him open his hotel, and if in twenty-four hours we can't plague the life out of him and make him sick of hotel proprietorship, put us down as idiots! Do you agree?

OMNES. We do! [*Enter Grimes, Teddy, and Dolly*]

GRI. The emperor's coming out and he's got something to say. [*To Gilly*] And I'll paralyze you!

TED. [*Rushes for Gilly, but is taken back by Dolly*] Let's both paralyze. [*Snaggs appears on balcony*]

SNAG. On deck!

TED. Grimes, mount the rostrum. [*Grimes gets on barrel*]

SNAG. Ladies and gentlemen, in accordance with the directions of the will, I propose to at once open the hotel and run it. I shall remain in possession until the first drummer arrives and designates which of you young ladies is the heiress. Teddy, Grimes, and Dolly have agreed to help me. Grimes, close the court. [*Grimes strikes gong*]

GIL. Rose, May, Tom, come here. [*Aside to them*] He has no business to open that hotel. Let us all go in and make him sick of hotel life.

ROSE, MAY, and TOM. Good! We will!

TED. Three cheers for the new landlord! [*Grimes, Teddy, and Dolly cheer. Rose, May, and Tom groan*]

GRI. Tiger!

SNAG. Whoo!

GIL. Mr. Snaggs, there's more to that will! There's a codicil!

SNAG. There is? What then?

MAY, ROSE, and GIL. We must see it.

TED. Don't you let 'em! You hold on to it!

SNAG. I mean to.

ROSE. You'll get yourself disliked.

SNAG. Thank you, I'm used to it.

GIL. Mr. Snaggs, now don't compel me to use force.

SNAG. There's no danger of that.

ROSE. Now, Gilly, if you're a man, go in and thrash him!

TED. Do you want to get Gilly hurt?

MAY. Gilly, go up and throw him down!

GRI. I reckon there's going to be some fun.

GIL. [*To Snaggs*] You're a swindler, sir!

SNAG. You're not! You're not smart enough!

TED. [*Doubles her fists at Gilly*] Don't be afraid, Snaggsy, I'm here!

SNAG. I afraid of that?

GIL. You had better be! If you come down here, I'll pull your nose!

SNAG. Then I won't come down.

GIL. Will you show us the rest of that will?

SNAG. No, sir. I have the will, and as I said once to a jury—[*Song and chorus*]

ACT II.

SCENE: *The office of the Grand View Hotel. Scene above on platform, ten feet above floor, twenty feet across, divided in center into two rooms. Room L. is a bathroom with bath, two chairs, a table, and a bell-pull. Room R. is a bedroom with a folding bed, two chairs, and a bell-pull.*

The office: boxed-in scene. Door R.E.2. Elevator facing audience, R.2.E. Ice-water cooler on stand R. Piano upstage R. under stairway. Bootblack stand near ice-water cooler R. Staircase R. running from C. to behind platform R.3. or 4.E. Counter L.2.E. Bells on flat behind counter. Safe, telephone, etc., key-board with keys. Bar shelves with bottles, glasses, towel, etc. Glass cigar-case on counter L. near 1.E. Kitchen door L.2.E. Door in back flat L. of and foot of stairs.

DISCOVERED: *Dolly in room R., singing. Grimes at bootblack stand polishing boot.*

DOL. Well, if this is a sample of hotel life, I've had enough of it. The guest who slept in this bed last night must have had two nightmares and tried to ride them different ways. He actually tied the sheets in a hard knot. [*Laughs, closes up bed, comes down*]

GRI. Well, that guest was a tough one. He kicked because the head of the bed was lower than the foot. He ought to be willing to give his feet a chance once in a while. If I'd been the old man, I'd spotted him in the eye for what he said 'cause breakfast was an hour late—only an hour! Reckon an hour of his time isn't so valuable he needs to make a whole neighborhood miserable about it.

SNAG. [*Outside R.*] Here! Back that train right up to the door and bring the provisions inside. Don't swear, sir! Don't swear! There is no reason for it. [*Enters R., carrying paper parcel which he puts on the counter; then goes behind. As he enters there is a noise and a laugh outside*] This is the meanest town I ever saw!

DOL. [*At counter*] What's the matter, sir?

SNAG. Matter? Everything! The boys in the street guy me. I don't see why they should. I'm sure I looked like a hotel-keeper on the top of that load of provisions.

DOL. You must have seemed rather a guy, sir.

SNAG. Go and bring in the provisions. Grimes, help Dolly. [*Grimes laughs and follows Dolly*] You laughing hyena! [*Snaggs takes off hat and puts on smoking cap*] Now I feel tony. [*Enter Dolly with basket. She goes to counter. Grimes carries other things to door L.*]

DOL. Mr. Snaggs, what are the other people in the town to do for food?

SNAG. What do you mean, Dolly?

DOL. Why, you've bought all there was in the town, haven't you?

SNAG. No; only a reasonable supply.

DOL. Reasonable supply! Why, here's a bushel of peas for two people.

SNAG. Is that too much?

DOL. Too much! Why, they'll spoil before half of them are eaten.

SNAG. Give them to Grimes. [*Grimes crosses with basket*]

DOL. Very well, sir. Then you've got eighteen quarts of strawberries. They'll spoil, too. [*Grimes crosses with box*]

SNAG. Give them to Grimes.

DOL. And there's milk enough to last a week. It'll be sour before morning.

SNAG. Eh? Will milk spoil?

DOL. Yes, dreadfully quick. [*Grimes crosses with milk-can*]

SNAG. Well, give it to Grimes.

DOL. But goodness, sir, Grimes can't eat everything.

SNAG. Dolly, you don't know Grimes.

DOL. But Grimes can't eat all this.

SNAG. He must, or I'll bring an action. [*Dolly exits door L. Grimes enters again*]

SNAG. Grimes, come here.

GRI. [*Touches pad on Snaggs*] What's that?

SNAG. Straw.

GRI. What's that for?

SNAG. To give the outside public an idea we keep a good table. [*They both laugh*] Ah, Grimesy, my boy, I've been looking out for you. I've got a bushel of peas, eighteen quarts of strawberries, and sixteen quarts of milk for you to consume. Can you get away with it?

GRI. I'll try.

SNAG. Grimesy, have a drink. [*Snaggs goes behind bar, places decanter and glasses on counter*] Grimes, help yourself. [*Grimes covers glass with his hand, turns back to counter and fills glass nearly full. Snaggs watches him*] I'll give you a towel and let you take a bath. [*Puts decanter and glass away*]

GRI. [*After drinking*] Good stuff, that.

SNAG. Well, it ought to be; it cost me a dollar a gallon. [*Grimes clutches his throat as if in pain; then rushes to water cooler, turns tap and drinks. Then goes to corner R., and pretends to be sick. Business*] Grimes, take that seven-dollar-and-a-quarter look off your face, do you hear, and pay attention. You'll tend bar, answer the bells, and build fires.

GRI. Yes.

SNAG. You'll run the elevator, black boots, wait on table, carry trunks upstairs, attend all trains, take care of the coat-room—and cook. [*Snaggs leans on counter and looks at Grimes through his spectacles*]

GRI. Is that all? Can't you hire me out to the neighbors?

SNAG. No, I don't want to work you too hard. Now, Grimesy, my boy, when I ring this bell [*Rings*]—and call "Front," you must come to the counter at once, understand! Now we'll try it. [*Strikes bell*] Front!

GRI. [*Rushes to the counter*] But why do you call me Front? Why don't you call me Grimes?

SNAG. I don't know. It's always done in first-class hotels. Can you shave? I may call on you to shave some of the customers. I don't care how you get the hair off, so long as you get it off. Say, can you build a fire?

GRI. I reckon I can.

SNAG. Then you can do more than most folks. Let me see you build a fire in that stove.

GRI. But it's a warm day.

SNAG. Never mind. It will be a cold day when I get left. [*Comes from behind counter. Enter Dolly*] Ah, Dolly, come here. Have you done all the work upstairs today?

DOL. Yes, sir.

SNAG. Did you make up the beds clean?

DOL. Yes, sir, and I've changed all the sheets.

SNAG. Tut, tut, tut! That's not the right way. To make up a bed clean, you must turn the sheets.

DOL. But after you've turned them once?

SNAG. Repeat it!

DOL. Will they stand it?

SNAG. By gracious, they've got to, or I'll bring an action! Now, go! Will they stand it in my hotel? [*Dolly exits. Grimes comes from stove, takes off Snaggs's cap, strikes match on his head, goes back to stove, and lights it. Then comes back to C.*]

GRI. Fire's built.

SNAG. Grimesy, you're an artist.

GRI. Then I'll take a cigar.

SNAG. So you shall. [*Snaggs goes behind bar; gives Grimes a cigar. Business*] Now, Grimes, I have here a nice black jacket and a bosom—a—a—what do you call it?

GRI. Front.

SNAG. Yes, a front; and here is something you never saw before, a collar, and a nice white necktie. Now, Grimes, you must fix up and look like a gentleman.

GRI. I don't want to be a gentleman. I want to be tough.

SNAG. There are a number of gentlemen who wear white neckties who look tough; so you're all right. [*Leans on counter*] Now, Grimes, this is important. When a guest arrives—if one should arrive—we want to give him a good impression. First impressions count for a good deal. We want to make him think there's a crowd in this house; so the moment he enters, you rush upstairs and ring all the bells in the house; then you rush down again and carry up pitchers of ice-water. Guests always require ice-water.

GRI. Some folks like something in it just to take out the cruelty.

SNAG. Well, take up a bottle, an empty one—a black bottle, so it won't show that it isn't full.

GRI. Why not take up a full one?

SNAG. Grimesy, my boy, I don't think you'd drink a drop, but then you might spill some and that would be a waste. Now go and see if anyone arrives by the train, and yell out "Grand View Hotel" as loud as you can at the station.

Gri. [*Takes package and goes to door*] Leave it to me. I'll yell loud enough to sour all the milk in the cellar. [*Exits R.*]

Snag. [*C.*] No, don't do that; I've bought sixteen quarts. Well, everything is going nicely. Teddy is willing to cook or do anything that is required. Teddy's a treasure, but I don't think I'd have discovered it if it hadn't been for the opportunity of getting this hotel with her. Queer how a rich girl's good points stand out more prominently than a poor one's. There was Matilda. I wonder where's Matilda. Teddy's a far prettier girl than Matilda. But Matilda was very handsome until that cursed bank broke. But away with thoughts of love. Business is the word. Hello, here's that will. I must put it in my safe. [*Puts will in safe*] Ah, the register. I must have names on the register. Well, I can get them, as I have signatures to a petition. [*Local. Writes names in register. Enter Rose and May*] Customers! [*Strikes bell*] Front! Oh, it's you, is it?

Rose. Yes, it's me, Mr. Snaggs, but you needn't look so cross. We are not going to eat up the place.

Snag. Eat! I wish you would help Grimes. He's got more than he can manage.

May. Mr. Snaggs, what have you done with that will?

Snag. It is in my safe.

Rose. Are you going to let us see it?

Snag. Quite impossible.

Rose. I insist that you let us see that will.

Snag. Yes, my dear girls, but if I won't, what does your insisting amount to?

May. Mr. Snaggs, you're a reprobate! [*Strikes counter*]

Snag. My dear ladies, after being blackguarded by some of the ablest lawyers on earth, nothing you can say can possibly wound me. As a learned friend of mine once said, that my mouth stretched across the wide desolation of my face, the sepulcher of rum and the fountain of falsehood. [*Enter Dolly hurriedly, L.*]

Dol. Mr. Snaggs! Mr. Snaggs, come quick! The kitchen boiler is going to explode! [*Exit Dolly*]

Snag. What? The new boiler! [*Breaks from them. Exits L.*]

May. We must see the will! [*Goes behind counter. Tries safe*] It's locked.

Rose. But we must see it!

May. Yes, but how?

Rose. Easy enough. Disguise ourselves and come here as guests. We will give him some packets which we will say contain jewelry, to put in the safe. Then one of us will want a certain packet and go to the safe to pick it out, and then get hold of the will.

May. That's a splendid idea. Do you know that Tom is here and Snaggs don't know him? He'll help us out. Ah, how I love that boy! [*Teddy is heard singing upstairs. May looks up*] There is Teddy. She mustn't see us. Come along!

Rose. Why, she's got up to stun. She has on a dress and train. She really looks pretty. She's coming downstairs. Come along! [*Exit both R. Teddy enters downstairs, richly dressed. She runs downstage*]

Ted. [*C.*] Where'll those sisters of mine be now, I wonder. I guess I'm as much of a dazzler as anybody. So this is fashion. You economize on the width to be enabled to furnish enough to sweep the ground. If this is style, I don't like it. How can anybody dance with a train like that switching about one's heels? It's the most uncomfortable dress I ever had on. I never could climb a fence in it, and I'm laced so tightly I can't draw a long breath. When I sent for the fashion plate, they sent me a fan with it. A fan is no use to cool one, but it's mighty convenient to flirt with. Now how do they curtsy to a partner? [*Curtsies and stumbles*] Why, one of these things in a ballroom with a thousand people carrying on a conversation must be worse than death. Fancy saying to Mr. Alphonso Jones: "Now, really, you don't mean it! You say that you do, but you don't! You men are such flirts. What's that? Will I dance with you? But I have just danced with you. Will I waltz with you? Then I will. Here's my card. Now, don't put down more than one! I waltz nicely? Ah, you say that to every girl in the room! You don't? Oh, you do! I see it by your face. No, I'm not blushing behind my fan. Is ours the next? [*Crosses*] I won't forget! [*Crosses back*] Oh, here comes Charley for the quadrille. [*Crosses to C.*] Yes, yes, I won't forget! 'The next!' I'll be here. [*Crosses to R.*] Excuse me. *Shall* I be here? Well, I should quiver!" [*Goes through last figure of the lancers, singing the music, calling the figures, ending with grand chain. Then laughs and sits down C. of stage. Enter Dolly, L.D., and Grimes, R. Grimes has on black jacket and white tie, and the word "Hack" printed on his hat. Dolly assists Teddy to rise*]

Gri. Great guns, what a belle she'd be at the B.U.M.S.'s grand ball! Oh, if I only had my pumps on! [*Waltzes a little*]

Dol. Why, Miss Teddy, how beautiful you look! It's a shame to wear such a lovely dress about this dirty old hotel.

Ted. Dolly, the hotel must have tone, even if I have to sacrifice my personal freedom and comfort. Oh!—

Dol. What's the matter?

Ted. There's another lace gone.

Gri. Miss Teddy's got the right idea. Mr. Snaggs said to me, "Grimesy, my boy, wash your face at least once a day! We must be high-toned."

Ted. Say! What makes him call you Grimesy?

Gri. I dunno. Reckon he cottons to me.

Ted. Don't you let him do it!

Gri. Why not?

Ted. Grimes, he's a lawyer, and you know what tricky fellows these law-yers are. If he calls you Grimesy, no good will come of it. He's probably after you for a witness or he wants to trick off a summons on you.

Gri. I believe you're right. I'll keep my eye on him. [*Teddy curtsies to Grimes, who bows, hat in hand*] Miss Teddy, I don't like this collar. It hurts my neck. I want to be tough.

Ted. Grimes, give us a step. [*Teddy pats for him. He dances. At the break she trips him with her train*] Now, escort me to the piano. [*Grimes rushes her to the piano; she plays. Grimes and Dolly sing and dance. Snaggs enters while they are dancing. He touches Dolly, who exits L. Then he kicks Grimes, who exits R., yelling "Grand View Hotel"*]

Snag. [*Sees Teddy at the piano*] What? A guest? And a lady? [*Goes behind counter; takes a drink; returns to C.*] Madam, do you require a room?

Ted. Why, Snaggs, are you above recognizing your own cook?

Snag. Why, bless me, it's Teddy!

Ted. [*Touches pad*] Why, what's that?

Snag. Snaggsy keeps a good table. Where did you get that rig?

Ted. It's one I borrowed.

Snag. Go take it off.

Ted. Never take off tomorrow what you can put on today. Say, let's give a ball. The bloods all do.

Snag. Give a ball? I'd be a nice party to give a ball, wouldn't I? [*Aside*] It would be just my luck to have a drummer come in while she's looking like Cleopatra or the Queen of Sheba. Teddy, you've no idea how much better you look in your old clothes with a black streak down one side of your nose. It is so charmingly conventional.

Ted. I want to be unconventional. I don't like anybody who is conven-tional. The last time we had a convention down here, they all got cham-pagne. [*Imitates drink*]

Snag. I remember. I was there. Teddy, will you marry me?

Ted. Promise me, if I do, that you'll not complain of the bread and say how much better your mother used to make it.

SNAG. Don't ask me to promise that.

TED. But you must. [*Throws herself into his arms. Enter Grimes with a rush*]

GRI. Mr. Snaggs! A customer!

SNAG. A customer!

TED. Where is he?

SNAG. Is he a drummer?

GRI. No, a lightning-rod man. [*Rushes off*]

SNAG. Teddy, go and get breakfast.

TED. What shall I cook?

SNAG. Mush.

TED. And for dinner?

SNAG. Mush.

TED. And for supper?

SNAG. Mush. [*Teddy rushes off L. Snaggs rushes behind counter; strikes a bell*] Front! [*Enter Grimes, and Tom disguised as lightning-rod man*]

GRI. This way, sir. Grand View Hotel—best house, sir. [*Tom goes to counter, puts rods on counter and satchel on floor*]

GRI. [*C.*] The bells. [*Rushes upstairs and down again*]

SNAG. [*Bell*] Front! Go answer 24. [*Grimes rushes up and down again. Bell*] Front! Pitcher of ice-water to 78. [*Business of Grimes rushing about. Bell*] Front! Ice-water to 123. [*To Tom*] Glad to see you, sir. How is everything down below?

TOM. Down below? Where do you think I come from?

SNAG. Why, down at the city. We always speak of it as down below. [*Grimes rushes down, panting; points to his mouth. Snaggs hands him black bottle on waiter. He goes upstairs. Enter Teddy, wearing white apron and carrying a rolling-pin in one hand and pieces of dough in the other*]

TEDDY. Where is the salt?

SNAG. I forgot the salt. Put in yeast.

TED. Where is the yeast?

SNAG. There's a barrel-full.

TED. That is enough to supply the whole country. [*Frightens Tom with rolling-pin*]

TOM. I guess I'll go. [*Goes toward door*]

SNAG. Take a drink. [*Tom drops rods on stage and goes back to counter. They drink*]

TOM. Pretty girl, that.

SNAG. If you call her pretty, you should see her sister.

TOM. I don't think May's pretty.

SNAG. Hey, what did you say?

TOM. I said—rods—all kinds of rods. Don't you want them on your house?

SNAG. Couldn't be hired to have them.

TOM. Do you want to get struck by lightning?

SNAG. Yes. I've been trying all my life to get struck by lightning. [*Holds up bottle*] Jersey lightning. Will you be struck?

TOM. Don't care if I do. [*They drink*]

SNAG. Excuse me, are you a drummer?

TOM. No, sir. I'm the boss of the lightning-rod factory. [*Enter Grimes*]

GRI. Mr. Snaggs, the man upstairs says that the black bottle won't do. He must have the decanter.

SNAG. Grimes, you must be mistaken.

GRI. No, I ain't.

SNAG. [*Aside*] This is a trick for him to get a drink, but I can't refuse before the customer. [*Gives decanter and glass*]

GRI. And he wants four good cigars.

SNAG. [*Drops tray—crash*] Now, Grimes, I'm sure you're mistaken.

GRI. No, I'm not. [*Crosses to counter. Gets cigars*]

SNAG. [*To Grimes*] I'll kill you when he goes.

TOM. Do I get a room?

SNAG. Show the gentleman to number 13. Take the elevator.

GRI. [*Holds up bottle*] I've got it.

SNAG. No! No! The passenger elevator. [*Comes from behind counter*] If everything is not all right, let me know. By the way, breakfast is ready.

TOM. Don't want it.

SNAG. Never mind breakfast, Teddy. [*Tom and Grimes go in elevator. Tom's coat catches in door and is torn off*]

TOM. [*Inside elevator*] Hi! Hi! Stop the car! Stop it! Stop it! [*Elevator descends. Tom jumps out and comes to C.*] Say, boss, see what your blasted car has done.

SNAG. What's the matter?

TOM. Look at my coat-tail. The house shall pay for this.

SNAG. Certainly. [*Examines catch of door*] But we shall have to charge you for the damage you have done to the door by your coat-tail catching in it.

TOM. I won't pay it.

SNAG. I'll bring an action.

TOM. [*Aside*] What's the use of disputing the bill. I don't intend to pay it anyway. [*Aloud*] Very well, sir. Show me up. [*Enters elevator and goes up*]

SNAG. Look out for the back of your trousers. Grimes, look out for that jay. He'll blow the gas out. [*C.*] We have a customer at last. [*Takes satchel*]

I took care not to send this up. [*Shakes it*] Gold, perhaps; old boots, more likely. [*Behind bar*] I'll make Grimes pay for that whiskey. That will be one point gained. [*Grimes and Tom enter room L.*]

GRI. Here's your room, sir.

TOM. How are you at seven-up?

GRI. Bang-up.

TOM. Got a pack of cards?

GRI. Why, certainly. [*Takes cards from pocket. They play*]

SNAG. [*Writing*] One elevator, $1.25. Still, I can't blame Grimes for taking that whiskey. I'd have done it myself, and he's a good, faithful fellow; always at work. [*Grimes takes drink from bottle*] And he thinks Teddy is the homeliest. [*Enter Rose and May. Aside*] More customers. This is affluence. [*Aloud*] Good day, ladies. [*Bell*] Front! [*Bell*] Front! I wonder where the devil Grimes is. [*Bell*] Front! I wonder if that man is killing Grimes.

TOM. They seem to be ringing for you.

GRI. It's no use while this lasts. [*Holds up bottle*]

ROSE. Is this the hotel?

SNAG. It is, madam. [*Bell*] Front! Where is Grimes to—to ring these bells?

MAY. Can you give us rooms? [*She runs scale up*]

SNAG. I beg pardon? [*She runs scale down*]

MAY. What are your terms?

SNAG. Our terms on the fourth floor are ten dollars a day.

ROSE. Isn't that rather high?

SNAG. Yes, of course. The fourth floor is rather high. It is three flights up.

MAY. Don't you give terms to the profession?

SNAG. What profession?

MAY. We will show you. [*Duet by Rose and May during which Dolly enters and dances behind them. At end of dance, Dolly exits*]

SNAG. Take the best room in the house, first floor front, a dollar and a quarter per day, bath included. [*Bell*] Front! I'll kill that Grimes!

TOM. See here, I want my trunk brought upstairs.

GRI. All right, I'll see to it. [*Exits from room. Comes downstairs. Sees ladies*] What, guests? [*Rushes up again to room. Upsets Tom. Rushes down again to counter*]

ROSE. By the way, Mr. Landlord, here are some packages of jewelry that we wish to put in the safe. They'll be perfectly safe there, won't they?

SNAG. As safe as though they were in my own pocket. Grimes, show the ladies up to the first floor, room number 6. Take the elevator.

GRI. But I ain't got through the other job yet.

SNAG. What do you mean? [*Comes from behind counter*]

GRI. Why, I rang the bells, but I haven't taken up the ice-water.

SNAG. Piano.

GRI. No piano, ice-water.

ROSE. What?

SNAG. [*To Grimes*] Sh! Never mind. Show these ladies up.

GRI. But you said when I rung the bells to take up pitchers of ice-water.

SNAG. Sh! Don't give it away. [*Assists ladies into elevator*] Take care of your coat-tails.

ROSE and MAY. What!

GRI. [*In elevator*] But you said when I rung the bells I was to take up ice-water.

SNAG. Yes, yes, that's all right. He's giving away all the ice-water. [*Enter Teddy with a pan of dough. Puts it on the counter*]

TED. Say, Mr. Snaggs, who are they?

SNAG. Two escaped prima donnas.

TED. Any more?

SNAG. Yes. A lightning-rod fiend. [*Enter Rose and May with Grimes, into room R.*]

ROSE. What a wretched room! [*Exit Tom from his room*]

MAY. Dreadful, my dear.

GRI. What! You're not satisfied? I should have showed you the other first and then you'd have liked this.

BOTH. Why?

GRI. The other is so much worse. Why, we have to make the bed in the bathtub. [*Exits downstairs*]

SNAG. [*Writes in account book*] Pitcher of ice-water, seventy-five cents. [*Comes to C. Meets Grimes*] Grimesy, my boy, as a hotel corps, you're a success.

GRI. Well, what you don't know about running a hotel ain't worth knowing.

SNAG. Grimes, you're splendid! How am I?

GRI. It ain't for me to say. Just ask your friends what I says about you. [*They embrace*]

TED. Look at 'em. You can't blame them for admiring each other. [*Teddy brings in clothes to make up dummy, which she does while Gilly is on the stage. Voices outside and sound of coach. Grimes exits. Snaggs goes behind counter*]

SNAG. [*Bell*] Front!

GIL. [*Outside*] It's a swindle, sir. I never pay more than twenty-five cents.

GRI. [*Outside*] You don't pay that very often, I reckon. [*Enter Gilly disguised as Colonel St. Clair Bray, followed by Grimes, who seizes Gilly's satchel and throws it into the coat-room*]

GIL. [*C.*] Check.

SNAG. [*Gives check to Grimes*] Check that man. [*Grimes fixes strap in Gilly's buttonhole*]

TED. That's right. He looks as though he'd get lost if he wasn't checked.

GIL. Boy, black my rubbers! [*Throws them to Grimes*]

SNAG. [*Bell*] Front! Attend to the guest.

GIL. I must have missed the committee. Not my fault, as I did not leave home till two hours after I'd started. [*Takes off hat; puts it on counter; goes to water cooler; takes off top; dips his hands in; then dips shoe-brush in; brushes hair, etc.*]

SNAG. That's ice-water. Grimes, give him the key to the bathroom. [*Gilly looks around for towel*] Grimes, give him a towel. [*Grimes takes off white necktie; offers it. Gilly takes bill from the counter, wipes his hands upon it, puts it into his pocket. Then he leans on the counter*]

GIL. Don't you know me?

TED. Of course he does. He's always in hard luck. [*Exit Grimes*]

SNAG. Know you? Certainly. You are—[*Aside*] Who the devil is he?—[*Aloud*] I recognize you as—

GIL. Colonel St. Clair Bray, a member of the 48th Congress, and a great humanitarian. Why, I've saved more lives in my ward than any other man has taken. [*During the speech Teddy has placed his hat on the floor in C. of stage and put a brick under it*]

TED. Why, colonel, how are you? [*Shakes hands with him, leaving a piece of dough in his hand*]

GIL. [*Disgusted*] That's a pretty deal to give a colonel! [*Throws piece of dough at Snaggs; sees hat on stage; kicks it; hurts his foot and limps to water cooler; puts foot in water bucket. Teddy is kneeling down by the counter with the piece of dough in her hand*]

TED. [*To Gilly*] Say, boss, two to one I hit!

GIL. Go it, my girl! [*Teddy throws dough at Snaggs's head and a large piece at his stomach. Snaggs picks it up from the cash register, on which it fell, and hangs it on the key-board*]

SNAG. [*To Gilly*] You're no gentleman, sir!

GIL. [*At counter*] What's that?

SNAG. [*Blows flour from register into Gilly's face*] You're no gentleman.

GIL. I'm no slouch.

SNAG. You look it. [*Snaggs is writing in register. Gilly takes walnut from his pocket and hammer from counter and cracks the nut on Snaggs's head. He tries to do it a second time. Snaggs prevents him and knocks off his hat. Grimes comes in and puts a cocoanut on Gilly's head and is about to crack it with an axe, when Gilly turns and prevents him. Gilly then shakes hands with Snaggs. During this scene Teddy makes up the dummy*]

GIL. Well, is the committee here to greet me?

SNAG. Haven't seen any.

GIL. Am I not to have a serenade?

SNAG. Haven't heard of it.

GIL. Am I not to address the crowd?

SNAG. We have no crowd.

GIL. Then get me a crowd and a serenade.

SNAG. [*Bell*] Front! Be a crowd and a serenade for this man.

GRI. Hooray! Hooray! Hooray! [*Exits*]

GIL. Do I get a room? [*Looks at register. Aside*] Fisk! That must be Tom. Room 13. [*Aloud*] Does Colonel St. Clair Bray, member of the 48th Congress, get a room? I want a room with a door and a window in it, and hot and cold gas.

SNAG. Do you want running water?

GIL. Yes, I want running water.

SNAG. Turn up the pitcher and it will run. [*Bell*] Front! Show the member for Congress up to 106.

GIL. [*To Grimes*] Young man, are you a voter?

GRI. I am.

GIL. Are you with me, or are you agin' me?

GRI. I am with you.

SNAG. [*C.*] Hold on, colonel. I vote in two precincts.

GIL. I'm looking for repeaters.

SNAG. You'll need them. [*Gilly takes Snaggs's arm; goes to elevator; Snaggs goes in, rings bell. Gilly goes back for his hat. Elevator goes up without him; Gilly comes back and finds it gone*]

GIL. I guess I'll walk. [*Exits upstairs*]

TED. Grimes, you got left that time.

GRI. I'll find out that fellow's name and get the B.U.M.S. to vote against him. [*Enter Matilda; goes to C.; looks around*]

GRI. Chase that out.

TED. [*To Grimes*] Who's this? Is it a sweetheart of yours?

GRI. [*Goes up to Matilda, winks at her; then goes to door*] Cuckoo! [*Exits*]

MAT. What's the matter with that young man? His face is ugly enough without twisting it like that. [*Teddy places chair. Matilda sits down C.*]

TED. Oh, you mustn't mind him. He's a poet, and we always allow him poetic license.

MAT. Well, I'm not looking for a poet. I'm in search of one of the meanest little miscreants that ever tampered with a woman's affections.

TED. What's he like?

MAT. He's like nothing. He's a little, short, nearsighted, peevish, cheeky lawyer, who never won a case in his life.

TED. Such men are plenty enough. What's his name?

MAT. Snaggs.

TED. [*Aside*] Our Snaggsy! [*Aloud*] What do you want of him?

MAT. I want him to repair the damage he has done my heart.

TED. How did he do it?

MAT. Six months ago when I had $30,000 in the Pacific Bank, he asked me to marry him; and as I loved him, I consented. Then the bank failed and he deserted me.

TED. He's not such a fool as he looks.

MAT. Eh? But I would not tamely submit. I sued him for $20,000 damages for breach of promise. He insisted on pleading his own case; so, of course, I won. Here's a copy of the judgment against him and I mean he shall pay every cent of it, or marry me.

TED. [*Aside*] The mercenary monkey! He asked me to marry him!

MAT. I hear he is in this house. Where can I find him?

TED. He just went up to the top floor. Room 106. [*Exit Matilda upstairs*] It's lucky I never loved this man. Shall I expose him at once? No. Better later. That man Snaggs would do more things that other folks wouldn't do than anybody else I ever saw. If I fall in love with him, they'll say I'm eccentric. [*Enter Snaggs with a jump from the elevator*]

SNAG. Well, I got here.

TED. Make me a lemonade.

SNAG. Got no lemons.

TED. Business is improving, isn't it? We shan't be more than fifty dollars out today.

SNAG. We shan't be any behind, Teddy. I don't know what the actual expenses for running a hotel will be, but whatever it is, that lightning-rod man will pay it in the way of extras.

TED. But suppose he doesn't have any extras.

SNAG. He's got to. Here's Dolly. I'll begin on him now. [*Enter Dolly*] Dolly, take a lot of towels up to 13.

Dol. That hog is loose again and rooting up the garden.

Snag. Great heavens! That hog loose again? That's the third time today. He must think that pigpen is a jail, he gets out so easily. [*Exits with Dolly, L. Enter Matilda, room R.*]

Mat. [*To Rose and May*] Mr. Snaggs here?

Rose. No, he's in the office.

Mat. Oh, indeed. [*Exits*]

May. Who is that?

Rose. I don't know. Let's go and see. [*Exit. Enter Grimes with a trunk on his shoulders. He tries to carry it upstairs, but Teddy stops him each time. At last he drops the trunk and sinks down on it*]

Ted. Hello, Grimes. What's the matter?

Gri. I've got to take this trunk upstairs.

Ted. How easy you carry it!

Gri. It's not so easy as it looks.

Ted. I should think you'd hurt yourself carrying such a heavy load. Even if a trunk does seem heavy at first, I should think it would appear heavier after you held it a while.

Gri. Well, it does. [*He weakens*]

Ted. Say, Grimes, how far has that trunk got to go?

Gri. Three flights. I shall never get there.

Ted. How much does the trunk weigh?

Gri. It weighed about two hundred when I picked it up. Now it weighs about four hundred.

Ted. Say, I'm real sorry for you, Grimes. I should think you'd break your back with such heavy loads.

Gri. I'm beginning to think so.

Ted. But you don't mind it.

Gri. Not much. But it's tough work.

Ted. Still you'd rather do it than work. [*Here Grimes drops the trunk. Enter Rose and May downstairs. Tom and Gilly from elevator*]

Rose. There's that homely sister of ours.

Gil. [*Crosses to Rose*] Dear Rosey!

Rose. Hush! Don't you see Teddy?

Gil. She'll recognize me. How can I avoid it?

Rose. Why, go and make love to her.

Gil. Of course. That always confuses a woman so that she don't know what is the matter. [*Crosses to Teddy*] Ah, fair young lady.

Ted. Yes, fair to middling. What do you want? [*Flicks duster in his face*]

Rose. [*To Grimes*] Be careful of our wardrobe.

MAY. What sort of a towel do you call this? [*Shows a very small one*]

GRI. You can only wash your face once a day in this hotel and that's law. [*Enter Matilda downstairs; she pushes Tom, who falls; she steps on him and crosses to counter. Grimes crosses to door*]

MAT. [*To Teddy*] Where's Mr. Snaggs?

TED. Gone to Somerville, fifty miles away.

MAT. I'd follow him if it were a thousand. [*Crosses to door, R.; pulls Grimes's nose; exits*]

TED. [*To Gilly*] Are you an opera singer?

GIL. No, I'm a politician.

TED. Well, you look as though you'd enjoy a good fight, but there are opera singers here. [*Crosses to Rose and May*] Maybe you're them.

ROSE and MAY. Yes, we are.

TED. You know something about music, I suppose.

ROSE and MAY. Yes, we do.

TED. Then sing something.

ROSE. We never sing.

TED. What! Opera singers and never sing?

MAY. [*Aside to Rose*] We must sing something or she'll suspect us. Come along. [*Enter Dolly. Medley. At conclusion of medley, all exit but Teddy. Dolly and Tom. Tom comes down C., takes out his handkerchief, wipes Teddy's cheek, kisses it, and exits slowly up the stairs*]

DOL. [*Laughs*] Oho! So you're just like other girls.

TED. Well, he's very much of a gentleman. His manners are much superior to the other guests', those opera singers. You'd think they wanted the earth and meant to put a fence around it. Now this gentleman was very reasonable. All he wanted was a little kiss.

DOL. Why, don't you know him?

TED. Yes, he's the lightning-rod man.

DOL. Why, no, it's Tom, and the two opera singers are your sisters. They've come here in disguise to make Snaggs sick of the hotel, and I'm going to help them. [*Business*] Good-by, Miss Teddy, good-by. [*Exits*]

TED. H'm. Ain't I mad! And Tom kissed me! I won't stand it! I'll have revenge! I know what I'll do. I'll fix up as a drummer, come here and worry the life out of all of them. I'll make them wish they were all dead. They shan't make a fool out of me! [*Goes behind counter; rings the bell in imitation of Snaggs. Bell*] Front! [*Enter Grimes; rushes to counter; sees Teddy; is disgusted*]

GRI. Ah, what are you giving me? [*Teddy whispers to him and turns his face towards the dummy; pantomimes to him to throw it out. He does so.*

Teddy laughs and exits. Grimes goes up and sits on trunk. Enter Snaggs, very drunk; reels against stove; puts his hand upon it and burns himself. He reels to trunk and sits down]

GRI. I've got to take this trunk upstairs.

SNAG. I'll help you. [*Business of lifting and dropping it*] Grimes, come and take a drink. [*Both go behind counter, drink, and return*] Let's haul it up. [*Grimes gets ladder and Snaggs gets ropes. Business with the ladder*] Tie this to the trunk. [*Grimes lets go ladder; ladder falls with Snaggs on it; Snaggs gets up, goes for drink, followed by Grimes; both return to trunk; try to lift it; then sit on it exhausted*] Oh, let them carry their own trunk up. [*Enter Teddy with piece of dough which she puts over Snaggs's mouth. He takes it and puts it in his pocket*]

TED. [*Aside to Grimes*] Don't you let him call you Grimesy. [*Goes to counter*]

GRI. All right, Miss Teddy.

SNAG. Grimesy, my boy—

GRI. I don't want you to call me Grimesy. If you call me Grimesy again, you'll have to hire other help. I'll quit!

SNAG. Grimes, are you crazy?

GRI. Miss Teddy put me onto your racket.

SNAG. Teddy? Don't name her! You acme of imbecility, pay attention. It's about the only thing you're able to pay. I love Teddy, but have every reason to believe she is not reciprocal. I don't think she loves me at all.

GRI. I reckon you're right.

TED. You bet he is. [*Exits*]

SNAG. Now I want to test her love. Will you help me?

GRI. What are you going to do?

SNAG. Hang myself.

GRI. [*Quickly*] You bet I'll help you.

SNAG. First, I shall propose to her. If she refuses me I will stab her to the heart [*Pause*]—with a look. I will then take a last fond adieu and proceed to hang myself with this rope. Then when I kick the trunk away, it is for you, my noble Grimesy, to rush from your concealment and save me by cutting the rope.

GRI. How shall I know when you are dead enough?

SNAG. You fool, I don't die!

GRI. Who does, Miss Teddy?

SNAG. I assume to die, when you cut me down.

GRI. Knock you down?

SNAG. Cut me down! This thing's got twisted.

GRI. How shall I know when to cut you down?

SNAG. When I say, "Farewell forever," you rush from your concealment and exclaim, "Master, I will save you!"

GRI. "Farewell forever. Master, I shall save you!"

SNAG. You hang me successfully, I will give you two dollars.

GRI. Two dollars, remember.

SNAG. Let me see. I shout, "Farewell forever." You rush forth and exclaim, "Master, I will save you." Perhaps we had better try it once. You hide behind the counter. [*Grimes goes behind counter and hides*] Homely beauty! Empress of my soul! Be my bride, ne'er so e'er what may betide. Then farewell forever!

GRI. [*Rushes out*] Miss Teddy, I will save you!

SNAG. You idiotic essence of insanity, you don't save Miss Teddy, but me!

GRI. Oh, I do, do I? Now I see.

SNAG. Now don't come too soon. [*Pause*] And for heaven's sake, don't come too late! [*Teddy heard singing*] By Blackstone, she's coming! Now, Grimes, conceal yourself! [*Grimes goes behind counter. Snaggs down C.F., kneeling. Enter Teddy*]

TED. [*Aside*] Now the ball begins. [*Aloud*] Mr. Snaggs, have you seen Dolly?

SNAG. Oh, Teddy, my soul's delight!

TED. Mr. Snaggs, you've been drinking.

SNAG. You shouldn't notice it. It is not good breeding to notice a man's been drinking.

TED. How well-bred the police are—sometimes.

SNAG. Teddy, I've been trying to drown my sorrows caused by your cruelty.

TED. Did you succeed?

SNAG. Hic! Pretty well. Teddy, tell me that you love me.

TED. Mr. Snaggs, I will be candid with you. I have tried to love you, heaven knows how often. But it is no use. Every time I think of you it recalls to my memory that dear delightful Mike, with whom you were so intimately associated, you know, and that drives all thoughts of love from my mind. It's no use, Snaggsy. I can never bring myself to love you. So farewell forever.

GRI. [*Rushes out with saw*] Snaggsy, I will save you! Two dollars!

SNAG. You are too soon. Wait till I hang. [*Grimes throws down saw, disgusted. Goes upstage to piano. Lies down on stage*]

SNAG. Teddy, you are cruel.

TED. And you are a fool.

SNAG. Teddy, will you marry me?

TED. N—no. [*Screams*]

SNAG. It's no use. I must try the hanging. [*Teddy leans on the counter. Snaggs crosses to her, crying*] You are wiping your feet on my heart. [*Goes to trunk, gets up on it, puts rope around his neck, looks anxiously around for Grimes*] I wonder if Grimes will remember. Teddy, you know not what I suffer. For your sake I seek a watery grave. [*Looks around for Grimes*] Farewell forever! [*Kicks trunk away and yells, "Grimes, Grimes, Grimes!" All rush on stage screaming. Teddy laughs*]

GRI. [*Rushes down C.*] Master, I will save you!

ACT III.

SCENE: *Same as Act II.*

DISCOVERED: *Gilly disguised as the Colonel in chair R. Tom as lightning-rod man behind counter. Rose upstage L. May at counter. Snaggs lying on bed in room R.*

ROSE. [*Comes downstage*] Where's Gilly? Oh, there you are. Now, Gilly, how long is this masquerading going to last?

MAY. Yes, Tom, are we to keep it up forever?

TOM. Why, we must continue until Snaggs gives up this hotel.

GIL. But he can't have the hotel.

TOM. Well, he's got it.

GIL. But he can't keep it.

TOM. But he is keeping it.

ROSE. It's not that I want the hotel. It doesn't belong to me anyway.

GIL. Now, Rosy.

ROSE. I tell you it don't, but I don't want him to have it.

MAY. That's what I say.

TOM. Now, May.

MAY. Don't you say it belongs to me. Rose and I are agreed that it belongs to Teddy. And if a drummer ever arrives it will be given to her and we don't mean to see her swindled out of it.

TOM. Oh, Teddy won't get it. She's pretty. And we'd better see that codicil, anyway, before deciding that it belongs to anybody.

GIL. Well, Snaggs shan't have it, if I have to lick him. [*All laugh*]

MAY. Why, you couldn't lick anything.

GIL. Then I'll hire somebody to do it. [*Enter Sam Potts*]

POTTS. Hello! Who's the boss of this shebang?

GIL. The fellow who happens to be the biggest man is boss around here.

POTTS. Then I'm the boss here and don't you forget it.

ROSE. Well, don't quarrel with my Gilly.

GIL. Quarrel? Say, can you fight?

POTTS. Can I? Feel that! [*Puts up fists*]

GIL. That's enough. I see you can. Would you lick a man for money?

POTTS. I'd try. [*Points to Tom*] Is that the man?

MAY. [*Frightened*] No, no, no!

GIL. I'll tell you what I want. You take a room here as a prize fighter, and knock the life out of Snaggs and Grimes. Can you give them a good licking for ten dollars?

TOM. Give him twelve and make a sure thing of it. You be here in an hour. [*Potts goes upstage and exits. Enter Dolly*]

GIL. Dolly, where's Snaggs?

DOL. [*To Rose*] Grimes put him to bed in your room. [*Exits*]

ROSE and MAY. What?

GIL. You wake him up with a chorus. [*Song and dance. Gilly goes upstairs and wakes Snaggs. Brings him down. At end of chorus, he goes behind counter*]

SNAG. [*Bell. And in a very weak voice*] Front!

ROSE. Mr. Snaggs, why don't you attend to your customers?

MAY. What time does the noon train for the West leave over the B.B. and G.?

SNAG. [*Hands her a book*] The noon train leaves at two P.M.

GIL. See here, I must write to the *Tribune* that I've had a good evening here and addressed the crowd. Give me some paper.

TOM. What time is dinner?

SNAG. [*Bell*] Front! [*Enter Grimes, slowly, downstairs*] Is anybody getting dinner?

GRI. Everybody but us.

ROSE. [*At elevator*] I wish to be taken up.

SNAG. Grimes, call a policeman to take her up.

ROSE. What!

SNAG. Never mind the policeman.

GRI. Nobody ever does.

MAY. Where's the Sangus Branch Road?

SNAG. Somewhere at the other end of the state.

GIL. See here, am I to have only one sheet of paper?

SNAG. Oh, have a thousand sheets of paper! Have a toothpick! Have a watermelon! Take the earth! Take 'em all! Get out! [*Throws sheet of paper at him. Enter Dolly*]

DOL. Mr. Snaggs, have you bought a rattrap?

MAY. Shall I ever know about that train?

TOM. Do we have any food in this house?

ROSE. Is the elevator running?

SNAG. [*At telephone*] Hello. What? Yes. No. I don't owe her a cent. I paid the wash bill last week. [*All commence to talk to him at once, confusing him*]

GIL. A pitcher of ice-water for Colonel St. Clair Bray.

SNAG. [*Bell*] Front! Take a pitcher of Jackass Bray to ice floor. Change cars at 13.

GRI. All aboard for the G.I.T., U.P., and G.I.T.

SNAG. Oh, you get up and get. [*All commence to talk again*]

GRI. Will you take Ella?

TOM. What Ella?

GRI. Elevator. [*Rose and May go into elevator; Tom upstairs; Gilly to piano; Dolly follows Snaggs*]

DOL. [*Loudly*] Mr. Snaggs!

SNAG. Oh, get out! [*Runs her out of the door. Gilly commences to sing and hammer at the piano. Snaggs shuts it; Gilly opens it; Snaggs shuts it again*]

GIL. Look here, if I can't sing and play down here, I want a piano in my room, and don't you forget it! [*Exits*]

SNAG. [*Bell*] Front! Take a piano upstairs, and don't you forget it! [*Lights a cigar, which explodes. He comes to C. Business with hat*] Grimes, get me a shoehorn. My hat has got smaller. Well, the fun in a drunk is not in the getting over it. I feel as if I had swallowed an alarm clock. [*Puts his hands in pockets and finds dough. Pulls it out and looks disgusted*] I wonder who put that in my pocket. [*Throws it at Grimes. Discovers pad gone*] Grimes, I've lost the straw. [*Grimes starts to look for it*] There, never mind. Where have you been, you ingrate? You have acted most shabbily in this affair.

GRI. Why, Mr. Snaggs, I thought you were dead and went for a burial permit, and also to get the B.U.M.S. to turn out for the funeral.

SNAG. When I go fishing, I'll take you along with me to record the catch —you are such a liar! [*Goes up and sits by stove*]

GRI. Mr. Snaggs, why don't you join that association?

SNAG. What? The bums?

GRI. No. The Brakemen's United Merciful Society.

SNAG. Where's the advantage?

GRI. Why, if you die, they pass a resolution that you are dead. Mr. Snaggs, how about that two dollars?

SNAG. What two dollars?

GRI. The two dollars for the hanging.

SNAG. What are you talking about?

GRI. [*Upstage*] The two dollars you promised me right up there.

SNAG. Then go right up there and get it. I never promised you two dollars.

GRI. Yes you did, and I want it.

SNAG. Well, you don't get it.

GRI. I'll bring an action. [*Goes behind counter. Enter Dolly with a telegram*]

DOL. Mr. Snaggs, a dispatch. [*Laughs at him. Exits L.*]

SNAG. [*Reads*] "Save me two rooms. Will arrive on first train. Lawrence Jenkins." [*Comes to C.*] Grimes, we'll boom here today. Grab things. [*Grimes grabs cigars*] Hold on! Hold on! Put those back! [*Grimes does so*] Anybody getting dinner?

GRI. No. She gave out.

SNAG. Who?

GRI. Miss Teddy. She won't be back for an hour.

SNAG. Then they must wait for supper. Turn that clock back two hours. [*Grimes does so*] Now then, they will miss the train and have to wait over twenty-four hours. There's diplomacy. Now go to the station and see if you can lasso something.

GRI. [*Goes to door, whistles, and holds up two fingers*] Two dollars!

SNAG. Well, you don't get it. [*Exit Grimes. Snaggs comes around counter; leans on it; looks at bottle; goes behind counter; takes up decanter and glass; pours out a drink; puts it to his lips; shudders; puts it back*] Ugh! Nasty stuff! [*Comes back to C.*] This is not the most pleasant pathway of roses in life. I wonder if I have to cook the dinner. [*Goes behind bar*] I begin to think Teddy is not the homeliest. [*Sound of a coach outside. Bell*] Front! [*Enter Teddy dressed as a drummer, coat on arm, sample case in one hand, grip in the other. Gives grip and coat to Grimes; puts sample case on counter. Grimes puts coat and grip in coat-room*]

TED. Boy, check my coat. Take my bag. [*Writes name on register; wipes pen on Snaggs's head*] How are you?

SNAG. Fair to middling. How are you? And how is trade?

TED. Booming. I'll match you for the cigars, heads I win, tails you lose.

SNAG. No, don't trouble. I'm sure to lose, been losing all day. [*Hands over cigar box; Teddy takes one and gives it to Grimes*]

TED. Here, boy. Here's my check. Send for my stuff. Brush me. [*Grimes brushes Teddy; waits for fee*]

SNAG. It's no use, Grimes. You won't get a cent out of him. He's from— [*Snaggs leans his head on his hands. Grimes whistles, walks to door, holds up two fingers*]

GRI. Two dollars!

SNAG. You don't get it.

TED. How are you—full?

SNAG. Not now.

TED. Do I get a room?

SNAG. Certainly. Fourth floor, $5.00 a day; first floor, $1.25; third floor, $4.00; second floor, two for a quarter, two children count as one, nurses half price; a fire escape in every room in the house. This house has been burned down five times, and not a soul escaped—I mean perished.

TED. Have you a sample room?

SNAG. Oh, yes. What is it? Whiskey? Help yourself.

TED. No, no. You don't understand. Have you never heard of the firm of Bilson Geer and Company?

SNAG. No, sir.

TED. Largest house in the country. We sell more hair restorer than all competitors. In fact, sir, in five years there won't be a bald-headed man in the country.

SNAG. Medicine pretty fatal then, eh?

TED. Might be fatal in your case. Softening of the brain is coincident with its use. Give me a towel. [*Snaggs hands towel; puts his head down for Teddy to rub*]

SNAG. When you get through with me, put me back. [*After Teddy gets through rubbing his head, Snaggs stands a moment and then commences to dance; he tears leaf out of register and fans his head*] Pretty hot, ain't it? [*Enter Grimes with trunk*]

TED. Handle that carefully, my man. Do you know what it contains!

GRI. Lead, ain't it?

TED. No. Hair restorer.

GRI. Well, all hair restorers contain lead. Still fools will use them.

TED. Here's my key. Open it. [*Grimes starts upstairs with trunk*]

SNAG. [*Bell*] Front! [*Grimes drops trunk downstairs; falls over it; picks himself up and goes to counter*] Take that trunk upstairs. [*Grimes takes trunk and turns it end on end upstairs*]

TED. Say, judge, any fun in town? Any dances? What's become of that little daisy that used to call out cash? [*Takes a handful of matches from box on counter*]

SNAG. Take as many matches as you want. They don't cost me a cent.

TED. [*Goes up to piano; touches it*] The piano's a little off, like everything else in this house. [*Goes to counter*] Got any pretty chambermaids?

SNAG. Yes, one. [*Rose and May enter room L.*]

TED. What's her name?

SNAG. Teddy.

TED. [*Aside*] So I am a chambermaid, am I? [*Rose pulls bell-rope. Bell rings*] Excuse me, do you hear those bells?

SNAG. Oh, that's all right. I know what that means. He'll take up ice-water in a minute.

TED. Say, have you a good lawyer in town?

SNAG. [*Excited*] A good lawyer? Yes, sir! A great man! Light of his profession! What sort of a case?

TED. Ever win a case?

SNAG. No, but he never got beaten so badly as he might.

TED. Well, I've got a case and want your advice. A man bought hair restorer, used it, didn't go according to directions. Always had black hair. Hair grew out red in bald spots. Sues us for damages.

SNAG. Well, I should advise him to shave his head clear and use the hair restorer all over it. As I once said to a jury—

TED. Excuse me, you talk more like a lawyer than a hotel-keeper. But I see—you are always at the bar.

SNAG. Never by your invitation, however. You see, in our business customers must have actions brought against them; so a man managing a hotel has to know something about law. [*Grimes enters downstairs with bottle of hair restorer and wig on with hair off in patches. Goes to counter. Snaggs looks at Grimes's head and then rushes to water cooler and lets water pour on his head. Grimes exits door R. Rose and May appear on stairs*]

ROSE and MAY. Do we have our bells answered, or do we not?

SNAG. You do—

ROSE and MAY. Very well.

SNAG. Not.

ROSE and MAY. Oh, very well. [*Exit upstairs*]

SNAG. You see, that's always the way. When you answer the bells, they say, "Very well," and when you don't answer them they say, "Oh, very well."

GIL. [*Enters room R. and gets into bed*] Empty is the cradle. Baby's gone. [*Bed turns up*] Help! Help! [*Grimes enters stage with very small trunk. Starts upstairs with it*]

SNAG. [*Bell*] Front! Go and see what's the matter upstairs. [*Exit Grimes*]

TED. Have you had the merry war here?

SNAG. Yes. All day.

TED. Do you know, the easiest way is the best.

SNAG. Dare say it is. Never tried it. We've done everything in a deucedly hard way. [*Enter Grimes*]

GRI. That man was nearly killed. The bed turned up.

SNAG. I'm glad something has turned up. [*Enter Gilly downstairs, covered with plaster; hat smashed*]

GIL. Now, I really must complain. As I was sitting in my room, cogitating, the ceiling fell down completely, mashing me. My hat is ruined and my mouth is full of hair and mortar.

TED. Very mortar-fying.

GIL. Then again I find a stone imitation of a cake of soap in the water to wash with, no towels, no anything. And every time I lie down on that combination bed, it closes up and insists on being a bureau. I've just crawled out of the drawer to have my head cracked by the plaster.

TED. Do I eat? Because I must go out and drum up customers.

SNAG. [*Aside*] Drum up customers? [*Aloud*] Are you a drummer?

TED. Yes, I'm a drummer.

GIL. [*Aside*] A drummer! I'll tell the girls. I must tell Rose not to look pretty. [*Goes to stairs; meets Tom; points to Teddy and whispers to Tom; Tom rushes out of door R.*]

TED. And I'm a stranger in this town.

SNAG. At last we have the man to give a verdict. Come and take a drink.

TED. Thanks. I don't drink.

SNAG. What? A drummer, and don't drink? Oh, come, that won't do!

TED. Well, just this time. [*Snaggs drinks. Teddy throws hers over her shoulder. Business of Grimes. Gilly enters room, R.*]

GIL. Rose! May! Don't look pretty! There's a drummer downstairs!

ROSE. A drummer? Then we must look our best.

MAY. Certainly. We don't want this old hotel.

GIL. You're real mean. [*Exit Gilly, followed by Rose and May*]

TED. Here, Grimesy.

GRI. I say, don't you call me Grimesy!

TED. Well, give us a shine.

GRI. Five or ten?

TED. Ten. A man can't afford to be mean with his feet. [*Sits on chair. Enter Rose and May*]

ROSE. Mr. Landlord, I want my room changed.

SNAG. Ladies generally do.

MAY. Will you change the carpet in my room? It does not suit my complexion. It's too green.

SNAG. I'll have Grimes whitewash it in the morning.

TED. [*Aside*] There's Rose and May. I'll fix them. [*Aloud*] I say, girls, what are you—dummies to a milliner?

ROSE. I don't know what you mean, sir.

TED. Oh, you don't? Too bad! Maybe you belong to a Pinafore Church Choir company.

MAY. Sir, we are from the Grand Opera de Paree! [*Runs scale*]

TED. Oh! Well, you do look Irish.

GRI. Change feet.

MAY. He's laughing at us.

TED. I say, giddy girls, you look too sweet for anything. Is your hair your own? [*They scream and put their hands to their heads*]

MAY. [*Crosses to R.*] I don't like that man. [*Exits R.*]

TED. Ta, ta, giddy girls!

ROSE. [*Crosses to R.*] Sir, you're no gentleman! [*Exits R.*]

TED. I'm well aware of it.

SNAG. [*Laughs*] It was very wrong to insult my customers, but it was damned amusing.

GIL. [*Appears in room L. Coat off; board on forehead*] This matter is growing serious. He is to dispose of the property, and it is to go to the homeliest. I'll go out, dress myself up as Rose, and personate her to this drummer and get the decision in her favor. [*Exits*]

TED. Thank you, Grimesy, my boy. Keep the change.

GRI. He's a dandy. [*Looks at money*] Keep the change out of a cent! [*Goes to door; whistles; holds up two fingers*]

SNAG. You don't get it. [*Enter Gilly downstairs; he is stopped by Teddy*]

TED. Hello. Haven't I seen you before?

GIL. No, sir.

TED. No? But I'm sure I've seen you. Didn't you once live in Abilene, Kansas?

GIL. No, sir.

TED. Ain't you the fellow that was tarred and feathered for tricky proceedings?

GILLY. No, sir. [*Snaggs crosses to door R.*]

TED. Ain't you the man that was rode on a rail for jumping bail?

GIL. No, sir. [*Goes to door. Is stopped by Snaggs*]

SNAG. Would you just as soon pay your bill now?

GIL. No, sir. [*Pushes Snaggs out of the way. Exits to change for a girl*]

SNAG. [*To Teddy*] Do you think he'll pay his bill?

TED. No, sir. Well, he may. He is not a drummer.

SNAG. But you are. And now to business. Well, this hotel belonged to a man who has just died, and by his will he left the property to the homeliest of his three nieces. Comprehend?

TED. Perfectly.

SNAG. Now the first drummer who arrived after the will was read was to decide which of the three should have the property.

TED. Was that all there was in the will?

SNAG. No, there was a clause, a codicil.

TED. [*Excited*] Yes— Well—

SNAG. Never mind that. Now you are the first drummer who has arrived.

TED. So I am to decide which girl gets the property! Where are the girls?

SNAG. Hold on a bit! I want you to give the property to Teddy.

TED. What!

SNAG. Oh, don't get excited! I'm rather in hard luck and have got to have money. I think I can get Teddy to marry me.

TED. [*Aside*] The conceited wretch! [*Aloud*] You're in love with Teddy?

SNAG. Oh, no. I'm in love with the hotel. Now you decide in favor of Teddy, and whenever you come this way, your bill will be paid for when you call for it. See? [*Aside*] Oh, if I could only borrow Grimes's face for Teddy! I'm sure she'd get the property! I must go and find Teddy. [*Enter Dolly*] Dolly, find Teddy!

DOL. I was just going out.

SNAG. Then go out and find her. [*Exit Snaggs*]

DOL. [*Looks at Teddy*] Oh, what a nice young man! [*Exits R.*]

TED. I wouldn't marry Snaggs now if he were the last man on earth! He merely wants me for money. Oh, there's no trusting a man. But he spoke of the codicil. I wonder what was in it. I must see it. [*Enter Matilda*]

MAT. I've looked all about the station and I cannot find Snaggs. Excuse me, sir. Where is he?

TED. He? Who?

MAT. Snaggs.

TED. He just went into the garden.

MAT. Thank you, sir. [*Exits C.D. Enter Rose, R.*]

Rose. [*Aside*] So this is the drummer? [*Crosses to counter. Looks at register*] His name is Lawrence Jenkins.

Ted. She's finding out my name. I'll sail in and mash her. [*Enter Snaggs from L. door. Goes upstairs*]

Ted. I beg pardon. You were pointed out to me as the heiress of this place.

Rose. I! Nothing of the sort! So you've heard about the will, sir! Very singular, isn't it? I'm not one of the family, but I know the girls very well. I beg pardon, you're the drummer, are you not?

Ted. The coarse and untutored call us drummers, but in polite language we are commercial tourists.

Rose. Then you'll be called upon to decide which of the three girls gets the property. Perhaps I can give you some information about them.

Ted. I hope the homeliest is as pretty as you are.

Rose. The prettiest one—decidedly the prettiest one—is Rose.

Ted. Oh, the prettiest one is Rose?

Rose. Yes, she's a delicious girl. May is very pretty, too; not so pretty a girl as Rose, but charming. [*Enter Matilda C.D. Exits L.D.*]

Ted. How about the other?

Rose. What? Teddy? Well, she's a nice girl, but there's no earthly excuse for calling her pretty. She's absolutely homely.

Ted. So Rose is the prettiest!

Rose. You'll, of course, give the property to Teddy.

Ted. I don't know. I might be so charmed with Rose I'd fall in love with her and give her the property out of favoritism.

Rose. Don't you do it! Don't you dare to do it, if you value your eyes, for they'd get scratched out. I know her. Be sure and give the property to Teddy. [*Exit Rose, R.D. Enter Snaggs from elevator. Exits C.D. Enter May, R.D.*]

May. Excuse me, but are you the drummer?

Ted. Commercial tourist, miss. Trade is my bride and I'm on my wedding tour. I believe I am to decide about the property. Are you one of the ladies? If so, you must be Rose. They tell me she is the prettiest.

May. Who told you so?

Ted. A young lady just here.

May. It is not so. May is the prettiest. Rose is pretty, but she paints and laces and wears false hair, and don't begin to be as pretty as I.

Ted. You!

May. No, no! May, I mean. Teddy is the homely one. [*Enter Matilda L.D. Crosses stage and goes upstairs*]

Ted. If I live long enough, I'll get even with her for this.

MAY. Ta, ta, I'll see you later. [*Exit May, R.D. Enter Gilly in girl's clothes*]

TED. Good gracious, what's that?

GIL. Peek-a-boo! [*Crosses to register*]

TED. Who asked you in here?

GIL. I asked myself.

TED. Then ask yourself out.

GIL. [*At register*] Lawrence Jenkins, I've been looking for you everywhere.

TED. That is just where I've not been.

GIL. Where?

TED. Everywhere.

GIL. Are you the drummer?

TED. Yes, I'm the drummer.

GIL. Well, I'm Rose.

TED. [*Aside. Laughs*] It's Gilly. This pays for all. I'd give my head if Rose could see him now.

GIL. Yes, sir, I'm Rose. Are you going to give me the hotel?

TED. [*Aside*] The wretch is doing this to get the hotel for Rose. [*Aloud*] Give it to you? Why, I can't. It was to go to the homeliest, and you must be the prettiest.

GIL. I! The prettiest? Oh, pshaw!

TED. We may as well be spoons. You are pretty, and I flatter myself a little on my own personal appearance.

GIL. Oh, sir, you are modest.

TED. That's because I'm an American. All Americans are modest, and they are worse in Ohio than anywhere else. You are quite young, I'll wager.

GIL. Guess how old I am.

TED. I should say about sixteen.

GIL. Oh, somebody must have told you.

TED. Yes, you are the prettiest girl I ever met. You are delicious. May I kiss you?

GIL. Oh, that would not be right. [*Aside*] If he kisses me, he'll discover my disguise.

TED. True; but that would make it all the more fun. It always does.

GIL. Are you going to give me the hotel?

TED. Are you accomplished? Can you dance? [*Gilly dances*]

GIL. Now do I get the hotel? [*Teddy rushes for Gilly, who runs upstairs. Snaggs enters and goes behind counter*]

SNAG. I can't find Teddy anywhere. [*Sound of coach arriving and voices outside*] Just my luck! Customers when I don't want them. [*Bell*] Front! [*Enter prize fighter; crosses to counter; writes name in register after dropping his satchel; wipes the pen on Snaggs's vest*]

P.F. Does John A. Sullivan Opera Slugger stop here?

TED. Slugger! [*Exits hurriedly*]

SNAG. No, sir. Do you require a room?

P.F. You bet.

SNAG. Single room?

P.F. Well, I should smile.

SNAG. If you sleep with another gentleman, it will be cheaper.

P.F. I'd sooner sleep with a wet dog.

SNAG. [*Bell*] Front! Get a wet dog for the gentleman.

P.F. Do I get a room?

SNAG. [*Bell*] Front! Yes, sir.

GRI. This way, sir. [*Grimes attempts to take grip from prize fighter, who pulls against him. Grimes's head goes through panel of the counter. Grimes goes back to chair, R., rubbing his head*]

P.F. No you don't! Those are my dumb-bells. I'm in training for a match.

SNAG. A match? Don't you know it's against the law to slug your neighbors?

P.F. No, it ain't, you old beat!

SNAG. Beat! Why this scurrilous pronunciamento? [*Enter Teddy*]

P.F. Here! You take that back! [*Prize fighter rushes behind counter. Snaggs jumps over it and lies down in front of it. Prize fighter leans over the counter and addresses Snaggs*] Get up! Lie down! [*Several times*] If I thought you meant anything, I'd—[*Comes to front of counter. Snaggs crawls through hole to back*] Do I get a room?

SNAG. [*Bell*] Front! Show this gentleman up to the bridal chamber. [*Hands Grimes key with large bell attached. Grimes rushes upstairs followed by prize fighter and into room R.*]

TED. Weren't you scared?

SNAG. [*Has picked up a gun*] No. Simply disgusted. He knocks people out in four rounds. [*Taps gun*] I'd knock him out in one. [*Prize fighter in room R. takes off his coat. Grimes kicks him behind; then rushes out and down the stairs, followed by the prize fighter*]

GRI. He's coming! He's coming! [*Grimes jumps through the window into the elevator. The prize fighter tries to follow him through, but falls down. Snaggs and Grimes beat him; then Grimes exits. Snaggs retires behind the counter. Grimes reenters with an axe*]

P.F. [*C.*] Say, boss, is there anybody here I can have a round with?

SNAG. A round what? A round steak? Around the block? Or what?

P.F. [*Puts up fists*] A square-off.

TED. [*C.*] I'd rather be a square off than in front of those. I never was partial to nobility. Dukes, for instance. [*Touches prize fighter's fists*]

P.F. [*At counter*] I want a five-cent cigar.

SNAG. I haven't got any under twenty-five cents.

P.F. [*Roughly*] Give me a five-cent cigar!

SNAG. [*Frightened*] Yes, sir. Yes, sir. [*Gives cigar*]

P.F. Give me another.

SNAG. [*Gives it*] Cost me fifteen cents apiece.

P.F. [*To Teddy*] Have a weed.

TED. Thank you, I don't smoke.

P.F. [*Threateningly*] What?

TED. Well—sometimes.

SNAG. Please smoke. [*Teddy gives the cigar to Grimes, who chops the end off with his axe*]

P.F. [*At counter*] Give me a match.

SNAG. A match?

P.F. Yes, I'm giving you the benefit of my trade, and I expect a match. [*While he is lighting his cigar, Snaggs pours hair restorer on his head. He scratches his head, and the hair comes off*] Now show me to my room.

SNAG. This way, sir. [*Prize fighter goes to stairs. Snaggs follows him; then hits him, and turns away. Prize fighter goes up to Teddy*]

P.F. I've a good mind to smash your head.

TED. Yes, I dare say you have a good mind, too, but that is not exactly the point. [*Snaggs hits the prize fighter on the head with the cigar box; then runs and crawls through hole in the counter; comes around to the front, is met by prize fighter*]

P.F. Show me to my room!

SNAG. Take the elevator.

P.F. No. No elevator. [*Exit both upstairs*]

TED. [*F. and C.*] Oh, dear, I wish I could get the decision and get rid of these—ahem! [*Gestures to her trousers*] What a fool a man must feel in his clothes! [*Enter Matilda, C.D.*]

MAT. Oh, dear me! I'm all tired out! When shall I find him?

TED. I'll help you, ma'am. Conceal yourself in the elevator until I call you. [*Matilda enters elevator to hide. Enter Dolly*] Hello! You're a pretty girl. Is your name Rose?

DOL. No, sir. My name's Dolly.

TED. Why, Dolly, how you've grown!

DOL. Grown? When did you ever see me before? I don't remember you. [*Looks sharply at Teddy's face*] Why, you look like—yes—it's Teddy, I do believe! [*Goes to door R.*] Miss Rose! Miss May! [*Enter Rose and May*] Miss Rose, it isn't a drummer!

ROSE. Not a drummer?

DOL. No! It's Miss Teddy!

ROSE and MAY. [*Both scream*] Teddy! [*Snaggs and prize fighter enter room R., and put on gloves*]

TED. [*Imitates Rose and May*] Teddy! Yes, you mean things! You were talking to me when you said I was the homeliest!

MAY. Teddy, this outrageous conduct!

TED. I know it. I wanted to seem like one of the family. [*They rush at her. She evades them and exits U.E.L., followed by May*]

ROSE. [*To Dolly*] Don't fail to get the jewelry. We *must* see the will. [*Snaggs, who has helped put the gloves on the prize fighter, tries to get out of the room. The prize fighter hits him in the face. Then he rushes downstairs, yelling*]

SNAG. Oh, I'm cut! I'm cut! Where's the drummer?

DOL. It was no drummer. It was Miss Teddy!

SNAG. What? Teddy! Oh, I'm a goner!

DOL. Mr. Snaggs, the opera singers want the smallest packet of jewelry in the safe.

SNAG. [*Unlocks safe*] All right. [*Prize fighter jumps and the stovepipe falls. All enter except Matilda, Gilly and Tom*]

ALL. What's the matter?

ROSE. Is anybody going to put the stovepipe together?

SNAG. Somebody'll have to put me together. [*Takes up pipe. Burns hands*] Oh, damn! Oh, damn! [*Gilly enters room L. and sits on edge of bathtub. Prize fighter strikes through the partition and hits Gilly. Gilly pulls out the plug from the tub and water runs through to the stage*]

ROSE. Haven't you had enough fun with this hotel?

TED. Let's get the will.

SNAG. [*Holds pail to catch water*] Do you think I'm doing this for fun? Hello, the place is leaking! Grimes, stop the water! [*He sees girls at safe*] Leave that will alone!

GIL. [*Comes downstairs*] Girls, read it! [*Enter Tom as drummer*]

SNAG. Stop! Are you a drummer?

TOM. I am.

SNAG. Which two of these three girls are the prettiest?

Tom. Is that one in man's clothes a girl?

Ted. You bet I am.

Tom. Then the other two are the prettiest.

Rose and May. I knew it!

Tom. Do I get a room?

Snag. No. We are full. [*Exit Tom*]

Ted. [*C.*] Who said I was homely?

Snag. Teddy gets the property! Teddy, embrace your future husband!

Ted. Get out! You're not old enough.

Gri. [*Whistles*] Two dollars!

Snag. You don't get it. Teddy, of course you'll marry me!

Ted. Of course I won't! I have found out you did not want me. You only wanted the property!

Snag. Teddy, the hotel is yours.

Ted. Not yet. Here's the codicil which says, "If my nieces object to the will, and prefer to divide the property equally between them, they may do so." And so we will!

Gil. Mr. Snaggs, you had better leave town!

Snag. What? Kicked out after all I've done for this family? But the guests shall pay!

All. We were the guests! [*Enter Tom and prize fighter*]

Snag. I will not stir from this spot! Possession is nine points of the law! [*Teddy brings Matilda from the elevator*] As I once said to a jury—[*Turns and sees Matilda*] Matilda! [*Rushes out R., followed by Matilda*]

Ted. Sisters, we shall divide the property equally and no one shall know which of the Bunch of Keys was the homeliest!

CHORUS

[*Before end of chorus, enter Snaggs and Matilda and stay on till the*

CURTAIN]

A MIDNIGHT BELL

The author begs to state that this is a legitimate Comedy. It is a legitimate Comedy because it is in four acts, and farce-comedies are always in three. Its presentation will doubtless result in crippling as many per night as does the average farce-comedy, but remember that it is four acts and that it has a plot. It may be agreed that it is not a strong plot, that it is not a particularly interesting plot, but, on the other hand, it is a modern and unassuming plot, and it may serve the purpose of giving some slight coherence to the proceedings. However, the author is not strenuous on the subject of his plot. If, when the agony is over, it has been found that the characters, scenes, and incidents have been presented in an amusing fashion, the author will be satisfied, and have no feeling regarding anything that may be said about the plot.

CAST OF CHARACTERS

The cast of *A Midnight Bell* for its New York opening on March 5, 1889, was as follows:

THE CLERGYMAN, REV. JOHN BRADBURY	RICHARD J. DILLON
THE DEACON, LEMUEL TIDD	THOS. A. SEABROOKE
THE CITY LAWYER, NAPIER KEENE	W. H. CURRIE
THE BANK CASHIER, STEPHEN LABAREE	W. J. HUMPHREYS
THE BANK TELLER, NED OLCOTT	HART CONWAY
THE BANK PRESIDENT, SQUIRE OLCOTT	T. J. HERNDON
THE COUNTRY BOY, MARTIN TRIPP	EUGENE CANFIELD
THE VILLAGE DOCTOR, HIRAM WING	JESSE JENKINS
THE VILLAGE FIDDLER, EZEKIAL SLOVER	PERCY GAUNT
THE SCHOOLMA'AM, NORA FAIRFORD	ISABELLE COE
THE MINISTER'S SISTER, DOT BRADBURY	MAUDE ADAMS
THE OLD MAID, MISS LIZZIE GROUT	ANNIE ADAMS
THE WIDOW, ABIGAIL GREY	MARIE UART
THE SOPRANO OF THE CHOIR, NELLIE BOWEN	ELVIA CROIX
THE VILLAGE MAIDEN, ANNIE GREY	BETH BEDFORD
THE VILLAGE HELP, HANNAH	BESSIE WEYL
SCHOOL CHILDREN AND VILLAGERS	

ACT I: DINING ROOM AT SQUIRE OLCOTT'S HOUSE.

ACT II: THE SCHOOL.

ACT III: THE PARLOR AT MISS LIZZIE'S.

ACT IV: THE MEETING HOUSE.

ACT I.

PROPERTY LIST: *Ground cloth down. Large rug. Snow cloth seen through window and door; back to snow drop. Old-fashioned bookcase or table and bookshelf. Haircloth sofa R.C. Plain white window for curtain R.C. Grandfather's clock up R. Old-fashioned clothesrack L. of window. Dresser L. of door. Dining-room table for five persons. One old-fashioned painting. Two or three old-fashioned engravings. Mirror over mantel. Mantel fireplace, old brass andirons, poker, etc. Mantel ornaments. Seven or eight chairs to match scene. Large rocker at fire. Knob both sides door in flat. Folding pieces crossed over mantel. One shaker chair. File newspapers hung near bookshelf R. Two candles lighted. Two plain kerosene lamps. Cloth on table L.C. spread and breakfast ready for five. Five plates. Five cups. Five saucers. Syrup pitcher. Coffeepot stand. Sugar bowl. Six forks. Five knives. Five spoons. Napkins. Blue delf displayed on dresser. Scalloped paper for dresser. Newspaper on chair by fire. Dictionary on table R. or on stand. Pen, ink, and paper on table R. Squire's hat and muffler on rack. Cloud on rack, or hood, for Nora. Butter dish for Hannah to carry on L.1.E. Snow on Labaree shoes up R. Papers for Labaree. Snow on Martin's shoes up L. Things for Martin's pockets. Yellow dime novel for Martin's pocket. School key for Nora R.2.E. Schoolbook for Nora. Snow for shoes, Squire up L. Ox goad for Deacon up R. Snow on shoes, Deacon up R. Snow on shoes, Lizzie up L. Worsted shawl work for Lizzie. Snow on Lizzie, Squire, Nora up R. Pancakes and coffee-pot L.1.E. for Hannah. Snow on back of Dot's jacket up L. Snow for shoes, Labaree and Deacon up R. Warrant for Deacon.*

MUSIC: *At rise.*

SCENE: *Dining-room at Squire Olcott's house. Large old-fashioned room: fireplace and andirons; tall clock; old-fashioned bookcase; dining-room table and two chairs; large rocker at fireplace below it; hat-rack C. Lights down for candlelight; bunches ready up R. and L.; on when curtains at window are drawn.*

DISCOVERED: *Squire stirring fire; Hannah laying cloth; Ned ready L.2.E.; Labaree ready up L.; Nora ready up R.2.E.*

SQUIRE.   Oh, but it's an awful cold morning and this pesky fire won't burn worth a cent. B-r-r-r! I wonder what the thermometer says. [*Hannah exits*

R.1.E. Squire goes up to window and looks at thermometer] Two above now and it's seven o'clock. B-r-r-r! That means twelve or fourteen below at four. A very cold morning! [*Comes down C.; looks off L.1.E.*] I smell coffee in the kitchen, and it smells good; but I suppose I shall have to wait for it until the others get up. [*Up C., and looks off L.2.E.*] Lazy critters! They'd stay in bed all day if allowed. [*Hannah returns*] There's my legal friend from Boston, growls about rising at the unearthly hour of eight. Oh, well, I don't know as I ought to blame him. I'd have lain an hour longer myself if I could have slept. But this trouble about the bank worries me and I lie awake. I do hope it will be straightened out soon. [*Down C. again and works over R.*]

HAN. I hope so, squire. Everybody thinks because I am your help I know all about it, and I'm sick of answering questions about it. [*Exits L.1.E.*]

SQUIRE. [*Back to chair R. of table*] I'd like to know what Mr. Keene discovered about the matter last night. I don't suppose I ought to wake him, but there's that nephew of mine. He shan't sleep any longer; there's no reason for his staying in bed, nor for getting up, either! But he shall! [*Crosses to door L.2.E. Shouts*] Ned! Ned!

NED. [*Upstairs, faintly*] Hello.

SQUIRE. Get up! It's late!

NED. Yes.

SQUIRE. [*Closes door*] There! I feel better. [*Crosses stage to R.*] I might call the schoolma'am, too, but no! It's her last morning in my house; she may sleep as long as she likes. [*Hears knock at door L.C.*] Hey, who's this? [*Door opens. Labaree enters; hat on*] What? Mr. Labaree? Good morning. Come in.

LAB. Good morning. Mr. Keene up?

SQUIRE. [*Seated R. of table*] Up? No. Nor won't be for an hour. Want to see him?

LAB. Yes. I've got some papers here for him. [*Significantly*]

SQUIRE. About the bank robbery? Is there anything new discovered?

LAB. [*Goes over to fire*] I can't say a lie. The papers are for him.

SQUIRE. Labaree, I hope we'll get at the facts of this robbery pretty soon. It worries me dreadfully. If we don't find the thief before long, folks will begin to suspect it was you or me. That would be a joke, wouldn't it? [*Forces a laugh in which Labaree joins*]

LAB. Yes, very funny. [*Rap at door*] Sh-h! [*Startled*] Who's at the door?

SQUIRE. [*Looks at Labaree; puzzled at his fright. Opens door; discovers Martin*] Oh, it's you, is it? Well, don't stand there. Come in. [*Enter Martin*] What brings you here?

MAR. Say, is the schoolma'am up? [*Down C.*]

SQUIRE. [*R.C.*] Of course not! Do you expect folks to get up in the middle of the night? What do you want anyway?

MAR. Say, I lost my key to the schoolhouse and 'less I can get hers [*Voice breaks*] I can't get in to build fires.

SQUIRE. Lost yer key, hey? Where did you lose it?

MAR. I don't know. If I did [*Voice breaks*] I'd go there and look for it. [*Crosses in front of table L.*]

SQUIRE. Martin Tripp, what is the matter with your voice?

MAR. Changin'.

SQUIRE. Well, I wish it would hurry up and get changed. Are you sure you lost that key?

MAR. I don't know. Maybe I hain't. All I know is I hain't got it and I don't know where it is.

SQUIRE. Did you look in your pockets?

MAR. Yes, sir. It tain't there. [*Labaree stealthily examines his papers*]

SQUIRE. [*R. of table; brings chair C.*] You look again. Let me see you empty your pockets and turn them inside out.

MAR. [*L. of table; takes out of pocket a knife, string, nails, coppers, and apples, and a vast quantity of things including a dime novel*] Say, you see I hain't [*Voice breaks*] got it.

LAB. I say, what's that book?

MAR. Oh, nothin'. [*Tries to conceal book in his pocket*]

LAB. Let me see it. [*Martin reluctantly obeys*] A dime novel: "Long-Haired Dave; or, The Terror of the Yellowstone!" Nice stuff for a boy to read! Does your mother allow you to read such stuff? [*Martin refills pockets*]

MAR. Oh, she don't keer, but dad said if he caught me readin' one of 'em again he'd lick the daylights out of me. [*Voice breaks*] And he hain't caught me. [*Enter Nora R.*]

NORA. Good morning, Squire Olcott. Good morning, Mr. Labaree. Good morning, Martin.

MAR. Good morning, Miss Nora.

SQUIRE. Why, my dear, you're up early. [*Takes chair up; sits center of table*]

NORA. Yes, squire. It's my last morning under your hospitable roof, and I didn't wish to be the one to keep breakfast waiting.

SQUIRE. Well, I'm sorry you're not going to stay longer. I'd be glad to have you.

NORA. Oh, I must go. Mrs. Grey and Annie would never forgive me. But I thank you.

SQUIRE. By the way, Martin wants to see you.

NORA. What is it?

MAR. I've lost my key to the schoolhouse. [*Martin goes over to Nora C.*]

NORA. Again?

MAR. Yes'm.

NORA. And I suppose as usual you want to borrow mine? Well, here it is. Run along now and build the fires or you won't have the schoolhouse warm by nine. [*Goes to bookcase; gets out dictionary; takes notes*]

MAR. Yes, I will. Say, squire, don't [*Goes up to door*] tell dad about— you know. [*Taps pocket; returns down C.*] Oh, say, squire, will you lend me your bear-trap that's out in the shed?

SQUIRE. What do you want to set it for?

MAR. The ghost up at the church. [*Ned ready L.2.E.*]

LAB. [*Comes to L. of table*] The ghost up at the church?

MAR. Yes. They say that the ghost of Print Bowen, the old sexton that was killed falling from the belfry, haunts the church. They say 'twas him that rung the bell at midnight last year. [*Nora overhears this and shows her amusement*]

SQUIRE. Nonsense! It was boys.

MAR. I dunno. If it'd been boys, I'd been one of 'em. My mother believes it was the ghost and [*Voice breaks*] I want to trap him. May I take the trap?

SQUIRE. Yes, you can take it. Do you know what a ghost is, Martin? [*Rises; puts chair back*]

MAR. No, but I'm going to catch him and see. Say, squire, how'd I better bait the trap?

SQUIRE. Well, from what I knew of the late sexton, I should say bait it with a jug o' cider. [*Goes towards Labaree, who assents, shaking his head*]

MAR. All right. I'll go set the trap now. [*Goes up to door*] Say, squire, do you like Injun stories? I'll lend you this if you do. [*Squire after him; Martin exits quickly; then is heard singing as he goes off*]

LAB. Say, squire, I want to see Mr. Keene privately. If you don't object, I'll just go up to his room. [*Starts for door*]

SQUIRE. All right, if you want to take the consequences of waking him up. [*Exit Labaree L.2.E.*] I wouldn't! [*Takes down hat and comforter from rack up C.*] I don't suppose Ned and Lawyer Keene will be down for some time. [*Stops to think*] I wonder if I've forgotten to call anybody? No, I'll go out to the barn to see if the horses are all right. [*Nora comes towards him, crossing over to fireplace*] Tell Hannah to call me if they come down before I return. [*Exits L.C. Music*]

NORA. [*Sits by fire*] How comfortable this house is and how good they all are here. How I wish I could accept the squire's invitation instead of going to Mrs. Grey's! Oh, dear, with this boarding around every week, a country schoolteacher's life is not a happy one. [*Turns to fire. Music stops. Ned looks in L., then enters and crosses to C.*]

NED. [*Front of table*] Nora! You here alone? Oh, I'm so glad!

NORA. [*Turns*] Glad? Why?

NED. Because I've got something I want to talk to you about.

NORA. Very well, Ned. What is it?

NED. Nora, you've always been the best friend I've had. [*Moves towards her*]

NORA. I'm glad you think so. But your uncle is a good friend to you.

NED. [*Faces front*] Yes, but it's because I'm one of his family. I'm a trial to him. He doesn't understand me as you do.

NORA. Well, what do you want to say to me?

NED. [*Stands by her, at her R.*] It's a secret and I want you never to tell. Promise?

NORA. Yes, of course.

NED. Well, you know how it is with Annie Grey and me?

NORA. I know you seem to be good friends.

NED. Oh, there's no use of beating around the bush. Nora, I want to marry her! [*Nora looks at him*] Now you may think I'm crazy, but I'm not.

NORA. In time I hope you will marry her.

NED. Yes, I mean to marry her in *time*. Before it's too *late*. You see, her mother's bound she shall marry Steve Labaree!

NORA. Her mother wishes that?

NED. Yes. Labaree has managed all the old lady's business for her and she thinks he's the only man on earth. He's courting the mother to get the daughter, and Mrs. Grey's going to make Annie marry him even if the poor girl does not want to.

NORA. Does Mr. Labaree know this?

NED. Yes, he does. Annie has told him that she can't love him, but he still tries to get her.

NORA. But Annie will never consent to marry him!

NED. You don't know what an old tartar her mother is! If Annie stays at home her mother'll make her marry Steve! I've no doubt!

NORA. That mustn't be!

NED. Of course it mustn't! [*Rises; turns chair*] Now, you promised you wouldn't tell!

NORA. Yes.

NED. [*Takes C.*] Well, we mean to elope!

NORA. Elope! [*Rises*] Oh, Ned! [*Follows Ned*] You must not!

NED. We've got to. There's no other way. And I'll tell you what I want you to do. You persuade Parson Bradbury to marry us!

NORA. I persuade Mr. Bradbury to marry you?

NED. Yes! He'd refuse if I asked him, but he'll do anything you want.

NORA. [*Confused*] Oh, you're wrong, Ned! [*Turns from him*]

NED. No, I'm not! And you know it! A girl knows when a man loves her even if he hasn't told her.

NORA. Stop, Ned! You have no right to talk so! [*Sits again R. of table*]

NED. Now, Nora, you know it's the truth, and you know that Liz Grout and Nellie Bowen and all that crowd of superannuated old fossils that are constantly tagging after Mr. Bradbury hate you as much as they can because they see he likes you! They make me tired! Why, Liz Grout's old enough to adopt him, and Nell Bowen will never see thirty-five again. She owns up to twenty-seven, and she's the youngest of the lot. Yet they think because John Bradbury's a minister that he isn't like other men, that he's going to pass by a bright, good girl to marry a peevish, sour, disappointed old maid. I guess they'll find out their mistake. It's a wonder to me he stands their pestering so patiently and treats them so kindly.

NORA. He is always kind to everybody. [*Leans head on her hand*]

NED. That's why I think he'll be kind to me, if you'll ask him. Will you?

NORA. No, Ned [*Ned over to R.C.*], and you must drop this wild scheme of eloping. [*Rises and goes to him*]

NED. Drop it? And let that poor girl be forced to marry Steve Labaree!

NORA. No, no! That doesn't follow. It may be possible to arrange the matter all right.

NED. I don't see how, and I'm not going to take any chances. [*Sits on sofa R.C.*]

NORA. Ned, listen to me. I would be glad to see Annie Grey your wife. I would do all I honorably could to make her so, but against this clandestine marriage I must set my face.

NED. Then what would you do?

NORA. Try other means. Get your uncle to go to Mrs. Grey and try to arrange it.

NED. Oh, but he wouldn't do that.

NORA. Indeed, he would! [*Stamping outside*] He's coming in now. Just tell him the story and see.

NED. It's no use. I can't. [*Rises and goes up to window R.C.*]

NORA. Then I will! Wait and listen!

SQUIRE. [*Enters L. Takes off muffler, hat, and mittens*] Hello, Ned. You up? [*Goes back of table. Sits L. Gruff to Ned*]

NORA. He's been up some time. I think he's trying to reform. [*Glances towards Ned*]

SQUIRE. [*Sits L. Dryly*] It's time!

NORA. [*Leans over Squire's chair*] Now, squire, I've got a plan to reform him completely and I want you to help me.

SQUIRE. Humph! What is it?

NORA. Have him get married! [*Ned a step or two from window*]

SQUIRE. What? That boy? [*Ned retires again to window, disgusted*]

NORA. Boy! He's no boy! He's old enough to vote for you! [*Squire looks at her suspiciously*] For member of the Governor's Council next month! How old were you when you married?

SQUIRE. Well, I wasn't much older, that's a fact! [*Ned crosses to back of table*] But he—[*Squire glances up at Ned, who goes over sulkily to fireplace*] why, he can't take care of himself! He'd make a pretty fellow to manage a wife!

NORA. Yes, but my scheme was to have his wife manage him.

NED. [*Down to fireplace E.*] Oh, Nora, it's no use talking to him. I told you it wasn't! [*Gesture of Nora to Ned—"Keep quiet!"—as she gets back of table*]

SQUIRE. Ain't, eh? You don't know as much as you think you do, young man. Go on, Nora.

NORA. Well, Ned and Annie Grey are very fond of each other.

SQUIRE. Are, eh? Well, she's a good enough girl, but I don't know's I'd care to have Ned marry into that family. I don't think much of it. Why, that woman's such an old scold, less than six months after Grey married her he ran away to sea. They ain't my style of folks.

NORA. Mrs. Grey feels the same way about your family; she has told Ned not to come to her house.

SQUIRE. [*Turns sharply to Nora*] She told Ned not to come to her house? Well, I declare!

NORA. Now we thought you might go and see Mrs. Grey and persuade her to let Annie marry Ned in a year or so. Don't you think you could make her believe your family is as good as hers? [*Nora glances over at Ned*]

SQUIRE. I reckon I could. [*Rises; crosses over C.*] Nora, I believe you've got the right idea of making something of this boy! [*Nora goes to window and watches the Squire. Squire C.*] Come here, Ned! [*Ned goes to him*] If I fix this matter for you, will you promise me to settle down to work, quit skylarking, and act like a man?

NED. Anything, uncle!

SQUIRE. Well, I'll go over and see the widow by and by. I'd like to have her tell me my nephew isn't good enough for her gal! [*Crosses to fire and pokes it*]

NORA. There, Ned, you see! Now I'll leave you to talk it over. [*Goes up C.*]

NED. [*Goes to her*] Nora, I never can thank you enough.

NORA. Nonsense. Thank him. [*Exits R.*]

NED. Uncle, I do thank you! [*Goes R. of table. Delighted*]

SQUIRE. That's all right, my boy. The idea that you're not as good as them Greys! Well, I'll see about that, my boy.

DEACON. [*Outside*] Whoa! Gosh darn ye, whoa!

NED. [*Up and to window*] There's Deacon Tidd—Old Practical—coming in.

SQUIRE. I wonder what he wants.

NED. Oh, he's got something to 'tend to. He thinks he's got to 'tend to everything that happens in this town. He 'tends to everybody's business but his own. Probably he wants to see you. I'll go call Keene. [*Exits L.2.E.*]

DEAC. [*At window*] Mink Jones, you keep that dog o' your'n away from my oxen or I'll spile the set o' your trousers for yer! [*Enters L. Goes to fire*]

SQUIRE. [*L.*] Good morning, deacon. I saw you coming.

DEAC. Good morning. Good morning. Purty sharp weather this morning. [*At fire; takes off mittens*]

SQUIRE. Yes; how was the thermometer?

DEAC. I didn't look to see. What's the use of wastin' time to look at a thermometer? Ye can't make it any warmer by doing so, and it wouldn't do me no good to know how cold it was. I knew it was cold enough to freeze my ears if I didn't rub 'em, and that was enough to know.

SQUIRE. [*L.C.*] You take a very practical view of things. [*Sits R. of table*]

DEAC. Wa'al, I try ter. I don't go in fer wastin' time on nonsense. My motto is, don't be frivolous. Where's the schoolmarm? [*Fires this last sentence off suddenly*]

SQUIRE. She's upstairs.

DEAC. Humph. Nice time o' day not to be up. I must 'tend to this. When it comes her week to board at my house she'll be up before this or she'll get no breakfast. You'd ort not to encourage her lyin' abed.

SQUIRE. Oh, she's been down already, but breakfast's got to wait anyhow till Lawyer Keene comes down and I'll defy the old Harry to make him get up till he's ready. But sit up! He'll sit up all night. Why, he was studying over that bank matter till three o'clock this morning.

DEAC. Any new developments?

SQUIRE. Not that I know of. We only know that thirty thousand dollars of the bank funds has mysteriously disappeared. I've trusted the affairs of the bank so much to Mr. Labaree that I really don't know much about its business and that's why I got this Boston lawyer to come down and help investigate it.

DEAC. Yes, and I don't admire your choice of an adviser. Nice lawyer he is! We get him down here to chase the bank robber and I hain't seen him chase nothin' but the minister's sister!

SQUIRE. [*Rises*] Well, don't be too severe on him, deacon. We used to chase the girls ourselves when we were his age.

DEAC. By gosh, we did! And say, squire, we could cut out some of them young fellers that's skitin' 'round here even now, I guess! [*Nudges Squire; both laugh, turn backs, and kick*] I say, squire, do you remember that little gal—? [*They laugh. As laugh subsides, Squire sighs, and then begins thus—*]

SQUIRE. I wish Keene would hurry up and find this bank robber.

DEAC. You don't suspect Labaree?

SQUIRE. Certainly not! None of the directors do. Why, I was in the bank myself after he left it on the night the money disappeared. I had occasion to open the safe, and all was right then, and next morning the bonds were gone, though the safe was locked all right and I had the only key to it myself.

DEAC. Well, it's a curious case. How soon will the schoolmarm be down, think? [*Back of table and over R.*]

SQUIRE. Oh, very soon. Do you wish to see her for anything important?

DEAC. Important? I should say I do. I want ter let her know I'm comin' 'round to examine the school today. [*Looks at bookcase wisely*]

SQUIRE. No doubt she'll be glad to see you. [*Sits L.*] Nora has given us a good school, I think. She's a fine girl.

DEAC. Yes, a fine girl, but she ain't so practical as she might be. [*Puts down dictionary scornfully*] She's been wastin' a heap of valuable time teachin' them youngsters manners, which ain't no good to anybody. I never had any. Why, she's got those ten-year-old children so that when a gal meets a boy on the street, she bows to him and he raises his hat. Did you ever hear of such darn nonsense?

NORA. [*Enters R. and comes C.*] Good morning, Deacon Tidd. I heard what you were saying, deacon, as I came downstairs. I shall be very glad to see you at the school today, and I hope that you won't think after all that my efforts to teach the boys to be gentlemen have been such a sad waste of time. I believe once last winter when you came to the school the boys pelted you with snowballs from behind the woodpile and drove you away. [*Squire quietly amused*]

DEAC. [*R.*] Drat 'em! They did. If I could have found what boys they were, I'd warmed their jackets for 'em, too. [*Sits on sofa*]

NORA. Well, I'm sure they won't be so rude this year.

DEAC. I shan't give 'em a chance. I shall come around when they are all in school. I'm practical, ye know. However, I don't mind ye teachin' 'em better'n to do sich things as that. [*Knock at C.L.*]

NORA. There's a knock. Shall I open the door?

SQUIRE. If you please. [*Nora opens door. Enter Lizzie with Scottish terrier led by cord. Nora looks quizzically at dog*]

LIZ. Good morning, everybody. Keep still, Spot. [*Down C.*] Very cold, isn't it? Any news about the bank?

SQUIRE. [*L.*] Yes, it *is* cold. [*Avoids her; goes over to fireplace. Nora places chair for Lizzie C.*]

LIZ. But the bank? Keep still, Spot, or I'll whip you, you naughty dog. [*Sits C. Nora sits L. of her*]

DEAC. [*R.*] What yer got yer dog on a string for? Can't ye trust him alone? [*Works back over to fireplace L.*]

LIZ. The boys plague Spot so I have to keep him near me. Only t'other day Martin Tripp glued feathers to his tail, and if you'd seen him whirling 'round, you'd thought he was a windmill. Squire, the Sewing Society meets at my house tonight and I called to see if you'd lend me a dozen of plates and cups and saucers? I'm afraid I hain't enough to go 'round, for this mystery about the bank is sure to make a large attendance.

SQUIRE. Certainly, I'll tell Hannah to send them over to you. [*Exits L.1.E.*]

DEAC. Miss Lizzie, as one of the committee you must be on hand at the examination today. [*Deacon discovers fire too warm for his back; takes newspaper from table*]

LIZ. Oh, certainly. I ought to have given the school more attention than I have lately. Will Mr. Bradbury be there?

DEAC. I hope so. I mean, as one of the committee he ought to be there.

LIZ. Has he visited the school often?

NORA. Not very—that is, several times.

LIZ. Mr. Bradbury's a very conscientious man. He's the best clergyman we ever had.

DEAC. Well, I ain't denyin' that. His sermons are strong, though he don't quite lay stress enough on the way the wicked'll roast. [*Has had back to fire all during scene and has been getting warmer; now takes newspaper from chair and holds it behind him; all of a sudden thinks he's on fire. Business*]

LIZ. [*Jumps up*] Deacon, are you afire? [*Women excited*]

DEAC. Gosh, I believe I am. [*Ad lib*]

Liz. I hope you ain't one of the wicked, deacon.

Deac. I guess that some of the good'll roast as well as the wicked.

Nora. Then maybe Mr. Bradbury is right.

Deac. Oh, don't think I'm complainin' o' Mr. Bradbury. I only wish he was a little more practical. He needs a wife to keep him straight. [*Stares first at Lizzie, then at Nora. They stare at each other*]

Nora. [*Looks down*] Perhaps so.

Liz. Indeed, a clergyman should always have a wife. She can do so much good. Not a young, frivolous girl, but an experienced woman.

Deac. Like yourself, say—?

Liz. [*Snappishly*] Oh, deacon, don't you be frivolous. Mr. Bradbury would never think of marrying me, I'm afraid.

Deac. No, I don't say as he would. [*Lizzie angry*] But he ought to have a wife to keep that sister of his in order. She's a tyke, that young one.

Nora. Oh, deacon, Dot is not a bad girl at all. She's a dear, good girl.

Deac. Wa'al, I'll allow all ye say in favor of the parson, but I consider her a pert minx. Why, the other day I asked her if she was trying to show disrespect for me, and she said, no, she was trying to hide it.

Nora. Dear me! I'm sure she was very sorry she said it.

Deac. Maybe she was sorry, but she gave no evidence of sorrow.

Nora. She doesn't mean to say or do saucy things, but she doesn't think.

Deac. Then she'd orter. That ain't no practical excuse for her. It's like the other day I was over at Lempster and a fellow fired a revolver at me and nigh on ter hit me. They told me not to mind him as he was an ijiot, but I told 'em the effects of a bullet in the head wasn't modified by the intellectual condition of the fellow that fired it, and I jest as soon be shot by a wise man as an ijiot. But what's the use of explaining these matters to you women? Ye don't want ter do what's practical. Ye'll work all day in a flower garden, but ask ye to hoe corn and you'd faint.

Liz. Why, deacon!

Deac. [*Crosses to Lizzie and stretches shawl she is knitting. This makes Lizzie nervous*] Look at that thing ye've got there! What good is it?

Liz. Why, that's a shawl I'm knitting for the church fair. I've been at work on it for three weeks. Ain't it pretty?

Deac. [*Examines the shawl again*] 'Tain't no practical use, but if it'll sell for money to pay the minister, it's all right.

Liz. Here, deacon, stop. You've got the worsted caught on your sleeve button.

Deac. [*Yanks arm away*] Get it off.

Liz. Well, keep still, won't you? Every move you make you unravel it. [*Enter Martin L.C.*]

Mar. Oh, deacon, come quick!

Deac. Me? [*Starts*]

Liz. [*Grabs him*] Wait a minute!

Deac. Well, get it off! What is it?

Mar. [*Laughs*] Mink Jones's dog went for your oxen [*Voice breaks*] and they're running away!

Deac. Great gosh! Stop 'em! [*Rushes off L.C. followed by Lizzie and others. Lizzie cries as she exits "Stop! Come back with my shawl!" Talk ad lib. Squire enters from L., excited, talking ad lib, and follows. Nora and Martin remain up R.*]

Mar. Come, Miss Nora, and see the fun! [*Nora and Martin exit C. Enter Keene and Labaree*]

Lab. It's a painful thing, Mr. Keene, but it must be done. As the squire remarked, if the thief isn't found pretty soon, people will begin to suspect him or me.

Keene. Yes. So you've taken good care to see that it shouldn't be you.

Lab. Hm! You don't doubt my motives, I hope, Mr. Keene.

Keene. Most emphatically, no!

Lab. I don't know, Mr. Keene. I never wronged a human being in all my life.

Keene. Oh, it's all right. The warrant is there. [*Labaree knows it*] Hunt up Deacon Tidd and have him serve it. But do me a favor! Don't have it done until after breakfast is over. [*Sits on sofa R.*]

Lab. Why not?

Keene. Because it will spoil my breakfast.

Lab. I'll go and find deacon and give him the warrant. [*At door*] Be sure, Mr. Keene, this is a very painful duty for me to perform. [*Exits C.*]

Keene. I wonder what I ought to do in this matter. This case against the squire is nothing more than a suspicion, and I think I know why Labaree tries to make so much out of it. By Jove, [*He rises*] I'll let things take their course. Give a villain rope enough and he'll hang himself. I'd like to spare them the trouble that's in store for them, but it will bring out the truth. [*Stands L. Enter Lizzie, Squire, and Nora L.C. Lizzie has worsted and remnant of shawl. She is angry. The squire is laughing*]

Liz. The old fool! I hope he never will catch them oxen. If that worsted hadn't broken, I'd have lost the whole thing. Think of it! Three weeks' work on that shawl, and look at it! [*Hannah enters L.1.E.*]

Han. Breakfast's ready.

SQUIRE. Well, never mind the shawl, Miss Lizzie. Sit down, all of you. Good morning, lawyer. Come all, sit down. [*They all sit in this fashion:*

Squire — Keene

Nora — Lizzie

Empty chair]

Hannah, take Miss Lizzie's dog to the kitchen and feed him. [*Business of Hannah trying to catch the dog*]

LIZ. [*Takes dog on her lap*] Spot won't eat unless I cut his meat for him. I'll feed him here. [*Exit Hannah. Change for Widow Grey*]

SQUIRE. Confound the dog! I didn't invite the brute to breakfast.

LIZ. He's a delightful little fellow, and very intelligent. Only last night he mistook our cow for a strange one and drove her half a mile up the road. If it had been a stray cow, it would have been very nice, you know. As it was, my brother had to go after her.

KEENE. A very intelligent dog! How your brother must admire him!

SQUIRE. Why do you call him Spot? There ain't no spots on him.

LIZ. No, but I once owned a spotted dog which I should hev named Spot, only it got used to the name of Skeezicks; so when I got this dog I called him Spot. By the way, Mr. Keene, I've got a new collar for Spot. Can't you suggest something to have engraved on it? [*Puts dog up to Keene's face*]

KEENE. Say a quotation from Shakespeare?

LIZ. Yes. That would do.

KEENE. There's a line in *Macbeth*: "Out, damned spot! Out, I say!"

LIZ. Now, that's very unkind. You don't like dogs, Mr. Keene. What shall I tell them at the Sewing Circle about the bank affair?

KEENE. Tell them what you like.

LIZ. But what shall I say became of the money?

KEENE. Do you know what became of it?

LIZ. No.

KEENE. [*Civilly*] Then tell them you don't know.

MAR. [*Outside with Dot*] Say, Dot Bradbury, don't you put that ice down my back.

DOT. [*Bursts in L.C., breathless and flushed. Comes down L.C.*] Good morning, everybody. I—oh, mercy, I came right in without knocking. Excuse me! I'll go back and knock now. [*Starts to go*]

SQUIRE. [*Good-naturedly*] Come here, you minx! Don't open that door and let in more cold air. What do you want? Some breakfast? Set down. [*Pats her on the cheek*]

DOT. No, thank you. We had a donation party at our house last night, but we had enough left to make a breakfast. Nora, I came over to walk to school with you. Are you ready to go? [*Sits on end of sofa R.*]

NORA. Very soon. Excuse me, please. [*Rises from table*] I'll go upstairs and get my wraps. [*Exits R.*]

SQUIRE. Miss Bradbury, do you know Mr. Keene?

DOT. Oh, yes, we are old acquaintances. I've known him nearly two weeks. [*Sits in Nora's seat*] I made it a point to get an introduction to him as soon as I heard Miss Lizzie say he was the most aggravating—[*Business of being embarrassed; gets up*] Oh, I didn't mean—exactly—[*Takes R. corner*]

LIZ. Mr. Keene, she's only a child. You mustn't mind what she says.

KEENE. Certainly not. No more than if I had heard you say it yourself. [*Over L.*]

LIZ. [*Looks indignant and rises*] Why, I don't suppose you'll tell me anything about the bank anyway; so I may as well go over and tell Mrs. Grey to be sure to come to the Society. Come, Spot. You'd better come 'round this evening, squire. Good morning. [*Starts for door*]

ALL. Good morning!

LIZ. Good morning. Come along, Spot.

ALL. [*Loud*] Good morning. [*Lizzie exits L.C.*] Good morning!

SQUIRE. [*Goes to window just as Lizzie passes*] Good morning! [*Very loud*] Durn your skin!

KEENE. Well, we're rid of the invincible. [*Dot starts to eat. Keene sees her and calls Squire's attention to her*] I see you're not hungry!

SQUIRE. There couldn't have been much left over from the donation party after all. [*Better as an aside. Pats Dot*] I must go and call Ned to breakfast again. He'll never come down if I don't make him. [*Goes to L.2.E. Keene watches Dot*]

KEENE. Squire, I want to see you this morning. I have something very important to say to you. [*Squire starts toward him*] No hurry for an hour or so. [*Sits in rocker by fire and puts one foot on other chair*]

SQUIRE. Very well, I'll be back soon. [*Exits L.*]

DOT. [*After business, crosses to Keene, offering chair*] Mr. Keene, don't you want another chair?

KEENE. What for?

DOT. For your other foot.

KEENE. Oh, excuse me. [*Offers rocker*] Permit me to offer you the rocker. So Miss Lizzie says I'm aggravating.

DOT. Well, I didn't exactly mean to tell that. It was a slip of the tongue. I hope you didn't feel badly about it.

KEENE. Oh, no. I'm hardened to having unkind things said of me. I'm a lawyer.

DOT. I should think it would be real nice to be a lawyer.

KEENE. To have unkind things said of you?

DOT. No, but to be able not to mind them. And then you have a chance to talk back, and a minister's sister doesn't. Oh, I'd like to be a lawyer.

KEENE. There are things about the practice of the law that must be very fascinating to the fair sex. For instance, a lawyer often has twelve men in a box, and they can't get away, and they have to sit and listen as long as he chooses to talk.

DOT. How dreadfully dull it must be for those men sometimes.

KEENE. H'm. Isn't that intended for a reflection on me?

DOT. Oh, dear no! I should think you might be very amusing—I mean instructive.

KEENE. [Aside] I believe this girl is laughing at me. [Aloud] And is the position of a minister's sister so very trying?

DOT. Awful! Everything you say or do is criticized, and you're expected to set a good example. Now I know of only one thing in this world so hard as setting a good example.

KEENE. And that is?

DOT. Following one. Just try it sometime and see.

KEENE. Where shall I find one to follow?

DOT. There's Nora Fairford. She's one of the nicest girls that ever lived. She never does anything to be sorry for. She's never rude or irreverent.

KEENE. [Sits R.] I should say Miss Fairford is a good example which all the young men would be glad to follow. Who is she anyway? I take a great interest in her.

DOT. [Goes over to him quickly] Well, you needn't now, not a bit. It won't do you any good if you do. That is—

KEENE. Oh, I understand perfectly.

DOT. I'm afraid you do. [Crosses L.]

KEENE. [To table] Well, tell me her history.

DOT. Oh, it's rather a sad one. Her father was a very rich man—[On arm of rocker] but four or five years ago he lost all his money and poor Nora was left without a friend or a penny. But she had a good education and she at once went to teaching.

KEENE. She's very popular here, isn't she?

DOT. Well, all the young folks like her and most of the old ones, too. But there are a few that don't. There's Miss Lizzie Grout and Miss Nellie Bowen and Widow Grey and Miss Sarah Jane Prouty [*Very fast*] and two or three others of that set are as mean to her as they can be. [*Crosses R.*]

KEENE. I suppose having no husbands to pick on they have to find a victim elsewhere.

DOT. Yes, and they don't seem to do much else but tell stories about her. They're running to our house all the time with them, but John doesn't believe a word they say against her.

KEENE. I suppose not.

DOT. Why, they've tried to get Deacon Tidd, who is the committeeman that engages the teachers, to take the school away from her! Oh, you've no idea how mean they are! Oh, dear, they're the bane of my life! But I suppose it's wicked to talk like that about my neighbors and maybe that's why it's such a comfort to do it.

NORA. [*Calls from upstairs R.*] Dot, come up here.

DOT. Yes. Mr. Keene, will you excuse me?

KEENE. With pleasure. [*Sits R. of table*]

DOT. [*Moves to door. Seriously*] Mr. Keene, I'm sorry if I've been annoying you. [*Seems hurt*]

KEENE. [*Jumps up and goes to her*] My dear Miss Bradbury, pardon me! You have not been annoying me. I did not mean to speak rudely.

DOT. Oh, I forgive you. [*Gives hand*] I suppose you didn't know any better. [*Turns and darts out R.*]

KEENE. Egad! She got the best of me, but considering I allowed myself to spat with a woman I may congratulate myself on coming on right well. [*R.*]

NED. [*Enters L.*] Good morning, Mr. Keene. Beastly cold, isn't it?

KEENE. Yes. Ned, sit down. I want to talk to you about this bank affair.

NED. [*Looks wise*] I'm ready.

KEENE. I've got some bad news for you. I want to prepare you for trouble. The thief, they think, is discovered.

NED. Why, that's not bad news. Who is it?

KEENE. Your uncle!

NED. My uncle! Why, what madness! Mr. Keene, is this another of your jokes?

KEENE. I was never more serious in all my life.

NED. Why, he's president of the bank!

KEENE. My dear boy, when money is missing from the bank, the president is the first man suspected.

NED. [*Rises and crosses L.*] But he's above suspicion!

KEENE. [*Follows him*] My dear boy, there never was anybody above suspicion except Caesar's wife, and I've no doubt she was very plain!

NED. [*Indignant*] This is an outrageous action, and whoever has been guilty of it shall answer for it to me! You don't believe uncle did it, do you? [*Sits L. of table*]

KEENE. [*Leans on table C.*] Ahem! Just briefly review the evidence. It seems, according to your uncle's own statement, that he remained in the bank on the night of the robbery after Mr. Labaree, the cashier, left it, as he often did. He had, he told Mr. Labaree, occasion to go into the safe to get some private papers, and not having his key with him, asked Labaree to leave his key, which Labaree did. This put the only keys to the safe in the possession of your uncle. It is admitted by your uncle that the bonds were in the safe then, as Labaree called his attention to them. When he left the bank he says he locked the safe and the bonds were in it; he also locked the outer door which fastens with a combination lock, the secret of which is known only to your uncle and Labaree. The next morning Labaree couldn't get into the safe till your uncle brought over the key and then the bonds were discovered to be gone. [*Ned starts to speak*] But the locks had not been tampered with. The safe had been opened by somebody who knew the secret of the combination and had the key to the inner door. Who was it?

NED. [*Rises and crosses*] But I can't believe it was my uncle. There must be some explanation to this. Couldn't it have been Laba—well, I won't accuse him. But what motive could uncle have? He's rich.

KEENE. The books of a certain broker in Boston show heavy losing speculations in his name.

NED. But couldn't his name have been used by somebody else? Me?

KEENE. Time will tell.

NED. [*Seated R. of table*] Oh, Mr. Keene, my uncle is an old man and this will kill him.

KEENE. I'm very sorry, but I don't see any way to help it. They'll come to arrest him this morning. Labaree has obtained the warrant and taken it to Deacon Tidd to serve.

NED. Labaree? I see it all. It's his plot to disgrace our family and ruin me with Annie Grey. I am the one at whom this cruel blow has been aimed, but my uncle shall not be made to suffer on my account. [*Enter Nora and Dot*]

NORA and DOT. [*Together*] Well, we're going to school. So good-by. [*Enter Deacon. Labaree seen looking through the window*]

DEAC. Where's the squire? [*Music*]

NED. [*Aside to Keene*] Oh, this will kill him!

KEENE. Keep quiet! [*Enter Squire L.2.E.*]

SQUIRE. What, deacon, back again?

DEAC.   Yes, squire. I've—I've got a little business with yer. [*Looks around*] 'Tain't pleasant for me and—

SQUIRE.   Well, what is it?

DEAC.   It's in my capacity as sheriff. Shall—shall we step outside to talk it over?

SQUIRE.   No. You have no business with me that I am ashamed of. Speak out, old friend, and tell me what you have to say.

DEAC.   Squire Olcott, I've got a warrant for your arrest! [*Business of Ned, Keene, and the girls*]

SQUIRE.   For my arrest?

DEAC.   Yes. You are charged with robbing the bank.

SQUIRE.   Me? Why—why, there must be some mistake.

DEAC.   I hope there is. But the warrant's here. That's what I've got to go by. I must ask yer to go with me.

SQUIRE.   [*Overcome*]   You're goin' to take me? You're goin' to lock me up?

DEAC.   That's my duty. I'm bound to arrest yer. [*Squire sinks in chair*] And I haven't the heart to do it! [*Enter Labaree*]

LAB.   Then you must have. As one of the officers of the bank I demand that you serve the warrant!

DEAC.   [*Puts hand on Squire's shoulder*]   Old friend, I've got to do it! Come! [*Squire rises feebly and starts for door*]

NED.   [*Aside to Keene*]   I can't stand this! [*Aloud*] Stop! That old man is innocent! [*Grabs warrant; tears it up*] I am the thief! Take me!

CURTAIN

[*Music continued for second curtain*]

SECOND CURTAIN

Labaree

Keene

Squire   Deacon   Ned

Dot   Nora

ACT II.

PROPERTY LIST: *Snow cloth outside school and back. Practical snow on roof to slide off. Snow balls; one to break. Sleds L. (rubber wheels), three to show wear. Watering can up back of schoolhouse. Two handfuls of snow for Martin, ready by doorstep. Teacher's desk on small platform R.C. Three chairs for visitors. Desks and stools for children. Maps, blackboards, vowel chart (cover walls with these as much as possible). Rack for caps and coats up L.C. Nora's shawl and hat hanging behind desk. Small gong bell on teacher's desk. Larger*

school bell on teacher's desk. Pens, pencils, ink, and paper on teacher's desk.
Schoolbooks on teacher's desk. Chalk at blackboard. Snow on Ned's shoes
up R. Schoolbooks for children to carry on. Six slates. Clock to strike nine
off R. Big apple for Martin L. "Back-hair" ready up R. Card for Ned. Train
whistle ready up R. Ready to cut shade cord up R. for end of act.
Music: *At rise.*
Scene: *The school and the cast. The scene shows the exterior and the interior*
of the schoolhouse. There is snow and a landscape drop at back. At R. of
stage is a schoolhouse set showing interior and all appurtenances of a country
school. The L. of the stage shows a schoolhouse yard. The stage should be
built up from the schoolhouse so that the third or fourth groove is three or
four feet above level. Here should be set a steel groove or track hidden by the
elevation on which sleds can be made to pass across from L. to R. There is
practical snow on roof to slide off. Another track for Deacon to come down,
steep and aimed to hit the schoolhouse and pass through a break-away fence.
Snow wings L. Fallen log L.1.E. Scene as realistic as possible. Lights all up
through the act. See that schoolhouse is not dark. Martin ready at top of slide.
Children ready L. entrances. Shouts ready. Deacon ready up R. Labaree ready
L.2.E.
Discovered: *At rise, children are sledding, playing in the snow, shouting, etc.*
Business of a boy taking a bellywhopper. All run off L.2.E. after pelting the
sliders with snowballs. Nora in school room with Annie Grey, who is crying.
Martin rushes on from behind house.

Mar. Here comes old Tidd! Get your snowballs. [*Kids get snowballs;*
rush off L. Deacon enters after peeking on from behind schoolhouse]

Deac. Drat 'em! I guess they've gone in. [*Comes down C. shower of*
snowballs. Deacon yells and runs L. Kids yell and disappear]

Nora. Don't feel so badly about it, Annie. It may not be so serious as we
fear.

Annie. [*Crying*] Oh, do you think they'll send Ned to prison, Miss Nora?
Shall I never see him again?

Nora. Not so bad as that, surely. Indeed, Mr. Keene told me he thought
it would all come right in time.

Annie. Where is Ned now?

Nora. Deacon Tidd took him over to his house and locked him up there.
I do think Squire Olcott acted very cruelly in refusing to bail him, but he'll
be treated well. Come now, Annie, it's almost nine o'clock. If you don't feel
able to stay in school, I'll excuse you. I think you'd better, perhaps, go home.

Annie. Oh, I don't care to. Mother would be so angry if I did.

NORA. [*Writes at desk*] I'll make that all right. I'll write her a note, telling her I took the responsibility of sending you home, because I thought you ill.

ANNIE. But she will scold you for it.

NORA. Never mind me.

MAR. [*Enters schoolhouse*] Say, Miss Nora, will you show me how to do the ninth example? I asked Dave Hamlin down to the store, and he tried it four times and he says the answer's wrong in the book.

NORA. I'll show you. [*To Annie*] Here's the note. Good-by, dear. [*Kisses her and Annie goes out L.2.E. Nora takes slate and ciphers with Martin. Enter Labaree. He meets Annie Grey as she exits L.2.E.*]

LAB. Good morning, Annie. [*Looks at note*] Where are you going?

ANNIE. Home. [*Puts note behind her. Starts to go. He detains her*]

LAB. I suppose you've heard that Ned Olcott has confessed that he robbed the bank and is arrested.

ANNIE. Yes, I've heard it.

LAB. I always told you that he was a bad fellow. You see, now, that I was right.

ANNIE. I don't believe that he is a bad fellow. I don't believe he did it, and I hate you, because you're so glad he's in trouble!

LAB. Glad? But I'm not. I'm very sorry for him. I'm on my way now to see what can be done to help him out of his difficulty.

ANNIE. Then don't let me detain you. [*Exits L.*]

LAB. That's all right, young woman, but you'll think differently some day. [*Exits R. Enter John with children L.1.E.*]

JOHN. And that is the end of the story—

CHILDREN. Oh, tell us another, Mr. Bradbury, please.

JOHN. Some other time. Run along and play.

NORA. There it is, Martin.

MAR. Thank ye. [*Exits. Meets John coming in*]

JOHN. Good morning, Martin.

MAR. Good morning. [*Crosses to L.*] Say, Mr. Bradbury, look out. That step is icy.

JOHN. I see it is. Why don't you put some ashes on it? [*C.*]

MAR. Well, Deacon Tidd's coming here today. [*Chuckles*]

JOHN. And what has that to do with it?

MAR. Oh, nothin'. But it may kinder give him somethin' practical to 'tend ter—

JOHN. You must do something to it. [*Knocks at door*]

MAR. Do something to it? All right. [*Goes off R.2.E. Returns with watering can, waters step, tries it, slips on it, exits L.2.E. with can*]

NORA. [*Meanwhile opens door*] Good morning, Mr. Bradbury. Come in!

JOHN. [*Enters*] Have I arrived too soon?

NORA. [*R.*] Oh, not at all. That is—the session begins in a few minutes. I hope you will pardon anything that may be wrong this morning. I am so distressed about Ned Olcott that I am not at all myself. The poor fellow!

JOHN. It is too bad. I never thought Ned a bad fellow, only spirited.

NORA. And I'm sure he is not bad. There is a mystery about this affair that is yet to be cleared up. Oh, Mr. Bradbury, don't you think you could persuade his uncle to try to do something for him?

JOHN. I don't know.

NORA. I am sure you could. Oh, do, please. Go and see Squire Olcott and ask him to do something for Ned.

JOHN. You seem very anxious for Ned!

NORA. Why, of course. Oh, Mr. Bradbury, he is a real good boy at heart and I am sure he is not the thief. Please go and see his uncle.

JOHN. I will, if you desire it.

NORA. You will find the squire at home now. [*Clock strikes nine*] There's the clock! I must ring the bell. [*Takes bell*]

JOHN. Let me ring it for you.

NORA. Oh, no. No thank you. Please hurry and see Squire Olcott. Think of that poor boy. [*They go to door. She rings bell. Children come on. All bow to John, who bows*] Beg of him to try and help Ned.

JOHN. I will say all that I can.

NORA. You are very good. [*Enters school. Dot runs on late, kisses John, and rushes in. All the children take seats*]

JOHN. [*Alone outside the building*] How very anxious she seems about Ned. Does she—she sympathizes with everybody who is in distress. I won't be jealous till I have cause and the right to be. [*Exits R.U.E.*]

DEAC. [*Head appears over fence L.*] Them dratted boys have gone in! I reckon it's safe. [*Enters R.2.E. followed by Lizzie and Keene. Goes to schoolhouse*]

LIZ. You seem mighty feared of these boys, deacon.

DEAC. No, I ain't. But it's undignified to be snowballed by 'em. Ye know I never lose my dignity. [*Falls on the icy step*] Land o' gosh! [*Rises and falls again. Keene picks him up. They enter building. Lizzie goes over the step very carefully*]

NORA. Good morning, again. Mr. Keene, you here?

KEENE. Yes, I went over to the deacon's house with them when they locked up Ned, and the deacon invited me up to see the school.

NORA. That was very wise and thoughtful of him. Please be seated. [*They sit*] Deacon Tidd, shall we proceed at once to the examination of classes, or will you say a few words to the children?

KEENE. [*Aside to Deacon*] Never miss a chance to make a speech. Give them some practical common sense.

DEAC. Wa'al, mebbe I'd better say a few words. [*Rises and goes to Nora's desk*] Children [*Starts his speech; then stops to look at Martin; business*], children, I'm glad to see ye here—I'm allus glad to see children in school, 'cause it keeps 'em out of mischief and other folks' dooryards. I hope yer study hard and try to behave yerselves, 'cause if ye don't, some on ye'll git lickens. [*Business*] Ye must appreciate yer advantages and not be frivolous [*Business*]—but study hard as yer can. Learn what is practical, learn the multiplication table, stick to the three R's—readin', writin', and 'rithmetic, and ye'll grow up to be good citizens. [*Turns to Nora; Keene starts applause; children join in; Deacon crosses R. to Keene*] Fine children this town raises!

KEENE. Yes, very fine children.

NORA. First class in geography, come forward. [*Dot, Martin, and one other start*] Deacon, shall I question them? [*He ʻods*] Dot, describe the equator. [*All put up hands*]

DOT. The equator is an imaginary line extending around the earth equidistant from the poles.

DEAC. Now, hold on. I must 'tend to this. [*Rises*] Hevn't I begged on ye to teach these children something practical? What's the use wasting time over imaginary lines? If the line was there, it would be all right to know about it, but it's imaginary.

NORA. [*Indignant*] Perhaps, deacon, you had better ask them a few practical questions.

DEAC. All right. Er—er—

NORA. Do you want the book?

DEAC. Oh, no—er—er—

KEENE. [*Aside to Deacon*] What's the largest city in the world?

DEAC. What's the largest city in the world? [*Class hold up hands*] Martin?

MAR. Chicago!

DEAC. Yes.

KEENE. [*Aside to Deacon*] No it isn't!

DEAC. I mean—no! Don't you know better'n that?

MAR. Wa'al, anyhow a Chicago man told me it was! [*Deacon looks inquiringly at Keene, who shakes his head*]

DEAC. Wa'al, don't you ever believe anything a Chicago man tells ye—er—er—

KEENE. [*Aside to Deacon*] Largest city in New England?

DEAC. What's the largest city in New England? [*Hands up as before*] Dot?

DOT. Boston. [*Hands down*]

DEAC. No.

KEENE. Yes, it is. [*Nods to Deacon that it is correct*]

DEAC. [*Aside to Keene*] Have you ever been to Nashua?

KEENE. Yes, but Boston's the larger.

DEAC. [*Pause*] Yes, quite correct. Boston's the biggest.

KEENE. [*Prompting*] For what is it noted?

DEAC. For what is it noted? [*Hands up*] Martin.

MAR. Its baseball club. [*Hands stay up and are frantically waved*]

DEAC. No, no. Dot?

DOT. John L. Sullivan. [*All hands down*]

DEAC. Yes, that's right. [*Looks at Keene. Gag for Martin*]

KEENE. Yes, better let that go. Ask what two rivers join to make the Ohio.

DEAC. What two rivers join to make the Ohio? [*Hands up*] Dot?

DOT. The Allegheny and the Monongahela.

DEAC. Not at all. Why, an Allegheny is one o' them critters they hev down South that bit Fin Never's leg off when he was in the army, and now he's gittin' a pension 'cause he said he had it shot off. Monongahela is whiskey—you can't fool me on Monongahela.

LIZ. You're wrong, deacon! You're wrong! The Monongahela has got you mixed up and you're thinkin' of alligators.

KEENE. It often affects a man that way. Not at all surprising. Go on, deacon.

DEAC. Wa'al—er— Where is the North Pole, Dot?

DOT. [*Slight hesitation*] I—I don't know, sir.

DEAC. Don't know? Don't know where the North Pole is? Now ain't you ashamed?

DOT. Why, sir, if Sir John Franklin and Dr. Kane and De Long and Greely couldn't find it, how should I know where it is?

DEAC. Wa'al, they hain't gone to look for it in a practical way. I wish they'd send me to look for it. I'd tend to it.

DOT. [*To Nora*] I wish they would. [*Deacon sits*]

NORA. The class is dismissed. [*Class sits*]

KEENE. [*Crosses over L. above desk*] Do you not instruct your pupils in oratory? [*Winks at Dot*]

NORA. The boys speak "pieces," as they call it.

DEAC. Well, if you've been teachin' it, let's hear some of it.

KEENE. Won't you oblige me, Miss Fairford, by having Martin speak a piece?

LIZ. Do. I so love a display of eloquence.

NORA. I submit. Martin, come forward and recite. [*Business of Dot catching Martin by the ear and bringing him up from bench*]

MAR. I'd rather not.

DEAC. I must 'tend to this. Come along, young man! [*Martin comes C.*]

DOT. [*Aside to Martin*] Now you'll catch it!

NORA. You may begin. [*Aside to Keene*] This is unkind. [*Martin holds up his hand*] Well, what is it?

MAR. Please, may I go out?

DEAC. No, sir. You stay right here and speak.

MAR. [*Sulkily*] What'll I speak?

DEAC. "Woodman, spare that tree."

KEENE. [*Crosses back R. Aside to Deacon*] That's a chestnut.

DEAC. What's a chestnut? Oh, yes. Go on, Martin.

MAR. [*Bows awkwardly*] "Woodman, spare that tree.
　　　　　　　　Touch not a single bough.
　　　　　　　　In youth it sheltered me,
　　　　　　　　And I'll protect it now.
　　　　　　　　'Twas my forefather's hand
　　　　　　　　That—" er—er—
　　　　　　　　"'Twas my forefather's hand
　　　　　　　　That—" —er—er—

NORA. [*Prompting him*] "That placed it—"

MAR. [*Stumbling*] "That placed it—placed it—placed—" Oh, blame take the whole business! [*Goes to his seat*]

DEAC. If I was your forefather, I'd know where to place my hand! I must 'tend to this! Ye hain't got the idea at all. Get down here! Say, young man, don't you know that you're tampering with one of the most beautiful poems Shakespeare ever writ? [*Martin is below Nora's desk*] Now take the first line: "Woodman, spare that tree." Now he means that particular tree. You command the woodchopper to spare that tree and you want him to spare that tree because it's a chestnut tree. Now take the next line: "Touch not a single bough." [*Bows*] That's a beautiful line. "In youth it sheltered me, and I'll protect it now." Ye mean that you'll pertect that tree. Yer want to take an attitude of perfect. [*Puts up fists as if for boxing. Martin sneaks to his seat. John has just entered as Deacon takes attitude and he smiles in spite of himself. Deacon wilts and falls into chair. Keene has put Deacon's hat on the chair. Deacon sits on it and crushes it. Comedy business*]

JOHN. [*Amused*] Don't let me interrupt. [*Sits above Nora*]

NORA. It is nearly time for recess, but before that I want you to hear the children sing.

DEAC. All right. [*Still annoyed*] Do something quick.

KEENE. [*To Deacon*] Don't you regard music as frivolous?

DEAC. No, sir. I sing in the choir myself.

KEENE. Oh! That's what Martin meant when he said you got off your bass every Sunday.

NORA. What shall they sing?

LIZ. "Jingle Bells."

NORA. [*Strikes bell*] Rise! [*Children rise. Nora strikes a chord and the children sing. After an encore, Nora rings a bell again*] Pass out, children. [*All the children rise and pass out except Dot. As soon as they are out, they grab their sleds and yell, and then exit L. Martin remains L.*]

JOHN. Let us go outside and see the sliders.

LIZ. [*Sidles up to John, who avoids her and gets over L. She follows him*] Yes, let's. [*All go out except Nora. Children go by on sleds and some cheer at them. Dot lingers to say a word to Nora*]

KEENE. Going to slide?

MAR. [*Comes on with sled*] Come on, Miss Lizzie.

LIZ. No, I won't. I don't dare to slide with you boys. You'd upset and break my neck, and if you didn't the depot's at the foot of the hill and you'd run under a train of cars or something.

MAR. No, I won't. Come on.

KEENE. Go ahead. It's safe enough.

LIZ. I won't do it. Now if I had some safe person to steer the sled—

KEENE. Wouldn't you go if the deacon steered?

LIZ. I don't know but I would.

DOT. [*She has come out of the schoolhouse*] There, deacon, you can't refuse. Martin will draw the sled up and ride behind.

DEAC. Martin don't ride behind me. I want him where I can keep my eye on him.

MAR. Come on, deacon. [*Keene and Dot retire upstage*]

DEAC. Wa'al, it's frivolous. But I don't keer if it'll oblige Miss Lizzie. It'll probably save her life, as she'd git killed slidin' with those boys. Come on, Miss Lizzie, I'll show 'em how to steer a sled. [*Exit Deacon, Lizzie L.2.E. Boy, Deacon, Lizzie, and Martin up to slide*]

MAR. [*Keene and Dot come downstage*] If they ever get to goin' they can't stop 'till they git to the depot. They won't git back in time for [*Voice breaks*] no more "Woodman, spare that tree"! [*Laughs, and exits L. with sled*]

KEENE. Let's wait here and see them come down.

JOHN. [*To Keene*] I'm afraid you're bent on making mischief at the expense of us poor country folks. It was hardly kind to torment Miss Fairford by inciting Deacon Tidd to make himself ridiculous.

KEENE. Oh, I'm sure I didn't mean to make her unhappy. I'll go and apologize to her.—No, I'd be sure to make the matter worse. Won't you do it for me?

JOHN. [*Crosses*] I will try. [*Goes into schoolhouse*]

KEENE. [*Aside to Dot*] I knew he was aching for an excuse to go in there.

DOT. How very clever you are. [*She runs L.2.E. followed by Keene. They remain up L. Music*]

JOHN. Miss Fairford!

NORA. [*Looks up from desk*] Oh, Mr. Bradbury, did you succeed in doing anything for Ned?

JOHN. No. [*She looks sad*] The squire declares that he has done everything for the boy and now he's disgraced him. He'll do no more for him.

NORA. [*L.*] Oh, poor Ned! I'm so sorry.

JOHN. [*R.*] But don't be distressed. I shall furnish bond for him.

NORA. You? Oh, how very kind of you.

JOHN. By the way, Mr. Keene tells me he has made mischief here today and begs me to ask your pardon for him.

NORA. Oh, I forgive him.

JOHN. I fear you have many trials in this school.

NORA. Oh, I sometimes get blue and discouraged, but it doesn't do any good. By the way, here is a new textbook. Please see what you think of it. [*Enter Keene with Dot L.2.E. and comes down. Music stops*]

KEENE. I wonder, Miss Bradbury, to find you in this little village school.

DOT. And I wonder that you can leave your large practice to come to this little village.

KEENE. But I haven't a large practice, only a few cases and those can wait. I don't suppose I'd have had any except for some wealthy friends of mine who, when I was admitted to the bar, went and sued somebody just to give me a few cases to begin on. But, really, a girl of your age should be beyond this school.

DOT. Indeed, how old do you think I am?

KEENE. Your sex has about three ages. A woman is either eighteen, twenty-nine, or sixty. I infer you're about eighteen.

DOT. Then you don't flatter me one bit. For I'm only sixteen. However, I've been through this school years ago. Why, I was away at boarding school two years, but I had nothing to do this winter, and I wanted to be with Nora as much as possible. So I thought I might just as well review the old studies. Here come the sleds. [*Rushes to schoolhouse*] John! Nora! Here they come! Hurry up! [*John puts shawl over Nora and they go out to door. Dot with Keene. Boy comes down on sled. Then Deacon and Lizzie. Then Martin. Deacon's hat and Lizzie's back hair fall off as they pass. Children cheer*]

MAR. [*Runs on R.U.E. with back hair and hat*] Miss Lizzie lost her back hair and the deacon's lost his hat. They'll both [*Voice breaks*]—git cold walkin' way back from the depot. Say, Mr. Keene, come up and try it once.

KEENE. Losing my hat and back hair? No, thank you.

MAR. Oh, come along. I'll steer and won't dump you. [*Exits L.*]

DOT. [*Comes from schoolhouse; has just looked at clock*] There is time for one more slide before recess is over. Come along, Mr. Keene, I'll go, too. [*Exits*]

KEENE. Very well. Will you go, too, Mr. Bradbury? [*Exits*]

JOHN. I don't think I'll slide, but I'll walk part of the way up the hill with you. [*Exits L.*]

NORA. Hurry up. There's only a few minutes left. [*Stands in door and waves them off; then enters schoolhouse*] Oh, dear, I suppose I may as well work away on these everlasting reports. [*Tap at window*] What's that? [*Goes to window. Ned looks in*] Ned! [*Music*]

NED. [*Outside*] Open the window, Nora.

NORA. [*Opens the window. Ned climbs in*] Why, Ned! How came you here?

NED. Sh! Can't you lock that door? I've escaped from the officers! There was no chance to build a fire over at the lockup and it was so cold that old Tidd locked me in a chamber in his house. And when they left me alone, I got out just as easy as could be!

NORA. But, Ned, what are you going to do? Why have you come here?

NED. Do? I'm going to run away. The train goes in about twenty minutes. If they don't discover my escape, I can get down the hill to the depot and away on the train. But, Nora, I couldn't go away without seeing you—and Annie. Isn't she here? Can't you fix it so I can see her for a minute?

NORA. No, Ned. She has gone home. Oh, Ned, tell me the truth. Did you really rob the bank?

NED. No, Nora. It was to tell you about it that I took the risk of coming here. I couldn't go away having you and Annie think of me as a thief.

NORA. But did your uncle?

NED. No. I'm sure it's all a plot of Labaree's. I would not be the cause of my uncle's disgrace; so I confessed the crime myself. I can't stay here now and plead not guilty, and I can't bear to go to prison. I must escape! Keene told me to get away if I could, and I must go, leaving my friends to think of me as a miserable, ungrateful thief! [*Sinks on chair. Music stops*]

NORA. Poor boy!

NED. You believe me innocent, don't you?

NORA. Indeed I do, Ned!

NED. And will you tell Annie? [*Rises*]

NORA. Everything! But where are you going?

NED. To Boston first. There is no telegraph station here. They can't telegraph to have me arrested on the train. Here—[*Hands her a card*] if you wish to communicate with me, write to that address. You will write, won't you, and tell me about Annie?

NORA. Yes, Ned! [*Enter John L.2.E.*]

NED. And now I must be off, for I must steal along behind fences and through the wood to board the train just as it leaves the depot! Good-by! [*Takes Nora's hands and kisses them as John quietly and unperceived opens the door and sees him*]

NORA. Good-by, dear boy! [*John goes out softly, shutting the door*]

JOHN. [*Crosses to L.*]   Ned Olcott! It is as I feared.

NED. Oh, Nora, I must write just a word to Annie. [*Grabs paper and writes*]

NORA. Hurry, Ned! It is almost time to ring the bell. [*She is nervous*]

JOHN. But how comes Ned here? He is under arrest. I understand! He has made his escape and is going to fly. He has come here to say good-by to her. Perhaps to make arrangement for her to join him somewhere. I can give the alarm and prevent that! [*Starts to do so; pauses*] No! [*After an effort, folds his arms and exits gate L. Remains L.1.E.*]

NED. Here, Nora. [*Gives note*] Kiss the dear, good girl for me! Good-by! [*Goes to window*] Mercy on me!

NORA. What is it?

NED. Here come Tidd, another officer, and Labaree! They are following my tracks in the snow! I'm caught!

NORA. Oh, you must not be! You must escape somehow!

NED. How?

NORA. Fly! Go out this way, get to the depot and board the train! [*They go into the yard. Train whistles. Music*]

NED. There's the train at the station now! Too late!

NORA. No! You can make it yet! Take a sled and slide down the hill to the depot! [*Ned up to slide*]

NED. Yes, it's my only chance! [*Grabs sled and runs off L.2.E. Enter Keene L.2.E. and looks after Ned*]

KEENE. By Jove, it's Ned and he's taking my advice and is running away! [*Enter Deacon with Labaree R.U.E. Keene to Deacon*]

KEENE. What's up?

DEAC. He's got away! I went back to get another hat and found out he'd got out the second-story window. We tracked him here and he got in the back window of the schoolhouse.

KEENE. The deuce he did!

DEAC. We must search the schoolhouse!

NORA. Stop! You shall not come in here!

LAB. [*Peers through the window*] He is not in the schoolhouse! He is yonder! Look!

DEAC. There he is! He's trying to get away on a sled! Well, I can slide, too. We must catch him! [*Exits L. followed by Labaree*]

NORA. Oh, Mr. Keene, save him! Save him!

KEENE. Calm yourself! [*Looks off*] Hurry, Ned! [*Enter John followed by Dot*]

JOHN. What's the trouble? [*Dot up to Keene*]

NORA. Oh, Mr. Bradbury, save Ned Olcott! The officers are on his track and they will capture him! I know they will! I know they—[*Faints*]

JOHN. She's fainting! [*Supports her*] Miss Fairford! Nora! Mr. Keene! Dot! Help me! [*Dot and John support her into the schoolhouse*]

MAR. [*On the slide*] What's the matter?

KEENE. Go head off the deacon!

MAR. You bet I will! [*Runs up the slide*]

KEENE. [*As Ned goes down the slide*] Hurry, Ned! Hurry! [*Ad lib. Business of great excitement. Music changes for second curtain. Deacon comes*] *down the short slide, strikes the schoolhouse. The snow falls off the roof and covers him*]

CURTAIN

SECOND CURTAIN

[*Keene up C. John, Nora, Dot inside schoolhouse*]

Martin

Keene

John	Dot	
with	on	*Deacon*
Nora	step	

ACT III.

PROPERTY LIST: *A Yankee old maid's "best room." Ground cloth down. Small plain rugs or rag carpet. Small table with cover R.1.E. Old-fashioned wax flowers on table. Horsehair sofa R. Tidy on sofa. Mantel, fireplace, etc. R. Coal fire. Shaker chair at fireplace. Rush-bottom chairs for eight people. One rush-bottom rocking-chair. Plain white curtain for window (closed). Old-fashioned clock on mantel. Candelabra with prisms on mantel. Center entrance (no doors) opening on hall, draped with old-fashioned, large-patterned stuff. Stand with plain pot of geraniums seen in hall. Table up L.C. (covered) with books, album, etc. Second sofa down L.C. Small table to L. of this sofa. Two kerosene lamps. Old-fashioned portrait. Crayon portrait. Knitting and sewing materials for women. Peacock feathers or bunch of dried grasses over picture. Motto, "Welcome, Stranger," in hall. Sampler. Tapestry picture (queer). Doorbell to ring off L.3.E. Plates for twelve people. Slice of pie on each plate. Twelve forks—one on each plate with napkin. Pan of doughnuts for Martin to carry on. Chrysanthemum for Keene.*

MUSIC: *At rise.*

SCENE: *The parlor at Miss Lizzie's. The Sewing Society: stage filled with women. Doors, R.U.E., L.C., and L.2.E. Fireplace R.2.E. Window R.C. Old-fashioned clock, etc. Rocker R.C. Fiddler. Sofa L.E.*

DISCOVERED: *All the women seated in groups. Lizzie C. Widow L.C. Martin ready L.4.E. Slover ready L.4.E. Doorbell ready up L. As curtain rises, the speeches are something like the following, delivered all together:* "I knew that boy would turn out badly." "I always predicted he'd end his days in prison." "I always mistrusted that Nora Fairford. She's one of the demure, sly kind." "I never could bear her." *Etc.*

LIZ. [*Comes out from up R.C.*] It was very unfortunate about young Tripp.

ALL. What was it? What did he do?

LIZ. [C.] Why, they chased about two miles through the fields after a boy they thought was Ned, and when they caught him, it was Martin Tripp. And in the meantime Ned had escaped!

ALL. That Martin Tripp is a very bad boy! [*Enter Martin C. Hat on*]

MAR. Good evening, everybody.

LIZ. Good evening, Martin. Come in and sit down.

MAR. No, I can't stop. I just dropped in to tell you I'd be here later; so's you wouldn't be worried.

LIZ. But where's Deacon Tidd?

MAR. Oh, he'll be here. He's been out to the cider mill all day, and you'd orter see him! [*Imitates Deacon*] Say, I'll be back in a little while. [*Exits C.*]

LIZ. I do hope that boy's voice will get settled sometime. It's awful.

WID. [*On sofa L.C.*] I hope the deacon hasn't had too much cider at the mill. It excites him so.

LIZ. [*Sits beside Widow to her R. Woman on Widow's L. gets up*] I hope not. Where's Nora Fairford—[*Spitefully*] that she's not here, Mrs. Grey?

WID. Oh, she's over at my house with Annie. You see Annie isn't very well today and Nora said she'd stay with her a while and come here later.

LIZ. And you allow her to associate with your Annie after her conduct this morning in helping Ned Olcott get away? I'm surprised!

WID. Why, I hadn't thought of that before, or I wouldn't have left her with my Annie a minute. I'll go right home now and send her away. [*Rises; puts away her sewing*]

LIZ. But the gentlemen'll be here pretty soon and if you go home now, you'll miss supper.

WID. [*Resumes seat, quickly. Those to L. and R. of Widow sniff at her*] That's so. Well, I guess it won't hurt Annie much to be with her a little while. Annie is a good girl and won't be influenced by bad companions. [*All shake heads dubiously*]

LIZ. I know Annie is a good girl, but I shouldn't run any risks. [*Goes over to sofa R.*]

ALL. No, indeed!

WID. Well, I shan't go home till after supper anyway. But hereafter I shall not let Annie speak to her. But what are we to do? She's the teacher. Miss Lizzie, you're on the school committee. Why don't you turn her off? [*Rather sharply to Lizzie*]

LIZ. I can't unless the deacon consents. But I don't think she's a proper person to teach the school and mebbe Mr. Bradbury will change his mind after this. [*Bell rings*]

WID. The deacon'll be here, won't he? Let's speak to him about it.

LIZ. Very well. The bell just rung. Mebbe it's the deacon now. [*Goes up to C. entrance. Enter Labaree, Squire, Wing, Slover. All the women greet them*]

LIZ. Mr. Labaree and Squire Olcott. So you joined us? I'm glad to see you. How comes the squire here? [*Dr. Wing has led the Squire over to the fire R.*]

LAB. The squire wisely has concluded to forget his nephew from this time forward and will not let it interfere with his life in any way.

LIZ. A very sensible idea!

LAB. Good evening, Miss Bowen. How do you do, Mrs. Walker? [*Bows and shakes hands, evidently very popular. Sits next to Mrs. Grey*] Am I the first of the gentlemen to arrive?

WID. Martin Tripp was here, but I guess he's gone up to the church to 'tend to his trap he's set for the ghost. [*All laugh*]

LIZ. I guess the others will be along soon. I'll go and see about the supper. [*Exits L.2.E.*]

LAB. [*Aside to Mrs. Grey. Others talk in dumb show*] Well, we're rid of that Ned Olcott. I hope you've talked to Annie and persuaded her what a rascal he is.

WID. Well, she's really been sick today; so I hain't said much to her. But she'll come around all right. She'll do as I say! She's my darter!

LAB. How very fortunate it turned out to be Ned instead of the squire who stole the bonds. [*Enter Lizzie L. Labaree takes the Widow to corner L. for confidential chat*]

DEAC. [*Outside*] Martin Tripp, when I spoke about sittin' behind a bobtail, I referred to a hoss. I don't know anythin' about cards. [*Enters L.C. All rise to greet him very cordially*]

LIZ. So you got here, deacon?

DEAC. [*Very jolly and beaming*] Well, this has been an awful busy day for me. Beside being at the cider mill, I had to referee a cow case, arrest two tramps, and lead in prayer. But I knew you couldn't get along without me; so I came over to 'tend to things. [*Labaree has whispered to the Widow who now crosses him*]

WID. It was very kind of you. [*She whispers to Lizzie as Deacon goes over*]

DEAC. Wa'al, I knew you'd say so. [*Crosses Lizzie to speak to people sitting on sofa R. Women and Deacon C. Lizzie, Widow, and Labaree L.*]

WID. [*To Lizzie*] Now speak to him.

LIZ. Deacon, we want to speak to you on a very important subject.

ALL. Yes, a very important subject. [*Ad lib*]

DEAC. Do, eh? What is it?

LIZ. We think Nora Fairford is just as bad as Ned Olcott and we want her turned out of the school!

DEAC. Wa'al, I dunno.

WID. If she isn't, I'll take my Annie out of school.

DEAC. Wa'al, ye ain't paid yer taxes fer two years and ye ought to take her out.

LIZ. And the school'll be broke up.

DEAC. I hate ter do it.

WID. Oh, very well. Break up the school!

LIZ. Now, deacon!

ALL. [*Coax him and chuck him under the chin*] Don't be contrary!

DEAC. [*Looks about, tickled*] Hold on! I'll 'tend to it. I guess she's too frivolous to be a good teacher anyhow, and it—won't do to break up the school. All right; she shall go.

WID. She's coming here tonight. Will you tell her then?

DEAC. Yes, I may as well. [*Widow and Labaree retire L.*] If I don't do it at once, I shan't hev the heart to do it at all. [*Faces front*] But I tell yer, Keene said she did not have anything to do with the escape of Ned. [*Enter Keene C.*]

LIZ. [*Does not see Keene. Tosses her head and crosses R.*] Mr. Keene don't know everything.

KEENE. True! [*All start. Deacon up L. enjoys Lizzie's embarrassment. Then he comes down C.*] I congratulate myself that I'm one of those persons who don't.

LIZ. Oh, you're here, are you? [*R.*] Well, listeners never hear anything good of themselves. [*Crosses L.*]

KEENE. That's so. The propensity of people to say ill of their neighbors behind their backs is too strong. [*Up L.C. Enter John and Dot C.*] Here are Mr. Bradbury and his sister.

[*Squire   Doctor   Deacon*
        John   Dot   Keene   Lizzie   Labaree   Widow]

JOHN. Good evening, everybody. [*All bow to him, rising*] Excuse me, Miss Lizzie, for being so late. [*Crosses with Dot. Very formal recognition of Widow and Labaree. Dot shows her dislike and takes John up L., where Deacon intercepts them*]

LIZ. Oh, you're in time for supper.

MAR. [*Enters L.*] And am I?

Liz. Yes. Did you catch the ghost in your trap? [*Attention everybody; even Squire turns in his chair*]

Mar. No, but I've baited it with a jug of cider and I guess I'll fetch him tonight. [*All laugh*]

Liz. Will the gentlemen please come out into the dining-room and get the plates? [*The men follow her off L. Deacon and others remain L.2.E. The ladies seat themselves around*]

Mar. Gentlemen? Am I a gentleman? [*Exits, head up, chest out*]

Deac. Say, widow, I hope you made the pies. [*Widow is pleased*] 'Cause you always put lots o' brandy in 'em. [*Widow displeased. Deacon exits L. Squire*

         John   Dot   Widow*]

John. He does seem pretty cheerful. [*Goes up to Squire at fireplace*]

Deac. [*Enters with large plate which he brings down to Widow. All the other men follow and help the ladies*] Here, widder, I got the biggest plate in the hull lot for ye. [*Comes around in front of her. She is on L. corner sofa L.C.*]

Wid. [*Snappishly. Puts plate on chair L. of her*] Indeed, ye'd better keep it yerself.

Deac. Oh, never mind me. Age before beauty! [*Down L.*]

Wid. What?

Deac. Why, age before beauty—no, no, I mean beauty before age! [*Sits on fork; yells; gets up. All laugh; then resume seats and eat. Keene has got a big pan of doughnuts from Martin and sits next to Deacon and keeps filling his plate with them. Comedy business. Martin back of table. Dot with people down R.*]

Mar. Say, deacon, what did you have on your wagon coming in from the cider mill today?

Deac. Didn't have nothin' on.

Mar. Mr. Keene said he seen you comin' in and he said you had a jag on.

Deac. See here, young man [*Martin retreats to R. while Deacon looks L.*] I may as well tell you right here. I've had enough of your sass. Don't you make any insinuations about me and don't you call me by my first name agin as you did yesterday, and if you do, you git it right. My name is Lemuel, not Lemeul. Now don't forget! [*Martin is now egging Dot on to worry the Deacon*]

Keene. What makes this boy so fresh to you?

Deac. In a moment of confidence I trusted him and he imposed on me.

Keene. How's that?

DEAC. [*Aside*]   Why, last spring when the tax assessors was 'round he hid a dog fer me and ever since he's been unduly familiar. They all get too sassy to me. There's that Dot. [*To Dot*] Look here, Miss Bradbury. [*Deacon takes a large doughnut*]

DOT.   I'm looking. Do you want me to see how you're devouring doughnuts?

DEAC.   Wa'al, no, I don't. But you know what you played on the organ Sunday while I was takin' up the collection? Mr. Keene said it sounded like a tune called "I owe ten dollars to O'Grady." [*Keene becomes very busy eating; laughs heartily; turns his back to Deacon*]

DOT. [*Indignantly; crosses to Martin C.*]   It was nothing of the sort. That's one of Mr. Keene's very funny jokes.

DEAC.   Well, I've got no confidence in ye.

DOT.   You should have faith.

DEAC.   Faith? You don't know what havin' faith means.

DOT.   Oh, yes, I do. Having faith is believing what you know isn't so. [*Turns upstage. All shocked*]

DEAC.   It is, eh? Then I've got faith in your good behavior. [*Keene slaps Deacon's shoulders. Deacon rises. Business. Deacon C. Martin sees him coming, gets over back to L.*]

DOT. [*R. of Deacon*]   But I'll tell you what Mr. Keene says. He says the Society ought to make you wear a bell punch and ring it every time you get a contribution.

DEAC.   Well, I don't think Mr. Keene's an authority on church matters, especially in giving contributions. [*Keene is about to speak. Dot to John and Squire R. Business*]

LIZ.   There, there! Let's don't have a wrangle. Friends, Mr. Slover is here tonight. I believe we might have a little music. [*Lizzie goes up C. Deacon takes her place beside the widow. He is eating coleslaw; gags. Song*]

MAR. [*Back of sofa L.C.*]   Say, hadn't we orter have some dancin'?

KEENE.   I'd like to, but wouldn't somebody object?

MAR.   Oh, I guess not. Mr. Bradbury won't; he's a real good feller.

KEENE.   But the deacon?

MAR.   Oh, he's been up to the cider mill all day.

KEENE. [*Aside to Deacon*]   Do you ever dance at these meetings?

DEAC. [*Jumps up*]   Dance? Oh yes, let's have a dance!

WID.   Why, Deacon Tidd!

ALL.   Well, I declare! [*Keene joins Dot*]

DEAC.   Oh, it's all right. Ain't it, parson? [*Turns to him*]

JOHN.   I certainly see no harm in it. [*John speaks to Labaree up R.C.*]

DEAC. Come on. [*Pushes sofa and chairs out of the way*] Slover, git out yer fiddle. Take partners for smash winders.

KEENE. *For what?*

DEAC. That's the name of the dance. Miss Lizzie, be my partner?

LIZ. No, thank you. I got enough o' your management slidin' down hill terday.

DEAC. Ain't yer ever goin' to quit flingin' that up to me? If I'd seen the widder here wasn't engaged I wouldn't been askin' on yer. [*Labaree is just about to ask the Widow when the Deacon cuts him out. Business. Then same business between Labaree and Martin. Widow accepts Deacon. They are down L.*]

MAR. Dance with me, Miss Lizzie? [*She accepts him*]

JOHN. [*Comes up to them*] Dot, my head aches. I'm going out to get a breath of fresh air. [*Goes up to door; turns*] Friends, enjoy yourselves. [*Exits C. Remains up L.*]

KEENE. Excuse me a minute, deacon. [*Down C. with Deacon*] How do you dance this?

DEAC. Have you lived all this time and don't know how to dance smash winders?

KEENE. I'm afraid I have.

DEAC. Why, you go down the center—down the outside—cast off one couple right and left—ladies change—turn partners—chassé between sides—forward and back—turn partners once and a half around—chassé between heads forward and back—turn partners—down the center again—down the outside—cast off one—and go it again. It's easy enough.

KEENE. Oh, yes. Very simple. You haven't a diagram of it, have you?

DEAC. No, I hain't got no diagram. Just keep your eye on me. Come along. [*All in place*] All ready? Let her go!

DANCE

DEAC. [*In midst of dance stops all of them*] Hold on! [*Pulls his suspenders out; ties them around his waist*] All right! Let her go! [*Dance as before, until Deacon and Martin get mixed up with Miss Lizzie and the three exit L.*] Of all the green fellers I ever seen, give me one of them city chaps.

KEENE. [*To Labaree, who falls in chair R.*] Are you feeling badly, Mr. Labaree?

LAB. Just a little touch of my old heart trouble. It's nothing. [*Martin enters L. Everybody makes fun of him. Martin engages in business, and then exits C. Deacon enters, Miss Lizzie on his arm, talking. Martin remains up L. Widow replaces sofa*]

KEENE. [*R.*] Deacon, you're not much of a dancer.

DEAC. [*L.*] Mr. Keene, you spiled it all. If you ain't no better counselor than you be dancer, you'll never catch that bank robber. [*All laugh*]

LIZ. By the way, speaking of counselors, isn't Squire Olcott going to be elected councilor or something?

LAB. He has been nominated for the Governor's Council, but this bank scandal may defeat him. [*Enter John C.*]

JOHN. Is the dance over?

DEAC. Yes. [*Goes down C. with John*] By the way, Mr. Bradbury, you hain't said a word about politics. Ain't you goin' to preach a sermon givin' them other folks fits and tell them if they don't vote our way they'll go to destruction.

JOHN. No, I am not!

DEAC. Ain't? Why not?

JOHN. Because I am a clergyman, not a stump speaker! [*Takes stage L. Enter Martin L.C., rushing down C.*]

MAR. Something's the matter! [*All crowd around him*]

ALL. What is it?

LIZ. Is the kitchen chimney afire?

MAR. Worse'n that!

WID. Is the cow chokin'?

MAR. Worse'n that!

DEAC. Well, what is it? Out with it!

MAR. Something's the matter with the moon!

ALL. With the moon?

MAR. Yes. 'Twas full tonight. [*Pauses and looks at Deacon*]

KEENE. What? Was the moon full, too?

MAR. Yes.

KEENE. Had it been to the cider mill?

MAR. I don't know. Maybe it had. Anyhow, something's knocked a fearful chunk out of it.

DEAC. Something the matter with the moon? I must 'tend to this! [*Turns upstage. Martin follows. To Martin*] I don't need none o' your help. [*Exits L.C. All turn to go*]

JOHN. I remember now. There is an almost total eclipse tonight. It can be seen from the back of the house. [*All but Keene rush off, talking as they go. John remains up left*]

KEENE. Pardon me, Mr. Bradbury, but is there any thing serious the trouble with Mr. Labaree?

JOHN. Dr. Wing told me that Mr. Labaree is far from being a well man. He's got heart disease and a sudden shock might end his life.

KEENE. Thank you. Don't let me keep you from viewing the eclipse. [*Exit John C.*] There is something more than heart disease troubling Mr. Labaree. [*Dot looks in L. Keene sits on sofa R. and yawns*]

DOT. [*Pauses at door L.C.*] Aren't you coming out to see the eclipse, Mr. Keene?

KEENE. No, I've seen lots of eclipses.

DOT. [*Comes down C.*] Oh, and I suppose you consider an eclipse down here in the country very inferior to those you've seen in Boston.

KEENE. Certainly. Boston eclipses the world!

DOT. I thought you would make one of your very funny jokes on it, though. You've made fun, or tried to, on about everything here.

KEENE. You are very severe on my mild jokes. Yet you have laughed at them. Consistency, my dear Miss Bradbury, is a jewel.

DOT. So I've heard.

KEENE. And yet they say—women love jewels.

DOT. Does it ever occur to you when you are going to make one of these very sharp remarks against my sex that your mother was a woman?

KEENE. No. For a man thinks of his mother not as a woman, but as an angel. [*Crosses and up C.*]

DOT. And don't you expect—don't you want the woman you marry to be an angel? [*Sits on sofa; Keene above it*]

KEENE. [*Turns*] Well, I don't know. I'm bound to admit that I think a bright, jolly girl will do me. [*Dot is pleased*] That's what I expect to marry. Do you girls expect to marry saints? Because, if you do, you'll be disappointed. [*C.*]

DOT. No, but I expect to marry a man I can love, honor, and obey.

KEENE. Obey? Would you promise to obey?

DOT. Why, of course!

KEENE. And would you obey? [*Crosses over to sofa*]

DOT. Yes, but I guess I'd have something to say about what the commands would be.

KEENE. That remark convinces me that I have done your sex wrong in suggesting that it was willful or capricious. I now resolve never to speak disparagingly of woman again.

DOT. Well, I suppose you won't stay in town very long now that the bank robber is found and the case finished.

KEENE. Not ex— — Can you keep a secret? [*Sits on arm of sofa. Dot turns on him*] But the question's unnecessary.

DOT. You do me proud. [*Extravagant bow*]

KEENE. Oh, no, I don't.

Dot. Then you mean that I can't?

Keene. I never contradict a lady.

Dot. Not if she's wrong?

Keene. Not even if she is wrong.

Dot. Why not?

Keene. It is quite unnecessary. Let her alone and she'll contradict herself.

Dot. Oh, indeed! I thought you were not going to say anything more that was sarcastic about the ladies. Consistency, you know, is a jewel.

Keene. True consistency is a jewel, but jewelry is vulgar.

Dot. You are so clever about getting out of scrapes. I don't wonder that you're so stupid about getting into them. But what was the secret?

Keene. On second thought I don't think I'll trouble you with it. [*Rises and takes C.*]

Dot. How extremely considerate you are! But aren't you going to tell me the secret? [*Spoken very quietly*]

Keene. I think I better not.

Dot. Under the circumstances I don't think you have a right to refuse.

Keene. A man has a right to keep a secret from anybody but his wife. Now you're not my wife. [*Sits on sofa*]

Dot. I am quite well aware of that fact.

Keene. Now, if my wife asked me—

Dot. [*Agitated*] Have you got a wife? [*Draws away from him*]

Keene. No. [*Dot appears relieved*] But I'm beginning to think I ought to have one. I need a wife to tell me when I'm making a fool of myself.

Dot. Wouldn't the lady lead a very monotonous life?

Keene. [*Rises; looks at Dot before speaking*] Perhaps so, but she'd enjoy it. A woman is never so happy as when she is telling a man he is making a fool of himself. Dot, can I speak the truth?

Dot. [*Nervously*] I'm afraid not.

Keene. Then let me try. [*Dot has picked up her sewing from the sofa and starts to take stitches in it. Keene leans over her shoulder and she pulls thread and needle through her sewing, raising the needle above her shoulder. Keene bobs his head up to avoid being stuck with the needle*] Dot!—[*Same business over the other shoulder*] Dot!—[*Same business. He grabs her arm*] Dot! I love you! [*She tears her sewing*] I—Oh, I wish you were a jury! [*C.*] I'd know what to say to you then! Will you marry me? [*Sits on sofa to her R.*]

Dot. Why should I?

Keene. Well—I—because I want you to.

Dot. Then I suppose I must?

KEENE. You will! [*Rises*]

DOT. Yes.

KEENE. Come here! [*Draws her to him and kisses her. John enters L.C.*] Come in. I wasn't looking for anything in her eye. It was a kiss! [*Dot releases herself*]

JOHN. I believe you. Well?

KEENE. The fact is, your sister wants to marry me.

DOT. [*Turns on him*] Ah—oh—eh—

KEENE. Well don't you?

DOT. [*Crosses to back of sofa*] Well, I said I had no objection.

KEENE. Neither have I. [*To John*] Have you?

JOHN. No. I had made up my mind to it a week ago.

DOT. Why, I hadn't thought of it then!

JOHN. No? Well, I'm not so sure of that. [*Crosses to Dot, then to Keene*] Mr. Keene, I'm glad to have you for a brother, for I think you'll make Dot a good husband. I believe you are an honorable man. [*They shake hands. John sits on sofa*]

DOT. I think so, though he is a lawyer. [*Leans over sofa and puts hands on John's head*] Poor, dear old John! I'm so sorry your head aches.

JOHN. Oh, I'm better, I hope. Dot, dear, don't you want to go out and look at the eclipse and let me say a word with Mr. Keene.

DOT. Yes, certainly. [*Runs to door L.C. Keene puts shawl around her; kisses her; she turns*] Mr. Keene, what was that secret?

KEENE. Why, that I was fond of you.

DOT. Oh, I knew that long ago! [*Exits L.C.*]

JOHN. Mr. Keene, I believe you'll make Dorothy happy.

KEENE. Dorothy? Oh, that's her name! I must remember that. [*Makes a note of it*] I will try, old man. [*Sits on chair L. of sofa*]

JOHN. I'm glad that I can speak with frankness to you in regard to this matter of Ned Olcott. At any cost, whether he is guilty of robbing the bank or not, he must be brought back a free man. Can it be done? Is he guilty?

KEENE. I am not sure he is not. Remember what I say is in confidence. [*John bows*] Ned told me after the arrest that he confessed to save his uncle.

JOHN. And his uncle is the guilty man?

KEENE. I—Well, it's hard to say. I have my own theory concerning the case. Somebody else must have had a key to that safe. There's one thing about it that's rather funny. If the squire did the job, it shows he knows a man's got to have money if he runs for office, for the robbery took place on the night of the day he was nominated for councilor.

JOHN. [*Rises excitedly*] That day? Then Ned is not the robber! [*Crosses L.*]

KEENE. No? Why?

JOHN. He was a delegate to that convention at Newport that day. We both stayed there that night and as the hotel was crowded occupied the same room and came home together on the morning train, arriving a few minutes after the robbery was discovered.

KEENE. A complete alibi. But see here. This puts the squire back in the box.

JOHN. But it clears Ned. I can bring him back to her. [*Faces front*]

KEENE. To her?

JOHN. There is a person that I know who is suffering very much on Ned's account. It is for her sake I take so great an interest in the affair. May I not say to her that she need fear nothing? If she is patient, she may see Ned again, safe and free? Do let me relieve the poor girl's anxiety!

KEENE. Say that much if you like, but nothing more.

JOHN. Thank you. There's no doubt we can clear Ned?

KEENE. Your testimony will do that. [*Crosses L. Nora enters C. John crosses to her*]

NORA. Good evening, has everybody gone? [*John and she converse together*]

KEENE. No, they're out looking at the eclipse. [*Aside*] I suspect in this party I make a crowd. [*Aloud*] I say, I think that if you'll excuse me—[*They don't notice him*] I say, I think I had better take a look at that moon myself. [*Exits L.C.*]

JOHN. [*L. of Nora*] Miss Fairford, I have joyful news. [*Music*]

NORA. Of Ned? [*R.*]

JOHN. Yes. But first I must make a confession. This morning, unnoticed by you I intruded into the schoolroom while he was there and overheard. before I could withdraw, a few words.

NORA. And you heard—?

JOHN. Enough to know that Ned has left a sweetheart who loves him, whose heart, I fear, is breaking now.

NORA. You're right, Mr. Bradbury. But, pray, not a word of this to anyone.

JOHN. Not one. But I have good news for her. Let her dry her tears and rest in patience. Ned is innocent, and he shall be brought back to her, free and without a blot on his good name. [*Goes up C.*]

NORA. Oh, Mr. Bradbury, will you do this? [*Follows him*]

JOHN. I will see that it is done.

Nora. Oh, you have taken a great load from my heart.

John. [*At door*] Then I am repaid. [*Exits L.C. Music stops*]

Nora. [*Goes R. Surprised somewhat at his leaving her*] I wonder why John seems so unhappy. I know of no reason for it. [*Sits on sofa. Enter the whole crowd, talking about the moon. Dot runs and sits on sofa and talks to Nora. Keene at fireplace R. Dot crosses R.*]

Wid. [*R. aside to Deacon*] There's that hussy! Now let her know she must go!

Deac. [*C.*] I hate ter do it.

Liz. [*L.*] It's yer duty, deacon. You promised.

All. Yes, you promised.

Deac. Miss Nora—[*Music for first curtain. Nora rises*] I've got a disagreeable duty, but I must 'tend to it. I'm sorry to say that after what happened this morning, we've concluded that you ain't the proper person to teach school and that you must go.

Dot. [*Rises*] Oh! [*Keene stops her; she sits again*]

Nora. Oh, deacon! You discharge me?

Deac. I've got ter. I hate ter, but I'm ableeged ter. [*Upstage Labaree L.C. nods his head in agreement*]

Liz. We've had enough of women who help thieves to escape. Please to leave my house. [*Enter John C.D.*]

Wid. And don't return to mine. I'll have no such person 'round!

Liz. [*Points to door L.C.*] Go!

Nora. But I have no money. No friends. Where can I go?

John. [*Down C.*] To my home! [*Takes Nora's hand. All surprised*]

CURTAIN

SECOND CURTAIN

Liz. Deacon, a pretty mess you've made of this!

Deac. Me?

All. Yes, you!

Deac. Me? It was jest ye women! You tried to chase this gal out o' town 'cause you was jealous o' her and wanted to get her away from the minister! And yer landed her right in his house! [*Falls in chair C. All disgusted*]

ACT IV.

Property List: *Ground cloth. Three pews each side of the organ. Cushions (to be handled and taken up). Bonds in cushion, second pew R. Hymn books. Windows draped. Dime novel for Martin. Stool for Martin. Curtain for choir rail. Hymn books for Dot to carry on R. Two kerosene lamps for organ. Trap (steel) back of organ. Jug of cider back of organ. Lantern (lighted) for Deacon. Large oil can for Deacon. Jackknife for Deacon. Rope in belfry to connect with bell. Clock in front of gallery rail.*

MUSIC: *Organ and singing.*

SCENE: *The Meetinghouse. Lights down. Special border ready up above belfry. Calcium ready L. window. The balcony and lower section of the tower of the Meetinghouse. In center small organ; pews on each side; lamp hung C.; tower L.; ladder from tower to belfry; bell above and rope coming down through section of the tower showing; hymn books, etc., about gallery. The roof is covered with snow and moonlight, the effect giving contrasts with the interior when dark. High old windows with small panes at each side of organ at back. There is an entrance behind the organ and into the belfry.*

DISCOVERED: *At rise of curtain the choir, including Deacon, Labaree, Lizzie, Nellie and others are singing "There is a Land that is Fairer than Day." Dot is playing the organ, Martin pumping it and reading a dime novel; as he grows more and more interested in what he is reading he pumps slower and slower, gradually stops, still reading. The choir stops singing, one by one, leaving the Deacon singing alone. He turns finally and sees Martin reading the novel; stops singing, chagrined and angry.*

DEAC. What's the matter here? Young man, what are you here for? [*Grabs book, throws it across stage L.*]

MAR. Now you made me lose the place just as Buffalo Bill was going to scalp him.

DEAC. Young man, you'd better leave those dime novels alone.

ALL. Well, I should say so! [*Lizzie leaves organ bench*]

NELLIE. There! I don't see but that goes as well as could be expected.

DEAC. Yes. [*Martin goes L. for book*] But if you didn't make the organ squeal on that high note it would be better.

NELLIE. I think, Deacon Tidd, the trouble is all on your account. You spoiled the whole thing by your roaring. [*Crosses L.*]

DEAC. Now, you look here! [*Follows her*] You said the whole thing went as well as could be expected.

NELLIE. Yes, with you in it!

WID. Well, I think you're both to blame. [*Labaree backs her up. General row ensues*]

DOT. [*Comes C.*] Oh, dear, don't have another quarrel. You've had three tonight. If you only had Nora to play it, it would go all right.

ALL. Nora!

Liz. If she were to play the organ, I wouldn't stay in the choir.

Wid. Nor I! [*Tilts her nose up; turns to Labaree, who approves*]

Liz. She's a mischievous woman and you'll find it out some day. [*Crosses Deacon to C., and he goes L.*]

Dot. She isn't! [*She and Lizzie quarrel ad lib. Deacon stops them*]

Deac. Here, here! If there's anything I hate it's wrangling in the choir. You never hear me say a word. I think your brother's made a mistake in letting you take that woman into your house. [*Lizzie up to organ*]

Dot. You told John he did just right.

Deac. That's so. But when the whole Sewing Society called on me and expostulated and brought me a lot of jelly and dried apples and stuff, I see my error. But I'll talk to your brother about that.

Dot. Well, you can't change *his* mind with a bushel of dried apples.

Deac. There, that'll do! [*Moves away from her to the L. She follows him*]

Liz. Well, where's the books with the other carol in 'em?

Dot. Oh, I forgot to bring them. They're over at the parsonage. I'll run over and get them. [*Exits C. at back*]

Wid. I'm glad she's gone. Now we can speak to the deacon.

Liz. Deacon, have you notified Parson Bradbury that he must not harbor that woman in the parsonage as the Parish Committee voted?

Deac. No, I hain't. He's been away all week, ye know.

Liz. He'll be home tonight.

Deac. Well, I'll 'tend to it, but 'spose he says he won't do it? [*Lizzie, disgusted, goes up R. back of the pew*]

Wid. [*Crosses L.*] Then let him go himself. [*Deacon shakes his head and retires L., sits down in his pew, the Widow after him*] We're the people he's got to please and he has no right to refuse to do as we say.

Lab. [*Goes to C.*] If he finds he's got to give her up or go, he'll give her up!

Liz. You're a sensible man. Mr. Labaree. We appreciate you. By the way, how shabby the cushion on your pew's gettin'. I'll take it home and put a new cover on it. [*Labaree grabs it from her, creating a sensation*]

Lab. [*Agitated. Deacon rises*] Don't touch that. I—I mean, I'm much obliged to you and I want it to sit on. [*Deacon examines his cushion*]

Liz. Then I'll take it home after church tomorrow. We want soft cushions for *sensible* men to sit on. [*Looks sharply at the Deacon*]

Deac. My cushion's gettin' kind o' shabby, too. I guess you're right about the parson. I'll have a talk with him.

Liz. Thank goodness, we're to get rid of that Nora Fairford at last. [*Crosses to organ C. Enter Keene C. from L., meets Lizzie, moves to organ*]

KEENE. [*Sharply*] Good evening. Miss Bradbury here? [*Remains L. of organ*]

LIZ. [*Guiltily*] She'll be back in a minute. [*Down L. to Deacon*]

KEENE. Well, deacon, I suppose you're happy over the recapture of Ned?

DEAC. [*L.*] Yes. O' course, I knew we'd git him. I writ the Boston perlice jest what ter do and they nabbed him.

LAB. It seems his uncle has come forward and given bail for Ned. [*Rises and moves down R. Enter Dot and John C. from R.*]

JOHN. Good evening, friends. [*All turn away from him*]

LIZ. Here he is now. [*Aside to Deacon*] Let's have the matter over.

JOHN. Why, how is this? Am I not welcome?

LIZ. Oh, yes. We're glad to see you again, Mr. Bradbury, but—

JOHN. But what? [*Dot stands with an armful of books*]

LIZ. [*Aside to Deacon*] Go on! Tell him!

DEAC. [*Crosses Lizzie*] The fact is, Mr. Bradbury, we been havin' a kinder serious consideration o' parish affairs.

JOHN. Well, is there anything wrong? If so, let us make it right, if possible.

DEAC. Well—

JOHN. Well, what is it?

DEAC. I don't know jest how ter say it—[*Turns toward Lizzie*]

JOHN. Say it frankly and honestly with no indirection.

DEAC. Mr. Bradbury, I've always liked you as a minister, but the best are liable to make mistakes, you know; even I do. We think you've made one in takin' into yer house this Nora Fairford.

LIZ. Very good. Go on, deacon.

DEAC. Now we—at least, I hate ter do it. But the committee want yer to see your error and has decided to ask you to send her away.

DOT. Oh! [*Drops books; picks them up. Keene crosses in front of organ to R. and helps her*]

JOHN. This is your request as a committee?

LIZ. We are all agreed, Mr. Bradbury, that it's your duty, your plain duty.

JOHN. I must myself judge of what is my duty and I respectfully decline to comply with your request. [*Dot jumps up from her knees*]

DOT. You dear, good brother. [*Embraces John*] They're a set of spiteful—

JOHN. Sh! Dorothy! [*Turns Dot over to Keene who takes her up R. of organ*]

DEAC. Don't say you won't, Mr. Bradbury, because—

JOHN. Because what?

DEAC. It was voted that you must send her away or go away yourself!
[*Dot restrained by Keene*]

JOHN. [*Indignant for a moment*] Your committee has dared to say this to me! [*Calms himself*] Pardon my harsh tone. I bow to your decree. Tomorrow I, for the last time, will speak to you as your pastor.

DEAC. What? You won't let her go?

JOHN. No! [*Deacon down extreme L.*] And now, my friends, let us terminate this painful interview. Let us part in peace and goodwill. [*All exit, shaking hands with John as they go. Just as Labaree is offering his hand, Keene interposes and takes John's hand instead. Labaree exits. Dot, John, and Keene remain. Dot has handkerchief out*]

DEAC. [*Last to go. Keene back to Dot at organ*] Mr. Bradbury, this ain't none o' my git-up. I was fer lettin' you do as you'd a mind ter, but the wimmen are dead set on it. I tell you, you can't run a Society unless yer keep the wimmen contented.

JOHN. Deacon, I believe you acted for what you thought was best.

DEAC. Wa'al, I try to be practical. [*Starts to say something; breaks down and moves off; returns; tries to speak; takes out handkerchief; goes off L., blowing nose*]

DOT. [*Comes down to John*] Oh, John, Nora will never allow this on her account!

JOHN. She must know nothing of it. We must go home. Come along. [*Exits L.*]

KEENE. [*Dot sits L.*] Dot, what does all this mean? [*Comes down from organ*]

DOT. I don't know—I—

KEENE. I understand well enough why all these women hate Nora, but how funny John and she act. If he loves her, why doesn't he tell her so and ask her to marry him, as I did you?

DOT. [*Half tearfully*] I suppose he hasn't got as much impudence as you have. [*Bursts into tears*]

JOHN. [*Enters L.*] Why are you crying? [*Crosses R. Footsteps below*]

DOT. Why, we—sh! Here's someone coming. [*Enter Deacon with lantern and oil can*] Oh, deacon, is that you?

DEAC. Yes. Do you recollect how the bell squeaked last Sunday? I've been meanin' to oil it all the week, but the wimmen pestered me so I ain't got 'round ter it. Now I've got ter do it tonight. [*Turns when up L.*] Don't lock the door, Mr. Bradbury. [*Enters tower L.*]

JOHN. All right. Good night. [*Sits R.*]

DEAC. [*In tower*] Help! Help! [*Appears caught in a trap*] Take it off! Take it off!

ALL. What is it? What's the matter? [*Great excitement*]

DEAC. Somethin's bitin' me! Take it off!

KEENE. [*Takes off trap*] Why, it's a trap!

DEAC. A trap?

KEENE. Yes. It's the trap Martin Tripp set for the ghost and baited it with a jug o' cider.

DEAC. Baited it with what?

DOT. A jug o' cider.

DEAC. Where's the bait? [*Runs off L.*]

JOHN. [*To Dot and Keene*] Well, run along home. You go ahead and I'll put out the light. [*Dot and Keene exit C. Moonlight*]

JOHN. [*Returns R. Puts out light. Music*] I must write my farewell sermon tonight. I did not know that I loved this church and these country people so much. Ah, well, at any rate she shall be made happy. [*Exits R. Music stops*]

DEAC. [*Comes up trapdoor into tower*] I got the bait. [*Climbs ladder*] By jimminy crickets, if I'd known how cold it was here, I'd got Martin Tripp ter do this job. I'll jest git home as soon as I can and pile inter bed with four comforters over me. [*Tries to raise trap into tower*] Why, how is this? Gosh darn it, I forgot I put a lock on this trap to prevent the boys from gettin' up. [*Climbs down*] They been playin' tricks on the bell. [*Feels for keys*] And I've left the keys to hum. Well, I'll jest let the old bell squeak tomorrow. It's too cold to fool around up here. [*Tries to lift trap*] Now what's the matter with this? [*Tugs with trap*] The hasp has caught on the under side. By gosh, I'm locked in! B-r-r! How cold it is! What am I to do? If I stay here all night I'll freeze to death! I'm pretty nigh onto froze now. 'Tain't no use hollering. Nobody'd hear me at this time o' night. [*Goes to window; looks out*] I don't see nobody 'round. Yes, I do! There's Martin Tripp! Martin! Martin!

MAR. [*Outside*] Is that you, deacon?

DEAC. Yes. I'm locked in the belfry. Come up and lock me out!

MAR. I dasen't. I'm afraid of the ghost. I'll come around in the morning.

DEAC. He's runnin' away! That's the drattedest boy! Martin! Martin! You know I always liked you. Hey, there!

MAR. Stay there!

DEAC. Well, if I war'n't in church—Well, if I ever get out of here alive, I'll swat that boy. Now, Tidd, be practical. [*Puts jug up to mouth*] By gosh! The cider's froze! This is a terrible situation for a human being. I don't see but one thing fer me ter do and that's to take my jackknife and cut a hole in that trap so I can get my hand through and unhitch the hasp. [*Gets knife out, kneels, and goes to cutting*] Of course, the knife's duller than a hoe! [*Cuts trap*]

LAB. [*Steals in C.*] All quiet now. Ugh, what a night! It's cold! [*Hears cutting*] What's that? [*Listens*] Only a rat. [*Music*]

DEAC. By hemlock, I'm blisterin' my hand all up! [*Resumes cutting*]

LAB. These cursed women came near spoiling everything. When Miss Lizzie wanted to take this cushion home she didn't suspect that the bonds stolen from the bank were in it! Lord, how she frightened me for a minute! My heart isn't done beating yet. I must dispose of these bonds at once! It seems that no hiding-place is safe for them. [*Takes bonds from cushion*] There's that false key. I must get rid of that somehow. I'm nervous tonight. I could almost believe the stories they tell of the church being haunted.

DEAC. What a fool I am! Why, it's easy enough to let people know I'm here. [*He rings the bell*]

LAB. What's that? The bell! My God! [*He drops the securities. Deacon keeps on ringing the bell until people run on stage. Labaree falls C. Martin runs up ladder and gets Deacon out from R. John from L., Keene, Dot, Widow, Annie, Lizzie from R.*]

JOHN. Here's Mr. Labaree! He's fainted!

MAR. You, deacon! I thought I'd caught the ghost! [*Enter Squire and Nora. Squire down L. to R. of John. Nora remains with Annie*]

KEENE. And here are papers. Hold a light. [*General explanation ad lib*]

DEAC. [*Behind organ; comes down*] Hold on! I'll 'tend to things. Wait for me! [*Rushes on with lantern*]

KEENE. Here are the bonds and papers which prove what I've long suspected, that the bank robber was Stephen Labaree!

ALL. Labaree! [*Squire turns, facing front*]

DEAC. By gosh! This jest takes me down! Labaree the robber! [*Goes up L. Martin peers over his shoulder*]

ALL. This is awful!

LIZ. Why, I thought Ned Olcott owned up he was the thief!

KEENE. Yes. To save his uncle. [*Enter Ned*] Here he is home again. [*Shakes hands*] And free, and there are the papers that will acquit him. [*John crosses Squire and takes Ned's hand. Keene retires down L. Dot joins him. Annie tries to, but restrained by the Widow*]

NORA. [*Down R.C.*] And now, Mrs. Grey, that you know the truth, you will no longer refuse to let Annie marry Ned?

SQUIRE. He's to be cashier of the bank!

WID. All right. [*Turns to speak to Lizzie. Ned and Annie embrace*]

JOHN. [*To Nora*] Why, I thought you were in love with Ned.

NORA. Then you were mistaken.

DEAC. I see it all now. We've all been fooled. [*Throws hat to floor*] Mr. Bradbury, as chairman of the Parish Committee, I ask yer humbly to forgive us and stay with us.

JOHN. You must ask her. [*Indicates Nora*]

NORA. [*Crosses to Deacon*] Is it left to me?

DEAC. Yes. [*Retires up L. Music*]

NORA. Then, John, you must stay!

CURTAIN

A TRIP TO CHINATOWN;
Or, AN IDYL OF SAN FRANCISCO

In Extenuation: The author begs to say that whatever
this play may be, it is all that is claimed for it.

CAST OF CHARACTERS

The cast of the New York opening of *A Trip to Chinatown* on November 9, 1891, was as follows:

WELLAND STRONG, *a man with one foot in the grave*	HARRY CONOR
BEN GAY, *a wealthy San Francisco bachelor,* *of the Union Club*	GEORGE A. BEANE
RASHLEIGH GAY, *his nephew*	LLOYD WILSON
TONY GAY, *his niece*	LILLIAN BARR
WILDER DALY	
WILLIE GROW, *proposed at the Bohemian Club*	BLANCHE ARKWRIGHT
NORMAN BLOOD, *chum of Rashleigh*	ARTHUR PACIE
NOAH HEAP, *waiter at the Riche*	HARRY GILFOIL
HOFFMAN PRICE, *landlord of the Cliff House*	FRANK E. MORSE
TURNER SWIFT	
SLAVIN PAYNE, *a servant to Ben Gay*	HARRY GILFOIL
WAITERS	
ISABELLE DAME, *a family friend*	GERALDINE MC CANN
CORA FAY	MAGGIE DALY
MAY WING	LUCY DALY
FLIRT	ALLIE ARCHMERE
MRS. GUYER, *a widow from Chicago, not too strenuous on culture but makes up for it with a "biff"*	ANNA BOYD

THE SCENE IS LAID IN THE CITY OF SAN FRANCISCO.

ACT I: RECEPTION ROOM IN THE HOUSE OF BEN GAY.

ACT II: "THE RICHE" RESTAURANT.

ACT III: BALCONY OF THE CLIFF HOUSE IN SAN FRANCISCO WITH A VIEW OF SEAL ROCKS AT BACK.

[NOTE: For comment on the text, see page XIV in the Introduction. The first version of Act III here printed is from a prompt copy of the play; the second version of Act III is from the copy of the play in the New York Public Library.]

ACT I.

SCENE: *Reception room in Ben Gay's house.*
DISCOVERED: *Slavin Payne.*

SLA. [*Reads the superscription on an envelope in his hand*] "Mr. R. Gay!"
I haven't a doubt that it's an "R," and it's meant for Mr. Rashleigh. Besides,
it's from a lady. The shape, the perfume—[*Smells it*] the handwriting, all
prove it to be from a lady, and the old gentleman never receives notes from
ladies. There's no doubt in my mind it's for Rashleigh. Still, the "R" looks
enough like a "B," I think, to warrant me in giving it to Uncle Ben. He'll
open it and I hope find out from it how the young man is going on. I'll give
it to the old man. [*Enter Wilder*]

WILD. Slavin, has Mr. Rashleigh come in?

SLA. [*R.*] No, Mr. Daly.

WILD. When do you expect him?

SLA. I don't expect him, sir. I would not dare take the liberty of expecting
him, sir. I know my place, sir. [*Enter Rashleigh*]

RASH. Hullo, Wilder, old man! You here? I was over at your house looking for you.

SLA. Is anything required of me?

RASH. Yes. Get out! [*Exit Slavin*]

WILD. Now, Rash, you know the masquerade ball tonight. Well—

RASH. I know! I'm going to be there.

WILD. Yes. But the girls are going. Flirt is up in Tony's room now. The
scheme's all fixed.

RASH. They going! Why, how? I can get out, but Uncle Ben'll hear of it
—and your father'll never let Flirt go.

WILD. To the ball, no! But we're not supposed to be going there. We have
got permission to go on a night tour of Chinatown. That will account for our
being out late. Well, instead of going to Chinatown, we all meet at The Riche,
have a jolly supper. Our masks will be sent there; we'll put them on and go
to the ball. Being en masse, nobody'll know us, and when we get home, the
old folks will never suspect we haven't been to Chinatown. See?

RASH. That's all very well, if it works. How did Flirt get your father to
consent to her going through Chinatown?

WILD. Oh, he consented when Mrs. Guyer said she'd go as chaperone. Didn't you get a note from her telling you all about it?

RASH. No. Did she send me one?

WILD. Yes. She sent it by messenger from our house.

RASH. I never got it. Very strange!

WILD. Now, does it all go?

RASH. Why, yes. If Uncle Ben will consent to Tony's going through Chinatown.

WILD. Leave the girls to coax him.

RASH. But, say, if the widow's going along, we'll need a third fellow to balance the party. You bet she doesn't go without a fellow all to herself.

WILD. The widow! Well, hardly! She's the one who got up this whole scheme, my boy. The trip to Chinatown story and all! And you bet she's taken care the party isn't short on men. She's got Towne Painter to go as Flirt's escort, so you can devote yourself entirely to the widow.

RASH. Well, that suits me! The widow's more fun than any girl I know. Say, Wilder, I don't believe a woman is ever at her best till she becomes a widow.

WILD. The boys all seem to think she's in her prime anyway. That's a great song Billy Parker wrote and dedicated to her. [*Starts to sing. Duet, Rashleigh and Wilder: "The Widow"*]

> Do you know her? Have you met her?
> If so, you'll ne'er forget her—
> The pretty little widow with the laughing eyes of brown.
> Demure in her sobriety,
> Severe in her propriety,
> But the life of all society,
> The jolliest thing in town.
> No giddiness or giggle,
> No shyness and no wriggle,
> That makes the budding maiden such a nuisance and a bore.
> So bright in conversation,
> So free from affectation,
> You can bear no hesitation,
> And you hasten to adore!

CHORUS

> But when you come to tell her how you love her,
> As never was a woman loved before!
> Do not think you can deceive,

Don't expect her to believe,
She has heard it in the days of yore!

Most likely she'll refuse you,
Most likely 'twill amuse you,
She's got so many clothes in black, to mourning she must cling;
But if your pray'r impresses,
And besides, she rather guesses,
But along with her addresses,
A husband is the thing;
She'll breathe hard for a minute,
But, my boy, there's nothing in it;
It's only strict propriety that makes her tremble so.
She long ago has brooded
On the question, and concluded,
Very likely before you did,
If you'd be the man or no?

CHORUS

But when you come to put your arms around her,
And squeeze her till you can't squeeze any more,
If you think she's going to faint,
She will fool you, for she ain't!
She has been there several times before! [*At end of song, voices heard outside*]

WILD. It's the girls and your uncle. [*Enter Ben, Flirt, and Tony*]

BEN. I don't care if night trips to Chinatown are the fashion! I say, no!

TONY. But, uncle, I've lived here in San Francisco all my life and have never been through the China quarter, and this is such a good chance. We'll have a whole party together, and of course a policeman. And we'll ask Mrs. Guyer to chaperone us.

BEN. I don't see that she'd make any difference.

FLIRT. Why, she's a widow.

BEN. Yes, and is always sniveling about it. Why doesn't she get married again? I suppose because no man's fool enough to yield to her blandishments. I know I wouldn't!

TONY. But if she goes—

BEN. She goes alone! I won't have you out all night chasing through Chinatown. That settles it!

Tony. [*Bursts into tears*]   I think you're just as mean as you can be! [*Exits crying*]

Flirt. [*Crying*]   Poor Tony! [*Exits crying*]

Rash.   Come, Wilder. [*They exit*]

Ben.   Now I'm an infernal old beast, I suppose. Well, I can't help it. They're my sister's children, and I'll do my duty as their guardian, if I earn their everlasting hatred! [*Enter Slavin with letter*]

Sla.   Letter left for you, sir, by messenger boy. [*Gives letter*]

Ben. [*Looks at it*]   For me!

Sla.   Yes, sir. Anything I can do for you, sir?

Ben.   Yes. Go away! [*Exit Slavin*] Looks like a woman's letter. What woman would write to me? [*Opens letter and reads*] "My dear old boy!" [*Look*] "You must take me to the grand masquerade ball tonight! Even if I am in mourning, I'm bound to go on the strict Q.T., and you are the only man I dare to trust. You get the masks—it wouldn't do for me to order them —meet me at The Riche, don our masks and drive to the ball, and nobody'll know anything about it. Don't fail, for I'm dying for a good time. Yours — —. P.S. If you want to make it a party of four, I can bring Flirt." [*Speaks*] Well, I'll be—! Well, that letter's plain enough. These widows know what they want and are not afraid to declare themselves. But this to me! Why, I know she's been running to the house to see Tony, but I never suspected it was me she was after! Damn bright woman, that widow! I'll not disappoint her. But how can I stay out all night without the family knowing it? Change my mind. Let 'em go to Chinatown! By jove, how lucky it comes! [*Orchestra begins*] There's that cussed street band. Playing dance music, too. That's suggestive. I hope I haven't forgotten how to shake my feet. [*Dances. At close, enter four young people and catch him*]

Tony.   Why! Uncle Ben!

Ben.   I—was only thinking. I've turned matters over in my mind.

Tony.   I should think you must have with such violent exercise.

Ben.   I've decided to let you go to Chinatown. It's highly proper that you should see it thoroughly. Promise me you will go. Go early and stay late!

All Four.   We will! [*Exit Ben, R.*] Well!

Flirt.   There's a change of mind for you. I wonder what did it.

Tony.   I don't know nor care. We go to the ball! That's the point! [*All burst into chorus during which Widow enters and goes to C.*]

Wid.   And for it all, you can thank me!

Two Girls.   Our chaperone!

Wid.   That will do, young ladies! Rashleigh, why didn't you answer my note?

RASH. Because I didn't get it.

WID. Didn't get it? How stupid of you!

RASH. Oh, I know what it said. And it's all right. So you can dispense with those black looks.

WID. Not for twenty-nine days. You must remember I'm a widow.

WILD. Still mourning for poor Jack?

WID. Bitterly! I shall wear a black mask at the ball. Wilder, don't forget that in ordering the masks. [*Enter Slavin with a letter*]

SLA. [*To Rashleigh*] Note for you, sir. [*Gives letter*] Can I oblige you, sir?

RASH. Yes! Go and hide yourself! [*Exit Slavin*] It's a note from Painter. [*Reads*] "Dear Rash:—May be a little late, but will join you at The Riche. Will inquire for Mr. Gay's room. Wait for me. Yours, Towne Painter." That settles it! Our party of six is complete! Of course we'll wait for him. You wouldn't care to go with the party one man short?

WID. Care to? I just wouldn't! [*Enter Ben*]

BEN. Now, Tony—Why, Mrs. Guyer! Good morning! How do you do?

WID. [*Rather surprised*] Good morning, sir!

BEN. [*Aside*] I see! Discretion!

TONY. Uncle, she's going to chaperone us!

BEN. Is she? That's nice! But if she changes her mind—[*Winks at Widow*] you can go just the same. [*Aside*] She's throwing 'em off. Fly woman! I must speak to her. [*Aloud*] Tony, I want you four young people to get 'round the piano and sing me my favorite quartette.

TONY. Anything to oblige. [*The four gather around. Business at the piano*]

BEN. Mrs. Guyer, sit down. [*Seats her. Aside to her*] Of course, you mean to keep your appointment tonight?

WID. Most surely! Why?

BEN. Oh, I shouldn't let the young folks go out, only for that.

WID. You flatter me! [*Aside*] What ails the man?

TONY. We can't find the quartette, but here's a quintette. Come, Mrs. G., help us out. [*Widow goes to piano to sing*]

BEN. [*Aside*] Rats! I asked 'em to sing so I could talk to her. Well, I'll be— —! [*Quintette sings "Push Dem Clouds Away"*]

> If you want to git to Heaven on de nickel-plated road,
> Just push dem clouds away!
> Bring along all yer baggage and check it to de Lord,
> When you push dem clouds away!

If de train am a-speedin' an' you can't catch on,
When you push dem clouds away!
You're a coon dat's gone, and wuss dan none,
When you push dem clouds away!

CHORUS

Just push!
Don't shove!
Just push dem clouds away!
Keep a-pushin', an' a-shovin', an' a-pushin', an' a-shovin'
Till you push dem clouds away!

Oh, de chickens up dere don't have to scratch,
When you push dem clouds away!
All green and yaller is dat water-million patch,
When you push dem clouds away!
If de people am a-yellin' for pie and milk,
Just push dem clouds away!
De angels dere all dress in silk,
When you push dem clouds away!

There'll be no boys a-puffin' cigarettes,
When you push dem clouds away!
They'll all have wings, those mammy's little pets,
When you push dem clouds away!
Old Gabriel's horn will toot and roar,
When you push dem clouds away!
There'll be no dudes around the stage door,
When you push dem clouds away!

FLIRT. Does that satisfy your craving for music?
BEN. Entirely! I don't care if I never hear you sing again!
WID. That's nice! Now, I must run home and get rested for tonight. Good-by, all.
BEN. [*Opens portières. Aside to Widow*] Everything's O.K.?
WID. I hope so.
BEN. You and I are all right, but no Flirt!
WID. Certainly not! [*Exits*]
BEN. Young ladies, there's a woman whose example you ought to follow.
TONY. You don't know how hard we try to, sir. [*Enter Slavin with a telegram*]

SLA. Telegram, sir! [*Hands it*] Any service I can perform, sir?

BEN. Yes. Leave the room! [*Exit Slavin. Ben reads telegram*] "You will probably see me before this reaches you, for I am at Oakland. Will reach your house in an hour. Welland Strong." Whew! I didn't expect him till tomorrow.

FLIRT. Who is he? A nice young fellow, or an old codger like—oh, lots of folks.

BEN. He is a dying man, an old and dear boyhood friend of mine on whom Death has fixed its clutch. He comes here as my guest in the hope that our glorious climate may prolong his existence. Poor fellow, he used to be the picture of health. I dread to see him, hollow-chested, cheeks hectic, flushed, and glassy-eyed. And he, my boyhood's dearest friend! Say, he's liable to be here any minute. We must—[*Rings*] make ready to receive him. Get a lounge ready. [*Girls obey. Enter Slavin*]

SLA. Did you ring?

BEN. Ring? I next thing to turned in a fire-alarm! Get a glass of wine ready on this table. Bring fans and smelling salts. Have a man help you bring him from the carriage. [*Everybody bustling and get everything fixed*] He'll probably faint after his long journey. Now, is everything ready? [*Enter Welland Strong with cat and parrot*]

STRONG. Ah, there! [*All turn to him*]

BEN. What? Welland Strong!

STRONG. Yes! Welland Strong!

BEN. Why, how do you do?

STRONG. I may die before night! [*Business*]

BEN. Sit down! Here, Slavin! Take the gentleman's wraps! Have a glass of wine? [*Exit Slavin with wraps*]

STRONG. I will! Wine is harmful to me. It shortens my life. But I'll take it! [*Drinks*]

BEN. You don't look badly, old man!

STRONG. No! That's the exasperating thing about it!

WILD. Which lung is affected, sir?

STRONG. Neither as yet. But the left one probably will be by Saturday night.

RASH. Do you cough much?

STRONG. Not at all! That's a very serious feature. My malady is so deep-seated that I can't bring the cough to the surface. But instead I feel a sensation which, in a well man, would be called a thirst for liquor.

TONY. And what do the doctors say?

STRONG. No two agree.

BEN. And who shall decide when doctors disagree?

STRONG. Usually the coroner. Why, I had seven of them. One fool said that nothing ailed me. Do you know, the only man who really understood my case was a horse doctor! He said if I stayed in Boston I'd die in sixty days. Out here I'd live two years if I obeyed certain rules. Here's the book of rules and it tells just how much I shorten my life each time I break one. That glass of wine shortened it nineteen hours. [*Enter Slavin*]

SLA. Shall I take the gentleman's game to his room, sir?

STRONG. He may as well.

SLA. Anything else I can do?

BEN. Yes! Keep out! [*Exit Slavin with pets*]

STRONG. By the way, can you give me the address of a good horse doctor?

BEN. Why, yes. But hadn't you better see our family physician?

STRONG. Oh, no! He's no good! None of these M.D.'s are! They're used to catering to their patients' whims. Giving them what they want to take. A horse doctor don't try to please his patients. He gives them what they need. I'll never trust any but a horse doctor.

BEN. Well! Well! I'll see you have one. I know a man who cured my mules of colic.

STRONG. That's the man I want. He'll keep me going along, if any one can.

TONY. What feature of our climate do you rely on to help you?

STRONG. The earthquakes!

ALL. Earthquakes?

STRONG. Yes. They're very invigorating.

BEN. Have you ever seen an earthquake?

STRONG. I was chased three miles by one once.

BEN. Now, old man, you've got two or three years anyhow and we'll try to make you comfortable. After dinner we'll sit down and talk over old times. [*Aside*] I forgot! I've got to be out tonight. What'll I do with him? [*Aloud*] We'll have the house all to ourselves, for the young people are going out to see Chinatown by night. You'd enjoy it if you were only able to go with them. [*The four young people look at each other, startled*]

TONY. But he isn't, uncle. It's a very fatiguing trip.

STRONG. I don't know! I have sworn to see Chinatown, and, fading daily as I am, I shall never again be so able as tonight. It will, of course, shorten my life, but I'll go if the young people will take me!

BEN. Why, of course! Just delighted to have you go! Aren't you?

QUARTETTE. Oh, yes.

STRONG. Then I'll sacrifice—[*Looks in book*] ten days of my life and go! [*Cats heard outside. Enter Slavin all scratched*]

SLA. Your cat's got at our cat, sir! You'd better come, sir! [*Exit Strong and Ben, excited. Brief cat fight outside. Four young people down C.*]

WILD. Damn!

FLIRT. M-m-m!

TONY. M-m-m!

FLIRT. This is a nice fix!

TONY. We're dished on going to the ball, and we've got to put in a night toting that old fool all over Chinatown!

FLIRT. It's bad enough to lose the ball.

TONY. But toting him around is such a cheerless task.

WILD. What's to be done?

OMNES. Ask the widow! [*Enter Widow*]

WID. What? How to get out of this new scrape?

GIRLS. You know—?

WID. Just met your uncle in the hall. He told me this Mr. Strong would go with us to Chinatown, so I need have no compunctions about not going. And then—then he winked most mysteriously.

TONY. Uncle winked at you! I can't understand what he meant!

WID. Neither can I, and I'm a widow!

FLIRT. But this dying creature that's tucked upon us! What are we going to do with him?

WID. Take him along!

ALL FOUR. To Chinatown?

WID. No! To the ball!

TONY. But if we tell him where we're going, he will go straight to uncle with the story.

WID. But don't tell him where he's going; just take him along.

TONY. But when he comes home he'll tell on us.

WID. Then he'll have to tell on himself, too! I don't know this Mr. Strong, but if he isn't as deep in this scrape as we are before we get home, then may I always remain a widow.

TONY. But he'll make four men to three ladies. Some girl will have to manage two beaux.

WID. I think somebody will prove equal to that emergency!

TONY. On the whole, I'm rather glad he's going. We'll have a lot of fun with him.

WID. He's got an exciting evening in store for him. [*Enter Strong*]

STRONG. The excitement of that cat fight has taken a week off my life.

TONY. Here he is. Oh, Mr. Strong, I want to introduce you to our charming young widow, Mrs. Guyer.

WID. [*Curtsies*] I am honored.

STRONG. [*Pathetically*] A widow and a woman!

WID. Those affiliations usually go together.

STRONG. How pathetic! In the flower of youth to be bereft of sweet companionship! To be doomed henceforth forever to tread life's pathway unaided and alone!

WID. Ye-yes. But, say—there's no law against her marrying again.

WILD. Well, if I left a widow—

WID. You'd be pig enough to want her to stay one. That's a man. He thinks it's a slur on him for his widow to marry. Nothing of the sort. It's a compliment. Shows he made married life so happy that she wants more of it.

RASH. When I marry, I think I shall marry a widow.

FLIRT. Oh, Rashleigh! Why?

RASH. I'm too lazy to do any of the courting myself.

WID. We will change the subject. Mr. Strong, is your visit to San Francisco for pleasure?

STRONG. I came here to die.

WID. To die!

STRONG. Yes! It's a sure thing. The remedy I am taking for my lung trouble contains dynamite. If the disease conquers the remedy, why, I die of the disease. If the remedy conquers the disease, I shall be so full of dynamite eventually that I'll go off with a bang—[*Widow startled*] like a torpedo dropped from the roof on a policeman's head! Think, I may suddenly vanish with a loud report—[*Widow screams*] before your eyes! [*Widow screams again*] And it may happen any moment! Now!!! [*Widow shrieks wildly and faints in chair*] Great heavens! She's fainted! Send for the horse doctor!

WID. [*Springs up and glares at him*] What!

ACT II.

SCENE: *"The Riche" Restaurant. The stage is divided into three compartments: C., private supper room; R., the office with desk, etc.; L., another private supper room.*

DISCOVERED: *Noah Heap in C. room.*

NOAH. Mr. Rashleigh Gay's party of six. Well, that means up all night for me and plenty of wine on ice. But it also means five dollars for a tip. Mr. Gay may sometimes forget some of the commandments, but he always remembers the waiter. He'll go to Heaven. [*Voices outside*] Here they are.

[*Opens door C.*] Right this way, Mr. Gay. This is your room. [*Enter three ladies, Rashleigh, and Wilder*]

TONY. Number 10, with a piano. I'm glad we've got that!

FLIRT. But what's that orchestra?

WILDER. They have one that plays every night in this restaurant from eight to twelve.

NOAH. [*Points to R.U.E.*] The ladies' dressing room in there! [*Points L.U.E.*] The gentlemen's here. The dresses are in the room.

FLIRT. Let's go and get dressed at once while they're getting supper so we'll lose no time. Come on, Tony. [*Exit Tony and Flirt, R.U.E.*]

WILD. [*To Widow*] What shall we order for supper?

WID. Oh, some Pommery. [*Exits R.U.E.*]

RASH. Mr. Painter's not here yet?

NOAH. No, sir.

WILD. We'll have to wait for him; he's got our tickets to the ball.

RASH. Couldn't we buy others?

WILD. No, none are sold at the door. So we've got to wait for him. We'll go ahead with supper—though—sa-say! Where's our dying companion, Strong? [*Enter Strong*]

STRONG. Here I am!

RASH. What's happened?

STRONG. The hackman said five dollars. I said two!

WILD. What did you agree upon?

STRONG. Five! Tell me! Do we stop here long?

WILD. Our friend, Mr. Painter, who is to meet us here, hasn't arrived and he has the tickets.

STRONG. Tickets! For Chinatown?

WILD. Ye-yes. Of course.

RASH. Oh, you're not let into Chinatown without tickets. [*To Noah*] Isn't that so?

NOAH. Yes, sir. Fifty cents, please. [*Rashleigh gives Noah a coin*]

STRONG. Supper! [*Consults book*] Eating at night shortens my life ten days!

RASH. Well, you can sit and see us eat.

STRONG. You're very kind. But I'll not impose upon your courtesy. Lend me a pencil till I put down—[*Writes*] "Late supper, ten days off." What's ten days' life to me? Here, waiter, my coat and hat! [*Exit Noah with wraps*]

WILD. Now, Rash, we must be getting dressed. But, say, we haven't ordered supper.

RASH. That's so. Mr. Strong, what would you like? Won't you give the order?

STRONG. I fear the taste of a dying man may not exactly suit your fancies.

WILD. I don't know. I never tasted one. But you go ahead and order the supper. [*Rashleigh and Wilder go to L.U.E.*]

RASH. The wines we get out here are harmless. [*Exit both, L.U.E.*]

STRONG. I don't quite understand all this! [*Enter Noah, C.*] Oh, waiter! I hope you were careful of my coat. There was a large bottle of medicine in each pocket.

NOAH. Yes, sir.

STRONG. If the medicines got mixed, they would explode.

NOAH. Why didn't you say so before? [*Grabs carafe and drinks*]

STRONG. Waiter, I will order the supper. Give us—[*He pantomimes business of ordering the supper*] And, waiter, could you give me a glass of whale's milk?

NOAH. Whale's milk?

STRONG. Why, yes. My doctor recommends it.

NOAH. Well, you tell him to go milk a whale and get you some. It ain't on our bill of fare.

STRONG. Too bad! Say, waiter, will you do me a favor? There's a porous plaster between my shoulders that's drawing me crazy. Will you kindly reach down my back and pull it off?

NOAH. Certainly, sir. [*Puts hand down Strong's back*] How do you like your agony, sir?

STRONG. Take it slow. There's not a bit of hurry.

NOAH. I know, sir. A hair's breadth at a time. I won't hurt you, sir.

STRONG. Easy! Easy! [*A bell rings in outer office. Noah bolts for the door, R.L.E., taking porous plaster with him. He leaves Strong quivering with pain. Noah enters outer office and looks at annunciator*] He took skin and all! [*Reenter Noah in room C. with plaster stuck to his fingers*]

NOAH. I'll swear I heard a bell ring. Didn't you? [*Business with plaster*]

STRONG. No, sir! I wasn't listening for bells.

NOAH. [*Bothered by plaster*] Here's your plaster, sir! [*Gives plaster to Strong. It sticks to Strong's hands*]

STRONG. I don't want it. I never save these things as souvenirs. You throw it out.

NOAH. Excuse me! I've got to get supper. [*Exits C. and reenters room R., the office*]

STRONG. [*Business with porous plaster. Gets badly stuck up with it and in desperation exits C., calling*] Waiter! Waiter! [*Meantime Noah has gone behind office desk. Enter Ben, office, R.*]

BEN. Has a lady been here inquiring for Mr. Gay?

NOAH. No, sir.

BEN. I'm in time. Show me to a private supper room for two.

NOAH. Certainly, sir. This way. [*Exit both from office. Enter Widow wearing Hamlet dress into room C., from R.U.E.*]

WID. It seems I am to go to the ball in the guise of a man. I was forced to it. A man among the women! Well, that's what I always wanted to be! What sort of a young fellow shall I be to catch the girls? The very English young man: "Good morning, dear boy. Awfully pleased, awfully! Beastly weather this—in London, you know. Come 'round to the club, old chappie! Have a brandy and soda. We've new windows in our club now—special glass, magnificent fog effect! Brightest day makes you feel right at home in London, dear boy." And there's the young freshman in college: "We boys— ha! ha! ha!—have lots of—ha! ha!—fun. We've had a cow in the president's chair twice, and—ha! ha!—we've had a cane rush—ha! ha! ha!—and three men had bones broken, and it was lots of fun, and—ha! ha! ha!—Let's waltz! What! Engaged for the next? And all the rest? And here comes Mr. Winner. Yes, he's a senior, and I'll have to excuse you! Oh!" Or I might be one of those dear, delightful toughs: "Say, dere, sis, come and do a toin! What's dat? Engaged, be blowed! If he says a woid, I'll t'row him out, see?" But I guess I'll do best as just the average young man right up to date. [*Sings "The Chaperone"*]

> A crisp young chaperone,
> Who is always bright and gay;
> And when they dare not go alone
> They always take a chaperone
> To take the curse away,
> To take the curse away.
> Although it's far from pleasing
> To be severe and hurt,
> I'm chaperone this evening,
> That all of you may flirt.
> A crisp young chaperone,
> Who is always bright and gay;

And when they dare not go alone
They always take the chaperone,
To take the curse away,
To take the curse away.

A gay young chaperone,
Who is always bright and gay;
And captivating at a glance,
Will set your sluggish heart adance:
And eyes that fire and flash,
And eyes that fire and flash.
But still she's oft demurely,
Quite shy, reserved and plain;
Perhaps you think so surely,
Her heart and hand you'll gain.
A crisp young chaperone,
Who is always bright and gay;
And when they dare not go alone,
They always take the chaperone,
To take the curse away,
To take the curse away. [*After the song, a dance, and then Widow exits R.U.E. Enter Ben and Noah, room L.*]

BEN. This will do. When the lady calls, show her right in. And, say, you'd better have supper all ready. I shan't have to wait long for her.

NOAH. Yes, sir. Champagne, and what else, sir?

BEN. The best of everything. A corking supper, my boy! Nothing's too good!

NOAH. Yes, sir. Like to look at the evening paper, sir?

BEN. No. No paper for me! [*Exit Noah*] I'll just sit and think of what a lucky dog I am. I wonder how Strong's enjoying Chinatown. [*Sits and smokes. Enter Widow and the two girls in costume, R.U.E.*]

WID. I think you are very unkind, girls, to make any such remarks. You know I won't be out of mourning for twenty-nine days yet, and it's the only black dress of the lot. [*Strong enters C., sees Widow; exits C. and coughs outside*] Here comes Mr. Strong! I—I—Where's my mask? [*Dons mask*] Now to win him over to our frolic. I wonder if he's got a mask. [*Strong looks out C.*]

STRONG. May I come in?

WID. Certainly, Mr. Strong. I want to ask you a question. Are you stuck?

STRONG. Not now!

WID. But you have been!

STRONG. [*Aside*] That waiter told her. [*Aloud*] Yes.

WID. And you may be again some day.

STRONG. Not if I know it!

TONY. [*Exhibits costume*] Will these do? [*Sees Strong*] Oh!

STRONG. Bless my soul! What does all this mean?

WID. Girls, we may as well throw aside all attempts at concealment. [*Strong turns to go*] Mr. Strong [*Removes mask*], we are not going to China-town. We are going to the masquerade! We expect you to go with us, to join in the fun with us—and when we get home, we rely on your sense of honor to swear that we've been to Chinatown!

STRONG. But, my dear—

WID. Swear as an honest man that you will do this.

STRONG. But I don't think your uncle would deceive me! [*The girls offer him a glass of wine*]

BEN. [*In the other room*] I wonder what Strong would say if he knew I was here.

WID. Swear it!

STRONG. I do!

TONY. Ah, I knew he was a thoroughbred!

Strong. Say! Come to think of it, it's a mighty good joke on the old fel-low! [*Laughs*] One moment. [*Produces book*] This means two weeks more off my life—but let her rip! [*Enter two boys, L.U.E.*]

FLIRT. Are you dressed at last?

RASH. We are! Now for the supper, and then we're ready to start.

WILD. Mr. Strong, perhaps we ought to explain.

STRONG. It might be as well, but if you've got a really good lie fixed up for me, I don't mind hearing it.

TONY. He knows, and he's with us.

TWO YOUNG MEN. He is? Good boy! [*One each side of him and sing, "We'll Show You 'Frisco!" Then they all sing, the girls between them, "Out for a Racket!"*]

> Out for a racket, racket up to here!
> Out for a racket, racket up to here!
> Out for a high old frolic,
> Strictly alcoholic,
> Wine or whiskey, ale or lager beer!
> Out for a racket, racket up to here!

Out for a racket, racket up to here!
Out for a high old frolic,
Strictly alcoholic,
Out for a racket up to here!

[*Widow sings*]

In me, a modest maid you see!
Of course you know I'm college bred!
I've learned to calm my ecstasy,
To worldly joys seem dead!
This air demure is all put on,
I love to romp and make a noise!
My mamma thinks I'm an angel, but—
You ought to see me with the boys!
I love to romp and make a noise,
And you should see me with the boys! Ah!

Although, you see, I'm scarce of age,
I love to have a high old time!
Just now this seems to be the rage,
To me it is divine!
A cigarette, a glass of wine,
With lots of fun and lots of noise!
I would not be an angel when
I have a night out with the boys!
I love to romp and make a noise,
And you should see me with the boys! Ah!

BEN. [*Looks at watch*] Ten minutes of ten! By jingo, she ought to be here. It's prolonging the agony. [*Rings. Enter Noah*] Waiter, are you sure that lady hasn't called?

NOAH. Sure, sir! Supper's ready to serve when you want it.

BEN. I don't want it till she gets here. She can't be long now.

NOAH. Patience is a great thing in these cases, sir. Don't you want the evening paper, sir?

BEN. No, no! I didn't come here to read the evening paper. Bring me a cocktail. [*Exit Noah*]

FLIRT. Say, let's not wait for Mr. Painter. I'm starved. [*Enter Noah, C., with tray*]

RASH. Waiter, you can bring the supper. [*Music begins*]

TONY. There's the orchestra. Say, we're losing time! What's the matter with dancing right here?

FLIRT. That's so! Come on! Mr. Strong, you'll dance?

STRONG. If you can bear the spectacle of a man with one foot in the grave trying to be merry with the other, I'll do my best. [*Minuet. To finish it, Noah, who has been setting table, drops tray. Strong falls in chair. Noah exits C.*] There goes that lung!

FLIRT. Why, no! The waiter dropped a tray of dishes.

STRONG. I thought that lung had busted, sure. It's likely to at any minute.

BEN. Some pack of hoodlums in that next room! By jove, this is getting monotonous. [*Enter to Ben, Noah with four cocktails*]

NOAH. You didn't say what kind of a cocktail, so I brought four.

BEN. You know your business.

NOAH. I can take three of them back.

BEN. Over my dead body! [*Takes tray*]

NOAH. Hadn't you better look at the evening paper, sir?

BEN. No, sir! I had not! [*Exit Noah. The three men gather about Widow, R.U.E. Tony and Flirt are left alone down L.*]

FLIRT. Will you look at that!

TONY. Excuse me! I'd rather not see it.

FLIRT. I don't know why men go crazy over widows! It's enough to drive one—

TONY. To marrying some man and then poisoning him. This man Strong's only going to live two years. I've a mind to make love to him. With what I'd keep him out nights, I think I could shorten his existence to six months.

FLIRT. And she—

TONY. She's doing her duty as chaperone. Taking care we don't get familiar with the gentlemen.

FLIRT. Yes, and taking great satisfaction in it. I can see she's laughing at us!

TONY. I vow I'll break it up. [*Aloud*] Mrs. Guyer, how long did Mr. Guyer last after you were married?

WID. Only six months. [*Men draw away*]

TONY. I—I heard he died from the effects of a blowing up!

WID. [*Unruffled*] Yes. Excursion boat. Dear boy! He was insured for fifty thousand dollars! [*Men right back around her*]

TONY. [*Aside to Flirt*] I wish I was a man or a parrot! I want to swear! Say, Flirt, sing a song. They'll have, in common decency, to listen.

FLIRT. I can't.

TONY. Then ask me to.

FLIRT. [*Aloud*] Say, everybody. Tony knows this song the orchestra's playing. I want you all to listen to it.

TONY. [*Sings song, "Never to Know." Business of weeping with the song*]

STRONG. Beautiful! So touching! How much we miss in this life by not daring to speak out. I went thirsty two days in a prohibition town because I didn't dare to ask the landlord for a drink. [*Weeps again*] Forgive these tears! But that song has turned all my thoughts to sadness. The separation of two fond beings makes me think of the fast approaching day when one of my lungs will be withered and vanished, leaving the other desolate, alone and overworked. I have often in the still watches of the night pondered on this and at last my sad musings took the form of a little poem.

TONY and WID. Oh, give it to us.

STRONG. [*Takes drink and makes memorandum in book*] It's called the "Lay of the Lingering Lung." I wish that band would play a soft, tuneful melody. [*Recitation with music by Strong. As they break up, Strong goes to Tony and Rashleigh to Flirt. Widow sizes up situation*]

WID. Ahem! Have you heard the latest scandal? [*Every man rushes up to her*]

THREE MEN. What is it?

TONY. What have you been doing today?

WID. That remark was contemptible! Now, you shan't hear the story. [*Tells story to men in dumb show*] It isn't long. [*To girls*] And I really am not trying to monopolize the gentlemen entirely. I shall probably insist, as a favor to me, that they devote themselves to you. [*Goes on with a cry. Makes gestures*]

TONY. There they are again! I vow I'll be a widow within a year.

FLIRT. I know what it is. It's the dress. [*Widow makes parenthetical gesture*]

TONY. Did you see that gesture? I'll bet I know what she said. A widow'll say anything. Come, Flirt. [*They rise*] Gentlemen, we wish to use your dressing room just a moment. [*Exit L.U.E. Ben rings*]

WID. I'll bet I know what they're up to. [*Rises*] Pray excuse me. [*Exit Widow R.U.E. Noah enters Ben's room*]

BEN. Fill 'em up again all 'round.

NOAH. [*Takes tray*] Yes, sir. I have the evening paper.

BEN. Keep it! [*Exit Noah*] By thunder, that widow takes her time! [*During the above, Rashleigh has filled glasses and passed them*]

STRONG. Gentlemen, you ought not to tempt me like this. [*Drinks and reaches for bottle*] Every glass of this stuff is a day off my life. [*Drinks*] You are aiding and abetting suicide. [*Produces book*] Has anybody kept tab on me?

WILD. That last one was seven, I think.

STRONG. A week gone! I've wasted five weeks of my life tonight, and I came here for my health. [*Enter Noah with note and four cocktails on tray, C.*]

WILD. What's that?

NOAH. Cocktails. The gentleman in the next room ordered them.

RASH. Very good of him. [*Passes glasses*]

STRONG. [*Takes glass*] That man's bent on my murder. [*All drink and replace glasses on tray*]

BEN. [*Rings*] I wonder what's become of my cocktails.

RASH. Tell the gentleman we're very much obliged.

NOAH. Yes, sir. A note, sir. [*Gives note and exits, C.*]

RASH. [*Reads note*] It's from Painter. "Unavoidably detained. See you very soon." [*Noah enters Ben's room*]

BEN. Where's my cocktails?

NOAH. Gentlemen in the next room drank them, sir, and sent in their compliments.

BEN. They did! Well, I like their nerve! You go back quick and get me four more. Stop! Make it eight! And, say! Are you sure that lady hasn't got here?

NOAH. Sure, sir. Only ladies here are with the party next room. I rather think, sir—

BEN. Think what?

NOAH. You're shook!

BEN. Shook?

NOAH. Hadn't you better eat your supper alone, sir?

BEN. No, sir. She'll be here, sir! You get those cocktails!

NOAH. The evening paper!

BEN. Damn the evening paper! [*Exit Noah*] Shook! Me shook!

WILD. Mr. Strong, this isn't the first time you've been out for a pleasant evening. I see by the way you handle that bottle.

STRONG. When I was on earth I was not obtuse to the redeeming features of wine, women, and song.

RASH. Well, be a boy again. We have the wine and the women. Give us the song.

STRONG. If you care to listen to a voice from the grave, I'll—let me see— give you a little story of the course of true love. [*Song, "2:15," by Strong. During this scene Strong and the two boys are drunk*]

BEN. I'm having a devil of a good time. This is what you get for trusting a widow. [*Enter Noah with cocktails*]

NOAH. Cocktails, sir! Shall I put them down? [*Strong, in other room, is getting a bit loaded*]

BEN. No, I'll do that. [*Takes tray*]

NOAH. The evening paper!

BEN. [*Somewhat jagged*] Give it to me! [*Takes paper. Tears it up*] Now, are you easy in your mind? I came here to have supper with a lady! Do you think I'll be satisfied with an evening paper?

NOAH. What about that supper, sir?

BEN. I'll eat it. Bring it up.

NOAH. The evening paper, sir, had a whole page about a scandal in high life.

BEN. [*Looks at fragments*] It did? Well, I'll be—! Have you got another copy?

NOAH. No, sir. [*Exits. Ben gets on floor and tries to piece paper together. Enter, into other room, the two girls in shape dresses*]

TONY. Now can we have a little attention? [*Enter Noah at C. Musical introduction. Tony and Flirt down C., and sing. Then the two boys join them. Then as they go up R. and L., Widow enters R.U.E. in white Chinese dress and does Chinese specialty. Then Strong, who is getting pretty drunk, down C., and sings with Widow, all joining in chorus and dance at finish*] The widow in white! Have the twenty-nine days gone by so soon?

WID. [*Bursts into tears*] Oh, Tony! How cruel of you! To think I'd forget the respect due poor Jack! Don't you see this is a Chinese dress, and the Chinese for mourning wear white. I know my business.

NOAH. Supper is served.

WID. Come on! Let's get it over before you boys get to making love to each other's girls and the quarrels begin. [*They sit at table, filling time while Ben speaks in the other room*]

BEN. I can't put it together. It's all mixed up with the market reports. [*Reads*] "The infuriated husband, revolver in hand, rushed madly after a drove of prime western hogs just arrived." Oh, rats! [*Rise, pretty drunk; kicks at paper. Falls in chair*] By jove, I'm drunk! [*Rises and tries himself*] Drunker'n a boiled owl! That's a good one! I'll just keep it up and get paralyzed. I'll have some fun out of this racket yet. [*Rings*]

WID. Please pass the salt.

RASH. With all my heart.

WID. Just the salt, please.

TONY. [*Rises*] Well, here's to all of us!

ALL. Drink hearty! [*Song: "Reuben and Cynthia"*]

Reuben, Reuben, I've a notion
If the men were sent away,
Far beyond the stormy ocean,
Female hearts would all be gay.
Cynthia, Cynthia, I've been thinking,
If the men should take that trip,
All the women in creation,
Right away would take that ship.

Reuben, Reuben, I've been thinking,
What a strange thing that would be,
If the streams of drinking water,
All turned salty as the sea.
Cynthia, Cynthia, I've been thinking,
You can safely take my word,
More than half the population,
Wouldn't know it had occurred.

Reuben, Reuben, I've been thinking,
Will you tell me where or when,
Women will be forced to stop this,
Doing things just like the men?
Cynthia, Cynthia, I've been thinking,
And can answer with dispatch;
She must cease her mannish methods,
When she comes to strike a match.

Reuben, Reuben, I've been thinking,
Why do people risk their gold,
Betting on the wicked races,
Knowing they are bought and sold?
Cynthia, Cynthia, I've been thinking,
That is where the laugh comes in;
Each man thinks that he has fixed it,
So the horse he backs will win.

STRONG. Anybody have some cold meat? Mutton or beef?
FLIRT. Which is the best?

STRONG. [*Smells each*] It appears to be a case of horse and horse! Waiter, this knife is very dull.

NOAH. Permit me, sir. [*Takes knife; gets behind Strong; imitates sharpening knife*] Try that, sir.

STRONG. [*Tries it*] Much better!

NOAH. Anything else you want, sir?

STRONG. What have you got?

NOAH. Anything on earth.

STRONG. If there's anything you have not got, I want it.

NOAH. I can give you anything from a train of cars to a dog fight.

ALL. Give us a dog fight! [*Noah's imitations. At start of dog fight, Ben in next room starts looking for it. Afterwards, exit Noah*]

STRONG. [*Rises*] Ladies and gentlemen—

WID. He's going to make an after-dinner speech! Stop him!

RASH. Head him off!

ALL. Come on! [*Medley. At end of medley, all off*]

BEN. [*Rings, after entering from hall where he has been looking for dog fight*] She's here! I've found this handkerchief in the hall and it's hers. [*Enter Noah*] You demented lizard, do you see that? It's her handkerchief! She's here! Now, trot her out!

NOAH. Was that the lady you were waiting for?

BEN. Yes! Well?

NOAH. Why, we thought it was your wife! We said you weren't here!

BEN. Well!

NOAH. And she went away!

BEN. [*Grabs him*] While I've waited, she's been here and you sent her away!

NOAH. I regret it, sir.

BEN. Regret it! Regret it! I'd kill you where you stand, only I don't want to become known as a foolkiller! But I'll make it cost you your job. I'll give you a character at the office! [*Bolts out. Noah exits after him. Strong enters L.U.E., and crosses to R.U.E.*]

STRONG. [*Bows*] Did any of you ladies bring a corn knife?

TONY. [*Looks out*] No. Will a curling iron do?

STRONG. No, thanks! I can't curl my corns. [*Exits R.U.E. Enter Ben at office, followed by Noah, who goes behind counter*]

NOAH. What is it, sir?

BEN. I want to see somebody in authority.

NOAH. Gaze right on me!

BEN. You! You're in authority! Well, I want to tell you that the waiter I've had is a blear-eyed tramp, a bandy-legged idiot, and a foul hedgehog!

NOAH. I'll make a note of it. Anything else, sir?

BEN. Yes. Your place is a dive, and I'll never set foot in it again. [*Starts to go*]

NOAH. [*Locks door*] Hadn't you better settle your bill first?

BEN. I forgot. How much is it?

NOAH. One hundred dollars.

BEN. One hundred dollars! What for?

NOAH. Well, there's sixty-five dollars for the supper.

BEN. But I haven't had supper.

NOAH. But you ordered it.

BEN. All right! I deserve it! I—I—[*Business of looking for pocketbook*] Why, I've—I've lost my pocketbook. I'll send you the money tomorrow.

NOAH. We don't do business that way.

BEN. But I'm perfectly good.

NOAH. What name?

BEN. Excuse me! But you shall have your money.

NOAH. I mean to—before you go.

BEN. But, my boy—

NOAH. Send home for it!

BEN. Send for the money to pay for a racket here! Impossible! Now, my dear boy—

NOAH. No! I'm a blear-eyed tramp, and I get that money, or you go to jail. See?

STRONG. [*Enters L.U.E.*] I'll see why they don't answer that bell! [*Exits C.*]

NOAH. Do I get it, or do I ring for the police?

BEN. My very dear boy, I'm a respectable citizen! Don't arrest me! The story'll be all over town.

NOAH. Yes, but you won't be all over to hear it. You'll be in the jail. [*Strong enters office*]

STRONG. You hyena, I want—[*Strong and Ben look at each other. Both yell. Strong turns to run*]

BEN. Here! I want you! [*Starts after Strong*]

NOAH. Here! Come back, you! [*Starts after them. Grand chase. As they rush through C. room, everybody on exclaiming: "What's the matter?," etc. Strong yells "Murder!" and "Help!" Ben and Noah ad lib. Everybody working up excitement. At finish Ben overtakes Strong in room C., and grabs him*]

BEN. Now, I've got you!

STRONG. I'm a dying man! Mercy!

BEN. Mercy! Not a damned bit! Lend me a hundred dollars!

ACT III.

SCENE: *Balcony of Cliff House, San Francisco, with a view of Seal Rocks at back.*

MUSIC: *Offstage at rise. Sounds of laughter off R.*

DISCOVERED: *Turner Swift running ice crusher; Landlord shoveling ice into glasses on tray, which Waiter, who is standing upstage C., is holding.*

LAND. [*Gives bowl with ice to Turner*] Keep it going, Turner. This dance they're doing now is the last but one on the list. This ball has been a corker. [*Goes down L.*]

TURN. [*Near ice crusher*] I never saw people want so much cracked ice.

LAND. It was lucky we brought the crusher up here on the piazza. The waiters never could have gone downstairs for it. [*Exit Turner L.3 with a bowl of ice. Enter Flirt R.U.E., laughing and throwing a flower off R. after kissing it. Then she runs down C.*]

FLIRT. [*To Landlord*] I must take off my mask and breathe for a moment. [*Removes mask*] Well, monsieur, have I earned a *douceur?*

LAND. [*L.C.*] You're a dandy. More men have tried to find out who you were than any other woman at a ball before. Haven't you enjoyed it?

FLIRT. In a way, yes. I have danced with all my mistress's beaux. That was fun, but it was stupid.

LAND. Stupid? Why?

FLIRT. If I spoke they would know me. So all ze time I had to hold my tongue—a very hard thing for a woman to do.

RASH. [*Off R.2.E.*] Come, let's have one drink.

FLIRT. They are coming. I fly. [*Exits L.3.E. very quickly*]

LAND. [*Crosses to R. to table*] She's been the life of the ball. Lucky thought of mine. [*Enter Rashleigh, Willie, and Norman R.3. They are laughing and fanning themselves*]

WILL. [*As he goes down L.*] It's out of sight, isn't it?

RASH. and NORM. Great!

LAND. [*R.*] You have enjoyed yourselves?

RASH. [*R.C.*] Indeed we have! We got here late but we've had fun enough in half an hour to pay us for coming. Say! [*Leads Landlord to R. Aside*]

Who's the girl that kicks so high? The one dressed as a magician, the one in yellow? [*Norman and Willie talking L.*]

LAND. How should I know? She's masked.

RASH. That's so. She came without an escort, didn't she?

LAND. I believe so.

RASH. She won't go home without one. That is, if I can get away from my party. I wonder where she went.

LAND. I think that way. [*Points R. Rashleigh goes up and looks off R.3.E.*]

NORM. [*Crosses to Landlord. Aside to him*] Say! [*Leads him to R.*] Who's the magician girl?

LAND. Everybody in a mask is a stranger to me.

NORM. Oh, I forgot that. Very appropriate dress for her—a magician. Any man she waves her hand at is gone.

LAND. I see. Very good.

NORM. Which way did she go?

LAND. [*Points L.*] I think that way. [*Norman goes up and exits L.3.E.*]

WILL. [*Crosses to C.*] Say, landlord—

LAND. [*Crosses to C.*] Yes, sir, the lady in yellow dressed as a magician is not known to me, but I think you'll find her on the beach. [*Landlord exits L.2.E. Willie goes up C. and looks over rail. Rashleigh and Norman back on, all three men waving handkerchiefs as if flirting with someone. Enter Tony, Widow, and Isabel, R.2. They see the three waving their handkerchiefs*]

WID. There they are. [*Each goes up to one of the men and takes him by the ear. Tony to Norman, L. Widow to Willie, C., and Isabel to Rashleigh, R. They bring them downstage*] What's all this waving of handkerchiefs?

RASH. Waving of handkerchiefs? Nothing of the sort. We had them out to wipe our fevered brows, and the sea breeze made them flutter. Don't you see how it sways the lights?

TONY. Oh! We thought you were flirting with somebody. Forgive us! [*All embrace. Willie goes upstage laughing*]

WID. [*Advances. Aside*] The innocence has not all gone out of the world yet. [*Aloud*] Oh, doesn't this sea air feel good after that hot ball room? [*Goes up C. Enter Landlord, L.3.E.*]

RASH. Let's not go in for the last dance, but have a cooling drink out here. Landlord, give us six lemonades and some of that cracked ice. And, Willie, you go order the carriages up. [*Exit Willie, R.U.E.*]

WID. And, landlord, the sea breeze is just a bit strong. Can't you give us a screen to break it?

LAND. I can. [*Exits L.3.E.*]

ISA. [*R.C.*] I should think you might feel the air.

Wid. [*C.*]   It was the only black costume in the lot. [*Laugh. Enter Willie, R.U.E.*]

Will. [*C.*]   Our carriages are gone!

All.   Gone!

Will.   Yes. The doorkeeper says it was my fault.

Rash.   I'll bet it was!

Will.   So we had to telephone to town, and we've got to wait till they get here.

Norm.   Did you telephone?

Will.   I didn't think to. But I will. [*Exit Willie, R.U.E., very quick*]

Isa. [*R.C.*]   We'll have to wait here an hour. [*Enter Landlord, L.3.E.*]

Wid. [*Aside*]   It will give Mr. Strong time to get here. [*Aloud*] Just time for breakfast. Landlord, breakfast for the party in a private room. [*Up C.*]

Norm. [*Goes up L.C. to Landlord*]   And say, landlord, have those professional dancers gone yet?

Land.   No, sir.

Norm.   Here's fifty for them, if they'll come here and dance for us.

Land.   I'll arrange it. [*Exits L.U.E.*]

Norm. [*Goes down L.C.*]   I wonder if Strong is still at The Riche. [*Enter Willie, R.U.E.*]

Isa.   Oh, what are we to tell uncle?

Rash. [*R.*]   Why, that we lost Strong at The Riche and had to go to Chinatown without him.

Isa.   He won't believe it. I'm afraid we're in for an awful scrape.

Will.   Here are the dancers! [*Exits L.U.E. All sit. Enter Dancers. Specialty and exit. Turner and Servant place a large screen C. Widow goes up to screen*]

Wid. [*C.*]   Oh, that's much better.

Rash. [*R.*]   How Strong would have enjoyed it! I'm almost sorry we shook him. [*Enter Strong, R.U.E., quick*]

Strong.   You didn't! [*All rise, greatly surprised and gather around Strong*]

Norm.   What! How did you get here?

Strong. [*C.*]   Ran! After I got away from The Riche, I rushed madly downstairs. Nothing but a nighthawk coupe stood there. I jumped in. "Drive to the Cliff House!" said I. "Drive like the devil!" He did so! As we turned into the park, the bottom of the rickety old vehicle dropped out. The driver didn't notice it. He kept on driving like the devil, and I had to run inside that hack all the way out here! [*All laugh*] I wouldn't have minded it though, if it hadn't been such a chestnut. But, bless my soul, what does all this mean? [*Girls a bit confused and hesitate. Then Widow blurts out*]

WID. [*R.C.*] Girls, we may as well throw aside all attempt at concealment.

STRONG. [*Looks at her*] Throw aside all attempt at concealment? Excuse me! [*Rushes upstage. Norman and Isabel stop him; then all downstage as before*]

WID. [*Business*] Mr. Strong, I might as well tell you my story. Instead of going to Chinatown, we've been to the ball. Hence these dresses. How am I as a harlequin?

STRONG. [*C.*] I appreciate the take-off—but—

WID. But if Uncle Ben knew of it, we'd be in an awful scrape; so we rely on your generosity not to tell him.

STRONG.. Me tell him? I'm in a worse scrape with him than you are. Say, you've all had a narrow escape. Your uncle was in another room at The Riche!

ALL. [*Astonished*] How do you know?

STRONG. Met him. We had a fight and a foot-race. He won the foot-race and I won the fight!

WID. Was he there looking for us?

STRONG. Not all of us. He was waiting for you, Mrs. Guyer.

WID. Waiting for me? What for?

STRONG. He somehow had the idea that you were to meet him there and go to the ball with him.

ALL. [*Guying*] O—o—h!

RASH. [*R.*] What's all this? Now I understand his actions towards you this morning.

WID. Absurd!

STRONG. Perhaps, but I've got his clothes on. [*Laughs*] And here's a letter that I found in the pocket. [*Takes out letter and reads*] "My dear old boy—"

WID. [*Grabs letter and goes R.C.*] Why, that's the letter I wrote to Rashleigh!

RASH. [*Takes letter*] And the letter I didn't get! [*Looks at envelope*] Say, was this meant for me?

WID. Why, of course.

RASH. Well that "R" looks a good deal like a "B."

WID. [*Takes letter*] Somebody has evidently changed it. [*Gives it to Strong*]

RASH. Changed it? It does look so. And it was in Uncle Ben's clothes? I'll bet Slavin did it and then gave it to Uncle Ben!

WID. That's just it. I understand now his behavior this morning. He thought that note was for him and went to The Riche to meet me! [*All laugh*]

STRONG. Yes, and he'll be out here to meet you—[*Pause*] as soon as he gets some clothes. [*Laughs*]

RASH. [*Serious again*] Then we'll be caught after all.

TONY. [*L.C. Serious*] Let's start for home, quick! [*All rush up to R.3.E.*]

WID. [*Turns to them*] Stop! Do nothing of the sort! Stay here and—

ALL. [*Turn to her*] Get caught?

WID. [*C.*] No! Catch him! [*All laugh*] We'll have it the talk of the town. [*Enter Landlord, R.2.E.*]

LAND. [*At door*] Breakfast is served.

ALL. Come on! [*Exit all but Strong, R.2.E., laughing*]

STRONG. [*Looks at letter*] I wonder if she did mean that letter for Rashleigh or for Ben. That does look like a "B." Well, if she did mean it for old Ben, she's going to make him bear the consequences to save herself. She's going to disgrace that old man before his family. And these are the creatures we love and trust. [*Goes upstage to R.3.E. Looks at sign over door—"To the Aquarium." Then looks across stage to L.3.E. Sees sign over door—"To the Bar." Rushes off L.3.E.*]

RASH. [*Off. R.2.E.*] We must find Strong! [*Flirt screams outside L.3.E. Then she runs on to R.3., meets Norman, who enters L.3.E. She screams again, runs around back of screen to L.3.E. with Norman after her. Meets Strong entering L.3.E. She screams and runs to door R.2., with both Norman and Strong after her. Rashleigh enters from door R.2. Flirt screams and runs around screen, men after her, to door R.2. Enter Willie, R.2.E. He catches her. All grab her and take her downstage to C. Rashleigh, R.C.; Willie, R.; Norman, L.C.; Strong, L. The men form group around her*]

ALL. Our little kicker! [*The men all hold hats as high as they can. Flirt looks at the hats. She shakes her head*]

RASH. [*Suddenly*] I forgot to tell you. She can't talk! She's dumb! [*All lower hats. Widow sneaks on R., and goes behind screen*]

NORM. [*L.C.*] Too bad, isn't it? Won't you just try to speak? [*She shakes her head. Widow advances*]

WILL. [*R.*] And won't you sing and dance? [*She shakes her head*]

NORM. You won't open your mouth? [*She negatives*] And such a pretty mouth, too.

STRONG. I know why she won't open her mouth. She's got no teeth.

FLIRT. [*Angry*] It's nothing of the sort! [*Then sorry she spoke*]

STRONG. [*Goes to L. corner*] I knew I'd make her speak.

RASH. That voice! I've heard it!

NORM. So have I!

WID. [*Advances to C. quickly*] So have I. I know who your charmer is—
my maid, Flirt! [*Snatches off Flirt's mask. Flirt, R.C.*]

STRONG. Great Scott! [*Men astonished*]

WID. [*C.*] So, young lady, you are the high kicker who has captured all
our beaux away from us. Who taught you to go to masquerade balls on the
quiet?

FLIRT. [*Demurely curtsies*] My mistress.

FOUR MEN. Good!

WID. Then I forgive you. On the whole, I'm glad you're here. I want you
to retie my shoes. Go in that room. [*Exit Flirt, R.2.E. Widow crosses to R.,
laughing*] Gentlemen, I congratulate you on your conquest of my maid. [*Exit
Widow, R.2.E., laughing*]

STRONG. [*Crosses to C., laughing*] Gentlemen, we are in the same fix as
the vigilance committee who hanged the wrong man by mistake.

ALL. How's that?

STRONG. The laugh's on us. Well, this is my first night in San Francisco,
but it's a great one. [*Business*] It reminds me of the first night I struck New
York.

RASH. What happened?

STRONG. I may say I have embalmed these facts in a little song.

ALL. Let's hear it.

STRONG. [*Sings. "The Bowery"*]

> Oh! the night that I struck New York,
> I went out for a quiet walk;
> Folks who are "on to" the city say,
> Better by far that I took Broadway;
> But I was out to enjoy the sights,
> There was the Bowery ablaze with lights;
> I had one of the devil's own nights!
> I'll never go there any more!

> CHORUS

> The Bow'ry, the Bow'ry!
> They say such things and they do strange things
> On the Bow'ry! The Bow'ry!
> I'll never go there any more!

> I had walked but a block or two,
> When up came a fellow and me he knew;

Then a policeman came walking by,
Chased him away, and I asked him, "Why?"
"Wasn't he pulling your leg?" said he;
Said I, "He never laid hands on me!"
"Get off the Bow'ry, you yap!" said he;
I'll never go there any more!

I went into an auction store,
I never saw any thieves before;
First he sold me a pair of socks,
Then, said he, "How much for the box?"
Someone said, "Two dollars!" I said, "Three!"
He emptied the box and gave it to me;
"I sold you the box, not the socks," said he.
I'll never go there any more!

I went into a concert hall,
I didn't have a good time at all;
Just the minute that I sat down
Girls began singing, "New Coon in Town."
I got up mad and spoke out free,
"Somebody put that man out!" said she.
A man called a bouncer attended to me.
I'll never go there any more!

I went into a barber shop,
He talked till I thought he would never stop;
I said, "Cut it short." He misunderstood,
Clipped down my hair as close as he could;
He shaved with a razor that scratched like a pin,
Took off my whiskers and most of my chin;
That was the worst scrape I ever got in.
I'll never go there any more!

I struck a place that they called a "dive,"
I was in luck to get out alive;
When the policeman heard my woes,
Saw my black eyes and my battered nose,

"You've been held up!" said the "copper" fly!
"No, sir! But I've been knocked down!" said I.
Then he laughed, but I couldn't see why!
I'll never go there any more!

The Bow'ry, the Bow'ry!
They say such things, and they do strange things
On the Bow'ry! The Bow'ry!
I'll never go there any more! [*After the song, exit à la militaire,
L.3.E. Widow enters R.2.E.*]

WID. They are taking Mr. Strong down to the bar. I don't understand it.
They can't want to put him to sleep and leave him there. Well, there's no
danger of their doing it, even if they try. [*Exit R.2.E. Enter Strong, L.3.E.*]

STRONG. [*Advances to C.*] Something's the matter. I don't feel like taking
a drink. [*Goes to steamer chair, R.*] Must be at the point of death. In the excitement of this night I have forgotten that I am a sick man. Somehow, I
always do forget it the moment my attention is called away from it. I don't
know how much I have shortened my life. I only know I feel a draught.
[*Picks up fur rug. Landlord crosses from R.3.E. to L.3.E. with a tray of beer*]
What's that?

LAND. Draught beer.

STRONG. [*Slips into steamer chair*] Take it away! Take it away! [*Lies
down, covering head with fur robe. Flirt enters R.2.E., and seeing men have
gone, goes to steamer chair*]

FLIRT. If those four men will let me alone, I'll sit out here and watch for
Mr. Gay. [*Sits down on Strong, who grabs her. She screams and runs off
L.U.E. Strong sits up, looks around, puts thermometer at the back of his
neck*]

STRONG. Well, this is simply devilish. [*Lies down again, covering face.
Flirt on L.U.E., sneaks over to the chair and looks under the robe. Then hits
Strong in the face hard. Jumps back. As Strong jumps up, she laughs*]

FLIRT. Oh, pardon, are you ill, monsieur?

STRONG. [*On chair*] My head! I must have eaten something that disagreed
with me.

FLIRT. I cure madame's headaches with my hands. Perhaps I can cure
yours.

STRONG. Try it. [*Flirt goes to back of Strong and begins to chafe his
temples*] That's the idea. That's just what I want. [*Widow enters R.2.E., and
crosses to C. upstage*]

FLIRT. My mistress taught me this.

STRONG. Your mistress is a very fine woman.

WID. [*Advances. She motions to Flirt to leave and resumes rubbing Strong's temples. Flirt exits R.2.E. Widow stands back of Strong and imitates Flirt's voice*] You think my mistress charming?

STRONG. You bet. [*Widow rubs harder*]

WID. You enjoy her society very much?

STRONG. More than any lady I ever met.

WID. You could devote yourself to her?

STRONG. With all my heart.

WID. And some day you might marry her?

STRONG. After last night? Not for gold and precious stones!

WID. [*Slaps his face, goes C. Strong springs up, sees who it is, turns and walks off R.U.E.*] That's what a woman gets for being a good fellow. It's all right for the time being, but they've no use for you afterwards. [*She sits on steamer chair and cries*]

STRONG. [*Reenters R.U.E. Sees her. Aside*] She's crying. I do believe she's in love with me. I don't see any reason why she shouldn't be. And if I thought —[*Aloud*] My dear Mrs. Guyer—why those tears?

WID. You cruel man! You've broken my heart!

STRONG. [*Sincere*] Say not so! Say not so!

WID. Am I so very bad?

STRONG. Why, I never hinted at such a thing.

WID. [*Crosses to Strong*] You said you wouldn't marry me for gold or precious stones.

STRONG. [*C.*] But I didn't say I wouldn't marry you for your own sweet self.

WID. [*R.C.*] Mr. Strong, is this airy persiflage, or do you mean business?

STRONG. [*Takes out thermometer. Business of taking his temperature*] It may shorten my life, but it's—

WID. What?

STRONG. Business. [*He kisses her*] This is business, isn't it?

TONY. [*Off R.*] Daisy! Daisy Guyer! Come to breakfast. [*Strong crosses to steamer chair*]

WID. [*C.*] Yes. [*To Strong*] That reminds me! I've got to get them out of their scrape, and old Mr. Gay may be here any moment! [*Calls*] Landlord! Landlord! [*Enter Landlord, L.3.E.*] Have you another private dining room?

LAND. [*Points L.2.E.*] Right here.

Wid. [*C.*] It's mine. And I want you to prepare breakfast for two. And I want it served here on the piazza. And when the gentleman arrives, show him in there.

Land. [*L.*] Yes'm. What name will he give?

Wid. Perhaps not any. But he's a nice-looking old gentleman with grey side-whiskers.

Land. How will he be dressed? [*Strong slips into steamer chair*]

Wid. [*Looks at Strong's clothing*] Good heavens! [*Turns back to audience. Strong puts end of robe to his face*] I hadn't thought of that. If he isn't properly dressed, don't let him in. [*Exit Landlord, L.3.E. To Strong*] Now, I'll go and await the coming of Mr. Gay. And you must keep out of the way till it's all over. See? [*Exits L.2.E.*]

Strong. [*Gets up and crosses to the ice crusher L.*] Engaged to me and going to breakfast with Ben Gay! And I'm to keep out of the way till it's all over. [*Leans against ice-box. Looks into the door*] I don't like it. [*Puts thermometer to back of his neck*] The thought chills me. [*Sees that he is leaning on the ice-box*] No, it's this ice-box. By jove, I've an idea. I'll hide in here and keep tabs on that breakfast. I have some little confidence in her but none in him. [*Gets into crusher. Three boys enter L.U.E.*]

Norm. What became of Strong? [*As they cross to R.*]

Rash. He's probably at breakfast. Come on. [*Exit R.2.E.*]

Ben. [*Enters R.U.E., running*] Landlord! Landlord! How am I to find her? Where's the landlord? [*Exits L.U.E.*]

Sla. [*Enters R.U.E., running*] Mr. Gay! Mr. Gay! Oh, where did he go? I knew when that boy came to the house for his clothes that something was wrong. Oh, what shall I do? [*Turns to go off L.3.E. Landlord enters L.U.E. and sees Slavin. Ben crosses behind screen from L.3.E. to R.3.*]

Land. [*Looks at Slavin*] Grey side-whiskers. Peculiar dress. That's the man! [*Aloud to Slavin*] Are you looking for somebody?

Sla. [*R.C.*] Oh, yes, sir.

Land. [*C.*] I know who it is. You just step in this room and you'll find the party.

Sla. Oh, thank you, sir. [*Crosses C. in front of Landlord and exits L.2.E. Widow screams from room L.*]

Land. [*Goes upstage*] And he's seventy if he's a day! [*Exits R.U.E. Strong looks out of ice crusher*]

Strong. I wish I could see into that room.

Land. [*Outside R.3.E.*] A lady in black? [*Strong closes crusher. Enter Landlord and Ben, R.U.E., Landlord on first*] The lady you describe is here, but she is taking breakfast with another man.

BEN. [*C.*] Another man! Well, this takes the cake. Heavens, how fast she catches them! I know. It's the fellow who got her card by mistake at The Riche. I wonder if it's Strong. By thunder, I won't stand it! You go and tell that man I want to see him.

LAND. I hope there'll be no trouble.

BEN. No, no. Call him out.

LAND. [*L.C.*] Would you like to look at the evening paper, sir? [*Ben looks at Landlord and then takes paper. Exit Landlord, L.2.E. Ben throws the paper on the floor in disgust*]

BEN. I want to know who the fellow is that cut me out so easily. [*Crosses to R. Enter two Waiters, R.3.E. The first with two bottles, the second with tray, etc. They exit, L.2.E. Ben looks on in astonishment*] Two bottles of wine with the oysters. He's a money spender, anyhow. I wonder who this dude can be. [*Enter Slavin, L.2.E. He coughs. Ben turns and recognizes him.* PIC- TURE] Merciful heaven! What, you the dandy masher? You the prodigal son giving wine suppers at The Riche and breakfast to swell women! It can't be! It's preposterous! It's a joke or a nightmare! I'm crazy! That's it!

SLA. [*Advances to C.*] You are, sir. That's it. [*Widow looks out from win- dow, L.3.E.*] Oh, Mr. Gay, forgive me, but you've been such a good friend to me for twenty years, I couldn't help it.

BEN. Help what?

SLA. Following you, sir. When you sent a messenger boy home at two in the morning for those clothes you've got on, I knew something was wrong. So I followed the boy to The Riche, and when you took a cab, I got on the seat with the driver. I remembered how many of our rich men have committed suicide. "If Mr. Gay tries it," I said, "I'll be there to save him!"

BEN. Is that what you came here for?

SLA. Yes, sir.

BEN. You dear, devoted, damned old fool! I'm not going to commit sui- cide. [*Goes toward him. Slavin crosses back of Ben to R.*] Go back to town. I don't want you here. [*Ben crosses to L.*]

SLA. [*R.C.*] That's what folks bent on suicide always say. I know my duty, sir.

BEN. [*L.C. Aside*] Great Scott! What am I to do? He mustn't know what I'm here for. [*Aloud*] See here. This has gone far enough. You go back to town or I'll discharge you!

SLA. Discharge me, sir, if you will, but while you're crazy, I'll stick to you!

BEN. While you stick to me, I'll be crazy! Slavin, what would you think if I told you the truth?

SLA. I'd know you were crazy, sir.

BEN. There is a lady in that room.

SLA. Yes, sir. Mrs. Guyer.

BEN. I'm out here to take breakfast with her.

SLA. You, Mr. Gay? And you're not crazy?

BEN. Crazy! No! You understand. One must have his little flirtations. [*Strong raises lid of ice crusher*]

SLA. You're just like me, sir. No fool like an old fool.

BEN. Now, if Strong isn't here, he will be soon. He mustn't see me, or her. Now, I'll forgive you for your cussed nonsense on one condition. Keep watch! If he comes around, drive him away.

SLA. How will I do it?

BEN. Threaten to shoot him with this. [*Takes revolver from his pocket. Strong slams down the lid. Slavin and Ben start suddenly*] Take this and keep your eyes open.

SLA. [*Goes up R.*] Will I shoot him?

BEN. No. Don't shoot him. Just make believe.

SLA. All right, sir. I'll make believe to shoot him, and maybe I will shoot him. [*Exits R.U.E.*]

BEN. [*Crosses to door, L.2.E.*] At last! [*Raps at door*]

WID. [*Off L.*] Come in. [*Exit Ben, L.2.E. Enter young folks, R.2.E. Rashleigh first, others following quickly*]

RASH. I saw him go in there. She said we were to hide behind this screen. [*All go behind screen. Sound of kissing heard off L.2.E.*]

WID. [*Outside L.2.E.*] Why, Mr. Gay!

BEN. [*Outside*] Now, Mrs. Guyer. [*Widow runs out of L.2.E. followed by Ben. Both go up front of screen C.*] My dear Mrs. Guyer!

WID. Mr. Gay, I'm astonished that you would do such a thing.

BEN. Didn't you ever hear of a gentleman's stealing a kiss?

WID. Not before the fish was served.

BEN. Now, don't be offended.

WID. Then swear you won't do it again.

BEN. Must I do that?

WID. Yes, or I'll go home this minute. Kneel! [*All look over screen at once. Rashleigh at L. and Norman at R. end. Ben kneels*] Now, look up! [*Ben looks up and sees the young folks laughing at him. He falls flat*]

ALL. Why, Uncle Ben! [*All come from behind screen and come down L. and R.*]

BEN. [*On knees again*] Mrs. Guyer, I can't tie that shoe. [*All laugh. Looks around and gets up*] Great Scott! My whole family! [*Down C.*] What does this mean? Why aren't you in Chinatown?

Tony. [*L.C.*]   Because we're here. [*Crosses R.*]

Ben. [*L.C.*]   I see you're here. I gave you permission to go to Chinatown and I catch you all at the Cliff House. [*Goes to L.*]

Wid.   You catch us? Pardon me, we catch you! [*Aside to others. Turns to Ben*] Mr. Gay, I may as well tell you the joke. I have won a bet. I wagered Tony a breakfast that any halfway pretty woman could get you out on a racket. Then I wrote you to meet me at The Riche. [*Aside*] Heaven forgive the story! [*Aloud*] Haven't you been at The Riche and all over town after me? [*All laugh*]

All.   Own up! Etc. [*Ad lib*]

Ben. [*Goes to L.C.*]   To win a breakfast, you've led me on to make a fool of myself before my whole family. This was a mean trick to play on an old man!

Wid. [*C.*]   Old men shouldn't run after young girls. [*Enter Landlord and Waiter, L.U.E.*]

Ben.   Everybody likes a good time once in a while. [*All laugh*]

Wid.   That's just it. Hereafter, when the young folks want a little fun, don't oppose it.

Ben.   No. I'll declare myself in on it. [*All hurrah*] And we'll begin right now. Landlord, some champagne! [*All hurrah and laugh*]

Land. [*To Waiter*]   You get the champagne and I'll crush the ice. [*Turns handles of the ice crusher. Exit Waiter, L.U.E. Strong torn up, comes out of the ice crusher. Girls scream. Then they laugh when they recognize Strong who goes down C. quick*]

Ben.   It's Strong! Revenge! Revenge! Strong, you're a sight!

Strong. [*C.*]   I don't care! They're your clothes! [*Enter Slavin, R.3.E., pointing revolver at Strong. Ben rushes up and stops him. Girls all scream. Ben then down R. Landlord, Slavin, and Waiter upstage*]

Rash. [*L.*]   Well, what's to be done?

Wid. [*C.*]   Have a bird and a bottle and go home! [chorus: *"Out For A Racket." Ben and Strong dancing. Isabel, R.; Flirt, R.; Tony, L.; Willie, R.*]

CURTAIN

ACT III.

Scene: *Private gymnasium in the house of Ben Gay.*
Discovered: *Tony and Flirt in wrappers.*

Flirt.   I think we're the first ones up. And I had a good mind not to get up at all!

TONY. This settles the "out for a racket" business for me, Flirt. Do you realize that we're in an awful scrape? Of course uncle can't do anything worse to you than tell your father.

FLIRT. That's so. He couldn't do anything worse. I'd rather he'd whip me. I guess it does settle the "out for a racket" business. Oh, Tony, isn't there anything to keep him from telling? I'll get killed.

TONY. I don't know of any. We'll all have to suffer except the widow. And she's the only one who had any fun. The way the men devoted themselves to her ruined my evening. Flirt, I've made up my mind. I'm going to be a widow!

FLIRT. Oh, Tony! But you've got to be a wife first, and your husband may live forever.

TONY. No, he won't! I shall marry Mr. Strong! Heaven has sent him here, I feel, to my relief. [*Enter Wilder and Rashleigh*]

FLIRT. Oh, Wilder, did you send word home that we were here?

WILD. I did. And, say, it's lucky we didn't go to the ball. It was closed by the police.

RASH. And Painter was arrested! That's why he didn't come to The Riche. [*Enter Widow*]

WID. Good morning, everybody!

ALL. Good morning.

TONY. To what are we indebted for this early call?

WID. I've come over, first, to have a little practice with the foils. [*Throws off cloak, disclosing fencing costume*] Second, to get you out of the scrape.

FLIRT. Oh, can you?

WID. Well, you know me! What do you think?

WILD. We'll bet on you every time.

WID. Last night after I reached home, I began to think that you were in a fix. "They've got to tell some story to get out of it," said I. "And they're not good at telling stories," said I. "They may lay the blame on me," said I. "Then my reputation will be in the laundry, and a widow has to be careful of her reputation. I must go over there and tell a story that will get us all out of it," said I. And here I am!

TONY. One word for us, and two for yourself! You're very good!

WID. Now, am I in time?

RASH. I think so. Neither uncle nor Mr. Strong are up yet.

WILD. That Strong's a thoroughbred, after all.

WID. A delightful man! It's a pity he's got to die so soon!

TONY. Nothing of the sort! I—I mean—perhaps he hasn't. [*Aside*] But I'm sure he has!

FLIRT. Well, say, what story are we to tell uncle?

WID. I don't know yet. But there's a way out of this scrape, and I know how to find it. I've only got one favor to ask. Don't mix in and spoil things. How soon will they be up?

RASH. Nobody knows.

WID. I've got to be at my dressmaker's in an hour. Can't you call them?

TONY. Not for worlds!

WID. Then we must make a racket so they'll have to get up! Where are their rooms?

TONY. [*Points R. and L.*] There and there! Come, Flirt, let's get our gymnasium suits on. [*Exit two girls*]

WID. We may as well start the racket! Come on! [*Medley, during which the two girls return in gymnasium suits. At finish, all exit. Enter Strong from R., Ben from L. They look like wrecks. Neither knows what to say. Strong has a bowl of ice and offers some to Ben*]

STRONG. Have a piece?

BEN. [*Takes ice*] Thanks! Don't you think a little absinthe would do us good? [*Rings*]

STRONG. It can't shorten my life much! [*Noah[1] heard singing below. Comes up stairs still singing "Out For A Racket"*]

NOAH. [*Pretty drunk*] Here I am!

BEN. Noah! Sirrah! What does this mean?

NOAH. I've been right with you. Drunk as a boiled owl! I knew everybody else was on a toot, so I filled up! Three very pretty jags we three gentlemen had! [*Exits*]

STRONG. What a beastly fellow!

BEN. This is strictly between us! My catching you was an accident. I went to The Riche to have supper with a lady.

STRONG. You old rascal!

BEN. But if my family knew that, I'd lose their respect forever.

STRONG. Why, you didn't do anything wrong, did you?

BEN. No, damn it! The widow didn't—

STRONG. The widow didn't what?

BEN. Why—er—that's—that's something you didn't understand. What I was going to say is this: That loan of a hundred dollars squares you, but in order to save my own reputation I must make these youngsters believe that I followed them there, and I must punish them accordingly. It's rough on them, but—

[1] In this second version of Act III, that was found in the New York Public Library, the servant is called "Noah" throughout. Obviously he should be "Slavin."

STRONG. Don't make it too rough. Remember we used to enjoy a little racket in the days gone by when we were their age.

BEN. By thunder, we did! [*Duet, "Days Gone By," Strong and Ben. Enter Noah with three drinks*]

NOAH. Here we are, brother sufferers.

BEN. [*Takes drink*] If you don't stop your impudence, I'll discharge you! [*Ben and Strong drink*]

NOAH. That's what I want! I'm drunk and I'm glad of it! I'm a whale!

STRONG. A whale? No!

NOAH. This is the first time in forty years I've dared to open my head and now I'm going to let 'er go. I'm looking to get kicked out of the house!

BEN. You shall be! [*Exits downstairs, kicking Noah*]

STRONG. He'll just give it to those children to prove his own probity. I think I'll take to bed till the affair's over. [*Enter Tony*]

TONY. [*In gymnasium dress*] Oh, there he is! Oh, if I can get him to marry me! Black is so becoming to me. Ahem! Good morning! Mr. Strong, how do you feel this morning?

STRONG. I think I shall live until dinner time.

TONY. Oh, I hope so. We should miss your cheery "Yes, thanks," when the wine is served. Oh, Mr. Strong, do you know, everything about you interests me? Have you got a wife?

STRONG. A wife? No.

TONY. Then you're a jolly bachelor!

STRONG. No! Not a bachelor!

TONY. Not a bachelor! Oh, forgive me if I've touched a tender spot in your heart. You are a widower!

STRONG. No, not a widower!

TONY. Excuse me, Mr. Strong, you say you're not a single man?

STRONG. I am not.

TONY. Nor a married man nor a widower! Will you kindly tell me what you are?

STRONG. Well, if you must know, I'm a divorced man!

TONY. A divorced man! How romantic!

STRONG. Yes, and very expensive.

TONY. And when are you going to—try it again?

STRONG. Never!

TONY. Never? Oh, don't say that!

STRONG. Why, I'm a dying man!

TONY. That's it! With such a glorious opportunity to make a woman a widow, you have no right to remain single a minute. You ought to marry the first woman you can lay your hands on!

STRONG. [*Puts his hands behind him and shies away*] But I don't want a wife!

TONY. You do! To wear mourning for you! Now, you must—

STRONG. But the divorce forbade me to marry. It would be contempt of court.

TONY. Then contempt the court! Positively despise it!

STRONG. And go to prison? Say, it's time to take my medicine! Excuse me! [*Exits L.*]

TONY. Well, I declare! [*Enter Wilder*]

WILD. Sweetheart, I want to—

TONY. Oh, go away!

WILD. What?

TONY. Go away! You weary me!

WILD. Weary you? Why, I thought you loved me!

TONY. I do, but you won't do! You're not going to die in two years!

WILD. I hope not!

TONY. Then that lets you out. You're not in it. So don't bother me! [*Rushes out*]

WILD. Well, I declare! [*Terrible crash below. Enter three ladies*]

THREE LADIES. [*Ad lib*] What's that? Etc. [*Noah enters, coming upstairs, singing. Girls much alarmed*]

NOAH. [*Has parrot and cat. To Wilder*] You're wanted below. [*Throws Wilder downstairs*] That's two! [*Girls scream*] I'm going to do 'em all! I've been discharged, and before I go I'm going to lick every man in the house! Then I'll kiss all the women! [*Women scream and exit; Widow into Ben's room*] I'm a whale! Where's that dying man? He's my pie! I'll make him eat his own game! [*Exiting*] I'll give you your medicine! [*Tremendous crash, R. Enter Tony, Flirt, and Rashleigh*]

RASH. What is it?

FLIRT. Noah is in there killing Mr. Strong!

TONY. Go save him! [*Crash R.*]

RASH. Give me something to hit him with! [*Grabs Indian club*] That's too heavy! [*Drops it. Crash R.*]

TONY. [*Hands him the same club*] Here, try this!

RASH. That's too light! [*Crash R.*] Where's my ball bat?

FLIRT. Locked up in the locker! The key's downstairs.

RASH. Go get it! [*Exit Flirt, downstairs. Tremendous crash R.*] Oh, wait till I get something to hit him with! [*Crash*]

TONY. Oh, he'll be killed! Take the Indian club!

RASH. No, I can't! I must have the bat! [*Crash*]

TONY. Oh, Rashleigh, save him! He'll surely be killed!

RASH. Then I'll avenge him! [*Enter Widow, L.*]

WID. What's the matter?

TONY. Noah is killing Mr. Strong! [*Grand crash. Widow and girls yell. Enter Strong, throwing Noah out, who is all torn up; handful of parrot feathers*]

STRONG. I have shortened my life one year!

NOAH. You've shortened mine fifty! I'll never be able to digest that parrot!

ALL. The parrot!

NOAH. He made me swallow it! [*All laugh*] That's right! And damn it! How I hate feathers! [*Spits some out*] Ladies and gentlemen, is there anything I can do for you?

ALL. Yes! Get out! [*Exit Noah*]

WID. Mr. Strong, you are a brave man!

STRONG. I know it!

WID. Hadn't somebody better go and see if the others are hurt?

STRONG. With pleasure! [*Exits C.*]

WID. Tell me, whose room was that I ran into?

TONY. Why, Uncle Ben's.

WID. [*Bursts out laughing*] I see it all. You're out of your scrape! Oh, this is funny! [*Laughs. Enter Wilder, C.*]

ALL. What *is* it?

WID. Only a letter I saw lying on his desk! [*Laughs*] But I shan't tell you a word more, only back me up in all I say to him, and I'll get you out of your scrape. But, listen, we must all seem very merry and when he comes in, all laugh at the good joke on him.

FLIRT. But what is the joke?

WID. You'll see! Come on. Start a chorus or something. What, must I start it? Very well! [*Specialty, Widow and quartette. Enter Strong, C.*]

STRONG. The servant has apologized to everyone but me. He says he hasn't done anything to me, and I agree. By the way, your uncle's coming. [*Enter Ben, C. All laugh at him*]

BEN. Oh, that's the way you feel, is it? I suppose you consider this affair of last night a laughing matter?

WID. Decidedly! With the laugh on you!

ALL. With the laugh on you!

BEN. On me? We'll see about that!

WID. Gently, now. Mr. Gay, we want you to settle a bet.

BEN. I never settle bets.

STRONG. How about loans? I have the check here as evidence.

WID. [*Grabs check*] Just what I wanted. Now, Mr. Gay, listen! Your niece here, poor innocent Tony, was telling us what a good man you were, and I laughed at her.

BEN. Very nice of you!

WID. I offered to bet her a supper at the Cliff House that if any decent-looking woman asked you to take her to the masquerade, you'd do it.

BEN. [*Aside*] I've been buncoed!

WID. She took the bet, and so I wrote this note which I have just picked up in your room—[*Shows note*] for you to meet me at The Riche. Then we all went to The Riche to see if you were there. And you were!

WILD. [*To Tony*] What a corking lie! She's a wonder!

TONY. Oh, uncle, I never thought it of you! [*Widow whispers to Tony, who exits L.*]

FLIRT. What will my father say when I tell him?

BEN. [*Yells*] Hold on! I—I—Why, that letter made me think that you had all gone to The Riche; so I went there to catch you, and I did! Ha! Ha!

WID. How did you happen to run up such a big bill? [*Looks at check*] What is this item for supper ordered for self and lady? [*All laugh. Enter Tony with masks*]

TONY. And what did you want of these two masks?

BEN. Why, I—you understand?

WID. Mr. Gay, don't you think I've won that bet?

BEN. Oh—I—don't think anything about it! Don't one of you dare to mention this affair again as long as you live! [*To Flirt*] Especially to your father!

WID. But about that supper at the Cliff House?

BEN. Oh, I'll pay for that and we'll all have a good time together. Eh, Strong?

STRONG. It will shorten my life a year, but I'm with you!

CHORUS—*"Out For A Racket"*

FINALE

CURTAIN

A TEMPERANCE TOWN

Which is intended to be a more or less truthful presentation of certain phases and incidents of life, relating to the sale and use of liquor, in a small village in a prohibition state. The author has endeavored to give all sides a fair show. But he is quite willing to be classed as protesting against the prohibitory laws of Vermont, where a man named Kibling is now serving a sentence of something like sixty years for selling about seven hundred glasses of liquor (less than most of our respectable city hotels sell in a day).

TIME: THE THANKSGIVING PERIOD OF THE YEAR 1882.

CAST OF CHARACTERS

The cast of the opening New York performance of *A Temperance Town* on September 17, 1893, was as follows:

LAUNCELOT (MINK) JONES	GEORGE RICHARDS
ST. JULIAN (BINGO) JONES	EUGENE CANFIELD
ERNEST HARDMAN	RICHARD J. DILLON
SQUIRE BELCHER	WILLIAM CULLINGTON
KNEELAND PRAY	JOSEPH FRANKAU
DR. CADWELL SAWYER	FRANK A. LYON
FRED OAKHURST	E. F. NAGLE
JOHN WORTH	W. H. CURRIE
UNCLE JOE VIALL	GEORGE OBER
WILLIAM PUTNAM	FRANK RUSSELL
WES PERRY	HERMAN A. SHELDON
WILL PEAK	HARRY LUCKSTONE
JUDGE GRAHAM DOE	GEORGE OBER
SHERIFF	MADISON COREY
SHERIFF'S OFFICER	CHARLES ADAMS
SPRAGUE	HERMAN SHELDON
FRANK HARDMAN	FRANK RUSSELL
MRS. PATIENCE HARDMAN	LAURA AYERS
RUTH HARDMAN	CAROLINE MISKEL
ROXANA	DALLAS TYLER
MRS. JONES	MARIE UART
ONE OF THE CROSSMAN CHILDREN	MABLE EARLE
WAITER	
JURY	
VILLAGERS	

ACT I.

Scene: *Exterior of parsonage. Set house with porch, balustrade, and stairs with three or four steps extending from L.1.E. to L.3.E. Set stable extending from R.1.E. to R.3.E. Large double practical doors of stable open. Practical pump with bucket by it near stable door. Horse-blanket hanging on stable door. Double shed extending from R.3.E. to R.C. Gate opening between stable and shed R.U.E. large enough for wagon to pass through. Watering-trough beside pump. Chopping-block, axe, and woodpile L.U.C. Washtub on stool beside stairs to house L. Bench large enough to hold two persons R.2.E. Grass mats, etc., around stage.*

Discovered: *At rise, Mrs. Hardman, Roxey, and Mrs. Jones. Mrs. Jones is chopping wood.*

Mrs. H. Don't do that, Mrs. Jones. You'll cut yourself.

Mrs. J. Why not? Who else will do it for me?

Mrs. H. Ask Mink. He is your husband. Surely he will not refuse to aid you, when you have so much work to do.

Mrs. J. Oh, bless your soul, he is too busy down at the saloon, attending political meetings and all that sort of thing.

Mrs. H. Well, I think he should take more interest in his family affairs. It seems to me that you are leading a very hard life.

Mrs. J. I know that Mink is dreadful shiftless and that he might do better; but he has never spoken a cross word to me in his life, and we have been married for over twenty years. If it wasn't for that saloon he might do better.

Mrs. H. Yes, it was through that saloon that my poor boy left home, and went to his death. It seems that saloons are nothing but a blight upon a community.

Mrs. J. Yes, but if folks didn't find some kind of consolation, they wouldn't go there. I don't want to hinder Mink from having all the pleasure he can find in this life, for it's mighty hard, anyway.

Mrs. H. Won't Bingo help you? He is young and strong and seems to have nothing else to do.

Mrs. J. Well, I don't know. It seems to me that work of any kind always went against the grain of the Joneses. Bingo has won a bet, and old Joe Viall has to wheel him a mile in a wheelbarrow today, as he is the loser.

Mrs. H. Why, that old man is ninety-four years old! He'll never be able to wheel that strong boy that distance!

Mrs. J. Well, he'll have to do it or pay some kind of a forfeit. These men arrange things to suit themselves, and I don't want to interfere.

Mrs. H. [*To Roxey*] Why, what are you doing with that sword?

Rox. Why, polishing it up for Thanksgiving. Ain't it nice and clean? [*Shoulders sword and sings*] Steady, boys! Forward march! Steady, boys! Steady! [*Marches and makes exit, L.2.E. Enter Dr. Sawyer, Pray, and Belcher through gate*]

Bel. Good day, Mrs. Hardman. Is the parson at home?

Mrs. H. Yes. I will send him to you directly. [*Exits L.2.E. into house*]

Bel. Gentlemen, I assure you that we have entered upon a crusade which I am certain will result in the greatest good to our fellow citizens.

Pray. Yes, there is no doubt of it whatever. Is everything arranged?

Dr. S. Yes. We have secured a witness who will swear to the purchase of liquor, and that will be certain to secure a conviction.

Pray. Think of it, gentlemen! What a blessing this will be! Look at our citizens who have been decoyed into wasting their time and means in this low brothel! Look at John Worth! He should be an example to the youths of this village. He had a fortune of $160,000 left him. Yet he insists on spending his time and money among the low associates he forms in the saloon.

Bel. Gentlemen, what I am about to do is not for a mercenary purpose, but on behalf of the welfare of the community. I ask no reward. My honest conviction forces me to the steps I am now taking.

Pray. Yes. Think of John Worth! His father wanted him to be a gentleman. He sent him to Europe to study Greek and Latin. Then he comes back here and talks about drinking wine and eating what he calls banquets.

Dr. S. And see what the consequence of tolerating this nuisance will result in. The man is not satisfied with his illegal traffic. He is now going to add gambling to his crimes. He is going to have a raffle and seek by a game of chance to empty the pockets of the community.

Pray. Hush! Here comes Hardman. He is with us heart and soul. He blames the saloon for his son's disappearance, and ever since the boy ran away he has devoted his life to the cause of temperance. [*Enter Hardman from the house*]

Hard. Welcome, gentlemen. I presume you came to report progress in our glorious cause. Blame me not if I appear too anxious, but they ruined my son and made my life desolate. These wreckers of our homes must be taught a lesson, and I will never yield in my warfare against their unholy traffic while I have strength left to battle with it! [*Shouts outside*] What means this noise?

PRAY.   Old Joe Viall has lost a bet made in the saloon and he is now wheeling Bingo a mile in a wheelbarrow in order to pay it. [*Enter Peak*] Ah, this is our man, the one who is to secure evidence against Oakhurst, the rumseller. Well, Peak, what success have you met with?

PEAK.   None at all. Our game won't work. He refuses to sell me any liquor.

PRAY.   Why?

PEAK.   He said I wasn't a proper person to have liquor.

DR. S.   Then what can we do?

PEAK.   I'll tell you what I can do. I'll go around to the back door. I'll bore a hole through and peep. I can see everything he sells.

HARD.   But are you sure you can identify the bottles?

PEAK.   Identify? What do you mean by identifying?

PRAY.   Why, pick out the bottles the liquor was sold from.

PEAK.   Well, I should say so. I know the contents of every bottle. But say, I get my ten dollars, don't I?

PRAY.   Certainly; we will attend to that. [*Exit Peak*]

HARD.   Now, in case this man should prove unreliable, are you prepared to furnish forth the proofs? Will anyone else swear to the purchase of liquor?

DR. S.   Ay, that's an important question. Can such a witness be found?

PRAY.   Leave it to me. I think I have a reliable person who will do so. But, hush! We may be overheard.

HARD.   Overheard? These are my premises, gentlemen, and I assure you no eavesdroppers frequent them.

PRAY.   Probably not, but—you have a daughter.

HARD.   I have. But I know her sentiments are mine and that she is heart and soul with me in this conflict against rum.

PRAY.   You may think so, but we have proofs that she is in the habit of visiting Oakhurst and his family. She has doubtless ere this warned him of our intentions.

HARD.   Gentlemen, you are mistaken! I will call her. [*Goes to door of house*] Roxey! Tell Miss Ruth to come here. [*Roxey enters from house and exits*] My daughter is incapable of falsehood and shall answer for herself. [*Enter Ruth*] Daughter, is it true that you have ventured into the house of Oakhurst, the rum-seller?

RUTH.   It is true.

HARD.   And what could have induced you to visit that place?

RUTH.   The child was sick and I thought it my duty to aid.

PRAY. And were there not others more worthy of your assistance than a rum-seller's child?

RUTH. None perhaps so much in need.

HARD. [*To Ruth*] Did you warn him that there was a possibility of a raid being made upon his place tonight?

RUTH. The thought never even entered my mind!

HARD. Gentlemen, I hope you are satisfied, but step into the house with me. We will talk the matter over. [*Exit Hardman and Belcher into house*]

DR. S. I will go and see Oakhurst at once. He owes me quite a bill and I had better get all I can from him before we raid his place. [*Exits into house*]

PRAY. Miss Ruth, don't blame me for this. It's not my fault. [*Exits into house*]

RUTH. What miserable hypocrites! [*Shouts outside. Enter Roxey and Mrs. Jones from the house. Old Viall wheeling Bingo in a wheelbarrow. Peak, Wes Perry, and rest of villagers*]

PERRY. Three cheers for Uncle Joe! [*Crowd gives cheers*]

BINGO. Gentlemen, the exercises are now over and I would advise the meeting to disperse at once or the parson will come out and run you off his grounds. [*Exit Perry and crowd. Bingo gets out of wheelbarrow*] A little while ago I was riding in this wheelbarrow. Now I've got to put it away! [*Wheels it into stable, R.*]

VIALL. [*To Mrs. Jones*] Mrs. Jones, are you cooking doughnuts?

MRS. J. Yes, I am. What do you want to know for?

VIALL. 'Cause I can smell 'em. I always was fond of doughnuts.

MRS. J. Well, what do you mean by coming around here and making such a disturbance?

VIALL. Well, you see we got a little excited and us boys will be boys.

MRS. J. Yes; and fools will be fools! [*Exits into house followed by Ruth*]

VIALL. Mighty fine gal, that! I like her! She seems to be so lively and full of ginger all the time. Guess I'll go in and sample them doughnuts. [*Exits into house. Enter Bingo from stable*]

BINGO. I've just had a lively time today. Guess I'll chase down to the saloon and see if old Joe is setting 'em up yet. [*Pauses and looks at Roxey, then at door of house, pointing*] Say, here comes the boss ramrod!

ROX. What do you mean by a boss ramrod?

BINGO. That's a name we give all these temperance cranks, and Deacon Pray is the boss. But he can't fool me. You just wait until the Fourth of July, and if I don't have his sign down and my name over the door for a saloon, my name ain't Jones. [*Exit both, Roxey into house, Bingo into stable. Enter Ruth and Pray from house*]

PRAY. And are you interested in this saloon-keeper, Miss Ruth, so much that you desire no harm to befall him? [*Downstage; Ruth R., Pray L. Enter Bingo from the stable*]

BINGO. Beg pardon, Miss Ruth. [*Bingo hands Ruth a peach on the end of a stick*] Can I offer you this?

RUTH. Certainly. But why do you give it to me in such a peculiar manner?

BINGO. Well, I heard them say down at the saloon that old Pray couldn't get near enough to you to hand you a peach on a stick; so I thought I'd try! [*Exits into stable. Enter Roxey from house carrying the sword*]

ROX. Oh, Miss Ruth, I've got it polished up so that it looks like new. There isn't a speck of rust on it anywhere. [*Enter Mrs. Hardman from the front door of house*]

RUTH. [*Taking sword*] My poor brother! [*Sorrowfully*] This is all we have left to remind us of you, the only token that you have lived and fought for the land that gave you birth. [*To Pray*] Pardon me, but this is a memento of my brother. A comrade brought it, and a message. Since then we have heard nothing from him. You know he went away to the war.

PRAY. You'll excuse me, Miss Ruth, but I have some business at my store. [*Exit Pray through gate*]

MRS. H. Come, Ruth. Are you ready? [*Exits into house*]

RUTH. Yes, mama, I'm coming. [*Kisses sword*] Now I will take you with me and you will fill my dear brother's place in his vacant chair. [*Exits into house*]

ROX. [*Throws herself full-length on the bench*] These relations of mine are a cheerful lot. [*Enter Bingo, who looks at Roxey. She rises*] You are the boy that does the chores, ain't you?

BINGO. Yes.

ROX. And your mother does the washing?

BINGO. Yes.

ROX. Let's see. Your name is Bingo, ain't it?

BINGO. No. It's St. Julian; St. Julian Jones.

ROX. What a peculiar name!

BINGO. You see how it was; when I was born, pop thought he'd christen me that, 'cause he saw the name on a bottle down to the saloon.

ROX. But why do they call you Bingo?

BINGO. Because they call dad Mingo; sometimes Mink for short; and his dad's name was Stingo. That's some kind of a drink. We all take to it.

ROX. Why don't you make them call you by your right name?

BINGO. 'Cause they won't do it.

Rox. Well, why don't you make them? Stand on your dignity!

Bingo. Stand on your dignity! Say, you don't know much about the Joneses!

Rox. Didn't anybody ever take an interest in you and talk to you kindly?

Bingo. Yes, lots of 'em. They come and tell me I ought to be ashamed of myself, that I'm going along the broad road to the wrong place, that I'm sure to land in State's prison or be hung, and all that sort of thing. They make me sick!

Rox. But if you took care of yourself, they would certainly show you respect.

Bingo. No, I'm not rich. It takes money to be respected in Vermont.

Rox. But if you took care of yourself and kept your face and hands clean, people would like you better. I know I would!

Bingo. Say, are you going to stay here long?

Rox. Yes, I live here and I'm going to stay here all the time.

Bingo. Oh, then you're the help?

Rox. No, *sir*. I'm a relation. My parents are dead and I came here to live with my relations, and I'm not supposed to receive wages!

Bingo. Gee, I'm glad I'm not an orphan! I got a mother to work for me.

Rox. My father was a minister at Crossing. He got six hundred dollars a year and never saved a cent.

Bingo. Whew![*Whistles. Enter Mrs. Hardman. She calls Roxey. They exit into house*] Make folks respect me! [*He goes to stable, fills bucket from horse-trough R. and washes face. He uses currycomb as brush for his hair and looks in water for a mirror. He dries hands and face on the horse-blanket. Enter Belcher, Pray, and Dr. Sawyer*]

Pray. The very person I want to see! Bingo, I want to talk with you.

Bingo. Temperance! Aw! Aw!

Pray. Do you know that, if you keep on your present course, you'll go straight to a place where the Devil rules?

Bingo. [*Starting*] Yes, I'm going right straight to your drugstore.

Dr. S. [*As Pray turns away*] Do you know the miserable fate that overtakes the drunkard?

Bingo. Yes. He's got to send for a doctor.

Bel. [*As Dr. Sawyer turns away*] Suppose that in your drunkenness you commit some horrible crime. What would you do?

Bingo. Send out of town for a lawyer. [*Going C.*]

Bel. [*To Pray*] It's a sad case.

Pray. Where are you going, Bingo?

Bingo. My name ain't Bingo. It's St. Julian.

PRAY. Isn't St. Julian a rather high-sounding name? Your clothes are hardly becoming to the name.

DR. S. How would you like a new suit of clothes?

BINGO. How am I going to get 'em?

BEL. I'll tell you. We'll give you some money. Then you buy some liquor with it and get drunk. Then go before a justice of the peace and swear where you got it.

BINGO. Well, when do I get the clothes?

PRAY. In about a month; say in December.

BINGO. Not much! Come around in December and we'll talk it over.

PRAY. Stay! Why do you want them so soon?

BINGO. Because tomorrow is Thanksgiving Day and I want to break them in at the raffle.

PRAY. You can have the clothes today if you promise to do what I tell you. I'll give you an order for a suit of clothes at Cooley's store.

BINGO. I'll do it. Give me the order. [*Pray gives it. Bingo starts out*]

PRAY. Wait! You must have some money. [*Hands him ten cents*]

BINGO. Ten cents! One drink only.

PRAY. How many do you want?

BINGO. Oh, about twelve or thirteen.

PRAY. Well, here's a dollar. Will that be enough?

BINGO. I guess so. I'll try and make it go. Now, you want me to go and get a certain number of drinks and then go to court and swear to it?

DR. S., BEL., and PRAY. Yes, that's it! Yes!

BINGO. [*Going to gate*] All right. You bet I'll make folks respect me. [*Exits*]

DR. S. Well, I think everything is working nicely. Come, Brother Belcher, will you walk over to my office? [*Exit Belcher and Dr. Sawyer. Enter Ruth. Pray advances and leads her to a seat on the bench*]

PRAY. Miss Ruth, do you know it is very melancholy to be compelled to live alone?

RUTH. I have no doubt of it.

PRAY. And I have been thinking of building a new house.

RUTH. Indeed?

PRAY. Yes, and I intend to have in it everything that goes to make life comfortable.

RUTH. A very sensible idea.

PRAY. I don't claim a large one and I've come to ask your advice. I wish to build one just large enough for two.

RUTH. I think you are right.

PRAY. The two should be—

RUTH. Yourself and your mother. [*Enter Worth*]

WORTH. Pardon me, Miss Ruth, I found this earring a few moments ago and remembered having seen it in your possession. Will you permit me to return it to you?

RUTH. Thank you, Mr. Worth. It certainly is mine.

PRAY. You have turned very honest.

WORTH. Yes, and therefore unlike my neighbors. But excuse me. [*He goes to stable door, picks up a cushion, returns to Ruth. Pray and Ruth rise. Worth throws cushion on the seat*] This makes a hard seat more comfortable. [*He sits quietly in Pray's place*]

PRAY. [*To Ruth*] I will go and speak to your father. [*Exits into house. Music. Enter Mink Jones driving an old horse and buckboard wagon containing a treadle and a bag of loose corn. Drives to C. of stage*]

MINK. Whoa, there! Whoa, there, Shoo-fly!

WORTH. Hello, Mink! Are you tired?

MINK. [*Standing up in wagon with the whip in his hand*] Tired? Tired ain't the word for it! Had to get up at four o'clock this morning. Killed two pigs for the butcher; doctored a sick horse for old man Smith; tarred and feathered a rat so he'd scare the others out of Fogg's grocery store; took down the schoolhouse stovepipes because they were stopped up, and fixed 'em up again; hauled a load of coal for Widow Wiggins; stopped a dog fight in Brody's store; started a balky horse for Ed Billings; and then Dad Hawkins died last night and I had to go over and shave the corpse.

WORTH. Well, I should think you would need a rest.

MINK. Rest? Why, there is no rest for the weary. And now I've brought this treadle home and I have to fix it up.

WORTH. Where is the treadle?

MINK. Here on the buckboard.

RUTH. Mink, old Joe is in the house.

MINK. Well, let him enjoy himself.

WORTH. But aren't you jealous of old Joe?

MINK. Jealous? Me jealous? Why, that's the only thing I have to tease Mrs. Jones about. I twit her on that so as to make her let up when she jaws me. [*Gets out of wagon*] Well, I must hurry up and fix this treadle so as to get to go to the raffle tonight.

WORTH. But will your horse stand?

MINK. Stand? No, I'm afraid he'll fall down. I'll take him over here where he can lean against the house. [*Mink leads horse to L.1.E. Exits with horse far enough to leave the back end of wagon on the stage*]

RUTH. Raffle? What does he mean?

WORTH. There is going to be a raffle tonight at the saloon for the benefit of Oakhurst. He is in trouble.

RUTH. Poor fellow! I feel sorry for him. I've heard he was a Union soldier. [*Enter Mink*]

MINK. Yes, Miss Ruth, and as brave a man as ever fought. [*Enter Hardman who listens at the door*] He lost the use of his arm while he was carrying a wounded comrade off the field of battle. Got a bullet for doing good. Now he's got no strength to do manual labor and deserves assistance from those who stayed at home while he was doing the fighting. I think Fred Oakhurst one of the squarest men that ever lived, and I've got a dollar and thirty-one cents put on that raffle, and it all goes. [*Turns; sees Hardman; grabs bag of corn by bottom of bag and lifts it on his back. As bag was not tied up, corn falls out in a stream as he crosses stage hurriedly to exit into stable. Hardman comes down to Worth*]

HARD. Do you think that if Oakhurst was a store-keeper, Mink would side with him? His poor wife is working here all day for a dollar, less than he will spend at that raffle tonight. I can forgive the drunkard, for he is weak. But the rum-seller, never! They were the cause of my poor boy leaving home and of leading him to an untimely grave. Cursed be he who puts the poisoned cup to his neighbor's lips! [*Enter Oakhurst*] What can you want in my place?

OAK. I wish to see the doctor. My baby is worse. [*Exit Ruth into house, returning immediately*]

HARD. Do you ever think of the thousands of children who are dying from the neglect of drunken parents? Do you ever think of the thousands of homes that are daily wrecked by men of your calling? Has it ever occurred to you that retribution must come for the tears of the innocent babes and the agonies of broken-hearted fathers and mothers and children that are dying when the money that should support them is spent in the rum-shop? [*Enter Dr. Sawyer followed by Pray*]

RUTH. Don't chide him, father. His child is sick.

DR. S. Well, Oakhurst, what's the matter?

OAK. My child is worse and we are afraid she is dying.

DR. S. See here, Oakhurst, you owe me quite a bill now and I must have money today.

OAK. [*Pleadingly*] Doctor, I cannot let you have it today. I have paid out every dollar I had in the house; but I'll let you have some tomorrow.

DR. S. No, no! I must have it today, or not a step do I go!

OAK. But, doctor, my child is dying!

DR. S. Well, go ahead. But remember! This is my last visit! [*Exit Oakhurst*] I'll never get a penny unless I see him at once. [*Exit Dr. Sawyer, C.*]

PRAY. Good, kind-hearted old doctor! He loses all thought of self when others are in need!

WORTH. I don't think so. Did the good Samaritan bring a lawsuit to recover his pay? [*He goes upstage*]

PRAY. Where are you going now? To look up your Bible, or to the saloon?

WORTH. Being a free-born American citizen, I go where I please! [*Exits C.*]

RUTH. Father, may I bring a few little comforts to Oakhurst's sick child?

PRAY. Why should you care for a rum-seller's child?

RUTH. Father, he was a Union soldier.

HARD. Well, go, daughter. It can do no harm. [*Ruth exits into house. Enter Mink with a basket of corncobs on his shoulders, places it on the tail of the wagon, which upsets, knocking him down, and the corn spills. Enter Mrs. Jones from the house with a basket of clothes full of clean linen. As she goes toward C. she sees Mink*]

MRS. J. So, Mink, here you are, drunk again!

MINK. Drunk again?

MRS. J. Yes, again, I said. Don't try to tell us it's the same old drunk. And what do you mean by coming home at four o'clock in the morning?

MINK. No, my dear, it was eleven o'clock. Won't you take my word for it?

MRS. J. No, I'll not! I looked at the clock and it was four. [*Exits C. with basket*]

MINK. Gentlemen, my feelings are hurt. My wife would sooner believe a damned old two-dollar alarm clock than she would me. [*He rises from the floor, gets his foot tangled in the harness, which is in the back of the wagon, and finally struggles across the stage towards the stable, looking at his feet*] What's this to be, a waltz or a schottische? [*Exits into stable. Enter Mrs. Jones with dry clothes in the basket*]

BEL. Mrs. Jones, you ought to be pitied, having such a husband!

MRS. J. Well, I'd a heap rather have him than you.

BEL. But he's such a shiftless fellow!

MRS. J. I don't care! I married him, and he's mine, and I don't intend to let anybody else run him down! [*Exits into house. Enter Ruth with a bundle which she hands to Roxey, who enters with her. Enter Dr. Sawyer*]

DR. S. Well, Oakhurst's child is likely to die.

HARD. Daughter, where are you going?

RUTH. This is a bundle of little delicacies for Oakhurst's sick child.

Pray. A saloon is no place for a lady to be seen. [*Going up*] Let me take it. I am going that way. [*He takes the bundle*]

Hard. Daughter, go into the house! [*Exit Ruth and Roxey*]

Pray. Oakhurst has seen us over here and suspects we are planning a raid. That is why he made an excuse to come here.

Hard. Do you think there is any chance of our plan failing?

Pray. None whatever. I have secured a witness who will swear that he purchased liquor in the saloon.

Hard. Who is it?

Pray. Bingo Jones.

Hard. Will he do it, think you? [*Enter Bingo, shouting, flashily dressed, and drunk*]

Pray. Here he is! Bingo, did you secure the liquor?

Bingo. Yes, you bet I did!

Pray. And will you swear that you bought it at the saloon?

Bingo. Saloon? No! I bought thirteen drinks over at your drugstore! Whoops! Hurrah! [*Consternation for all*]

CURTAIN

SECOND CURTAIN

Rox. [*Enters from house and stands R.C.*] St. Julian, how could you? [*Bingo throws hat on steps and looks crestfallen*]

ROXEY	BINGO	
HARDMAN	DOCTOR	PRAY

ACT II.

Scene: *Interior of Oakhurst's saloon. Set bar at back with small arch opening door in flat behind bar. Door in flat R. and L. in each end beyond bar. Set window open L.3.E. Table and three chairs L.C. Bottles and glasses on table. Chair in front of fireplace R.2.E. Shovel and broom near fireplace. Bottles and glasses and cigar boxes on bar. Treadle stands against wing, R.1.E.*

Discovered: *At rise, Bingo on chair R.C. Worth, Wes Perry and others at table L. Oakhurst at bar looking despondent. Newspaper on table.*

Worth. Where are all the boys?

Perry. Don't know. Some of 'em ought to be around before this. I hear Mink had some trouble with his buckboard today.

WORTH. I guess that's what's keeping him away. He generally makes this place his home.

BINGO. Yes, that runs in the family, you know.

WORTH. But where's Uncle Joe Viall? [*Enter old Joe Viall*]

VIALL. Here I am. Always on time and as slick as they make 'em!

WORTH. How are you feeling, Uncle Joe?

VIALL. Pretty tolerable fine for an old man. Can't you see I am?

PERRY. Old Dave Walton was pretty sick last night. The doctor thinks he's going to die.

WORTH. He must be the oldest man in town.

VIALL. What? He's a mere boy! He's only seventy-eight. Why, I used to spank his mother!

OMNES. Ha! Ha! Ha!

OAK. [*To Bingo*] What is it worth to pick up the ashes around the shop?

BINGO. About five dollars.

OAK. Five dollars! I'll give you twenty cents.

BINGO. I'll take it! [*Oakhurst gives him broom and pan and goes behind bar. Exit Bingo*]

WORTH. I hate to see Fred looking so blue.

PERRY. Well, these ramrods have been making it pretty hot for him lately.

VIALL. I seen old Doc Sawyer, Deacon Pray, and Belcher up to the parsonage this morning. Don't think they're getting ready for another raid, are they?

PERRY. I shouldn't wonder. Pastor Hardman is very bitter in the prohibition cause. He blames the rum-shop for being the cause of his boy running away.

WORTH. [*Standing*] And could you blame the boy for going? Was his home a happy one? Did Hardman ever speak a kind or encouraging word to any of his family? I have known him for twenty years and never heard him speak a kind word to his wife or daughter. Did you ever hear him utter a cheering word to his wife? Did he ever offer to buy her a new dress or tell her that her dinner was good? Did he ever return from a walk and bring her even a bunch of wildflowers? Did you ever hear him praise her in the presence of others? I vow I never did. Does he ever bring her a few ribbons, or exhibit in any way the little tokens of affection a woman loves so well? No! Poor woman! Her heart is broken for the loss of her boy who was driven away by a cold-hearted father. And she, like all around her, is literally starved for want of affection and sympathy!

PERRY. [*Going to bar*] Well, gentlemen, what will you have to drink? [*All rush to the bar, old Viall tottering the last of all*]

VIALL. Hold on! You're not going to leave me out! [*Enter Mink*]

MINK. Mine's the same as last year. [*All drink and return downstage*]

WORTH. I hear that you met with an accident this morning.

MINK. Yes. You see, I greased the buckboard this morning and forgot to put the nut on the off hind wheel. The damned thing broke down before I got a hundred yards. [*Picks up towel from chair Bingo was sitting in and dusts himself*]

OAK. Hold on! There's varnish on that towel! [*Mink tries to throw it out-of-doors, but it sticks to his fingers. Enter Bingo who snatches towel and tries to throw it out-of-doors, but it sticks to his fingers also and he exits disgusted. Mink, in the meantime, tries to rub his hands off on his clothes, but apparently makes matters worse. In despair he goes to treadle and wipes his hands on it; it is leaning against wing R.1.E. Mink falls backward against it as he wipes his hands on it and falls to floor as it revolves. All laugh*] Come, gentlemen, have a drink. [*All go to the bar. Enter Bingo through door in flat with a pail of water, which he throws out of the open window. Will Peak is outside window and is wet. He shows head in window and throws another pail of water into the room; it had been standing outside. Bingo is wet*]

WORTH. Who threw that water in here?

PERRY. Will Peak? He's spying around against Oakhurst. You had better look out for a raid tonight.

OAK. I hope not. I've trouble enough lately.

WORTH. Bingo, are you coming to the raffle tonight?

BINGO. No, I'm going to church.

MINK. Yes, he's fallen in love with that new gal up at the parsonage. He got a quarter this morning and what do you suppose he did with it?

OMNES. What?

MINK. He bought a toothbrush! [*All laugh*]

VIALL. Well, that's what I call squandering money.

BINGO. Well, it would be in your case. Say, paw, maw wants you to come home right now.

MINK. I'll come home when I get good and ready.

BINGO. Well, you'll get ready soon enough if she comes after you. [*Goes toward door*] Say, here comes old Pray!

OAK. Boys, cover up the drinks quick! [*Business of hiding the drinks. Enter Pray; he speaks to Oakhurst*]

PRAY. Miss Ruth Hardman requested me to give you this parcel for your children, as she was unable to come herself. The string broke as I was carrying it here; so I could not avoid seeing what it contained. Lots of nice things!

OAK. Won't you thank her for me and tell her I am deeply grateful. [*Exit Pray. Oakhurst comes down C.*] And I always thought she had been taught to hate a saloon-keeper. Bingo, will you tend shop a minute? [*Exits C.D.L.*]

PERRY. Say, boys, did you see the tears in Oakhurst's eyes?

VIALL. Yes, that little act of hers has broke him all up.

PERRY. That circumstance reminds me. Speaking of Ruth Hardman—

WORTH. Hush! Suppose we don't mention a lady's name in a barroom! [*Bingo has small stove-shovel and scuttle. Takes ashes out of stove; then goes to every one of the characters who are smoking and knocks ashes off their cigars into the scuttle; all look surprised. Bingo exits quietly, whistling, out of door. Mink, who is sitting on chair R., rises and dashes his cigar on the floor; then he sits down, disgusted*] Why do they call these temperance folks ramrods?

PERRY. I suppose it's because they are so straight.

MINK. I don't think it is a very appropriate name. A ramrod puts in a load; that's something they don't do.

VIALL. I see by the papers that there's a fellow out West who has invented a scheme to make it rain.

MINK. Well, I wish I could invent a scheme to raise the wind.

WORTH. Mink, is it true that married men live longer than single men?

MINK. No. Married men don't live any longer. It just seems longer.

VIALL. What paper is that?

WORTH. The Springfield *Reporter*.

VIALL. Well, read us the news of the town.

WORTH. All right. "Weatherfield notes: The entertainment at the school-house was liberally patronized last Saturday evening."

MINK. Yes. Eight women, six children, a dog, and myself.

WORTH. "Street fakers are becoming numerous of late and it is proposed to place an additional tax on lightning-rod agents."

VIALL. Yes. Them confounded lightning-rod agents is a nuisance. They ought to be stopped from coming around. They are the curse of the country.

WORTH. "Vandals have lately been stealing the flowers from the graves in the country."

VIALL. Gol darn it! I'd like to catch them stealing flowers from my grave! I'd fix them!

WORTH. "Elder Whizzle is now eighty-two years old. He looks well, but he is a little lame in the left knee."

VIALL. Only eighty-two? Why, he ought to be spry! When I was eighty-two I could walk ten miles and never stop for a rest.

WORTH. "The person who took the hoe from Abner King's barn is respectfully requested to return the same at once." [*Mink starts to leave. Worth runs after him and pulls him back*] What's the matter?

MINK. I don't want the damned old hoe anyhow. I'll bring it back right away. [*He sits down again*]

VIALL. I call that Springfield *Reporter* the best paper in the country for news. They say it stands next to the New York *Clipper*. I took it for two years. [*Enter Bingo; he goes to bar as if to buy a drink*]

MINK. Hello! Going to buy liquor? Don't do it. Lend it to me.

BINGO. Not much!

MINK. Haven't I always given you the benefit of my example, how not to act? How much have you got?

BINGO. Twenty cents.

MINK. Well, if you're going to spend it, don't let it go out of the family. [*Goes to bar with Bingo*]

BINGO. As I was coming up the street, I was met by old Mother White. She says to me, "If you go into that place"—meaning here, "you'll surely be damned!" Then I said, "I'll be damned if I don't!" [*Raises glass to drink*]

PERRY. I say, Bingo, what does that little gal up to the house say to you?

BINGO. [*Dropping glass from mouth slowly*] She said if I stopped drinking and took care of myself, folks would respect me and wouldn't call me Bingo any more. [*Sets glass of liquor untouched on the counter*]

MINK. Ain't you going to drink?

BINGO. [*Going to door*] No, I ain't. I'm going to take this money home to mother. Any fellow that lets his mother work as hard as mine does and don't try to help her is of no account. [*Exits*]

WORTH. If that boy had been raised right, he'd have made a good man.

MINK. Yes, and learned to despise me. That's the way. He'll bring it home to his mother and waste it buying flour. [*Enter Oakhurst*]

OAK. Come, gentlemen, and look at the turkey we are to raffle tonight. [*Shows turkey*]

MINK. Ain't it a beauty?

WORTH. I'll have a few throws for that anyway.

PERRY. So will I.

MINK. Say, won't we just whoop things up here! [*Enter Mrs. Jones*]

MRS. J. You'll just come home and whoop things up in the woodshed! You're a nice man to leave me home doing all your work besides my own, while you come here and drink up all both of us can earn. You ought to be ashamed of yourself! [*Cries*]

MINK. My dear, this language!

Mrs. J. Don't talk to me, but come right home.

Mink. Gentlemen, I know you will excuse my wife. This is the first time she has ever been in a barroom, and—and—

Mrs. J. Yes, and it's all your faults. You're nothing but a set of drunken brutes!

Mink. Once more, gentlemen, I apologize for my wife's actions. It is nervous prostration. She is unaccustomed to these surroundings. You must excuse her. There, my dear, show them that you are a lady by birth and education. Let them see that you are still the same beauty and wit they all used to admire.

Mrs. J. You ought to be ashamed of yourself.

Mink. I know I am to blame, my dear. I appreciate your delicate feelings and understand that you wish to retire from this place which does not befit a lady of your attainments to be seen in. [*Urges her slowly to door*]

Mrs. J. Then you will come home at once?

Mink. Yes, my dear. [*Kisses her*]

Mrs. J. Oh, Mink! Mink! [*Kisses him*]

Mink. [*At door*] Now hurry, my dear, hurry. Let no one see you leaving this place. I will follow. [*Kisses her again as she exits. He kicks his leg at crowd inside*]

Mrs. J. [*Outside*] Be sure and come home.

Mink. Yes, my love. Take care now. Don't fall down. [*Shuts door and comes downstage*]

Worth. Mink, you're a wonder.

Viall. If I had a wife like that, I'd lick her.

Mink. Oh, you would? Boys, Uncle Joe's going to treat!

Viall. No, I ain't! I said, "lick her"!

Mink. Well, that's what we want, "liquor"!

Viall. You're a liar! You—you—damned fool! Don't you know the difference between "lick her" and "liquor"?

Mink. You bet I do!

Perry. The idea of a woman talking like that to her husband!

Mink. What did she say that was unbecoming a lady?

Perry. She called you a drunken brute!

Mink. Well, ain't I? See here! I've been married to my wife for twenty-two years. She's put up with my faults all that time, and anybody that says a word against her—well, I'll lick him! [*Squaring off*]

Worth. Hold on there, Mink. Wes meant no harm. [*Enter a little girl, one of Crossman's children*]

CHILD. [*To Oakhurst*]   Father sent me down here and told me to ask you to fill this bottle.

OAK.   He sent you here after whiskey?

CHILD.   Yes, sir.

OAK.   Go right back and tell him if he wants it to come for it himself! A saloon is no place to send a little girl! Here's a nickel for you to buy some candy with.

CHILD.   But he says he'll lick me if I come home without it.

MINK. [*Jumping up from chair*]   Will he? Come, little girl, I'll go home with you! [*Takes girl's hand and exits with her F.R.*]

VIALL.   Well, if he hadn't gone, I would have. [*Enter Bingo*]

OAK.   Gentlemen, I have never sold liquor to a minor yet.

PERRY.   Well, here's Bingo. Say, Bingo, ain't you a minor?

BINGO.   No, I ain't. I got a vote and I ain't going to sell it for no three dollars, neither.

VIALL.   That's right! Don't vote at all if you can't get five dollars for it!

BINGO.   I've made up my mind I'm going to be a brakeman, a detective, or a Negro minstrel.

PERRY.   Why, what would you do as a detective?

BINGO.   Don't you remember the night I caught you down at the mill?

PERRY. [*Jumping up quickly and putting his hand over Bingo's mouth*] Not a word about that, or there'll be trouble! I'll lick you! Come on, will you have a drink?

BINGO.   I guess I'll not drink just now.

VIALL.   Well, if you're going to be a minstrel fellow, you ought to give us a song.

BINGO.   Excuse me, I don't sing for nothing.

WORTH.   We'll take up a collection.

BINGO.   I guess I'll take up the collection first. [*He passes the hat around, going to Viall last of all. Viall pretends not to understand what is going on. Bingo stands looking at him. At last, business of Viall feeling for money, which he grudgingly drops in hat. Bingo counts out money, two dimes, a quarter, and a copper penny. He looks at old Viall disgustedly; then goes to door*]

WORTH.   Hold on! Where are you going?

BINGO.   Going to take this home to mother.

WORTH.   But we want the song first.

BINGO.   All right. [*Goes to Viall who is sitting on chair R. Business of both trying to strike proper key. After a while Bingo does song and dance after the style of a country boy who has been to a minstrel show and who endeavors to imitate song and dance man: "When Pop Was a Little Boy Like Me." Exits D.L.F.*]

WORTH. That boy has improved wonderfully of late.

PERRY. Yes, and it's all due to that little gal in the parsonage. She's bound to make a man of him.

WORTH. Heaven bless such girls! If these temperance folks would talk less and import more pretty girls, their cause would prosper more. [*Enter Dr. Sawyer*]

PERRY. I bet I know what he's after: money!

DR. S. Oakhurst, it's about time you settled that little bill. I've waited long enough.

OAK. You'll have to wait a little longer. I haven't got it about the house at present.

DR. S. Oh, that's nonsense! You're a business man. You're never without money. I'll wait no longer. [*Enter Pray D.F.*]

PRAY. Oakhurst, let me have a pint of whiskey! My mother is sick and I must have it at once!

OAK. But why don't you go to your own drugstore for it?

PRAY. Because I have no time. Come, Oakhurst, let me have it quick! Suppose your wife or child was sick and I refused to let you have medicine at my store?

OAK. Mr. Pray, I cannot. You know how I am situated.

WORTH. Your mother must have been taken sick very suddenly. I saw her driving toward Springfield an hour ago.

PRAY. She had to turn back. Oakhurst, for mercy's sake, let me have it!

OAK. [*Goes to bar; hands bottle to Pray*] Here then, Pray.

PRAY. And here is the money.

OAK. No, it is a present; I give it to you.

PRAY. But you must take it! I take money from you for what you purchase.

OAK. No. I will not take it.

DR. S. What, man! Refuse money and owing it to me? Take it, I say! That is my money, not yours, that you are refusing, and I want it! [*Oakhurst takes money. Exit Dr. Sawyer and Pray*]

WORTH. I'm afraid you did wrong then, Fred. [*Rises and looks out of window*] See, there goes his sick mother now!

VIALL. I'm afraid the ramrods are after you, Fred.

OAK. I hope not. I've had trouble enough already. What will become of my poor children?

WORTH. [*Shakes Oakhurst's hand*] Never mind, old fellow. I'll become your bondsman. [*Enter Mink D.F.*]

Oak. Welcome. Let's have one more round for luck! [*All go to bar*]

Mink. Just in time.

Viall. No, boys, don't get me drunk. [*Enter Bingo D.F.*]

Bingo. Fred, here comes the sheriff!

Oak. Quick! Hide the stuff! [*Everybody hides the liquor. Enter Sheriff, Pray, Belcher, Dr. Sawyer, Hardman, Peak, and officer*]

Sher. I have a warrant for your arrest, Oakhurst, on the charge of selling liquor. Shall I read it?

Oak. It's unnecessary.

Sher. Very well. I have also an order to search the premises. Keep your eye on that man. [*Points to Mink*]

Mink. That's right. Cast a slur on an innocent man!

Sher. Officer, do your duty! [*Officer searches Worth. He snatches a bottle off the table. Officer grabs it as he passes it to Perry. Officer rushes to him; he passes it over head to Viall; officer grabs at it; Viall snatches it away. Funny struggle among them all. Viall squares off with fists as if to fight. Sheriff eventually gets bottle*]

Pray. Take him away to the lockup! [*Officer seizes Oakhurst*]

Bel. Stop! [*Oakhurst is released*] While I have no sympathy for a rum-seller, I am here to enforce the law. I will do my duty and prosecute this man, but I will not persecute him! If bail is offered, it must be accepted.

Worth. I will go his bail!

Perry. And so will I!

Sher. Has every place been searched?

Pray. Search the cellar! You may find liquor there. [*Goes down into the cellar with Dr. Sawyer, Peak, and an officer*]

Worth. [*Aside to Oakhurst*] Is there anything in the cellar?

Oak. Yes, a fresh barrel of beer.

Hard. [*Advances to Oakhurst*] This may seem hard to you, but think of the many crimes you have caused! Think of the unhappy mothers and children you have caused to suffer! Will this not be a glorious Thanksgiving to them?

Oak. Yes, and think of my wife and children! What sort of a Thanksgiving have you made for them when this, their only sustenance, is taken from them!

Mink. You think you are right when you deprive a people of their personal liberty. Suppose we had the making of the law and passed one compelling you to drink two glasses of liquor a day, would you like that?

Hard. No.

Mink. Then let me tell you! You could drink it a damned sight easier than I could let it alone! If a man ain't born a man, you can't make him one by law! When I quit drinking, I'll do it because I want to, and not to please the whim of a lot of cranks like you! As long as you try to reform me by law, I'll drink! And I'll get it, too, and no darn country legislature can stop me, either! [*Great noise in cellar as keg of beer explodes. Peak is thrown over mouth of trap with face disfigured, coat torn; Pray with hat off, face blackened; Dr. Sawyer with one side of his whiskers blown off*]

CURTAIN

SECOND CURTAIN

Everyone off except Oakhurst, who is discovered with head down on bar counter, crying. Enter Mink D.F., on tiptoe. When he sees Oakhurst, he puts his hand in his pocket, takes out coin, and places it slyly on the counter in front of Oakhurst. Then he quietly exits.

ACT III.

SCENE 1: *Dining room in parsonage. Door L.3.E. Door R.2.E. Table C. Organ L.1.E. Tablecloth on table. Three chairs beside table.*
DISCOVERED: *Mrs. Hardman, Mr. Hardman, and Roxey.*

MRS. H.   I wonder what is the matter. I told Mrs. Jones to come early.

ROX.   Well, everything is ready.

HARD.   This will indeed be a happy Thanksgiving, not alone for ourselves, but for others, on account of the glorious results of our work last night. The rum-shop has been closed and the proprietor has been arrested. Another victory in the cause of temperance! [*Knock on door outside. Enter Mink, drunk*]

ROX.   Why, it's old Mr. Jones.

MINK.   Oh, yes; it's old Mr. Jones, and young Mr. Jones, old Mr. Jones's son.

HARD.   Mr. Jones, are you in your natural condition?

MINK.   Yes. As large as life and as natural as ever! Old Mr. Jones and young Mr. Jones!

HARD.   You appear to be under the influence of liquor.

MINK.   Well, that's my natural condition! Old Mr. Jones and young Mr. Jones!

HARD.   How did you procure the liquor? I thought that all Oakhurst possessed was seized last night and destroyed!

MINK.   Yes, I had to drive ten miles over to Springfield to get this load. They emptied everything poor Oakhurst had in the gutter last night. Infernal shame! Some of it mighty good stuff, too! [*Enter Mrs. Jones*]

Mrs. J. Hello, Mink! [*Astonished*] You here? Did you tell them?

Mink. No. Just got here.

Mrs. J. Just got here?

Mink. Yes, I'm all here. [*Hugs her*] Old Mr. Jones and young Mr. Jones!

Mrs. J. And I declare! You've been drinking, too!

Mink. Couldn't help it, my dear! So lonely without you!

Mrs. J. Well, I suppose, poor fellow, you were! For you know, Mrs. Hardman, I'm just that tuckered out I don't know what to do. They raided poor Oakhurst's saloon last night and that poor woman ill in bed with a sick child to look after! I had to go and sit till four o'clock this morning with them. But I must hurry now. You won't have to wait long. I'll have dinner ready in a few minutes. [*Exits hurriedly R.2.E.*]

Mink. I'm going over to Oakhurst's place to try and fix that damned old treadle. [*Exits L.3.E.*]

Hard. That man is ruining her husband; yet she sits up all night to nurse his sick family. [*Enter Viall with a telegram*]

Viall. They sent me up here with this from the depot. They calculated as how it was something you'd want to know about right away.

Hard. [*Reads telegram*] I shall exchange pulpits with the Reverend Hale on Sunday.

Viall. Where's Mrs. Jones? I'd like to see Mrs. Jones.

Mrs. H. You'll find her in the kitchen.

Viall. Mighty fine gal, that Mrs. Jones. I guess I'll go and see her. [*Exits into kitchen R.2.E.*]

Mrs. H. How stupid! The idea of sending the oldest man in the village with a telegram! [*Knock outside. L.3.E. Enter Dr. Sawyer and Pray*]

Pray. I wish to see you, Mr. Hardman, in regard to Belcher. From what occurred last night and from what we have learned today, we are led to believe that he is siding with the enemy and that he does not intend to assist us in our moral warfare.

Dr. S. We are fully convinced that he is lukewarm in the glorious cause of temperance!

Pray. Yes. Lukewarm is the word! He had no desire to see Oakhurst go to prison last night and insisted that he should have bondsmen.

Hard. Hush! I think matters can be arranged. I will write to my brother in Boston and request him to send an able lawyer to assist in the prosecution.

Dr. S. and Pray. A good idea!

Hard. [*To Dr. Sawyer*] Will you inform Belcher of our decision?

Dr. S. Oh, no! My patients are so numerous at present that I cannot find the time. Perhaps Deacon Pray will undertake that duty?

PRAY. Me? No! Decidedly not! [*To Hardman*] Will you speak to him?

HARD. I have it! I will prepare a note informing him of our decision and requesting his resignation. We will each sign it.

DR. S. and PRAY. That will be perfectly satisfactory.

DR. S. I have a patient to visit, but I'll return directly. [*Exit Dr. Sawyer L.3.E.*]

HARD. Come, Mr. Pray, we will step into the parlor and prepare the note. [*Enter Ruth with sword*]

PRAY. Surely you are not going to war, Miss Ruth?

RUTH. Sir, I keep this sacred as a relic of my poor, dead brother!

PRAY. Pardon me! I meant not to offend.

HARD. As I said before, Mr. Pray, you can speak to my daughter for yourself. I will abide by her wishes. But come into the adjoining room. We will talk the matter over. [*Exits, followed by Pray*]

RUTH. Probably not, but he always does seem to offend. [*She places the sword on a chair and decorates it with ribbons*] Dear old sword! Although the hand that wielded you is withering in an unknown grave far away from home and those who yearn to feel its honest clasp; although your owner's form has returned to the dust from whence it came; may his spirit come on this Thanksgiving Day, as we place you in his vacant chair and with gentle memories solace those who loved him! [*Enter Worth with package containing roses*] Ah, Mr. Worth, I am so glad to see you!

WORTH. I have taken this privilege to bring you some flowers.

RUTH. Oh, how kind of you! You always seem to guess what I want. Are they Maréchal Niel?

WORTH. No; they are real American Beauties.

RUTH. But surely you could not have obtained them in this neighborhood! You must have sent to Boston for them!

WORTH. I did.

RUTH. Then they must have cost quite a fortune.

WORTH. Surely ten dollars is not a great deal of money.

RUTH. It is, if it is squandered on useless articles.

WORTH. I don't think I am in the habit of squandering money.

RUTH. Not even in a saloon?

WORTH. Believe me, the few dollars I spend there bring as much calm joy and sunshine into the lives and the hearts of those old men as these roses do to you.

RUTH. Then they must love liquor very much!

WORTH. They do, and I am almost certain that I do as much good in lightening the lives of those poor old fellows as you do by going to church.

Ruth. By the way, do you go to church very often?

Worth. No. Dickens is my Bible, and among those old fellows I at times fancy that I am Nicholas Nickleby, that Pickwick is my intimate friend, and that Micawber is waiting for something to turn up in the drink line. This world would be much poorer if deprived of the creations of Dickens. Could we stand to lose Sam Weller, Mrs. Gamp and old Scrooge, Tiny Tim and Tabby Becks, Mr. Boffin and Silas Wegg, Captain Cuttle and Jack Bunsby? These are the people who have lived and moved and we know them. These are characters that will live and do live in memory and literature, in their laughter. If you desire to study character, there is no place like a country barroom.

Ruth. You surely do not expect to find Dickens in a barroom!

Worth. I sometimes think Dickens must have spent more than one day in a barroom.

Ruth. Yes; but he probably made use of it. You don't!

Worth. I will struggle along and probably may find use of it some day.

Ruth. Well, see that you don't struggle very hard. Industrious men frequently overtask themselves, and you seem to waste a good deal of your ten-dollar time in doing nothing.

Worth. Who ever heard of a woman falling in love with a man because he was industrious?

Ruth. I didn't speak of love. [Laughs] But I have no right to question your method of living. Pardon me!

Worth. It is not necessary. I rather like it. Come, tell me my shortcomings.

Ruth. Do you mean it?

Worth. Yes.

Ruth. Then ask my father.

Worth. Ah, no. I'd rather not!

Ruth. A woman likes to know that the man she loves has some definite purpose in life. But come, let us change the subject. This is Thanksgiving Day, and on every anniversary of this day, I take this sword and place it on my brother's chair. Poor fellow, he went away to war on Thanksgiving Day!

Worth. Was he killed?

Ruth. We have no reason to believe otherwise. This was sent home by a comrade who brought a short message. Since then, we have heard nothing of him and can only suppose that he rests upon some Southern battlefield among the unknown dead. If he were only buried here, it would be some comfort and a blessing to mother!

Worth. And to you also?

RUTH. Yes.

WORTH. If he had died upon the field while in active service, some trace of him could be discovered by communication with some member of his corps.

RUTH. Father sent to Washington and searched the records, but he could find no clue that was of any service.

WORTH. [*Aside*] I wonder if it is possible? [*Pause*] By Jove, I'll try! [*Aloud*] Well, Miss Ruth, I regret that I have to leave you today.

RUTH. Surely you are not going away?

WORTH. I have very important business which will take me from this village for a time, but before I go I will bring you around this month's *Harper's* and call to say good-by. [*His actions show that he wants to embrace and kiss Ruth, but he restrains himself. Ruth takes both his hands in hers. Worth speaks with great self-control*] Adieu! For the present! [*Exits L.2.E.*]

RUTH. [*After a pause*] I forgot to thank him for those roses! [*She runs to the window and looks out after Worth. Enter Roxey*]

ROX. Miss Ruth, do you know that old man came into the kitchen to talk to Mrs. Jones and he sat square down on a hot mince pie!

RUTH. Did it hurt him?

ROX. No, but it ruined the pie! [*Enter Viall pursued by Mrs. Jones*]

MRS. J. Don't you ever dare show your nose in that kitchen again, or I'll scald you, you old fool, you! [*Exits into kitchen R.2.E.*]

VIALL. Ah, she don't mean it! She's only a little bit mad! By gosh, that pie was hot! She's a mighty fine gal, I tell you!

ROX. I hope you've had your lesson and that you'll stay out of the kitchen now! You ought to be ashamed of yourself running around after girls at your age!

VIALL. What's age got to do with it? A woman is as old as she looks, but a man is as old as he feels! I'm just as spry as I was sixty years ago. Why, everybody talks of my being so spry, and I can sing a better song than any of your milksop fellows that's running around this town!

ROX. Sing, Uncle Joe, and let us hear you!

RUTH. Yes. Do I know your favorite? [*Goes to organ and starts to play "I'm Just as Young as I Used to Be." Old Viall clears his throat and sings, after several false starts. At close of his song, he tries to dance. At that moment, enter Hardman accompanied by Pray*]

HARD. What is the meaning of this?

RUTH. [*Embarrassed*] Uncle Joe was only singing. [*She rises*]

HARD. It seems my house is getting very gay. Daughter, go to your room! I have business with Mr. Pray. [*Ruth exits D.F.*]

VIALL. I guess I'll go, too! [*Exits L.2.E. Roxey exits R.2.E.*]

HARD. As I was saying, Mr. Pray, I do not wish to interfere with my daughter's happiness. I will leave the matter entirely in her hands. As for me, I cannot withhold my consent from one who has been so earnest a worker in the glorious cause of temperance.

BEL. [*Shouting from outside. Much noise*] I will see them face to face! [*He rushes in, furious. Mink follows*]

HARD. What is the meaning of this conduct?

BEL. [*Furious*] It means I'm on to you! You, sir! To write a letter and discharge me! I won't give you the chance! No! I'll fool you! [*Angry*] I'll resign! You're going to send to Boston for a lawyer, are you? Well, I'll give you all the law you want! I will appear in behalf of Oakhurst, who is a victim of oppression! I will offer my services free and defend him against your vile conspiracy! In the cause of the downtrodden and the oppressed I am ever ready to do my duty. Furthermore, we are going to form a Personal Liberty League in this village, and Mink Jones there shall be president. We intend to prosecute you for conspiracy! I know your records! Every one of you! [*To Pray*] You want the saloon closed up so that you can get all the rum there is in town to sell in your drugstore! You sneak! You hypocrite! [*Pointing and shaking his finger at Dr. Sawyer*] You want people to pay you for prescriptions to get it! And as for you, [*Pointing at Hardman*] it is a personal grudge that you hide under the cloak of religion! Your cloth protects you, but you're a fraud, a mossback, and a shellback! And don't you forget it, you whited sepulcher! [*Exits L.2.E. in great haste*]

PRAY. This is really a most unpleasant affair.

HARD. Never mind. He is not worth noticing! Dismiss him from your mind! My daughter is in the parlor, if you wish to see her.

PRAY. This scene has quite unnerved me. Perhaps I had better defer—

HARD. Not at all! There is no time like the present! [*Pray bows to Hardman. Exits D.F.*] Well, Mr. Jones, what have you to say?

MINK. Not a word.

HARD. What do you mean by a "Personal Liberty League"?

MINK. All I know is, I'm to be president.

HARD. I know that you're opposed to prohibition.

MINK. No, I'm not, so long as they don't enforce it.

HARD. [*Going to door in flat*] So Belcher is going to defend this rumseller. Well, I'll have the best lawyer in Boston to prosecute him in the glorious cause of temperance! [*Exits door in flat. Enter Mrs. Jones and Roxey with dishes R.2.E.*]

MRS. J. Why, Mink, what are you doing here now?

MINK. Say, Belcher has been here and scared the life out of old Pray and the parson!

MRS. J. Mink—Mr. Jones—

MINK. Excuse me—*President* Jones of the Personal Liberty League!

MRS. J. Well, President Jones, will you just help me with that table?

MINK. Certainly! I'm not going to stand by and see my wife do any hard labor! [*Enter Bingo L.3.E.*] Bingo, help your mother with that table! I've got to go over to the saloon and help. [*Exits R.3.E. Bingo helps with the table downstage with Mrs. Jones, who then exits*]

ROX. St. Julian, will you help me with this tablecloth?

BINGO. Certainly, I will.

ROX. Now take hold of the corner and help me fold it. Keep folding until you come up to me, just like this. [*Bingo drops the cloth when he gets close to her and turns away*] Why, what's the matter?

BINGO. Say—do you smell whiskey?

ROX. Why, you haven't been drinking again?

BINGO. No, but I've been around dad all day. Say, are you going to church tonight?

ROX. Why, yes.

BINGO. I'll be there. [*He keeps his hand up before his face*]

ROX. Don't you always go to church?

BINGO. Not when there's good fishing.

ROX. Don't you ever go to Sunday School?

BINGO. Just before Christmas, and because you go.

ROX. But you shouldn't go on my account. Don't you love the Lord?

BINGO. Don't know him! [*Enter Mink in time to hear last remark*]

MINK. Yes, church is a mighty good place to go to make love in! But if you think all the folks that go to church love the Lord, you'll get left. Please give this to Mrs. Hardman, Roxey. [*He hands her a small paper bundle*]

ROX. Carry the bundle for me, will you, St. Julian?

BINGO. All right. Is it heavy?

MINK. I carried it, didn't I? [*Bingo looks at the bundle, and hefts it*]

ROX. [*Disgusted*] Oh, give it to me! [*She picks up the bundle and exits R.2.E.*]

MINK. [*Stands watching Bingo, who has look of amazement on his face*] Sparking, are ye? Well, she's a mighty nice gal. It's natural for the Joneses to talk to the gals. I've a good mind to cut you out, if I had the time. [*Goes to door L.*]

BINGO. But you can't do it.

MINK. Why can't I do it?

BINGO. Because you'd have to give up what I did, and you couldn't! [*Laughs and pushes Mink out of door before him. Enter from flat L.C. Ruth and Pray*]

RUTH. I have already told you, Mr. Pray, that your entreaties are in vain. My decision is final, and I cannot consent to become your wife!

PRAY. Then we are to be enemies?

RUTH. I see no reason for that! [*Enter Worth L.3.E.*]

WORTH. [*Grabbing Pray by the shoulders and forcing him to the door*] There's a customer over at your store and you must go there immediately! [*Pushes him out and closes door*]

RUTH. Why—how will Mr. Pray feel?

WORTH. I presume he feels very much put out. But before I say good-by, I want to ask you a little question. Do you think you will regret my absence?

RUTH. I—I—think—that I will miss you. [*Coming down*]

WORTH. I hope so. [*Drawing near Ruth*]

RUTH. Why?

WORTH. Because—[*He puts his arm about her waist*] because I want to be your husband!

RUTH. Dare I trust my happiness to you?

WORTH. You may! I will be glad to see the day we love each other! Will it ever come?

RUTH. But is that all you want to know?

WORTH. For the present, yes. When I have proved to you that I have a definite object I will ask you another question. But I must hurry to catch my train. By the way, I have brought you *Harper's* for this month. Look it over. You may find something of interest in it. And now I must say good-by. [*Holds both of Ruth's hands*]

RUTH. Good-by, and I wish you a pleasant journey. [*Worth exits door in flat. Business of Ruth at window as before*] He's gone! He's gone, and now I'm so sorry! Why did he give me this magazine? I wonder if there is anything in it of interest to me. Let's see. [*She turns pages of magazine*] "Life in Alaska." No, no. Rather a chilly subject. "Account of the Australian Gum Tree." That's not very interesting. Why! [*Astonished*] Here is the exact picture of our house! And here is a picture of the saloon, too! What is this? "How Mink Jones Always Holds Four Aces. By John Worth." Then he hasn't been wasting his time! Oh, how glad I am to know it and to think that this story was written by him! [*She sits on the piano stool, propping the open magazine on the music rack of the piano, and becomes greatly absorbed in the story. Enter Roxey and Mrs. Jones with the dinner R.2.E.*]

Mrs. J. Miss Ruth, dinner is ready. [*Pause*] Miss Ruth, dinner is ready! [*Ruth takes no notice*]

Rox. Miss Ruth, dinner is ready! [*Very loud*] Miss Ruth, dinner is ready!!!

Ruth. [*Startled*] Oh, very well.

Mrs. J. Roxey, call dinner, will you?

Rox. [*To doors*] Dinner! [*She calls it louder several times and then exits door in flat. Enter Hardman and Mrs. Hardman. Ruth crosses to chair R. of table. Mrs. Hardman stops by chair where sword rests and leans on the chair*]

Hard. My poor boy! Gone but not forgotten! [*Enter Pray in excitement*]

Pray. I've come on an errand. I felt it my duty to deliver this letter. It is in your daughter's handwriting. This was intended as a warning to Oakhurst of our raid last night. I caused it to be intercepted. It was in the bundle of things she was taking to Oakhurst's children.

Hard. Daughter, is this true?

Ruth. [*Defiantly*] Father, it is!

Hard. [*To Pray*] Well, sir, I presume your errand is done?

Pray. [*Going*] I don't seem to get much thanks.

Hard. Virtue is its own reward. [*Exit Pray*] Daughter, why did you do this? Why did you seek to shield the rum-seller?

Ruth. Because he was a Union soldier like my brother!

Hard. And are you not sorry?

Ruth. No! I'd do it again!

Hard. You must retract those words, or you cannot remain in my house! [*The Hardmans stand rigidly. Ruth looking at her father. Final business of Ruth walking with quiet determination towards the door as slow curtain falls*]

CURTAIN

SECOND CURTAIN

Tableau—Mr. and Mrs. Hardman stand alone in their dining room. Ruth has gone.

Hard. [*Pointing to her chair*] Another vacant chair!

Scene 2: *Full stage, showing exterior view of church. Set church running across stage from R.1.E. to R.3.E. Steps leading to door of church R.2.E. Illuminated window of stained glass in church. Banks covered with grass mats scattered around stage with white slabs to represent gravestones.*

Discovered: *Mink on steps of church singing "They Called Her Lovely Mary, the Lily of the West." Enter Sheriff; sees Mink.*

SHER. What are you doing here? Why don't you go home?

MINK. I can't. I've got to go to the saloon to help Fred cut some wood. But what are you doing here? This ain't Sunday.

SHER. There's to be a temperance meeting here tonight and, as Ruth has gone, I've got to play the organ instead.

MINK. Where is she?

SHER. I don't know, and I don't care. Nobody will take her in.

MINK. Why not? Well, there's more damned hogs in this town than I ever knew. [*Exit Sheriff into church. Exit Mink singing "Lovely Mary." At the same time Dr. Sawyer and Belcher enter R.1.E. They look at each other contemptuously. Belcher says "Quack! Quack!" and crosses to L.U.E. and exits. Old Viall enters L.U.E. and goes into the church. Bingo enters L.U.E., crosses to church, runs up steps, looks in, and runs down again. He hides R.1.E. Mrs. Jones and Roxey enter L.U.E. Mrs. Jones goes in first and as soon as Roxey gets halfway up, Bingo calls "Roxey!" She comes down and they go to R.U.E. Then Hardman and Mrs. Hardman enter L.U.E. Behind them enters Ruth. She pantomimes sadly, comes down quietly and kisses the hem of her mother's dress as she ascends the steps. Ruth staggers over to C. of stage and falls on the ground in churchyard. The two Hardmans enter the church*]

RUTH. I don't know where to go for shelter! I am so tired! I must lie down here on this cold grave! [*Enter Pray. He discovers Ruth reclining on the gravestone. She screams and faints*]

PRAY. I guess I must have frightened her. She's fainted. So the new house wasn't good enough for her, eh? Well, let her lie there! [*Exits into church. Enter Mink R.U.E. with the treadle. He stands in C. of stage, holding it*]

MINK. Well, I've carried many a load in my time, but this is the toughest I ever tackled. It weighed over a hundred when I started; now it weighs a thousand. Gosh, I've got to rest.

HARD. [*From inside the church*] Friends, we are assembled here tonight that we may give thanks that we have been freed from the grasp of the demon drink. [*Mink listens to Hardman's voice*] His clutches have been loosened from the throats of our unfortunate brothers who were beguiled by his devilish snares and who allowed themselves to fall into his hands. We should rejoice that the evil of drunkenness has been banished from our midst and that the majesty of the law has been upheld in our peaceful community. Rum makes a man ruin his life. It is the cause of poverty throughout the land. It makes homes unhappy. It destroys the sanctity of family life. It causes children to be crippled by their drunken fathers and the hearts of wives to be made desolate. It makes the strong cruel to the weak, parents cruel to their children, and virtue a slave to vice. Let us rejoice that we are freed from this terrible monster, drink! [*The organ is played inside and the congregation sings a hymn. During the sermon Mink has discovered Ruth. First he covers her with his coat. Then he lifts her in his arms. At the end of the sermon he carries her tenderly offstage R.1.E. As the people come out of the church, they fall sprawling over the treadle that Mink left on the church steps. Old slippery day business*]

ACT IV.

SCENE 1: *Interior of anteroom in courthouse. Two large practical sliding doors open into courtroom. Chair C., also R.1.E. and L.1.E. Shelves L.1.E.* DISCOVERED: *Hardman, Mrs. Hardman, and Judge Doe.*

HARD. Now, judge, that you are ready, I suppose we will not have to wait any length of time before court opens.

JUDGE. No. We will waste no time. The witnesses for the prosecution will soon be here. But come into my private office and wait there until court is convened. [*Mrs. Hardman exits into Judge's office. Enter Dr. Sawyer, Pray, and Sprague, the Boston lawyer*]

HARD. Ah, gentlemen, we have been waiting your arrival. Judge Doe, permit me to introduce to you Mr. Sprague, the attorney for the prosecution, a famous lawyer from Boston.

JUDGE. I am delighted to meet such a distinguished member of the legal fraternity and trust that our relations will be amicable during the progress of this trial.

SPRA. [*Very suave*] I have no doubt they will be. I had the honor of quoting your decision on at least one occasion.

JUDGE. I trust you found it in consonance with the law. But excuse me, gentlemen, I must prepare for court. [*Exits L.*]

SPRA. Ha! Ha! Peculiar old gentleman! Yes, the opposing counsel, in a case I had at one time, quoted one of his decisions and the case was decided against him as being entirely at variance with the statute. [*Enter Peak*]

PRAY. Well, Peak, are you ready to go on the witness stand?

PEAK. Oh, yes, I'm ready, but I ain't seen that ten dollars yet that you promised me.

PRAY. Oh. That'll be all right. [*Exit Peak*]

DR. S. By the way, do you know that John Worth is coming here?

PRAY. Yes, I heard of his arrival today.

DR. S. They say he has become a famous man. He has written a book and has lots of townsfolk in it. I guess you're one, for he speaks of a mighty mean druggist. He must mean you.

PRAY. Do you think so? Well, I heard of it, and he also mentions a rascally doctor who kills all his patients. I think he refers to you.

DR. S. Does he? Well, I wish I had gotten even with him when I had the chance.

PRAY. How was that?

DR. S. Why, let him die of the whooping cough and the measles.

PRAY. Here comes the counsel for the defense. [*Enter Belcher with about twenty law books; he places them on a chair*]

SPRA. Indeed? Well, I'd like to meet the man.

BEL. [*Pointing to the books*] Here I have a few copies of Judge Doe's decisions.

PRAY. Mr. Belcher, this is Mr. Sprague, the opposing counsel.

BEL. [*Looks at him*] And is that the little runt? [*Sprague makes motion as if to answer*]

DR. S. Don't rile him up.

BEL. Watch those books! [*Exits L.*]

SPRA. Pardon me, I'd like to see those books. [*Looks at them*] *Judge Doe's Decision, Judge Doe's Decision.* Why, they're all Judge Doe's decisions. Ha! Ha! Ha! [*Reenter Belcher*]

BEL. Another of Judge Doe's decisions. [*Lays book on top of others. Glares fiercely at Sprague*]

SPRA. *Judge Doe's Decision!* I'll go at once and secure every copy there is in town. [*Exits with Dr. Sawyer and Pray R.1.E. Enter Hardman*]

HARD. Mr. Belcher, I must give you thanks for sheltering my daughter in your house.

BEL. Yes. I thought Mink's house was no place for her; so I took her to my residence where my wife and I can care for her. The fact that she is your daughter cuts no figure. We don't keep that stored up against her. She's not responsible for the accident of her birth.

HARD. Where is she now? Can I see her?

BEL. She is talking outside with my wife. When she's through I'll ask her to meet you. [*Exit Hardman, bowing*] Weakening! Weakening! He's got to give in at last. How I hate an obstinate old man. Well, I'll wait till Hardman gets through his prayers; then I'll go in. [*Enter Mink*]

MINK. Say, Belcher, I want an injunction.

BEL. An injunction for what?

MINK. My boy, Bingo, is going to sign the pledge.

BEL. What's the matter? Don't you think he'll keep it?

MINK. That's what I'm afraid of. He will keep it! Then what's going to become of him? I want an injunction to stop him from taking the pledge.

BEL. You ought to be glad that he will.

MINK. Glad? What? Do you think I want to see all the sunshine and roses taken out of his life? It's not in the nature of the Joneses to do without liquor!

BEL. Well, then the Joneses should stop their nature! That young man will be infinitely better off by making the change.

MINK. Now, see here, Mr. Belcher, put yourself in my place. Imagine the feelings of a father who sees his son go to ruin all on account of that damned gal! She made him do it!

BEL. Then she deserves credit. The woman who can reform a man where temperance lectures and legislatures fail, and who can in her own quiet way silence the mouths of fanatics and cranks by rescuing a fellow creature from the vice of intemperance, is an ornament to society and deserves a monument. A few earnest women can do more than all your loudmouthed orators in settling the temperance question. May Heaven bless her! Come into the court.

MINK. When Hardman is through saying the Lord's Prayer I'll come in. [*Enter Roxey, Bingo, and Mrs. Jones, R.*] Oh, you came to sign the pledge, did you? Well, you're too late. The judge has gone in, court is in session, and you're going to get left.

BINGO. I guess not. I can wait until recess.

MINK. Oh, this is too much! [*To Roxey*] And you're the cause of it!

BINGO. No, she ain't! I'm doing it of my own free will.

MINK. Free will! Who ever heard of a man in love having a free will?

MRS. J. Father, why don't you let him alone? You know our boy is much happier than he was before, and you can thank Roxey for it.

BINGO. Yes, father, and everything is settled; so you might just as well grin and bear it!

MINK. I suppose I'll have to bear it, but I'll be damned if I grin. [*Exit Roxey and Mrs. Jones. Bingo starts to follow*] Say, Bingo, what are you going to do with that gal?

BINGO. Get married.

MINK. What! To that insect! Why, she'd never be able to do a day's washing! She never could support you!

BINGO. I don't want her to. I mean to support her. [*Exits L.*]

MINK. It's a mistake. That boy is no Jones! [*Exits L. Enter Hardman and Ruth L. Ruth crosses and Hardman stands L.*]

RUTH. Father!

HARD. You have left my house and disobeyed my wishes, but your mother is ill and desires your return.

RUTH. My mother! [*Affectionately*]

HARD. You have given help to one who has caused misery to others, to one who drove your own brother away to fill an unknown grave. I now ask you to return for your mother's sake. I feel that her life depends on it. Woman is a creature of instinct, and I believe that sympathy led you to your foolish act. I cannot forgive, but I will condone! And now, I ask you if you will return.

RUTH. For my mother's sake, yes! Where can I find her?

HARD. In Judge Doe's private office. [*He points L. Ruth exits. He looks after Ruth*] Ruth once more under my roof! But still, for me, there will be two vacant chairs. [*Exits L.*]

SCENE 2: *Courtroom. Judge in high stand C. Jury R. Table and two chairs in front of judge's stand. Prisoners' box near jury. Flats draw off to make this scene.*

DISCOVERED: *Jury in jury box R. Witnesses L. Belcher and Sprague at table C. Judge Doe in his place. Hardman, Peak, Dr. Sawyer, Mink, Bingo, Roxey, Mrs. Jones, Pray in spectators' places at opening of flats. Noise.*

JUDGE. Order! Order! [*Pray is on the witness stand*]

BEL. [*Coming down C.; to Pray*] You say you purchased liquor from the defendant?

PRAY. Yes.

BEL. What means did you employ to get this liquor?

SPRA. [*Excited*] I object! I object!

BEL. [*Excited*] Shut up! Shut up! I know my business!

JUDGE. Order! Order! Order!

BEL. Did he not say to you that he could not and would not accept pay for the liquor?

SPRA. I object! [*Excited business with Belcher*]

JUDGE. Order! Order!

BEL. Did you not work upon the defendant's sympathy by saying that the liquor was intended for your sick mother? And don't you know she was out riding at the time and you were guilty of a deliberate lie?

SPRA. I object! I object! [*Same business of running up and down in excited manner. Both Belcher and Sprague shout to each other ad lib and slap hands*]

JUDGE. Order! Order!

BEL. That man worked on my client's sympathy to obtain the liquor!

SPRA. I object! I object!

BEL. Your Honor, I claim the right to speak in this court and do not propose after fifteen years' experience to be dictated to by a mealy-mouthed, pie-eating Boston dude!

JUDGE. Order! Order!

SPRA. Your Honor, I request that the counsel for the defense will allude to me as the opposing counsel.

BEL. Opposing counsel! Why, you're no opposition at all! [*Same business as before*]

JUDGE. Order! Order!

SPRA. I didn't come here to be bulldozed by a Vermont pettifogger, whether his name is Belcher, Welcher, or Squelcher.

BEL. You'll think it's Squelcher before you're through!

SPRA. Is this court going to be conducted according to law or according to the rush rules of the London prize ring?

JUDGE. This court will be conducted according to my decisions.

BEL. [*To Pray*] Now—how do you know that this bottle contains liquor?

PRAY. Well, I thought so.

BEL. You thought so! Did you taste it?

PRAY. No; that's against my principles.

BEL. Oh, then you are not sure! You merely thought so!

PRAY. Well, I think I thought so.

BEL. Oh, you think you thought so! Well, if you think that you thought so, what made you have any reason to think that you thought? You should have thought so!

SPRA. I object! I object! [*Business with Belcher as before*] Your Honor, with all due respect to you, I think this man is the biggest fool in town!

JUDGE. With all due respect to me—!!! With all due respect to me—!!!

BEL. Your Honor, when this man speaks of fools, he forgets himself.

JUDGE. Order! Order! You're no lawyer!

SPRA. You're no judge! [*Noise*]

JUDGE. Order! Order! I've a good mind to fine everybody present ten dollars for contempt of court.

SPRA. Well, I'm glad to be put on record as having contempt for this court!

JUDGE. I'll fine you ten dollars!

SPRA. Oh, very well. Do as you please. [*Aside to Judge*] Judge, can you lend me ten dollars. I have no money with me at present.

JUDGE. Very well; the fine is remitted.

BEL. Now then. I am through with this self-confessed liar who swears he obtained liquor and yet cannot swear to its being liquor. Is there anyone here present who will consent to taste it? [*Several in the audience of spectators, including Mink, spring to their feet to offer, but the jury, in consternation, rise as one man and protest]*

JURY. NO! NO!

MINK. And I was damn fool enough to get out of serving on that jury!

JUDGE. Yes, and if you don't keep quiet, you'll get out of this courtroom!

BEL. Now, Your Honor, and gentlemen of the jury, I will review the character of the evidence against my client. In the first place, look at these men who, under the guise of temperance reformers, wish to attain their own selfish ends. This man, [*Pointing to Pray*] who has been so active in the prosecution, wants to sell liquor and have all the money come to his drug-store. Oh, I know them! I know their records! I've been one of them myself! This hoary-headed sinner [*Pointing to Dr. Sawyer*] wants to write his pre-scriptions for liquor and receive a fee. The parson thinks he is honest in his convictions, but he has motives of personal revenge! Gentlemen, show me a prohibitionist and I will show you a crank, or a man with an axe to grind. They all have a purpose in view, and that purpose is their own selfish inter-ests. Look at the difference between my client and his opponents! They, under the guise of temperance, persecute him! What was he? A Union soldier, struck down by a bullet while trying to help a wounded comrade off the field of battle! Unable to do manual labor, he resorts to a certain calling which is legal in many states, but is considered a crime in Vermont. Working upon his sympathies under the pretense of having a sick wife, this interested deacon of the church and would-be pillar of society induces my client to break the law that he may secure a benefit from it; and he hired a mean, low, measly sneak [*Pointing to Peak*] to bore a hole through his back door and watch his movements. Now, gentlemen of the jury, picture to yourselves my client Oakhurst on the field of battle, wounded by the bullet of an enemy, seeking to shield a dying comrade in the cause of our glorious Union, and then think of this mean, conniving scoundrel peeping through a hole in the back door!

SPRA. Gentlemen of the jury, you have heard the arguments of the counsel for the defense. They are simply vituperation! This man [*Pointing to Oak-hurst*] has been an offender against the laws of the State. His crime has been proven. The fact of his having been a Union soldier does not prevent his being a criminal and an offender against the laws which he is supposed to have sworn to protect. I ask you to consider the evidence adduced fairly and to allow your sympathies to be antagonistic to your verdict. The fact of his having been a Union soldier does not acquit him of his crime. [*Sits down*]

JUDGE. Gentlemen of the jury, you have heard the evidence of both parties. In this case, I would advise you to treat the arguments of both counsels with the utmost contempt! [*Sprague and Belcher both jump up*] If you believe from the evidence you have heard that the prisoner sold liquor, your verdict must be guilty. If, on the other hand, you consider the evidence unreliable, your verdict must be favorable to the prisoner. The jury may now retire. Is my lunch ready?

SCENE 3: *A corridor in the courthouse. Pray, Dr. Sawyer and Sprague enter L.*

PRAY.   Well, what is your opinion of the case, Mr. Sprague? Do you think we'll win?

SPRA.   The Lord only knows. I expect anything of that judge. [*Enter Peak*]

DR. S.   Well, Peak, your memory seems to have been very good from the way you gave that testimony.

PEAK.   Well, I can't say much for your memory. You forgot to give me my ten dollars.

DR. S.   Oh—ah—yes. [*Fumbling in his pocket*] Mr. Pray, have you got ten dollars about you?

PRAY.   Well, no—[*Same business as Dr. Sawyer*] but I have five.

DR. S.   I have five, too.

SPRA.   [*Grabs both bills*] Gentlemen, let me settle this case. Come, Peak, follow me. [*Exits with Peak R.*]

PRAY.   A very clever fellow, I must say. Got Belcher quite excited every time.

DR. S.   Yes, I noticed that. But I believe our side will win in spite of the efforts of the rum crowd. [*Enter Sprague*]

SPRA.   Well, gentlemen, I fixed it with him for five dollars.

PRAY.   Whose five dollars did you give?

SPRA.   I believe it was yours.

DR. S.   Then I suppose I may ask you to return mine.

SPRA.   Oh, no! That's my fee for the settlement! Excuse me, you don't seem to know much about lawyer's methods.

PRAY.   Well, I believe I'll have time to step over to the store for a few minutes.

DR. S.   And I think I'll step into the court and find out how the case is coming on. [*Pray exits D. Dr. Sawyer crosses to D.L., meets Sprague. Sprague crosses, turns quickly, takes Dr. Sawyer down R. and whispers to him*] Only by prescription.

SPRA.   Very well, let me have one.

DR. S.   Here! [*Produces book*] I keep them all ready made out. You'll find the drugstore right across the street.

SPRA.   Thank you! Thank you! [*Going*]

DR. S. Excuse me please, five dollars!

SPRA. But I thought—[*Looks bewildered; then hands over money*]

DR. S. Excuse me, but you don't seem to know much of doctors' methods. [*Exits L.*]

SPRA. Well, I'll be damned! [*Exits L. Enter Judge and Hardman L.*]

JUDGE. Yes, Brother Hardman, I must decline with regret your kind invitation to lunch, as I have already ordered mine. I must also take the opportunity of informing you that I heartily approve of your noble and disinterested efforts on the part of temperance. Ah, here is my lunch. [*Waiter enters with the lunch on a tray covered with large napkin. He drops two bottles of wine to the floor; picks them up quickly, but in such a manner that Hardman sees them. Exits L. Judge is embarrassed*] Ah—the fact is—I am compelled to take a little claret at mealtimes. Doctor's orders, you know; severe stomach trouble! [*Enter Mink with a large whiskey bottle in his hand*]

MINK. The jury wants more evidence.

JUDGE. More evidence? What do you mean?

MINK. They require more evidence. They want Exhibit A filled again.

JUDGE. What, sir? Were you in the jury-room? How did you get that bottle?

MINK. No, I wasn't in there. They lowered it by a string from the window.

JUDGE. [*Winking at Mink and pointing to the door L.*] Well, sir, if I found you in that jury-room, I'd fine you a hundred dollars. [*Exits L. followed by Mink*]

HARD. Well, this passes belief. I could scarcely have believed that such things are occurring daily under my very eyes. [*Enter Worth and a stranger. This is Frank Hardman, the son thought dead. Hardman shaking hands with Worth*] Mr. Worth, I am delighted to see you again. I have heard of your success and tender my congratulations in conjunction with a kindly welcome home.

WORTH. I thank you for your kindly interest, but here is an old friend of mine whom I met in Montana. He lived here a number of years ago and was very well acquainted with many of our townspeople. See if you cannot remember him.

HARD. My memory is somewhat defective of late years, but his face is very familiar, and his name is—

FRANK. Frank Hardman! Father, don't you know me?

HARD. My boy! Returned at last! But tell me, why did you stay away all these years and not inform us of your whereabouts?

FRANK. When I left home, I joined the army. I was severely wounded in battle and was carried off the field by a comrade at the risk of his life; he received a bullet in his shoulder while he was saving me. As I lay in the hospital, I reflected on my past life and considered that I might as well be dead as to return and live it over again. On my return, I went to Washington and found that I had been listed as incurable; hence, probably, the rumor of my death. I then went West, where I have accumulated a fortune and where I was discovered by my friend, Worth, who induced me to return and to whom we must all be thankful for this meeting after so many years. [*Shakes hands with Worth*]

HARD. And are you a temperance man?

FRANK. The best kind of one, for I have learned to use and not abuse the good things of this life. Can you give me your hand on that, father?

HARD. All the theories of my life are breaking down, my boy. But I'm glad you're home, and here is my hand. [*They shake*]

FRANK. But tell me, where are my mother and my sister? Can I not see them?

HARD. Come with me. You will find them in Judge Doe's private office. [*Exit both L. Enter Mink. Shakes hands with Worth*]

MINK. How do! How do! I heard you arrived in town, John. Folks say you are a big man now, and I didn't know whether you'd want to shake hands with us little cusses. So I thought I'd get around here and see you.

WORTH. Friend Mink, you'll find that I have just as firm a grasp as ever for an old friend. Prosperity will never make me vain.

MINK. Well, I never thought it would. But you do look well. It's no use talking. [*Enter Bingo*]

BINGO. Say, dad, your horse is running away! [*Exits L.*]

MINK. [*Surprised*] Well, this is the age of miracles! [*Exits L. Enter Ruth*]

RUTH. [*Gives her hand to Worth*] How can I thank you, Mr. Worth, for your untiring efforts in securing my brother? He has told us all the difficulties you encountered, and I feel that I can never find it in my power to repay you. Still, I assure you that you have my thanks.

WORTH. Yes, that's what an author always gets.

RUTH. Can I do more?

WORTH. Yes! Let me know if the day has come when we have learned to love each other!

RUTH. I—I think it has!

WORTH. [*Embraces and kisses her at the door as they both exit L.*] My darling!

MINK. [*At this moment he is thrown through the door of the court C. and stands outside door as it closes. He looks surprised, but takes it as a matter of course; very nonchalant*] Guilty! It's no use talking! That's what the verdict will be after the jury tackles that last bottle of exhibit. It's a crime for any man to sell such stuff! They'll be putting a tax on every man next year. [*Stage darkens momentarily as side flats are drawn quickly, showing courtroom again. Mink drops into a seat*]

CLOSE IN

SCENE 4: *Courtroom.*

JUDGE. Order! Order! The jury having found the prisoner guilty of the crime charged against him, it now remains for the court to pass sentence on him. There are fifty counts in the indictments, and the fines for each count, together with the costs, amount to the sum of $6,190, which sum must be paid into court at once or, in default, the defendant shall be confined in prison for twice the number of days that there are dollars in the fine.

BEL. But, Your Honor, this is excessive! My client is a poor man and cannot pay the fine. He would have to serve over fifty years in jail at this rate to settle it!

JUDGE. Such is the law of the state of Vermont.

FRANK. Stay! Is not your name Fred Oakhurst?

OAK. It is.

FRANK. Were you not a member of Company K, Eighteenth New York Volunteers? And did you not carry a wounded comrade off the field of battle at Shiloh, risking your life and being wounded in the attempt?

OAK. That is a fact. I was wounded in the shoulder.

FRANK. Well, I am the man! [*Shakes Oakhurst's hand*] Your Honor, I will pay the fine for this man. I am rich and have the money. He is my comrade and a Union soldier and a brave man, and I will stand by him!

HARD. [*Steps over to Oakhurst and shakes his hand*] We are all guilty of mistakes in our lives. I have made a serious one! I regret that I should have been the cause of injury to one who saved my son's life. May I ask your pardon?

OAK. It is freely granted.

MINK. Yes, and you'll find that a man may have many a noble thought and do many a good action even if he is a rum-seller!

CURTAIN

A MILK WHITE FLAG

*And Its Battle-Scarred Followers on the Field of Mars
and in the Court of Venus*

*A Tribute to Our Citizen Soldiers by One Who Would Gladly
Join Their Ranks if He Knew How to Dance*

*The Field of Battle is not necessarily St. Albans, Vt., or Har-
risburg, Pa., but a town of that deliciously provincial character
was in the author's thoughts as he wrote. Visitors from the West
may imagine Zanesville, Ohio, or Oshkosh, Wis.*

THE ROLL CALL

[The opening performance in New York on October 8, 1894]

THE COLONEL, CHRISTIAN BERRIEL, *a retired coal merchant*

CHARLES STANLEY

THE MAJOR, PAUL BARING, *a prominent life insurance man*   LLOYD WILSON

THE JUDGE ADVOCATE, HOWLAND HOOPER, *a well-known young lawyer*

ARTHUR PACIE

THE SURGEON, MARK TOMBS, *leading physician of the town*   ED GARVIE

THE BANDMASTER, STEELE AYRES, *who is also a popular music teacher*

FRANK BALDWIN

THE PRIVATE, WILLING SINGER, *a hired man*   SAM WESTON

THE DANCING-MASTER, GIDEON FOOTE, *who also has a school for children*

FRANK LAWTON

THE LIEUTENANT, PHIL GRAVES, *also a prominent undertaker*

JOHN S. MARBLE

A

B

C   } VIVANDIÈRES

D

TOMA HANLON

LILLIAN MARKHAM

ROSA FRANCE

ETTA WILLIAMSON

THE STANDARD BEARER, CARRIE FLAGG   ALICE CAMPBELL

ALL OF THE ABOVE BELONGING TO AND BEING PART OF THE RANSOME GUARDS

THE GENERAL, HURLEY BURLEIGH, *an officer of the regular Army and guest of the Guards*   NEWTON CHISNELL

THE DEAR DEPARTED, PIGGOTT LUCE, *a successful railway contractor*

R. A. ROBERTS

THE ORPHAN, PONY LUCE, *daughter of the contractor*   LOTTIE MOORE

THE PARTICULAR FRIEND OF THE BEREAVED WIFE, "LIZE" DUGRO

RILLIE DEAVES

THE BEREAVED, AURORA LUCE, *who either is or isn't the contractor's wife*

ISABELLE COE

THE DRUM CORPS

THE MESSENGER BOYS

THE BAND

ACT I: PRIVATE QUARTERS OF THE OFFICERS OF THE RANSOME GUARDS.

ACT II: THE RECEPTION ROOM AT THE HOUSE OF PIGGOTT LUCE.

ACT III: GRAND HALL OF THE ARMORY.

ACT I.

Scene: *The armory—officers' quarters. Bandmaster seated L. at piano, play-ing accompaniment. Judge Advocate at his back with glass in hand. At rise of curtain the Judge is singing and the Bandmaster playing. The members of the band are seen in the R. alcove drinking, throwing dice, etc., at the bar. Cur-tain after about sixteen bars of Judge's song. At end of song Judge speaks.*

Judge. A beautiful song, Mr. Bandmaster. Everything you write bears in-disputable evidence of having been composed by a great musician. [*Turns to chair L. of L. table*] Will you put the song in your new opera? [*Drinks from glass in hand. Judge sits; lights cigarette*]

Band. [*Turns on piano stool to R., gets glass, and drinks. Goes up L.C.*] Certainly. It may be a little over the heads of the public, but I shall sacrifice popularity to art. [*Places glass on top of piano; picks up music book; crosses stage to C., front of table L.*]

Judge. The armory seems very quiet this morning. Where are all the boys?

Band. Oh, it's early yet. They are all down in the barber's shop.

Judge. Say, by the way, who is that stranger that the doctor is showing all over the armory and paying so much attention to?

Band. Why, don't you know? That is General Burleigh of the *regular* Army.

Judge. Not General Hurley Burleigh?

Band. The very same.

Judge. Why, he has got a great reputation in the regular Army. They say he is wonderfully brave.

Band. He is. He's come to town to visit his mother-in-law, and as a mili-tary organization, of course, we are bound to entertain him. The doctor has him in charge. [*General heard to speak outside, L.: "Marvelous, doctor! mar-velous!"*] Sh! Here they come! [*Crosses to R. Enter Doctor and General, L.3.E. Come down C. Doctor first, then General*]

Doct. Walk right in, general! Walk right in! [*R.C.*] Now you are in the officers' private quarters. [*General L.C.*] And here are two of them. General Burleigh, let me introduce Mr. Howland Hooper. [*General crosses to Judge; Judge rises and crosses to General; they shake hands*] He's our judge advo-cate, general. And this gentleman is Mr. Steele Ayres, our bandmaster. [*Gen-eral crosses to R., and shakes hands with Bandmaster*] Now, general, be seated. [*General crosses to chair at R. of L. table. Doctor down R.C. Band-master goes to chair R. of R. table and sits. Judge sits L. of L. table*] I think you have seen everything now. The banquet hall, the ballroom, the card rooms, the billiard room, the bowling alley, the drill room, and the bar. Now what do you think of it as an armory?

GEN. I can truly say that during all my service in the Army, I never saw an armory like it. [*Sits*]

DOCT. I thought you'd say so. [*Crosses to back of L. table and sits*]

JUDGE. With the possible exception of the Union League and the Manhattan Athletic, it's the best equipped armory in America, and those are not exactly armories, as the members don't wear uniforms.

GEN. How does it happen that you gentlemen wear uniforms?

JUDGE. Why, we're soldiers!

GEN. [*Rises*] I beg your pardon! What I meant was, why did you make the organization military? [*Sits*]

DOCT. Why, that's the beauty of the whole thing. A man in this country who doesn't belong to the militia is a bilin' idiot. It relieves you of so much that is disagreeable. In the first place, a member of the militia doesn't have to serve on the jury; that's why most of our members joined. And then it gives us all titles. We're colonels and majors and captains, and we wear swell uniforms for which the State pays, and that gives us fifty per cent the best of it over a man in plain clothes in mashing the girls. [*Rises and crosses to C.*] Oh, it's a big thing to be a soldier!

GEN. But are there no responsibilities that go with these advantages?

DOCT. Don't know of any.

GEN. Supposing the nation became involved in war and you were called on to take the field. What would you do?

JUDGE. Disband.

GEN. [*Rises quickly and looks at Judge*] But suppose you didn't have time to disband! Suppose it was just a case of riot! You wouldn't want to disband to avoid one day's service! [*Crosses R.*]

DOCT. [*Goes upstage L. to desk*] That's all fixed. [*Picks up a package of certificates from desk in L. arch. Then goes downstage to L.C.*] Here is a certificate for every member that he is sick and unfit for military duty. All they need is to be dated.

GEN. But you'd do something in case of riot?

JUDGE. Why, of course. We'd meet the day after the riot and pass resolutions. Do you see that big book? [*Points to book L.*] It contains the resolutions we passed last year, and we've begun another for '96.

GEN. [*C.*] But what *is* the "out" about this beautiful arrangement? Even the best of things have their disadvantages. You must have some annoyances.

DOCT. [*L.C.*] Only one.

GEN. And what is that?

DOCT. The other regiment. [*Goes upstage to desk and places certificates on it*]

GEN. The other regiment? [*Crosses to chair R. of L. table and sits*]

JUDGE. Yes. There's another regiment in town called the Daly Blues, named for a man named Daly, who pays 'em for the honor. They are a case of daily blues to us. They try to outdo us in everything. If we have a picnic, they have one. If we have a ball, they have one. It's maddening!

DOCT. [*Down C.*] Of late we have done 'em, though. We've let 'em do things first, and then we've gone 'em one better. Why, our performance of *Hamlet* did theirs out of sight, and we're going to keep doing them. [*Bandmaster wanders over to piano, around back of tables. Doctor then goes to chair L. of R. table, lights pipe and smokes it*]

JUDGE. You bet we are!

GEN. Then you do have your battles after all. [*Sits*]

JUDGE. I should say we do! Why, we'll get up in the middle of the night to hate those fellows. But don't worry! They'll get the worst of it. Our colonel's equal to the emergency.

GEN. I haven't met him yet.

JUDGE. You must. [*Rings bell on table*] Why, our colonel is the greatest commander of the age. [*Rings again. Rises*] Confound that private! Where is he?

DOCT. He's been sick a couple of days and doesn't get down early.

JUDGE. Well, if he can't get here to attend to business, we'd better fire him and get another. We can't run this regiment without a private. [*Sits*]

GEN. Pardon me, do I understand there is only one private in this regiment?

DOCT. Oh, we have more than three hundred members who attend the balls and turn out for parade. To be accurate, our membership is three hundred and ninety-nine, and Mr. Johnson, as honorary member, makes four hundred; and we've got one private that we *pay* to do military duty. 'Tend the door, you know, and run errands.

GEN. Oh, I see.

BAND. [*Seated at piano*] And this one is the best private we ever had. He's got a splendid voice.

GEN. Voice? Excuse me, but what the devil has his voice got to do with it?

DOCT.   Oh, let me explain. Our bandmaster here, Mr. Ayres, is writing an opera.

GEN.   That is a very warlike proceeding.

JUDGE.   Yes, it's a war opera.

GEN.   Oh, indeed?

JUDGE.   Yes. We've had war plays like "Across the Potomac" and "A Fair Rebel." But no war opera yet; So Mr. Ayres determined to supply the want.

GEN.   Very patriotic. What does he call it?

JUDGE.   "Hell with the Enemy."

GEN.   "Hell with the Enemy." That's good. That's the way I found it at Bull Run.

DOCT.   And Lieutenant Graves, the undertaker, is writing the libretto.

GEN.   An undertaker writing a comic opera libretto! I think I've seen more or less of his work. But what has the private's voice to do with all this?

DOCT.   Why, he sings well, and we've got four vivandières, same as they have in the French Army, to serve drinks.

GEN.   But girls on a field of battle would be absurd.

DOCT.   But we're not going on any field of battle.

GEN.   Oh, I forgot that.

DOCT.   And the vivandières sing well. Mr. Ayres has made them learn the songs to see how they go. Would you like to hear some of the music?

GEN.   I would.

BAND. [*Rises from piano stool*]   I'll go and call the girls. We don't need the band. [*Exits L.3.E.*]

GEN.   You have a band?

JUDGE.   Oh, yes. Don't you see them in there standing up against the bar?

GEN. [*C. Rises and looks at band*]   Oh, yes. What are they celebrating to-day?

DOCT.   Nothing. When not playing, they are always standing up against the bar. It is a great convenience. We always know where to find them.

GEN.   Don't they get drunk, though?

DOCT. [*Rises. Crosses C. to General*]   Yes, pretty drunk. But what if they do? I've noticed that the average brass band plays just as well when drunk as when sober. [*General looks at Doctor; then crosses to R. Sits*] Here come our messenger boys. [*Doctor crosses to L.C. Music. Enter Bandmaster L.3.E. Enter Captain of Drum Corps and four Messengers. They all march C., turn, face audience, and salute. Bandmaster goes to piano*] And here come the vivandières! [*Doctor crosses to back of L. table. Sits. Enter Vivandières to music. Specialty for Vivandières and Messengers. During specialty General sits R. After it Vivandières, Captain, and Messengers exit L.3.E. During spe-*

cialty Bandmaster conducts. Doctor crosses to C.] Now, general, will you take a drink?

GEN. [*Rises*] Will you gentlemen drink, too?

ALL. You bet!

GEN. Then you do *some* things we do in the *regular* Army! [*Judge rings bell on L. table. Enter four Vivandières, L.3.E. They form C. upstage*]

DOCT. Oh, yes. What shall it be?

GEN. A little rye, please.

DOCT. [*Addresses first Vivandière*] A, rye for the gentleman.

A. C has the rye. [*C advances to General and serves liquor*]

DOCT. Mine's Bourbon. [*A advances and serves him*]

JUDGE. I'll take some Old Tom. [*B advances and serves him*]

BAND. A pony of brandy. [*D advances and serves him. The four men drink. Vivandières then take their emptied glasses, salute, turn upstage, and march off L.3.E. Music pp. till they are off. General follows them upstage. Business*]

DOCT. Now, general, you will be in town for several days. Judge Advocate, you're one of the Board of Governors. See that the general has a two-weeks' card of invitation to the armory. That will give you all the privileges of the club—I mean armory—you know, just as though you were a member. [*Enter Major L.3.E., excitedly*]

MAJ. [*L.C.*] Look out the window quick! There she goes! [*All but General rush to window R.2.E. General turns C. and looks at group at window*]

DOCT. The one in lavender and white?

MAJ. Yes.

JUDGE. The one with the French sailor hat?

MAJ. Yes.

ALL. She's a corker. [*All grab opera glasses and look out of window. Pause*]

DOCT. [*To General*] Come and take a look at her.

GEN. Well, I—[*Starts to go*]

JUDGE. [*Goes to C.*] You're too late. She's turned the corner. [*All hang up glasses. Major and Bandmaster go upstage to C. Doctor goes down R.C.*]

GEN. Why do you have those glasses in the window?

JUDGE. For just what you see them used for. All the pretty girls in town promenade past this window when it is pleasant. [*Judge crosses in front of General to L. of L. table*]

GEN. And they know you have those glasses? [*Bandmaster goes to piano and sits*]

Doct. [*Crosses to General in C.*] I think they must. The number of girls who pass by has doubled since we put the glasses in. [*General looks and crosses to R. Doctor to L.*]

Judge. [*To Major*] Who is she? [*Judge in front of L. table*]

Maj. [*Comes down C.*] My mash.

Judge. Since when?

Maj. Ten minutes. I caught her away from the major of the Blues.

All. Good boy!

Judge. Tell us all about it.

Maj. Why, he was standing in front of Mose Gunst's cigar store and she came down the street looking at him—thought he was pretty, and he was so absorbed and forgot himself and his leg itched and he did this—[*Scratches one leg with his other foot*] and she looked around to laugh and saw me and never looked back at him. Oh, our uniforms knock theirs silly. [*Crosses to R. corner*]

Judge. Well, what happened?

Maj. [*Crosses back to C.*] She crossed the street and passed me and dropped this glove. [*Shows glove. They all look at it*]

Gen. [*R.*] Why didn't you return it to her?

Maj. Oh, no. This is an excuse to call at her house and get acquainted.

Gen. How do you know where she lives?

Maj. Here's her address marked inside the glove. 999 Four Hundred Avenue. [*Crosses to R. corner, kissing glove. All but General and Major mark address on their cuffs. General watches them. General follows Major across stage. Doctor, Bandmaster, and Judge all watch General*]

Gen. [*Aside to Major*] Where's Four Hundred Avenue?

Maj. Never mind! [*All laugh*]

Judge. Come, let's drink on that. Now, Baring, my boy—by the way—General Burleigh, Major Baring. [*Major and General shake hands*] A soldier, every inch of him. [*General crosses to chair R. of L. table; Major to chair C. back of L. table; Judge to chair L. of L. table; Doctor sits R. of Major; Bandmaster L. of Major. All sit; pass bottle around; fill glasses*] Now, Baring, do you know who that girl is?

Maj. No. Do you?

Judge. Yes, Let me tell you. She's the daughter of the rich railroad contractor, Piggott Luce.

Doct. I know the man. They are building a new railroad here. He came here as a sort of promoter. He got over a million dollars of the capital placed in this town. Now the road is in the hands of a receiver, but the promoter has built a beautiful house.

MAJ. I know him. He's insured in my life insurance company for $100,000. [*To General, who rises and goes C.*] I'm Vice-President and General Manager of the Great American Mutual Life Insurance Company. I can insure you—

DOCT. [*Rises and gets between Major and General*] Stop! No business talk in the clu—armory! [*Crosses to window R.2.E. General returns to chair R. of L. table*]

JUDGE. Say, I must tell you about the Luce family affairs. Luce's wife—that's the girl's mother—is suing her father for a divorce, and I'm her mother's attorney.

BAND. You are her mother's attorney?

JUDGE. Yes. We had the case tried in private chambers yesterday. The court reserved his decision. I think, though, I'll win the case.

MAJ. And you know the daughter?

JUDGE. No. She was kept out of sight. We wanted her mother to make a mash on the judge so as to get a favorable decision, and it wouldn't do to let him know she had a daughter aged sixteen, especially as she is very well preserved and doesn't look it.

DOCT. [*At window R.2.E.*] There she goes again. [*All except General rush to window and use glasses as before. General jumps up and looks at them. Picture*]

MAJ. [*Drops glass and comes to C.*] I guess she is coming up on the show-off stand. [*Judge crosses to L. of C. window; Doctor and Bandmaster to R. of C. window*]

GEN. The show-off stand! What's that?

MAJ. Why, you see this armory fronts on the park that runs down to the lake. Well, just opposite this window we have built a lookout stand. The girls go up on it to get a view of the lake.

GEN. [*As Major goes up to R. of C. window*] And is the view so fine from the lookout?

DOCT. [*At C. window*] I don't know. It's great from here. Try it. [*All grab glasses. Major draws curtains. Discovers Orphan on lookout stand C., back of window. She has a pair of opera glasses in her hand and returns the gentlemen's gaze. Picture. General down in L. corner, astounded. Music pp.*]

GEN. I see. On the principle of living pictures.

MAJ. [*Closes curtains*] Not too much of a good thing, gentlemen. [*All put glasses down. Judge goes to L. of L. table; Doctor L. of R. table; Bandmaster R. of R. table. All sit*] Oh, I almost forgot! [*Produces four notes*] Here, boys! [*Enter four Messenger Boys, L.3.E. All reading. Salute*] Tuesday! Wednesday! Thursday! Friday! Boys, deliver these notes! [*Gives notes to Messengers who salute and exit L.3.E.*]

GEN. [*Upstage C. to Major*]   Military orders?

MAJ. [*C.*]   No. Notes to four young ladies.

GEN.   What do you do Saturday?

MAJ.   Call at 999 Four Hundred Avenue.

GEN.   I see clearly that this regiment was organized for purposes of slaughter. [*Aside*] Lady-killing. [*Aloud*] And you make it a rule to aim for the heart?

MAJ.   Why, our leader here has composed a song that exactly states our position. Will you listen?

GEN.   With pleasure. [*Sits R. of R. table*]

MAJ. [*Sings "Warriors Bold"*]

We are warriors bold
In blue and gold,
The ladies' eyes delighting;
We are right on hand,
To march with a band,
When there is no chance of fighting.
But when there's a job
Of scrapping a mob,
And we hear the wild crowd trample.
To quell the riot
We keep very quiet,
And set 'em a good example.
The time we shine
Is when in line
On the Day of Decoration;
And all the girls will cry
As we march by,
"They're the bulwark of the nation!"

Our thirst for blood
And our love for mud
Cannot be called extensive;
And we don't like storms,
For our uniforms
Are horribly expensive.
But the Fourth of July
When the sun is high,

No street parade can tire us;
For well we know
Wherever we go,
The ladies must admire us.
So with all our will
We'll gain in skill,
And cultivate our sinews.
And we're one and all
At our country's call
As long as peace continues! [*At finish of song, Major goes upstage to bar*]

DOCT. [*At R. table. Then crosses to back of L. table and sits*] Now you know what we are here for. [*Judge shows Doctor the picture of a girl. Lieutenant Graves enters L.3.E. Goes to closet L. end. Business of changing into uniform. General is attracted by his action and watches him very intently. Graves then crosses to R. table. He rings bell and Vivandière, A, enters L.3.E. She crosses stage and serves him a drink. She then hands him the check-pad which he signs and returns to her. She salutes and exits L.3.E. He rises, crosses to closet, and changes back to street clothes; exits L.3.E. The General, who has been watching this very closely, turns to audience. Then he looks at the whiskey bottle on the table, and sits down*]

GEN. I don't think this whiskey is so bad that a man need fear to tackle it without his sword. [*Drinks. Enter Private L.3.E. Private salutes twice. General scrutinizes him*] Well, when did the cat find that and bring it in?

JUDGE. That's the private. Well, what do you want?

PRIV. [*C.*] The colonel has come in, and the dancing-master has just arrived. [*Goes upstage C.*]

GEN. The dancing-master!

DOCT. Yes, of course. We have a dancing-master come twice a week. Why, we know more about waltzing in a minute than the Blues do in a year! [*Crosses to C.*]

GEN. Indeed!

JUDGE. But you must meet the colonel.

DOCT. [*C.*] I'll miss my dancing lesson this morning, boys, and go and introduce the general. Come, general. [*Doctor starts R. General rises and follows Doctor. Doctor stops General in C.*] General, you are about to see a great man. Perhaps it would be wise for you to prepare yourself. [*General looks at Doctor. Then turns to table L. Takes a drink. Then turns to Doctor, who has gone behind L. table*]

GEN. Certainly. [*Drinks*] I'm prepared. [*Goes upstage L.C.*]

DOCT. I mean, prepare yourself by looking at his picture. Here it is. [*Crosses L. and draws curtain which covers picture on closet door*]

GEN. Why, he looks very much like the great Napoleon.

DOCT. [*Crosses to General*] It is often remarked that the great Napoleon looked like him. Come, general. [*Exit Doctor and General, L.3.E.*]

PRIV. [*Advances with two cards to L.C.*] Judge Advocate, here's two cards for you. [*Hands cards to Judge, who has advanced to him. Private salutes. Goes upstage C.*]

JUDGE. [*Looks at cards*] My client, Mrs. Luce, and her particular friend. Gentlemen, I know it's against the rules to receive ladies in the armory before noon—but—it only lacks ten minutes.

MAJ. As one of the house committee, I say receive them. [*Rises and motions to Private. Private exits L.3.E.*] Mr. Ayres and myself will nominally retire. [*Bandmaster and Major start upstage; stop; look at bottles on table; they go back and Bandmaster takes bottle from L. table and Major takes one from R. table. Judge watches them. Then both go upstage C. and hide behind curtains*] Will this do?

JUDGE. Admirably. [*Enter Private, L.3.E., escorting Widow and Friend in*]

WID. [*Extends her hand to Judge*] Ah, good morning, Mr. Hooper. [*Private exits L.3.E. Friend goes down L. Judge places chair for Widow R.C. She sits*] I know it is rude to intrude upon you in the privacy of your club, but I had to come to ask you about the state of my divorce suit.

JUDGE. Madam, I can only tell you what you already know. The judge has taken the case under consideration. He has gone to the Adirondacks fishing and has promised to send it this evening by mail. I hope he will grant you the divorce.

WID. I don't see how he can help it. [*Rises*] They grant divorces in this state for cruelty, and what can be more cruel than a man who makes his wife fifth in his affections?

JUDGE. Fifth?

WID. Yes, he cares more for four queens than he ever did for me. Think of a man so devoted to poker that he talks of it in his slumbers! Does a wife want to awaken from a sound sleep by the information that she is a few chips shy?

JUDGE. Of course, she doesn't.

FRIEND. Of course not! Whatever else Aurora has been, she was never shy.

WID. No, modesty was my limit. But that's not all. He has come home at daybreak and, when he couldn't get the key in the keyhole, has sworn to the policeman that someone has plugged up the kitty. Is that right? I tell you, sir, a woman is better off married to a grizzly bear than to a man that plays poker. [*Crosses to chair R. of L. table and sits*]

JUDGE. All that was carefully explained to the judge.

FRIEND. [*Crosses to Judge, R.*] And you don't think there is any doubt he will grant the divorce, do you?

JUDGE. Well, I hope not. Still, the judge himself knows the value of three of a kind.

FRIEND. Don't all men? [*Crosses to back of Widow*]

JUDGE. Not always. I didn't last night.

WID. I can't help considering it singular that you don't know what the decision will be?

JUDGE. But, my dear madam, you ladies don't altogether understand law.

WID. Well, if we don't, we make up for it by our practical common sense.

JUDGE. [*Sarcastically*] I forgot that.

WID. [*Rises. Crosses to Judge*] Well, there is one thing certain. Divorce or no divorce, I detest him, and I'll never, never, never live with him again!

FRIEND. [*At table L.*] Not if I can help it! [*Goes to piano L.*]

JUDGE. [*To Widow*] And yet you once loved him.

WID. Never!

JUDGE. Then why did you marry him?

WID. [*Aside*] Why, he was engaged to her, my particular friend, and we were such good friends I couldn't resist cutting her out! I almost wish now I hadn't done so.

FRIEND. [*Advances to Widow*] Come, Aurora, we must hurry to the store so as to match this silk—[*Shows sample*] before dark. Come. [*Goes upstage to L.3.E.*]

WID. You will let me know the minute you hear from the judge?

JUDGE. The very instant.

WID. [*Goes up to L. arch*] If the divorce isn't granted, I'll never forgive you. [*Exits L.3.E.*]

FRIEND. [*Goes to Judge, R.C.*] If you get the divorce, I'll double your fee!

JUDGE. You? Why?

FRIEND. If she gets the divorce, then he'll be free and can marry—oh, never mind. [*Goes to L. arch. Turns to Judge*] Good morning! [*Exits L.3.E. Major and Bandmaster stick heads out from behind curtains*]

JUDGE. I think I drop. A beautiful illustration of woman's friendship for woman. When you see two women display great affection for each other, you can bet they both have an object. [*Bandmaster with two bottles enters, goes to bar, places one bottle on bar; then he goes to table R. and places the other bottle there. Judge R.C.*] Major, I congratulate you on your prospective mother-in-law. [*Enter Lieutenant Graves, L.3.E. Goes to closet; changes clothes as before*]

MAJ. Ah, Graves, after another drink?

LIEUT. Yes. Have one?

MAJ. No. We're going down to have a game of pool. Come, gentlemen. [*Judge and Bandmaster exit R.3.E. Major hesitates; then turns to Lieutenant*] Say, Graves, you seem nervous today.

LIEUT. Yes, some stock speculations of mine are worrying me.

MAJ. I'm sorry. [*Exits R.3.E.*]

LIEUT. Private! [*Enter Private L.3.E.*] If a man named Luce calls to see me, he isn't a member; but let him up.

PRIV. Man named Luce is here. [*Beckons to L. Enter Piggott Luce, L.3.E. Goes to R. of L. table. Lieutenant goes to L. of L. table. Private exits L.3.E.*]

LIEUT. [*Sits down*] Ah, Luce, sit down! We are all alone. We can talk freely.

LUCE. I shouldn't have disturbed you at your club.

LIEUT. Armory, please.

LUCE. All right. [*Sits down*] But there's something you've got to know. You remember we've been speculating in mining stocks?

LIEUT. Yes. You let me put up the money to go in on a good thing.

LUCE. Well, I may as well come to the point. Read that telegram. [*Offers telegram, which Lieutenant does not take*]

LIEUT. I don't have to. I know what it says. I felt for some time that everything had gone wrong.

LUCE. You're right. The mining speculations in which you and I have engaged have gone to pot. The mine has clean played out, and we are $100,000 worse off than nothing.

LIEUT. So bad as that? The profits of burying thirty thousand people all gone! It's bad!

LUCE. And, furthermore, we have used some other people's money and are in a fine way to get into State's Prison!

LIEUT. Dreadful! Dreadful! Is there no way out of this fix?

LUCE. Only by getting $100,000.

LIEUT. Even if yellow fever struck this town, I couldn't get that much!

LUCE. There is one way to get it, but it's a pretty nervy thing to do. Are you game?

LIEUT. It seems so. I've been game for you. However, if I'm game, you're fish.

LUCE. What do you mean?

LIEUT. You're very scaly. I'm game enough to keep out of State's Prison, if I can. What must we do?

LUCE. I must die!

LIEUT. You die! Damn good idea! But why?

LUCE. You know my life is heavily insured. When you put up the money for this scheme of ours, I got my life insured for $100,000 in your favor, as a protection to you.

LIEUT. You did? At the same time you got yourself insured in another company in your wife's favor, and used my money to pay both premiums.

LUCE. Well, cheer up. Cherries are ripe! Now I want to do the right thing by you. If I die, you get $100,000. Don't you drop?

LIEUT. And to get this money and save me from prison, you are going to die! [*Rises and crosses to embrace Luce*] My dear, dear friend! How can I thank you?

LUCE. [*Rises and stops Lieutenant*] Hold on! Not so fast! I'd see you in Sing Sing for life before I'd really die for you! Sit down and listen! [*Both sit*] Haven't you read in the papers lately of the swindles of life insurance companies? Of people pretending to die to get the insurance on themselves? That's the game we must play!

LIEUT. I begin to see.

LUCE. Now, I've got it all planned. The fact that you're an undertaker makes it dead easy.

LIEUT. Do you mean that for a joke?

LUCE. Good heavens, no! Let me proceed. I must be accidentally killed. I've got that part of it all fixed up. You, as an undertaker, take possession of my body. Nobody else sees it. You take me to your shop. That night I escape to Canada. You have a hurry-up funeral over an empty coffin the next day. Then you get your money later and send me my bit to Quebec. Now, have you got the courage to tackle it?

LIEUT. If you can go through with it, I can.

LUCE. Me? Why, I'll just stay hidden in your shop and have a champagne racket while you do the work! It'll be a picnic for me!

LIEUT. And I'll give you a funeral you'll be proud of. But how about your family?

LUCE. My family be hanged! Don't you know my wife is suing me for a divorce and my daughter sides with her? Besides, she gets a $100,000 insurance policy on me, too.

LIEUT. And are they to know you're not dead?

LUCE. Not on your life! Aurora wouldn't keep the secret to get $100,000.

LIEUT. Now when does the deplorable accident occur?

LUCE. At noon, while the men are at dinner. Be on hand. I must go now to perfect things. [*Rises and starts for L.3.E.*]

LIEUT. [*Rises and crosses to L.C.*] And I'll go and get ready. Say, old man, we're playing a desperate game!

LUCE. [*Turns to Lieutenant*] Desperate diseases require desperate remedies. Cheer up, cherries are ripe! [*Exits L.3.E.*]

LIEUT. I've been an undertaker for thirty years, but this kind of a corpse makes me shudder. I don't know what it will do. [*Exits L.3.E. Enter Judge, Major, and Bandmaster, R.3.E. Judge crosses to L. of L. table; Major to R. of L. table; Bandmaster to R. of table*]

MAJ. Poor old Graves seems all broken up over his stock speculation. [*Enter General and Doctor, L.3.E. General crosses to table R. Doctor goes down to table L.*]

DOCT. The general has met the colonel, just caught him as he was going out, and says he never saw such a man in his life.

GEN. I never did. [*Crosses R. Enter Private, L.3.E.*]

PRIV. The dancing-master has completed the dancing specialty for the finish of the first act of Mr. Ayres's opera. I'm all ready to rehearse. So are the girls. [*Turns quickly and exits L.3.E.*]

GEN. [*R.C.*] Are you gentlemen going to produce the opera?

BAND. [*R. of R. table*] We are. I at first intended to give it to the Bostonians, but it's so mighty good I don't dare trust it to them.

JUDGE. [*Crosses to R. table*] Barnaby himself told me he thought that we had better do it ourselves.

BAND. Wouldn't you like to hear a rehearsal of it?

GEN. [*R.*] I don't know much about music. I'm used to fighting Indians. [*Aside*] It'll keep me near this good rum, anyway. [*Sits by R. table*]

BAND. [*Crosses to C.*] Come on! Call everybody! We'll rehearse that finale now. Here, drum corps! [*Beckons to Drummers off L.3.E. Then goes to piano, L. Enter Captain, Standard Bearer, Drummers, and Messenger Boys from L.3.E. Music. All march to C., turn, and salute. Medley, during which Bandmaster conducts from near piano*]

MAJ. [*Before song*] The last is a tribute to the bandmaster, written by himself: "Without Him, What's the Band?" [*Hands field glass to General. At end of medley all exit L.3.E. This is to be arranged according to music. Positions to be arranged accordingly after medley*]

GEN. Well, this is a new kind of warfare to me. [*Gentlemen all return laughing and talking. General R. of R. table; Bandmaster back of R. table; Major to L. of L. table; Doctor to back of L. table; Judge to L. of R. table*]

JUDGE. Now then, let's have a drink. [*Enter Private, L.3.E.*]

Priv. Attention! Here comes the colonel! [*All turn and look towards C. as curtain opens. The Band has entered R., the Drummers and Messengers L. All cheer. A Drummer draws curtains, disclosing the Colonel on a horse. When Colonel is in C., he removes his hat. The shouting ceases*]

Col. Ransome Guards, I salute you! [*Exits. All cheer and up C.*]

Maj. Attention! [*Cheers stop again*] He comes! Ransome Guards, give proper attention to the greatest military chieftain of the age! [*Band plays. All salute as Colonel enters dejectedly L. and goes C.*] Colonel, we rejoice to have you with us. But you seem sad.

Col. I am. I have bad news to tell you. [*Band and Chorus and others look at him anxiously*] Leave us! [*They exit R. and L.*]

Maj. Is it serious?

Col. Very! They have stolen a march on us?

All. Who?

Col. The Daly Blues, of course.

Judge. Are they having a picnic?

Col. Worse than that!

Maj. Or a fox hunt?

Col. Worse than that!

Gen. Or a game of football?

Col. Worse than that!

All. What is it?

Col. They're having a funeral! [*Picture: all dejected. Pause*] Yes, gentlemen, with shame I admit it. I never suspected it, but one of their men has died and they are giving him a funeral today and tearing the town wide open doing it.

All. Terrible! [*All dejected*]

Col. [*Braces up*] But it's not too late yet! Are they to enjoy any festivities that we don't have?

All. No, sir!

Col. We'll have a funeral!

All. We will!

Doct. Three cheers for the funeral! [*All cheer*]

Col. The officers will resolve themselves into a council of war. [*All but General move toward L. table; Judge to R. of L. table; Doctor back of L. table; Colonel C. of L. table; Bandmaster R. of Colonel; Major L. of L. table. All stand and look at C. of L. table as though looking for something. Private goes to bar quickly and gets decanter of whiskey which he puts in C. of table. All show satisfaction and sit. During all this time the General is R. of R. table watching closely the proceeding. He sits down when others do*]

The private will guard the door. [*Private stands C.*] Now, then, it's decided to have a funeral. What is the first thing to be done?

GEN. Get a corpse! [*All look at General; then at Private, who exits L.3.E.*]

DOCT. That's right. A funeral without a corpse would be absurd.

COL. I know that! We'll get one! Private! [*Private enters L.3.E. and goes to C.*] Private, is anybody in the regiment dead?

PRIV. No, colonel.

COL. Anybody likely to die?

PRIV. No, colonel, I'm feeling splendid.

COL. This regiment is always in hard luck. [*Private goes upstage*] Who's dead in town? Where's the paper? [*Enter Lieutenant Graves, L.3.E., excited*]

LIEUT. Gentlemen! Gentlemen!

ALL. What is it?

LIEUT. [*C.*] There's been a terrible accident over at the new railroad. A derrick fell and killed the contractor!

COL. A man killed! Hooray!

ALL. Hooray! [*Rise and dance with joy*]

COL. Just what we wanted!

LIEUT. Luckily I was on the spot; so no other undertaker got the job!

COL. The Ransome Guards are always on hand.

LIEUT. I had him removed to my shop at once. As he was an old friend of mine, I shall have to take full charge of the funeral. I just came to let you know I wouldn't be around here for a couple of days. Good-by! [*Starts to go L.*]

JUDGE. Say, what was his name?

LIEUT. Piggott Luce. [*Exits L.*]

JUDGE and MAJ. [*Both jump up*] Merciful heavens!

ALL. What's the matter?

MAJ. [*Stands agitated*] He's the man whose life I insured for $100,000! [*Falls in chair*]

JUDGE. He's the father of that girl in the red dress. He's the man I'm suing for a divorce! [*Falls into chair*]

COL. Well, what of it? Isn't his death as good as a divorce?

JUDGE. But you don't understand. He was insured for $100,000.

COL. Well?

MAJ. And it's my company that's got to pay it. I'm ruined! My father and I are two-thirds of the company!

COL. Well, take your medicine. [*To Judge*] What's your holler?

JUDGE. Well, don't you see, if the judge has granted the divorce, my client isn't his wife and won't come in for the life insurance! It'll go to his daughter.

[*In despair*] Think of it, gentlemen! My grief, it is terrible! If I have won that case, if the judge has decided it in her favor, I have deprived her of a fortune! Gentlemen, it is terrible!

COL. [*Consoling*] Oh! Well, don't worry. You probably didn't win it. You only win about one case in ten.

JUDGE. Yes, but this is the tenth. I've just lost nine.

DOCT. Can't you see the judge and stop the case?

JUDGE. No. He took the case under advisement and went off into the Adirondacks, fishing. Nobody knows where to find him, and he said he'd mail his decision to the clerk of the court. We can do nothing but wait for his decision and hope for the best.

COL. Well, the interesting fact remains that, divorced or not, he's dead. [*To Major*] And as you've got to pay the insurance anyway, I don't see why you should care who gets it.

MAJ. I suppose you're right, and there's one consolation: he had another policy in the Equitable. They got soaked, too.

COL. Then you ought to be happy. And don't you see, his death is luck for the Ransome Guards. We want a dead man and he will do.

GEN. But he wasn't a member of your regiment, was he?

COL. That's all right. We'll elect him. The Board of Governors is here.

DOCT. But he hasn't been proposed.

COL. Private, give me the proposal book. That matter's easily fixed. Now get the voting box. [*Private hands him the book; Colonel writes in it; Private gets voting box and basket from the desk and stands back of table L.*] He's proposed now. Major, second it. [*Major writes in book; then passes it to Judge*]

DOCT. But the rules require names to be posted two weeks.

COL. We can't wait that long. He won't keep. Here, I'll set the date back. Now we'll vote. [*Colonel writes in book again; then closes it and passes it to Bandmaster. Private places box and basket on table and then exits L.3.E.*]

DOCT. Hold on! This man was once proposed for membership and rejected! I voted the blackball on his name. To be consistent, I must vote a blackball now.

COL. Vote a blackball! I should hope you would! Decency demands it. The man's dead! Mourning's in order! Blackballs elect! [*All take blackballs from basket and drop them into voting box*] All blackballs! He's unanimously elected a member of the regiment.

MAJ. Now we pass some resolutions, don't we?

COL. Of course. I never miss a chance to pass resolutions, do I? [*Rises and removes his hat*] Now, gentlemen, it is moved and seconded that,

Whereas, It has pleased Fate to take hence our well-beloved friend and fellow-soldier, Piggott Luce, *Resolved,* That he shall be buried with all due military honors as a member of the Ransome Guards. All in favor of this resolution say "Aye."

ALL. Aye.

COL. It's a vote. Now we'll drink to the health of our newest member. [*All rise, pick up glasses, and drink; then all resume seats*]

DOCT. Say, supposing his family don't want us to bury him?

COL. I hadn't thought of that.

GEN. And supposing the Daly Blues try to get him?

COL. [*Rises*] They shan't have him! Not if I have to buy him!

MAJ. That's the best way anyway.

COL. That's what we'll do. But say, what ought we to pay for him? Doctor, what's a fair price?

DOCT. What do you take me for? How do I know?

GEN. There! There! Don't get mad! What do you say to fifty dollars?

DOCT. Dead cheap!

GEN. [*Crosses to table L.*] I call it a stiff price.

COL. It's certainly enough. He wasn't young. He wasn't handsome. He's been hit by a derrick and all stove in. He's damaged goods. She's in luck to find a market for him at any price.

MAJ. Still, we must have him. So don't haggle. Get him as cheap as you can, but get him.

COL. [*As General crosses R.*] We'll try to get him, though, for the honor of the thing. And in order to impress the widow, I shall call upon her, accompanied by the entire regiment and headed by the band. Gentlemen, we'll go tomorrow. Major, issue the necessary orders. [*Colonel rises and crosses to C.*] Now, gentlemen, we must outdo the Blues at any cost. I suppose they are using the town hearse; we'll have it repainted!

MAJ. What color?

COL. Why, black, of course. You don't want a red hearse, do you? If they have got their cut flowers in town, we'll send to Boston for ours. We'll have a sumptuous funeral.

GEN. [*Rises and crosses to Colonel*] Sir, you are a revelation in military life.

COL. Thanks. Have a drink? [*General, Colonel, and Doctor cross to R. table; sit, and have a drink*]

JUDGE. [*R. of L. table*] See here, major, do a brother officer a favor. Your company has got to pay that insurance anyway. Settle this trouble in my favor by paying it to the widow.

MAJ. [*Seated L. of L. table*] Not yet! I admit I've got to pay the money, but I have a strong notion to marry the daughter, and if the divorce is granted, the daughter gets the money, and if I marry her I keep it in the family. [*Drinks*] I shall await the judge's decision. [*Great cheering heard off R. Everybody rises quickly and looks upstage. Judge rushes to window, opens curtains, and goes out on balcony. Bandmaster stands at his back. They both look down into the street. Private enters; goes to C. window*]

COL. What's that?

JUDGE. [*On balcony*] It's the Daly Blues! They are having their funeral procession and the crowd is cheering them! They're going to march right past our armory! [*Wild cheering heard again off R.*]

COL. [*Crosses to C.*] Well, damn their impudence! But I'll fix 'em! Mr. Ayres! [*Bandmaster comes to him*] Get out the band! Go out on the portico of the armory and play!

BAND. A dirge?

COL. A dirge? No! Something derisive! Something that will make the corpse turn over in his coffin! [*Exit Bandmaster quickly, R.3.E.*] Here, private! [*Private advances to L.C. Judge drops down back of R. table*] Go get out the hose and wet the street! Make it mud a foot deep and let 'em wallow in it! [*Exit Private quickly, L.3.E.*] I'll fix those fellows! [*Band begins playing "Ta-ra-ra" off R.3.E. Then Bandmaster enters, followed by the band playing very forte. They march to C. of stage, face audience, and play about sixteen bars; then left face and exit L.3.E. Music drops to pp. Colonel, Major, Doctor, and Judge dance up and down R. and L., changing hands*]

GEN. That will make the corpse turn in his coffin! [*All dance around the General, forming a circle. At discord they stop dancing. Band begins to play forte again. Then suddenly a terrible discord is heard again. Everybody on the stage suddenly turns from delight to consternation. Major rushes to the C. window, followed by Judge and Doctor. General is in R. corner, Colonel C. Private rushes on wildly from L.3.E. All surround him*]

PRIV. The funeral procession is licking the band!

ALL. What! [*All rush to C. window, out on balcony, and shout to crowd below*]

COL. Let that band alone! [*A shower of bricks, vegetables, dead cats, tin pans, etc., are thrown at the individuals standing in the windows. The crowd offstage begins to jeer and yell. The throwing of bricks, etc., continues as long as anyone stays on the balcony. Directly after the first shower of bricks, Doctor rushes from window, jumps over bar, and hides. Judge rushes downstage and hides behind chair, L. Major crawls under L. table. Colonel rushes downstage and into closet. During all of this, the General has been standing*] *in the R. corner, looking on. When all are hid, he rushes to C. of stage, takes in the situation, shows disgust, rushes up to C. window. At once the throwing of bricks, etc., is resumed. The General picks up the brick and such stuff as he can find and throws it back at the crowd outside. The crowd continues to jeer. Private has been hiding behind curtain, L.3. arch. General draws pistol from his hip pocket. Another great volley of bricks are thrown at him. He opens fire on the crowd. In an instant all is quiet. The crowd is heard to run from the armory calling "Help!" and "Don't shoot!" General empties his revolver. After a good pause, General up C. fires one last shot]*

GEN. [*Laughs*]   Run, damn ye, run! [*Down C. Pause*] Gentlemen, they're gone. [*Comes downstage*]

COL. [*Opens closet doors*]   Gone? Are you sure?

GEN.   Yes. Come out. [*All crawl out from their hiding-places and rush up to the window and look out*]

COL. [*In C. of window on balcony*]   They're in full flight. It isn't a retreat. It's a rout! [*Rushes downstage. Doctor R. of Colonel; Major and Judge L. of him. General R. corner*] Victory again perches on the proud banners of the Ransome Guards! Call in the band! [*Exit Private, L.3.E.*] Let it pour forth strains of triumphant joy! [*Colonel crosses to R. Private enters L.3.E.*] Here comes the band! [*Enter the Bandmaster followed by the Band, all torn up and in a horribly dilapidated condition; their instruments broken. They stagger to the C. of the stage and look at the various characters in the most appealing way. Colonel falls in chair R. of R. table. Consternation on the part of the officers. Picture*]

CURTAIN
SECOND PICTURE

The entire Band at the bar striving to get a drink. Characters all about L. table, looking on in holy horror. General crosses L. and sits in chair L. of L. table, laughing heartily.

ACT II.

SCENE: *A room in Piggott Luce's house. Private discovered standing C. Lively music at rise.*

PRIV. [*C.*]   It takes them long enough to answer a note in this house. I suppose the fact of the owner being brought home dead has kind of upset things. Here comes somebody now. [*Enter Particular Friend from L.1.E. Private salutes*]

FRIEND. Good morning. You brought a note from Colonel Berriel. Say to him that his communication stating that himself, escorted by the entire regiment, will call upon Mrs. Luce to express sympathy is delivered. She is prostrated by this shock, but will endeavor to receive them. They had better not come, though, until about three o'clock, as she is busy with her dress-maker and will not see anybody until her mourning dress is done. Can you remember?

PRIV. Yes, mum. [*Salutes and exits through gate to L.U.E.*]

FRIEND. What can this call by the regiment mean? Oh, poor, poor Piggott! And in a few days you'd have been divorced and free to marry me! [*Widow heard to cry off L.1.E.*] She's coming! [*Music pp. Friend places chair L.C. Goes to meet Widow and leads her to chair. Widow sits crying. Friend drops down R. of Widow*] What do you want, dear?

WID. Tell me—Tell me the truth!— Does my dress fit? [*Rises*]

FRIEND. Perfectly.

WID. And give me the particulars. I can bear them now.

FRIEND. Well, you see, my dear—

WID. Stop! Does black become me?

FRIEND. Wonderfully!

WID. [*Looks at herself*] I think it does. This being a widow isn't so bad after all.

FRIEND. This ends the divorce suit, doesn't it?

WID. [*Rises suddenly*] Divorce suit? Don't mention it! The odious thing! Thank the Lord I am still his wife! Here is his policy of life insur-ance for $100,000 payable to his wife. [*Shows policy*]

FRIEND. But supposing you are not his wife?

WID. Not his wife? What do you mean? There's my wedding ring!

FRIEND. Well, you know how the divorce case stands. Supposing the judge granted you the divorce before your husband died?

WID. [*Crosses to R.C.*] I never thought of that! Merciful heaven, if it should be so! But no, I won't have it so! Why do you add to my grief by such horrid suggestions? I am his wife, and no court shall deprive me of that honored title, and the life insurance! [*Crosses to C.*]

ORPH. [*Outside, L.*] Mama! Mama! [*Enters*] Mama! Oh, there you are.

WID. My child! My only comfort now! Kiss me! [*Embraces her*]

ORPH. Mama, here's the evening paper with an obituary of papa in it. Shall I read it to you?

WID. [*Crosses back of chair and sits*] Yes, dear, I am calmer. I can bear it now.

ORPH. [*Reads from newspaper*] "Prominent citizen dead."

WID. Prominent citizen. Good. Go on.

ORPH. [*Pause*] "In another column will be found an account of the death of one of our most respected residents, the Honorable Piggott Luce."

WID. Beautifully written. I must thank the editor.

ORPH. "His age was forty-six. He leaves an interesting family, a widow—"

WID. [*Rises*] Does he tell my age?

ORPH. [*Pause*] No. Only mine. [*Widow sits*] "—a widow and a daughter, aged seventeen."

WID. [*Rises*] Seventeen! He says I've a daughter aged seventeen? Give me that paper! [*Takes it and tears paper. Then throws it to ground and crosses R.*] If it's the last act of my life, I'll horsewhip that editor! Oh! Oh! [*Half-faints in Friend's arms R.C.*]

ORPH. [*Crosses to R. to window*] Why, mama, I *am* seventeen!

WID. [*Recovers quickly and crosses to Orphan*] What do you mean by saying that? You're nine! Barely nine at that! What do you mean by running around in that long dress and your hair done up?

ORPH. Why, mama!

WID. Don't call me mama while you look like seventeen. You tell people I'm your sister!

ORPH. Heavens, no!

WID. If you call me mama, people will think I'm forty.

ORPH. Well, you are forty, pretty near.

WID. You atrocious brat! Go and put on short dresses at once.

ORPH. Why, mama, I want to put on my mourning dress as soon as it's done.

WID. A child of nine doesn't need mourning. I'm forty, am I? Go and cut your hair! [*Shoves Orphan toward door L.2.E.*]

ORPH. [*Turns to Widow*] Oh, mama, don't make me cut my hair!

WID. Cut it, I say! And when you come back, bring a doll! Go, I say! [*Hustles Orphan off L.1.E. As Orphan exits, she is crying, "I won't bring a doll! I shan't bring a doll!," etc.*] I'm forty, am I? I'll see to cutting that hair myself! I want it dyed the color of mine for a switch. [*Enter Lieutenant Graves from R.3.E. Coughs. Goes to C. arch*]

LIEUT. [*C.*] Excuse me. May I come in?

WID. [*Turns to him*] Certainly. You are the undertaker?

LIEUT. [*Down C. He carries small black satchel. Inside it are a bottle of beer and two pretzels*] Yes. I came over to see how His Lateness stands the heat.

Wid. All right. [*Lieutenant starts to go R.*] By the way, when this accident happened, you seemed to be laying for it and at once took charge of things. I've let you go ahead, but you haven't yet told me how much you are going to charge for burying him. I'm a business woman and want figures.

Lieut. You want him put the usual depth?

Wid. Of course. Deeper, even. I don't want him to ever come to the surface again.

Lieut. Six feet will hold him and he won't freeze.

Wid. I never thought of him as freezing.

Lieut. The price is three hundred dollars.

Wid. Three hundred dollars! Outrageous!

Friend. [*R.*] I think so, too.

Wid. He only weighed a hundred and fifty-two pounds, and a dollar a pound is all it's worth to bury anybody.

Lieut. We don't bury people by the pound, but by the foot. Six feet deep at fifty dollars a foot is three hundred dollars.

Wid. Well, you can send in your bill for three hundred dollars, but I won't pay it.

Lieut. Then he comes up.

Wid. I'll get another undertaker. I don't think you amount to much in the business anyway. I never saw anybody who said he'd like to give you a job. Come, Lize. [*Widow and Lize cross to door L.1.E.*]

Lieut. [*Aside. Crosses to R.*] What a fool I am! I'll spoil everything. [*Aloud and turns to widow*] Stop, ma'am! Your last remark settles it. I'll bury this man if I don't get a cent for it, just to show you how neat a job I can do. Now you must leave me. I've got work to do. Don't disturb me or let anybody come here until I call. [*Exit Widow and Friend L.1.E. Lieutenant goes to C. arch and pulls curtain rope. Curtains close on all arches. Lieutenant then crosses to R. chair and puts satchel on it*] Now to give Piggy his lunch. This isn't the champagne supper—[*Takes from his satchel the bottle of beer and two pretzels*] he counted on, but it will keep him alive. [*Crosses to door R.1.E. and calls*] Piggy, are you there?

Luce. [*Inside*] I'm here.

Lieut. The coast is clear. Come out, old man. [*Lieutenant crosses to R.C. Enter Luce R.1.E., dejected. He wears long frock coat, stockings, Boston garters, and drawers, no necktie. He looks at Lieutenant a minute; then turns away disgusted*] I've brought you your lunch.

Luce. [*Takes beer and pretzels from Lieutenant*] Beer! It would have been just as easy to have brought a bottle of champagne.

Lieut. You shall have that the next time.

LUCE. There won't be any next time.

LIEUT. Why? Don't you enjoy your picnic?

LUCE. Picnic? I never went through such an experience in my life! [*Angrily*] Why did you let them put me on ice?

LIEUT. My assistants did that.

LUCE. I've got a cold that will last me for life. Twenty times I came near sneezing while they were bringing me here. Say, have you got a pocket handkerchief?

LIEUT. I have not.

LUCE. Of course, you wouldn't have! What the devil did you bring me here for?

LIEUT. Your wife would have it, and I didn't care to oppose her, and I must do just as she says. If I don't, she'll get another undertaker, and then you'll go back on ice.

LUCE. You're right. Where did you get that man that drives your hearse?

LIEUT. Why?

LUCE. He stopped at eight saloons on the way. I had to lie there on ice while he drank. After the fifth drink, he was drunk. He ran into ditches, into a cow, stopped on the railroad track to light a cigar, and I heard a train whistle! Oh, what a ride I had!

LIEUT. It won't happen the next time.

LUCE. You bet it won't! I told you before there'd be no next time! How about my pants?

LIEUT. Your pants?

LUCE. Yes. When you brought me this coat and vest, you forgot to bring me my pants.

LIEUT. Oh, they were brought to you, but I suppose my assistant took them. They are never seen, you know, and he considers it a shame to bury ten-dollar trousers. He regards the trousers as his perquisites.

LUCE. But I must have a pair of pants!

LIEUT. All right, you shall have a pair.

LUCE. Say, Phil, I'm beginning to weaken.

LIEUT. It's too late to back out. Now get back in your box. [*Pushes Luce towards door, R.*] Don't worry. I'll stand by you all the time. It'll soon be over. [*Lieutenant gets satchel from chair, R.*]

LUCE. Say, Phil, can't I have something to read?

LIEUT. Yes, I've got a book in my satchel. [*Gives book*]

LUCE. Ella Wheeler Wilcox, *Poems of Passion*. Nice stuff for a man in my fix to read. [*Exit Luce R.1.E.*]

LIEUT. Poor old pal! He's having a hard time of his picnic. [*Opens curtains. Music pp.*] Good heavens, here comes the regiment! [*Exit L.2.E. Music heard in the distance. Band plays march pp. off R.4.E. As regiment enters, music becomes forte. Grand entrance of the Ransome Guards, R.4.E. Order of march as follows: (1) Captain of Drum Corps followed by Drummers. They march to C. and form in L. arch. (2) The Standard Bearer followed by four Messenger Boys. They march on to C. Standard Bearer marches on through C. arch and stands in front of R. arch. Messenger Boys form back of arch R. (3) The Bandmaster followed by the Band. They march on to C. Then divide and march R. and L. of C. gate. Bandmaster stands R. of C. arch and conducts. (4) Judge and Major enter, followed by Doctor, General, and Private. They all march in through C. arch and form a group inside of room R. Then enters the Colonel, followed by the four Vivandières. Colonel marches in through C. arch and strikes a picture C. The four Vivandières form in C. arch. Band forms again in C. and marches down in back of Vivandières; Bandmaster at their head. Regiment continues marching and forms R. and L. of C. gate. At command from Captain they "front face." When all have reached this position, Band stops playing at end of strain*]

COL. [*Looks L. and R. and upstage. All do same*] I wonder if they know we are here.

GEN. I don't know. People usually notice it when a brass band and a drum corps enter their house, but it might be wise to fire a cannon.

COL. Where's the private? [*Private in citizen's clothes advances*]

PRIV. Here, colonel.

COL. Why! Why! [*Fainting*] Somebody support me! [*Doctor and General support him*]

GEN. What is it?

COL. This man hasn't his uniform on! [*All groan*]

JUDGE. Cut him down!

MAJ. Run him through!

DOCT. Dissect him!

COL. Heavens! This is appalling! But I'll be equal to the emergency. [*Braces up*] Infamous hound, why are you in this condition?

PRIV. I fell off a bicycle and bust the stuffing out of my pants.

COL. Wretched whelp! Get thee gone! Get back to the armory and don't show your head outside! Go! [*All groan. Exit Private C.*] What an outrage! To make people think we were short on uniforms! He shall suffer for this!

DOCT. Sh! Here she comes! [*Band plays "The Heart Bowed Down" pp. All look towards door L.1.E. Enter Friend*]

FRIEND. Gentlemen, she's here. [*Enter Widow, L.1.E. She faints. All lean towards her. Music stops. Picture. Then she revives*]

WID. Gentlemen, such welcome as a house of mourning can afford is yours.

COL. Madam, it is a mourning in which we claim the right to participate. You have lost a faithful, devoted, affectionate, and adored husband.

WID. [*Sobs*] He was.

COL. Others, also, are bereaved. Our country has lost a gallant defender, these brave soldiers, a beloved comrade.

BAND. One moment. [*Turns to Band and directs. Band plays one chorus of "Comrades." Everybody on the stage except Widow and Friend mark time with the music*]

COL. Madam, your husband was a member of the Ransome Guards.

WID. He was a member of the Guards?

COL. He was!

WID. And he never let me know it!

COL. He didn't know it himself! He was only elected yesterday. Madam, it is my distinguished honor to present to you this set of resolutions of sympathy, and to say that we are prepared to take charge of our dear brother, Piggott Luce, for the purpose of giving him a military funeral.

WID. What! Take my poor darling away from me! Never! [*Rises*]

DOCT. [*Aside to Colonel*] I told you so!

COL. But, madam—

WID. It's cruel. I thank you, gentlemen, for your resolutions, but I cannot part with him.

COL. But consider: he was a comrade of ours!

BAND. One moment. [*Band plays "Comrades." All mark time. Colonel stops them*]

COL. He was a ——— of ours. We have claims. He is to have a funeral that will beat the one the Daly Blues had yesterday out of sight. [*Colonel turns to Doctor*]

WID. Oh, I don't know what to say. Let me advise a moment with my friend.

COL. Certainly, madam. We deeply respect your agitation. Beauty in distress ever appeals to a soldier's heart. You command and we obey. [*Widow joins Friend. Colonel speaks to officers*] Gentlemen, leave us. [*Band plays "March"; turns upstage and marches toward gate. Major, Judge, Doctor, Bandmaster all bow and exit through C. arch. Messenger Boys, Standard Bearer, Captain, and Drummers back upstage. Vivandières face upstage and exit through C. arch in advance of officers. Band stops playing at end of strain. Widow stands L. General up C., watching widow*]

COL. [*Up C. to General*] A fine woman!

GEN. A mighty fine woman! [*Exits C. Colonel looks at Widow. Closes curtain*]

WID. Isn't he lovely? Now, Lize, what would you do? Let 'em have him?

FRIEND. I certainly would!

WID. It'll save having the house all cluttered up, and, of course, they'll pay all the expenses. Why, on the whole, it looks like a good thing. I'll accept the offer.

FRIEND. Shall I call the colonel?

WID. Yes. But wait a minute. I must be becomingly agitated and reluctant. Where's my handkerchief? [*Finds it*] All right.

FRIEND. [*At curtains*] Colonel! If you please! [*Enter Colonel*] It is all right.

COL. She has consented?

FRIEND. Yes. [*Exits L.1.E.*]

WID. Colonel Berriel, I have sacrificed my personal feelings to a sense of duty. Those who, like my beloved husband, have risked their lives as defenders of their country, belong in a way to their comrades. [*Band plays "Comrades" behind curtain C. Colonel stops them*] I feel that I have not the right to deny you the privilege of paying the last tributes to one who in hours of peril stood shoulder to shoulder with you. I only stipulate that I shall be permitted to occupy at the funeral a position sufficiently prominent to emphasize the fact that I also mourn for him.

COL. You shall be the star of the whole business. [*Calls at curtains*] Gentlemen, this way. [*Enter officers C. Go down R.*] It's all right. [*Aside*] Didn't cost a cent. [*Aloud. Crosses to Widow*] Now to prepare for the funeral. We'll break the hearts of the Blues!

WID. [*Advances to L.C.*] But before you do go, you'll accept some slight refreshments?

ALL. Refreshments? You bet we will! [*Officers all smile and bow*]

WID. This way, gentlemen. [*Music pp. Bandmaster and Doctor, followed by Judge and Major, cross to L. Widow goes to door L.1.E. and motions to them to precede her. The four men exit L.1.E. General crosses to Colonel, L.C., takes his arm; both cross to C. Widow motions them to precede her. They bow and insist upon her going first. She smiles and exits L.1.E. Colonel and General cross to L.1.E.*]

COL. A fine woman!

GEN. A mighty fine woman! [*Exit General, L.1.E. Colonel is about to follow, when he turns and sees Bandmaster*]

BAND. Colonel, can I have half an hour's leave of absence?

COL. Why?

BAND. All the rest of the regiment have taken one. [*Pulls curtain rope. Colonel surprised at seeing, after curtains open, that all are gone*] The band discovered a beer tunnel. The girls saw an ice cream joint. And the soldiers got into a rum saloon, and they all broke ranks!

COL. Where do you want to go?

BAND. I thought I'd visit all three places.

COL. Go along. [*Exit Bandmaster through C. arch off L.3.*] When shall we get a commander great enough to lead his ranks unbroken past a saloon? [*Crosses to R. Enter Widow L.*]

WID. Oh, colonel, I thought you had deserted me.

COL. Me a deserter? Never!

WID. [*Gloomily*] I am glad to hear you say so. To one who has so lately been left alone, there is a shudder in the very thought of a deserter.

COL. [*Seats her*] But, my dear madam, you cannot think of him—our dear brother-in-arms—as a deserter. He didn't die on purpose. Come! Come! Cheer up! You're young yet. [*Gets chair from R.*]

WID. [*Business with chair*] That's very true.

COL. Have you never thought of marrying again?

WID. Well, I won't say that the thought has not occurred to me, but I haven't dwelt upon it. You see, I've only had since yesterday to look around.

COL. Sometimes you discover a thing when you least expect it. Have you kept your eyes open today?

WID. Well—I—I guess I have.

COL. You have no objection to military men?

WID. Objection? Oh, no! I think General Burleigh is perfectly delightful.

COL. [*Aside*] Damn General Burleigh! [*Aloud*] It is getting late. [*Widow puts Colonel's chair up R.*] We have stayed here altogether too long. We came up here on business. It is transacted and we will go. Where are the others?

WID. They went into the garden to smoke.

COL. It is getting late. We must go back to the armory. I'll rally them. [*Starts to go. Turns. Business. Exits*]

WID. What a perfectly delightful man! [*Enter Orphan dressed like a child, R.*]

ORPH. Well, I hope I look sufficiently juvenile to satisfy my dear *young* mama!

WID. It's a great improvement. Only don't look as though you knew so much. It makes me feel positively girlish. I don't care who sees you now.

ORPH. You don't? Well, I do! I wouldn't have Major Baring see me for the world!

WID. Oh, but I want him to. I want them all to. They may have heard you were seventeen. I shall show you off to them to prove to them that you're only nine! And if you don't act like an infant, look out!

ORPH. Oh, mama, I can't! I'd die of shame!

WID. If the colonel thought you were seventeen, I'd die of shame. Have you got a doll?

ORPH. Yes, darn the thing!

WID. Go and play with it out in the yard. Make mud pies for it! [*Widow puts chair up L.*]

ORPH. Oh, please, mama! I won't make mud pies!

WID. If you don't do as I command, I'll—I'll spank you.

ORPH. All right—all right. You see if I don't get even with you for this. I'll be a kid all you want me to. [*Starts to go up. Meets six officers entering. Screams as she sees officers. Business of being scared*] Oh, mama!

ALL. Who's this?

WID. [*R.C. of Orphan*] Gentlemen, my little girl.

MAJ. [*To Judge*] It's the girl who dropped the glove! My grief, what a change!

ALL. How do you do, little girl?

WID. Pony, can't you say "How do you do?" to the gentlemen?

ORPH. I can, but I won't.

MAJ. Dear me, that's unkind. Why, other little girls, when I call, come right up and kiss me.

ORPH. Do you know little blind girls? [*Widow shocked and confused. All men laugh heartily. Judge, Major, Doctor, and Bandmaster sit R. Colonel crosses back of Widow to General, L. Both sit L.*]

MAJ. [*Aside to Judge*] I know it's the girl that dropped the glove. [*Aloud*] I'm awfully fond of children. Come, little girl, and sit on my lap.

ORPH. No. There's too many looking.

WID. I have forbidden it. She's too young to sit in gentlemen's laps.

ALL. Too young?

COL. They begin very young nowadays.

WID. I mean too old.

ALL. Too old?

GEN. Do they ever quit?

ORPH. I don't intend to.

WID. [*Somewhat confused*] That is, she's just at that intermediate age when she's both, but there are other things she can do. She can recite.

COL. [*Rises quickly*] We must be going. [*All rise and start to go away*]

WID. [*Quickly*] And she does skirt dances. [*All resume seats quickly*]

COL. Well, we have got a moment to spare. Let the little lady oblige.

WID. Well, under the circumstances—[*All insist strongly on song and dance*] Oh, gentlemen, very well, since you insist so strongly. Dearie, do a skirt dance for the gentlemen.

ORPH. I don't want to.

WID. [*Aside*] If you don't act like a child and do as you're told, you'll go to bed—

ORPH. [*Aside*] To bed at sundown? Never! [*Aloud*] All right. I'll sing and dance. But, remember, you told me to.

WID. Gentlemen, pardon a mother's pride in her baby. But she's so bright for a child only nine, I can't resist showing her off. Come, dearie.

ORPH. [*Sings "Wouldn't You Like to Fondle Little Baby?"*]

> In me you see a very little lady,
> A baby yet, I've heard my mama say.
> Too young to interest
> Whoever is our guest.
> They pet me, but they wish I'd go away.
> The men that call are not a bit attentive;
> When mama's in the room I'm never seen.
> I wonder if they'd find it an incentive,
> If I, instead of nine, was seventeen.

CHORUS

> Wouldn't you like to fondle little baby?
> Wouldn't you like to take me on your knees?
> Don't you think that you would do it—maybe,
> If mama wasn't there to raise a breeze?

> My Uncle Freddie bought a box of roses
> To send his sweetheart, a pretty Kitty Lee.
> In the box he put a note,
> And this is what he wrote:
> "My dearest, when you wear them think of me."
> He left the box alone for half a minute;
> The roses I was mean enough to sneak,

And a pair of papa's trousers I put in it.
Now Uncle Fred and Kitty never speak.

CHORUS

Wouldn't *he* like to fondle little baby?
Wouldn't he like to have me on his knee?
Don't you think that he would do it—maybe,
If mama wasn't sitting there to see? [*At end of song, Orphan works into dance, and then exits L.1.E.*]

WID. Remember, gentlemen, she's only a baby.

GEN. What will she be when she grows up?

COL. [*Rises and crosses to C.*] Gentlemen, an inspiration! The Ransome Guards have no daughter of the regiment. She shall be installed as such!

ALL. Good!

COL. And now we must go back to the armory and prepare for the funeral. [*All rise*] Mr. Bandmaster, go to the beer tunnel and drag out the band. You, judge, go to the saloon and rally our men. And you, doctor, go to the ice cream parlor and bring the girls.

DOCT. Why not let the major go after the girls and I'll go to the saloon.

MAJ. Not on your life! Don't dispute orders! Obey them! [*Judge, Doctor, and Bandmaster salute Colonel and pass out through C. arch and exit L.3.E. Widow passes through C. arch and works around to L. back of the General. She carries on silent flirtation with him*]

GEN. I suppose we wait for them here. [*Turns to Widow*] My dear madam, bravely as you bear up, I see your heart is heavy. I have had great experience in offering consolation to the widows of my men who have fallen in battle. Won't you come out into the garden, and let me see if I can't say something to cheer you?

WID. Your offer is so kind I cannot refuse you. [*She takes General's arm and crosses with him to C. arch. Colonel advances from R. and offers his arm. She addresses Colonel*] Excuse us. [*Widow and General go upstage and off L.3.E.*]

COL. [*C. to Major*] Confound his impudence! But I'll do him for it. I have an idea. Major, do me a favor. I want to serenade this lady tonight.

MAJ. Well?

COL. Now, I can't sing. Napoleon couldn't, but you can, and I want you to sing for me. By the way, I sent a basket of champagne up to your house today. Will you do it?

MAJ. Why, I don't see how I can refuse you and keep the champagne. [*General and Widow reenter L.3.E.*]

COL. Good! We'll come back here when all are in bed. You do the sing-ing, and when she comes down, you cut and run; and I'll do the love-mak-ing. [*Widow and General down C., laughing*] Sh! [*Major crosses to R. Colonel turns to Widow and General who appear in C. arch, laughing*] Has the general succeeded in consoling you?

WID. He has poured balm upon my wounded heart, but some sorrows are too great to be obliterated in a moment.

COL. I'm pretty good at offering consolation myself. Let me have a whirl at it. [*General crosses to L.*]

WID. Perhaps I'd better. [*Takes Colonel's arm and starts to go through C. arch. General advances to her. She turns to him*] Excuse me! [*Colonel and Widow go upstage and exit L.3.E.*]

GEN. [*L.C.*] I'll not let him get the best of me. Major, can I trust you?

MAJ. Every merchant in town does.

GEN. I want you to do me a favor. I want to serenade this lady tonight.

MAJ. And you don't sing?

GEN. I do not.

MAJ. And you want me to do the singing for you, and then cut out and run and let you do the love-making?

GEN. You're a mind reader.

MAJ. General, did you send a basket of wine up to my house today?

GEN. No, but I will.

MAJ. Then as a consistent man I don't see how I can refuse.

GEN. You'll do it? [*Major nods "Yes"*] Good boy! [*Widow and Colonel enter, L.3.E., laughing*] Sh! Not a word of this! [*General crosses to L. Major to R. Widow and Colonel pass through C. arch, laughing*] Well?

COL. Well! I think the lady is very much cheered up! [*Band heard play-ing off L.3.E., "We Won't Go Home Until Morning." All turn and look in that direction*]

GEN. What's that?

COL. Ah, hear that martial sound! [*Music grows forte*] Here come my brave guards. [*Music forte. Enter Friend, L.1.E. Enter regiment. Order of march: (1) Captain with regiment enter from L.5.E. and march to C. of stage; at command, halt and front face; (2) Bandmaster with Band enter from L.4.E., march to C., halt and front face; (3) Captain and Drummers, followed by Doctor and Major, who are followed by four Vivandières and Standard Bearer and four Messenger Boys, enter from L.3.E. At command from Major, all halt and front face. Judge joins Major. All officers are smok-ing. Everybody singing, "We Won't Go Home Until Morning." They show considerable spirit. Band stops playing when in this position at the end of a strain. Colonel marches upstage to C.*] Madam, we salute you and bid you au revoir. [*Turns to regiment*] Attention! Right face! Forward march! [*Band repeats "We Won't Go Home Until Morning." Everybody sings and marches offstage R. Private enters from L.3.E. with wheelbarrow and beer keg. He marches offstage and exits R.3.E. Music and singing gradually become pp. and die out. Widow goes downstage C. General crosses up to Colonel, C. Both turn and look at Widow. She holds out her hands to them. Both go to her, take her hands, squeeze them; then go upstage to C. arch*] A fine woman!

GEN.   A mighty fine woman! [*They lock arms and exit R.3.E. The Widow goes to C. arch and waves her handkerchief. Then she slowly walks downstage*]

WID.   They both squeezed my hands. [*Kisses both hands*] It was very presumptuous of them, of course, but I'm not a bit sorry, and now that they are gone, it's very lonely. [*Friend exits, L.1.E.*] Oh, I don't care much which, but I wish one of them would come back. [*She sings. At end of song, darken house and stage. Moonlight works on. Widow exits L.1.E. Enter Lieutenant Graves, R.3.E., very quickly and excitedly. Closes curtains. Turns up lights. Then goes to door R.1.E.*]

LIEUT.   Piggy! Come out! [*Enter Luce, excited, looking pale; hair disordered*] I must speak to you a moment. What do you suppose your wife has done?

LUCE.   I know! I overheard it all! She's given me to your cursed regiment to save funeral expenses! But I suppose I ought not to complain. She might have sold me to medical students!

LIEUT.   Then, I suppose, you would be all cut up.

LUCE.   Is that one of your jokes?

LIEUT.   Well, you must see it through!

LUCE.   And be buried alive! I'll be smothered if I do!

LIEUT.   Ha! Ha! Very good! But don't joke. This is serious. I've got it all fixed. As a member of the guards, I demanded to be left in charge of the funeral, and they've agreed. Now, instead of burying you, we put you in a tomb, and let you out after dark. That's what I came to tell you.

LUCE.   Great Scott! This is an awful experience! By the way, have you brought my pants?

LIEUT.   I forgot.

LUCE.   Look here, Graves, I begin to think you're at the bottom of this pants business.

LIEUT.   Is this another of your jokes?

LUCE. Jokes? Do you think a man in my fix would make jokes? No, sir, I believe you've held my trousers out, so if I weakened and wanted to run away, I couldn't do it!

LIEUT. Oh, Piggy, you do me an injustice!

LUCE. Well, I hope I do.

LIEUT. Say, Piggy, this hasn't turned out just as you expected.

LUCE. No. I'm in an icebox!

LIEUT. A nice box? Oh, yes, another of your jokes.

LUCE. Jokes? Don't be a fool! When do you take me to the armory?

LIEUT. Tomorrow at ten.

LUCE. Well, for heaven's sake, don't send a hearse after me! I was brought here in a hearse, and I've had enough of it. I can't stand riding in a hearse.

LIEUT. Is that another of your jokes?

LUCE. Jokes?

LIEUT. Why, of course, you can't stand riding in a hearse. You'll have to lie down.

LUCE. Damn!

LIEUT. By the way, I collected the life insurance today.

LUCE. You did? Hooray!

LIEUT. Yes. I have two checks for fifty thousand dollars each.

LUCE. Give me mine now!

LIEUT. Don't you want me to take care of it for you?

LUCE. No, sir, I don't! [*Grabs check*] Graves, this looks good! This wasn't such a bad scheme after all.

LIEUT. As you often say, "Cheer up. Cherries are ripe!" Good night, old fellow. Pleasant dreams.

LUCE. Pleasant dreams? Rats! [*Rushes off R.3.E.*]

LIEUT. I'll have to leave His Hasbeens alone in the dark. [*Puts out lights and opens curtains. Then exits L.3.E. Enter Colonel quietly, R.2.E. When about C., he beckons Major, who enters R.4.E. Colonel passes into room through C. arch to L. Looks about. Major follows Colonel into room rather noisily. Colonel cautions him to be quiet. Stage quite dark. Moonlight very bright*]

COL. [*L.*] I've reconnoitered. All is still. Now, major, cut loose!

MAJ. [*Sings "Love's Serenade"*]

> In the silvery moonlight rays,
> While sweetly the nightingale sings,
> Up to thy lattice a song I raise,
> Secrets of love it brings.

Longing for thee, I am waiting here,
The roses have all gone to sleep;
Open thy window, none else is near;
And none but the stars may peep.

Smile, and the night is turned to day,
Already the moonbeams fade.
Ah, Queen of my Heart, forever and aye,
Oh, list to love's serenade.

Dream, my darling, oh, dream of me!
Here I am waiting alone!
Love's serenade I am singing to thee,
Kneeling before thy throne.

Turn not from me in careless scorn,
I cannot live without thee.
Here, while I wait the coming morn,
Ah, dream, ah, dream of me! [*After the song the Colonel, who has been seated during it, motions to Major to go. Major exits through C. arch and off R.3.E. Colonel pulls curtain rope; curtains close. Then he looks towards L.*]

Col. Now, I must be caught just escaping. [*Starts to rush violently through C. curtain. Then stops and looks towards L.*] Why the gollywash doesn't she come? [*Then suddenly he hears her approaching*] Ah! [*Starts to go through C. curtain. Widow enters quickly through L.1.E. She turns electric light button near door. Footlights up. Then Widow rushes toward Colonel; catches him; throws him around to R. He tries to hide his face*]

Wid. [*C.*] You naughty man, I've caught you! [*Suddenly she recognizes the Colonel*] Why, it's Colonel Berriel!

Col. I cannot deny my identity. The resemblance of Napoleon to myself would betray me.

Wid. Why should you deny it? Be sure I am not offended.

Col. Then I don't get a chance to apologize?

Wid. Apologize? Sing it to me again!

Col. [*Consternation*] What!

Wid. Sing it to me again!

Col. I—well, you see—some other time will do.

Wid. If you don't care enough for me to oblige me, why did you come here at all? [*Turns away from him to L.*]

COL. Because I— Have you ever been told that the Empress Josephine looked like you?

WID. Only by my mirror.

COL. Then, I tell you so. And this resemblance means predestination!

WID. [*Turns slightly away from him*] Oh, colonel, this is so sudden!

COL. Everything is so sudden nowadays.

WID. Don't have the engagement ring less than two carats. [*Rushes into his arms; they embrace*]

COL. "Was ever woman in such humor wooed?
    Was ever woman in such humor won?
    Richard's himself again."

WID. [*Moves to L.*] Oh, I don't understand it all. I cannot tell why I have yielded so easily. But, oh, that song! It seemed to enthrall me! [*Turns to him*] When shall I hear it again?

COL. [*Takes her again in his arms*] Perhaps later, I will come back and sing it under your window. [*Crosses to R. Aside*] I wonder if I can find that shyster insurance agent.

WID. [*Moves to L.*] Oh, it was so exquisite! It was not so much the song as your voice that seemed to thrill me! The song is running through my brain now. [*Judge back of C. curtain begins to sing "Serenade" pp.*] It seems to me I do hear it! Listen! [*Colonel on hearing the song becomes horrified and very nervous*] I—I—I—I—do hear it! [*She rushes up to curtain rope. Pulls it. Curtains open. She discovers Major, singing. He stands, cigar in hand, one foot on champagne basket. General is seated on champagne basket R. of Major, smoking. Widow, on discovering them, staggers back, surprised. General rises in consternation. Colonel dances frantically, R. Major looks on amused and continues singing. Picture*]

QUICK CURTAIN

For second picture: Colonel, R.; General, L.; both singing. Widow looks on amused and knowingly. Judge, R.C., with champagne basket. He is laughing heartily. Sits on basket.

ACT III.

SCENE: *Drill room in the armory of the Ransome Guards. Curtain rises on court-martial in progress.*

DISCOVERED: *Colonel standing, C. Doctor and Judge seated, L.C. Bandmaster, R.C. Widow and General, R. Two Messenger Boys and Standard Bearer, R. Friend, L., back of Widow. Private and Major down L. Two Drummers down L. and two R.2.E. Four Vivandières on stairs C. Roll of drum at rise. Large bass drum C. covered with American flag. Officers seated on camp stools.*

COL. [*Standing*] Gentlemen of the court-martial, I understand that you unanimously approve of the findings of the court and of the sentence to be imposed.

OFFICERS. We do.

COL. Officer of the day, let the prisoner step forward. [*Major pushes Private to L.C.*] You are charged with the commission of a most heinous offense against the dignity and discipline of your regiment. You are accused of appearing on a public occasion without your uniform. You have admitted the crime, but have pleaded, in defense of it, insanity. The plea is manifestly absurd. The more insane you were, the more you'd wear your uniform. The finding of the court is that you are guilty, and the sentence of the court is that you be stripped of your uniform, your head be shaved, and you be ignominiously drummed out of camp. Officer of the day, remove the prisoner. [*Major leads Private off R.*] This court stands adjourned. [*Doctor, Judge, and Bandmaster cross L. Messenger Boys, Captain, Standard Bearer, and Vivandières exit R. and L. Drummer carries off drum L. Friend exits L. Bandmaster moves Friend's chair up C.*] Thank heaven, that court-martial is over! Now we can proceed with the funeral.

WID. Don't you think it's pretty severe on the old fellow to shave his head? [*Reenter Major R. up C.*]

COL. We've got to do it. When the Blues court-martialed their fencing-master, they drummed him out of camp. We must do more than they did.

WID. But this leaves you without a private.

COL. That's so.

BAND. And we must have one that can sing and dance, or my opera will be ruined. Hadn't I better go out and look for a good man?

COL. Indeed, yes. Go at once. We need him for the funeral. [*Exit Bandmaster L.3.E.*] Officer, tell us the program for the day.

MAJ. [*Down R.C.*] First will come the exercises in this hall, the coronation of the daughter of the regiment, and other things. Then we proceed to the big hall for the funeral, where the populace will be let in to admire the show. [*Goes up R.C.*]

COL. Now, how do you like the program?

WID. It seems to be good as far as it goes, but where do I come in? I don't seem to cut any figure in this display.

COL. Why, you'll be there.

WID. Yes, that's it. I'll just *be* there.

COL. And where you are, must necessarily be the center of attraction. The remains won't be in it with you.

WID. [*Rises and crosses to Colonel*] You're a dandy. [*Major, Judge, and Doctor all up C. General moves chairs up R. Widow takes Colonel's hand. Then she turns to General, who advances toward her*]

COL. By the way, another piece of good news. We have never had a regimental flag, and General Burleigh has designed one and is to present it to us today. Now, then, remember that the fun begins at three sharp.

WID. I must go and put on my bonnet. Wouldn't it be the funniest thing if I forgot to wear my bonnet to the funeral? [*She laughs heartily, turns upstage, takes General's and Colonel's hands and the three exit arch 2.E.*]

DOCT. [*Aside to Judge*] She seems all right with both of them today. How did they fix up that serenade of last night?

JUDGE. Oh, we all lied about it and managed to make it all right. [*Doctor exits L. Band heard off R. playing "Rogues' March" pp.*]

MAJ. [*Upstage*] Hi! Here they come with the private! [*All upstage. Enter from R. arch Captain and four Drummers followed by Private with head shaved. Band follows Private. When Private is C. he stops. Band and all stop*]

PRIV. Courage, comrades! I will have revenge! Revenge! I go to join the Daly Blues! [*All march again. Band plays and procession exits L. Private makes quick change to Tramp*]

MAJ. Here comes the daughter of the regiment! I will bet it's the "Ta-ra-ra" girl, and I'm going to find out.

JUDGE. I'm with you! [*Enter Orphan downstairs*]

ORPH. Good evening, gentlemen.

JUDGE. Good evening. The daughter of the regiment is welcome.

ORPH. I thank you, gentlemen.

JUDGE. I trust you will duly appreciate the honor conferred by your becoming the daughter of the regiment.

ORPH. The honor conferred on the regiment? Oh, yes!

MAJ. It's a great responsibility for one so young—only nine, I believe your mama said.

ORPH. That's what mama said. I hope you don't doubt her word.

JUDGE. We would not dare to. The Colonel would kill us.

MAJ. But you have an older sister—a sister who looks just like you—a sister who lost this glove—haven't you?

ORPH. You'd better ask mama. I mean, you'd better not!

JUDGE. Why?

ORPH. Because she'd faint, or else scratch your eyes out!

MAJ. But have you not an older sister?

ORPH. Indeed, I have not.

MAJ. And you are only nine?

ORPH. That's what mama told you.

MAJ. When will you be seventeen?

ORPH. The day after mama's married again.

MAJ. If I know anything about arithmetic, that will be eight years from now.

ORPH. If you know anything about women, you'd know that it won't be more than eight weeks from now.

JUDGE and MAJ. You're a daisy!

ORPH. Pardon me, a peach! You gentlemen are not up-to-date at all. [*Captain and Standard Bearer enter downstairs*]

CAP. [*To Orphan*] Your uniform as daughter of the regiment awaits you.

ORPH. Gentlemen, excuse me.

MAJ. Don't go yet. There's lots of time.

ORPH. Time for what?

JUDGE. To stay here and make us happy.

ORPH. It's one's first duty to make those about him happy. But, gentlemen, what can I do for you? I possess neither whiskey nor cigarettes.

MAJ. Now don't be sarcastic. That was a very pretty song you sang us at home. You must know another. Won't you favor us?

ORPH. Oh, certainly. Anything to oblige. [*Turns to Vivandières*] The military amuse us; we must amuse them. Girls, help me out. [*Song. Exit girls*]

MAJ. Ain't she great?

JUDGE. Well, I guess.

MAJ. And I drop to the whole business. She's seventeen if she's a day, and I can tell you by the way she looked at me that she knows I'm right in it. It's a good thing—having a daughter of the regiment.

JUDGE. Umm—yes—I could suggest an improvement.

MAJ. What is it?

JUDGE. This daughter of the regiment ought to be twins.

MAJ. Oh, cheer up, old sport! You'll get a sweetheart some day, if you'll only take my tip and shave those whiskers. [*Voices heard outside. Enter Colonel, General, and Doctor down C.*]

COL. That widow is a fine woman.

GEN. A mighty fine woman!

COL. And now, general, that the dignity of our regiment has been maintained, let's have a brandy and soda. [*General, R.C. Colonel, L.C. Doctor and Judge, L. Major, R.*]

GEN. I'll be glad to take a drink, but why not straight whiskey?

COL. Oh, but brandy and soda is more English.

GEN. Exactly. And whiskey is more American. And I happen to be an American.

JUDGE. But wouldn't you rather be English?

GEN. No, sir! I have worn the uniform of the United States for thirty years and have never been ashamed of it. The English are good people and all right, but the American whose country isn't good enough for him, doesn't deserve to have any country. And he generally hasn't. [*Enter Lieutenant, L.*]

LIEUT. Gentlemen, good morning. Everything's all right. I've got him here. They are just bringing him up the front stairs. [*Terrible crash off L. Enter Bandmaster, L., excited. All rush upstairs*]

BAND. They let him fall! He's gone end over end down the stairs!

LIEUT. I must see to this! [*Exits L.*]

COL. I hope no damage has been done.

MAJ. Jiminy, what a fall, though! He's mighty lucky to be dead before he got it!

BAND. I think I've got track of a good man to take the private's place. Ah, here he is!

COL. Let him in. We'll look him over. [*Enter Tramp, L.*]

TRAMP. Ah, there! The compliments of the seasons, gentlemen!

COL. Well, he's a beauty!

JUDGE. Well, who the devil are you?

TRAMP. My name is Dodge Shotwell.

GEN. Dodge Shotwell? A splendid name for a soldier!

TRAMP. [*Aside to General*] I'm a good thing. Push me along.

MAJ. What do you want?

TRAMP. It would be easier to tell you what I don't want, take less time.

COL. Let me give you some good advice.

TRAMP. By jingo, you guessed it the first time. That's the one thing I get plenty of.

MAJ. Why did you come here?

TRAMP. I want to be the private of this regiment. I want the honor of wearing the uniform of the Ransome Guards.

GEN. It would be an improvement on your present regalia.

COL. It's a noble ambition. I begin to like this man.

Doct. But we want a private that can make music.

Tramp. Well, I can do that. It's my stronghold.

Col. We may as well see what he can do. We must have a private at once. Go ahead.

Tramp. We'll see if you call this music. Time. [*Tramp specialty. After it, Tramp exits*]

Col. Gentlemen, will he do?

All. He will.

Col. Major, go put him into his uniform at once. [*Exit Major, L. Enter Lieutenant, L.1.E.*]

Lieut. Colonel, are you all ready?

Col. We are. Was he much hurt by the fall?

Lieut. I haven't asked him. I—I mean—Oh, no! He was put in his room all right. He'll do. I saw him myself. By the way, colonel, I've arranged, instead of burying him, to put him in a tomb. It's more swell.

Col. A good idea. A tomb is just the place for him.

Lieut. Then go forward and form the procession. I'll take a last look at His Goneness. [*Exit Colonel and others, L.3.E. Lieutenant looks about; then goes to door L.1.E.*] Piggy, old boy, come out! [*Enter Luce dressed as in Act II, L.1.E.*] Everything's all right.

Luce. Is it?

Lieut. I got at the colonel. You're to be put in the tomb just the same, and tonight I'll let you out, just as we originally planned. Oh, by the way, a telegram came for you today. [*Gives telegram*] Not being appointed your executor, I didn't open it. [*Luce opens telegram. Reads it. Gives wild yells and dances with joy. Runs upstairs. Lieutenant follows up and down the stairs*] What's the matter? Keep still! What is it?

Luce. It's from the mine. They've struck the richest vein of gold ever found in this country! We're millionaires! [*Both up and down stairs again*]

Lieut. Millionaires?

Luce. [*Hilariously*] Yes, you old geezer! You coffin trimmer! You hearse driver! We're bonanza kings! Give three cheers! [*Upstairs*]

Lieut. Hooray! Hooray! [*Runs up and down stairs*]

Luce. We'll paint this old town red! Cheer up! Cherries are ripe! Now, old sport, get me a pair of trousers and we'll go out and get drunk! [*Crosses R.*]

Lieut. But the funeral!

Luce. There won't be any funeral! Damn the funeral! We don't need the insurance money, and I've gone through all that nonsense I mean to!

Lieut. But stop! You must! It's too late to back out now!

Luce. Too late? Why?

Lieut. Because we've taken the insurance money. We have committed fraud!

Luce. I never thought of that.

Lieut. And now if you tell what you've done, they'll send us to State's Prison.

Luce. Good heavens! You're right.

Lieut. And if you come to life you'll have to go back to your wife!

Luce. Not on your life!

Lieut. And if she gets her divorce, she'll take a lot of your new-found wealth for alimony. There's no help for it. You must see the funeral through now!

Luce. Confound it! You're right. Ugh! How I dread it! You blamed old idiot, what did you want to take the money for? Ugh! And why did you get me into this scrape?

Lieut. Me?

Luce. Yes, you!

Lieut. Excuse me, you suggested the whole thing.

Luce. Did I? Then kick me!—Stop! On second thought, I'll see the whole thing through.

Lieut. Now get back in your box, Piggy, and look dignified.

Luce. What other infernal thing is going to happen before I get through with this job?

Lieut. Oh, nothing more is going to happen. It'll all be over in two hours. And tomorrow you'll be away, away from your troubles, away from your wife, and with a million dollars to spend!

Luce. And in ten days I'll be in Paris spending it!

Lieut. And I'll come over and help you.

Luce. Bully for you! We'll have the hurrah time of our lives! Remember, I see you at the tomb tonight! By the way, do I have that tomb all to myself?

Lieut. You'll be the only living creature in it.

Luce. Don't forget me and leave me locked up there!

Lieut. I will not!

Luce. [*Turns at door L.1.E.*] And don't forget to bring me a pair of pants! [*Exits L.1.E.*]

Lieut. We'll make a million out of this, and I wouldn't go through it again for five million! [*Private enters from under the stairs*]

Priv. They drummed me out of the armory, but I'm back again. They never knew me in this disguise, but here I am back again as private of the Ransome Guards. Now I'll get even with them for the way they've mutilated me. I'll mutilate their corpse and ruin their funeral. I'll paint his face black and when the public are allowed to view him, they'll think the Ransome Guards are burying a nigger. A nigger in the Ransome Guards! [*Exits L.1.E. Loud crash heard off L. Reenter Private. He is all torn up, his face partly blackened. He rushes to C. Luce appears at door L.1.E. with face partly blackened. He rushes at Private, who runs offstage R.2.E. with Luce after him. Luce returns immediately; crosses back to L. in a state of wild excitement. When he is able to make himself heard, he speaks*]

LUCE. I guess that fellow will know enough to let a corpse alone in the future. [*Band heard to play a march pp. off L. Luce rushes up to the stairs*] Good heavens! Here comes my funeral! [*Rushes off L.1.E. Funeral procession from L. Band enters through arch at head of stairs and forms R. and L. on balcony. Then four Messenger Boys march down the stairs and form R. and L. Then Standard Bearer enters carrying flag and marches to R. Then Lieutenant escorting Friend enters. Friend passes to L. and sits. Lieutenant goes to R. corner. Then Major and Judge; Major to R., Judge to L. Doctor and Bandmaster come in next; Doctor to L., Bandmaster to R. Doctor carries velvet box containing crown. Then four Vivandières march down C., two going to R. of stairs, two to L. Then Tramp, dressed as a private, carries musket and marches to L. of stairs. Then the Widow enters leaning on the Colonel's arm. He escorts her to chair R. Then enter the Captain and the four Drummers, drumming. Captain goes to L. Drummers remain on stairs, R. and L. When the Band stops playing, everybody cheers. Women wave handkerchiefs. The Colonel crosses to C. and turns to face the assembly*]

COL. Ransome Guards, attention! Ladies, our honored guests, we are about to participate in one of the grandest events in the annals of military events in the history of America—the adoption of the daughter of our gallant regiment. [*Band plays march. Enter Orphan at arch at head of stairs, dressed as daughter of the regiment. When at head of stairs, she draws sword, salutes, and marches downstairs to C. All look towards her. Chorus sings "Hail to the Daughter." Band plays and everybody sings. Women wave handkerchiefs. During chorus Colonel crosses to Doctor L., takes crown from box, crosses to Orphan C. Major crosses from R. to Orphan, takes her helmet off and passes it to Bandmaster. At end of chorus, Colonel speaks. Music from band, pp., during Colonel's speech*] Child of our departed comrade—[*Band plays "Comrades." All mark time. Colonel stops them*] By virtue of the authority invested in me, I place this jeweled chaplet on thy fair brow in token that thou art and ever shall be Daughter of the Ransome Guards! [*Places crown upon her head. Everybody cheers loudly. Orphan looks R. and L. and gradually works into chorus of "Wouldn't You Like to Fondle*

Little Baby?" All nudge one another and repeat chorus, at end of which Colonel and Major escort Orphan to chair R. of Widow. She sits. Colonel then crosses to C., Major to R.] Now you are about to be made the victim of a great honor. You are about to receive at the hands of a brave soldier your future Regimental Banner. Salute him as he crosses! [*Colonel crosses to L. Band plays a march. Enter General from L. through arch at head of stairs carrying white silk flag. He wears the uniform of a major general of the United States Army. He marches down the stairs to C.]* Three cheers for the general!

ALL. Hurrah! Hurrah! Hurrah!

GEN. I thank you all. You have distinguished me by permitting me to design and present to you a Regimental Banner. I have selected one which I believe is distinctly suited to this regiment. It is simple in design. No cheap device defaces its pure field, but it means much. It will be recognized and respected by all civilized nations. Borne at the head of your columns, the very sight of it will still the firing of the enemy and bring the battle to an end. Behold your banner! [*Unfurls flag. Chord from Band. Wild cheering from everybody on the stage. Women wave handkerchiefs. The officers show wild delight*]

WID. [*Rises and crosses to General*] Why, that's a white flag! It's a flag of truce!

GEN. Madam, I promised them a banner that they would never desert on the field of battle. They've got it. Listen to the anthem of "A Milk White Flag." [*Sings*]

Of all the flags that wave
To nerve men's hearts to fight,
None ever made a man so brave
As the flag of snowy white.
Beneath its folds so fair
No coward e'er would lag;
Up to the cannon's mouth, I swear,
I'd follow the milk white flag.

CHORUS

Hurrah! Hurrah! For the milk white flag!
For the milk white flag, hurrah!
We give three cheers for the milk white flag
That hasn't a stripe or bar!

GEN. Colonel Berriel, I offer you this banner as a sacred trust. Defend it well! [*Hands banner to Colonel*]

COL. [*L.C.*] Defend it we will! For as sacred trust I do accept it. On the field of battle it shall ever be our guiding star. The hotter the fight, the closer 'round it we shall rally. And should disaster seem inevitable, I, myself, will grasp the staff and under the very folds of the flag meet the enemy!

ALL. [*Applaud*] Bravo, colonel! Bravo! [*All repeat chorus of "A Milk White Flag." Band plays. Judge exits L.2.E. Colonel hands banner to Captain of Drum Corps. General crosses to R. of Orphan*]

COL. [*Crosses to C.*] Now on with the funeral! [*All start upstage*]

MAJ. [*In R.C., suddenly*] Say, gentlemen, I've got an inspiration! [*All stop and look at Major*]

ALL. What is it?

MAJ. Instead of putting him in a tomb, let's cremate him!

ALL. Cremate him! [*Enter Luce very quick from L.1.E.*]

LUCE. [*Rushes to C.*] I'll be damned if you do! [*Women all scream and with men start to rush offstage R. and L. in wild confusion. Picture*]

WID. [*Realizing*] He's alive! [*Screams*]

ALL. He's alive!

LUCE. You bet I'm alive!

MAJ. Hurrah! My company don't have to pay the life insurance! [*Crosses to R. corner. Widow screams*]

COL. And you're not a widow, and I can't marry you! [*Falls on Doctor's shoulder. Widow faints*]

DOCT. And without the corpse we can't have the funeral!

COL. We are dished on everything! [*All groan*]

JUDGE. [*At head of stairs*] Attention, everybody!

ALL. What is it?

JUDGE. I've won a case.

ALL. Hurrah!

JUDGE. [*Comes downstairs to C.*] The judge has been heard from.

ALL. [*Interested*] Heard from?

JUDGE. Yes. And the divorce is granted! [*Crosses to L.*]

ALL. Granted? [*Widow revives; shows great delight*]

COL. [*Turns to Widow and crosses to her at C.*] Then you are free! You can be mine after all! [*They embrace*]

FRIEND. [*L.*] Piggott! Piggott! And you are free to marry me!

LUCE. [*Upstage, L.C. Turns to her*] Lize, do you love me still?

FRIEND. Do I love you still? You bet I do! [*She rushes into his arms, L.C.*]

COL. [*Crosses with Widow to Friend and Luce. Draws Luce towards him C.*] Accept our hearty congratulations! [*Luce and Colonel shake hands. Widow crosses to Friend, L.*]

WID. I'm so glad, dear! [*Kisses Friend*]

COL. [*To General*] She's a fine woman!

GEN. A damn fine woman! [*Widow crosses to Colonel, C. Luce goes to Friend, L.C.*]

DOCT. That's all right about your love affairs, but how about the funeral?

GEN. [*R.C.*] Let me make a suggestion. If we can't have a funeral, we can have what the Daly Blues never had—a Resurrection Ball!

ALL. [*Enthusiastically*] Good!

COL. That's what we'll do! Send word to the populace that the funeral is postponed, and all take partners for the Grand March of the first annual Resurrection Ball of the Ransome Guards! [*Chorus: "A Milk White Flag." Everybody to sing and Band to play*]

CURTAIN

THE BANKER'S DAUGHTER
AND OTHER PLAYS

The Banker's
Daughter

& Other Plays

BY BRONSON HOWARD

EDITED BY ALLAN G. HALLINE

INDIANA UNIVERSITY PRESS

BLOOMINGTON

Requests for authorization of the use of any of the plays in this volume on the stage, the screen, or for radio or television broadcasting, or for any purpose of reproduction, will be forwarded by Princeton University Press to the proper persons.

PREFACE

IN KEEPING with the purposes of the present series, the following plays of Bronson Howard are now published for the first time; heretofore these plays have existed only in manuscript form or in privately printed editions. All of these plays but one have been produced and are thus a part of our stage history; at least two of the plays were outstanding hits in their time, one was a success, and two others had recurrent performances. Three of the plays were produced abroad.

Like most other successful playwrights, Howard wrote for production and not for publication. In fact, he was averse to the public printing of his plays.[1] An examination of Howard's manuscript materials reveals how consistently the idea of stage production dominated his methods of composition; the plays themselves are evidence of this approach.[2] The present volume, therefore, will appeal primarily to those interested in the drama; but the general reader as well may find value in the story, in the character presentation, or in the social commentary of the various plays.

The editorial policy has been to provide factual material relative to each play, and to minimize critical interpretation. Accounts have been given of the first performances, of subsequent productions, and of prominent casts; the bases of the present texts have been described; a bibliography of Howard's plays and a general bibliography have been provided; and, where possible, sources of the plays have been indicated. With respect to the latter point, it may be noted that a play is presumed to have no specific external source unless otherwise shown. The reason for this is that Howard was exceptionally scrupulous in acknowledging every borrowing or influence. As an illustration of his care in this regard, we have the *Moorcroft* incident related by Brander Matthews: Howard "was always most scrupulous in declaring whatever indebtedness he might be under to any predecessor. He printed on the programme of *Moorcroft* an acknowledgment that he had derived the suggestion for the play from a short story by John Hay, although what he had borrowed

---

[1] See Brander Matthews, "An Appreciation," *North American Review,* Vol. CLXXXVIII (October 1908), p. 511; also in *In Memoriam* volume described in bibliography.

[2] Howard wrote one play, *Kate* (1906), specifically for reading purposes; the particular combination of novel and drama forms here used is, as far as the present editor knows, unique.

was so insignificant that Mr. Hay told me he would never have suspected his own share in the work if Bronson Howard had not called his attention to it."[3]

This is a fitting place for the present editor to acknowledge his own indebtedness at many points to the extensive researches of Professor Arthur Hobson Quinn in the field of American drama. He also wishes to state that the approach, the play texts, and many data have been provided by Mr. Barrett H. Clark, general editor of the series.

A. G. H.

Bucknell University, 1941.

[3] Brander Matthews, *op. cit.*, p. 506.

CONTENTS

THE BANKER'S DAUGHTER
AND OTHER PLAYS

BRONSON CROCKER HOWARD

1842-1908

BRONSON CROCKER HOWARD was born October 7, 1842, in Detroit, Mich. His mother, Elizabeth Vosburg, was of Dutch descent, and his father, Charles Howard, came from an English ancestry that numbered dukes among its members. Charles Howard was a man of prominence: he was a prosperous commission merchant, he was elected mayor of Detroit in 1849, and he was publicly eulogized at his death in 1883.

After attending schools in Detroit up to 1858, Bronson Howard entered Russell's Institute in New Haven, Conn., with the intention of continuing his studies at Yale; however, he changed his plans and went into newspaper work. While working on the *Detroit Free Press,* Howard wrote humorous sketches and several plays, all but one of which were discarded. *Fantine,* based on an episode in Hugo's *Les Misérables,* was produced in Detroit in 1864. The following year Howard went to New York, where he became a reporter on the *New York Tribune* under the editorship of Horace Greeley.

For four years Howard wrote plays for the wastebasket. In 1870 he sent a play to Laura Keene, who thought so highly of it that she recommended it to Augustin Daly for production. Acting upon her suggestion, Daly produced Howard's *Saratoga* December 21, 1870; it had an exceptionally long run of one hundred one nights and was subsequently produced in London as *Brighton.* The success of this play materially encouraged Howard and launched him upon his long, prosperous career as a dramatist; his later plays included such hits as *The Banker's Daughter* (1878), *The Henrietta* (1887), and *Shenandoah* (1888).

In London, in 1880, Howard married Miss Alice Wyndham, sister of Sir Charles Wyndham.

Travel in Europe provided Howard materials for such international contrasts as *One of Our Girls* (1885) and *Aristocracy* (1892). Other activities of Howard included lecturing on the drama and campaigning for stronger copyright laws. He was founder and president of the American Dramatists' Club and a member of several other literary clubs. He died August 4, 1908, at Avon-by-the-Sea, N.J.

SURVEY OF HOWARD'S PLAYS

THOUGH Bronson Howard's development as a dramatist was continued and gradual, yet his career falls readily into two parts: from 1864, when his first play, *Fantine,* was produced, to about 1882, most of his work was either farce or melodrama; from 1882 on, his plays became more realistic in technique and increasingly attentive to problems in contemporary life.

Fantine, produced in Detroit in 1864, is a dramatic sketch based on episodes in Hugo's *Les Misérables.* Howard's first New York production was *Saratoga,* a brisk farce concerning the watering place, staged by Augustin Daly in 1870; this piece shows an early interest in the contemporary American scene. *Saratoga* was produced in London as *Brighton* and in Germany as *Seine Erste und Einzige Liebe.* Howard's next play, *Diamonds* (first produced in 1872), is a comedy of manners and continues Howard's interest in the current scene as dramatic setting. *Moorcroft; or, the Double Wedding* (1874) is a melodrama dealing with a slave situation; it is based in part on a short story by John Hay.[1] *Lilian's Last Love* (1873) pictures the danger in marrying for duty instead of love; this drama is of especial interest because it is the first phase of a three-version play, analyzed in Howard's *Autobiography of a Play.*[2] The second stage of the play, *The Banker's Daughter,* was produced in New York in 1878; the third version, *The Old Love and the New,* appeared the following year in London.

Howard's only one-act play, *Old Love Letters* (1878), is a sentimental treatment of reawakening love. It was first presented as a curtain-raiser to Howard's "comic drama," *Hurricanes* (1878). The next year saw the production of *Wives,* a comedy adapted from Molière's *L'École des maris* and *L'École des femmes. Baron Rudolph,* a melodrama of poverty, riches, and villainy, had its *première* in England in 1881. The last of Howard's farces was *Fun in a Green Room,* produced early in 1882. Probably belonging to this same period is the sentimental comedy of English life, *Knave and Queen* (at first entitled *Ivers Dean*);[3] according to the title-page of the manuscript, this play was written in collaboration with Sir Charles L. Young, Bart.

---

[1] See the Preface of this volume for a note on Howard's borrowing.

[2] *The Autobiography of a Play.* Dramatic Museum of Columbia University. First Series, New York, 1914. With an Introduction by Augustus Thomas.

[3] Though this play was not produced, and though no date of composition is indicated, the technique, mood, and manuscript style all suggest the earlier period of Howard's work.

The second part of Howard's career shows a greater attention to realism in technique and a growing concern with the problems of contemporary life.[4] *Young Mrs. Winthrop* (1882) reveals how absorption in business and society can ruin the family. *One of Our Girls* (1885) contrasts American and French ideas relative to maidenhood and marriage. The ruthlessness of big business, more particularly Wall Street, is exposed in *The Henrietta* (1887);[5] this satire on money-making was highly lucrative to Howard. *Met by Chance* (1887) involves an international contrast, a theme in several Howard plays. The next play was the popular romance of the Civil War, *Shenandoah* (1889). A second historical play is *Peter Stuyvesant* (1899) written in collaboration with Brander Matthews.[6]

Howard made one of his most extended studies of society and social climbing in *Aristocracy* (1892). An unpublished and unproduced play, *The Title* (wr. 1895), is an early discussion of woman's suffrage. The novel-drama, *Kate* (1906), reveals Howard's modernity in its theme of love versus ritual as the sanction for marriage.[7] Though not in true drama form, *Kate* epitomizes the main features of Howard's continually maturing art.

[4] Montrose J. Moses says that Robertson's example in *Caste* did much to suggest to Howard the treatment of contemporary life.

[5] An unfinished play by Howard, probably belonging to this period, has as its central object of satire a prosperous railroad magnate; although the play is set in England, this character is an American. The title of the play is *The Railway King;* it exists in manuscript only.

[6] An unpublished and unproduced play of Howard's, *Ladysmith,* deals romantically with the Boer War.

[7] An unnamed comedy, in manuscript outline form, concerns a virtuous young Englishman who is almost ruined by false gossip. The English setting both in this play and in *Kate* suggests that they were written about the same time.

HURRICANES

HURRICANES

First produced at Hooley's Theatre, Chicago, May 27, 1878, with the following cast of characters:

Mrs. Lucy Batterson		MARIE WAINWRIGHT
Mrs. Partridge Compton		MRS. ALLEN
Blanche	*four weak women*	ROSE OSBORN
Julia		AGNES ELLIOTT
Alfred Batterson		JAMES LEWIS
Gen. Partridge Compton		W. H. BAILEY
Sartewelle	*four strong men*	ED. J. BUCKLEY
Frederic Randolph		J. G. SAVILLE
Mrs. Stonehenge Tuttle, *one strong woman*		MRS. G. H. GILBERT
Mrs. Dalrymple McNamara, *a wise woman*		SYDNEY COWELL
Cutter		WM. CULLINGTON

Produced at the Park Theatre, New York, August 31, 1878, with the following cast of characters:

Mrs. Lucy Batterson		AGNES BOOTH
Mrs. Partridge Compton		MRS. LOUISE ALLEN
Blanche	*four weak women*	MINNIE PALMER
Julia		ALICIA ROBSON

ALFRED BATTERSON		FRANK HARDENBERG
GEN. PARTRIDGE COMPTON		
SARTEWELLE	*four strong men*	JAMES LEWIS
FREDERIC RANDOLPH		FRANK SANGER

MRS. STONEHENGE TUTTLE, *one strong woman*   MRS. G. H. GILBERT

MRS. DALRYMPLE McNAMARA, *a wise woman*   SYDNEY COWELL

CUTTER   WM. CULLINGTON

The New York production, with its *première* on August 31, 1878, ran approximately one month; it was presented again on the nights of October 18 and 19.

Hurricanes was produced as *Truth* at the Criterion Theatre, London, February 8, 1879.

TEXT AND SOURCE

The present text of *Hurricanes* is based on a photostatic copy of Howard's own typescript with manuscript corrections. The title-page reads as follows: Hurricanes/ A Comic Drama/ In Three Acts/ By Bronson Howard/ Act First/ Copyright./ 1878. Written diagonally across the upper left-hand corner is the following notation, not in Howard's hand: Bronson Howard's own/ MS, with MS corrections in his/ own hand.

With the exception of the note following the cast of characters, the corrections in Howard's own hand have been incorporated into the text. The present editor has made changes in punctuation, spelling, and other details of form where emendation was obviously necessary; otherwise he has left the text untouched. To list in detail these corrections would serve no useful purpose.

No source of the plot has been discovered. It could hardly be said that the quotation from Bryant's "The Battlefield" is a specific source; it may be stated, however, that Bryant, whom Howard described as "America's greatest poet," exerted a general influence on the playwright's mind and character. The use of this particular quotation is here probably more of an embellishment than an indication of borrowing. The theme of the "detained business man" is one readily taken from life.

CHARACTERS

Mrs. Lucy Batterson

Mrs. Partridge Compton

Blanche

Julia

four weak women

Alfred Batterson

Gen. Partridge Compton

Sartewelle

Frederic Randolph

four strong men

Mrs. Stonehenge Tuttle, *one strong woman*

Mrs. Dalrymple McNamara, *a wise woman*

Cutter [The following note in Howard's hand appears in the typescript copy at the end of the cast of characters: "At the 'Park Theatre,' New York, Mr. Cullington played the part of Cutter as a colored servant—quiet old man—in dress coat. This is better, perhaps, than as an English servant as in ms. B.H."]

[FOR PROGRAMME—To follow List of Characters]

Scene: *Honeysuckle Villa, Alfred Batterson's summer residence at New Rochelle, near New York.*

N.B. *In connection with this play, the author respectfully calls the special attention of the audience to the following facts:*

"Truth crushed to earth shall rise again;
The eternal years of Heav'n are hers.
But error, wounded, writhes with pain,
And dies among his worshippers."

ACT I.

SCENE: *The drawing-room of Alfred Batterson's summer villa at New Rochelle. Center doors leading to hall or a second apartment, from which an outer door leads to veranda, R.U.C. The hall or second room extends out L.U.C. A bay window to veranda up R.C. Door R.3.E. Door L.3.E. A sofa down R. A table with bell further up R.C. This scene remains unchanged through all three acts unless the manager desires more variety of scenery. In this case, follow instructions of Act III. The furniture, etc., may indicate any degree of wealth considered desirable, but should not be too elaborate and massive for the country residence of a rich New Yorker.*
Bright music as curtain rises. "We Won't Go Home till Morning." Cutter enters L.3.E., crossing up to window R.C. and looking out. Bright music for a moment after curtain rises.

CUTT. 'Ere they come—h'up the drive. So far h'as I can judge from the pile of boxes and h'extra packages, my master's wife's mother 'as come to stay h'at least six weeks. There's h'another box—on behind [*Moving to hall*] h'at least two weeks more. [*Opens door and looks off under his hand*] She's full h'inside too—ten weeks h'at the very least. Ten weeks visit from a mother-in-law! In h'England, where I come from, such a thing wouldn't be h'allowed, by h'Act of Parliament. This h'is a blasted country h'anyway. 'Ere's a young married man's mother-in-law settlin' down on 'im for three months. They calls this a free country. [*Sounds of approaching carriage. Coachman's "Whoa," etc. Cutter disappears through door R. Enter Lucy Batterson L.3.E. She runs to window*]

LUCY. Oh—mamma is here already. The train was early. [*She runs up to hall and meets Mrs. Stonehenge Tuttle on veranda. They enter*] Dear mamma!

MRS. T. My daughter! [*They embrace and come down C.*]

LUCY. I'm *so* glad to see you, mamma—in our new home. Sit down here, mamma, you must not go to your room yet. It is all ready—but I know you are tired.

MRS. T. Thank you, my dear Lucy [*Sitting C.*] I *am* tired. Three hours travelling since breakfast, and the railroad men were all so very uncivil. They didn't answer more than six questions in every hundred I asked them, and the baggage men growled at the baggage as if they expected extra compensation besides the wages they get from the company, and the air in the cars was simply abominable. Two old ladies in the seat before me insisted on having their window shut. They didn't like the dust, they said. I accidentally stuck my umbrella through the glass. That settled the question.

Lucy. My own darling, sweet mamma!—I am *so* glad you have come. [*Dropping to a hassock at her feet, during Mrs. Tuttle's speech above, Lucy has been removing her mother's bonnet, wraps, etc. Cutter and other servants have been trailing in through C. door and out at R.3.E. with boxes, packages, etc. Lucy continues*] I am sorry you had so many annoyances on the trip, mamma.

Mrs. T. They made as much worry about the baggage, my dear, as if I were a travelling theatre company—with all the scenery for "The Black Crook." When I changed cars at Bridgeport Junction I *gave* the hack driver ten cents over the lawful fare, and the man actually looked at me as if he wanted more. Such ungrateful creatures, my dear!

Lucy. But you are now here, my dear mamma, the trouble is all over— and—oh—Cutter! [*Cutter enters at C. door from R., loaded with boxes, shawls, and packages*] Did you tell the coachman to return immediately to the station, Cutter, to meet Mr. Batterson and the other gentlemen by the ten o'clock train from New York?

Cutt. Yes, mum. He drove back at once. [*Lucy brings down hassock and sits L. of Mrs. Tuttle*]

Mrs. T. His name is "Cutter," my dear? Cutter—[*Cutter approaches her*] Here is a quarter of a dollar.

Cutt. [*Pleased, taking it*] Thank you, mum. [*Aside*] Rather a nice old lady arter h'all.

Mrs. T. For you and the other servants. [*Cutter looks at the quarter, then at Mrs. Tuttle; moves up; looks back. Servants pass through with another large trunk, packages, etc.*]

Cutt. H'I'll divide it h'equally, mum. [*Aside*] We'll h'all of us h'invest our capital in Wall Street. [*Exits R.3.E.*]

Lucy. I'm so glad—so glad—you are here, mamma. Alfred and I have talked it over very often. We have so many plans to make you comfortable. This is your first visit in our new home, you know—your first visit to us since we have been married. We shall all have such a delightful time together. Alfred and I are very, very, very, very happy with each other. He has been looking forward to your coming as eagerly and as anxiously as I. You and he used to be such good friends—before we were married.

Mrs. T. Yes—my dear, Alfred and I were the best of friends—before you were married. I heard you tell the servants by the way, to have the coachman meet Alfred at the New York train.

LUCY. Yes, mamma—Alfred will be here in a very few minutes, now. He is coming from New York with two young friends of ours, Mr. John Sartewelle and Mr. Frederic Randolph. They are engaged to Blanche and Julia, you know, the two pretty orphan cousins of my husband, who are visiting us. I wrote you about them. They are charming girls. I know you will like them.

MRS. T. M'm. Are they *very* pretty, my dear?

LUCY. They are both sweet girls—and one of them—you ought to hear Alfred rave about her hair!

MRS. T. M'm—rave, my dear?—Ah—

LUCY. Ha, ha, ha! I get fearfully jealous sometimes, and I pull his ears, when he gets talking on that subject.

MRS. T. M'm. [*Significantly*] I'm very glad she's engaged, my dear.

LUCY. Ha, ha, ha! So I tell Alfred, mamma. I am sure you will love them both as much as I do, when you meet them.

MRS. T. I dare say I shall—quite as much. By the way, Lucy, dear—Alfred must have got up very early in the morning—to be "returning" from New York in the ten o'clock train.

LUCY. Oh, dear, no. Ha, ha, ha! Alfred went up to the city yesterday afternoon.

MRS. T. Ah, he went up to the city yesterday afternoon. M'm. Does Alfred *often* spend the night in New York?

LUCY. Oh, no indeed. This is the very first time Alfred has been away from me for a whole night since we were married.

MRS. T. Oh—m'm. There is an old saying, Lucy—"There is a time for everything."

LUCY. Yes, mamma.

MRS. T. The saying would be equally true, as I have learned by experience and observation, if it ran "There is a *first* time for everything."

LUCY. [*Eagerly*] What do you mean, mamma?

MRS. T. Nothing, my dear—in particular.

LUCY. Alfred sent me back a note last evening by General Partridge Compton's servant—

MRS. T. General Partridge Compton! Is General Partridge Compton one of Alfred's friends?

LUCY. Yes, mamma. General Compton and Mrs. Compton live in the next villa, you know.

MRS. T. M'm. [*Thoughtfully*] General—Partridge—Compton.

LUCY. Why, mamma! What is there about General Partridge Compton? He is a nice jolly old gentleman—what *are* you thinking about?

MRS. T. Nothing, my dear—in particular. There are a great many "nice, jolly old gentlemen"—like General Partridge Compton—in this world. I know him by reputation. Nice, jolly, old gentlemen, like General Partridge Compton, very frequently spend the night in New York.

Lucy. [*After a puzzled look at her mother*] Do they, mamma? It must be very uncomfortable for them, at a hotel.

Mrs. T. Yes—it is, my dear—at a hotel. They generally manage to make themselves comfortable, however—in *some* way.

Lucy. Well, Alfred sent me a note by General Compton's servant yesterday afternoon, saying that he was detained in New York on very important business—and he could not possibly return until this morning.

Mrs. T. Oh—m'm. "Important business." What time does the last train out leave New York, my dear, at night?

Lucy. Eleven forty-five! Saturdays at twelve-thirty.

Mrs. T. M'm. Just in the midst of "business" hours.

Lucy. [*Puzzled*] Why—what do you mean, mamma?

Mrs. T. Mr. Stonehenge Tuttle, your dear father, was once detained in New York at night—on "business"—my dear. [*Thoughtfully*] M'm—"important business."

Lucy. [*A little anxiously*] I do not understand you at all, mamma.

Mrs. T. "Business," with a married man, my dear, is like "love" with an unmarried man.

Lucy. Business—like *love,* mamma?

Mrs. T. It is "the old, old story." [*Lucy starts to her feet, crosses to R., looking off*] Take a loving mother's advice, Lucy. [*Lucy drops her face in her hands*] Nip it in the bud, my dear.

Lucy. [*Sobbing*] Nip—what—in—the—bud, mamma?

Mrs. T. All the "business" that your husband has in New York after eleven o'clock at night.

Lucy. O-o-o-o-oh—[*Sobbing*]

Mrs. T. A man can generally finish all necessary business in New York in time to catch the midnight train. [*Rising*] Nip it in the bud, my dear.

Lucy. Oh, mamma! [*Sobbing*] I—I—I was so happy—until—until—

Mrs. T. [*Drawing up*] Until *I* came.

Lucy. Un-until just a moment ago. O-o-h. [*Weeping*]

Mrs. T. I hadn't been married as long as you have, my dear, when I had just such a crying time as this. Ah—heigh-ho—[*Taking out her handkerchief*] How well I remember that first rude breaking of my youthful dreams! [*Wiping her eyes*] Your father—he was *afterwards* your father—he—we—we had only that morning agreed together that we would call you—Richard— but fate ordered it otherwise!—your father sent me word from New York that he was detained over night on business. We—you—I was alone that night.

Lucy. Mother!

Mrs. T. My child! [*Lucy falls upon her neck, both sobbing*] Your father returned from New York on the morning train.

Lucy. Yes.

Mrs. T. Mark what followed! He was *yawning* all day, *yawning,* my dear, and he fell asleep in his chair at the supper table!

Lucy. Oh—mamma!

Mrs. T. My child! [*They sob on each other's shoulder*] I afterwards discovered that he had been up till half past four—and all the "business" that he had accomplished was to settle sundry bills—at Delmonico's and elsewhere.

Lucy. Mother! [*They walk up R., Lucy encircled in her mother's arms and weeping on her shoulder. They pause up R.C.*]

Mrs. T. Cling to your husband, Lucy, like the ivy to the oak—heigh-ho—that is the way I always clung to Mr. Tuttle—but don't let any parasitic bunches of mistletoe share with you its branches. Notice if your husband *yawns* when he returns. My dear—notice if he yawns.

Lucy. Mother! mother! mother!

Mrs. T. My child, notice if he *yawns*. My child, notice if he *yawns*. [*Exit R.3.E. A sound of carriage wheels. Cutter reappears from R.3.E.*]

Cutt. [*Looking through window*] Master and the young gentlemen—business in New York! Ah—m'm—h'exactly. H'I've assisted a new married couple through the 'oneymoon and the first year or so, before. H'I've been rather surprised that master could postpone his business engagements in New York so long. H'I really began to fear that master was *neglecting* his business in New York—business is business. [*He walks out through door R. Sound of carriage drawing up—"Whoa," etc. A moment's pause. Enter Batterson, Sartewelle, and Frederic. Music—"Won't Go Home till Morning." All move in languidly. Cutter follows them in. The three gentlemen take off their light overcoats, etc., and toss them into the arms of Cutter up R.C. They move down languidly, Sartewelle L., Batterson C., Frederic R. A yawning chorus follows*]

Batt. Ah—oo—ooh.

Fred. Ah—oo—ooh.

Batt. Ah—oo—ooh.

All Three. Ah—oo—ooh.

Cutt. [*Yawning up R.C.*] Ah—oo—ooh. [*The three gentlemen having dropped into seats turn sharply and look at him*] H'I beg your pardon, sir, but h'it's catching. H'I dropped the word to Mary, sir—this morning. The rooms are h'all ready h'if you and the h'other gentlemen wish to lie down—

BATT. [*Rising*]   Lie down, Cutter!

SART. and FRED. [*Rising*]   Lie down?

CUTT.   H'I beg your pardon, gentlemen—but h'I thought perhaps, 'aving business in New York last night, you might be a trifle sleepy. Gentlemen generally is.

THE THREE GENTLEMEN. [*In succession*]   Sleepy? Sleepy? Sleepy?

ALL TOGETHER.   Sleepy, Cutter?

BATT.   Do we *look* sleepy, Cutter?

CUTT.   Oh—not in the least, sir—not h'in the least. Only h'I thought, sir—h'I thought—business in New York is so very tiresome, sir—h'I thought, if you *were* sleepy, you might like to take a nap.

BATT.   Take a nap! at ten o'clock in the morning? Absurd!

FRED. and SART.   Absurd!

BATT.   That will do, Cutter. [*Cutter walks up; stops in hall and looks back*]

THE THREE GENTLEMEN.   Ah—oo—ooh.

CUTT.   Ah—oo—ooh. [*Exits L.U.E.*]

BATT. [*Leaning on the back of a chair, solemnly*]   Young gentlemen—I wish to speak to you very *seriously*.

SART.   Serious? Certainly. [*Sits*]

FRED.   Certainly. [*Sits*] Ah—oo—ooh.

SART.   Ah—oo—ooh.

BATT.   Ah—oo—ooh. You are both young men. *I* am a married man. Within less than one month, *you* will be married men. You are about to lead two fair young creatures—two innocent and confiding maidens—to the altar.

FRED and SART.   Ah—oo—ooh. We are.

BATT.   Ah—oo—ooh. My own experience, young gentlemen, will be of value to you. I lived for many years the life of a bachelor in the city of New York. *You* are just beginning to know what the life of a bachelor in the city of New York is, young gentlemen. Towards the end of my solitary career, I was rapidly becoming what the world calls an *"old* bachelor." Young gentlemen, a man who becomes an old bachelor, in the city of New York, lays up a large store—a very large store—of experience—varied experience—concerning which, young gentlemen—the less said the better. The day after tomorrow will be the second anniversary of my marriage to the most delicate, the most charming, the most affectionate, the most modest and the sweetest woman that ever lived. [*Sartewelle and Frederic start up slightly and look at him, then fall back languidly*]

BOTH.   Ah—oo—ooh.

BATT. Ah—oo—ooh. I am confining myself to plain, hard *facts*, gentlemen. Until yesterday I have never been absent for a single night from her whom I led from her mother's protecting arms two years ago—a timid blushing bride, trembling like an aspen leaf, but resting upon my arm with all the trusting faith of perfect love.

SART. and FRED. Ah—oo—ooh.

BATT. Ah—oo—ooh. Yesterday afternoon, gentlemen, I was tempted for the first time—for the first time—to forget my duty as a husband. I remembered some of the wild delights—delights, gentlemen, as I used to think them —of my bachelor days. I determined to enjoy them again. I wrote a *lie*—a lie, gentlemen, on paper and sent it to my wife. I drank again of the forbidden cup. I have discovered that the once fascinating draught is composed of nothing but froth and dregs. The froth was utterly insipid to me and the taste of the dregs remains in my mouth. Ah—oo—ooh.

SART. and FRED. Ah—oo—ooh.

BATT. Remember what I say, young gentlemen. I have gained one thing, at least—I had become so accustomed to the ring of the true metal, I had forgotten how dull and leaden the sound of counterfeit pleasure really is. A single smile of a loving wife is a coin from the mint of happiness more precious than all the imitation smiles that form the currency of vice. Ah—oo—ooh.

SART. and FRED. Ah—oo—ooh.

BATT. Remember my words, young men. [*He walks up C. Enter Lucy R.3.E.*]

LUCY. [*Stopping suddenly*] Alfred!

BATT. [*Earnestly*] Lucy! My wife! [*Extending his hands. She moves towards him eagerly but stops as if doubtful*] My darling wife!

LUCY. You—you—you were detained in New York, Alfred—on—on business? [*Doubtfully*]

BATT. Yes, my love—on—on important business. [*Aside*] Oh, Lord! I thought the lying was all over. [*Aloud*] I haven't had a comfortable moment since I left you, Lucy. [*Aside*] *That's* the truth anyway. [*Aloud*] I am delighted—delighted, my darling—to be with you again.

LUCY. Oh, Alfred!—I believe you. [*Running to him and dropping her head on his breast*] I *do* believe you.

BATT. Believe me?—my *darling!* [*Resting one hand on her head and the other about her waist*] Could you doubt me? I have never been so glad to get back to you in all my life. Rest on this bosom, my pet, like a wandering lamb returned to its fold.

LUCY. [*Glancing up*] I, Alfred?—a wandering lamb?

BATT. I mean—I—I mean—the wandering fold has returned to its lamb—my love. [*She drops her head on his breast*] Ah! like a weary pilgrim you have straggled back to your home. [*She glances up*] I mean your weary home has straggled back to you, my dear.

LUCY. A-h—*dear* Alfred! [*Dropping her head on his breast again*] *This* is indeed *my* home.

BATT. [*Resting his hand on her head*] It *is* my love—it *is* your home—and it will never desert you again. A-h! [*Tenderly*] A sense of calm comes over me, the calm of domestic tranquillity—the serene happiness of perfect restfulness, in a faithful and confiding love. Ah—oo—ooh. [*Lucy starts, looking up at him suddenly and stepping back*]

SART. and FRED. Ah—oo—ooh. [*Lucy looks from one to the other*]

BATT. Ah—oo—ooh.

LUCY. O—h! Alfred! [*Drops her face into her hands, sobbing*]

BATT. [*Moving to her*] Lucy—my dear Lucy! [*His arms about her waist. She draws up suddenly and with dignity*] My darling Lucy!

LUCY. What time did you get to bed last night, Mr. Batterson? [*Sartewelle and Frederic start around interested*]

BATT. Bed?—I—oh—I—why—[*Aside*] More lies! More lies! [*Aloud*] My lawyers live so far from the depot you know. We finished our business by a quarter past eleven—but I knew I could hardly catch the last train at that time, and besides, I didn't want to disturb you, my dear, and *you doubted* me, Lucy! It is very odd—but yawning is very *catching*. I've been riding from New York with these *young* fellows. Boys will be boys, you know—they were up *very* late last night. [*Sartewelle and Frederic look at each other*]

FRED. [*Aside*] Well—I'll be blowed!

SART. [*Aside*] Cool—decidedly cool.

BATT. The boys have been yawning all the way from New York.

LUCY. [*Dubiously*] Oh—

FRED. Yes—I—I—I had a very difficult case to work out for a *young* lawyer. I didn't leave off till after four o'clock.

SART. [*Deliberately and distinctly*] I—was—with—Frederic—in—the—case—he—refers—to.

FRED. [*Aside*] Hang him! Sartewelle always sneaks in under one of my lies. Jack always dodges the truth by telling it.

BATT. You know yawning is very contagious, my dear.

FRED. Ah—oo—ooh.

SART. Ah—oo—ooh.

BATT. Ah—oo—ooh.

ALL. Ah—oo—ooh.

LUCY. Ah—[*Starting to yawn*] Why—ah—why, isn't it funny? Ah—oo—ooh. [*Yawns*] It *is* catching, isn't it, Alfred? Forgive me! [*Throwing herself on his breast*]

BATT. I do, Lucy—I do forgive you.

ALL. [*Including Lucy*] Ah—oo—ooh.

LUCY. Oh—I haven't told you, Alfred; mamma—*dear mamma* is here.

BATT. She has arrived then?

LUCY. In the 9:40 train.

BATT. We shall have a charming visit. I *love* her for your sake, Lucy—you remember those beautiful lines of Edgar Allan Poe, addressed to his wife's mother: [*Drawing her to him and quoting with tenderness*]

"My own mother . . .
Was but the mother of myself; but you
Are mother to the one I love so dearly,
And thus are dearer than the mother *I* knew
By that infinity with which my wife
Is dearer to my soul than its soul-life." Ah—oo—ooh. [*Ending the quotation with a yawn*]

ALL. Ah—oo—ooh. [*Batterson walks L. with Lucy and shows her out L.3.E. Batterson pauses*]

BATT. [*Pausing and looking after her*] Domestic bliss; it is the one bright thing on earth for which the angels envy us. [*Enter Mrs. Tuttle unperceived R.3.E.*] A-h—oo—ooh—[*Exit Batterson L.3.E.*]

SART. and FRED. Ah—oo—ooh.

MRS. T. [*Unperceived up R.C.*] I thought so! Business in New York! [*She disappears R.3.E.*]

FRED. I say, Sartewelle—

SART. Frederic.

FRED. Somehow, whenever you and I get into a scrape together, *I* always do all the lying, to get out of it—you only drop in a perfectly truthful remark, every now and then, and you come out of it just as well as I do.

SART. My dear Frederic, the religious poet, Herbert, has expressed my own sentiments in very beautiful language. "Dare to be true. Nothing can need a lie." In other words, stripped of poetic exaggeration, lies are not nearly as necessary in this world as people think they are—I consider it in good taste to avoid them.

FRED. Y-e-s—by utilizing other people's fibs.

SART. One well-told lie—and I can always depend on you for that—is like a family umbrella; it can cover two as well as it can one. When a shower comes on, my dear Fred, I merely accept your hospitality.

FRED. [*Rising and moving*] Well—I'll tell you what it is, Jack. I'm going to insist hereafter on your carrying your own umbrella.

SART. [*Rising and moving C.*] Just as you like, old boy; if you object to my using your lies after you've got through with them—but I consider it's damned uncivil. You must let me borrow an old umbrella, now and then.

FRED. Ha, ha, ha! All right—but I say, Jack—Ha, ha, ha!—poor Alfred!

SART. Ha, ha, ha! Poor Alfred!

FRED. He's fearfully used up this morning.

SART. Ha, ha, ha!

FRED. Ha, ha, ha! He was lively enough at the ball last night. Ha, ha, ha!

SART. Yes. Ha, ha, ha! He was lively enough at the ball.

FRED. When he was dancing a Highland fling. Ha, ha, ha!

SART. Ha, ha, ha! With the girl in the blue gaiters—ha, ha, ha!

FRED. Ha, ha, ha!

MRS. T. [*Appearing R.3.E. Aside*] Girl in the blue gaiters! Business in New York!—[*Disappears*]

FRED. It was about the liveliest masquerade I ever attended.

SART. Particularly lively. Ha, ha, ha!

FRED. Ha, ha, ha! By the way, [*Glancing about*] we're not in our own room, you know. [*They walk up, look R. and L. in the hall, etc. They turn down C.*] Some walls have ears—

SART. I've heard of such walls—devilish long ears, sometimes. Eyes, too—wall-eyes.

FRED. When walls *have* ears, they never keep a secret.

SART. Curious, too; they belong to the Masonic order.

FRED. No human being shall ever hear from *my* lips what went on last night.

SART. Nor from mine. [*They grasp hands and shake with solemn confidence. Then each puts his finger to his lips*]

FRED. [*Confidentially*] But wasn't it comical when General Compton—Ha, ha!—

SART. Ha, ha, ha, ha! I wouldn't have believed the old gentleman could be so lively. Ha, ha, ha!—when the sylph in pink satin knocked off his hat with the toe of her slipper—Ha, ha, ha!

FRED. Ha, ha, ha! He kicked it up and caught it on the top of his bald head as easily as if he were a hired dancer at the Jardin Mabille in Paris. Ha, ha, ha!

SART. Ha, ha, ha! The little witch in white, that you were waltzing around with! [*Punching him*]

FRED. The gazelle in violet you were with, in the corner!

BOTH. Ha, ha, ha, ha! Ah—oo—oo—oo—ooh. [*They look mysteriously over their shoulders R. and L., then at each other. They grasp hands and put their fingers to their lips*]

FRED. Mum's the word.

SART. Mum. [*They move R. and L. front. Enter Blanche R.U.E. She looks down through window*]

BLANCHE. [*Seeing gentlemen*] Oh—Jack!

SART. Blanche!

BLANCHE. Frederic. [*Looks out R. and calling*] Oh, Julia! They are both of them here. [*Comes in through door and down L., extending her hand frankly*] I'm real glad to see you, Jack. [*Julia appears in hall from R.*]

FRED. Julia!

JULIA. [*Coyly, without moving, but extending her hands*] Fred! [*Frederic runs up and walks down with her R.*]

SART. We were just talking about the girls—[*Frederic glances at him, startled*] weren't we, Fred?

FRED. [*Aside*] Jack tells the truth in a way that *would* shame the devil. [*Aloud*] Yes—we were just talking about *you* girls.

SART. [*Aside*] What an utterly unnecessary fib! Why can't Fred tell the truth, now and then—as I do.

BLANCHE. You and Fred were coming down yesterday evening with Cousin Alfred. *He* was detained on business [*Pouting*] but you *might* have come without him.

JULIA. Yes, we girls were so disappointed. You *might* have come without Alfred.

SART. Certainly—we—we— might have come without Alfred.

FRED. Yes, we might have come without Alfred, but—

SART. But—[*Hesitates and looks across to Frederic*]

FRED. [*Aside*] He's waiting for me to tell a lie. [*Aloud*] I—I—stayed up to work out a law case that comes up tomorrow—ah—oo—ooh.

SART. Ah—oo—ooh.

FRED. I—I—was reading in my room until after 4 o'clock—so that I could spend all today with you—

JULIA. Oh, Fred! You are *so* good.

FRED. I was all *alone* in my room. [*Glancing at Sartewelle. Aside*] I've locked the door on *him*.

BLANCHE. And can *you* plead so good an excuse, sir truant?

SART. I was detained for exactly the same reason that Frederic was.

BLANCHE. Oh! Dear Jack! You worked all night, too, so as to be with *me*.

FRED. [*Aside*] Jack's under *my* umbrella again! [*Aloud to Julia*] And now I shall claim my *reward*.

SART. [*To Blanche*] Yes—we claim our *reward*.

JULIA. [*Coyly*] Oh—but—not when we're—not while we—

BLANCHE. Not while we're all together, you know. Not for the world!

JULIA. Not for the world! [*Mrs. Tuttle reappears R.3.E. Moves down a few steps and stands up R.C. unperceived*]

FRED. But we're all of us *engaged*.

SART. Certainly; we're all engaged to each other.

BLANCHE. Yes, of course, we're all engaged—but—if—of course, if it were all at once.

JULIA. If it were all at once—so we couldn't see each other.

SART. One—two—

FRED. and SART. Three! [*They kiss the girls simultaneously—not suddenly, but holding the girls in their arms, and enjoyably, the girls facing away from each other R. and L.*]

MRS. T. Ahem. [*The girls start up and look around, chagrined*]

BLANCHE. Oh!

JULIA. Oh!

SART. Oh!

FRED. Oh! [*Enter Lucy L.3.E. followed by Batterson*]

LUCY. Mamma, dear!

MRS. T. Lucy! My child! [*With feeling, encircling her in her arms C.*] My *darling* child.

LUCY. Alfred and I are so happy to have you here—we have just been talking over your visit.

MRS. T. [*Still embracing her*] My darling child!

LUCY. Here is Alfred himself, mamma.

BATT. [*Advancing cordially and extending his hands*] My dear mother—[*Mrs. Tuttle draws up and looks him coldly in the eye*] I—I—I assure you—[*Advancing—hesitates*] I—my dear mother—I—I—[*He looks at her, then glances at the others, dumbfounded; turns and walks up L.C., bewildered and confused. Lucy looks at them completely puzzled and anxious. She looks at Batterson, then at her mother; moves to Batterson, confused*]

MRS. T. Lucy!

LUCY. [*Turning back to her*] Mother.

MRS. T. You have forgotten to introduce me to your friends.

LUCY. Oh—[*Glances back at Batterson*] Certainly. Miss Julia Douglass—one of my husband's wards—my mother, Mrs. Tuttle. [*They bow with due formality. Mrs. Tuttle suddenly moves to Julia, putting her arms about her and kissing her forehead*]

Mrs. T.   My poor child! [*Julia puzzled*]

Lucy.   Mr. Frederic Randolph, mamma. [*Frederic starts to bow pleasantly. Mrs. Tuttle draws up and looks at him fixedly*]

Fred. [*Confused, half bowing, hesitating, etc.*]   I—I am sure—I—very much honored—I—I—[*He makes a last effort to bow; glances around nervously; walks up R. and across to Batterson, up L.C.*]

Mrs. T. [*Turning L.*]   And this is your husband's *other* ward?

Lucy.   Miss *Blanche* Douglass, mamma. [*They bow. Mrs. Tuttle moves to her suddenly, takes her in her arms and kisses her forehead*]

Mrs. T.   My poor child! [*Blanche bewildered*]

Lucy.   Mr. John Sartewelle, mamma. [*Mrs. Tuttle draws up and stares at him. He stares; tries to bow several times but meets no response except a stony gaze and rigid form. He suddenly turns up L. and joins the other gentlemen. The three gentlemen put their heads together and appear in animated conversation, with lively gestures*]

Mrs. T. [*Turning*]   My daughter—I wish to speak with you—in—private. [*She sails up with great dignity and exits R.3.E. The gentlemen straighten out into a line and stare at her. Lucy moves up to door, looks back at the girls and at the group of gentlemen; exits R.3.E. The gentlemen again gather in a cluster with a sudden motion, gesticulating and talking. Blanche crosses to Julia R.*]

Blanche.   Julia! What *can* it all mean?

Julia.   What *do* you suppose *has* happened? [*They turn and look up at the gentlemen, who are gesticulating vigorously with their heads together*]

Blanche. [*Looking up across*]   A-h-e-m. [*The gentlemen stop suddenly. Sartewelle turns and looks at Blanche. He immediately turns back and the three go on gesticulating with heads together*] What *do* you think, Julia?

Julia.   I—I can't think anything. [*Looks across*] A-h-e-m. [*The gentlemen stop. Frederic looks around a moment, then back, and the gentlemen go on as before*]

Blanche.   *Something* has happened, *Julia!*

Julia.   I'm *sure* there has!

Blanche.   I'm dying of curiosity.

Julia.   So am I—just dying. [*Reenter Lucy R.3.E. She sails in with the air of an injured princess. She comes to a full stop up R.C. and looks at the party up L.C. The three gentlemen straighten out into a line, Batterson in the C. A moment's pause, Lucy looking at them with a queenly air*]

LUCY. [*Breaking down*] O-o-o-h. [*She moves down across L. Sobbing, with her face in her hands, she stands extreme L. Batterson starts down C.*]

JULIA. Lucy!

BLANCHE. Why, Lucy!

BATT. My wife! Lucy! [*Stepping towards her*] My dear wife! [*Lucy turns suddenly towards him. He stops abruptly*]

LUCY. Stand back, sir! [*He moves a step back, looking around, confused and troubled*] Important business in New York! [*With a lofty air*] Dancing the Highland fling [*He staggers back*] with a girl in blue gaiters! [*Batterson drops back upon sofa, R.C., limp and lifeless—in another second Frederic does the same in a chair up L.C.—Sartewelle the same up L. The girls start. A house bell is heard. Cutter comes in from hall L. and passes out R.3.E. Lucy moves up C. with a stately stride and to L.3.E.*] I go to my apartment, sir. Leave me alone with my grief. It is too sacred for such as you to disturb. [*Exit L.3.E.*]

BATT. [*Still limp on the sofa*] Domestic bliss! The angels don't envy me, now.

BLANCHE. Julia!

JULIA. Blanche! [*Enter Cutter R.3.E.*]

CUTT. Mrs. Tuttle sends her compliments—and will the young ladies do her the honor to visit 'er in 'er own h'apartment. [*Sartewelle and Frederic start to an erect sitting posture*]

BLANCHE. I—Cutter?

CUTT. Yes, miss.

JULIA. I—Cutter?

CUTT. Yes, miss—in 'er own h'apartment—h'immediately. [*Exits L.U.E. Blanche and Julia pass their arms about each other's waist and walk up R. Sartewelle and Frederic rise and look at them in a hopeless way*]

BLANCHE. [*Pleasantly, looking across*] We'll be back presently, Jack.

JULIA. [*Pleasantly*] We'll be back presently, Fred. [*Exit R.3.E. Sartewelle and Frederic walk down side by side to front of stage L., their hands thrust into their pockets and with a disconsolate air. They look at each other dismally*]

FRED. Jack.

SART. Fred.

FRED. *Some* walls have ears.

SART. And as you previously remarked—heigh-ho—when walls *have* ears they never keep a secret.

FRED. I—I am afraid—the—girls *will* be back.

SART. Heigh-ho—presently. [*Frederic passes to extreme L. Sartewelle strolls across to extreme R. dismally. Batterson starts suddenly from his limp position to a rigid, erect, sitting posture with a savage look, the others start and look at him*]

BATT. [*Sternly*] What—*does*—this—mean? [*The others turn away R. and L., scratching their heads. Batterson looks from one to the other*] How in the name of all that's miraculous, did my mother-in-law find out that I was dancing the Highland fling with a girl in blue gaiters, last night?

FRED. [*With deliberate distinctness*] I haven't the remotest idea.

SART. [*Quietly*] She undoubtedly overheard something. [*Frederic and Sartewelle glance at each other*]

BATT. [*Rising, with a tragic manner and raising his arm*] Hear me!—Ye mysterious powers of the air! Ye that whisper scandal through every zephyr, playing about the eager ears of the daughters of Eve. Hear me! Ye poisonous vapors—miasmatic exhalations that destroy domestic happiness!—I vow eternal enmity against every mother of every man's wife! Implacable hostility against the numberless legions of mothers-in-law that infest the planet Earth! —Against!—[*Thrusting his hands into his pockets*] my own mother-in-law in particular. [*He strides upstage, C. Stands up C. with his back to the audience, his head dropped. Reenter Blanche followed by Julia R.3.E. They walk slowly. They are struggling with pride and grief, looking down to the floor and catching their breath. When they arrive at C., they turn and walk down, side by side, their eyes still cast down. Blanche L., Julia R., they pause front, the picture of grief-stricken young creatures, striving to choke down their emotion, on account of their pride. They do not look up but turn partly, Blanche facing Frederic L., Julia facing Sartewelle R.*]

BLANCHE. I—I—[*Chokes*]

JULIA. I—[*Chokes*]

BLANCHE. [*Pathetically*] I was engaged to become your wife. I—[*Chokes. Frederic looks at her*]

JULIA. I—I promised to be your wife. I—[*Chokes. Sartewelle stares at her. Blanche raises her eyes mournfully; sees Frederic. Julia does the same—sees Sartewelle. They exchange glances—quietly, demurely and silently*]

BLANCHE. [*Pathetically*] We have discovered our mistake.

JULIA. Our—our bright young dreams—are—over.

BLANCHE. [*In tearful tones but not weeping*] A—a—gazelle in violet.

JULIA. Little witch in white.

BATT. [*Turning suddenly, up C.*] By the ghost of a French dressmaker! The old lady had all the particulars. She must have been there herself. [*Sartewelle and Frederic stand R. and L., abashed and silent*]

BLANCHE. We—we shall—never—marry anybody—now.

JULIA. Never! Anybody. [*They turn round and walk up C., side by side. They turn L. Blanche follows Julia out L.3.E. Each stops, looks back and gulps down her emotion before disappearing. The gentlemen look at each other, standing in a triangle. Batterson walks down to Frederic L.C. front lugubriously. Sartewelle crosses front, Batterson grasps the hands of both*]

BATT. Boys! We are all in the same boat.

SART. The boat is sinking.

FRED. And we three rats can't desert it.

BATT. Heigh-ho! The old cat has found us out. [*Sepulchrally*] I have murder in my thoughts—[*Looks from one to the other. A vigorous ring of doorbell. They all start*] The knocking at the gate—Macbeth. [*Cutter passes through hall from L. The gentlemen wheel back and look upstage. Cutter opens the door. Enter Mrs. Compton*]

MRS. C. [*Bowing*] Gentlemen.

BATT. Mrs. Compton.

FRED. and SART. Mrs. Compton. [*She passes down, stopping up R.C. Enter General Partridge Compton*]

COMPT. [*Standing in doorway and nodding cheerfully*] How are you, Batterson—Jack—Fred—boys! [*He is a red-faced, jolly-looking old cove*]

BATT., FRED. and SART. [*Lugubriously in succession*] General—General—General.

COMPT. [*After winking at them vigorously, still standing in doorway*] Ah—oo—ooh. [*Yawning. The three suddenly gather in a clump, with their heads together, conversing violently. Mrs. Compton stands up R.C., getting a card from her case. Cutter has passed in and stands L.C. General Compton walks down C. Looking at gentlemen*] A-h-e-m. [*They straighten out into a line. General Compton winks at them twisting up the side of his face very significantly. They only stare at him lugubriously*] Ah—oo—ooh. [*He winks again. They stare solemnly. He walks R. Aside*] Oh, I see. He, he, he! Conscience! The boys aren't used to it yet; it was the same with me at first—worse than a headache—that was a great many years ago—Ah—oo—ooh.

MRS. C. Cutter, [*Handing cards*] take our cards to Mrs. Stonehenge Tuttle. [*The three gentlemen suddenly gather into a clump again, talking vigorously. Cutter goes out with cards R.3.E.*] Of course, I needn't be formal with Lucy. I never send her a card.

COMPT. [*Looking across*] What the devil are those lunatics talking about now? [*Mrs. Compton moves down C. Stops; looks at the gentlemen*]

MRS. C. Ahem. [*The gentlemen straighten out*] How delightful for you and Lucy to have your mother with you, Mr. Batterson!

BATT. Yes—certainly—delighted.

FRED. and SART. Delightful.

MRS. C. Ah—heigh-ho—my own dear mother—the general was always so charmed to have her visit us.

COMPT. [*Moving to her*] I always loved her for your sake, my darling.

MRS. C. Ah—Partridge, *dear*!

COMPT. My own sweet pet! [*He pats her under the chin, she resting her head on his shoulder*]

MRS. C. [*Looking around*] Pardon us, gentlemen—but the general and I have never ceased to be lovers. [*Looking up at him*]

COMPT. A—h! [*Embracing her. Reenter Cutter R.3.E. General Compton walks R.*]

CUTT. Mrs. Stonehenge Tuttle sends her compliments to Mrs. Compton and to General Partridge Compton. She will see Mrs. Compton in her own h'apartment. [*The gentlemen gather in a clump*]

MRS. C. Her own apartment? Oh—Mrs. Tuttle and I were always such dear old friends. [*She moves up, Cutter holding open the door. She stops near door looking back at the clump of gentlemen*] Au revoir, gentlemen. [*They straighten out and bow. She bows. They all bow in line*] Back again presently, Partridge, dear.

COMPT. My love! [*Exits Mrs. Compton R.3.E. Cutter follows her out. General Compton R. winks and twists his face, putting a finger to his nose, etc. The others stare at him gloomily. General Compton stops and looks at them; repeats his winks, etc.*] Ah—oo—ooh. [*They stare solemnly. He walks C., looks at them a moment, and then bursts into laughter*] Ha, ha, ha, he, he, he, ho, ho!—[*Drops upon sofa, sitting back at his ease, looking at the others and laughing*] He, he, he, he, he! Ho, ho, ho!—why boys! You take it hard—you take it hard, boys. He, ho, he, he, he, ho, ho! You'll get over it, boys—you'll get over it—as you get older. Even I was that way once—that was a great many years ago. Ah—oo—ooh. He, he, he, he! Troubled conscience, boys?—he, he, he!—take my advice. The most inconvenient thing in this world for a man to carry about with him is a clear conscience. It is always in the way. A clear conscience gives a man as much trouble as a sensitive tooth. Get rid of it, boys! You all have a great many years before you—take the advice of an elderly man. You have a long and weary journey through life—don't burden yourself at the outset with the dead weight of a clear conscience. Ah—oo—ooh. Ha, he, he, ho, ho, ho! [*Rises and looks at them*] Oh—I see. A mortal terror of being found out. That is what I mean by the term "clear conscience." Listen to words of experience and wisdom, boys, from a joyous, light-hearted old reprobate. The surest way to be found out is to be in continual fear of it, and to wear an expression like that. *I* have never been found out in my life! [*The three gather suddenly into a clump. General Compton looks at them puzzled*] What the devil do you mean by that performance? [*They straighten out and look at him solemnly as before*] Ah—oo —ooh. He, he, he!—I'll give you a point, boys. Twenty years ago, I got into a chancery suit, about some railroad property in New Jersey. I've been down to New York, ever since, as often as I liked, to consult my lawyers about it. He, he, he, he! Five years ago, they came within an ace of deciding the case in my favor. I told my lawyer I wouldn't have that happen for fifty thousand dollars. We continued it indefinitely. He, ha, he, he! A railroad suit in New Jersey is a very convenient thing to have in the family. He, he, he, he! Ah— oo—ooh. [*Pauses and looks at them. They are still in a straight line staring dismally*] Oh—you'll get over this, boys—he, he, he!—In twenty years from now, you will laugh about these things as heartily as I do—ha, he, he, he, he! [*Glances at them*] He, he, he, ho, ho! Ho, ho, ho, ho!—[*He walks R., laughing heartily and unctuously. Mrs. Compton enters R.3.E. and walks down C. She stops C., drawing up with suppressed indignation and looks sternly at General Compton, he still laughing, not seeing her. He turns, sees her and stops laughing abruptly*]

BATT., SART. and FRED.   Ha, ha, ha, ha, ha, ha! [*Laughing in the semi-sepulchral, fiendish way of misery enjoying company, with sardonic expressions. Still standing in straight line. Mrs. Compton turns her head and looks at them. They stop abruptly*]

MRS. C. [*Turning on General Compton and speaking with dignified severity*]   A sylph in pink satin knocked off your hat with the toe of her slipper. [*General Compton falls back into sofa R.*]

BATT., SART. and FRED.   Ha, ha, ha, ha, ha! [*Mrs. Compton turns her head and looks at them. They stop abruptly*]

MRS. C. [*Severely*]   As for *you*, gentlemen—[*They face around with a common impulse and walk upstage in single file, passing out R.U.E. They stop on veranda and look in through window. To General Compton with dignity*] You kicked up your hat, and caught it on the top of your bald head, as easily as if you were a hired dancer at the Jardin Mabille in Paris. [*She turns, walks up C. and then to door L.*] Farewell, General Compton, farewell. [*Exits L.3.E. A pause, General Compton lying motionless on sofa R. Batterson's head appears at door C. He steps in and beckons back. Sartewelle and Frederic step in. The three move down L.C., looking at General Compton. The latter springs suddenly to his feet and faces them. He strides across, takes Batterson by the arm, leads him R. and faces him squarely*]

COMPT. [*Excitedly*] How did your mother-in-law, Mrs. Stonehenge Tuttle, find out that a bald sylph—a pink sylph in—a sylph in pink satin—knocked the toe of my—knocked the top of my bald hat off, sir!—with the toe of her slipper, sir?

BATT. The air! A bird whispered it to her—I haven't the remotest idea. [*Turns up R.*]

COMPT. A bird! Some damned parrot, sir—[*He strides across, leads Frederic R.*] perhaps *you* can solve this mystery?

FRED. [*Distinctly*] I haven't the faintest idea how the accident happened. [*General Compton strides across and stands face to face with Sartewelle L.*]

SART. I know as much about it as Frederic does. [*General Compton turns up L. Batterson strikes bell upon table up R.C. A moment's pause. Enter Cutter R.3.E.*]

BATT. Cutter, say to Mrs. Stonehenge Tuttle, that her daughter's husband and three other gentlemen desire to speak with her in the drawing-room. [*General attention to Batterson. Exit Cutter R.3.E. Batterson moves C. and continues in a stern tone*] Gentlemen: I am most sincerely grieved to take the course to which I have been forced. Under the circumstances, however, no other line of action is left open to me. Mrs. Stonehenge Tuttle arrived about half an hour ago. There is a return train for Bridgeport Junction at 11:10 this forenoon. [*Looking at his watch*] I shall request Mrs. Tuttle to have her baggage ready for that train. Her trunks are not unpacked, yet, I presume, and it will put her to but little inconvenience. It is a hard duty, gentlemen—but my resolution is taken.

COMPT. [*Stepping to Batterson and taking his hand*] Batterson, my boy—I am with you. I shall never hear the whistle of the 11:10 train without a thrill of delight. As to the 9:45 train this way—in which that woman arrived—it'll wake me up every morning with a shudder. I shall order my servant hereafter, to bring me my soda and water regularly at that hour, instead of 12:30. [*Walking L.*]

FRED. [*Moving to Batterson*] I will stand by you, Alfred. [*Moves L.*]

SART. You may depend upon me, Alfred. [*Moves L. Reenter Cutter R.3.E. The three other gentlemen stand L., Batterson C.*]

CUTT. Mrs. Stonehenge Tuttle wishes me to say that she will be h'in the drawing-room—h'immediately. [*Batterson springs to the others, standing extreme L. Exit Cutter L.U.3. The four gentlemen stand in a line down L. facing the door R.3.E.*]

BATT. [*Folding his arms*] I am resolved.

COMPT. We are resolved.

FRED. and SART. [*Quietly but firmly*] Resolved. [*Enter Mrs. Stonehenge Tuttle R.3.E. The gentlemen straighten up stiffly. She moves sternly down and stands C. looking them firmly in the face. A moment's pause. The four gentlemen suddenly gather in a clump, with heads together, and converse in dumb show as if consulting on what to do first—being taken without sufficient preparation*]

MRS. T. Well, gentlemen! [*They straighten out, facing her. She draws up majestically and folds her arms*] I am at your service, gentlemen. [*They stare at her a moment, look from one to the other, show increasing signs of nervousness. General Compton sneaks upstage and goes out R.U.3., passing out beyond window. Light music. Sartewelle follows; then Frederic. Batterson tries to speak to Mrs. Tuttle, weakens; moves up, turns, tries again; exits R.U.E. Mrs. Tuttle has turned towards him and stands C. with back to audience as curtain descends. If curtain is called, Mrs. Tuttle should stand alone in C. of stage, facing audience, her arms folded, mistress of the situation. All the others gone*]

N.B. The following handwritten note appears at the end of the text; it is not certain whether it is intended to be a substitute for "Light music" above, or is to accompany curtain call: "Music heavy. 'Hail to the Chief,' or, 'Hold the Fort'."

ACT II.

SCENE: *Same as in Act I. At rise of curtain stage is empty. Serious music. "Heart Bowed Down," with a burlesque tinge, till end of first business. Batterson appears at side of the center door R. He looks about, as if to see that the coast is clear. He steps in and moves down. Frederic appears and steps in. Sartewelle appears; he steps in. General Compton follows. The four seated down front, General Compton R., Batterson R.C., Frederic L.C., Sartewelle L. They look at each other alternately a moment lugubriously. Batterson rises, walks up C., closes the center doors and locks them. He moves to door, L.3.E., locks it, crosses and locks door R.3.E. The music ceases as Batterson resumes his seat.*

BATT. [*Sepulchrally*] Have you any remarks to make, gentlemen?
COMPT. *I* don't think of anything in particular to say.
FRED. Nothing occurs to *me*.
BATT. Gentlemen—we are all in a very uncomfortable position.
ALL THE OTHERS. Very.
BATT. My respected mother-in-law—
THE OTHERS. M'm.

BATT. I never had the pleasure of seeing Mr. Stonehenge Tuttle—but I feel justified in saying that my wife takes after her father. I am convinced, gentlemen, that the position of *Mrs.* Stonehenge Tuttle in this house is impeccable, until we—we—until we arrange matters pleasantly with our respective wives and sweethearts.

COMPT. Yes—certainly—pleasantly.

SART. and FRED. Pleasantly.

BATT. Our recent defeat—

COMPT. Rout.

FRED. and SART. Panic.

BATT. Our recent failure was the necessary result of the untenable position which we then occupied. There is another train for Bridgeport Junction [*Looking at his watch*] at 12:15—but it is useless to proceed in that direction, until we have come to a complete and perfect understanding with the ladies —the—the ladies to whom—we—we are—respectively—

SART. and FRED. Attached.

COMPT. Fettered.

BATT. By all the laws of honor and affection.

COMPT. By the laws of New York.

BATT. I am sorry to say, gentlemen, that I see but one way to accomplish the desired result. Heigh-ho—[*sepulchrally*] I grieve to say it, gentlemen, but we must tell more lies.

COMPT. [*Cheerfully*] By all means.

FRED. [*With alacrity*] Of course. More lies.

COMPT. The only thing that puzzles me is what kind of a lie to tell.

FRED. That's the only thing.

COMPT. I've depended on my railroad suit in New Jersey so long—I'm a trifle rheumatic. At your age, young gentlemen, my invention was as light in the legs as a three-year-old colt. I could take in a five-barred gate just for exercise. Heigh-ho. I can't lie as I used to—heigh-ho—[*Shaking his head*] I'm growing old.

SART. [*Quietly*] I would suggest [*All turn towards him giving marked attention*], merely a suggestion, gentlemen—the only light accomplishment on which I pride myself is telling the truth; but in case you think it absolutely necessary in the present instance to vary from the strict letter of the truth—I would suggest that the first object of your solicitation is to come to an exact and perfect agreement as to the precise story you are all to tell.

THE OTHERS IN TURN. [*Looking at each other*] True—of course.

SART. The day after tomorrow is the anniversary of Mr. Batterson's wedding.

Batt. Heigh-ho—it is!—the anniversary of the day on which I pledged myself to love, honor, and cherish the admirable woman whom I have so deeply wronged. [*Bowing his head on his hand*]

Sart. I would suggest—merely a suggestion, gentlemen—that we *might* have been preparing a surprise for Mr. Batterson's wife on the occasion of that anniversary. [*Batterson looks up suddenly, the others start*] We *might* have been rehearsing a parlor vaudeville—a dress rehearsal—at the house of some friend in New York.

Batt. [*Starting to his feet*] Mrs. Dalrymple McNamara! She is a member of the Murray Hill Dramatic Club.

Compt. [*Starting up*] A dress rehearsal!

Fred. [*Starting up*] A vaudeville! We can do *anything* in a vaudeville! Ha, ha, ha! [*Walks up L., pleased*]

Compt. Certainly—once get the vaudeville in—and we can lie indefinitely. Ha, ha! [*Walks up R., pleased*] Ha, ha!

Batt. A surprise for my wife! Mrs. McNamara is my best friend in New York. A dress rehearsal—the Murray Hill Dramatic Club—at her house! I'll write her a letter—tell her all—she will sustain everything we say when she meets the other ladies. A vaudeville! We have all the characters. I was dancing a Highland fling, with a girl in blue gaiters. Quite possible in a vaudeville.

Compt. Ha, ha, ha! Nothing more natural—in a vaudeville.

Fred. Perfectly natural—in a vaudeville. I was in a corner, with a little witch in white. Nothing more simple—in a vaudeville.

Compt. Ha, ha, ha! Perfectly simple—in a vaudeville. Ha, ha, ha!

Sart. I might have been—I don't say I was, gentlemen, but I might have been—waltzing with a gazelle in violet in a vaudeville.

Batt. and Fred. All perfectly natural—in a vaudeville.

Compt. Ha, ha, ha! Nothing more likely, perfectly natural—in a vaudeville! Ha, ha, ha!—and I—I—[*pausing suddenly, scratches his head*] a sylph in pink satin, knocked off my hat with the toe of her slipper!

All. [*With sudden seriousness*] Ah—oh—m'm—ah.

Batt. That *isn't* quite so natural—in a vaudeville.

Fred. That *is* a trifle awkward.

Batt. Very.

Compt. We can do *most* things in a vaudeville, but how the deuce can I get a sylph in pink satin to knock off my hat with the toe of her slipper—in Mrs. McNamara's drawing-room?

All. [*Except Sartewelle*] Ah—m'm—ah.

Sart. [*Quietly*] Possibly, General Compton was dancing with a lady dressed in pink satin, he may have stumbled and fallen. [*General Compton starts*] The lady in pink satin may have knocked off his hat with the toe of her slipper—by an accident—in a vaudeville. [*General Compton rushes across L. and grasps Sartewelle's hand*]

COMPT. My friend—my dear young friend! You have lifted a load from my shoulders—or rather from my head. You have enabled me to get my hat off without carrying the hair with it. I couldn't have done it better, myself, at your age. For a straight out-and-out, well-constructed lie—

SART. I beg your pardon—it is merely a suggestion.

COMPT. Call it what you please, my boy. Spell it any way you like. Authorities differ. [*Walking across R., Batterson strikes the bell on table R.C.*]

BATT. Gentlemen—I will meet you in the billiard-room, presently. [*The others walk up, Batterson drops into a chair, the others find themselves locked in*]

COMPT. I say, Batterson—

BATT. Eh! [*Looking back*] Oh—I beg your pardon, gentlemen. [*He moves up, takes a key from his pocket; opens the door. Cutter is standing in hall C.*]

CUTT. Ring, sir? [*He steps aside R. General Compton, Frederic, and Sartewelle pass out L.U.E. Cutter steps in and stands L.C.*]

BATT. [*Moving down and dropping into seat R.C.*] Say to Mrs. Batterson, Cutter, that her husband—her husband—desires to meet her in the drawing-room.

CUTT. Yes, sir. [*He moves to door L.3.E. Finds it locked*] H'I beg your pardon, sir—

BATT. Eh? Ah. [*He moves up, takes a key from his pocket; unlocks the door, Cutter passes out. Batterson moves down and drops into a chair R.C.*] A lie lays as many eggs as a spider; and they are all hatched with more certainty. I little dreamed, when I wrote to Lucy, yesterday afternoon, and told her I was detained in New York on business that I should be obliged to go on, from the point I began, and construct an entire cobweb of falsehood. And worst of all—I've got to *act* a falsehood, now. [*Enter Lucy L.3.E. As she enters, Batterson glances at her and springs up, assuming a rigid and composed attitude R. Lucy walks down L.C. sadly with bowed head and slow step. When down front she raises her head, draws up, looks at him and then away*]

LUCY. You wished to see me—Mr.—Batterson? [*He glances at her, then slowly thrusts his hands into his pockets and walks up R.C. as if thinking. He turns, glances at her; moves down scratching his head, glancing up at her, once or twice as he comes down*]

Batt. [*Aside*] I'm so unused to this kind of business—I hardly know how to begin. [*Aloud*] I—I—I am at a loss how to address you, madam.

Lucy. [*Looking steadily before her*] I do not wonder at your embarrassment.

Batt. I—I wished to say, madam—that—that (*Hesitates—then aside*] Oh, hang it!—I've got to do it—my entire future depends on it!—[*Aloud*] that your recent conduct surprised me—surprised me, madam, surprised me! [*Aside*] I've *begun* with a truth, anyway. I was never more surprised in my life.

Lucy. You *were* surprised—I doubt not—at learning your perfidy was discovered.

Batt. [*Aside*] She has hit it exactly. [*Aloud, drawing up*] Perfidy, madam? [*He walks up R.C.*]

Lucy. You were surprised, perhaps, that she whom you had deceived, should show the natural indignation of a betrayed and outraged woman.

Batt. [*Aside, up R. lugubriously*] I wish there was a dose of prussic acid within reach.

Lucy. And what of *my* "surprise," sir?—the surprise of a confiding young wife?—

Batt. [*Aside*] If I had a revolver in my hand at this moment—

Lucy. To find that he who had pledged to her his honor and his love— [*Batterson groans*] had spent the idle hours of the previous night—in a place of debauchery and vice!—[*Her head in her hands and sobbing*]

Batt. Debauchery—vice!

Lucy. [*Choking*] A—a—dancing a Highland fling, sir—with a girl in blue gaiters! [*Sobbing*]

Batt. Blue!—[*Springing towards her with a tragic air*] gaiters—*vice*— ha!—I see it all!—I see it all. [*He staggers R. and falls into a chair R.C., as if overcome with emotion. She turns and stares at him. He continues—aside*] I flatter myself I did that pretty well for an amateur liar. Compton, himself, couldn't have done it better—in *his* professional way.

Lucy. Alfred!—I—Alfred!—[*Moving towards him*] you see it all?

Batt. I—see—it—all! [*Aside*] I'm glad *she doesn't*. [*Aloud, waving his hand backwards towards her*] To think that a mere whisper—a mere accidental coincidence of words—I see it all!—should destroy the confidence which years of devotion had created between us!

Lucy. Alfred—do speak! *Have* I misunderstood the truth?

Batt. [*Aside*] I wish she had.

Lucy. Speak, Alfred, tell me everything!

BATT. [*Aside*] Tell her everything! Lies!—lies! I *taste* them now in my throat.

LUCY. Alfred! Our future happiness—

BATT. [*Aside*] Our future happiness! She has administered the necessary emetic. [*Aloud and rapidly*] We were all at the house of Mrs. Dalrymple McNamara last evening. We were preparing a vaudeville—to surprise you on the anniversary of our marriage—day after tomorrow—it was a full dress rehearsal—I danced a Highland fling with one of Mrs. McNamara's lady friends—she had blue gaiters on! [*Aside with a sigh of relief*] I feel better now.

LUCY. Alfred!—Alfred!—[*Tearfully*] Forgive me!—Alfred! my husband [*dropping on her knees, and burying her face in his lap sobbing*], forgive me!

BATT. Oh, hang it, I wasn't looking for this, I can never stand this. Lucy! [*She sobs*] Lucy—[*Starting to his feet and throwing her back and staring down at her*] Lucy!

LUCY. [*Starting up and looking up into his face*] Alfred?

BATT. If you love me, Lucy—[*Crossing L.*] don't ask *me* to forgive *you*. [*Aside*] If the woman keeps on that sort of thing I shall certainly blow my brains out.

LUCY. But, Alfred—

BATT. Yes-yes-yes-yes! That's all right, my dear—you forgive me—that's all right—you forgive me—I understand.

LUCY. I? Forgive you?—for what?

BATT. For—[*Glancing at her—then away*] for deceiving you.

LUCY. Oh! ha, ha, ha!—you were doing it all for my happiness, Alfred. You rogue! Business in New York—and I—to think what a return I was making for your kindness—you—you did it all for me, Alfred—[*Wiping her eyes*] I misunderstood you entirely. You were doing it all for me.

BATT. [*After a sheepish, conscience-smitten look—glancing over his shoulder*] Say you forgive me, Lucy.

LUCY. I—forgive—*you*?

BATT. Say you forgive me.

LUCY. Why—I—ha, ha, ha, ha, ha!—of course, if you will insist, Alfred—I—ha, ha, ha!—*dear* Alfred! [*Going to him*]

BATT. My love!

LUCY. [*Resting in his arms*] You spent all the long weary night away from your comfortable home—and *me*—just to make me happy. [*Batterson looks away uncomfortably*] I *thank* you, Alfred—I *thank* you.

BATT. Don't mention it, my love.

Lucy. And you are quite sure that *you* forgive—[*Batterson puts his hand over her mouth quickly*] You are certain you for—[*He covers her mouth again; kisses her*] Ah—*dear* Alfred!—you are such a kind generous *faithful* creature.

Batt. Y-e-s. [*Turning with her and walking up C., his arms about her waist*]

Lucy. We shall be *so* happy, after this.

Batt. Y-*e-s*—so happy—heigh-ho—after this.

Lucy. [*Starting suddenly as they get up C.*] Oh—I will run and tell mamma about it, at once. [*Runs to door R.3.E.*]

Batt. Ah—my dear—

Lucy. Why—the—door is locked. [*She looks at Batterson. He looks at her a moment, then draws the key out of his pocket and hands it to her. She looks from him to the door and the key, puzzled, moving towards him*]

Batt. I thought best that we shouldn't be interrupted—when I sent for you, my love.

Lucy. Oh, yes—I see. [*Taps him on the cheek and kisses him. He receives her caresses with a guilty look. She returns, puts in the key and opens door*] Mamma will be delighted to hear the truth.

Batt. Ah—Lucy. [*She looks at him*] It has just occurred to me—that—the —the young folks haven't made it up yet, you know. You might tell your mother—afterwards.

Lucy. Oh—why, certainly! Their happiness must not be delayed an instant. [*Runs across L.*] I will send them to the drawing-room at once—you must go for Jack and Frederic!—[*Runs to him, throwing her arms over his shoulders*] You darling generous fellow!—you are quite sure you forgive— [*He covers her mouth and kisses her. She runs L.*] I'll send down the girls for *their* happiness at once. You dear, good, innocent man! [*Kisses her hand and runs out L.3.E. Batterson looks after her a moment. Then looks front, dolefully*]

Batt. Somehow—I—I don't feel much better than I did before it was all settled. [*Walking down*] I shall send for the coachman and order him to kick me out of the house. I'm half inclined to do it myself. Heigh-ho—now I must write a letter to Mrs. Dalrymple McNamara, elucidating the entire conspiracy and throwing ourselves on her mercy. [*With a sudden thought*] By the way—there's still another lie!—I forgot that. I must ask her to write me a letter, in reply, saying that one of her lady friends is taken suddenly ill, and the vaudeville cannot possibly come off. Heigh-ho—I suppose I shall have to keep on lying about this, one way and another for the rest of my natural life. The original lie will go down to posterity as an heirloom in the family. I am an utterly disgusted man. [*Exits hall L.U.E. Enter Blanche and Julia L.3.E.*]

BLANCHE. What *can* Lucy mean by—

JULIA. She wouldn't tell us a thing!

BLANCHE. Only to come down to the drawing-room and meet Fred and Jack for ourselves.

JULIA. She seemed *so* happy, herself—and before that she had done nothing but cry.

BLANCHE. Yes—that's—what—all of us have been doing. [*Crying*]

JULIA. Yes—we—we—we've all been—crying to—to—to—together. [*Crying*]

BLANCHE. I—I—I don't intend to stop crying—

JULIA. Nor—nor—nor I—

BLANCHE. Until—until—something very—remarkable—and—and unexpected—happens.

BOTH. [*Half up R.C.*] O—o—o—o—h. [*Sobbing. Enter Frederic and Sartewelle L.U.E. They stop up L.C., looking at the girls. The girls see them; stop crying suddenly; draw up with dignity, and move down together R. They stand side by side, facing the audience squarely, erect and firm, holding back their tears, as in Act I. Frederic nudges Sartewelle to proceed. Sartewelle nudges Frederic*]

FRED. [*Apart*] Go on, Sartewelle—*you* begin. This is *your* lie, you know. You constructed it.

SART. I beg your pardon. It was merely a suggestion on my part. Proceed.

FRED. I'll be hanged, if I'm going to do all the lying—for both of us—any more. Besides, your way of telling the truth is so much more certain to conceal the facts.

SART. My dear Fred—if I find your lie doesn't cover the whole ground, I'll piece it out with the truth—and make the deception complete. [*The girls suddenly face around, standing shoulder to shoulder and looking straight across at the gentlemen*]

BLANCHE. *Well*—young gentlemen?

JULIA. *Well*—young gentlemen.

FRED. We both wanted to meet you girls, so that we could explain to you— [*Sartewelle pulls his coat sleeve and whispers in his ear*] I mean—so that *you* could explain to *us*—your very remarkable conduct towards us.

SART. [*Coolly and quietly*] If you have any explanation of that conduct, young ladies, we shall be very glad to hear it.

FRED. We do not wish to be severe with you.

SART. Certainly *not*.

FRED. We know that you are thoughtless, quick-headed young girls—

SART. [*Complacently*] Only *young* girls.

FRED. —And we are perfectly ready to forgive you.

SART. We are quite willing to forgive you. [*The girls look at each other, taken aback and bewildered. They suddenly fall on each other's neck*]

BOTH GIRLS. [*Sobbing*] Oh—oh—oh—o-o-h! [*Frederic and Sartewelle walk upstage, with an air of conscious triumph. They turn down with the manner of pretentious magnanimity. Choking and sobbing on each other's neck*] M—m—m—o—o—o—o—h.

FRED. These tears—these tears convince us that you feel the wrong you did us.

SART. They convince us that you are truly repentant. [*The girls both draw up indignantly, dashing the tears from their eyes with their handkerchiefs. Blanche moves quickly to Sartewelle and draws up before him as if to express herself, choking with indignation. He looks at her steadily and quietly. She returns, R.C., and stands facing the audience. Patting her foot, Julia then does the same business with Frederic and returns R. standing like Blanche*]

BLANCHE. [*To Sartewelle*] You were in a corner, sir—with a "gazelle in violet."

JULIA. [*To Frederic*] *You* were waltzing around, sir—with a "little witch in white."

BLANCHE. Repentant, indeed—*we* repentant!

JULIA. The wrong *we* did *you*!

FRED. O-h!—precisely!—Ha, ha, ha, ha, ha, ha, ha!—

SART. O-h!—exactly—Ha, ha, ha, ha, ha, ha, ha!—

BOTH. [*Looking at each other, etc.*] Ha, ha, ha, ha, ha, ha, ha!—

FRED. Julia!—you're not *really jealous*?

SART. You're not really *jealous,* Blanche?

BLANCHE. Jealous!—jealous of such creatures as those!—No!

JULIA. Certainly *not*!

THE GENTLEMEN. Ha, ha, ha, ha, ha!—

FRED. Why—Julia! Ha, ha, ha! I confess it. I *was* waltzing around last night with a "little witch in white."

SART. And I was in a corner with a "gazelle"—if you like—"in violet."

BOTH. Ha, ha, ha!—

FRED. I confess it, Julia—and so *you* are *jealous*! Ha, ha, ha! My little witch was a beautiful brunette—her hair and her eyes as black as ebony—her skin! —of that rare olive hue, which so seldom blooms under an American sun. Ha, ha, ha!

SART. [*Aside*] She was the lightest kind of a blonde. How utterly unnecessary to change her entire complexion. [*Aloud*] *You* were *jealous,* Blanche? I confess to the gazelle. Ha, ha, ha—she had auburn hair—of a delicate golden tint—[*Frederic starts and looks at him*] brushed smoothly over the forehead, with a little curl or two peeping out above the ear; their sister curls fell over her neck in a cluster. Her complexion—a dainty blending of white and pink—her eyes were blue; her nose a trifle aquiline, pearl earrings in her ears; her dress—"violet," as you say—was cut—

FRED. [*Moving to him suddenly and seizing him by the arm*] Hang it, Jack—you're giving an exact description of the girl!

SART. Why not?

FRED. You're edging too near the facts.

SART. My dear Frederic, the nearer we come to the facts the more certain they are to overlook them.

FRED. Well, don't get too near.

BLANCHE. Gentlemen, we have heard you.

JULIA. We have heard you.

BLANCHE. You, Mr. John Augustin Sherbrooke Sartewelle, confess to the gazelle in violet.

JULIA. You, Mr. Frederic Effingham Randolph, confess to the little witch in white.

BLANCHE. You have described them accurately.

SART. Accurately.

BLANCHE. Possibly you can also inform us, gentlemen, what these have to do with certain law cases—

JULIA. Certain law cases!

BLANCHE. Which are to come up tomorrow.

JULIA. And you were both engaged upon them until four o'clock in the morning.

BLANCHE. So you could spend today with us.

GENTLEMEN. Ha, ha, ha, ha, ha!

FRED. Oh, certainly!

SART. By all means!

FRED. But we—we *did* hope to keep it a secret.

SART. We didn't *intend* to tell you.

THE GIRLS. We dare say—not.

SART. You absolutely insist?

THE GIRLS. We certainly do.

SART. Oh—very well then—I will—

FRED. [*Stopping him, apart*] Let *me* do that, I'm afraid you *will* tell the truth—through the sheer force of a bad habit. [*Aloud, crossing to Julia*] You see, Julia, we were going to give you a surprise.

THE GIRLS. You did.

FRED. [*R.C.*] What we said to you before was only a blind, Julia.

JULIA. [*R.*] That's just what we thought it was.

SART. [*L.*] We weren't studying law at all.

BLANCHE. [*L.C.*] We suspected as much.

FRED. We were at the house of Mrs. Dalrymple McNamara in Thirty-fourth Street, New York, last evening—rehearsing for a vaudeville—to be performed at Honeysuckle Villa—the day after tomorrow—for Cousin Lucy's wedding anniversary! [*The girls have turned towards them joyfully*] We were only keeping it from you, because we thought you would enjoy the vaudeville more if you weren't expecting it.

SART. We thought you'd be happier if you didn't know what we were really doing.

JULIA. Oh, Fred! Forgive me! [*Running to him*] Forgive me for suspecting you.

FRED. I *do* forgive you.

BLANCHE. [*To Sartewelle*] Jack—dear Jack!

SART. I forgive you, Blanche. [*They walk up with the girls*]

FRED. Julia!

SART. Blanche! [*They embrace their girls respectively up C., shaking hands with each other as they do so. Exit R.U.3. General Compton appears in hall from L.U.E.; he looks out R. after the others, then front, then out again*]

COMPT. By Jove!—Ha, ha! It is working to a charm. [*He walks down with a confident air; strikes the bell on the table R.C.*] Ha, ha! Mrs. Dalrymple McNamara—[*Walking L.*] Vaudeville—full dress rehearsal—[*Walking R.*] Ha, ha! All I have to do, is to get my hat knocked off—naturally and gracefully—by the toe of the slipper—of one of Mrs. McNamara's lady friends. Ha, ha! It is working to a charm. [*Enter Cutter L.U.E.*] Cutter—say to Mrs. Compton—that General Compton—her *dear* Partridge, Cutter—[*Winking at him, Cutter winks back*] wishes to see her in the drawing-room at once—her *dear* Partridge, Cutter.

CUTT. [*Going*] Her *dear* Partridge. [*Exits L.3.E.*]

COMPT. Ha, ha! I rather enjoy this. Vaudeville—Mrs. Dalrymple McNamara—full dress rehearsal. I enjoy this. It reminds me of my youthful days before I settled permanently into the railroad suit. It wakes me up—Ha, ha! It sets the blood stirring in my veins. I was getting rheumatic. Ah—those youthful days! Those halcyon days of early matrimony! Ha, ha! I could get into more scrapes and get out of them sooner than any other man the entire length of Fifth Avenue. Ha, ha! That night young Hackencrest and I—Ha, ha, ha, he, he, he! What a terrific scandal that created among the friends of Mrs. Hackencrest, for ten years afterwards! Hackencrest was a bungler. I was in the same scrape. On the next Sunday the parson referred pathetically in his sermon to the melancholy accident that had detained Colonel Partridge Compton in New York—Mrs. C. had been summoned to the city by telegraph. Ha, ha, ha, he, he! Those delicious days! I positively enjoy this—I feel twenty years younger than I did this morning. [*Rubbing his hands and skipping lightly to R. Enter Mrs. Compton L.3.E. He turns and draws up with dignified composure and watches her, she hesitates up L.C., looks at him, moves down with a rigid step L.*] I asked the servant to express my desire that you should come into my presence—in order that we might—ah—in reference to a matter—concerning which—it is evident—you—have—at present—an erroneous impression. We misunderstand each other, madam.

MRS. C. On the contrary, sir—we understand each other perfectly. [*General Compton winks, aside to the audience*] I have no erroneous impression, whatever.

COMPT. [*Aside*] Mrs. General Compton is correct. [*He walks up R.C., turns*] From the few words—the very few words, madam—which you addressed to me at our last meeting—and from your manner, madam, I conclude that you imagine—you imagine, madam—that I have been guilty of conduct and association unbecoming to myself—both as a man—and as your husband.

MRS. C. Your conclusion is correct, sir.

COMPT. I can recall nothing whatever in my previous life, madam, to justify you in reaching such a conclusion. Notwithstanding the utter groundlessness of your suspicion, madam—I will explain—I will so far demean myself as to explain, madam—the—the—the somewhat peculiar—I will even say—the *very* peculiar—circumstances, to which you so briefly referred.

MRS. C. Very peculiar circumstances, indeed, General Compton!

COMPT. Mr. Batterson and myself—with the two young gentlemen—were present last evening—

MRS. C. At a full dress rehearsal of a vaudeville, at the residence of Mrs. Dalrymple McNamara in New York. So I have been "informed."

COMPT. Oh!

MRS. C. Mrs. Lucy Batterson has just been giving me the "facts" as recited by her own husband. I was about to ask her, if her husband had explained *your* connection with the story—as well as his own—when we were interrupted by the servant with your message. There *are some* things, General

Compton [*Drawing up*] which cannot be done—by a lady in good society— even when she is rehearsing for a vaudeville. The story is a very ingenious one—but *I* find it quite impossible—to put this and that together.

Compt. Madam—my dear madam—my dear Mrs. Partridge—my dear Maria—is it for this, that I have been an example among men, for the last quarter of a century, of conjugal devotion, and fidelity? Is it for this, that I have cast aside those pleasures of the world—so dear to less constant husbands? Is it for this—Maria!—is it for this, that I have interested myself in nothing that did not contribute to our mutual happiness; is it for this—is it for this, madam, that I have spent the long and weary hours of last night, poring with a lawyer over the musty documents of our railroad suit in New Jersey?

Mrs. C. [*Turning suddenly upon him*] Our—railroad—suit—in New Jersey. [*General Compton taken back; looks confused and crestfallen*]

Compt. After we left the rehearsal, my love. [*Walks down R. Aside*] I shouldn't have made a stumble like that, twenty years ago. Heigh-ho—I'm growing old. [*Aloud*] I went to our lawyer's *after* we left the rehearsal, my love. By the way, my dear—now that you know all about the matter, we— we intended it for a surprise, you know—we didn't intend to let any of the ladies here know anything about it—but now that you have discovered—I— he, he, he! I must tell you about a very funny incident that happened at the rehearsal—He, he, he! It was *such* a joke on me! He, he, he! The vaudeville is an original one written for the occasion by Sartewelle; [*Aside*] I must tell Jack of that so *he'll* say the same thing—[*Aloud*] We all have to dance and sing in it. He, he, he! You ought to have seen me dancing around the room with—with—Mrs.—Mrs.—Grafton Chipchase—wife of Captain Chipchase of the regular army.

Mrs. C. Ah—m'm—Mrs. Captain Chipchase was there. She is about your age. She was in the cast?

Compt. Yes, my dear. [*Aside*] I must drop a line to Mrs. Captain Chipchase. [*Aloud*] Mrs. Captain Chipchase and I were dancing an Irish jig near the end of the second act—the scene is laid in Ireland—[*Aside*] I must tell Sartewelle of that. [*Aloud*] He, he, he, he, he, he! It was such a joke on me. He, he, he, he! [*Dropping upon the sofa*] Everybody laughed so—they put it into the play! He, he, he, he! I was dancing down the center and—he, he, he, he, he, he—and Mrs. Captain Chipchase was doing a double shuffle down in the front. [*Aside*] I must tell Mrs. Captain Chipchase of that. [*Aloud*] And —and—he, he, he—I—I—I—I stumbled and fell! He, he, he, he—but that wasn't the fun of it—he, he, he, he—Mrs. Captain Chipchase didn't see me— he, he, he, he, he—and she—he, he, he, he—she knocked off my hat with the toe of her *slipper!* He, he, he, he—[*Mrs. Compton turns suddenly and looks at him*] The shoemaker hadn't finished her Irish brogans—ha, ha, ha, ha—It was *such* a joke on me!

MRS. C. General Compton!

COMPT. My love.

MRS. C. You—you really say that—that—

COMPT. [*Innocently*] Yes, my love—and I jumped up and I kicked the hat up in the air—and I caught it on my bald head—he, he, he—they put it in the play.

MRS. C. My poor, darling, dear Partridge! [*Running to him. He springs up and catches her in his arms*]

COMPT. [*Aside, over her shoulder*] I never had such a time making two ends meet in my life. [*Reenter Lucy L.3.E.*]

LUCY. [*Seeing them embracing*] Oh, I'm *so* glad! *You* are happy, too!

MRS. C. Oh—my darling Lucy! [*Going to her, they kiss*] General Compton has explained everything.

COMPT. Everything.

MRS. C. It was only Mrs. Captain Chipchase that kicked off my husband's hat.

COMPT. [*Aside*] Captain Chipchase will challenge me to a mortal combat.

MRS. C. My *dear* Partridge [*Going to him*], *can* you forgive me?

COMPT. I can, my dear—I am the soul of magnanimity. Ladies, I must leave you to congratulate each other. [*Aside*] I must go and tell Sartewelle he is the author of that play. [*Going*]

MRS. C. *Dear Partridge.*

COMPT. [*Stopping up C. and she goes to him*] My love. [*They embrace. He moves upstage. Aside, as he goes up*] The scene is laid in Ireland. [*He steps aside at door to let Blanche and Julia pass. They come tripping in from L.U.E., joyfully*]

BOTH GIRLS. [*Nodding*] General Compton!

COMPT. Girls! [*Aside*] I feel twenty years younger. [*Exits R.U.E. The girls trip down and kiss the other ladies. A general kissing scene. Every lady kisses every other*]

LUCY. We're all so happy!

THE TWO GIRLS. So happy!

BLANCHE. Everything is explained.

MRS. C. Everything.

BLANCHE. What fools we all were, to be sure!

ALL. Ha, ha, ha, ha!

MRS. C. To suspect such darling creatures—

LUCY. When they were sacrificing themselves for *our* happiness.

MRS. C. Doing it all for us.

ALL. The darling creatures!

LUCY. I—I feel so happy! I—I—can almost cry.

JULIA and BLANCHE. I, too.

MRS. C. So can I. [*Dashing tears from their eyes*]

LUCY. [*Suddenly listening*] Carriage wheels! Someone is coming up the drive. [*Moving up*] We are not expecting anyone today. [*She looks out of the window upstage*] Someone by the train. Oh! Why, it's Dalrymple McNamara herself! [*All the ladies turn, looking up*] Ha, ha, ha! [*Coming down*] We hear the flutter of the angel's wings. Oh! All of you! We mustn't breathe a single word to Dally about our discovery—

THE OTHERS IN SUCCESSION. Oh, of course not, of course not—of course not.

LUCY. It has been so kind of her to take all the trouble.

THE OTHERS. So kind of her.

LUCY. We must pretend, on Saturday, it was really a surprise to us, ha, ha, ha—I'll run up and meet her. [*Runs up and exits R.U.E. Coachman's sounds*]

MRS. C. Not a single word, girls.

JULIA. Oh—not a look.

BLANCHE. Not so much as a glance of the eye.

MRS. C. We mustn't let her suspect for a moment that we know about it. [*Reenter Lucy with Mrs. Dalrymple McNamara R.U.E. They kiss in the hall and then come down. The others kiss Mrs. McNamara eagerly. They put a chair C. and seat her in it as they run on. They sit about her. Mrs. Compton at her side R., Lucy at her side L., on a hassock, Blanch L.C., Julia L.*]

LUCY. We are real glad to see you, Dally.

THE OTHERS. Delighted, Dally.

LUCY. And it is such a surprise to us. I didn't dream of seeing you for a month yet.

THE OTHERS, SUCCESSIVELY. Not for a month. Not for a month. Not for a month.

MRS. MC. Oh—I should be here on Saturday anyway—Lucy, my dear, did you think I could forget your wedding day? Ha, ha, ha—you haven't invited me this year, but I shall be here on the great anniversary anyway.

LUCY. Oh—of course.

THE OTHERS. [*In succession*] Of course. Of course. Of course. [*They look from one to the other significantly*]

BLANCHE. [*To Julia*] Not a word.

JULIA. Not a look.

MRS. C. [*After putting her finger to her lips and looking across to the girls*] Not a sign.

LUCY. Of course, you would be here on Saturday.

MRS. MC. I count myself as one of the family, you know. Invitation or no invitation—I know *something* will be going on. [*The others look at each other significantly*]

LUCY. Of course—*something* will be going on.

BLANCHE. Of course!

JULIA. Of course!

MRS. C. Of course! *Something* will be going on.

MRS. MC. Why, you are all so mysterious.

BLANCHE. [*To Julia*] Not a word.

JULIA. Not a look.

MRS. C. [*After putting her finger to her lip*] Not a sign.

MRS. MC. [*Having watched them*] He, he, he! Upon my word, I begin to fear I am an intruder. Ha, ha, ha, ha! Well keep the mystery to yourselves, girls. Only I promise you this—I shall be out from New York by an early train Saturday—and if you keep anything secret from Dally McNamara all day—you will do more than anyone else ever did for so long a time, not even her poor, dear, dead and gone husband—he, he—heigh-ho—poor darling, and he had so many secrets to keep from me. He, ha, ha, ha! Keep your own secret—ha, ha, ha—till I find it out. I was on the way back to New York from New Haven today. [*A slight start from the other ladies*]

LUCY. On—your—way—from—

BLANCHE. From—

MRS. C. On—your—way—from—

LUCY. From—New—Haven?

MRS. MC. Yes, I was running up home from New Haven. I couldn't pass New Rochelle you know—so I ran in for lunch—I will go onto New York in the next train. [*Lucy rises and moves between the two girls at the back*]

BLANCHE. That's just a blind.

LUCY and JULIA. Oh. [*Relieved, Mrs. Compton crosses to the others. They converse in a close group*]

MRS. MC. Ha, ha, ha! [*Aside*] There is something going on. They can't deceive *me* long. *One* might—but four women certainly can't keep a secret.

LUCY. [*To Mrs. Compton*] It is only a blind, you know.

MRS. C. Oh—ah—exactly—I see. [*She recrosses to R.*]

MRS. MC. Aunt Mary Plummerton has another little boy—had you heard of it? That's the seventh, you know. I have been with her in New Haven for the last three weeks. [*The other ladies start and look at each other as if the truth were forcing itself on them*] Such a rousing boy—ha, ha! [*Jumping up*] Twelve pounds and a half! Ha, ha, ha! [*Giving a turn up the stage*]

ALL THE OTHERS. [*Suddenly in chorus*]   M-m-m— Oh-o-oh! [*They sob and cry vigorously; Mrs. McNamara gives a start and looks on in astonishment*]

MRS. MC.   Well!—for a reception of good news!— Aunt Mary has five girls —are you all crying because she has another boy?

ALL THE OTHERS. [*In chorus, rising*]   No! O-o-o-o-o-o-oh!

MRS. MC.   Then, what on earth can it—are you crying because I've been in New Haven for three weeks?

ALL THE OTHERS. [*In chorus*]   Y-e-s-! O-o-o-o-h!

MRS. MC.   Are *you* mad?—or am I?

BLANCHE.   We're all of us mad.

MRS. C.   Mad as hornets!

JULIA.   Oh, Blanche.

BLANCHE.   Oh, Julia! [*They fall upon each other's necks and then move upstage encircled in each other's arms*]

JULIA. [*At door*]   O-o-o-h! [*Exits L.3.E.*]

BLANCHE. [*At door*]   O-o-o-o-o-o-o-oh. [*Exits L.3.E.*]

MRS. MC. [*Having watched them*]   Where—am—I?

LUCY. [*L.C.*]   Mrs. Compton!

MRS. C. [*Crossing to her*]   Lucy! [*They move up L. At door*] O-o-o-o-o-o-oh! [*Exits L.3.E.*]

LUCY. [*Speaking through her sobs*]   Come—come—come into my—my— own room—Dally! O-o-o-o-o-o-oh! [*Exits L.3.E. Mrs. McNamara stands a moment looking up—looks front, puzzled—moves up C. and looks after Lucy L.*]

MRS. MC.   Honeysuckle Villa has suddenly become an asylum for female lunatics. [*Starts*] Lucy! Lucy, dear! [*Exits L.3.E. Slight pause. Stage empty. Enter Mrs. Stonehenge Tuttle R.3.E. She passes across stage majestically. Exits L.2.E. Reenter General Compton, Frederic and Sartewelle R.U.E. They come dancing down C. General Compton between the others. Broad smiles on their faces*]

COMPT.   Ha, ha, ha! [*Dancing*] Beautiful—beautiful!

FRED.   Beautiful!

SART.   Beautiful!

COMPT.   The ladies are perfectly satisfied—and we are all happy again.

ALL. [*Dancing*]   Ha, ha!

COMPT.   Ha, ha! [*Rubbing his hands with satisfaction and crossing to L.C.*] I never enjoyed anything so much in my life.

ALL. [*Dancing*] Ha, ha! [*Reenter Batterson L.U.E.*]

BATT. Heigh-ho—gentlemen. [*Calls back from hall*] Cutter!

FRED. [*Apart to Sartewelle*] Poor Batterson! *He* doesn't seem to enjoy it. [*Enter Cutter L.U.E.*]

SART. No, he takes it hard, poor fellow—he is like myself—he feels that a falsehood is a very serious breach of etiquette.

BATT. Heigh-ho—gentlemen— We have still a melancholy duty to perform. [*Looks at his watch*] Another train passes for Bridgeport Junction at 12:15.

COMPT. Are you sure that's the *next* train?

BATT. Absolutely. I have just consulted the latest time-table. [*Taking out time-table, they all gather and look at it*]

COMPT. *All* the trains stop at the next station.

FRED. And it's only a short drive over.

BATT. Heigh-ho—I have considered that. The next express train doesn't pass till three o'clock.

COMPT. and THE OTHERS. Ah—ah—m'm.

BATT. Gentlemen; it has become more essential than ever to take this—this very disagreeable step. My respected mother-in-law may overtopple, at any moment, the elaborate structure which we have erected with so much care—and such consummate skill—for our defense. Heigh-ho—it is a melancholy duty.

COMPT. *Sacred duty!* As I have frequently remarked—one should always do his duty. [*Crosses R.*]

FRED. One ought never to shirk a duty. [*Moves R.*]

SART. "To hallow'd duty, here with a loyal and heroic heart, bind we our lives." [*Moving R.*]

BATT. Cutter, say to Mrs. Stonehenge Tuttle that the husbands of two of the ladies in this house—and the affianced lovers of the others desire to meet her in the drawing-room.

CUTT. Yes, sir. [*Going L.*]

BATT. Ah—Cutter! Mrs. Tuttle is in her own room. [*Motioning R.*]

CUTT. H'I beg your pardon, sir, but—Mrs. Tuttle is in the h'other part of the 'ouse—with the h'other ladies. [*Batterson glances at the others, moves a few steps down R.C., thrusting his hands in his pockets and having an anxious thoughtful air. Cutter continues*] Mrs. Tuttle joined them h'only a moment ago, sir.

BATT. [*Quickly*] Only a moment ago? [*Speaks rapidly*] Tell her we wish to see her at once, Cutter—immediately—*at once!*

CUTT. H'immediately—h'at once. [*Exits L.3.E.*]

BATT. [*Sternly and rapidly*] Gentlemen—I am a desperate man! I shall give my mother-in-law an apparent *reason* for her course, if she presumes to attack our truthfulness. We shall give her a self-evident motive for assaulting us—our wives must choose between us! Remember, gentlemen, it is only one woman.

COMPT. Certainly, only one woman.

FRED. Only one woman.

BATT. And our position, now, is very different from that which we occupied at our previous meeting.

SART. Very different.

FRED. Entirely different.

COMPT. [*Behind chair*] Our position now—is impregnable. [*Reenter Cutter L.3.E.*]

CUTT. [*At side of door, stepping back*] Mrs. Stonehenge Tuttle h'is coming. [*Batterson moves suddenly to the others*] H'at once. [*They stand in a group down R.*]

BATT. Only one woman, gentlemen.

FRED. Only one woman.

COMPT. One woman! [*Reenter Mrs. Stonehenge Tuttle, L.3.E., followed at short distance by Lucy, Blanche, Julia, and Mrs. Compton. The gentlemen stare at them astounded. The ladies move down L. solemnly in single file. Mrs. Tuttle comes to a full stop and folds her arms looking straight before her. The others come down with bowed heads as if in grief. They all draw up indignantly and face the gentlemen, the latter still astounded and staring at them. Cutter has moved up to hall C. He looks back at both sides. Exits L.U.E. The gentlemen gather into a globule, their four heads together; they gesticulate rapidly*]

COMPT. One woman!—It's an avalanche of women.

BATT. Nevertheless, gentlemen—[*They all gesticulate and mumble*]

SART. Certainly!

FRED. By all means!

COMPT. Undoubtedly; we can't retreat, now. [*They straighten out and face the ladies*]

BATT. [*Sternly*] Mrs. Stonehenge Tuttle!

SART. Mrs. Stonehenge Tuttle—

COMPT. Mrs. Stonehenge Tuttle—

BATT. You are my wife's mother—

THE THREE OTHER GENTLEMEN. [*Together*] You are my wife's mother. [*They check themselves, Mrs. Tuttle suddenly turns her head and glances at them. The gentlemen gather in a clump, shaking their heads, etc. They again straighten out*]

BATT. [*Sternly folding his arms*]   I desire to remark to you, Mrs. Tuttle—[*Reenter Mrs. McNamara L.3.E.*]

THE THREE OTHER GENTLEMEN.   We desire to—[*They stop abruptly and stare at Mrs. McNamara, who stops before them, C.*]

MRS. MC. [*Smiling pleasantly and making a low curtsy C.*]   Gentlemen.

THE FOUR GENTLEMEN.   Mrs. McNamara! [*Music, "Whoa, Emma," very vigorously. They scatter in all directions. Frederic moves up and out through bay window, Sartewelle through hall. Batterson jumps over the sofa and out R.3.E. General Compton across stage and out L.3.E. Mrs. McNamara bursts into hearty laughter, looking at them R.C. Mrs. Tuttle drops into chair, L.C., looking grimly before her; the other ladies grouped about her and sobbing. For second tableau, if curtain is called, the gentlemen absent, and Mrs. Mc-Namara in sofa, R., laughing. The other ladies sobbing*]

ACT III.

SCENE: *Same as that of Acts I and II. If variety of scenery be desired, another apartment may be set, with conservatory or any other arrangement that may be thought best. The business as here given applies to the arrangement of furniture as in the other acts, but may be easily modified for another arrangement. The entrances, however, should be about the same—R.2. or 3.E., L.3.E. and up C. Music at rise of curtain, "Hope Told a Flattering Tale." Mrs. McNamara is heard laughing merrily without. She enters C. She is in same costume as before, but she may be without bonnet, etc.*

MRS. MC.   Ha, ha, ha, ha, ha! [*Coming down, she strikes bell on table*] Ha, ha, ha, ha! Four weak women—weeping and sighing—in one room—four strong men—groaning and growling—in another room! Ha, ha, ha, ha! [*Sits*] Never knew a house so completely divided against itself. It is likely to come tumbling down about my head at any moment. Ha, ha, ha, ha, ha! [*Resting back in her chair and laughing. Enter Cutter L.U.E. He moves down to L.C. and stops. Looking up at him*] Oh—Cutter.

CUTT.   H'at your service, ma'am.

MRS. MC.   Where are the four gentlemen, Cutter?

CUTT.   H'in the billiard-room, mum!—h'all four of them, mum. They 'ave just h'ordered brandy and water, mum—for h'eight.

MRS. MC.   Ha, ha, ha! Brandy and water for eight. Ha, ha, ha!

Cutt. The gentlemen are very quiet, mum—but they seem h'uncomfortable.

Mrs. Mc. They are quiet, Cutter?

Cutt. Very—very quiet, h'indeed, mum. The h'absence of conversation in the billiard-room is h'absolutely painful, mum—h'except every now and then, one of the gentlemen makes a brief remark, mum, and the h'other gentlemen h'immediately make the same remark.

Mrs. Mc. Indeed? And what may that remark be, cutter?

Cutt. H'I shouldn't like to repeat it, mum. H'it begins with a "D"—and finishes with—"nation."

Mrs. Mc. Ha, ha, ha, ha! [Rising] You may say to the gentlemen, Cutter, that Mrs. Dalrymple McNamara desires to see them all—immediately—in this apartment.

Cutt. Yes, mum. H'all four, mum—h'immediately. [Exits L.U.E.]

Mrs. Mc. What great, innocent, stupid creatures men are, to be sure! Ha, ha, ha! They go off and do something wicked—and they come home and flounder about like so many hippopotamuses in a tank—trying to be shrewd, and not let their wives and sweethearts know anything about it. Ha, ha, ha! When poor, dear McNamara was alive—the delightful, great big idiot, poor darling! Heigh-ho, ha, ha, ha! I sometimes used to pat him on the cheek and pretend to believe all the awkward fibs he told me—ha, ha, ha—and he was just as happy, poor dear!—as if he really *had* deceived me. The great blundering darling! Heigh-ho—I wish he was alive now—and in this scrape with the rest of them; it *would* be such fun, seeing him trying to get out of it. Ha, ha, ha! [*Batterson's head appears at left of door, up C. He looks at Mrs. McNamara, then around; then steps in and walks lugubriously down R. Mrs. McNamara looks up and sees him, she rises, assumes a melancholy expression and looks at him. He stops and looks at her gloomily. Lugubriously looking at him*] Heigh-ho!

Batt. Heigh-ho. [*He sits*]

Mrs. Mc. [*C.*] Ha, ha, ha, ha, ha, ha, ha, ha! [*Stops suddenly, looking at him*] Heigh-ho.

Batt. Heigh-ho. [*Frederic's head appears. He steps in. Sartewelle's head appears. He steps in; they walk down L. Mrs. McNamara turns, sees them, and curtsies low*]

Mrs. Mc. [*With mock mournfulness*] Gentlemen.

Fred. and Sart. [*Gloomily*] Mrs. McNamara.

Mrs. Mc. Heigh-ho.

Sart. and Fred. Heigh-ho. [*They sit. Sartewelle L. and Frederic L.C.*]

Mrs. Mc. Ha, ha, ha, ha, ha! [*She whirls up L.C. laughing. General Compton's head appears. He looks around and then steps in. He comes down R.C. Mrs. McNamara stops laughing and watches him. Mournfully*] General!

Compt. [*Lugubriously*] Mrs. McNamara.

Mrs. Mc. Heigh-ho.

Compt. Heigh-ho. [*Sits R.C.*]

Mrs. Mc. Ha, ha, ha, ha, ha! [*The gentlemen sit, motionless and lugubrious. She stops laughing suddenly and looks from one to the other, sighs*] Heigh-ho.

The Four Gentlemen. Heigh-ho.

Mrs. Mc. Poor, injured innocents! Ha, ha, ha, ha! Gentlemen—you are four utterly wretched creatures.

The Four Gentlemen. [*Limp and dejected*] Utterly.

Mrs. Mc. You basely deceived your wives?

Batt. and Compt. We did.

Mrs. Mc. And your sweethearts.

Sart. and Fred. We did.

Mrs. Mc. Your wives and sweethearts discovered your perfidy.

The Four Gentlemen. They did.

Mrs. Mc. You have added to your previous infamous conduct the crime of concocting a fictitious story?

The Four Gentlemen. We have.

Mrs. Mc. Involving myself, by the way—and a number of my friends. *One* of my personal lady friends, I believe—in my own drawing room—was a little witch in white. [*Frederic turns away in his chair, guiltily*] Another of my eminently respectable associates—was a gazelle in violet. [*Sartewelle turns away guiltily*] A third lady acquaintance of mine was a girl in blue gaiters—[*Batterson same*] who danced a Highland fling! While my very particular dear friend, Mrs. Captain Chipchase—[*General Compton half rises and turns away*] Ha, ha, ha, ha! There!—I will forgive you all for *my* share of the fiction. You have been punished enough already.

The Four Gentlemen. Heigh-ho, quite.

Mrs. Mc. You are now—as you sit in my presence—four great, stupid— ha, ha, ha—pardon my bluntness—donkeys.

The Four Gentlemen. We are.

Mrs. Mc. Without wit enough in the lot to contrive another plan. I will heap coals of fire upon your head. I will get you out of your trouble—[*The four gentlemen turn suddenly and eagerly toward her*] on one condition— that you obey me implicitly.

Batt. [*Rising*] Get—us—out—of—

FRED and SART. [*Rising*] Out—of—our—

COMPT. [*Rising*] Out of our trouble!

BATT. Oh—yes—we'll obey you.

FRED and SART. Certainly—

COMPT. We'll obey you.

BATT. We will follow you like a flock of sheep.

COMPT. Like four pet lambs.

MRS. MC. Be seated, gentlemen. [*They all sit*] There is one direct and simple way out of your dilemma. Your wives and sweethearts will fly back to your manly bosoms—and all will be happy again. *My* plan is this—

BATT. [*Starting up*] Ah—one moment. [*He starts up with cautious motion to lock the center door. General Compton, Sartewelle and Frederic start to lock the doors R. and L.*]

MRS. MC. Oh—no—you need not lock the doors.

BATT. But the ladies might—

COMPT. Certainly.

FRED and SART. They might—

MRS. MC. They might overhear the plot. That would do us no harm whatever.

THE THREE GENTLEMEN. No harm? [*Returning to their seats*]

MRS. MC. That is the advantage of *my* plan—over *yours*. There is no necessity for locks or secrecy; and after you have carried out my plan—there will be nothing whatever to conceal from your wives.

THE FOUR GENTLEMEN. [*Puzzled*] Nothing—to—conceal? [*They look at each other dubiously*]

MRS. MC. Nothing whatever. You remember the words of America's greatest poet, gentlemen?

> "Truth crushed to earth, shall rise again;
> The eternal years of Heav'n are hers.
> But error, wounded, writhes with pain,
> And dies among his worshippers."

Note, gentlemen, the fine distinction in gender which the poet has made. Truth! The eternal years are *hers! Error*—dies among—*his* worshippers. A woman—a representative of eternal truth—will help you out of your trouble. My plan is this [*All attention*]; tell your wives and sweethearts—the honest truth. [*The gentlemen start to their feet*] The truth, the whole truth, and nothing but the truth! [*A slight pause, in which the gentlemen look from one to the other. They then give a united long drawn whistle*]

THE FOUR GENTLEMEN. Wh-e-e-w!

BATT. That never occurred to me.

FRED. It never entered my head.

COMPT. I never thought of that.

BATT. The idea is original—at all events.

MRS. MC. Ah, gentlemen; it is a very wise man that has wit enough to tell a woman the truth.

SART. In the right place.

MRS. MC. Ah, you men! You men! If you only knew us women as we know ourselves—a little word of truth from our husbands, now and then, would heal so many wounds. You have promised me, you know—I will go and tell the ladies you wish to see them. [*Going up*] Remember, gentlemen— the naked truth! [*Exits L.E. The four gentlemen move to a row down front. Sartewelle L., Frederic L.C., Batterson R.C., and General Compton R. They stand a moment scratching their heads in thought; look at each other; again relapse into thought*]

BATT. What do you think of Mrs. McNamara's plan, gentlemen?

COMPT. I think it will be devilish hard to execute.

FRED. Very.

SART. Telling the truth? The simplest thing in the world. Try it, once.

FRED. I—I—you don't happen to think of any more lies, do you, general?

COMPT. No—the—the fact is—as I said before—I'm sorry, boys—but—I've depended so long on my railroad suit in New—

BATT. Yes—exactly.

SART. There's no other way out of it, gentlemen. You positively must adopt Mrs. McNamara's plan—and my own—tell the exact truth. [*Strolls up toward R.*]

COMPT. Hard—very hard—for a man to stoop to telling his wife the truth —at my age.

BATT. Yes, he'd better begin it younger—if he wants it easy.

FRED. Oh, very well—if we must, we must. Of course, the first thing to do is to get our heads together and decide upon what the truth is.

COMPT. Certainly. [*He and Frederic coming together*]

BATT. [*Between them and putting them apart*] Oh, no—gentlemen! That's the great advantage of Mrs. McNamara's plan. Men who speak the truth never put their heads together. [*General movement towards R. Reenter Mrs. McNamara L.3.E.*]

MRS. MC. They are coming—all of them. Remember, gentlemen, the naked truth.

SART. Nude as the Venus di Medici.

Mrs. Mc. Ha, ha, ha, ha! [*Moving up to door, C., and looking back*] You poor unhappy, injured lambs! Remember, the naked truth. Ha, ha, ha, ha, ha, ha, ha! [*Exits L.U.E.*]

Compt. It'll be about the nakedest truth the ladies ever saw. [*The gentlemen stand R. and R.C. but not in line this time, looking up to L.3.E. Enter Lucy followed by Blanche, Julia and Mrs. Compton L.3.E. They come in with heads and eyes dropped and countenances of grief; as each gets in L.C. she looks up at the gentlemen, catches her breath and moves to her seat. Lucy sits L. near C. Blanche passes her, sitting further to L., and further down. Julia sits between them. Mrs. Compton passes down to extreme L. after they are seated, all draw handkerchiefs from their pockets, put them to their eyes; sob, wipe their eyes, and finally draw up, folding their hands and sitting erect. The gentlemen, in the meantime, have stood R. watching them. They now take chairs respectively and sit in a similar line R. General Compton extreme R., Batterson next, Sartewelle next and Frederic near C.*

Frederic	Lucy
Sartewelle	Julia
Batterson	Blanche
General Compton	Mrs. Compton

The four gentlemen take their handkerchiefs, touch their eyes, then straighten]

The Four Gentlemen. Heigh-ho.

The Four Ladies. Heigh-ho. [*Pause. Frederic punches Sartewelle to begin. Sartewelle punches Batterson, Batterson punches General Compton, General Compton turns away in his seat, shaking his head. General Compton turns again and punches Batterson to begin, Batterson punches Sartewelle, Sartewelle punches Frederic. Frederic shakes his head turning away in his chair. A thought strikes Frederic. He takes a coin from his pocket, tosses it and claps it down on Sartewelle's knee*]

Sart. Tails. [*Frederic removes his hand and sits back with a relieved air. Sartewelle takes the coin, tosses it and claps it on Batterson's knee*]

Batt. Heigh-ho. [*Sepulchrally*] Heads. [*Sartewelle removes his hand and sits back. Batterson takes the coin, tosses it and places it on General Compton's knee. Sartewelle touches Batterson's arm and whispers to him. Batterson leans over to hear him, uncovering the coin. General Compton looks down at it, then up at the ceiling. Batterson turns, again covering the coin as he does so, and looks up at General Compton inquiringly*]

COMPT. Tails. [*Batterson looks at the coin, sees he has lost; puts the piece in his vest pocket, rises. Frederic extends his hand. Batterson gives him the coin*]

BATT. A-h-e-m.

THE OTHER GENTLEMEN. A-h-e-m—hem.

THE LADIES. Heigh-ho.

SART. [*Apart*] The naked truth, Batterson.

BATT. Not a stitch. Ladies, there has evidently been—a—very—a—there has been a—a misunderstanding—between—between us gentlemen—and—and yourselves! [*The ladies look at each other*]

COMPT. [*Half rising*] A misunderstanding.

FRED. [*Half rising*] You have misunderstood us.

SART. We have failed to make ourselves clear to you.

BATT. You have received the impression—

COMPT. The impression.

FRED. You have received the impression—

BATT. That—that we—spent—last—evening—at the residence—of Mrs. Dalrymple McNamara—in New York. That impression—is—erroneous.

COMPT. Erroneous.

FRED. and SART. Erroneous.

BATT. When we—conveyed that impression to your minds—

COMPT. Conveyed.

BATT. We—we were speaking metaphorically.

COMPT. [*Half rising*] Metaphorically.

BATT. So to speak.

SART. Poetry.

BATT. We have desired your presence now—in order to—to—acquaint you with—the—the exact—facts.

FRED. [*Half rising*] Stripped of all metaphor.

SART. Prose.

BATT. The true circumstances of the case were—as—follows—

FRED and SART. [*Turning in their chairs with their backs to the ladies*] As follows.

COMPT. [*Turning same*] As follows!

BATT. Frederic, Jack Sartewelle and myself were met on Fifth Avenue yesterday afternoon—about four o'clock—by General Partridge Compton. [*General Compton whirls about and looks up at him*] General Compton proposed that we accompany him. [*General Compton springs up and pulls Batterson's sleeve*] The naked truth, general!

COMPT. Sit down! [*Batterson drops into his seat*]

FRED. [*Rising*] General Compton suggested—

SART. [*Half rising*] He suggested that we should all—

COMPT. Sit down!

FRED. and SART. [*Dropping back*] The naked truth, general.

COMPT. Damn it! I prefer to undress the goddess of truth myself.

MRS. C. [*Sternly*] Proceed, General Compton.

LUCY. [*Plaintively*] Go on.

BLANCHE and JULIA. [*Wiping their eyes with little sobs*] Go on.

COMPT. We went to a public masquerade ball last night.

ALL THE LADIES. [*Sobbing*] O-o-o-o-o-o-o-o-oh.

COMPT. All four of us—together.

THE LADIES. O-o-o-o-o-o-o-o-oh.

COMPT. We didn't get away from it until half-past four this morning.

THE LADIES. O-o-o-o-o-o-o-o-o-o-oh.

COMPT. We've been telling lies about it ever since we got home—all four of us.

THE LADIES. O-o-o-o-o-o-o-o-oh.

COMPT. [*Aside*] I'm getting the clothing off pretty fast. [*Aloud*] Mr. Alfred Batterson was dancing a Highland fling with—[*Batterson starts to his feet, Lucy sobs aloud*]

BATT. [*To General Compton*] Sit down, sir! We may each of us confine ourselves to our own affairs, sir. [*General Compton sits*] We—we—well—we —to begin at the beginning—Mr. Frederic Randolph was waltzing with— [*Frederic starts to his feet*]

JULIA. O-o-o-o-o-oh.

FRED. Sit down, sir. [*Batterson sits*] I really don't see that we need say more in this matter than concerns ourselves—each individually. As to myself—I—I—while I say it with deep sorrow—I—I—freely confess—that—that Mr. John Sartewelle—[*Sartewelle springs to his feet, places his hand on Frederic's shoulders, forces him into his seat. Blanche sobs*]

SART. [*Turning to the ladies*] General Partridge Compton—

COMPT. [*Starting up*] Sit down, sir. [*Sartewelle drops into his seat*] These three young gentlemen—[*The other three start to their feet, the four look from one to the other a moment, then all resume their seats in silence. All start up nervously once or twice as if watching each other. Sit. A pause*]

JULIA. [*Rising slowly*] Frederic!

FRED. [*Rising*] Julia! [*He stands with a penitent expression looking down*]

JULIA. [*Tearfully*] You—you told me—you were—in your own room—all night, Frederic.

FRED. I did.

JULIA. Working on a—a law case—for tomorrow—so that you could spend today—with—with—me.

FRED. I told you a lie!

JULIA. You—you—were really—you were waltzing with a—with a—little witch—

FRED. In white.

JULIA. A—beautiful brunette—

FRED. She was a blonde, lies, all lies!

JULIA. Oh, Frederic! [*Sobbing*] O-o-o-o-o-o-oh. [*Dropping in her chair, Frederic sits*]

BLANCHE. Mr. John Sartewelle.

SART. [*Rising*] I wish to confess—frankly and fully, that I was at a public ball last night; a masquerade ball. In making this confession—I take great pleasure in the consciousness—a consciousness dear to every upright gentleman—that I have said nothing whatever, in connection with this affair, that was not absolutely and exactly true. [*Blanche springs to her feet. The other gentlemen move in their chairs with exclamatory groans*] If there is anything which a gentleman prizes more than another, it is the proud consciousness of truth. A clear conscience—

BLANCHE. Silence, sir! [*Drawing up and breathing hard with suppressed indignation*] The truth, indeed! You—you—*you*—were "with Frederic," sir!

SART. I was, all night.

BLANCHE. You—you—you were "detained for the same reason that Frederic was?"

SART. The same reason, precisely. I have told you all that frankly.

BLANCHE. Frankly! You did not tell me this, sir!—a gazelle, sir!

SART. That subject did not come up.

BLANCHE. In violet.

SART. A gazelle in violet.

BLANCHE. Auburn hair, of a delicate golden tint—brushed smoothly over the forehead—

SART. With a little curl or two peeping out above the ear—her eyes were blue—pearl earrings—her complexion—

BATT. A perfect photograph.

COMPT. An exact description.

SART. My witnesses! Blanche! [*Earnestly clasping his hands*] I cannot tell a lie.

BLANCHE. O—o-o-o-o-oh. [*Sobbing and dropping into her chair, Sartewelle sits*]

LUCY. [*Rising*] Alfred. [*Batterson rises*]

BATT. I confess to everything, Lucy, I have grossly deceived you.

LUCY. [*Tearfully*] She—she had—she had—

BATT. [*Dismally*] Blue gaiters.

LUCY. O-o-o-o-o-o-o-oh. [*Dropping into her seat. Batterson sinks into his, dejected. Mrs. Compton arouses herself and looks over to General Compton. He draws up uneasily, glancing at her, then away, etc.*]

MRS. C. Ahem!

COMPT. [*Rising*] Our railroad suit in New Jersey—[*Derisive groan from other gentlemen. Mrs. Compton springs to her feet*]

MRS. C. General!

COMPT. I beg your pardon, my dear. I forgot we were telling the truth. A pink sylph, my dear—I would say, a sylph in pink satin, my love—she knocked off the top of my bald head—I—that is—she kicked up the bald hat —of—a vaudeville in New Jersey—Mrs. McNamara's railroad suit—in—I—I —knocked off the—her slipper—my hat—somebody's bald head—it was the last dance of the evening, my dear—and I can't recall the exact facts with any degree of accuracy.

MRS. C. [*Severely, resuming her seat*] Evidently not, General Compton.

SART. and FRED. Evidently not, General Compton.

COMPT. That is the truth. [*Sits. A pause*]

THE FOUR GENTLEMEN. Heigh-ho.

THE FOUR LADIES. Heigh-ho. [*Batterson is sitting, turned away with his head dropped in a dejected attitude. Lucy rises and walks to near him*]

LUCY. [*Earnestly*] Alfred!

BATT. Lucy!

LUCY. You—you have deceived me, Alfred.

BATT. I have.

LUCY. It is the first time.

BATT. And the last time. [*Earnestly, looking up without looking around to her*]

LUCY. I—I *believe* you, Alfred—I believe you! My husband! [*He starts up and embraces her*]

BATT. My wife! [*They go up C., lovingly, she in his arms, and pass out L.U.E.*]

COMPT. [*Having watched them out*] By Jove! Mrs. McNamara's plan is a success. I shall always tell the truth hereafter.

BLANCHE. [*Rising*] Jack!

JULIA. [*Rising*] Frederic!

FRED. Julia!

SART. Blanche! [*The girls rush into their arms. The two couples embrace and move upstage R. and L.*]

COMPT. The truth is great! I wish I'd known this years ago. [*General Compton turns and faces Mrs. Compton with an expectant air. She sits bolt upright L., looking front. He crosses to her, extends his arms as if expecting her to fall into them. She continues rigidly in her position. He turns and recrosses front*]

COMPT. [*R.*] Mrs. McNamara's plan is a d—d failure. I'll be hanged if I ever tell the truth again.

FRED. Dear Julia!

SART. Darling Blanche! [*The two couples go up C. and pass out L.U.E. General Compton turns in time to see them going. He starts up*]

COMPT. Here, I say—[*He turns when half upstage and extends his hands towards Mrs. Compton. She continues looking sternly away. General Compton runs up and calls out after the others*] I say, boys, we aren't through yet. We've got to see each other through, you know—I say, boys! [*Beckoning. Sartewelle and Frederic reappear R.U.E. They come down a few steps with General Compton L.C. The three talk together, glancing at Mrs. Compton. General Compton walks down and stands near her. Batterson reappears in center door from L.U.E. Mrs. Compton rises stiffly, swings away upstage and across R. The General watching her and moving after her at a little distance. Frederic and Sartewelle move down L.C. Mrs. Compton sails across to L.3.E. General Compton up C., watching her. She stops, hesitates, then turns suddenly*]

MRS. C. Partridge!

COMPT. Maria! [*She rushes into his arms. Jack and Fred embrace*]

MRS. C. Dear Partridge!

COMPT. My love! [*They move to the door, lovingly, his arms about her waist*]

BATT. [*Moving down*] Ah—general! [*General Compton stops and looks back; Batterson, up C., beckons to him*]

COMPT. [*Turning to Mrs. Compton*] My darling. [*Kisses her*]

MRS. C. Partridge, dear! [*Exits L.3.E. Compton kisses his hands after her*]

COMPT. Gentlemen, I have sown my wild oats.

BATT. Sown? It's been harvest time—the last thirty years.

COMPT. [*Moving across down R.*] My days of youthful folly are past. I am a reformed man.

BATT. A regular stage reformation. [*Moving down R.C.*] Gentlemen— [*Sartewelle L., Frederic L.C., General Compton R., the four stand in line front*] I am deeply grieved to say it—I am painfully impressed with the delicate nature of my position—but—[*Taking out his watch and looking at it*] there is another train for Bridgeport Junction at 4:25. [*They look from one to the other significantly*]

COMPT., SART. and FRED. M'm—y-e-s!

BATT. The common enemy is still within the camp. No man in the United States has more profound respect for the preceding generation than myself. But the present generation has *some* rights which its predecessors are bound to respect—and in justice to the next generation, if not to the present.

CURTAIN

OLD LOVE LETTERS

OLD LOVE LETTERS

First produced at the Park Theatre, New York, August 31, 1878, as a curtain-raiser to *Hurricanes*. The cast of characters was as follows:

MRS. FLORENCE BROWNLEE   AGNES BOOTH

THE HON. EDWARD WARBURTON   JOSEPH E. WHITING

Old Love Letters ran for one month with *Hurricanes* and was also produced October 15, 16, 17, 18, 19, 24, and 25.

Old Love Letters was produced at the Madison Square Theatre, New York, March 30, 1886, in conjunction with *Broken Hearts*. The cast of characters was as follows:

MRS. FLORENCE BROWNLEE   AGNES BOOTH

THE HON. EDWARD WARBURTON   HERBERT KELCEY

This production ran to April 19, 1886.

Old Love Letters was produced at the Madison Square Theatre, New York, November 3, 1890, and ran to November 24, 1890.

A benefit performance of *Old Love Letters* for Mrs. Harriet Holman was given at the Star Theatre, New York, April 25, 1893, with the cast as follows:

MRS. FLORENCE BROWNLEE   AGNES BOOTH

THE HON. EDWARD WARBURTON   EUGENE ORMONDE

TEXT AND SOURCE

The present text of *Old Love Letters* is taken from a typescript of the play bearing the following title-page: Old Love Letters/ A Comedy in one act/

by/ Bronson Howard/ Copyright, 1878. This manuscript is almost identical with a privately printed copy that bears the same title-page except that in place of the earlier copyright notice, a later one is added.

A few typographical errors in the above text have been corrected, and the note on p. 65, which in the original appeared in the body of the text, has been moved to the bottom of the page.

The well-known couplet from Whittier's "Maud Muller," quoted in Mrs. Brownlee's opening monologue, describes the situation at the beginning of the play; it is possible, therefore, that Howard took a definite suggestion from this poem, but it is likewise possible that the quotation is only an embellishment, as is the subsequent extract from Longfellow's "The Rainy Day." The resurgence of an old love in the presence of reminiscent circumstances is, of course, a theme often employed in literature.

It may be of interest to note that Bret Harte in 1870 wrote his version of the Maud Muller situation; Howard's play, obviously owes nothing to this.

CAST OF CHARACTERS

Mrs. Florence Brownlee

The Hon. Edward Warburton

Henry, *a servant*

OLD LOVE LETTERS

SMALL PROPERTIES: *Lot of old letters from cabinet drawer. (Before curtain.) Two bundles of letters wrapped in faded tissue paper and tied with faded ribbon—letter in each (see pages 65 to 77). One to Warburton—other in cabinet drawer. Photograph album—portrait of Florence, 1878, on back. Call bell on center table. Small rosewood box to contain letters of Warburton (to servant, before curtain). Sheet music on piano. Song, "The day is cold and dark and dreary," on top. Two photographs and note case to Warburton before curtain. Salver to servant at L. entrance. (Ditto with card portrait.)*

FURNITURE: *Upright piano. Square center table. Old cabinet and secretary. Hat-rack. Hall bench. Two arm chairs, two back chairs, all leather-covered. Piano stool. Flower table. Looking-glass over mantel. Glass candelabra. Limoges vases for mantel. Glass chandelier for room. Same for entry. Brass and iron fender. Tongs, etc., in stand. Heavy curtains for window and door. Brass curtain rods and rings. Three small Turkish rugs—one at fire, one at piano, other at door.*

COSTUMES AND APPEARANCES: *Mrs. Brownlee is a widow of thirty-two, dressed quietly but richly, either in second mourning or very subdued colors. Her general manner is demure and gentle. When excited, animated but dignified. She is still in the early prime of womanly beauty; Warburton is a man of forty, with much dignity of manner; dressed elegantly and stylishly, but in keeping with his years and his position as foreign minister of the United States. His hair, mustache, iron-gray, and his personal appearance somewhat beyond his years, as described by himself on first meeting Mrs. Brownlee.*

SCENE: *Rain at rise. The residence of Mrs. Brownlee at Cambridge. Apartment of an old New England family mansion. The general appearance of the apartment that of which the modern so-called "East Lake" style is an imitation. The furniture rich and old, but not too florid, as if an old European house—general tendency to plainness. Evidences of a woman's taste in the way of bric-a-brac, flowers, embroidery, rugs. A mantel and fireplace L. at about 2nd entrance with fire. A mirror over it. A window L. upper corner. If there is a view beyond, the artist should bear in mind that according to the text it is a rainy day. An old-fashioned cabinet up C. A table, C. front. One of the drawers of the cabinet on this table with old letters in it. A portrait of an old gentleman on*

*the wall, up R., or on an easel up R.C. A chair near mantel. An upright piano.
down R. Door R.3.E. Door L.1.E. Low music. Rainy day.*

DISCOVERED: *Mrs. Brownlee sitting at left of table, down C. She is reading
old letters from the drawer on table, crumpling them up and throwing them
into the fire. As the curtain rises she crumples one letter and takes another from
the drawer, opens it, glances at its contents quickly, crumples it and tosses it
into the fire. As she looks at another she bursts into a merry laugh, crumples it
and throws it after the others. As she reads another, she stops laughing
abruptly, puts her handkerchief to her eyes and rests her head on her hand.
Music ceases.*

MRS. B.   Old letters! Old letters! They are like faded rose leaves in a book!
The thoughts in them are withered now; even the loving wishes have long
ago lost their fragrance. How many of the hands that wrote them are lying
over still hearts today! Heigh-ho! [*She takes the letter in her hand and throws
it into the fire. Several more from the drawer follow it, after rapid glances,
with alternate laughter and sighs. She pauses over another*] Helen Thomaston.
Fourteen years ago—is it so long? We were both eighteen. [*Reads*] "Arthur
and I are to be married next month. We are both so happy and oh! Florence,
I feel perfectly sure that we shall always love each other." Married and separated—more than ten years ago. [*Crumpling the letter and throwing it into
fire*] Go, and keep company with a young girl's hopes—I—I remember—I
wrote such a letter as that—when—when—Edward Warburton and I were—
Pshaw! [*Brushing her eyes*] What has a widow of thirty-two to do with the
silly dreams of a young girl? [*She takes another letter and bursts into hearty
laughter as she looks at it*] Ha! Ha! Ha! Ha! [*Reads*] "Henry Layton Jarvis."
Ha! Ha! Ha! Ha! Why did I keep that letter? Ha! Ha! Ha! Ha! Harry
swears—Ha! Ha!—dear good-natured, awkward Harry Jarvis—he swears he
will never love any woman but me, and will surely die if I refuse him. Ha!
Ha! He will surely die if I refuse him! Ha! Ha! Ha! This was barely thirteen
years ago. Harry's eldest boy is nearly twelve years old now. Ha! Ha! Ha! I
must show this letter to his wife. Laura is my best friend and Harry is the
jolliest, fattest man in the neighborhood. Ha! Ha! Ha! Ha! Ha! Heigh-ho!
Laura and I are such good friends now—I could never believe she meant any
wrong—and she was so sorry for it afterwards; but if Laura Malvern had not
come between Edward Warburton and me—I—we—[*Looking thoughtfully*]
—Heigh-ho!—

> "Of all sad words of tongue or pen,
> The saddest are these: It might have been."

[*She brushes her eyes and straightens up, suddenly*] Those silly dreams again! One would think I was a romantic schoolgirl still, instead of a subdued and practical widow. [*Takes another letter from the drawer*] Oh, poor, darling John! Heigh-ho! My husband. [*She glances over her shoulder at the portrait on the wall, up R.; kisses the letter*] Six years ago tomorrow. So it is. Since Mr. Brownlee died. Six years a widow. How rapidly time does fly! [*Glances at the portrait*] Poor, dear John! [*She touches her eyes daintily with her handkerchief. Reads*] "My darling little birdie!"—Ah!—John always called me his little birdie as if I were only a child. John was a little over fifty when this was written. I was nearly twenty; he always treated me as if I might have been his daughter. [*Reads*] "My darling little birdie." Heigh-ho! [*Kissing letter and then looking up at portrait*] There is no one to call me his "little birdie" now! [*She places her handkerchief to her eyes and rests her face in her hand, with her elbow on the table. She crumples the letter and tosses it back of her to the fire, sighs, brushes her eyes and is about to take another letter. She suddenly starts up*] Oh! No! I forgot! [*She hurries to the fireplace; stoops down and secures the letter; returns and stands at the table, smoothing it out as she proceeds*] John is looking down upon me from the canvas. [*Puts away the letter; walks up to L.C., stops before the portrait and looks up at it with a sad expression*] Dear John! [*She turns up to the window, leaning against the casing, L., and looking out*] Rain—rain—rain! I shall die of ennui! A widow always misses her husband so much on a rainy day. [*Looking up at portrait over her shoulder*] Mr. Brownlee used to be such company for me—when I couldn't get out of the house. [*Again looks out of the window, now becoming deeply serious*] Rain—rain—rain! It was on just such a day as this—will it always come into my mind when it rains? And I try so hard to keep it out! [*Buries her face in her hand, silently moves down. Raises her face; goes to piano, wearily; plays an accompaniment and sings*][1]

> "The day is cold and dark, and dreary;
> It rains, and the wind is never weary;
> The vine still clings to the mouldering wall,
> But at every gust the dead leaves fall,
> And the days are dark and dreary.

[1] If the lady is not a particularly good singer, this song should be omitted. The first stanza, in this case, should be recited during the preceding speech, after the words "I try so hard to keep it out," and she should move down, slowly, during the remainder of the speech, dropping into the chair at table with her face in her hands at the words "I have not lived at all since then." Very low, accompanying music by the orchestra, which should begin at the second "Rain—rain—rain" and continue until she drops into the chair at the table. Mrs. Booth did this instead of singing, in the original production, and it is probably the better way, even if the lady is a good singer.—B.H.

"My life is cold and dark, and dreary;
It rains, and the wind is never weary;
My thoughts still cling to the mouldering past,
But the hopes of youth fall thick in the blast,
And the days are dark and dreary."

It was just such a day as this—thirteen years ago. Edward and I—we—parted for the last time—in this very room. People have called me frivolous. I am— what can a woman be? What must a woman be? I have never lived my own life. I have done the best I could in a life that should have been lived by another woman. My own life—he was a part of it. I have not lived at all since then! [*She leans listlessly on the piano a second; rises, moves to the table and stands fumbling through the old letters with an absent air. She raises a package from beneath the pile, done up in faded tissue paper and tied with a faded ribbon*] Why, what are these tied up so carefully? The wrapper is old and faded and the ribbon [*About to untie it*]—Why I—I— [*Turns over the package; reads*] "June 12, 18—.[2] When love begins to sicken and decay"—I thought —I—I thought—I had destroyed those letters. No—I—I—mean—I—I thought I had returned them to him. No—I remember! Oh! I—should have destroyed them before my marriage. It was neither respectful to Mr. Brownlee, nor consistent with my own dignity as his wife. [*She walks to the mantel with dignity and makes a motion to throw the package into the fire. She withholds her hand and hesitates, looking down at the package. She repeats this motion, and then slowly unties the outside ribbon; takes off the wrapper, which she crumples and throws into the fire*] Of—of course it isn't wicked for me to keep them now. [*She looks at the letters a moment, then turns her head slowly and looks over her shoulder at the portrait of her husband. Again makes a motion to throw the packet into the fire; hesitates again. She finally places the letters in the bosom of her dress, then yields to her real feelings, drops her face into her hands and sobs. Enter a servant, Henry, R.U.E. He has a card upon a small silver salver. He steps in stiffly and stops, down R.C. Mrs. Brownlee draws up, dashes the tears from her eyes quickly, and extends her hand with dignity. He moves to her. She takes the card; starts slightly as she looks at it. Draws up*] Show the gentleman into this room, Henry. [*He moves up to retire*] Ah! Henry. [*He stops and turns back*] You may place that drawer in the cabinet. [*He proceeds to obey, and Mrs. Brownlee continues aside*] A distinguished visitor—the minister plenipotentiary of the United States to a foreign court. [*Aloud*] Henry, you may say to the gentleman that Mrs. Brownlee will be

---

[2] The typescript from which the present text was printed shows two or three erasures and date markings. It was evidently used more than once as a prompt script.—Editor.

down presently. [*Exit Henry, R.U.E.*] Thirteen years. [*She moves to the mantel and looks into the mirror, draws back*] It is not the same face—it is not the same. [*Moves L.*] Has he, too, changed so much? [*Exits, L.1.E. Henry re-enters, R.U.E. Warburton, who enters L. glances back, with a slight inclination of the head to Henry, who immediately retires. Warburton casts his eyes around the room for a moment; then he glances about a little nervously, though his general manner is composed and dignified. He looks into the fire, slowly removing one of his gloves*]

WARB. Rather out of season for a fire—very comfortable though. It is hardly colder than this in Vienna, in the middle of December. How my heroic ancestors, who came over in the Mayflower managed at first to endure the climate of Massachusetts is a profound mystery to me. I should hardly be willing to endure as much for the benefit of my posterity. My wife, poor dear, succumbed to the moderate chills of Paris. Even the warm skies of Southern Italy failed to restore her. Heigh-ho! Poor darling! [*He looks around the apartment*] Surely this room—I cannot be mistaken—now that I see the inside of the house. It must be the same—[*Looking at the room*] and yet—Ah! I see, Mrs. Brownlee probably returned to the old family mansion after the death of her—her husband. [*He stops, R.C., looking down thoughtfully*] It was in this very apartment—eighteen hundred and—² [*He takes a wallet from his breast pocket, opens it, looks through the folds and takes out a card photograph*] Ah! Mrs. Warburton! A good, gentle, sweet creature. [*Kisses it and returns it. He looks through the folds, takes out another card wrapped in white paper. He unfolds the paper and looks at the picture steadily*] Florence. She was a girl of nineteen, then—luxuriant hair—complexion as delicate and as brilliant as the tint of an apple blossom. It is only a fading memory. She is very differ-ent now, I suppose. [*Looks at paper*] Ah! Here it is. [*Reads*] "June 12, 18—"² Thirteen years ago. [*Reads*]

> "They sin who tell us love can die;
> With life, all other passions fly,
> All others are but vanity."

Southey. What nonsense great poets can write! [*He looks at the picture a mo-ment, then suddenly starts; looks as if hearing a sound; hastily returns the paper, pictures and wallet to his pocket. Straightens up and stands in an ex-pectant attitude to receive Mrs. Brownlee. She does not enter. He sees his mis-take, turns upstage and then down L.C. to mirror. He looks at himself, running his hand through his hair, etc., etc.*] Thirteen years make a very marked difference in the appearance of a human being. There was not a gray hair in my head at that time—not a wrinkle in my face. Ah! well we must all grow old—[*Walking to table*] men and women alike. [*Throwing open the album*] Mrs. Brownlee's father. A fine-looking old gentleman. [*Turns a leaf*] Florence herself. [*Pauses; looking at it steadily*] Evidently taken only a year after our—our—after our last meeting. Heigh-ho! There is a fuller and deeper womanhood in that face, but she hardly looks older than when I last saw her. Do women shed their early griefs so lightly, then? Perhaps there is a date. [*He takes the card from the album; looks at back; starts*] Eighteen hundred and —² The present year! [*He stands a moment, staring at the card, turning the face and back alternately. He then walks before the mirror, where he looks at his own face, then at the picture. He repeats this action several times. He then returns to the table, tosses the cards into the album, shuts the cover with some force, and moves to and fro, thoroughly piqued. He turns up C., sees the portrait on the wall; stops; looks at it with his eyeglasses*] A portrait of her husband, I suppose. I never met Mr. Brownlee. At least forty years her senior— M—m—I don't like his face. [*Shaking his head*] I don't like the expression. [*Reenter Mrs. Brownlee, L.1.E. He still stands criticising the picture, not hearing her. She stops, down L., looking at him, quietly*] Something about the lines of the mouth. [*Shaking his head*] The eyes have a certain cold, hard look!

MRS. B.   Mr. Warburton! [*He starts, turning towards her*]

WARB.   Mrs. Brownlee! [*He extends his hand, frankly, and walks down to meet her. She extends her hand. He takes it*]

MRS. B.   I am so glad to meet you again, after so long a time, Mr. Warburton.

WARB.   Thank you, madam. [*A slight pause, in which he looks at her steadfastly, returning her hand*] Thirteen years! [*They look at each other a moment in silence. She droops her eyes. He releases her hand and moves R. She looks after him. He stops, R.C. She moves to the table, L.C., and strikes bell*]

MRS. B.   Pray remove your coat, Mr. Warburton. [*He bows acknowledgment and proceeds to comply*] We should hardly have known each other, Mr. Warburton, if we had met elsewhere.

WARB.   I can be more complimentary, madam. Old Father Time has shown you more gallantry than he accords to the majority of ladies. He has politely touched his forelock, apparently, and passed by on the opposite side.

MRS. B.   Your politeness compels me to remember that you are a diplomatist, Mr. Warburton.

WARB.   I am an American diplomatist, madam. We usually keep on the truthful side of facts, even when politeness lies on the other. [*Enter Henry, R.3.E.*]

Mrs. B.   Henry—Mr. Warburton's hat and coat. [*Henry takes hat and coat, and retires, R.3.E.*] Be seated, Mr. Warburton.

Warb.   Honestly, then, Mrs. Brownlee—[*Placing a chair for her at L. of table. She sits*] as a diplomatist and friend—[*Sitting at R. of table*] you look almost as young as you did—as—when—when—as you did thirteen years ago.

Mrs. B.   Honestly, then, I am sincerely glad you think so. A woman ninety years old is quite willing to be mistaken for eighty-five. I confess to the most durable weakness of my sex. I will not flatter you, Mr. Warburton. The arduous duties of public life, I will not say time—

Warb.   Say it frankly, madam. Father Time has shown himself a severe creditor in my case. I have been borrowing my years of him at a very high rate of interest. Like the unjust steward, he has insisted on his own, with usury. Ha! Ha! My hair is nearly as gray at forty as it should be at sixty. Ha! Ha! Ha!

Mrs. B.   Oh! sir—I—

Warb.   And other men of forty bow with reverence to my gray mustache.

Mrs. B.   You are entirely too severe.

Warb.   Truth is usually severe, madam; and she becomes more and more so as we grow older.

Mrs. B.   I did not intend to—

Warb.   To be as severe as the truth. Ha! Ha! Ha! I acquit you of any such intention. You are a woman of society, madam; the most graceful and the most skillful of diplomatists. By the way, Mrs. Brownlee—this house—as I was coming up the street, following the directions I had received—the trees outside had grown so much, and the ivy so covers the building now—but as I entered this room—the fact is—I am a trifle confused. Everything looks so very natural to me, and yet—

Mrs. B.   It is the same house in which I resided with my father, when—

Warb.   I thought it must be the same—the same in which you resided when —when—

Mrs. B.   When—

Warb. [*Seriously and slowly, looking front*]   When you and I last parted.

Mrs. B. [*Looking down*]   The last time we met.

Warb.   Thirteen years ago!

Mrs. B.   Last June!

Warb.   The twelfth, in the afternoon.

Mrs. B.   Half-past three!

Both.   Heigh-ho! [*Looking front*]

Warb.   It was very much such a rainy afternoon as this.

Mrs. B.   Yes—I—remember—it did rain.

WARB. Heigh-ho!

MRS. B. Heigh-ho! I have always resided in this house.

WARB. Indeed?

MRS. B. You see—when I was—when—when I was—

WARB. Married.

MRS. B. When I was—married—[*She pauses in reverie. They both look before them, thoughtfully and in silence. He turns and looks at her a moment, seriously*]

WARB. As you were saying, madam—

MRS. B. Eh? Oh—[*Starting from her reverie*] yes—as I was saying—[*Hesitates, as if trying to collect her thoughts*]

WARB. When you were married—

MRS. B. Oh—certainly—when we were first married, we came here to live. My father died afterwards, and my—my—Mr. Brownlee and I continued to reside here. Little or nothing has been changed.

WARB. I never had the pleasure of meeting Mr. Brownlee. [*Glances over his shoulder at picture; rises; walks up R.C.*] This is your husband's portrait, I presume.

MRS. B. Yes.

WARB. M—m—about your father's age.

MRS. B. My father and Mr. Brownlee were old schoolmates.

WARB. M—m—I was looking at the picture before you entered the room; a fine face. I like it. A gentle, fatherly expression in the eyes.

MRS. B. Mr. Brownlee was always kind to me.

WARB. Undoubtedly. Every line in his face would convince me of that. Ah, madam! [*Moving down to her, and taking her hand, which rests upon the table, in his own*] Heigh-ho! I, too, have loved and lost. [*Presses her hand a moment, gently; releases it and resumes his seat. They look at each other across the table, mournfully; then both look down before them a moment*]

MRS. B. You have been a widower several years, I believe, Mr. Warburton?

WARB. About four years—no—six years—yes—four—four years last March —I would say—next October. Mrs. Warburton died exactly five years ago— last November. She was an admirable woman. I was devotedly attached to her. I really could not have been more warmly attached to Mrs. Warburton if she had been my own sister instead of my wife. [*Mrs. Brownlee glances up at him, quickly, then away*] Poor, dear woman. She was hardly fitted for the gay official life of a European capital; extremely domestic in her tastes. You never met Mrs. Warburton? [*He takes wallet from his pocket; takes out card; is passing it to her; she raises her hand to receive it. He suddenly withdraws it*] No. [*Returns it; takes another*] This one.

Mrs. B. A sad, sweet face. There is something in that face—a suggestion of hopes that were unfulfilled—[*Looking earnestly and sadly at picture*] We women can understand each other so well.

Warb. I frequently noticed the rather—melancholy—expression to which you refer—while Mrs. Warburton was living. I—I tried to do everything I could to make life cheerful for her—but—

Mrs. B. You loved her as devotedly as if she were your own sister?

Warb. Quite—quite—I assure you. No one who knew her could help loving her.

Mrs. B. She should have been very happy in such a love.

Warb. I really wish you could have known Mrs. Warburton. We often spoke of you—

Mrs. B. You—spoke—of me?

Warb. Frequently! Ha! Ha! Ha! [*Beginning a pleasant but somewhat forced laugh*]—Ha! Ha! Of course, I told her about the—the—the—Ha! Ha! Ha!—the desperate flirtation—you and I once had. Ha! Ha! Ha!—

Mrs. B. Oh! Ha! Ha! Ha! Ha! Ha! Ha! [*Joining with him in a merry ripple of laughter. He continues to laugh. She suddenly checks herself, and turns partly away, biting her lips*]

Warb. Ha! Ha! Ha! Ha! You and Mrs. Warburton could have laughed over it together.

Mrs. B. Certainly; Mrs. Warburton and I could have laughed over it together.

Warb. Ha! Ha! Ha! Ha! I dare say you and Mr. Brownlee laughed over your early love affairs, as frequently as Mrs. Warburton and I did over mine.

Mrs. B. Mr. Brownlee and I laughed over them quite as frequently, I dare say. Heigh-ho! [*Suddenly assuming a sad tone*] Mr. Brownlee and I were very happy together. In spite of the difference in our ages, we were so perfectly congenial. My heart had never known another love.

Warb. I—I beg your pardon, madam—but I—I—

Mrs. B. Sir? [*Looking at him, with an innocent air*]

Warb. I don't think I exactly caught your last remark.

Mrs. B. I was speaking of Mr. Brownlee and myself. I had never experienced anything more than—the mere—the mere thoughtless flutterings, so to speak, of a young schoolgirl's heart, you know.

Warb. Y—e—s, precisely.

Mrs. B. Mr. Brownlee was my first true hero.

Warb. Y—e—s?

Mrs. B. We—were—were very happy together. But it could not last. [*She averts her head, drawing her handkerchief from her pocket, and quietly press-*

ing it to her eyes. He regards her, half puzzled, half incredulously, but with a respectful and serious demeanor]

Warb.   Pardon me, madam, if our conversation has recalled unhappy recollections. I did not intend to intrude upon the sacred feelings of a devoted wife. Permit me to change the subject. I will mention the particular object, aside from a natural desire to meet an old friend, the immediate object of my present visit. I have called to render an act of justice to yourself, and to offer you an apology. On my arrival from Europe, about a week ago, after an absence of several years, I visited the old family residence of the Warburtons in the vicinity of Concord. It is the first time I have been to the place for years. The estate has but recently returned, in fact, to my possession. Day before yesterday—in the afternoon—I was rummaging among a lot of musty papers in a long-deserted room of the old mansion, and I came across a bundle of old letters. [*Taking packet from his pocket*] They were carefully wrapped in tissue paper, and tied with a blue ribbon.

Mrs. B.   You found them among some other old rubbish, in a deserted room?

Warb.   A sort of storeroom. They had been very carefully put away in a secret drawer of an ancient mahogany cabinet, which one of my ancestors brought over in sixteen twenty. Imagine my surprise, madam—I was positively startled—to discover that they were your own letters to me—written during our—our—

Mrs. B.   Our flirtation.

Warb.   Our flirtation—thirteen years ago. [*He lays the packet on the table*]

Mrs. B.   You will pardon me, Mr. Warburton, if I say I have been at a loss to understand why you had never returned those letters before.

Warb.   That question puzzled me, when I first found them. It is for that, madam, I owe you an apology—though I confess it is now very late to offer one. I removed the dust from a neighboring chair and sat down to ponder over the subject. I thought about it an hour or more. There was no one in the house to disturb my thoughts. It seemed almost as if it were this morning that I tied those letters in a packet, intending to return them to you. I recalled our last meeting distinctly. We—we—if you remember—we—we—had quarreled.

Mrs. B.   Yes. We had quarreled.

Warb.   On the previous evening. Of course, we can both of us—[*Very seriously*] laugh over the matter now.

Mrs. B.   Of course. We can both laugh over it, now.

Warb.   Those early lovers' quarrels are so amusing to look back upon in after years.

Mrs. B. Perfectly ludicrous.

Warb. How little you and I dreamed at that time that we could laugh over the affair so heartily, now.

Mrs. B. We wouldn't have believed it.

Warb. Heigh-ho!

Mrs. B. Heigh-ho!

Warb. I am still at a loss, madam, to explain how I happened finally to retain those letters in my possession. I trust, however, that you will accept my apology without that definite explanation which it is now impossible for me to give.

Mrs. B. Certainly, Mr. Warburton, I accept your apology. I will also return to you your own letters to me.

Warb. You have—retained them—so long—madam?

Mrs. B. In the expectation that my own might eventually be returned to me. [*She strikes bell on table*] I am a housekeeper, Mr. Warburton. It is a disgrace to a woman not to understand where everything is, in her house. I know precisely where your letters are at the present moment. [*Enter Henry*]

Warb. Indeed!

Mrs. B. Henry, you may ask Martha to look in the old black walnut bureau in the spare bedroom—second floor front—the third drawer from the top. She will find a small rosewood box, inlaid with mother-of-pearl, in the outer left-hand corner of the drawer. You may bring it to me. [*Exit Henry, R.U.E.*]

Warb. Permit me to compliment you, madam; I have never known a more accurate housekeeper.

Mrs. B. Thank you. A careful housekeeper becomes so accustomed to keeping everything in perfect order. She does it instinctively—without giving any one thing in particular a second thought.

Warb. Exactly. Precisely. [*A slight pause*] As I was just saying, when I found this packet of letters—I sat down by myself—in the old mansion, and I recalled every circumstance of our—our—last meeting—distinctly. You were then a young girl of barely nineteen—and a young girl of that age, of course —as you know—as we all know—[*Complacently*] a young girl of nineteen is the most—Ha! Ha! Ha!—the most unreasonable thing in the world. Ha! Ha! Ha!—[*Sitting back in his chair, calmly trifling with his watchguard and looking front. She draws up and looks across at him, then away. She sits bolt upright as he proceeds, in an attitude suggestive of slowly rising indignation*] Ha! Ha! Ha! A hot-headed young girl, who imagines herself in love, is a more formidable creature to deal with than any one of the six great Powers. Ha! Ha! Ha! I have never met anything in my diplomatic career so difficult to treat with. I had no connection with the Alabama difficulty, but I dare say that was a mere bagatelle—compared with the successful unraveling—of an —emotional entanglement—with a girl of nineteen. Ha! Ha! Ha! [*Mrs. Brownlee rises in a stately way; looks down at him with great dignity and with suppressed indignation. She turns and walks to the mantel; glances back at him; then looks down into the fire, tips of her toes resting on the fender. He proceeds, still looking front, and with the same low, complacent laugh*] Ha! Ha! Ha! Ha! I remember what desperate efforts I made to explain to you how entirely you misunderstood the real situation. [*She taps the fender with her foot and looks back at him over her shoulder, biting her lips*] Ha! Ha! Ha! Ha! It was of no earthly use, however. You would not listen to reason for a moment. Ha! Ha! Ha! Ha! Ha! [*Throwing back his head and still trifling with his guard*] Girls will be girls! [*She utters a quick, spiteful growl between her clenched teeth, turning to the fire again. He glances at her over his shoulder*] Eh? [*He rises, turns towards her, and continues, inquiringly*] I beg your pardon?

Mrs. B. [*Looking up, trying to smile and keep her temper down*] I—I—made—no—remark—Mr. Warburton.

Warb. Oh! Excuse me. [*He pauses a second, looking at her. She looks into the fire. He turns quietly up R.C.; puts up his eyeglasses and looks at the portrait of Mr. Brownlee. They stand a moment in silence*]

Mrs. B. Mr. Warburton!

Warb. Madam?

Mrs. B. Have you ever found any use for such a thing as memory during your experience as a diplomatist?

Warb. A—memory?

Mrs. B. A memory. If such a faculty is ever demanded in diplomatic life —I—you will pardon my frankness—but—I—I really wonder at your success.

Warb. [*Pleasantly*] I do not understand you.

Mrs. B. On second thought, I am wrong. The art of forgetting with accuracy requires an excellent memory.

Warb. Really, madam—I—

Mrs. B. You were speaking of a—a certain—misunderstanding—in which you and I were concerned—about thirteen years ago. The remarkable distinctness with which you have forgotten your own relations to that affair convinces me that you have an unusually good memory.

Warb. Upon my soul, Mrs. Brownlee, I—

Mrs. B. You remarked that a young girl of nineteen is the most unreasonable creature in the world. May I ask, sir, whether every young man of twenty-seven is an infallible philosopher?

WARB. Yes, my dear madam, I trust nothing I have said in reference to that affair has given rise to the slightest unpleasant feeling on your part.

MRS. B. Oh! Certainly not, sir. Not in the least, sir. Quite the contrary. The manner in which you have referred to our mutual associations has been calculated to arouse a particularly pleasant feeling on my part! [*She taps the fender with her foot*]

WARB. I assure you—I—I merely intended to recall—in a good-natured way—an incident which can have no serious interest, of course, for either of us, at the present time. And yet it is one which must be always more or less interesting to both of us—as a part of our early personal experience. I meant to say nothing about yourself in particular, as a young girl, which we should not both recognize as characteristic of young girls in general. I can say with perfect frankness, indeed, that I really think—you—never appeared to greater advantage than on that occasion. Your appearance, in fact, has lingered in my memory from that day to the present. You had on a plain white dress, trimmed prettily with a few fresh violets, which I had just gathered for you in the garden. You were standing near the window—I remember your exact attitude—when you first began the quarrel. [*She turns suddenly, drawing up and looking at him indignantly*] You remember? [*She sails across to extreme R. front, where she folds her arms and pats her foot*] As a young man of twenty-seven being an "infallible philosopher"—[*Moving down across L.*] certainly not, my dear madam—certainly not—Ha! Ha! Ha! On the contrary, I regard a young man of twenty-seven, in love, as the greatest dunce in the world—Ha! Ha! Ha! I speak from experience! I was a dunce at twenty-seven!

MRS. B. For the first time, Mr. Warburton, since we have been indulging in these—pleasant—reminiscences—your memory has assumed its normal functions. It was the fact that I was not a "dunce" that compelled me to regard your relations to Laura Malvern as the proper subject of an explanation. [*Moving towards R. of table, and speaking with increasing vehemence*]

WARB. [*Quickly approaching L.*] My dear Florence—[*She draws up*] Mrs. Brownlee—you would persist that I was in the wrong. [*Half angrily*]

MRS. B. Indeed! And which of us was the most obstinate, sir? You would persist in being in the wrong! [*Sitting R. of table, provoked and excited*]

WARB. I assured you of my perfect willingness to forget and forgive everything. [*Sitting L. of table with similar manner*]

MRS. B. Y-e-s? [*Patting her foot more and more violently, her temper getting the better of her*] I—I—remember—your condescension!

WARB. You would not listen to me.

MRS. B. Silence, sir!

WARB. I—

MRS. B. Not another word!

WARB. Any more than you will, now.

MRS. B. I, an unreasonable creature! I—indeed!—I would not listen to you! Laura Malvern afterwards confessed to me herself, that you were both in the wrong!

WARB. Well—really—I—you will excuse me—but I don't know that I am obliged to recognize a confession of my sins—by proxy.

MRS. B. Laura cried about it—in my own room—for two hours—and I forgave her.

WARB. [*Assuming a self-repressed and complacent air*] Laura Malvern was a good girl; pretty, too. Laura was a charming girl.

MRS. B. Very. Laura had so many charms she could afford to waste them.

WARB. There was a stately air about her—an air, so to speak of—

MRS. B. An air of—superiority—to those about her!

WARB. There was at the same time a certain—simplicity—a freshness—

MRS. B. Her simplicity was fascinating. She hadn't enough of it to become—your wife—apparently.

WARB. I have often thought—of course, I never received any assurance—of my—my—possible hopes—in that direction; but I have often thought—I dare say—that is—I have always had a lingering feeling—heigh-ho!—Laura Malvern might have made me—happy.

MRS. B. Ha! Ha! Ha! Ha! Ha! Ha! [*Bursting suddenly into a peal of laughter, and rising. Warburton rises, and regards her, without smiling*] Ha! Ha! Ha! Ha! Ha! You'd better cross the street—and—Ha! Ha! Ha!—discuss the matter with Laura herself. She is the mother of five boys. [*Moving up R.*] Ha! Ha! Ha! Ha! Ha!

WARB. Ha! Ha! Ha! Ha!—[*Joining her in the laugh, and moving down L.*] Ha! Ha! Ha! Ha! [*He turns and extends both his hands towards her. She extends her hands towards him. He moves up and later takes her hands in his own, up R.*] A widower of forty.

MRS. B. Quarreling as if we were mere children.

BOTH. [*Swinging their hands*] Ha! Ha! Ha! Ha! Ha! Ha!

WARB. Beginning again precisely where we left off.

MRS. B. Thirteen years ago. [*Warburton looks into her face, earnestly. She drops her eyes. Enter Henry, R.U.E. They drop each other's hands as if interrupted*] Eh? Henry? Oh—yes. [*She moves to mantel, L., he to piano, R. She receives a small box of rosewood and mother-of-pearl from Henry*] That will do, Henry. [*Exits, R.U.E. Mrs. Brownlee glances at Warburton, who is looking over the music at piano. She stands turned away from him, and takes the packet of letters from the bosom of her dress, glancing back at him over her shoulder once or twice as she does so. She places the letters in the box, closing the lid, deliberately, and locking it; then looks over at him]*

WARB. [*Reading from sheet of music*]

> "My thoughts still cling to the mouldering past,
> But the hopes of youth fall thick in the blast,
> And the days are dark and dreary.
>
> "Be still, sad heart, and cease repining;
> Behind the clouds is the sun still shining."

MRS. B. [*Walking to L. of table*] My servant has brought me the box which I instructed him to get.

WARB. [*Moving to R. of table*] Ah! [*She deliberately unlocks the box, throws the lid open and takes out the letters*]

MRS. B. Your letters to me, Mr. Warburton. They were exactly where I thought they were.

WARB. I see. [*He takes up the packet of her letters from the table. They look down a moment from the respective packets in their hands*] What curious creatures young lovers are. It takes so slight a thing to make them quarrel.

MRS. B. Mere trifles set them off. [*Sits*]

WARB. It all seems to come back to me as vividly as if it happened yesterday. After our—misunderstanding—I returned home in a very excited state—frame of mind. I remember distinctly, I could not sleep all night. I tossed about till morning.

MRS. B. I cried myself to sleep. Comical to think about, now.

WARB. I remember—I arose next morning, fully determined to return your letters at once—as you had commanded. I did them up carefully in a paper, but I lingered over each so long it took me all the morning.

MRS. B. It was noon before I finally had the ribbon on your packet.

WARB. I failed to send them to you; somehow, I could not find it in my heart to part with them at that time; some foolish, longing fancy. How curiously our feelings alter with time! All such fancies, of course, have passed away long ago—and we—we can now exchange these same letters—face to face—without the slightest emotion on either side. Permit me, madam. [*Passing her the letters*]

MRS. B. We are like different people now. Allow me, Mr. Warburton. [*Passing him his letters*]

WARB. Ha! Ha! Ha! Ha! [*Laughing quietly, in a half-amused manner*] What a harmless pair of simpletons we were, to be sure, when we wrote those letters—Ha! Ha! Ha! [*Running his fingers over the letters*] We might amuse ourselves, Mrs. Brownlee.

MRS. B. Amuse ourselves?

WARB. Ha! Ha! Ha! Ha! I will sacrifice myself. My hair is gray now. You may laugh at me to your heart's content. I will read aloud some of my youthful nonsense. Ha! Ha! Ha! Ha!

MRS. B. Ha! Ha! Ha! Excellent! And I haven't the slightest objection to reading you some of mine. I am a widow now—staid and sensible. We can laugh at each other. It will be rare sport—for both of us—at our age.

WARB. Ha! Ha! Ha! Ha! We can have a merry time over the romantic absurdities of our own youth. Ha! Ha! Ha! Ah, here is one. You remember that evening, Florence, we were walking in the grove and lost our way?

MRS. B. Oh—yes. I remember it perfectly, Edward.

WARB. It was the first time, if you remember, Mrs. Brownlee, that I mentioned to you—the fact—that—I—ah—entertained—serious views.

MRS. B. I recall the incident, Mr. Warburton—and the old stone wall, Edward, where we sat so long together, wondering which was the way home. Proceed, Mr. Warburton.

WARB. This letter was evidently written on the following day. [*Reads*] "My darling rosebud"—Ha! Ha! Ha! Ha! Ha!

MRS. B. Ha! Ha! Ha! Ha!—[*She stops laughing abruptly; looks at him as he continues to laugh; turns away, with a slightly nettled air. She tries to join him again, but stops, piqued*]

WARB. "Rosebud."—Ha! Ha! Ha! Ha!—

MRS. B. Really—I—really fail to see anything so very amusing in that, Mr. Warburton. [*He stops laughing and looks across at her*] I was barely nineteen at that time. As you have yourself recalled, I dressed in simple white. I don't see anything so particularly inappropriate on your part in comparing a young girl—who—who was not positively ugly—in comparing a young girl at that age, with a rosebud.

WARB. Certainly not, my dear madam, nothing could have been more appropriate. [*Reads*] "My darling rosebud"—Ha! Ha!—[*Checks himself again, glances at her, and continues his reading*] "The skies seem brighter to me this morning, darling Florence. All the melodies of nature more delightful to my ears; life a grander thing—a more glorious reality—more full of golden promises—"

MRS. B. Ha! Ha! Ha! Ha! Ha! Ha!—[*Bursting into a ripple of merry laughter. He starts to laugh with her, but soon stops and looks at her, seriously, across the table. She finally restrains herself and speaks demurely*] Go on.

WARB. Allow me to observe, madam, that while the language which I have just read is—ardent—unusually ardent—and—to a certain extent laughable—perhaps—on that account—allow me to remark—there is something so intensely earnest—something so deeply serious, madam—in the naturally exuberant feelings of a young man, under such circumstances—of course, we might laugh—to a certain extent—at the form in which those feelings are expressed—at the same time—

MRS. B. Pardon the interruption. Proceed, Mr. Warburton.

WARB. Certainly. [*Returns to letter*] "The skies—melodies of nature—golden promises." Ah—Here it is: "Life seems brighter to me, et cetera—since you gave me the tender assurance, last evening, that you would be mine—all mine—mine only—mine to love and to cherish—forever."

MRS. B. Ha! Ha! Ha! Ha! Ha! Ha! Ha! Ha! Ha! [*Again bursting into a merry laugh. He looks across at her, sternly; puts down letters on the table with some emphasis; rises; walks upstage; looks out of window, L.U. corner; turns back; pauses and looks up at portrait, up R. He returns to his seat, sits, looks across at her, sternly; turns away and folds his arms, assuming a rigid attitude and a stern expression. Mrs. Brownlee checks her laughter and regards him with an amused look*] Go on, pray, go on, Mr. Warburton.

WARB. I don't think there is anything more of special interest in the letters.

MRS. B. Oh—I am really beginning to feel interested. But it is only fair that I should give you a chance to laugh at me, now. Ha! Ha! Ha! [*Opening her own packet*] They are only the silly fancies of a young girl. You may laugh at me as heartily as you like; I will laugh with you. Ah—this one—oh! Edward!

WARB. [*Turning towards her*] Florence!

MRS. B. You remember that day we rode over to Minnehousic Falls together, in my little pony phaeton?

WARB. Yes—Ha! Ha! Ha!—the pony shied.

MRS. B. At another pair of geese. Ha! Ha! Ha! I nearly fell out, you know.

WARB. I was obliged to hold you in the phaeton during the rest of the journey.

MRS. B. Nearly seven miles. This letter was written the next morning. I am telling you how much I enjoyed the drive.

WARB. It was a pleasant drive.

MRS. B. Ah—[*Taking another letter*] This was written on the evening of the day after our first engagement. I had just received yours—the one you were reading a moment ago. This is an answer to it.

WARB. M-m.

MRS. B. [*Reading*] "My own dear life."

WARB. Ha! Ha! Ha! Ha! Ha! Ha!—[*Laughing heartily. She looks across at him sharply. He checks himself abruptly*]

MRS. B. If you see anything so very absurd in the girlish enthusiasm which dictated—

WARB. Nothing whatever, my dear Florence.

MRS. B. "My—own—dear—life." [*With deliberate and spiteful emphasis, looking straight in his face over the letter*] You can hear that without a smile. I will proceed. [*Reads*] "Your dear, sweet, nice letter has just come." [*A movement from Warburton as if trying to keep from laughter. She looks at him, sharply, a moment, then continues*] "I have read it over and over a dozen times already. I cannot tell you, Edward, dear, how happy I have been all day. My—" Oh! yes, it is blurred— "My soul"—that's it— "My soul has always yearned for a far-off, unattainable something in the dim hereafter of life."

WARB. Ha! Ha! Ha! Ha!—umph! [*Straightening his face, with nervous struggles in his chair. He finally succeeds, and looks at her, soberly*]

MRS. B. [*Reading*] "A far-off, unattainable something in the dim hereafter of life. The cravings of a woman's nature for that heart-food—which —which—which—oh!—which love—the cravings of a woman's nature for that heart-food which love alone—can supply."

WARB. Ha! Ha! Ha! Ha! Ha! Ha! [*Bursting into merry and continued laughter. She draws up, biting her lips; puts down letters with emphasis; rises, moves upstage to window, looking back at Warburton, then out of window. Warburton stops laughing; looks up at her over his shoulder; rises, moving to R.C.; turns and looks up at her, seriously. She turns down L.C., stops before mantel, glances over at him, then looks into the fire. He crosses to her*] Florence! [*Extending his hand. She glances back at him, averts her head and slightly extends her hand towards him. He takes it in both of his own, with a quick but earnest manner, and continues*] We were both of us writing the truth in those days. We have been trying to act a falsehood in these calm, practical days of middle life. Let us acknowledge, now, that we were wiser, then. I came to return your old love letters—I have brought you back my heart. [*She hesitates, looking away; then turns and drops her head upon his breast; his arm about her waist. Music same as at rise of curtain*]

CURTAIN

THE BANKER'S DAUGHTER

THE BANKER'S DAUGHTER

Fɪʀsт produced as *Lilian's Last Love* at Hooley's Theatre, Chicago, September 4, 1873.

Produced under the present title at the Union Square Theatre, New York, November 30, 1878, with the following cast of characters:

Jᴏʜɴ Sᴛʀᴇʙᴇʟᴏᴡ	CHARLES R. THORNE, JR.
Lᴀᴡʀᴇɴᴄᴇ Wᴇsᴛʙʀᴏᴏᴋ	JOHN PARSELLE
Bᴀʙʙᴀɢᴇ	J. H. STODDART
G. Wᴀsʜɪɴɢᴛᴏɴ Pʜɪᴘᴘs	J. B. POLK
Bʀᴏᴡɴ	W. J. LE MOYNE
Cᴏᴜɴᴛ ᴅᴇ Cᴀʀᴏᴊᴀᴄ	M. V. LINGHAM
Hᴀʀᴏʟᴅ Rᴏᴜᴛʟᴇᴅɢᴇ	WALDEN RAMSAY
M. ᴅᴇ Mᴏɴᴛᴠɪʟʟᴀɪs	C. W. BOWSER
Dʀ. Wᴀᴛsᴏɴ	H. F. DALY
Jᴇʀʀᴏʟᴅ	W. S. QUIGLEY
Lɪʟɪᴀɴ Wᴇsᴛʙʀᴏᴏᴋ	SARA JEWETT
Fʟᴏʀᴇɴᴄᴇ Sᴛ. Vɪɴᴄᴇɴᴛ Bʀᴏᴡɴ	MAUD HARRISON
Mʀs. Fᴀɴɴʏ Hᴏʟᴄᴏᴍʙ	MRS. E. J. PHILLIPS
Lɪᴢᴇᴛᴛᴇ	SARAH COWELL

NATALIE $\left\{\begin{array}{l}\text{LITTLE EFFIE BARRET} \\ \\ \text{LITTLE LELIA GRANGER}\end{array}\right.$

This production ran for one hundred thirty-seven performances, closing April 16, 1879.

Produced as *The Old Love and the New* at the Court Theatre, London, December 15, 1879.

Subsequent productions of *The Banker's Daughter* include:

1. A short run at the Union Square Theatre, beginning December 15, 1880, with Frederic de Belleville as Count de Carojac, and Owen S. Fawcett as G. Washington Phipps.
2. One week at the Grand Opera House, New York, beginning February 21, 1881.
3. Two weeks at the Grand Opera House, New York, beginning August 15, 1881. The cast included: Joseph Whiting, Mr. and Mrs. Charles Walcot, W. S. Daboll, Edward L. Tilton, Joseph A. Wilkes, Archie Cowper, Adele Belgarde, and Rose Graham.
4. One week at the Union Square Theatre, New York, beginning January 30, 1882, by A. W. Palmer's Company.
5. One week at the Windsor Theatre, New York, beginning February 20, 1882.
6. One week at Booth's Theatre, New York, beginning April 9, 1883; the cast included: Sara Jewett, George Clark, Frank Mordaunt, John W. Jennings, W. J. Ferguson, Barton Hill, H. A. Weaver, Sr., Nettie Guion, Mrs. E. J. Phillips, and W. T. Harris.
7. One week at the Apollo Theatre, New York, beginning February 8, 1886.
8. One week at the Apollo Theatre, New York, beginning April 5, 1886.
9. One week at the People's Theatre, New York, beginning February 7, 1887.
10. One week at John Thompson's Eighth Street Theatre, New York, beginning February 7, 1888.
11. The Grand Opera House, New York, June 18, 1888; the cast included: Herbert Kelcey, Frazer Coulter, Robert Hilliard, W. J. Ferguson, B. T. Ringgold, John W. Jennings, George Woodward, Georgia Cayvan, and Ethel Greybrooke.
12. One week at the Columbus Theatre, New York, beginning May 30, 1898.

13. One week at the American Theatre, New York, beginning March 11, 1901.
14. Reported playing in stock as late as 1914.

TEXT AND SOURCE

The present text of *The Banker's Daughter* is taken verbatim from the privately printed edition of the play bearing the following title-page: The/ Banker's Daughter/ by/ Bronson Howard/ Copyrighted, 1878, by Bronson Howard.

Several typographical errors in the above text have been corrected in the present edition.

In his *Autobiography of a Play* Howard gives a long, circumstantial account of the writing of *Lilian's Last Love* and its change into *The Banker's Daughter,* then into *The Old Love and the New.* In this discussion he is scrupulous about acknowledging indebtedness; referring to a certain scene, he says:

> This scene, in my opinion, is one of the most beautiful scenes ever written for the stage. At the risk of breaking the tenth commandment myself, I do not hesitate to say, I wish I had written it. As I did not, however, I can express the hope that the name of Mr. A. R. Cazauran, who did write it, will never be forgotten in connection with this play as long as the play itself may be remembered. I wrote the scene myself first; but when he wrote it according to his own ideas, it was so much more beautiful than my own that I would have broken a law of dramatic art if I had not accepted it. I should not have been giving the public the best play I could, under the circumstances. Imbued as my own mind was, with all the original motives of the piece, it would have been impossible for me to have made changes within a few weeks without the assistance Mr. Cazauran could give me; this assistance was invaluable to me in all parts of the revised piece.[1]

Professor Arthur H. Quinn states that this "scene for which Howard thanks Cazauran probably owed its original inspiration to the interview between Rodolphe and Armande in Boucicault's *Led Astray,* but the tone was altered."[2] Other differences in Boucicault's *Led Astray* are: the reconciliation is more mechanical; the reunion is effected by a grown daughter; it is the husband who has despised the faithful wife's love and who now changes his attitude.

[1] "The Autobiography of a Play," *Publications of the Dramatic Museum of Columbia University,* First Series, New York, 1914.

[2] Arthur H. Quinn, *A History of the American Drama from the Civil War to the Present Day,* New York, 1936, p. 49.

CHARACTERS

John Strebelow

Lawrence Westbrook

Babbage

G. Washington Phipps

Brown

Count de Carojac

Harold Routledge

M. de Montvillais

Dr. Watson

Footman

Lilian Westbrook

Florence St. Vincent Brown

Mrs. Fanny Holcomb

Lizette

Natalie

Time: 1869.

ACT I.

Set: *Handsome extension room in the house of Lawrence Westbrook, New York. Rich furniture, including handsome Japanese screen in L.U.C. At rise of curtain, enter Westbrook, R.U.D., followed by Footman.*

West. [*Crossing and sitting at L. table*] A poached egg, some anchovy toast, a little Chetna, some tea—in the meantime the papers and whatever mail there is. [*Sitting at table*] I feel a sort of shivering sensation; I seem to feel a draught; pull that screen around here. [*Footman does so*] That will do; what time is it?

Foot. Half past two, sir; the papers are on the table.

West. Very well! Get the mail.

Foot. Yes, sir. [*Exits R.U.D.*]

West. [*Yawning and shivering—opening Herald*] I think Babbage is right. I must be a fool to sit up listening to gossip of a society I really take no interest in; what the deuce is it to plain Lawrence Westbrook, banker and broker, who the best swordsman in Paris is, that he should sit up till five in the morning to hear it discussed? That Carojac must be a wizard though, if he performed half those feats; I suppose now that fellow would rather run a man through the body than inherit a fortune. He is about the only foreign nobleman that never asked me to cash a note for him. [*Enter Footman R.U.D.*] He says he has a greater favor than that to ask me.

Foot. [*At table*] The mail, sir.

West. [*Taking letters off salver*] Very well. [*Places letters on table*] See to my breakfast.

Foot. Yes, sir. [*Exits R.U.D.*]

West. [*Fixing on particular column in the Herald*] More failures! London catches it sometimes as well as New York. None of these can affect us, however; the gold balance at the Clearing House—two—four—twenty-nine—five. Hm! Hang it! I can't get up any interest in anything. [*Throws paper down*] Let me see these. [*Opens letters*] Babbage ought to have this. [*Takes up another*] The regular quarterly bill of Lilian's dressmaker. [*Takes up another*] From Strebelow! What can he write about? I saw him yesterday. [*Opens letter—reads*] Permission to address my daughter as a suitor. [*Looks pleased*] This is gratifying. I know few men that I respect more than John Strebelow. I'm sorry; it would not be May and December, but it would be

May and October. Strebelow must be forty—rich, honored, well-born, a man of unusual intellect. I wish he were but ten years younger. [*Looks at letter*] Will call for my answer this afternoon. He can have my permission; he'll never gain hers.

LILIAN. [*Heard laughing outside, R.L.D.*] Serious! Why, count! I can't be serious.

CAROJAC. [*Outside, speaking with French accent*] When will you be?

LIL. [*Bursting into room—riding habit, whip*] Whenever you are merry.

CARO. [*R., following in riding dress—whip*] But, mademoiselle, you always treat me the same way; you will never give me the answer. You parry all my attacks with a laugh.

LIL. [*C., laughing*] With so expert a chevalier, I must fence as best I may. No shield so safe against the point of a proposal as a lady's laugh, you know. That's your Balzac's aphorism. Do not look so sad; you seem like a Don Quixote, holding your whip as a small sword.

CARO. [*Vexed*] But—

LIL. Some other day, count, some other day.

CARO. I cannot wait; I must return to Paris.

LIL. [*Archly crossing to R.H.*] Good-by. Send me some gloves.

CARO. [*Bitterly*] You would not mock yourself of Mr. Routledge so.

LIL. Sir! You have no right—

CARO. I offend you—I beg your pardon; but I offer you—

LIL. [*Aside*] What I don't want.

CARO. The hand and title for a gentleman, and you will not give me an answer. But I will wait, and call tonight.

LIL. Tomorrow.

CARO. Tonight.

LIL. Indeed! I say now next week—next month—next year, if I wish. And, till then, Count de Carojac, *au revoir*. [*Exits laughing, snapping her whip, R.U.D.*]

CARO. She mocks herself of me. A week ago she was with Routledge when I call. She makes sport of me then, too, and he laugh; if I catch [*Clutching his whip*] M. Routledge in Paris, I may find a chance to make him smile wiz de oder side of him mouth. [*Going off R.L.D.*]

WEST. [*From behind screen, laughing*] Come here, count, come here. [*Rises, comes forward*] You must not be offended with Lilian; she is a spoiled child. But to be frank with you, I must tell you I am pretty certain you have no chance with her; with all her giddiness, if she at all entertained your proposal, she is naturally too true to so receive it.

CARO. Zen I will go back to Paris. I only wait here for her answer; when I hear her engagement with M. Routledge was what you call broke, I flatter myself I might—[*Enter Fanny R.L.D.*] Ah, Madame Halcomb! [*Bows*]

FANNY. [*R.*] I hope, count, you and Lilian had a pleasant ride.

CARO. [*C.*] Mlle. Westbrook enjoyed it vera much. She laughed all ze time [*Aside*] at my expense.

FANNY. A bad augury for you, count.

CARO. Oh, yes; I have my conje, and now will take me back to Paris. M. Westbrook, you will soon, I hope, geeve me an opportunity to repay there ze hospitality you tendayr me here.

WEST. [*L., shaking hands with Carojac*] I shall be only too happy, count, believe me.

CARO. [*Crossing to R.*] Zen, good-by.

WEST. A pleasant voyage.

FANNY. [*C.*] Good-by, count.

CARO. [*To Westbrook*] Much thanks. [*To Fanny, bowing and shaking hands*] Good-by. [*Exits R.L.D.*]

FANNY. So Lilian has refused the count.

WEST. [*Laughing*] She merely laughed at him; I had to do the refusing.

FANNY. [*Sitting on ottoman, C.*] Well, I'm glad it's over. She and Routledge fell out about him, and while he remained here it seemed impossible to know what might happen.

WEST. [*Laughing*] I certainly did not wish the count for a son-in-law; and I'm very glad my little girl had too much sense to be caught by his title. His character is not exactly what I like—ready to quarrel, a duelist!—and seeming to inherit but one ingredient of his ancestors' chivalry, its courage, and but one quality of their wit, its cynicism. A charming club acquaintance, but no son-in-law for me. Better Harold Routledge even.

FANNY. [*Approvingly*] Much better. [*Enter Footman R.U.E.*]

FOOT. Your breakfast is ready, sir.

WEST. Very well. [*Footman puts screen upstage. Exits R.H.*]

FANNY. [*Rising*] Your breakfast at three in the afternoon?

WEST. [*Crossing to R. and U.P.*] Yes, I was up late at the club; but I have a better husband for Lilian than either a French count or a poor artist.

FANNY. A better husband—who?

WEST. John Strebelow.

FANNY. A noble gentleman, but he is old; too old for a wife of eighteen.

WEST. Not forty yet!

FANNY. But I'm sure Lilian loves Harold Routledge.

WEST. Pshaw! I'll bet she has forgotten him already. Boys and girls of eighteen have whims, not love. You thought your heart would break when you married comfortable John Holcomb instead of romantic Alfred Harcourt. Yet you made a splendid wife, and a happy one.

FANNY. [*Dryly. Sits L.H.*] Did I? You judge by what you see, and all you see is the outside; where a woman is concerned, the blindest thing on earth is a man.

WEST. Well, well, sister, I'm not going to sell the girl. We'll talk of her again—after I've had my breakfast. [*Exits R.U.D.*]

FANNY. [*Solus*] Sell the girl! No, not so much a pound, I suppose, but like other fathers, you'll supply her a mentor where she wants a husband, and give her a stone where she asks for bread, on the plea that the stone is a diamond. [*Enter Lilian R.U.D.*]

LIL. [*Laughing*] Is the count gone? Good morning, aunt. [*Kisses Fanny*]

FANNY. Yes, pet. So you refused him?

LIL. Of course I did—courtship, castle, chivalry, and all. It was so very funny to see him. [*Laughs*]

FANNY. [*Looking at her steadily*] I thought you would.

LIL. You knew I would, when I laughed at him, which was from the door to Mount St. Vincent, and from Mount St. Vincent to the door again. He looked as if he'd like to call me out. [*Laughs*]

FANNY. This is the fourth offer you have refused in two weeks.

LIL. Is it? I don't want to marry. I'm as happy as a lark, and just as gay. I've done nothing but laugh all the morning. It was such fun. [*Laughs hysterically*]

FANNY. [*Rising and going to her, taking her by the waist*] Lilian, you are very miserable.

LIL. [*Looks up at Fanny; her hysterical laughter gradually becomes hysteric sobbing, and as she sinks on the chair, L.H., to which Fanny leads her, she bursts into tears*] My heart is breaking.

FANNY. [*Sighing*] I know, dear; I know! Harold Routledge sails for Europe tomorrow.

LIL. [*Sobbing*] I've tried so hard—so hard to forget him. I sent him back our engagement ring. I've done all I could to drive him from my mind. I stayed up half the night, reading all his letters before I—I b—burned them.

FANNY. My poor darling, listen to me; I lost my poor Alfred just in the same way! Don't repeat my mistake; write to Harold; tell him to come to you.

LIL. [*Rising and crossing to R. quickly*] Never! never! If my heart were to break a thousand times over, I would not do that. It is his place to write to me. He was in the wrong. [*Walks up and down the stage*]

FANNY. In the wrong?

LIL. He should have known me better than to fly at me about a mere flirtation with the Count de Carojac. He knew well enough it was all in fun; mere amusement.

FANNY. Well, well, dear, let me write to him. Let me tell him you have refused the count.

LIL. [*Demurely*] But, Aunt Fanny, he must not think I asked you to write.

FANNY. [*Smiling*] Certainly not. [*Crossing to R.*]

LIL. And you'll tell him I refused three other offers!

FANNY. [*Smiling*] Indeed I will.

LIL. And—ask him to—to call and see—and see you!

FANNY. Exactly.

LIL. [*Takes Fanny's head in her hands and kisses it*] Oh, you darling, good aunt!

FANNY. [*Kissing Lilian*] I am doing what I know your mother would do if she were alive to do it—what [*Sighing*] she would have done for me had I been wise enough to let her. I'll go to my room and write the letter.

LIL. You'll let me see it?

FANNY. Certainly not. It is none of your business, you know. [*Laughs*]

LIL. [*With frank, hearty laugh this time*] Ah—oh! Of course not—I forgot—I'm so happy.

FANNY. Heaven grant you may continue so, my darling. [*Exits R.U.D., R.2.E.*]

LIL. [*Solus*] Will he come? [*In affected doubt*] I rather think he will. I wonder how my eyes look—[*Goes to glass on mantel, L.H. Looks at herself; touches up her hair; turns from mirror*] I am pretty sure he will come. [*Enter Florence St. Vincent R.C.R.*]

FLOR. How de doo, Lilian?

LIL. [*Turning from glass*] Florence.

FLOR. [*Both sitting on ottoman, C.*] Riding with the Count de Carojac, eh? I saw you ride by our house. You to be a countess? Isn't the count magnificent? They say he's fought six duels, and he's a real nobleman, fresh from Paris, like the new spring bonnets just imported. I've been on the Boulevard driving with G. Washington Phipps, behind his new team—chestnuts—2:37. I suppose you've heard the news?

LIL. What news, dear?

FLOR. I'm going to be married.

LIL. [*Astonished*] Married! To whom?

FLOR. Mum! To old Mr. Brown, the millionaire.

LIL. To Mr. Brown! Why, he is nearly seventy!

FLOR.   Exactly sixty-nine the twenty-eighth of last February. He says he's only fifty-nine, but I know better. I would not marry him if he were only fifty-nine; fifty-two years between us. There always ought to be some difference, you know.

LIL.   Surely, Florence, you are not serious; your father cannot consent to such a sacrifice.

FLOR.   My father is delighted! It is not every man that has a son-in-law old enough to be his father-in-law. My youngest son will be thirty-eight years old. When the minister pronounces me Mr. Brown's wife, I'll be a grandmother. [*Laughs*] One of my granddaughters is nearly as old as I am already. Brown is a millionaire three times over at least. Father is president of a life insurance company, and he knows about such things. He says the average life over seventy is about five years; allow five years more, for untoward accident; ten years, I'll be only twenty-nine. That's young, you know, for a rich widow.

LIL.   Oh, Florence! Marriage is not a joke.

FLOR.   Then I should like to know what it is. [*Laughs*] I haven't been able to keep my face straight five minutes at a time since I told old Brown I'd be his wife. [*Laughs. Enter Footman followed by Babbage R.L.D.*]

FOOT.   I'll speak to Mr. Westbrook, sir. [*Exits R.U.D.*]

LIL.   Oh, Mr. Babbage! [*Goes to him pleasantly as he moves downstage and gives him both her hands*]

FLOR.   How do you do, Mr. Babbage?

BAB.   [*With Lilian's hands in his, nods his head at Florence, then taps Lilian under the chin*] I su—I sue! Heigh-ho. [*Kisses Lilian*] Now run away both of you and play with your dolls. [*Florence and Lilian look at each other and laugh*] I have important business with your father, Lilian. [*Moves to L.H. Looks at papers in large pocketbook*]

LIL.   [*Going*] Come, Florence.

FLOR.   [*Aside to Lilian, as they go*] Brown is at least fifteen years older than he is. [*Laughs*]

LIL.   Florence! [*Lilian and Florence exit C.U.D.*]

FLOR.   [*Beyond the door, laughing*] It is such a joke on both of us. [*Her laugh is heard dying away in the distance*]

BAB.   [*Solus, sitting R. of L. table*] Fifty thousand and a hundred and fifty—sixty-five—the registered bonds—Third National. [*Enter Westbrook, leisurely and yawning, R.U.D.*]

WEST.   Ah, Babbage.

BAB.   Just up? Three P.M.! Excuse my disturbing you so early in the morning.

WEST. [*Sits on ottoman, C.*] Right from the office, I suppose. For heaven's sake, don't talk business to me today, Babbage. I was out late last night, and I have a wretched headache.

BAB. You have a headache. Well, I've got something to cure your headache.

WEST. Eh!

BAB. Westbrook, you're a fool!

WEST. Thank you.

BAB. How much is this house worth?

WEST. Seventy-five thousand—why do you ask?

BAB. Is it free from incumbrance?

WEST. [*Embarrassed*] Y-e-s, that is—no—I put it in for a collateral yesterday—a private speculation of my own—a mere temporary matter.

BAB. How much?

WEST. Fifty thousand dollars.

BAB. Have you heard the news?

WEST. What news?

BAB. Do you want it sudden, or do you want it gradually? [*Pauses*] Westbrook, the firm of Babbage & Westbrook, Broad Street, will go into bankruptcy at three o'clock tomorrow afternoon. [*Rising—Westbrook is about to start to his feet, Babbage holds him down by the arm and resumes*] The firm of Traphagan & Traynor, London, went into bankruptcy this morning—news by cable. We hold their paper for three hundred and seventy-five thousand dollars. [*Westbrook falls back stunned in his chair*] How's your headache? [*Crossing to R.H.*]

WEST. My poor daughter!

BAB. Your own doing, Westbrook. The life of a quiet and respectable banker did not satisfy you; you must play the Rothschild, the merchant prince, live in imperial style, entertain foreign nobles, make your daughter—

WEST. Don't, Babbage—don't.

BAB. With your extravagance and private speculations, you've compelled the firm to run too near its capital, and now—

WEST. My poor daughter.

BAB. And mine! I have three daughters, four sons, and damn it, I've got a wife. Would to Heaven that were all. But our ruin involves others—you know what I mean.

WEST. Our depositors!

BAB. The earnings of the poor; of the legacy of the widow, the inheritance of an orphan.

WEST. My God! It is terrible! [*Rising, crossing to L. corner and back to L.C.*]

BAB. We need thirty thousand to fully meet our paper tomorrow. I've strained everything—everybody! We can't raise it. If this house were only free from incumbrance.

WEST. It is not, it is hopelessly involved. [*Sits R. of L.H. table; his hand falls on a letter*]

BAB. Then ruin must come to you and yours, to me and mine, to thousands of poor, honest, hard-working—

WEST. [*Rising in agitation*] There is a way.

BAB. A way!

WEST. [*Taking Strebelow's letter*] Here, read this—I can't.

BAB. [*After putting on spectacles, reads*] John Strebelow—Miss Westbrook's hand in marriage! I see—having pawned your house, you would pawn your child! Westbrook, you're a fool. [*Returns note to Westbrook*]

WEST. But—

BAB. [*In great agitation*] Damn me, but I'd rather see the firm of Babbage & Westbrook go to the devil, than see the happiness of that girl sacrificed to it. Besides, your daughter, like your house, is encumbered.

WEST. What do you mean?

BAB. I mean that Harold Routledge holds a mortgage on the property.

WEST. But Lilian and Mr. Routledge have had a serious disagreement. [*Rings bell*]

BAB. Of course they have. A woman never quarrels with a man she does not love, and damn it, never tires of quarrelling with the man she does love. You have been married—I am married, we both know it. [*Enter Footman R.U.D.*]

WEST. Let Miss Lilian know I wish to see her without delay.

FOOT. Yes, sir. [*Exits R.U.D.*]

WEST. I take a different view of my daughter's happiness. I can hardly hope to avert the terrible calamity you announce through the wealth of Mr. Strebelow, though it may possibly so turn out. I certainly shall not ask him for a check convertible tomorrow in exchange for my daughter's hand; but with John Strebelow her future is safe, whatever comes to us. To give her to such a man is not to sacrifice, but to shield her from the storm. This is what I wish to do. If you care to hear the result, I will join you presently in the sitting room.

BAB. [*Going*] Yes, I'll wait. But if the credit of Babbage & Westbrook cannot be saved without the sacrifice of a young girl's heart, I'd rather see it crumpled to the dust, and act as assistant bookkeeper to a peanut stand for the rest of my natural life. [*Exits R. lower D.*]

WEST. [*Solus*]   It is not for my sake, it is for her own. No girl could be the wife of a man like Strebelow and not learn to love him. She will be provided for; she will keep her rank in society. What father could do otherwise? [*Enter Lilian R.U.D.*]

LIL.   You wish to see me, father?

WEST. [*Not looking at her*]   Yes, I—I received this note a while ago. What answer shall I send, or rather give, for Mr. Strebelow will soon call?

LIL.   Mr. Strebelow! [*Looks at letter*] Oh, papa!

WEST. [*His face still averted*]   What shall I say to him?

LIL.   It quite takes my breath away.

WEST. [*At the table, pretending to look at papers*]   It is a grand offer.

LIL.   Of course it is.

WEST.   And you may well be proud of it.

LIL.   Indeed I am proud, very proud.

WEST. [*Eagerly turning to her*]   Then I may answer, yes.

LIL.   Oh, no—no!

WEST.   No, why?

LIL.   I do not love Mr. Strebelow, papa. I esteem, revere him, like him very much; but I—I—I never thought of him in—in that way, you know.

WEST.   You have broken off your engagement with Harold Routledge?

LIL. [*Agitated*]   Yes, I—I have.

WEST.   You would soon learn to love Mr. Strebelow; why, when you were but twelve years old, you know, you used to call him your sweetheart. Oh, your old liking for him will soon return, after you are married to him.

LIL. [*Starting*]   After I am married to him. Why, papa!

WEST. [*Leading to ottoman, C.*]   Listen, my child. I am ruined! In a few days I will have no home of my own, no roof to cover you.

LIL. [*Bewildered*]   You, poor!

WEST.   Worse than poor—bankrupt. I would see you sheltered from wants, from humiliations you have never yet known.

LIL.   I'm not afraid, so long as I am with you. [*Kneeling at his feet*]

WEST. [*Putting her back on the ottoman, kissing her*]   Brave girl! But it is not only poverty, it is shame, disgrace. It is not only ourselves, it is hundreds, thousands, will find their ruin in mine! Who will heap upon your father's head the curses of the poor, the wail of the widow, and the tears of the orphan. I cannot survive it. [*Rising, taking L. corner*]

LIL. [*Rising*]   I see it! I see it! [*With forced calmness*] And this marriage would avert all this?

West. [*Back to L.C.*]   It would save us all. Thank God, your mother was spared this misery!

Lil.   Mother! Father, I—I will—I—

West.   Make the sacrifice—I mean—give your hand.

Lil.   My mother's last words to me were, "Do all you can to make your father's old age happy."

West. [*Averting his head again*]   One word will save it from infamy.

Lil.   Then I say it. Yes. [*Embrace*] But before you repeat that word to Mr. Strebelow, you must promise me one thing.

West.   Anything.

Lil.   It is this. You will tell Mr. Strebelow that I will be his—his wife. [*Pause*] That I accept him, if he will accept my hand without the heart I cannot now give him; and be satisfied with gratitude and respect instead of love. [*Crossing to L.H. Enter Footman, R. lower door, gives card to Westbrook*]

West.   Mr. Strebelow. Certainly, certainly. Show him in. [*Footman about to exit*]

Lil. [*To Footman*]   Stop—one moment. You [*To Westbrook*] will do what I asked?

West.   Yes.

Lil. [*To Footman*]   You can go. [*Exit Footman R.L.D.*] I could not trust myself to make such an explanation to Mr. Strebelow. I will leave you with him, father, and take with me your promise to be as frank with him as I have been with you. Then, if he will, he can take all I have left to give—my hand. [*Staggers*]

West. [*Leading her to a chair L.H.*]   But sit down, the suddenness of this has made you faint.

Lil.   Only a little; I—I don't think I will sit down—I might lack strength to rise again. [*Stands, leaning against chair. Enter Footman announcing Mr. Strebelow. Enter Strebelow R.L.D.*]

West. [*Going to meet him, they shake hands*]   My dear Strebelow, I'm delighted to see you, and to see you looking so well.

Streb.   Thanks. [*Crossing to Lilian, bowing*] Miss Westbrook. [*Goes toward her; she takes a feeble step to meet him; he holds out his hand, she places hers in it, her left hand clinging to the chair, L.H., for support*] May I hope my visit is equally welcome to you?

Lil. [*With calmness evidently voiced*]   So old a friend cannot be otherwise than welcome.

Streb.   I was in hopes your father had placed me in a more—I mean a different light than that of a mere friend.

LIL. My father has handed me your note, Mr. Strebelow. [*Stops short*]

STREB. Not, I trust, without the endorsement of his approval. [*Looking at Westbrook*]

WEST. I believe that Lilian can best tell you how much I approve of it.

STREB. [*To Lilian*] Let me hope to your father's approval, your own is added, and that—[*Seems embarrassed by Lilian's attitude*] and that I may expect an answer. [*Stops to take her hand*]

LIL. [*Giving her hand mechanically*] I must refer you to himself.

STREB. And after I have seen him, may I not see you?

LIL. [*Feebly*] Certainly. Father.

WEST. [*Crossing to Lilian, she takes his arm, lets go the chair, and walks to door R.U.E., turns, bows to Strebelow*] You will excuse Lilian and myself a moment. [*Exit, supporting Lilian, R.U.D.*]

STREB. [*Solus, crossing to L.C.*] Is my suit accepted under protest or is the strangeness of her manner the effect of mere timidity, a timidity probably increased by my formality? Still, there was an expression of suppressed emotion that may be either flattering or fatal to my affection. Those rumors, too, that I have heard upon the street. I will know the truth from Westbrook. I must in justice to her, in justice to myself. [*Enter Westbrook R.U.D.*]

WEST. [*Goes to Strebelow with outstretched hands*] John, I congratulate you.

STREB. Then I am accepted.

WEST. Why, certainly. Sit down.

STREB. [*Sits on ottoman, C.*] Westbrook, at such a moment frankness is a duty, and you will excuse it in a man to whom you entrust your daughter's happiness, and who trusts his own to her.

WEST. [*Embarrassed*] Certainly—certainly.

STREB. My proposal, though long contemplated by myself, must have appeared sudden to you—still more sudden to your daughter. Permission to address her as a suitor was all I expected. Her timid manner and her—

WEST. [*Trying to make light of it*] Tut! Tut! A girl of eighteen—besides she has been riding all the morning. Her nerves are out of order, and she is tired.

STREB. [*Watching him*] And she is yielding to no influence of yours?

WEST. [*Embarrassed*] Why should you think so?

STREB. Frankly then, because I have heard today that the firm of Babbage & Westbrook is likely to go to protest tomorrow.

WEST. [*Rising*] Mr. Strebelow!

STREB. Is it true?

WEST. We—we are—a little driven for ready money.

STREB. How much will be necessary to make your paper good?

WEST. Only thirty thousand dollars.

STREB. [*Rising*] May I write here? [*Sits at L.H. table*]

WEST. [*Feigning astonishment*] Why not?

STREB. [*Sits at table—writes*] This is the seventeenth—[*Taking pocket check-book from pocket*]

WEST. Of November—yes.

STREB. I will meet your deficiencies, Mr. Westbrook.

WEST. What! You?

STREB. Yes. Here is the check for the amount you need. You can give me what security you please, and at your own convenience. Did your daughter know of your financial troubles?

WEST. [*With effort*] She did not.

STREB. Then I wronged you both. Calm and formal as I am, I have long loved your daughter. I was her knight, her champion in the old days. She used to say I would be her sweetheart. She would lay her head on my breast, and go to sleep there; the little thing would nestle there, and I believe she has never fairly grown out of it, and I—and I did not wish—but you are free now, and your free answer is—

WEST. Yes.

STREB. [*Shaking hands with Westbrook*] Pardon my frankness and accept my thanks. May I see her?

WEST. [*Crossing to L.H., rings bell on L.H. table*] Of course.

STREB. It will be the endeavor of my life to render her happy—a solitary man, she will have all my care, all my love, and if her father needs my aid, he has only to speak. [*Enter Footman R.U.D.*]

WEST. Tell Miss Lilian Mr. Strebelow is waiting for her. [*Exit Footman R.U.D. Westbrook to Strebelow*] There is not a man in the world to whom I would so confidently entrust her—and I know that in giving her to you, I do all a father can to insure her happiness—and it is in that belief I do what I am doing. [*Enter Lilian R.U.D.*]

LIL. [*Down R.*] Mr. Strebelow!

STREB. [*Meeting her R.C.*] Lilian! I may call you that now?

LIL. My father has told you—

STREB. Your father has told me all. [*He holds out his hand*]

LIL. So be it then. [*Gives him her hand—he kisses it. Enter Aunt Fanny R.U.D.*]

FANNY. Mr. Strebelow. [*Bows*]

STREB. Mrs. Holcomb. [*Bows*]

FANNY. Will you excuse me? I have a word to say to Lilian.

WEST. Mr. Strebelow, if you will accompany me to the sitting room, Mr. Babbage and myself will explain how this sudden strain has arisen, owing to failure of a firm in London whose papers we largely hold. [*They cross and exit R.L.D., Strebelow bowing to the ladies*]

FANNY. He's come! I knew he would.

LIL. Harold!

FANNY. Yes. He's in the reception room. He kissed me for joy.

LIL. [*Wringing her hands*] Oh, what have I done? What have I done? [*Crosses to R.*]

FANNY. I told him I would send you to him. He cannot sit still a moment —not one moment.

LIL. See him—I will—I will. [*Goes toward door—at door rings bell*] But now, heavens, I dare not. [*Enter Footman R.D.*] Tell Mr. Routledge that Miss Westbrook cannot see him. [*Goes to Aunt Fanny*] I have concluded not to see—never again to see Harold—Mr. Routledge!

FANNY. [*Surprised*] Why?

LIL. Because, [*Steadies herself*] Aunt Fanny, Mr. Strebelow is to be my husband. Oh, Aunt Fanny, my heart is broken! [*Falls on ottoman. Quick drop of curtain*]

ACT II.

Salon. As curtain rises Lilian is discovered seated at piano L., Natalie standing by her side.

NAT. Oh, no, no! I want you to sing some more.

LIL. But there is no more, dear.

NAT. [*Imperiously*] Then make some more.

LIL. My dear, I am not able to do that.

NAT. [*Laughs, throws her arms around her mother, kisses her*] Then sing how much you love me. Oh, see, in the book [*Drags Lilian over to R., takes volume of Moore's Irish Melodies off table R.H., holds it up to her. Opens it haphazard*]

LIL. [*Taking book, sits R.C.*] This, this tells the story.

NAT. Oh, do sing.

LIL. [*Sings*]

> "I'd mourn the hopes that leave me,
>   If thy smile had left me, too.
> I'd weep when friends deceive me,

If thou wert, like them, untrue. [*Holding Natalie out before her*]

"But while I've thee before me,
    With heart so warm and eyes so bright,
    No clouds can linger o'er me,
That smile turns them all to light." [*Catching Natalie in her arms and lifting her to her lap*] So it does, darling, so it does! [*She kisses child. Westbrook has entered, C.R., at the last line of the last verse and stops at threshold looking at mother and child*]

WEST. Thank Heaven! I wish Fanny Holcomb could see this falsification of her prophecies, this justification of my wisdom.

NAT. [*Sees him over her mother's shoulder*] Oh, mamma, a gentleman. Is this grandpapa?

WEST. [*Coming down as Lilian puts Natalie down*] Yes, grandpapa come at last. [*Opens his arms to her. Natalie rushes into them. Kisses her, etc.*]

LIL. Oh, father! [*They embrace*]

WEST. Natalie has almost forgotten me, eh?

NAT. Your hair has grown so white.

WEST. [*Patting Natalie's head*] It is a long time since it looked like yours. [*To Lilian*] But you seem surprised to see me. Did you not receive my telegram? [*Putting her down*]

LIL. No. Nothing but your letter announcing your departure by the *Europa*.

WEST. I wrote you from Liverpool, and telegraphed you from Dover. But how is John? [*Enter Strebelow, R.3.E., with letter and telegram in hand*]

STREB. [*As he enters*] A letter from your father, Lilian, dated Liverpool. He ought to be here.

WEST. He is here! [*Strebelow crosses to him*]

STREB. [*As they shake hands*] So you have come at last, after three years promising.

WEST. Business was such I could not get away.

STREB. And prosperity has waited on attention.

WEST. Yes. Thank Heaven, we have steered over all the breakers and stand on a firm shore at last.

STREB. And Babbage?

WEST. [*Smiling*] Just as happy and just as surly as he can be.

STREB. [*Laughs*] But what do you think of Natalie and Lilian?

WEST. As I look at both I think John Strebelow must be the happiest man on earth.

LIL. Oh, father! [*Taking Natalie*] But I must go dress the child. I suppose you and Mr. Strebelow have a good deal to say to each other, so I'll leave you for a while. Come, dear.

NAT. But can I come and see grandpapa again after I'm dressed?

LIL. Certainly.

STREB. [*To Lilian*] Why not let Lizette dress her, dear?

LIL. [*Hesitating*] Yes—but—

NAT. No, no. Mamma promised to dress me herself to see grandpapa. Come, mamma, come. So I can come back soon. [*Pulls Lilian out R.3.E.*]

LIL. [*Turning at door*] Is she not lovely? [*Kisses her. Exit*]

WEST. [*Visibly affected, L.H.*] I should like to thank you for the happiness you have conferred on me and mine. But I—I can't, my son—I can't.

STREB. [*R.H.*] I've done my best to make her happy. I believe she is so. Though at times I cannot help noticing a sadness of look and tone that seldom leaves her save when with her child.

WEST. They were both gay enough when I came in—laughing, singing, kissing.

STREB. [*Thoughtfully*] Her whole heart is wrapped up in her child. If I were a younger husband, I might be jealous of the absorbing love she bears it.

WEST. [*Laughing*] The law of nature! The husband is number one till baby comes. Then he becomes number two; and, after all, a husband may well content himself with the second place in his wife's heart, when he knows 'tis only a miniature of himself that fills the first. [*Gives him bundle of New York papers. Enter Lizette*]

LIZ. [*Announcing*] Monsieur and Madame de Browne. [*Enter Florence C.D. from R. Lizette remains standing at door. Florence deep curtsy to Strebelow*]

FLOR. [*Down C.*] How is the Duke de Strebelow this morning? Where is the duchess? Is Lilian well? Ah! The Marquis de Westbrook. So you have arrived at last. How de doo? How is everybody in New York?

WEST. [*Shakes hands with her*] Delighted to see you looking so well.

STREB. [*Laughing*] My dear Mrs. Brown, you lavish your titles with such princely generosity that we poor republicans—

FLOR. "We republicans!" How I hate that word. Americans in Paris are at such a disadvantage in society! I am presented to Madame La Comtesse de Pompadilli, Cora Lacabella de Pontville, for instance, as plain Mrs. Brown. Mrs. B-r-o-w-n-e! I had to add the *e* myself. I want to keep in aristocratic practice. Browne is nearly seventy-six years old, you know. Perhaps I'll marry a duke some day or a Russian prince or an Italian nobleman, fresh from the almshouse.

STREB. [*Humoring her*] How is his highness—your royal consort—the Prince de Browne, this morning?

FLOR. The Prince de Browne is in his usual health; that is, he has the gout; he is coming upstairs now. Brown has the gout in its most aristocratic form. If he were a lineal descendant of William the Conqueror's entire army, he couldn't have it worse. [*Goes to the door, looks out*] Here comes the prince himself. [*Enter Brown, D.R., extremely senile. Hobbles on a cane. One leg bound up in bandages. He is richly, juvenilely dressed. Florence pats him*]

BROWN. He, eh, eh! My dear, [*Patting Florence under chin. Kisses her*] you got upstairs before me, didn't you? Strebelow, my dear fellow! Ah! Westbrook, [*Crosses to him*] got in at last, eh! Well? [*Shakes hands with Westbrook*]

WEST. Very well, thanks. But I'm sorry to see you so lame.

BROWN. Only a temporary attack, my dear boy. I'll be over it in six weeks. When such a thing attacks very old men they lack vitality to throw it off. [*To Strebelow*] But with a man of your age and mine, you know, [*Strebelow turns to hide a laugh as Florence nudges Westbrook*] the energy and elasticity of nature soon overcome its force. These premature attacks make some people think I'm old. It makes it appear as if there were some inappropriate difference, so to speak, between my wife's age and my own. [*Pats Florence under the chin*] We know better, don't we, my love? There isn't a better matched couple in the world. He, he! But time will fly, I suppose. Heigh-ho! Florence and I will soon be growing old together.

FLOR. Brown, my dear, you haven't had your afternoon nap yet. [*Goes to D.L.3.E.*]

BROWN. He, he, he! Yes, yes! During these temporary attacks I do like an afternoon nap, now and then. I'll go into the smoking-room and drop down on the lounge. I say, Westbrook, come with me and tell me all the news from New York, and put me to sleep. [*Moving up L.*] We regard this as Liberty Hall, Westbrook. Strebelow likes it. [*Strebelow courteously assents in dumb show*] Really I am getting as much attached to these afternoon naps as if I were a decrepit old man. If I don't get well soon, I dare say the habit will become so confirmed I'll keep up my nap for the next fifty years. [*Hobbles out L.3.E., followed by Westbrook*]

FLOR. [*In alarm down L.C.*] Fifty years! Strebelow, I'm really anxious about the prince.

STREB. No need to be anxious, my dear Mrs. Brown. I dare say he'll last for twenty years yet. He comes of a long and lingering family.

FLOR. [*With wry face*] That's comforting. [*Goes to easel*] But how do you like Lilian's portrait, now it is finally finished?

STREB. [*Going up L.C.*] The expression is, I think, too sad.

FLOR. You cannot blame the artist for that. I have not heard a hearty laugh from Lilian since she has been married.

STREB. That's very comforting.

FLOR. Only tit for tat. You have invited M. Montvillais, the art critic, and the Count de Carojac to see the picture this afternoon.

STREB. Yes, before it disappears forever from profane eyes in Lilian's boudoir.

FLOR. By the way, I suppose you know the Count de Carojac has been making desperate love to your wife lately?

STREB. Has he?

FLOR. Has he? Is that all you have to say about it? I expected—

STREB. [*Laughing*] What?

FLOR. That you would fly into a passion, tear your hair—seconds—pistols.

STREB. [*Laughing*] I have no desire to face the most dangerous duelist in Paris. Besides, de Carojac is a friend of mine, and as a French gentleman considers it his duty to prove his friendship by making love to my wife, in compliment to my taste.

FLOR. And what do you consider your duty as an American husband?

STREB. [*Seriously*] You forget I have an American wife.

FLOR. I wonder if Brown has the same confidence in my nationality.

STREB. [*Laughing and going towards D.R.*] I will inform the Duchesse de Strebelow that you are here. Speaking of female nationality in connection with the duties of a wife, I find it very hard to realize that Mrs. Brown is not a born Frenchwoman. [*Exits R.3.E.*]

FLOR. [*Sitting on piano stool, yawning*] Strebelow is too phlegmatic for a fight. [*Yawns*] I shall die of ennui. There is no getting a sensation out of anybody. If Carojac would make love to *me,* now. There might be some fun in that. But Brown has the gout, and he's too old for a row. It's very stupid.

LIZ. [*Entering C.R.*] The Count de Carojac. [*Exits. Enter Carojac C. from R.*]

FLOR. Oh, so delighted to see you!

CARO. [*Down R.C.*] Madame Brown, I am surprised.

FLOR. And sorry to find me here. I know it.

CARO. [*Sardonically*] I am too polite to contradict a lady.

FLOR. [*Going up L.C.*] You are as polished as a razor, and just as sharp.

CARO. Thank you.

FLOR. Well, there's the picture. [*He crosses to easel*] I hope its beauty will console you for the loss of the original.

CARO. I do not understand.

FLOR. Oh, yes, you do. She gave you the mitten.

CARO. The mitten. [*Coming down L.C.*] Zee gloves wizout fingers, wot is dat, eh?

FLOR. Mr. Routledge was too much for you in New York. Better make good use of your time now, for he has just arrived in Paris, and may turn the joke against you once more.

CARO. [*Suppressing vexation*] M. Routledge eez een Paree, eh? [*Aside*] If he zhoke weed me here, he may have to pay for zee zhoke. [*Goes to portrait*] Dayre is much melancholy in dee face.

FLOR. [*Watching him*] She's pondering over the past—the rides in the park, you know. [*Laughs*]

CARO. Zay mock zemselves of me altogether. Sac—

FLOR. [*Laughing still*] Now, don't be angry. Mrs. Strebelow will be here in a moment. Make love to her picture. I must go to the Prince de Browne and put a handkerchief over his old head or he will wake up sneezing. [*Runs off L.3.E. Reappears, watching Carojac*]

CARO. [*Before portrait*] The laugh is gone from the face now. I like it so much the better. I deed loof her. I think I loof her still. [*Enter Lilian R.3.E.*] She eez beauteeful! How lovely is the poise of the head, the outline of the face.

LIL. [*Coming forward*] I beg pardon, count.

CARO. Ah, madam, I was admiring.

FLOR. [*Peeping in and laughing*] The poise of the head, the outline of the face. [*Crosses to C. Lilian smiles*]

CARO. [*L.*] Zay laugh at me again.

FLOR. [*C.*] Better transfer your devotion to me, count.

CARO. I'll do any penance for my indiscretion, even that. [*Aside*] Zee she-devil!

LIZ. [*Announcing from C.R.*] M. de Montvillais! [*Exits as Montvillais enters*]

MONT. [*General bow*] Delighted, I am sure.

LIL. It is kind of you to come and give us the benefit of the acumen of so celebrated a critic.

MONT. [*Crossing to picture*] M-m-m! Ah, yes! Fine feeling! Le Rabiteau's usual precision of drawing—lacks tenderness in the flesh tints—richly toned, very.

FLOR. We know all about it now. [*Glancing at Carojac*] You French gentlemen are such excellent judges of pictures, eh, count?

CARO. [*Suppressing his vexation*] Yes, in art as in the politesse of life, zee French are the Greeks of our day.

STREB. [*Entering R.3.E.*] And the outer world barbarian, eh? [*Shakes hands with Montvillais and Carojac*]

MONT. Not exactly that, but—

STREB. Something very like it. But, Lilian, I forgot to tell you that your old friend and playmate arrived in Paris yesterday on his way back to Rome. I prevailed on him to stay over a day and give us at least one call.

LIL. Who?

STREB. Mr. Harold Routledge. I should think Mr. Routledge's success as an artist a fair reply to M. de Carojac's contempt of all art but French art.

LIL. [*At fireplace, R.H., with suppressed emotion*] Is Harold—is Mr. Routledge here?

LIZ. [*Announcing C.R.*] M. Routledge. [*Exits C.R. Enter Harold C.R.*]

STREB. [*Moves to meet Harold, shakes hands*] This is kind of you, Mr. Routledge.

FLOR. [*Going to him*] I am very glad to see you. [*Cordial shaking of hands*]

ROUT. Florence, Mrs. Brown, I should say. This is an unexpected pleasure. [*Advancing*] Mrs. Streb—Mrs. Strebelow!

LIL. Mr. Routledge.

FLOR. [*Laughing*] Mrs. Strebelow, Mr. Routledge, why don't you shake hands? [*They shake hands*]

LIL. I am glad you did not pass through Paris without calling on us, Mr. Routledge.

ROUT. You are very kind, madam. [*To Carojac*] Ah, Count de Carojac.

CARO. Mr. Routledge.

STREB. [*To Routledge*] M. de Montvillais. I beg your pardon, he is so celebrated a critic that I supposed you already knew him.

ROUT. [*Carojac sits on piano stool*] I had not the pleasure.

MONT. [*Condescendingly*] I know M. Routledge, by reputation. I had the honor to criticize his Dante and Beatrice, now in the Salon. In my private capacity I may say here in confidence it is a noble work, faultless. Of course, I could not say that in public, you know.

ROUT. [*Smiling at Montvillais*] I shall respect your confidence, monsieur.

CARO. [*Meaningly*] I see zee picture, and like all Paree I recognize the original of the Beatrice. It must be unpleasant for Madame Strebelow. Veree unfortunate.

ROUT. [*As if stung, glances at Carojac, then at Lilian*] Really, sir—

STREB. [*Sitting on chair, L.C., looking at picture*] I have heard of the likeness, and must go to the Salon and see your picture, Routledge.

ROUT. [*Seated L. of R. table*] The resemblance is purely accidental. Seeing Mrs. Strebelow now after six years, I must admit that it does exist. I knew Mrs. Strebelow in our young days, and I dare say that memory unconsciously took the place of inspiration.

CARO. Ah, zee memory must often be an annoyance to zee artist, eh? Mixing the disappointments of zee past with zee hopes of the future.

ROUT. [*Quickly*] Not in this case, sir. The suggestion—

CARO. Oh, it is more than a suggestion. It really might be accepted as a portrait of Madame Strebelow.

STREB. [*To Routledge*] Then you have been more successful than Le Rabiteau, here. [*Points to picture*] Completed but yesterday. Indeed, our little conclave today was to pass upon its merits. [*Rises*]

ROUT. [*Crossing to L.C.*] Rabiteau is an excellent artist.

STREB. Perhaps so. But in this case he has seemed inspired with a spirit of sadness.

CARO. [*At Routledge*] With him it could not have been memory.

MONT. [*Down C.*] I do not know about that. You recollect the scandal caused by his picture of the young Marquise de Pauliac?

FLOR. [*Quickly crossing to R.C.*] A scandal about a marquise. Oh, do tell it. [*Strebelow down L.C.*]

MONT. It is said that Rabiteau fell in love with her during her sittings, and she with him. But they very properly married her to a rich old nobleman instead of to a poor artist. Rabiteau had his revenge. He bestowed upon her face an expression that seemed to tell the story.

FLOR. [*Eagerly*] What story?

MONT. The story of a broken heart. Of a woman bearing in her bosom a secret that must not live, yet cannot die. A sadder story than that of the Spartan boy who let the cub eat his heart out ere he would reveal its guilty presence beneath his tunic. Some memory of this may have guided Rabiteau's pencil, suggested by a passing look on Mrs. Strebelow's face—a look of sorrow at the premature crushing of a new bonnet, perhaps, which memory idealized. [*Florence goes to Lilian. Lilian holds Florence as if for support. Harold's eyes and hers meet. She turns away her head*]

STREB. [*Seeing all this*] And you think Mrs. Strebelow's face suggested his own experience?

MONT. Perhaps—as a child sees faces in the clouds. [*Going up C., talking to Florence*]

STREB. Tut, tut! Let us go to the smoking-room. [*To Lilian*] Mr. Routledge will tell you the latest fashionable news from New York. Come, gentlemen. Carojac, come. [*Exit R.3.E. Carojac follows to the door and returns*]

FLOR. And I will return to Brown. [*Lilian tries to stop her. She looks knowingly from one to the other and crosses to L.H.*] I'm afraid the handkerchief has fallen off his dear old head. I'm a mother to Brown.

CARO. [*In low tone to Routledge*] An excellent opportunity to refresh your memory for future inspirations.

ROUT. I do not understand—

CARO. [*Bowing*] I shall be happy to give zee explanation when and where you will. [*Bows and exits R.3.E. To Lilian*] Madam!

LIL. Mr. Routledge.

ROUT. Madam.

LIL. My husband tells me you have just returned from the United States. But pray be seated. [*Harold brings forward chair L.C. Sits L. Lilian sits R.*]

ROUT. My first visit to America in seven years. During that time I scarcely ever left Rome.

LIL. The reputation you have acquired is proof of the good use you made of your time. [*Awkward pause. With the air of one who has made up her mind to do something she feared*] Mr. Routledge, I am glad to have this opportunity to refer to a subject, the—the delicacy of which, time has in—in some sort lessened.

ROUT. Really, madam, I am at a loss to understand what in the past can require an explanation between us. When you closed that past, you explained it.

LIL. No, sir! Nor could I then trust myself to do so. I feel now, have never ceased to feel, that the explanation is due to you.

ROUT. [*Rising*] I do not feel so, now.

LIL. [*Positively*] Then, sir, it is due to me. And in justice to me, I am sure you will hear it.

ROUT. [*Inclining his head*] Madam.

LIL. You and I were engaged to be married.

ROUT. [*Standing C.*] I thought so.

LIL. After our foolish quarrel I sent for you to return to me.

ROUT. So I understood the letter I received from Mrs. Holcomb. In obedience to that letter, I did return. I returned full of joy and happiness, and when my heart was at its fullest. I was discarded through the mouth of a lackey.

LIL. And you never knew why, never guessed why?

ROUT. [*Bitterly*] You are mistaken. I knew why the very next day. I knew why when I heard from Mrs. Holcomb that you had accepted the hand of Mr. John Strebelow, who is a very rich man.

LIL. But you did not know why I accepted him?

ROUT. [*Bitterly still*] Because he, as I said, is a very rich man.

Lɪʟ. Mr. Routledge, that is true. [*Rising*]

Rout. You see, madam, no explanation was needed. [*Taking L. corner*]

Lɪʟ. No explanation I could then make. But Mr. Strebelow and myself have now been married and been happy together for seven years, and I can, I believe without injustice to him, explain why I did marry him for his money. I state it plainly and truly.

Rout. I have no doubt the purity of your motives equalled the frankness of this confession.

Lɪʟ. Those motives I think it is just to you to state, due to myself to make clear. [*Invites him to sit R.C. She sits R.H.*] Ten minutes after, with my consent, Aunt Fanny wrote you to return, my father told me that he was ruined, that in his ruin was involved the ruin of hundreds of others who had trusted their all to him. He besought me to save him from infamy, spoke of the curses of the poor, drew so appalling a picture that in pity, in fear, scarce knowing what I did, I consented before I had even time to think of what I had done. Mr. Strebelow came and I accepted him. I had scarcely done so, when you called. I—I tried to go to you, Harold. I tried, I could not, and so—so—

Rout. [*Rising*] Sent that message which condemned my heart to bitterness of isolation forever. [*Crosses to L. Sits*]

Lɪʟ. Can you forgive me?

Rout. I have already done so. And you are happy?

Lɪʟ. I am content. [*Music*] And you, Harold?

Rout. I suffered much, for I loved much. Had I loved less, the wound to my pride would have healed more quickly.

Lɪʟ. But you are happy now. Say you are. Say it.

Rout. Lilian, I would not add to the burden you have borne, the weight of a single reproach, but I cannot say what you ask me. [*Up C.*] Work as I may, do what I will, the feeling of the past clings to me. It tinges my every thought, steals into my every canvas, makes the present wearisome, robs the future of every rainbow tint that makes work a consolation.

Lɪʟ. Oh, Harold, don't, don't!

Rout. I should not say this to you, Lilian, but I have suffered so, cherishing a secret I dare not tell, and brooding over a love that would not die.

Lɪʟ. [*Weeping, goes to him*] Poor Harold!

Rout. [*Puts one arm around her waist*] And you have not forgotten me, Lilian?

Lɪʟ. I have never ceased to sympathize with the sorrow I knew, I felt you were suffering. For I knew what it cost me to inflict it upon you.

Rout. [*Madly rising*] And you—you love me still?

Lɪʟ. [*Starting back*] This is cruel of you. Unkind, Harold.

Rout. [*Catching her again*] I know not what I say, what I do. Let me carry away with me some word of affection—some.

Lil. [*Breaks from him*] Leave with me untainted the respect I have always entertained for you, Harold. I was foolish thus to trust you—to trust myself.

Rout. [*Following her*] You shall, you must.

Lil. I must remember what you seem to forget, that I am the wife of John Strebelow. One word more, and I ring. [*Hand over bell on table. Enter Carojac R.D.*]

Caro. [*Sardonically*] I thought so! You need not ring, madam. No scandal! [*Lilian screams, hangs her head*]

Rout. Sir!

Caro. [*To Lilian*] Mr. Routledge's memory of where he stands will calm the ardor of his inspirations. [*Routledge bows. Count bows. Quick curtain*]

ACT III.

Set: *Vestibule and stairway of the American Embassy at Paris. Guests coming up and going down stairs. Servant coming downstairs from L. off R.U.E. Strebelow and Carojac from cloakroom R.U.E. to C. French officer and lady enter R.2.E., go off R.U.E. Servant from R.U.E. goes upstairs and off L.U.E. with card.*

Caro. Madame Strebelow is with you this evening, of course.

Streb. She will be down presently. You frequently honor our receptions at the American Legation, M. le Comte.

Caro. Yes. The American ladies are so very beautiful.

Streb. And in the presence of female beauty, a French gentleman is never blind; eh, M. le Comte? [*Laughs. Enter Florence R.U.E. downstairs*]

Flor. M. Strebelow, you are late. How is Lilian this evening? M. le Comte. [*Nods*]

Caro. Madam.

Streb. [*R.H.*] Mrs. Strebelow was detained with her daughter.

Flor. [*C.*] Lilian is a slave to that child. [*Looking R.U.E.*] Why, here comes the prince. I just left him on the sofa in the back hall room talking with Mrs. Gordon; I thought I'd got him fixed for two hours at least. [*French officer enters from cloakroom, goes upstairs and off L.U.E., then servant comes from L.U.E. Exits into cloakroom. Enter Brown, L.U.E., hobbling with cane downstairs from R.U.E.*]

BROWN. Ah, you are here, my dear—he, he! You lost me, didn't you? He, he, he! [*Patting her under chin*] I have been talking with young Mrs. Gordon, my dear. You mustn't be jealous. I'm not a Don Juan, my love, I'm not a Don Juan. [*Crosses to Strebelow. Laughs*] I say, Strebelow, old boy. [*Apart to Strebelow, who has crossed to R.C. Florence talks with Carojac*] These young women are jealous creatures. [*Laughs*] They keep their eyes on their husbands. [*Laughs*] It's fun to tease them now and then, [*Laughs*] isn't it? [*Poking Strebelow in the ribs*] Just for a little spice, you know! It's wicked, I know it's wicked, but [*Laughs*] I believe they love a man all the more for a touch of—of deviltry—now and then—you know. [*Laughs, punches Strebelow. Gentleman enters R.D. Exits into cloakroom, after glancing at Brown and looking as if new to him*]

FLOR. [*To Carojac*] Wait till I get Brown fixed nice and comfortable somewhere. [*To Brown*] My dear, don't you want to come into the next room? There's a sofa and an easy chair. We'll have a nice visit, you and I, all by ourselves. [*Gentleman and lady enter, R.D., are going toward cloakroom. Servant enters with salver from cloakroom, one card upon it; gentleman places his card upon it. Servant goes up and off L.U.E. Gentleman and lady into cloakroom*]

BROWN. [*Laughs*] Yes, my dear. I say, Strebelow, she's a little jealous, do you see? She likes to be alone with me. Come, my love. [*Going with Florence, looks back at Strebelow*] Try it Strebelow, try it with your wife. It works to a charm—a little deviltry, you know. A trifle jealous, eh, Florence? Try it, Strebelow. Come, my love. I'm not a Don Juan, my dear, I'm not a Don Juan. [*Exits L.H.2.E.*]

FLOR. [*Finger to her lips*] Sh! I'll have the prince asleep upon the sofa in less than five minutes. [*The Count bows and waves his hand. She returns it. Exits after Brown L.H. Enter Montvillais R.2.E. Austrian officer. They bow to each other. Officer goes into cloakroom. French officer and lady come down L. stairs, go up R. stairs*]

MONT. Good evening, gentlemen. Dropped in at the opera this evening. Ortalini's voice is splendid, but the chorus is execrable. Ah, a new bit of bronze since the last reception—Hymen; rather too full about the torso. [*Enter G. Washington Phipps R.2.E. He is crossing the stage rapidly. Stops suddenly. He is an energetic young American business man in manner and appearance; dress suit*]

PHIPPS.   Eh, Strebelow!

STREB.   Mr. Phipps.

PHIPPS. [*Crossing to Strebelow*] Glad to see you. Heard you were living here. How is your wife? [*Gentleman and lady enter from cloakroom, go up and off L.U.E. Servant comes down from L.U.E. and exits to cloakroom*]

STREB. Well, thank you. When did you arrive in Paris?

PHIPPS. This evening—half past seven train. Paris is a very pretty city. Streets well lighted. Magnificent opera house. The inside is particularly gorgeous. Dropped into the Palais Royal on the way. The Comedie Fransaze is considerably larger, but the Opera Comeek—

MONT. [*Suddenly*] Pardon, monsieur—pardon!

PHIPPS. [*Looking at Montvillais, then at Strebelow*] Friend of yours?

STREB. Monsieur Montvillais, a fellow townsman—Mr. Phipps of New York City.

PHIPPS. G. Washington Phipps—dry goods.

MONT. Dry—gudes?

PHIPPS. Eighty-seven Church Street.

MONT. Eighty-seven?

PHIPPS. [*To Strebelow, pointing back at Montvillais with his thumb*] What line?

STREB. Stationery.

PHIPPS. Ah!

STREB. The Count de Carojac, Mr. Phipps. [*The Count bows very low and formally. Phipps crosses to Count, nods quickly. He sees the Count is still bowing, and bows low himself*]

PHIPPS. [*L.C. to Strebelow*] Same business?

STREB. [*R.C.*] Cutlery and firearms.

PHIPPS. Oh!

MONT. [*R.H.*] Your pardon, Mr. Phipps. I owe you an apology for having interrupted your remarks. Pardon, but you have been to the Grand Opéra; and to the Palais Royal, and the Comédie Français, and the Opéra Comique; and you arrived in the city of Paris at half past seven this evening?

CARO. [*L.H.*] You have seen considerable of the metropolis, Mr. Phipps, during your comparatively short visit.

PHIPPS. Not as much as I had hoped to see by this time. I have been in the city of Paris *four* hours. Delayed at the Grand Hotel. It took me at least fifteen minutes, sir, to persuade the chambermaid who brought me candles that I did not require her presence while I was changing my travelling suit for a dress coat and black pantaloons. These French chambermaids are slow to take a hint—in that direction. The Tuileries, by the way, presents rather an imposing appearance in the snow and moonlight. I had the driver go round by the way of the Tuileries and the Palace of the Louvre on the way to the legation. The Ark dee Triumph is rather neat in its way. When we got to the Champs Elizas, I told the driver to take a half hour's turn to the Ark, and we came back by the way of the Foburg St. Honory and the Church dee Philipee. Tourists generally lose a great deal of time unnecessarily. I've got everything I want to see in Paris written down in my notebook. Bought a guide to Paris in London. [*Takes a small guidebook from pocket*] Pronunciation all spelt out in English. Carry a map of the city in my coat pocket. [*Takes map from one of his pockets and unfolds it. Enter English officer, and gentleman with lady from D. Exit into cloakroom*]

STREB.   When did you leave New York, Mr. Phipps?

PHIPPS.   November thirteen, two o'clock P.M. Arrived in Liverpool November twenty-third, half past ten A.M. Exactly one week and a half ago. Spent four days and a half in the city of London and vicinity. I saw London thoroughly.

MONT.   Voilà l'Américain. He'll see all Paris in a fortnight.

PHIPPS.   I shall be in Paris precisely three days. Detained till Friday on account of business—figured silks. I shall then run over to Switzerland. They tell me I can see Mont Blanc from the windows of the hotel in Switzerland. [*Enter Footman from cloakroom, English officer, gentleman, lady. Exit L.U.E. Gentleman and lady from L. stairs, to R. Footman comes down again and exits into cloakroom*]

CARO.   Mon Dieu!

PHIPPS.   That will save considerable time. Berlin, by the way is a very beautiful city—wide streets. Came from London by way of Berlin; remained there thirty-six hours. Missed a train; delayed five hours. Stopped over at Dresden on the route from Berlin, and at the Cologne Big Cathedral; bones of eleven thousand virgins in the church of St. Ursula. I didn't count 'em but my guide swore to the fact. He wouldn't let up on a single rib. Guides never lie in Europe.

MONT.   You visited the Dresden Gallery, monsieur? You admire works of art?

PHIPPS.   I like pictures. I spent nearly twenty minutes in the gallery at Dresden.

MONT.   Diable! [*Servant starts downstairs to meet Phipps*]

PHIPPS.   Oreveoar, gentlemen, as you Frenchmen say. See you again, Strebelow; my regards to your wife. [*Going up, hands card to attendant*] There's my card, sir—G. Washington Phipps, N.Y., U.S.A. [*Exits L. upstairs, preceded by servant. Phipps bounds upstairs three steps at a time; is going off R.U.E. Servant calls, "This way, sir," pointing off L.U.E. Phipps says, "Oh! very well," bounds off L.U.E.*]

STREB. Whatever faults my countrymen may have, gentlemen, you will own that wasting time is not one of them.

CARO. Oui, mon ami, c'est vrai, c'est vrai. [*Moving to R.C.*]

MONT. Boom—whiz—z—chick! Mr. Phipps is a bullet. He is here and he is gone. [*Enter Lilian through arch R.U.E.*]

STREB. My wife. [*Goes to her*] But where's your father, dear?

LIL. Natalie insisted he should return to her. He said he felt too tired for a formal reception like this; but would, perhaps, call at a circle to see an old New York friend. In which case he will not be here till late. [*Seeing Montvillais*] Ah! M. Montvillais. [*They bow. She takes Strebelow's arm*] Come, let us make our bow upstairs, and return home. [*Going up C., they pass Carojac. Routledge is seen coming downstairs from L.U.E.*]

STREB. [*Up C.*] You overlook the Count de Carojac, my dear.

LIL. [*Laughing and turns, bowing slightly*] So I did. Pardon me, count! [*Count bows L.H. Routledge now on the steps, meets Strebelow and Lilian preparing to go upstairs. Awkward getting out of each other's way*]

ROUT. [*On steps L.C.*] I beg your pardon—

STREB. [*At foot of steps*] Ah, Routledge, glad to see you here.

LIL. [*Bowing formally*] Mr. Routledge.

ROUT. Mrs. Strebelow.

STREB. And you still persist in starting for Rome tomorrow?

ROUT. I must take the early train.

STREB. Then we must say good-by this evening.

ROUT. Yes, indeed. Good-by, sir. Madam, farewell. [*Bows. Strebelow and Lilian mount the first three steps. Strebelow, his wife on his arm, turns suddenly*]

STREB. Mr. Routledge.

ROUT. [*L.C., foot of steps*] Sir.

STREB. You must afford me an opportunity to bid for your Dante and Beatrice.

ROUT. Pardon me, but I do not intend to sell that picture.

STREB. Then at some future time. Good-by once more.

ROUT. Good-by. [*Exit upstairs Strebelow and Lilian. Routledge crosses to R. corner, turns and watches Mrs. Strebelow till off, then strolls off R.3.E.*]

MONT. [*Coming forward with Carojac*] But why?

CARO. Because I hate him. He made a laughingstock of me in New York. He came between me and—and—

MONT. But not here—not here in the legation.

CARO. Yes, here and now. He goes away tomorrow.

MONT. You will make a scandal. It will be said that Madame Strebelow is the cause of the fight. You have been dining. You are flushed.

CARO. [*Still more excited*] What do I care? Both he and she have always provoked me. I gave him his cue at Strebelow's house today. I will give him good cause to fight if he will face a sword. I'll teach him to laugh at Alphonse Carojac—

MONT. Well, but one moment. Come here where we can talk. [*Draws him off L.2.E. As they exit, Florence, who has been listening at the arch, L.U.E., enters*]

FLOR. [*Aside*] A sensation at last. A fight! Swords! The whole colony will be alive. I must tell Lilian. [*Runs to stairs, meets Phipps*]

PHIPPS. Mrs. Brown. [*They try to pass each other; finally she goes up, he comes down*]

FLOR. [*Up a few steps*] Don't stop me, I'm in a hurry.

PHIPPS. So am I. But I think I have something to say to you.

FLOR. What is it?

PHIPPS. Brown still alive?

FLOR. Yes.

PHIPPS. In good health?

FLOR. Nothing but the gout.

PHIPPS. Then I don't think I have anything to say. Good evening. [*Florence rushes upstairs and disappears. Coming down C., with back to audience*] Ah! Is this Hymen? [*Taking out notebook*] Knew him by his torch. Let me see? [*Writing*] That's the seventeenth statue of Hymen I've seen since I've landed in Liverpool—this one, I presume, is Diana. Diana comes under the D's. No, it can't be Diana. I have noticed Diana always wears the moon as a headdress. It must be Venus. I'll put it in the V's. [*Writes*] American Legation—Venus, number— I have seen ninety-seven Venuses since I landed in Liverpool. Venus is more popular than Hymen in Europe. American Legation—Venus number— [*Looks at statue again*] No, it can't be Venus either, too many clothes for Venus. Venus in full dress is not popular. In Europe I'll call it Juno. She goes under the J's. Patroness of marriage, the guidebook says. Juno, [*Writes*] number three. I'm short of Junos. Juno is not popular here as Venus. Let me see! [*Pulls out map*] I can instruct the driver to return to the hotel by way of the Maddyleen and the National Library. [*Holding map*] Perhaps we can dodge round by the way of the Cathedral of Noter-Dam. [*Goes up R., meets Routledge, who enters from cloakroom*]

ROUT. Ah, Phipps, I heard you were here. Are you in a particular hurry?

PHIPPS. No, I'm in a general hurry.

ROUT. Do you know the Count de Carojac?

PHIPPS. That black fellow in the cutlery and firearms line. Just been introduced. [*Looks at his watch*] Just nine minutes ago.

ROUT. He has been trying to provoke me—almost insulted me today.

PHIPPS. Punch his head.

ROUT. He insinuated a challenge to a duel.

PHIPPS. What for?

ROUT. Come into the anteroom. It is a very delicate matter; this place is too public. I would avoid it if I can honorably. [*As they go off, R.U.E.*] The reputation of an American lady is involved in the— [*Exit, R.3.E., through arch. Florence comes downstairs quickly*]

FLOR. I cannot find her anywhere. I've been through all the rooms. [*Enter Lizette from R.U.E.*]

FLOR. Ah, have you seen Mrs. Strebelow?

LIZ. Not for a quarter of an hour.

FLOR. [*Gives her money*] You will find Mr. Brown asleep on the sofa in the retiring room. Please go and sit by his side till he wakes up. [*Lizette, going*] Stop; when he does wake up, tell him—that's it, I'll go home with Lilian—tell him his wife has gone, and say he must go right home. And please help him on with his things. [*Lizette curtsies, and starts again*] And please [*Lizette stops again*] see that his handkerchief is on his head, and if his poor leg slips off the sofa, put it back, gently, so as not to disturb him. [*Lizette curtsies again, and exits L.H.*]

FLOR. Poor old Brown. I have as much care of him as if he were a baby; I have taken the place his mother occupied seventy-five years ago—but where can Lilian be? She must know of this. I'm sure Carojac will do what he threatened. It will be magnificent in all the papers. They will hear of it in New York; the *Herald* will interview me as a friend of the lady whose name was involved—what Mrs. Brown says—what Mrs. Brown thinks—description of the combatants—Mrs. Brown, wife of the millionaire, now residing in Paris —all in big type. I wonder what they'll think of it all on the Avenue? Mrs. Brown—that horrid name! If it were only Livingston, or the Countess of Brownatille. But where can Lilian be? I *must* find her. [*Goes upstairs quickly —from L.H.2. Enter Carojac, Montvillais with him, from the R.H. arch. Routledge, Phipps with him*]

PHIPPS. [*To Routledge*] You are right; the fellow must be a scoundrel. For Strebelow's sake as well as for his wife's— [*Routledge and Phipps have their hats in their hands. Routledge has cloak, Phipps coat on his arm. They are going off R.2.E.*]

CARO. [*R.H., meaningly*] You are not running away, M. Routledge? [*Music*]

ROUT. [*Stopping short*] Not from you, M. de Carojac.

CARO. I thought you would not, without giving me the opportunity to give you an explanation.

MONT. [*To Carojac*] Allons donc, Carojac.

CARO. [*Stopping Montvillais with gesture*] Laisse moi faire!

ROUT. [*Quietly*] I think, sir, I understand you without an explanation.

PHIPPS. [*To Routledge, aside*] The fellow has been drinking.

MONT. [*Coming to C.*] Permit me, M. Routledge, to offer the explanation. The count is a little irritated at the unfortunate resemblance to Mrs. Strebelow, which, in your Beatrice, is placed on exhibition.

ROUT. [*Quietly*] And why does the count concern himself about the matter, sir?

MONT. Oh, as a friend—an old and dear friend of Madame Strebelow.

CARO. [*Crossing to C.*] I think such things may be done in America—done in France they are an insolence which no French gentleman would be guilty of to a French lady. [*Enter Mrs. Brown and Lilian on stairs from L.U.E.*]

ROUT. [*A little more warmly*] If you seek a quarrel, sir, I beg you will find a cause unconnected with the name of any lady, American or French, and a place in which an American in accepting will not be forced to forget the respect due to the flag under whose protection you are speaking.

CARO. [*Insolently*] Zat is the first time I ever heard that a flag protected anything or anybody.

MONT. [*Expostulating*] Carojac, mon cher!

PHIPPS. [*To Routledge*] If you don't slap his face, I will.

ROUT. [*Waving Phipps aside*] That flag protects you now.

CARO. [*Still more insolently*] I beg your pardon. 'Tis you appeal to it. The Count de Carojac needs neither the American rag nor the American petticoat to protect him.

ROUT. [*Bursting out*] You are either drunk or a blackguard.

CARO. [*Rushing to Routledge*] Enfin! You are one liar—one coward! [*Throws his glove in Routledge's face*]

PHIPPS. [*Mad with excitement*] Knock him down! [*Routledge does so, when Carojac strikes him. Quick drop of curtain*]

ACT IV.

SCENE 1: THE DUEL. *The curtain rises on an empty stage. After a few seconds of silence, enter Routledge in circular cloak, followed by Phipps in overcoat from terrace.*

ROUT. [*Looking round on steps*]   This *is* the spot.

PHIPPS. [*R.C., looking round*]   Solemn, splendid, and icy. [*Pulls out notebook*] What do you call it?

ROUT.   All that the Russian bullets left of a once royal château.

PHIPPS. [*Making note*]   It makes me shiver.

ROUT. [*Thoughtfully*]   How calmly the feverish city seems to sleep! Phipps, [*Phipps comes down R.C.*] I feel a strange sense of ominous awe— I feel as if I were destined never to leave this spot alive.

PHIPPS. [*Comes forward*]   Nonsense! It's the first effect of the place— you'll soon shake that off.

ROUT.   Maybe so, but this man is said to be the best swordsman in Europe.

PHIPPS.   Do you know nothing of the smallsword?

ROUT.   I am a pretty fair swordsman. I learned its use in the university in Germany and, in Europe, no artist's studio is complete without a pair of foils.

PHIPPS.   I should fancy that fencing with foils for amusement is a very different thing from carrying on a serious discussion with buttonless swords.

ROUT.   Not with me, I think. I am generally coolest in the moment of danger. But before they come, there is one thing I want you to promise me.

PHIPPS.   What is it?

ROUT.   That you will do all you can to prevent the real cause of this quarrel from being known. Remember, I fight to avenge an insult to our country simply. For Lilian's sake, for Strebelow's sake, let no suspicion get abroad of—

PHIPPS.   You may depend upon me.

ROUT.   Deliberately and persistently this man's jealousy and irritated vanity have forced this fight, and whatever way it ends, I would have his attempt to avenge himself for his rejection baffled as far as Lilian and her husband are concerned. You understand?

PHIPPS.   I do. What you are doing, I would do, though practically I don't know a revolver from a jacknife, or a smallsword from a corkscrew. Hush! [*Listens*] They are coming. [*Pause. Enter Montvillais, Carojac, and Dr. Watson, R.1.E. They are all in overcoats. Montvillais carries three smallswords, the doctor, a box*]

MONT. [*To Routledge and Phipps*]   Your servant, gentlemen. You will pardon the delay. The swords were at my apartments and we stopped on the way for Doctor Watson, [*Bows all round*] an old London friend of mine, who willingly agreed to offer his professional services to whosoever may need them.

DR. WATSON. [*To Routledge*] Pleased to make your acquaintance, sir. I shall be as happy, believe me, to attend you as to attend my friend's friend.

PHIPPS. Happy either way—strictly impartial.

ROUT. [*To Doctor*] I thank you, doctor. [*Doctor goes up*]

CARO. [*As if tired of the delay*] Allons, Montvillais. [*Montvillais advances C., presents the handles of the swords to Phipps, who takes them, looks at them—moves over to Routledge*]

PHIPPS. [*To Routledge*] I'm to take my choice, I believe.

ROUT. Certainly.

PHIPPS. [*Staring at each sword in turn, moving to C.*] About the same length apparently. [*Feels points with his finger, pricking it*] I never saw two bolts of black silk more like each other. I shouldn't have the least choice as to which of them was passed through my body. [*He reverses the swords, presenting the handles crossed to Montvillais. Montvillais takes one, places the point on ground, bends the blade each way several times. Phipps, watching him, imitates with the other sword*]

MONT. Are you satisfied, Mr. Phipps?

PHIPPS. Perfectly. [*Aside*] Mine seems to bend as much as his does. [*Routledge and Carojac take off their coats—stand in shirt sleeves. Phipps to Doctor*] Won't this be a trifle chilly?

DOC. They will be warm enough after their swords are crossed. The exercise will make them comfortable.

PHIPPS. [*Aside*] D——d comfortable. [*Montvillais holding up sword C., with point to front*]

MONT. Messieurs! [*Carojac and Routledge cross swords*] Allez! [*Carojac and Routledge fence—after some passes, Carojac springs suddenly back*]

CARO. [*Springing back*] Sacristi!

ROUT. [*Lowering his sword*] Pardon me! I believe you are wounded. [*The seconds cover their principals with overcoats*]

CARO. [*Holding his left hand*] Sanks, M. Routledge, for zee courtesy. A mere scratch. It will not detain us a moment, doctor! [*Doctor and Montvillais go to Carojac on side of stage. Routledge joins Phipps on other side of stage. Doctor wraps bandage round Carojac's arm*]

PHIPPS. [*To Routledge*] First hit for our side! Bravo!

ROUT. [*Shaking his head*] More luck than skill. His arm is made of steel and his wrist of India rubber.

CARO. [*To Montvillais*]   It was his awkwardness, not his skill. I'll finish him in two passes now.

PHIPPS. [*To Routledge*]   Are you cold?

ROUT.   I'm hot as fire.

CARO. [*To Montvillais*]   Finissons! [*They fence again. Enter Strebelow as Routledge is disarmed*]

STREB. [*On bridge*]   Stop, gentlemen! [*Carojac runs his sword through Routledge as Strebelow cries "Stop"*]

ROUT. [*Falling into Phipps' arms*]   Too late! I knew it! [*All turning round to look at Strebelow. Montvillais and Carojac exchange looks. The Doctor is puzzled*]

ALL.   M. Strebelow!

STREB. [*Coming forward C., goes to Routledge*]   Too late! Is there no doctor here?

DOC. [*Coming forward*]   I beg pardon. I— [*Goes to Routledge, kneeling behind him*]

STREB. [*Dropping Routledge's hand*]   Count de Carojac!

CARO. [*Resuming his coat*]   M. Strebelow!

STREB.   The cause of this quarrel?

PHIPPS.   Of this murder, Strebelow!

MONT.   Murder, sir.

PHIPPS.   Ay, wilful, deliberate murder. The fellow forced the fight because he knew his superior skill. I call it murder.

CARO.   Sir, you will answer to me for this.

STREB. [*Calmly*]   Not till you have answered me. The cause of this quarrel? [*Phipps, Montvillais and Carojac look meaningly at each other*] Well, count, are you ashamed to tell it? [*Enter Lilian, R.U.E., over terrace followed by Florence. Lilian in disordered dress. Rushes across to L.C., sees Routledge lying on the ground, the Doctor over him*]

LIL.   Too late! Too late! Oh, Harold. Harold! My poor Harold! [*Throws herself beside Harold*]

ALL.   Madame Strebelow!

DOC.   Be careful, madam. You must not stir him.

LIL.   Oh, Harold, speak! Speak to me.

STREB. [*In astonishment*]   My wife!

LIL.   Dying—dying—dying for me, who blighted his heart! Harold! Harold! I've killed him, killed him.

CARO. [*To Strebelow, pointing to Lilian*]   Well, M. Strebelow, do you understand the cause of the quarrel, now?

STREB. [*Raising Lilian, assisted by Florence*]   I do not, sir.

CARO. He compromised your wife. He make her love for him public.

STREB. You lie, sir!

CARO. [*Smiling sardonically*]   Look for yourself. [*Indicating Lilian. Pause. Strebelow draws Lilian to him—draws cloak round her fondly and carefully*]

STREB. [*Slowly*]   Gentlemen, this lady is my wife. For her truth, her faith, and her honor, I pledge my life. Again I say, this man lies, and for this lie I will hold him accountable at the proper time and in the proper place. [*Quick drop of curtain*]

SCENE 2: "THE SEPARATION." *In the boudoir. At rise of curtain, enter Lizette L.C., followed by Strebelow, Lilian on his arm, then Mrs. Brown. Strebelow half leads, half supports Lilian to sofa, R.C., on which she sinks exhausted.*

STREB. [*To Mrs. Brown*]   Believe me, I am very grateful for your kind attention to Lilian. She seems better now. [*Crossing to Lizette*] Let the carriage wait. [*Exit Lizette L.3.E.*]

FLOR. [*Approaching Lilian*]   All she needs is a little rest—a little sleep. [*To Lilian*] You do feel better now?

LIL. Yes, yes, much better, thank you. It was the shock—the shock. Is Harold—is Mr. Routledge dead?

STREB. I trust not!

LIL. For heaven's sake, send and see!

FLOR. Dr. Watson promised to come here as soon as he had ascertained that Mr. Routledge had been safely moved.

LIL. The suspense will kill me! [*Rises and walks across to L.H. During this scene, up to the entrance of the Doctor, Strebelow is intently watching Lilian*]

FLOR. [*Follows Lilian*]   Do calm yourself, Lilian. Do not look so wild. You frighten me. I'm sure we all share your horror.

LIL. But who can share my feelings? Did you see the look of reproachful anguish his eyes cast upon me ere they closed—closed perhaps, forever? I shall go mad, mad, mad! [*Crossing back to sofa*]

STREB. [*Aside*]   "Reproachful anguish." [*Aloud*] I will send—there, there, dear! [*Rings bell on table L.H.*] Sword thrusts are not always fatal. Sit down, compose yourself. [*Sits at L.H. table and writes. Enter Lizette*] Send to this address, and inquire as to the condition of Mr. Routledge. Let the messenger take the carriage and return at once. [*Exit Lizette L.3.E. To Florence*] You must not be surprised at the extreme agitation of Lilian. Harold Routledge and she were old playmates; and the sensibility of—

FLOR. [*C.*] My dear Mr. Strebelow, I'm fairly astonished at being alive myself. The snow, the moonlight, the gray ruins of the historic château, the suddenness of the strife, the romantic aristocracy, and aristocratic romance of the affair made it all like a novel, till I saw Harold Routledge's blood on that man's sword. [*Lilian starts up from the sofa, crosses to L.H.*] Oh! Then I felt as badly, as horrified as Lilian herself. But [*To Lilian*] do calm yourself, dear.

LIL. Yes, yes, when the news comes I'll be calm—calm!

FLOR. I always liked Routledge; there was none of the plebeian about him. I recollect how glad I was when it was reported that you and he were engaged.

STREB. Engaged! Engaged to what?

LIL. [*Stops short, her back to audience and to Strebelow*] Engaged to be married.

FLOR. Why, Strebelow, you don't mean to say that you did not know Lilian Westbrook and Harold Routledge were once considered the Lucia and Edgardo of New York society? Why the match was—

LIL. [*Crosses to C., back to audience*] Please say no more about the— [*Turns round, looks at Strebelow, at Florence, totters. Strebelow runs and catches her in his arms as she is about to fall, crosses with and places her on sofa R.C.*]

STREB. Take courage, take courage, I'm sure your old friend is safe.

LIL. [*Looking at Strebelow piteously*] It was never right. [*As Strebelow is bending over Lilian, his back to the door, enter Dr. Watson, seen only by Florence. Florence goes quickly to him, catches him by the wrist*]

FLOR. [*L.C. aside to Doctor*] Is he dead?

DOC. [*L.H. to Florence*] No, but he cannot live an hour.

FLOR. If you say that here, you'll kill Mrs. Strebelow. Be careful! [*Aloud*] Here is the doctor.

LIL. [*Springing to her feet*] At last! At last! [*Going toward Doctor*] Tell me the truth—the truth. Is Harold Routledge dead?

DOC. No, no! He is badly wounded—but not dead.

LIL. Is there any hope?

DOC. While there's life, science sees hope.

STREB. [*Encouragingly*] There, there! I told you so. [*Passing her over to sofa*]

LIL. Thank Heaven! [*Sinks on sofa R.H.*]

FLOR. [*Behind sofa*] Now, dear, you must rest. The doctor will take me home. I'm sure poor Brown must be in a dreadful state. I'll call early tomorrow. Now go, and be sure you take a good sleep. Good-by! Good-by! Don't rise!

STREB. [*Crossing to C.*] Good-by—and thank you.

DOC. Good-by, Mr. Strebelow; and if there is any change for either the worse or the better, I will come and let you know. I'm going to him as soon as I have left Mrs. Brown at home.

LIL. Do—do!

STREB. Good-by. [*Exit Florence and Doctor C.L. Strebelow closes C. doors. Strebelow and Lilian solus*] Well, Lilian! You had best retire.

LIL. 'Tis no use, John, I could not sleep.

STREB. Will you go to Natalie?

LIL. Not yet. Before I go to her, I must—

STREB. [*With forced calmness*] Speak to me? Better postpone it till tomorrow. You are exhausted. I can wait.

LIL. No, every moment of doubt, of anxiety, would but exhaust me more. I will hear you now.

STREB. Hear me? I thought it was *you* who wished to speak.

LIL. It is! It is! But I fear to begin.

STREB. Let me help you. You love Harold Routledge. Do you not?

LIL. I do not know. I did love him.

STREB. And were engaged to him?

LIL. [*Surprised*] Yes, certainly I was.

STREB. And he loved you?

LIL. Yes.

STREB. What broke the engagement?

LIL. A lover's quarrel.

STREB. And you have loved him ever since?

LIL. I do not know.

STREB. You do not know! Yet, except myself, everybody seemed to know it. The painter saw it on your face and placed it on his canvas. The shallow critic read it, and declared it, and I—I, your husband, living by your side every day, every hour, for six years—I—I did not see it—did not feel it. [*Bitterly*] Love is blind indeed! Oh fool! Fool!

LIL. But John, you knew?

STREB. I knew! Knew what? What I know now, what it has taken me six years to know, is that the heart on which I reposed, in which I shrined a man's truest love, has been veiled to me as a sanctuary to whose religion I was a stranger. Yet I worshipped at it with the devotion of a saint; trusted it with my man's faith, my all.

Lil. [*Drawing herself up with pride*] Nor has the trust been betrayed. My duty and your honor—

Streb. Duty! Honor! Who spoke of duty or of honor? I spoke and speak of love; of that love which in a wife is the sole invulnerable armor of a husband's honor; of that love without which honor is valueless, and life a blank; of the love in which honor dwells as unconsciously as flowers bloom and water flows. God help the husband whose honor is guarded by duty alone.

Lil. You should have said all this before.

Streb. Before! Before what?

Lil. Before we were married.

Streb. Believing that with your hand I received your heart, why should I have said it?

Lil. You knew I had been engaged to Harry Routledge; that but a few days before you proposed to my father for me, it was settled I was to be his wife.

Streb. [*Surprised*] How should I know it? You never mentioned him to me.

Lil. But my father told you.

Streb. Never! Never!

Lil. Then my father deceived me.

Streb. But why—why?

Lil. That I cannot tell, unless it was to—

Streb. To what?

Lil. Unless it was to avoid any delay in our marriage. Immediate ruin—

Streb. Immediate ruin. Then you knew of the threatening bankruptcy?

Lil. [*Astonished*] Certainly.

Streb. [*Staggered*] And—and you accepted me to avert it?

Lil. To save my father; yes.

Streb. Then your father deceived me—deceived us both!

Lil. [*Frightened*] Oh! Father! [*Sits on sofa R.C.*]

Streb. Then I did not marry you. I bought you. I became not your husband, but your owner. This marriage was not a union, but a sacrifice—a sacrifice not of one, not of two, but of three lives. O Heaven! what have we done? [*Falls into chair L.C.*]

Lil. [*Rises, goes to Strebelow*] Can you forgive me? [*Kneels*]

Streb. [*His face in his hands*] Wait! Wait! [*Pause. Lilian is kneeling by Strebelow's chair—both are weeping*] We must not forget our child.

Lil. [*Raises her head in alarm*] Natalie! But tell me you forgive me—for her sake—for her sake!

STREB. I have nothing to forgive but my blindness. I should have thought for both. I will do so now. Tell me, and tell me frankly—for frankness now alone can save us—do you still love Harold Routledge?

LIL. I don't know. [*Rising*]

STREB. [*Rising and following her*] Do you not know your own heart? Don't sob so; be calm.

LIL. I did love Harold Routledge, I believe, with the love of a school-girl. We had a silly quarrel—broke our engagement. I wrote him to come back to me the very day I accepted you. He came back, doubtless full of joy, of hope, of love—for he did love me. [*Sobs*]

STREB. [*Thoughtfully*] I recollect.

LIL. I refused to see him. [*Piteously*] What could I do? He went away, and we were married. Regret at the pain the sudden blow must have given him remained with me long; but our Natalie was born—my heart turned to her—to—

STREB. I understand.

LIL. I could not understand. I never did! Your kind love, your watchfulness, your devotion won upon my mother's heart, but I feared to show it. I scarcely understood my own feelings, till—till he returned. But when I saw him whose life I knew I had blighted, lying there dying, as I feared, remorse, shame took possession of me—possesses me still. I—[*Sits R.C. on sofa*]

STREB. Spoken and acted like the noble woman that you are.

LIL. And you do forgive me? [*Kneeling*]

STREB. Again I say, there is nothing to forgive but my own blindness, and your father's folly.

LIL. And you will forget it all?

STREB. And continue our mutual sacrifice? That were to punish you—not that!

LIL. What would you do?

STREB. Leave you, for a time maybe. Natalie—poor child of a loveless union.

LIL. [*Screams*] Leave me, and—take Natalie?

STREB. [*Bitterly aside*] Oh, how little she knows me yet! [*Aloud*] No, poor mother! You shall keep your child. I would remain with you, too, were I a stronger man than I am. I can read clearly what is passing in your heart, but after seeing you sacrifice it to your father, I will not weakly tempt you to sacrifice it again to your child.

LIL. [*Piteously*] And you will leave me?

STREB. With your father—

LIL. And when will you return?

STREB. When your heart calls me. When it calls the husband as well as the father.

LIL. Remain with me and trust me.

STREB. Near or far, 'tis not you I fear to trust, 'tis myself. To live beside you day by day, to hear you every hour, construing each heave of your bosom into a sigh for another, each moment of abstraction into a dream of him! No! No! I'm not strong enough for that.

LIL. Then be it as you will.

STREB. It must be so. Go to Natalie. [*Lilian goes to R., pauses, then exits R.1.E. Solus, sitting in armchair L.C.*] 'Tis all over. [*Before picture L.*] How plain its story seems now! That face, so long to me the sun of earthly beauty, the object of all my pride in the past, the prefiguration of all my hopes in the future, now tells me only the suffering victim carrying in her heart a secret that must not live. [*In agony*] A love that cannot die! [*Pause, while Strebelow looks at picture in silence. Enter Lizette*]

LIZ. A letter, sir. [*Strebelow still looking at picture, Lizette places letter in his hand, which rests on his knee. Exit Lizette L.3.E.*]

STREB. I will look at it no more. Let the face be veiled to me in the future, as the heart has been in the past. [*Draws curtain over picture, as he does so drops letter, picks it up, opens letter, continuing*] Harold Routledge dead! Dead! Leaving her a widow with a living husband, and leaving me a wifeless husband and a childless father! [*Drops into chair. Quick drop of curtain*]

ACT V.

Set the same as Act I. At rise of curtain, Babbage and Westbrook are discovered seated at table. Papers, etc.

BAB. The papers are all right, old boy. This one is mine, and that one yours. [*As he speaks spreads two written sheets of legal cap on table, pushing pen toward Westbrook, who takes it and signs each, throws down pen and turns away*] Is that all the fuss you make about it, old fellow? It takes but a single clip to cut the longest chain. [*Wipes his eyes*]

WEST. [*In evident emotion, shakes hands with Babbage*] Staunch friend and partner of thirty years, I—I—

BAB. That's all right, Westbrook, all right. Don't mind me. I'm a stupid old fool, I suppose. Here goes! [*Signs the papers in turn, hands one to Westbrook, putting the other in his pocket*]

WEST. And now—

BAB. And now the last papers are signed that dissolve the firm of Babbage & Westbrook after an existence of twenty-nine years, eleven months, and fifteen days. Well, are you satisfied? We retire with a little over two million and a half apiece, owing no man a dollar.

WEST. If figures never lie, we are two highly successful men.

BAB. Both our shares securely invested; government bonds, real estate. A number one, two copper-fastened, iron-bound, solid business men. Is that success?

WEST. If figures never lie?

BAB. Hm! Figures are the biggest liars in the world. Give a boy a one dollar bill and tell him to multiply the amount of happiness he can get out of it by two millions five hundred thousand. He will hardly believe that you and I envy him the happiness he extracts from the first ten cents he spends, knowing he has enough left for the circus and all the side shows. Heigh-ho! Westbrook, the bigger the figures, the bigger they lie.

WEST. [*Sighing*] Rather late to take that view of them now.

BAB. [*Rising*] Hm! Westbrook, there is one more document—I—I— [*Aside*] Some people would call me an old fool, I suppose, if they knew it. [*Aloud*] There is one more document I want to transfer. It isn't a very sharp financial operation. [*Takes paper out of his pocketbook, hands it to Westbrook*] But it will ease my conscience a little.

WEST. [*Reading outside of paper*] A warrantee deed to Lilian Westbrook Strebelow! [*Opens paper, glances over it*] Grand Street property! My dear Babbage, what do you mean? This property is worth over half a million. We allowed that much for it in the division of our assets.

BAB. It's only the odd half million, old boy. You and I own five millions of dollars between us. Take it, Larry. Forgive me for bringing it up. But— but it's been on *my* conscience for the last nine years. By rights, we owe it all to Lilian, poor girl! I know it isn't money she needs. She has enough of that. But an old brute like me has nothing but money to give her. It won't help *her* any, I know, but it may help to ease my conscience a little. It's only the odd half million, Larry.

WEST. [*Much affected*] Ah, old friend and wise partner, you seem better than I.

BAB. There, there, old fellow, forgive me for bringing it up. But how is she today?

WEST. Just as she was yesterday, as she was last week, last month, last year, as she has been every day since John Strebelow gave her back to me in Paris with the words: "Take back your daughter, Mr. Westbrook and be it your task to soften to her memories of the past you made for her and me."

You know how I brought her home; how John Strebelow made her practically mistress of the bulk of his fortune, now settled on their child; how since then he has resided in Rome. I do not believe he ever returned to Paris after his terrible duel with the Count de Carojac.

BAB. And he never writes to you?

WEST. Never. But I believe he corresponds regularly with Fanny Holcomb. Oh, Babbage, had I but heeded your warning on that dreadful day!

BAB. We should not be sharing five millions today, but I should feel a happier and a better man.

WEST. I'd give every penny of it to bring Harold Routledge back to life, to compensate John Strebelow.

BAB. The latter, at all events, is possible.

WEST. How?

BAB. Listen. Just as sure as John Strebelow loves your daughter, just as sure your daughter now loves him, and hungers for him today.

WEST. Would to heaven it were true.

BAB. It is true. Since we commenced winding up our business, I have been here every day. I have repeatedly seen Lilian and Natalie together. I never heard them talk that they did not talk of Natalie's father, that Lilian did not tell the child how great and good her father is. Natalie writes to him regularly; and Lilian oversees the correspondence.

WEST. [*Eagerly*] How do you know this?

BAB. About a month ago, the day that Illinois Central bounded up to ninety-two and tumbled back to eighty-seven, Natalie came to me with a curious little letter in her hand, the day Perkins & Johnson went under, you know, short on Erie and Wabash; Pacific Mail went clean out of sight. Natalie asked me to put a little picture, as she called the stamp, on her letter and drop it into the box that goes to Rome. The letter was addressed to John Strebelow. It is exactly five weeks ago. Take my word for it, Lilian is trying to woo her husband, and the child is writing the love letters.

WEST. Heaven grant it. But, Babbage—[*Holding out paper*]

BAB. Well?

WEST. This gift really I cannot—

BAB. Let me have my own way about that, old boy. It is a private speculation of my own. [*Goes toward door*] It's only the odd half million. [*Reaches door, turns round*] Here comes another who has retired from business too, only to resume an active partnership pretty soon, [*Laughing*] I think.

WEST. Who is it?

BAB. [*Laughing*] The relict of the late Mr. Brown. I hear her in the hall.

WEST. [*Going*] Then come this way [*To upper door*] to my room. [*Westbrook leads off by upper door. Babbage turns to follow that way, going last, talking as he goes*]

BAB. I've kept the other two millions. What a heartless, grasping set we solid business men are. [*Going up R.*]

FLOR. [*Entering lower door*] Mr. Babbage! [*Crossing to L.H.*]

BAB. [*Turning back*] Mrs. Brown.

FLOR. How is Lilian today? [*Rings bell on L. table*]

BAB. [*Down R.C.*] The doctor was here half an hour ago.

FLOR. What did he say?

BAB. Nothing.

FLOR. Pshaw! If I were not a woman I could say that myself. [*Enter Lizette L.D.R.*] Excuse me one moment, Mr. Babbage. [*To Lizette*] Tell Mrs. Holcomb I will run up to see her. I want to see her on business.

BAB. Business! [*Exit Lizette upper door R.*]

FLOR. [*To Babbage*] I was on my way down town to order some new cards. [*Takes out a card with a wide black margin*] I came in to ask Aunt Fanny how wide I ought now to have the margin.

BAB. You call that business?

FLOR. Certainly. Aunt Fanny is a widow, like myself. What do *you* think, Mr. Babbage? [*Hands Babbage card. He takes it, gravely looks at it through his spectacles*] The two years are up tomorrow.

BAB. [*R.H.*] Westbrook and I bought and sold stock for Mr. Brown for upward of twenty years. Brown always liked a pretty wide margin himself. [*Hands card back to Florence*] Always allowed a wide margin, too. One good margin deserves another.

FLOR. [*L.H.*] Poor dear old Brown! [*Runs her finger round card*] I'll keep it wide. Heigh-ho! How do you like my new dress, Mr. Babbage? Neat, isn't it? Madame Raypangsay is so very artistic! It is a very delicate matter for a dressmaker to guide a young widow through the various stages of her affliction with good taste: absolute wretchedness, deep grief, profound melancholy, Christian resignation, sentimental sadness.

BAB. I trust your physician has hopes of yet pulling you through?

FLOR. The immediate danger is past. First, he prescribed retirement from the world. Severe as it was, I took the dose. Second he prescribed change of air.

BAB. You took the dose at Saratoga?

FLOR. No, Saratoga was too gay. Heigh-ho! I retired to Newport. I am now a promising convalescent. The doctor told me he had one more prescription. Really—I—

BAB. [*Dryly*] A second husband.

FLOR. Yes.

BAB. Will you take it?

FLOR. [*Laughing*] With all my heart!

BAB. You have something more *substantial* than that to offer your second husband.

FLOR. Thanks to my first, I have. Heigh-ho! [*Crosses to R.*] Don't you think there is a delicate suggestion of subdued grief in this corded trimming, Mr. Babbage? [*Without waiting for an answer, Florence looking at her dress, goes to lower door, looks at her train over her shoulder, at door kisses her hand to Babbage, and exits, lower door*]

BAB. [*Looking after her a moment*] Poor Brown! Always so anxious about his margin! There is nothing but a margin left of him now! Brown was one of us, a solid business man! [*Goes to upper door as he talks, exits, shaking his head*]

FANNY. [*Outside upper door as if meeting Babbage in the hall*] Ah, Mr. Babbage. Mr. Westbrook is upstairs.

BAB. Yes, I know. [*Enter Fanny, crossing to L.H.*]

FANNY. [*Looking round*] Not here.

LIL. [*Enters upper door*] Looking for me, aunt? I heard you come downstairs.

FANNY. [*Sits down L.C.*] Yes, dear, sit down. [*Lilian gets stool, sits by Fanny L.C.*] Have you thought of what I have said to you?

LIL. I have never ceased to think of it.

FANNY. You are growing more and more listless. Your health must give way at last.

LIL. [*Dejectedly*] I am so wretched, so miserable, have been all these years.

FANNY. I knew it all the time. Why do you not write to him?

LIL. I dare not.

FANNY. [*Coaxingly*] Why, dear?

LIL. Oh, aunt, if you had seen, had heard him, that terrible night, when he in his anger and disappointment, revealed to me the depth of his affection, the nobility of his manly nature—revealed to me what I would not confess to myself, that I did love, had long loved him, who I believed married me without a single thought of love—if you had seen that, heard that, you would understand why I dare not write to him now.

FANNY. Could he see what I have seen, heard what I have just heard, John Strebelow would be at your feet, the happiest of husbands, the proudest of fathers. Once more I tell you, child, you are repeating my mistake and your own. [*Enter Lizette U.D.*]

LIZ. Mrs. Brown is waiting to see you in your own room, Mrs. Holcomb.

FANNY. Tell her I will be there in a moment. [*Exit Lizette U.D.*] I wish she had chosen some other time. [*Rising*] I would again, I do again urge you, for your own sake, for your child's sake, Lilian, above all for your husband's sake, to write to him. Unveil your heart, let him see himself there beside his child, and the past will be atoned for by a peaceful and happy future, believe me. [*Goes to upper door*]

FLOR. [*Outside. Calls*] Mrs. Holcomb!

FANNY. I must go. I hear Florence.

FLOR. [*Calls again*] Mrs. Holcomb!

FANNY. Coming. [*Louder*] I'm coming up, Mrs. Brown. [*Exits R.U.D.*]

LIL. [*Solus, rising*] No, I dare not write to him, I dare not ask him to return to me, though I know my heart will break if he remains away. [*Stops as if in thought. Calls*] Natalie!

NAT. [*Running in from U.D.*] Here I am, mamma! And here is dolly. We've been putting her house to rights.

LIL. [*Sits in chair used by Fanny, places Natalie on the stool she herself had used*] Tell me, dear, how long is it since you sent the letter to papa?

NAT. The one you spelt for me?

LIL. Yes.

NAT. [*Timidly*] I—I sent another since.

LIL. [*Astonished*] Another?

NAT. Yes, I asked Mr. Babbage to put the post office picture on for me and put it in the box. Was it naughty?

LIL. It is never naughty for you to write to dear papa. But you showed me all your other letters.

NAT. [*Assuming importance*] Oh, I wanted to say something important to papa.

LIL. You need never show me your letters to him unless you please. But how did you direct it?

NAT. Aunty Brown wrote on the envelope.

LIL. Would you like to write to papa today?

NAT. [*Clapping her hands*] Oh, yes, yes. [*Rising*]

LIL. And let me tell you what to write?

NAT. Oh, that'll make it so easy. [*Runs to drawer of secretary, C., gets paper, envelopes, takes them to table, L.H., Lilian puts hassock on chair and lifts Natalie to enable her to sit on it. Natalie takes pen*] Now, mamma, what am I to say?

LIL. "Dear papa."

NAT. [*Writing*] That's easy. Now?

LIL. "I do hope—" On the line below, dear.

NAT. [*Writing*] "Do ope."

LIL. Hope—that's it—"you will come back to America."

NAT. [*Spelling as she writes*] K-u-m, come.

LIL. Oh, dear, no! Let me guide your hand. [*Guides Natalie's hand, speaking the words as she causes the child to trace them*] Come back to America. [*With emotion*] Mamma wants you very much. [*Sobbing*] So very much she—will—die if you do not come. Come back to her, to me. [*Lilian, sobbing, falls on ottoman*]

NAT. Why, that's just what I wrote in the letter I did not show you.

LIL. [*Turning her face from child*] What you wrote?

NAT. [*Looking at letter*] Yes. I knew you wanted him to come back. I told him what Aunty Brown told me when she helped me to write.

LIL. [*Controlling herself*] What did she tell you?

NAT. [*Going to her*] That the doctor said you might go away if he did not come back soon, and then, you know, he could not find you at all.

LIL. [*Catching the child to her breast*] Oh, my darling! My darling! [*Kisses her*]

NAT. I put the picture of you that you gave me last Christmas into the letter for papa to see.

LIL. [*Turning away from Natalie as Lizette enters lower door*] Oh, John! John! If you but knew my heart today as well as you know my face! [*Sees Lizette*] Well?

LIZ. [*With letters on salver*] The mail, madam. Two letters from Mr. Westbrook and one for Miss Natalie. [*Natalie runs to Lizette, who gives her letter and then exits U.D.*]

NAT. [*Looking at letter*] Oh, what a dirty letter! That isn't from papa.

LIL. Let me read it for you. [*Takes letter, looks at it*] It is from papa. [*Stops*]

NAT. What makes it so ugly?

LIL. [*Looking at letter*] It is stained with sea water. Steamship *Hanover!* The steamer that was wrecked. Natalie, this letter was at the bottom of the big ocean.

NAT. And they got it out again?

LIL. Yes, and sent it on to you.

NAT. Oh, they knew it was from my papa. Do read it.

LIL. [*Opens letter; picture falls out*] What is that?

NAT. [*Picks it up, looks at it*] See, mamma, papa's picture?

LIL. [*Takes picture, looks at it in deep emotion*] His hair is almost white now—and in three years! [*Kisses picture*]

NAT. Read the letter!

LIL. [*Reads*] "My little darling, I will take the next steamer for America!" The next steamer for America.

NAT. I'm so glad, so glad! [*Clings to her mother's dress*]

LIL. [*Looks at date of letter*] August the eleventh. Natalie, Natalie, papa may be in America now. [*Enter Florence, upper door R.*]

FLOR. [*Stopping upstage*] Why, Lilian, what's the matter?

LIL. Florence! Natalie's father—my—Mr. Strebelow is coming home.

FLOR. Oh, he's found his senses at last, has he?

LIL. The news has excited me a little, and I must tell my father.

NAT. [*Pulling her mother upstage*] Yes, yes, we must tell grandpa and Uncle Babbage.

LIL. [*To Florence*] You'll excuse me a few minutes.

FLOR. Certainly. [*Lilian and Natalie exit upper door R. Solus*] Now, I am really glad of that. Lilian was breaking her heart. Poor thing! I don't wonder at it. What's the use of a husband two thousand miles away? [*Enter Phipps preceded by Lizette*] Phipps!

PHIPPS. Brown.

FLOR. Returned from Europe.

PHIPPS. Just off the steamer. [*To Lizette*] Give this card and this note to Mrs. Holcomb and tell her I am at her service. [*Lizette exits. To Florence*] Just reached the dock. Business tour in Europe this time. Wasted no time on sight-seeing as I did three years ago.

FLOR. What steamer did you come in?

PHIPPS. *Veal de Paree*—less than half an hour ago! Strebelow and I jumped into a carriage as soon as we touched the pier.

FLOR. John Strebelow?

PHIPPS. Left baggage to the curiosity of the officials of the Custom House; only a small valise, box or two of collars, a few neckties, half a dozen shirts.

FLOR. Mr. Phipps, please give my imagination some chance. But Mr. Strebelow?

PHIPPS. Is at his hotel! He was in such a hurry to see his child he could scarcely wait for the *Veal de Paree* to swing to. The note I brought was from him. He wants me to take Natalie to him in the carriage I have below. He's crazy to see the child.

FLOR. Indeed! and Lilian, his wife? Has he forgotten her?

PHIPPS. Thinks and talks to me of nothing else. Did all the voyage. I tried him on dry goods—no use! He took no more interest in the new styles of imported brocades—that reminds me! [*Takes out watch, then notebook*] I must not forget to—[*To Florence*] Excuse me, but I must get to the bank before three o'clock. Let me see. [*Reading notes*] Arnold, Matthison & Company, Axminster carpets, five and ten off. [*Enter Fanny U.D.*]

FANNY. [*R.*] Mr. Phipps.

PHIPPS. [*C.*] Ah, glad to see you—just back from Europe—get Strebelow's note?

FANNY. Thank you, yes; you will pardon me, but I came to tell you I sent the answer to Mr. Strebelow directly.

PHIPPS. And Natalie—is she ready?

FANNY. I have asked Mr. Strebelow to call here to see her.

PHIPPS. [*Nods*] Right. I understand—and Mrs. Strebelow?

FANNY. I am now going to tell her. You will excuse me?

PHIPPS. Certainly. [*Exit Fanny U.D.R.*] Mrs. Holcomb has what I call horse sense—most women have.

FLOR. [*Sits by fire*] You think so?

PHIPPS. [*Returning to his notes*] Yes—old women.

FLOR. Oh!

PHIPPS. [*At his notes*] Long Island Manufacturing Company. I wonder if I can run over to Greenpoint! It will do tomorrow. By the way, Mrs. Brown, while I think of it—Merrill, Cook & Company—half past—draft on London—must not forget that. [*To Florence*] You have now been a widow upward of two years, I believe.

FLOR. Two years tomorrow.

PHIPPS. [*At his notes*] Whitbeck, Oldhanger & Company, order filled per samples. [*Looks at his watch*] Half past two. [*To Florence*] Will you be my wife, Mrs. Brown? [*Looking at her as he closes his watch, puts it into pocket, and then returns to his notes*]

FLOR. [*Starting up*] Sir!

PHIPPS. Will—you—be—my—wife? [*At notes again*] Sorry I could not get those goods for Jones & Cunningham. [*To Florence*] I will drop in and see you this afternoon. [*Florence staggers; he catches her in his arms. Places her on ottoman. Pause. She jumps up quickly*]

FLOR. I have concluded not to faint, Mr. Phipps. Have you ever been struck by a cannon ball?

PHIPPS. No; I was hit by a baseball once.

FLOR. Then you cannot appreciate my feelings at the present moment. [*Surveys him*] I rather like you, Phipps. You're not handsome, but you interest me. The doctor has prescribed a second husband.

PHIPPS. Of course that is the only prescription that can cure a widow of her widowhood.

FLOR. I might as well take the dose in one form as another. I will swallow it with my eyes shut.

PHIPPS. I'm not a sugar-coated pill, madam—but—

FLOR. [*Laughs*] Phipps, there's my hand.

PHIPPS. [*Kisses her hand, returns to notebook*] September second—suppose we call it thirty days after date? [*Writes*]

FLOR. Thirty days from date?

PHIPPS. Yes—by the way, what is your middle name?

FLOR. Florence St. Vincent Brown. Have *you* a card about you? [*He gives her card*] Thank you. [*Reads card*] George Washington Phipps. [*Crosses to R.*] I shouldn't like to forget your name before the happy day.

PHIPPS. Easily remembered. Father of his country Phipps.

FLOR. Now, don't forget, Phipps—October second.

PHIPPS. October fifth!

FLOR. Eh?

PHIPPS. Three days' grace you know. [*Florence laughs. Phipps, writing in books*] October second and fifth; we shall both fall due on the same day— say half past three P.M.

FLOR. Half past three P.M.

PHIPPS. Sharp!

FLOR. Sharp! [*Laughs. Exits U.D.R.*]

PHIPPS. [*Solus, looks at his watch after Florence*] Hm! I can give her seventeen minutes more. [*Exits after Florence. Stage remains empty for a few seconds. Enter Lizette and Strebelow, R.H., lower door*]

STREB. I will wait. [*Exit Lizette R.U.D. Solus, looking around him*] The very room! Here, on this very spot, it was she gave me her hand. As I stand here, it seems but yesterday—yesterday it seemed an age! [*Enter Fanny R.U.D.*]

FANNY. [*R.*] Mr. Strebelow!

STREB. [*Turning to her*] Mrs. Holcomb! [*They go to each other and shake hands*]

FANNY. I am very, very glad to see you here—here in this house, once more, Mr. Strebelow.

STREB. I know you are—I understand, and thank you.

FANNY. Mr. Phipps brought me your request to send Natalie to you. In justice to Lilian I could not do that. I felt, as you must feel, that the proper place for you to see your child was where her mother is.

STREB. Tell me of her. How is Lilian?

FANNY. As well as she has been any day since she returned here. The news of your arrival has excited her a little. But you shall see her for yourself.

STREB. See her! See her!

FANNY. I will send her to you.

NAT. [*Running in*] Oh, Aunt Fanny, when will papa be here? [*Sees Strebelow, catches hold of Fanny's dress; hides behind it, peeping out at Strebelow*]

STREB. [*Holding his arms out to her*] Natalie, don't you know me?

NAT. [*Comes forward a little, looks at Strebelow, utters a cry, rushes to him*] Oh, papa! Papa!

STREB. [*Taking her in his arms*] Natalie, my child! My own darling! [*Aunt Fanny steals silently to door*]

NAT. Oh, I'm so glad.

STREB. [*Sitting and holding the child out in front of him*] And you did not know me?

NAT. Oh, yes, I did; but your hair is so white, just like your picture. Oh, I'm so glad—and mamma will be so happy.

STREB. [*Kisses her, then looking at her*] How you have grown—and your hair is darker. How like her mother. [*Kisses her again. Fanny steals out upper door*]

NAT. It was naughty of you to stay away so long. I knew you'd come when I wrote you how much mamma wanted to have you here— And how unhappy she was without you. But what are you thinking about?

STREB. I came as soon as I received your last letter.

NAT. I knew you would.

STREB. [*Thoughtfully*] You wrote me a great many letters.

NAT. [*Proudly*] Didn't I? It was hard at first; but mamma told me what to write, you know.

STREB. [*Eagerly*] Yes, yes. Mamma told you what to say to papa. And— and—and—in the last letter, she told you to say how unhappy mamma was without papa? The words came from her—

NAT. Mamma did not know anything about the last letter. Aunty Brown helped me to write that, and Uncle Babbage put it in the box to Rome.

STREB. [*Rising and turning away from Natalie*] And—and your mamma knew nothing about what was in it.

NAT. [*Proudly*] Not a word. I did it myself. [*Goes up for doll*]

STREB. [*To himself*] And I thought her hand had guided hers, and that she called the husband while the child called her father! [*Pause*] "Mamma is very unhappy without you." It was not she who said it—not she. Her heart is silent still! [*Rising, rings bell*]

NAT. [*Coming down to him*] What's the matter, papa? You're not going to cry; mamma cries, but papas never do, do they?

STREB. They often have most cause. [*Crossing to C. Enter Lizette*] You may say to Mrs. Strebelow that I cannot wait at present. I have an engagement. I may call—I mean, I will return. [*Exit Lizette L.D.*] Good-by, Natalie, [*Taking child in his arms*] good-by. [*Kisses her*]

NAT. Good-by?

STREB. Yes, papa must go now.

NAT. Why, papa, you've not seen mamma yet!

STREB. I know, dear—I know—but I must go now—I must. [*Places child on ground, goes toward lower door as Lilian enters upper door*]

LIL. [*At door*] John! [*Strebelow turns quickly*] Mr. Strebelow.

STREB. Lilian! [*Pause. Child looking at both in wonder*] Lilian, I am glad to see you. [*Goes to meet her, extends hand to her frankly; she takes it timidly*]

LIL. You were going—without—without seeing me!

STREB. [*Embarrassed*] Believe me, I am—am—glad—more than glad to see you. But I felt I had no right to bring about such a meeting without your own express desire. When last we parted I pledged myself to that. I understand your long—long silence perfectly, and so—so we meet only to part again.

LIL. Part again! [*Crossing to L.H. Aside*] I knew it!

NAT. [*Who, by her mother's side, has been wonderingly listening*] Oh, papa, don't go away.

STREB. [*Taking her up*] Papa must go—Good-by, Lilian. [*Holds out his hand to Lilian. As Lilian steps to take it, her head averted, Natalie, who has one arm, tries to draw them together*]

NAT. Kiss mamma! [*Lilian and Strebelow, eyes meet. Her eyes are full of tears; they avert their heads from each other. Natalie looks from one to the other. Pause*]

STREB. [*Mastering his emotions. Putting down Natalie*] There, there, Natalie, good-by. Farewell, Lilian, forever.

LIL. Forever!

STREB. For three years your heart has been silent; will it speak later, think you? [*Lilian is sobbing*]

NAT. Oh, papa, I forgot—my last letter. [*Runs to table, takes letter*] Here it is [*Crosses to C.*] Mamma and I wrote it this morning; she held my hand. [*Gives him letter*]

STREB. [*Takes letter, about to put it in his pocket*] I'll answer it soon, dear.

NAT. Oh, read it now, papa.

STREB. [*Reading*] "Dear papa—mamma wants you very much." [*Reads letter, stops, looks at Lilian*] Lilian! Lilian! Can you repeat these words with your own lips?

LIL. With my whole heart. [*Throws herself into his arms as Fanny enters stealingly U.D.*]

STREB. [*Embracing*] My own wife—my wife! [*Enter U.D., Westbrook and Babbage following Fanny and Phipps; at L.D. follows Florence*]

FANNY. [*Demurely*] I beg your pardon. I was looking for Mrs. Brown.

FLOR. [*Same air*] I beg your pardon. I was looking for Mrs. Holcomb.

PHIPPS. Ah, Strebelow, let me present my future wife, Mrs. George Washington, the mother of her country, Phipps! [*Lilian goes to table, sits down. Natalie runs over to H.*]

WEST. [*To Babbage*] My conscience is at rest at last!

BAB. Mine is more easy.

STREB. [*Goes to his wife, turns round, holds out his hand to Westbrook*] In the future before us, let us forgive and forget the past.

BAB. And retiring from business, speculate no more in human hearts.

CURTAIN

BARON RUDOLPH

BARON RUDOLPH

First produced at Royal Theatre, Hull, England, August 1, 1881, with Mr. and Mrs. George S. Knight.

Produced at the Grand Opera House, New York, September 12, 1881; this first American production ran for two weeks. The cast included: Julian Magnus, Alfred Becks, Lysander Thompson, James Dunn, Maud Granger, Ida Vernon, Mrs. M. A. Farren, Ida Jeffreys, and Virginia Buchanan.

Ran for one week at Windsor Theatre, New York, beginning October 17, 1881, with George S. Knight.

Ran for one week at Windsor Theatre, New York, beginning October 30, 1882, with George S. Knight.

Produced at the Fourteenth Street Theatre, New York, October 24, 1887, with the following cast:

Rudolph Wiegand, *Baron Hollenstein*	GEORGE S. KNIGHT
Whitworth Lawrence, *a man of iron—and gold*	FRANK CARLYLE
General Benjamin Metcalfe, *a man of love and law*	CHARLES BOWSER
Judge Merrybone, *a man of justice and fun*	M. A. KENNEDY
Geoffrey Brown, *a man of tender years*	HARRY WOODRUFF
Allen ⎱ *professional men*	GEORGE D. FAWCETT
Owen ⎰	LIN HURST
John Henry Thomas, *a footman*	WILL C. SAMPSON
Overdeck, *an iron founder, a man who has a memory*	SAMUEL W. KEENE

THE COUNTY SHERIFF, *the right man in the right place*   FRANK COLFAX

RHODA, *a woman who yields, loves, and suffers*   CARRIE TURNER

ERNESTINE, *a baby, a girl, and a woman*   JANE STUART

MRS. NELLIE DASHWOOD   MRS. GEORGE S. KNIGHT

Produced at the Windsor Theatre, New York, January 9, 10, and 11, 1888, with Mr. and Mrs. George S. Knight.

TEXT AND SOURCE

The present edition of *Baron Rudolph* is taken verbatim from a photostatic copy of a typescript of the play; a title-page is missing. Obvious errors in spelling and punctuation have been corrected, and the full spelling of names has been substituted for abbreviations.

The typescript referred to above is substantially the same as a manuscript-typescript version of the play with detailed revisions in Howard's hand. There are several words, passages, and stage directions in the typescript that do not appear in the manuscript-typescript, and there are a few in the latter that do not appear in the former. Space does not here permit a detailed collation of these revisions, but a careful study of them should reveal much regarding Howard's methods of composition. Nine manuscript pages of revisions, in Howard's hand, dated "2 Mar., 1882," represent a succeeding stage in the form of this play; but since these revisions are directions for action and setting, rather than dialogue changes, they could not readily be incorporated into the present text.

William Winter, in his *Life of David Belasco,* states that: (1) *Baron Rudolph* belongs to the category typified by *Struck Oil;* (2) Nellie Dashwood in *Baron Rudolph* is like Mrs. General Gilflory in *The Mighty Dollar;* (3) *Baron Rudolph* bears some resemblance to *Belphegor; or, the Mountebank,* played by Charles Dillon, and *The Music Master,* by Charles Klein. It will be noted that the above plays are spoken of as parallels, not sources. The last named, of course, appeared many years after *Baron Rudolph.* Although Howard acknowledges no indebtedness to these plays, he was undoubtedly familiar with *The Mighty Dollar,* for it played at least twenty-five hundred performances before 1889, and its principal actor, Wm. J. Florence, was the one for whom Howard originally wrote *Baron Rudolph.*

CAST OF CHARACTERS

RUDOLPH WIEGAND, *Baron Hollenstein*

WHITWORTH LAWRENCE, *a man of iron—and gold*

GENERAL BENJAMIN METCALFE, *a man of love and law*

JUDGE MERRYBONE, *a man of justice and fun*

GEOFFREY BROWN, *a man of tender years*

ALLEN
OWEN } *professional men*

JOHN HENRY THOMAS, *a footman*

OVERDECK, *an iron founder; a man who has a memory*

THE COUNTY SHERIFF, *the right man in the right place*

RHODA, *a woman who yields, loves and suffers*

ERNESTINE, *a baby, a girl and a woman*

MRS. NELLIE DASHWOOD

IRONFOUNDERS, POLICE OFFICERS, ETC.

SCENES

ACT I: WINTER; EVENING OR NIGHT. RUDOLPH'S HOME IN NEW YORK.
    (An interval of sixteen years)

ACT II: SEPTEMBER; DAY. LAWRENCE MANSION, LAWRENCEBURG.

ACT III: SEPTEMBER; NIGHT.
    Scene 1: Drinking den of the ironfounders.
    (The curtain drops for change of scene)
    Scene 2: Lawrence mansion. Interior.

ACT IV: SEPTEMBER; DAY. MAPLEGROVE VILLA.

ACT I.

SCENE: *Rudolph's home in New York. Marks of great poverty, in the furniture, walls, etc. But a general appearance of neatness, so far as a good housewife can give it under the most disadvantageous circumstances. Railing and stairs from below, L.U. corner. Old, broken child's cradle, L. One of the rockers patched up, back end of the cradle to audience. A table R.C. One leg of the table loose, but in its place. Old chairs R. and L., mended and patched. One with a leg gone and bottom out, standing against wall L. A cheap looking-glass frame with one piece of broken glass, on wall L. Dormer window in flat R.C. with numerous panes patched up with paper; an old straw hat through one. Pots of flowers on the sill. A poor shawl and bonnet hanging on wall R.C.*

DISCOVERED: *Rhoda. She is sitting at right of table sewing a patch on a coat, already well patched in different shades; rocking the cradle with one foot. She is dressed very poorly, but neatly; looks worn and hungry.*

RHO. Heigh-ho! Rudy and I were getting along so nicely—and we were so happy—before this long strike began. Hush! [*Looking towards the cradle*] Poor baby! How can its mother give it food, when she gets hardly enough to keep her own soul and body together? H-s—h! [*Sings to the baby*] There! [*Finishing her work*] That looks very nice! [*Rising and displaying patched coat*] Rudy's best coat! I've patched and mended it so that there is very little of the original coat left. [*She lays the coat over a chair up R.C. She then turns down C. thoughtfully. Takes a note from her bosom, reads*] "I have told my sister, Mrs. Allison, of your unhappy position. She has commissioned me to say to you that she will gladly provide for yourself and infant and will give you remunerative employment in her own household. Whitworth Lawrence." There are a hundred other women as near starvation as I am, among the workmen's wives. [*Returning note to her bosom*] The rich Mr. Whitworth Lawrence takes a peculiar interest in my welfare? [*Runs to cradle R., kneels and rocks the cradle*] H—s—h! So hungry, poor little darling—[*Drops her face into her hands weeping over the cradle. A knock at the door L.C.*] Come in. [*Knock repeated*] Come—[*Enter John at door. He is a spruce young footman in plain, but handsome livery. He steps in with a dainty air, looking about him with a contemptuous manner. A note in his hand*] Well, sir? What now? You have come again. I sent an answer to your master on your previous visit.

JOHN. [*Handing her note*] My master requests an h'immediate h'answer, madam. [*Aside, scanning her impudently, as she stands R.C., reading note*] Devilish pretty woman—if you dress her h'up. H'on the 'ole I h'approve the change. My master's present lady is getting monotonous. We gentlemen like variety in these matters.

RHO. You may say to Mr. Whitworth Lawrence—

JOHN. H'I beg your pardon. H'in writing h'if you please. My memory is defective.

RHO. You may say to Mr. Whitworth Lawrence—there is no answer.

JOHN. H'oh!

RHO. I think you can remember that.

JOHN. Yes. [*Turning to door*] H'I think I can remember that. [*Exits*]

RHO. Riches! Velvets, diamonds! Food for myself and child—Why has this man pursued me with attentions in spite of my many refusals of him— When I accepted Rudy for my husband he should have known that was an end of it—[*Song. Hold for song*] There is my Rudy now.

RUDOLPH. [*Off*] How are you, Mrs. Finnigan—

MRS. F. [*Off*] Very well, thank you.

RHO. I hope the coat will suit him—[*Finish song and land in C.*] All for a pretty face! [*She drops her head and stands in thought. Rudolph enters at door. She starts and turns to him*] Oh—Rudy! I am glad you have returned. [*Eagerly moving towards him. Rudolph has an old empty basket in his hand*]

RUD. I—I was afraid, you wouldn't be glad, Rho. I—I went out to get something to eat, you know.

RHO. Oh! Heigh-ho—yes. Something for supper. [*Rudolph turns the basket upside down; tosses it up and catches it*]

RUD. [*Handing the basket to Rhoda*] There's the supper, Rho. [*She looks in the basket, shows its emptiness; walks sadly to table; sits*] That's all I could find, Rho. There's lots of that in the market—piles of it. Cook it any way you like, Rho; and warm it over for breakfast. Broil it.

RHO. Oh, Rudolph! The baby will turn her little head to me in vain. It will die—it will die. [*Dropping her head upon the table*]

RUD. Babies are sent from Heaven, they say. I wonder what they were thinking of, up there—when they sent off that one to such a place as this. The shipping clerk must have made a wrong entry. It would have been so much better for her, if she'd stayed there and waited for us. Heigh-ho! I'm afraid they've discovered the mistake—and ordered her back. [*He walks down L. Takes chair with broken leg, etc., from wall; sets it down. It falls over. He picks it up*] Rho, our furniture is getting out of repair. It needs varnishing— and—and so forth. It ought to be upholstered, too. I wonder whether we'd better have plain satin or brocatelle. [*He puts back chair; tries to hang hat on a nail L. It falls to the floor*] Oh!—I forgot. I used that nail to mend the baby's cradle with. [*He takes the piece of broken glass from the looking-glass frame*] Rho, we ought to purchase a new pier glass! This one has ceased to be an ornament to our drawing-room. [*Returns glass. He turns, walks R. Stops C. and looks at Rhoda, who remains with her head upon table*] That woman would adorn the mansion of a millionaire. Plenty of women can do that. She adorns the home of a poor man. Very—few—women—can—do—that. [*He throws his arms over his head and turns upstage; standing before window R.C. with his back to the audience*] Rho—[*Turning*] We'll have to get some new French plate for our conservatory. [*He moves down near her; looks at her a moment*] She's thinking of the baby. The baby will be thinking of her, in a few minutes. Then they'll both be miserable. [*Moves to cradle*] H-u-s-h! There's a smile on the baby's face. She's dreaming of the place she came from. I wonder if she sees the messengers coming for her. [*Looks around*] Perhaps they're here, now, waiting for her. [*Rhoda rises and walks L. where she stands with back half to the audience in an attitude of sorrow. Rudolph raises the child's coverlet*] How that woman has worked to keep things together. That coverlet is embroidered all over—with gold. She's an accomplished woman— Rho is. Heigh-ho. [*He lays back the coverlet; turns; walks toward Rhoda, stops, looks away*] She's trying to keep back the tears, for my sake. Any woman can cry. It takes a heroine not to cry. There are more heroines in this world than there are books to tell about them; and their husbands never know it. [*He returns to chair at table, R.C. He sits, in a dejected way, leaning back. As he stretches out his leg the table-leg falls. He picks it up hurriedly and looks over to cradle*] H-u-s-h. Rho, I've been thinking of getting a chattel mortgage on the furniture. [*Rises*] One of the banks might lend us a basket of cold victuals on that security.

Rho. [*Coming C.*] Rudolph! [*Moves to him*] You—You have been drinking again, Rudy.

Rud. [*Guiltily*] I—I did take just a drop or two of whiskey, Rho.

Rho. Oh—Rudy!

Rud. I—I met Bill Overdeck as I was coming in—

Rho. Bill Overdeck!

Rud. Bill Overdeck offered me some—some—consolation. I did take two or three swallows. Bill Overdeck often consoles me now-a-days.

Rho. Rudolph! You know what your habits once were. This will be worse than no food. It will be worse than an empty cradle. Rudolph, you know what your past life was—before we were married.

Rud. Yes, Rhoda. I know. My autobiography would make a good Sunday-school book. Rich father—title—the young Baron von Hollenstein, of Munich —University education—two years travel in Europe— Twenty thousand a year— Berlin—Vienna—Heidelberg—Paris! It would make a beautiful novel, Rho—and it would have a first-class villain in it, too. A novel ought to have a villain. Whitworth Lawrence and I—

Rho. [*Aside*] Whitworth Lawrence!

Rud. Whitworth Lawrence and I made light of half my fortune in Paris, in one season. I visited New York with Whitworth Lawrence. The day I accepted his invitation was the happiest day of my life, Rho.

Rho. No, Rudolph. He was your companion in dissipation. He helped you on the downward path.

Rud. Helped me? Yes— When I finished my visit to my old schoolmate, the part of my fortune that he hadn't helped me to spend was in his pocket. Whitworth Lawrence robbed me of the last remnant of my fortune, Rho— but I bless him for it!

Rho. Bless him for it? He would rob you now, if he could.

Rud. He can't! I am protected from him at last. I haven't anything left— only you, and the baby, Rho. He can't take them! I bless him! If Whitworth Lawrence hadn't robbed me of what I had left, I should never have found you, Rho—I should never have found you—! the daughter of an humble mechanic —such as I am now. I'm happier as a poor working man, than I ever was in the drawing-room of my own family mansion.

Rho. Ah, Rudolph—you have sacrificed everything for my sake. Your rich uncle in Berlin would have forgiven you everything else; but for your marriage, you might still have been rich.

Rud. Rich?—without you, my darling! My uncle, Johannes von Hollenstein, himself, isn't so rich as I am—he's a bachelor. I disown him. I—I've tried my best to keep you and our little Ernestine comfortable, Rho—and until this long strike—that reminds me; I received a notice from the "Honorable Committee." There is a meeting of us common workingmen this evening. I'm late, now. The meeting will be over. Where's my best coat, Rho? I'll attend the meeting in my most elegant attire. [*She gets the coat and gives it to him*] They'll pass another resolution, I suppose—about fundamental principles. Whereas! Resolved!— That it is our sacred right to do nothing—for eight hours a day—and support our families on the wages we don't get. Fundamental principles, Rho. [*He looks at the coat in his hands*] Bless you, little girl! [*Kisses her*] When I wear that coat—I—I can see Joseph—and go him two patches better.

RHO. Ha—ha—ha—ha—

RUD. [*Kisses her again and runs up. At door*] I'll make a speech, Rho—if I get there before the meeting breaks up. I'll deliver a scientific lecture on the art of supporting life—by voting three times a week on a new resolution. Principles, Rho!— Fundamental principles! I'll bring you back some for breakfast. [*Exits*]

RHO. Breakfast!— Poor Rudolph— It is saddest of all to see his light-hearted humor struggling to the surface, through misery and hunger. I do hope they will vote to put an end to the strike. [*She goes to cradle; kneels; drops her head wearily over the child*] Breakfast! [*A light knock at the door. Rhoda does not hear it. It is repeated. She raises her head, listens, rises, moves C.*] Come. [*The knock is repeated*] Come! [*Enter Whitworth Lawrence. Rhoda starting back—aside*] Whitworth Lawrence!

LAWR. I ask your pardon for intruding, Mrs. Wiegand. On the return of my servant without an answer, I sprang into my carriage and drove here, myself, at once.

RHO. [*Dropping into a chair R.C.*] Well, sir?

LAWR. May I be seated, madam?

RHO. As you please, sir.

LAWR. [*After sitting L.C.*] You strangely misunderstand my motives, Mrs. Wiegand. I offer you kindness, when you are most in need of it. I insist upon my good offices. You return my servant without an answer. I am not a man, however, to be turned so easily from a purpose. This long strike, as I happen to know, will continue. [*Rhoda starts anxiously*] I am a director of the company. We positively refused the last terms offered us this afternoon. I received word, just before my arrival here, that the meeting of workingmen, called for this evening, has already voted to continue the strike. [*Rhoda drops her face into her hands*] You and your child are suffering for the bare necessities of life. I offer you, through my sister, Mrs. Allison, the means of supporting yourself and your child comfortably, decently, respectably.

RHO. Respectably! [*Rising*]

LAWR. [*Rising*] Not otherwise, madam—upon my honor. You are the wife of my old friend and schoolmate, Rudolph Wiegand.

RHO. Your—friend?

LAWR. I intend to provide more liberally for your husband than for yourself.

RHO. [*Starting*] Indeed!

LAWR. I have offered you all that a man can offer a woman whom he respects—and whom he sincerely desires to respect. I shall offer your husband an important position in the service of our company—with a salary of five thousand dollars a year. I will be frank with you, Rhoda—[*She starts, looking at him. He bows*] Mrs. Wiegand. I will be honest with you.

Rho. If—you—please.

Lawr. In case of a certain contingency—I shall transfer thirty thousand dollars worth of the company's stock—now held in my name—to your—present—husband—

Rho. My—present—husband!—and that contingency?

Lawr. Our marriage. [*She starts back aghast; covers her face with her hands*] I love you, Rhoda Wiegand; devotedly—honestly! A legal divorce—[*She starts*]

Rho. Divorce!

Lawr. A legal divorce shall give me the right to call you mine.

Rho. Right!

Lawr. Mine!—right or wrong! By the law of the land. Rhoda! [*Earnestly*] My wealth—my name—my honor—shall be yours. Your present husband—[*She starts away from him*] shall be rich again. A gentleman again, raising his head in the society to which he was born. Your child—[*She starts away*] shall be raised in luxury—a pretty child of wealth—she shall be my daughter, Rhoda!

Rho. Never—never—[*Rudy sings offstage*]

Lawr. [*At window*] Come look—

Women. [*Off*] Oh—Rudy—Rudy—give us a kiss.

Lawr. You see he sings to the mob and kisses the women while you have not the necessities of life.

Rho. You are right. I can't stand it. [*Crosses to table*]

Lawr. Why not come to my sister— She will give you honorable employment—

Rho. I will.

Lawr. Then write—[*Gives her paper and pencil*] I am leaving you to save our child—[*Rhoda writes and repeats lines*] You will find my sister's carriage at the door—it is at your command. [*He exits. Rhoda hurriedly puts on the shawl and bonnet, hanging on the wall R.C. Goes to cradle; takes out the baby, wrapping it up hastily, in the coverlet. Hurries up to the door; opens it and exits*]

Mob. [*Riot offstage*] Good-by, Rudy— Come again— We like you—etc.

ACT II.

An interval of sixteen years has elapsed.

Scene: *Lawrence mansion. The home of Whitworth Lawrence, in the suburbs of Lawrenceburg. Lawn before the house. Corner of the mansion R.2. extending to R.4., with steps. Garden seats R.C., L.C., and L. A low balustrade with post, and urn of flowers, extending from L.4. wing to L.C. Foliage rises gradually from top of balustrade near post, until it mingles with foliage of wing. Limb of tree L.C. Hammock from limb to wing L.*
Discovered: *Mrs. Nellie Dashwood in hammock, L.C., singing.*

Mrs. D. [*After song, picking the petals of flower*] Loves me, loves me not. Judge Merrybone, governor-elect of the state of New York—General Benjamin Metcalfe, famous criminal lawyer—and probable future senator. It is really very embarrassing. General Benjamin Metcalfe will propose to me this evening. Judge Merrybone will also propose to me this evening. The widow of a United States senator—with thirty thousand dollars a year—can predict a proposal with as much accuracy as an astronomer can predict an eclipse or the transit of Venus. The only question is—which shall be the eclipse—and which the transit of Venus? The late senator asked me, one day, whether I should ever marry again in case he departed this life. "Senator," said I, "I haven't the remotest idea." "Widows generally do marry," said he. "Senator," said I, "they do." [*Resumes the picking*] Metcalfe—Merrybone. Widower—bachelor. Fate! [*Holding up the last petal. Enter Rhoda from mansion R.*]

Rho. All by yourself, Nellie?

Mrs. D. I've been gambling, my dear: a game of solitaire.

Rho. You have been gambling?

Mrs. D. Tossing dice for a second husband and my future happiness.

Rho. Heigh-ho—I trust you may find it.

Mrs. D. A second husband? He's trying to find me.

Rho. Future happiness, my dear Nellie.

Mrs. D. That's a very different thing. As to second husbands—they grow in clusters, like cherries. The only difficulty with a rich widow is to obey the laws against polygamy. One mustn't pick but one cherry at a time.

Rho. I suspect our jolly bachelor, Judge Merrybone—

Mrs. D. Judge Merrybone squeezed my hand in a highly prophetic way, last night. General Metcalfe squeezed my other hand at precisely the same moment. Were you ever thrilled by an ardent passion for two men at the same time, my dear?

Rho. Never, my dear Nellie—never!

MRS. D.   The two electric currents met in the center—exactly over my heart. I thought I was in a railway accident. There was an awful smashup inside.

RHO.   It is lucky I know you so well, Nellie. Other people say you have no soul.

MRS. D.   I get along very nicely without one in this world—and I might find a soul inconvenient in the next.

RHO.   Ah, Nellie! Your deeds have betrayed your tongue—you have a soul—and a heart, too. Since you have been visiting me, every poor creature in the neighborhood has learned to bless you.

MRS. D.   That is one of the luxuries I can buy with my money. So is a second husband, by the bye. But, Rhoda, dear! [*Suddenly changing her manner*] Those old sad spirits have been coming over you again. [*Moving to Rhoda, who has dropped into a seat L., and standing over her*] Pardon me, if I speak too frankly, Rhoda—but I fear—I fear—if I should find happiness in a second marriage, I—I shall find more than you have found, I suspect.

RHO.   Whitworth Lawrence has always been a kind husband to me—and a good father to my daughter, Ernestine.

MRS. D.   Oh—speaking of Ernestine—why will Mr. Lawrence insist on marrying the girl to that human icicle, Mr. Northcote Chillblood?

RHO.   Mr. Lawrence thinks that Mr. Northcote Chillblood will make Ernestine a good husband.

MRS. D.   Ernestine's own father died when she was an infant, did he not? [*Rhoda starts to her feet and passes R., Mrs. Dashwood watching her. Aside*] I have struck the nerve. [*Then aloud*] Forgive me, Rhoda!

RHO.   I do not know whether Ernestine's father be dead or living. [*She buries her face in her hands. Mrs. Dashwood goes to her, and places her arms about her waist*] I left him, sixteen years ago—with our child. I never saw him again. I only heard, that, without me by his side, he was going from bad to worse. I—I at least refused the proffered assistance of another—and struggled to support myself and child, with my needle. But I gave up the struggle at last. After two years, I was divorced. He disappeared—I never knew how nor where. But I often seem to see him in my dreams. Only last night, a weary and broken form stood at my bedside, ragged, forlorn, prematurely old; I dreamed that it was my husband. It seemed like reality. For aught I know, he may be a wanderer upon the face of the earth. I am miserable, Nellie— miserable!

MRS. D.   There, my dear!—You mustn't believe in ghosts. The late senator often appears to me in my dreams. "Dashwood," I always say—"get out."

That's the last of his ghost for that night. [*Turns upstage. Enter Ernestine, from mansion R.*]

ERN. [*Nearly crying*] Mamma, dear! [*Rhoda rouses herself, wiping her eyes and moving L. where she drops into a seat*] Mamma, dear!—I—I wanted to speak with you. I—I am miserable today, mamma. [*Dropping in seat R.*]

MRS. D. [*C.*] Both of them miserable! I shall be miserable myself, if I don't get out of this. [*To Rhoda*] Remember, my dear—you mustn't mind that ghost. Be firm with it, my love. Put your foot down. I always do—exactly as I did when Dashwood was alive. He hasn't forgotten it, to this day. My late husband's ghost and myself understand each other perfectly. [*Turning upstage. Judge Merrybone heard whistling a lively air up L.3.*] Judge Merrybone! We always know when the judge is coming—as we do a locomotive—by his whistle. [*She walks up to balustrade post L.C.—motions with fan and curtsies to the Judge without, L. She looks on the other side of the post and starts; a little scream escapes her*] Oh! The general, too! There's going to be another collision! I can't switch them off. I'll signal them. [*She makes coquettish motions, opening her fan, etc., etc. first towards one side and then towards the other*] No use! [*Stepping back R.C.*] There will be a collision! [*A little mock scream*] Oh! [*She covers her face with her fan, as if waiting for a catastrophe. Enter Judge Merrybone L.4.E. and General Metcalfe L.U.E. at same moment. Both advancing to meet her. They suddenly face each other, as they are extending their hands to her, and draw up with annoyance. Mrs. D. looks timidly from behind her fan*] Nobody killed!

MET. [*Offering his arm*] Will you allow me the privilege, Mrs. Dashwood?

MRS. D. [*Aside*] First to recover. [*Aloud*] Certainly, General Metcalfe. [*She drops her arm into his and moves up with him. She looks back over her shoulder at the Judge*] Ta-ta, judge—ta-ta. [*Exit, R.U.E. beyond mansion, she nodding her head to Metcalfe. Metcalfe glances back at the Judge. Judge Merrybone stands looking after them, and resumes his whistling. He comes down*]

JUDGE. [*Aside L.*] I don't say it in my official capacity as a judge—but I would if I could—Metcalfe be hanged! [*Whistles. Exits L.3.E.*]

ERN. [*R.*] Mamma, dear!

RHO. [*L.*] Ernestine.

ERN. Father is so determined that I should marry Mr. Northcote Chillblood. What I wanted to speak to you about, mamma, was—I—I—you know Geoffrey—Mr. Geoffrey Brown—would you feel very badly—mamma if—if I—if it should happen that I—that I should marry Geoffrey—instead of Mr. Chillblood—would you, mamma?

RHO. Marry?— Geoffrey? Would I feel badly? Certainly not, my child, but—

ERN. [*Joyfully*] Oh, mamma! [*Running to Rhoda and throwing her arms about her neck*] I love you more than ever! [*Kissing her*] More than ever, ever, ever, ever, ever! [*Then with gaiety*] The last time I saw Geoffrey—

RHO. Geoffrey has not been here in more than a month. Mr. Lawrence requested Geoffrey not to visit the house.

ERN. I—I—I saw Geoffrey this morning, mamma.

RHO. This morning?

ERN. I—I took breakfast with him.

RHO. Took breakfast with him?

ERN. Under those two old beeches by the brook yonder—[*Pointing it out*] near Maplegrove Villa, mamma. It was an accident.

RHO. An accident?

ERN. I—I'll tell you how the accident happened, mamma. I ran out yesterday morning for a walk before breakfast. I was running along by the brook—and there sat an old man—at least he wasn't really so very old—it seemed as if he looked older than he really was. His hair was gray and his beard was sort o' scraggly—and it flew about in the wind.

RHO. [*Sadly, turning away, aside*] How often such a figure has stood at my bedside, in my dreams.

ERN. I ran home as fast as I could, and took him some of the warm breakfast the cook had just got ready. I gave him what money I had in my pocket too. That was yesterday, mamma. I told him I'd take him another breakfast this morning, at the same place. So I went down to the brook early this morning, but the queer old fellow wasn't there. And when I was coming home, I—I—I met Geoffrey—under the beeches. Geoffrey was out for a walk before breakfast, too. Geoffrey has—he—he has happened to take a walk every morning before breakfast—for the last four weeks—at just the same time that I take my walk. That's the way the accident happened, mamma. Geoffrey and I sat down under the beeches and we ate what I had in the basket ourselves.

RHO. [*Awaking from a long reverie*] My darling Ernestine!—I trust you will always do exactly as you have done in this case.

ERN. [*Eagerly*] I shall be delighted, mamma!

RHO. Whenever you meet a poor, afflicted, world-worn creature—

ERN. Oh, I thought you meant about Geoffrey. Yes, mamma, I will. You have always told me that.

RHO. Always treat them gently and lovingly—as you did this time, my darling. [*She brings Ernestine's face to her own and kisses her. She walks sadly upstage. Ernestine walks R. turns and watches her mother. Rhoda walks out L.4.E. with bowed head*]

ERN.   Poor mamma!— She is so sad sometimes. [*Brightens*] Mamma said she wouldn't feel badly at all, if I should marry Geoffrey. I'll run away with him now just as soon as he wants me to. [*Enter Lawrence from mansion R. A newspaper in his hand*]

LAWR.   Ah—Ernestine!

ERN.   Yes, sir?

LAWR.   Have you thought over what I said to you yesterday about your marriage with Mr. Chillblood? I should like you to become his wife as soon as possible. Have you decided?

ERN.   Yes, sir.

LAWR.   Well?

ERN.   I won't.

LAWR.   [*In a firm tone, looking at her steadily*]   You—will—not—?

ERN.   I will not.

LAWR.   [*Firmly*]   We shall see. [*Crossing her to R.*] You may reflect upon the subject further, Ernestine.

ERN.   [*Aside*]   I'll write to Geoffrey that I'll run away with him this very day. [*Exits into mansion R.*]

LAWR.   Chillblood will make the girl a kind husband. Above all, Northcote Chillblood is the only man who knows all my transactions as president of the Lawrenceburg Iron and Steel Company. That last operation of mine would be accounted forgery in a court of law. It weighs upon my mind. [*Sitting R. and reading his paper*] What's this? [*Reads*] "We recorded last April the death of a prominent figure in the financial world, Johannes von Hollenstein, of Berlin." M-m—the Hollenstein estate holds two hundred and fifty thousand dollars of our stock. [*Reads*] "The deceased financier belonged to a distinguished German family, and was the uncle of that wild young Baron von Hollenstein of Munich, whose disappearance in America, nearly twenty years ago, created no little talk at the time." M—m— Rudolph Wiegand! People long ago ceased to talk about him. [*Reads*] "The executors of Johannes von Hollenstein, we now learn, have sent two agents to this country to enquire into the conditions of his American securities." Agents! They will insist upon examining our books. [*Reads*] "The agents referred to arrived in Lawrenceburg on Tuesday morning"—on Tuesday morning!—and they have not presented themselves to me. Do they already suspect the truth? [*Enter John from beyond mansion R.U.E. A note in his hand. He is crossing down L.*] Where are you going, John?

JOHN.   Miss Ernestine requested me to carry a note for her.

LAWR. Miss Ernestine? Let me see it. [*John hands him the note. He reads the envelope*] Geoffrey Brown, Esq. That will do, John. You may return to the house.

JOHN. Yes, sir. [*He goes up. John up C. looks L. and stops. Enter Allen accompanied by two Foundrymen, L.U.E.*]

ALLEN. [*Apart to John*] I may need you this evening. You had better call around.

JOHN. I'll call around. [*Exits R.U.E. beyond mansion. Lawrence puts the letter in his pocket*]

ALLEN. [*Coming down*] Mr. Whitworth Lawrence, I believe.

LAWR. Yes. What do you want?

ALLEN. President of the Lawrenceburg Iron and Steel Company. We are a committee, sir.

LAWR. Committee?

ALLEN. I am chairman of the committee. We represent the Lawrenceburg Branch of the National Ironfounders Union.

LAWR. This is no place to speak with me on business.

ALLEN. We aren't particular about the place, sir; you needn't apologize. We sent a letter to you last week. [*Enter the County Sheriff L.U.E. He pauses up C. looking at party*]

LAWR. I did not answer it. You demanded twenty per cent advance in your wages. The demand is absurd.

ALLEN. You refuse it?

LAWR. Definitely. Yes. You have your answer.

ALLEN. That is all we came for, sir. This meeting is adjourned. [*He bows and turns up. The Sheriff moves down R.C. quietly; faces Allen. They look at each other a second. Allen speaks aside to one of his companions*] The county sheriff.

SHER. Mr. Lawrence. [*Passes Allen, crossing down L.*]

LAWR. Mr. Goodhold. [*The three men go up C. Allen looks back at the Sheriff who eyes him quietly but steadily. Exit Allen and Foundrymen L.U.E.*]

SHER. So Allen is chairman of their committee. If his honest fellow working-men who are going on strike knew as much about their "Chairman" as I do, his position would soon be vacant. Allen completed a term for burglary two years ago. He was "converted to religion," immediately after his release.

LAWR. It might be well to inform his fellow workmen.

SHER. No!—hang it—no! We'll give the man a square chance. It's bad enough to kick a man when he's down!— To kick him when he's trying to get up is still worse. You have refused the foundrymen's demand.

LAWR. Positively.

SHER. I'll have a couple of policemen detailed to walk around your house at night, for a few weeks.

LAWR. A good suggestion. Thank you.

SHER. The men will be here about eleven o'clock tonight. By the way, Mr. Lawrence, my object in coming here today is—I suppose it's a rather weak thing in a sheriff—but I'm obliged to levy an execution in one of your cases tomorrow noon—on young Mr. Hackleton, in Maplegrove Villa. He's got a young wife and two babies. It isn't my business as a sheriff, but—

LAWR. You are right, Mr. Goodhold; it is not your business. By the way, have any suspicious characters come into town?

SHER. We locked up an old tramp last night, but he was such a jolly old fellow, sang songs until nobody would appear against him, so we let him go.

LAWR. You ought to arrest all suspicious characters and hold them. [*Starts to go. Judge Merrybone heard whistling without, L.*]

SHER. There is his Honor, Judge Merrybone. [*Enter Judge Merrybone L.1.E.*] Judge!

JUDGE. Sheriff! How are you Lawrence? [*Shakes hands with him, crossing him to C.*]

LAWR. Judge Merrybone.

JUDGE. I say, Goodhold—[*Apart*] about young Hackleton's case in Maplegrove Villa?

SHER. [*Apart*] I have just been speaking with Mr. Lawrence—no go.

JUDGE. [*Apart*] Come around to my house this evening. I'll invent some sort of a judicial paper to put off the execution a few weeks. [*Sheriff shakes his hand*] It's crooked law—but it's straight human nature. [*Punches him in ribs and turns away C., whistling*]

SHER. [*Going L.—stops*] By the bye—you have heard the news, judge?

JUDGE. News?

SHER. My prisoner, the president of the Blackhart Coal Company—

JUDGE. A case of forgery.

SHER. He committed suicide in his cell about two hours ago. [*The Judge emits a long low whistle*] Good day gentlemen. [*Exit Sheriff L.1.E.*]

LAWR. Suicide!—in his cell!

JUDGE. The best thing he could do. The case was a clear one against him. I don't mind telling you, now, Lawrence. I intended to charge the jury straight against him on every point. When the president of a great corporation defrauds his stockholders and brings ruin upon hundreds of innocent families— I'll sentence him every chance I get to as many years hard labor as the law allows me—and damn any governor of the State, and I'm to be the next—

that will let such a man out before his full time! [*Lawrence has listened with close-shut teeth, and with a slight shudder at the end*] I can't swear on the bench—I must do it off, now and then.

LAWR. [*With deliberate emphasis*] I quite agree with you, Judge Merrybone—the president of the Blackhart Coal Company has done the best thing he could do, under the circumstances. I have only one thing to criticise him for. If I had been in his place, I should not have waited for the trial. I should have committed suicide; but not in a cell.

JUDGE. You'd save the State the expense of a trial. That's patriotic. [*Mrs. Dashwood heard laughing without—enters with Metcalfe R.U.E., coming down L.C.*]

MRS. D. Ah, General Metcalfe—you criminal lawyers are so cynical in your opinion of other people.

MET. Not in our opinion of the ladies. [*Bowing. She flirts with him L.C.*]

LAWR. [*Moving to Metcalfe*] May I speak with you a moment, Metcalfe?

MET. Certainly. [*He moves up L.C. with Lawrence. Judge crosses to Mrs. Dashwood L.C. She flirts with him*] Important legal matters connected with your company?

LAWR. I wish to consult with you. Can you call this evening?

MET. I'll be here at eight.

LAWR. Thank you. I shall be expecting you. [*He passes up L. and exits L.3.E. in deep thought*]

MET. [*Down R.C. aside*] Merrybone's on the bench. I'm out of court.

MRS. D. Ah! [*Suddenly—a slight scream*] Judge! [*Jerking away her hand from his*] Really—you mustn't. My ring hurts my finger, when you do that. [*The Judge starts. Metcalfe starts around in his seat. They look at each other. The Judge sits C. Mrs. Dashwood moves to hammock L. Enter Rudolph L.U.E. He is a weak, weary-looking man, prematurely old, with iron-gray hair and beard; his dress is in tatters; one sleeve of his coat almost torn away; one leg of his trousers in shreds to the knee; an old torn, gray slouched hat in his hand. He has an old shoe on his left foot, the toes protruding from a hole, and the top caught together with a thong; it is covered with dust and dry mud. On the other leg he has a heavy top-boot, perfectly new and shining as if recently polished. His manner, as he enters, is a mixture of the pathetic and comic. He walks in with hesitation and some timidity, mingled with a touch of the tramp's peculiar impudence and a quizzical leer as he looks about. As he comes down, he stands a moment unnoticed. The Judge is looking away. Metcalfe first sees Rudolph, who puts out his hand for charity. Metcalfe turns abruptly away from him in his seat. Rudolph moves to the Judge, holding out*]

*his hand for charity. Judge, on the first impulse, moves his hand to his pocket;
then withdraws it, with a shake of the head*]

JUDGE. [*Aside*] No. We mustn't encourage these tramps. [*Aloud*] Well,
my good fellow, what do you want?

RUD. What—do—I—want? [*Scratches his head and looks himself over*]
Perhaps you can suggest something that I don't want. If you think of anything
I don't want, you will gratify my curiosity by telling me what it is.

JUDGE. Let me give you a piece of good advice—

RUD. You've hit it, judge, first time. Good advice is the only thing in this
world I'm not in immediate want of. Good advice comes within my means.

JUDGE. Ha, ha, ha! Say, Metcalfe—there's humor in this fellow. [*To Rudolph*] You called me, "Judge," I am a judge. The laws against vagrancy in
this state, by the way, are very rigid.

RUD. You are a judge? I hope you will excuse me for intruding, judge, out
of business hours, but, I'm a regular customer in your line.

JUDGE. Haven't I seen you before?

RUD. Oh, yes, judge— Do me a favor—couldn't you send me up for thirty
days, judge?

JUDGE. Ha, ha, ha! There's a man that can be of service to you, perhaps—
[*Indicating Metcalfe*] He's a criminal lawyer. [*Rudolph crosses to Metcalfe
and holds out his hand. Metcalfe turns persistently away*]

RUD. I beg your pardon, sir. I have been a tramp for nearly twenty years.
I am an old and respectable member of the profession; I flatter myself I am
an ornament to it—but I have never yet done anything to encourage a criminal
lawyer in his profession. I haven't any claims on you, sir. [*He walks upstage—
turns*] Gentlemen— let me give you a piece of good advice. Let me warn you
against the sin of envy. I dare say you both envy me. But you mustn't encourage it. Be contented with your lot. [*He walks up—turns*] Gentlemen—
the boys call me "Singing Rudy." If either of you finds yourself in trouble,
in the next world, mention my name. [*Walks up—turns*] Lazarus and I will
talk it over with Father Abraham. [*Walks up*]

MRS. D. Oh—but—I say! You've forgotten me. [*Coming C.*]

RUD. [*The Judge moves L. and sits*] I beg a thousand pardons. It is inexcusable for a gentleman to overlook the claims of the fair sex. [*Coming down
and removing his hat with gallantry. He bows with grace, and continues, with
elegance of manner*] La beauté sans pitié est une fleur sans parfum. Mais vous!
—vous avez l'une et l'autre,—madame—

MRS. D. Oh! Merci, monsieur. [*Aside*] French! He's the only gentleman
present who can speak it. He must be a prince in disguise. [*She looks at him
again. He has become the poor beggar again*] No!—princes never disguise

themselves by hunger. Here! [*Gives him a bank note*] And there is my card. [*Gives him card*] You may pay it back to me at your own convenience.

RUD. Ah—thanks, madam—it is a very long time since anybody lent me anything. Five dollars! I can't offer you any security, for so large an amount.

MRS. D. I will take the word of a gentleman for it. And see!—the other gentlemen have changed their minds. [*Judge Merrybone and Metcalfe look up suddenly*] They are both of them putting their hands in their pockets. [*They suddenly do so*] Each of them is going to pay you a dollar for your good advice. [*Rudolph walks to Metcalfe R. His manner again that of the beggar. Metcalfe gives him a fifty-cent coin. Rudolph looks at it sharply; then walks L., stops C., looks at the coin again; then over his shoulder at Metcalfe. He goes to the Judge; receives a dollar note, and returns up C., near Mrs. Dashwood*]

RUD. [*Pointing to Metcalfe*] That one owes us fifty cents.

MRS. D. and JUDGE. Ha—ha—ha—ha—ha—ha—

JUDGE. Pay your honest debts, general! [*Rudolph goes to Metcalfe and receives another coin. Tests it*]

MRS. D. You say the boys call you "Singing Rudy." You are a singer then?

RUD. I often sing and dance for the boys.

MRS. D. You shall sing for us. I insist.

RUD. Oh, no—no—I haven't practiced this morning. No gentleman can refuse a lady anything—can we general?—Can we judge? But the boys always whistle for me, and pat on their knees.

MRS. D. Oh, the judge can whistle and so can I—just as well as "the boys" can; and we can pat on our knees, too. How does it go?

RUD. It goes this way. [*Song and dance, light orchestral accompaniment. The rest of the party whistle and pat. Mrs. Dashwood calls on the others— "Judge! General!" She bursts into a hearty laugh, dances first around Rudolph, then with the Judge R. Rudolph seizes Metcalfe and dances with him. Mrs. Dashwood laughing merrily, falls back exhausted, caught by the Judge*] Boys! You did splendidly—you did it almost as well as the other boys.

MRS. D. Ha, ha, ha. Come, judge! [*Taking his arm and moving L.*] Good-by, Rudy.

RUD. Adieu, madame. Vous serez toujours présent à ma pensée. [*With gentlemanly dignity*]

MRS. D. Adieu, mon ami. [*Aside*] He is a prince in disguise. [*To Judge*] Judge—we will wander by the brookside. I was walking by a brook with the late senator one day—he was trying to propose to me that day—"Dashwood," said I, "Go on! We will wander by the brookside." Ta-ta, general—ta-ta.

[*Exits on the arm of the Judge, L.1.E. The Judge glances back at Metcalfe R.C.*]

MET. Judge Merrybone be—no—a lawyer must never allow himself—to be angry. It ruins the case. I'll go to my office—and—and I'll write her a letter! I'll be ahead of the judge yet. [*Starts upstage. Rudolph stands C. looking at his money. Metcalfe draws up haughtily before him. Rudolph steps aside and bows with polite dignity, waving his hand gracefully. Metcalfe looks at him superciliously and exits L.3.E. Rudolph drops into seat C.*]

RUD. Seven dollars. I'm a capitalist. What curious ups and downs a business man does have in this world. Ten minutes ago I was a pauper. Now!— How shall I invest my surplus capital? I'll continue the reorganization of my wardrobe. This coat will do very nicely for a few seasons yet—and there's considerable service in that left shoe; but the pantaloons begin to show wear. The knees begin to look shiny. The nap is worn off. They'll do very well for every day, but they aren't full dress. How I would shock the Lord—and His worshippers—if I should appear in church—His worshippers more particularly! I'll continue the reorganization of my wardrobe. [*Rising; he takes a step, staggers a little, rests on the chair*] Somehow that dancing—I feel a little weak. Oh!—I remember. I haven't had anything to eat since yesterday morning. How careless one does get about such trifles. I'll have to squander part of that money on something to eat. The human stomach is the most persistent dun in the world. [*Walking down L.*] My stomach finds it so difficult to collect its bills—its always on the verge of bankruptcy. [*Reenter Ernestine, from mansion R.*]

ERN. Oh! Why! [*Stopping C. as she sees Rudolph*] Rudy! Here you are.

RUD. Why?— Do you live here? [*Ernestine extends both hands, smiling and nodding. Rudolph goes to her and takes her hands*]

ERN. I'm real glad to see you again, Rudy. I thought I had lost you.

RUD. You're the little girl that brought me such a nice warm breakfast yesterday morning. You didn't tell me your name? I want some name to remember you by.

ERN. My name is Ernestine! [*Rudolph turns away. A pause. He looks off with a distant air, running his fingers through his beard*]

RUD. Ernestine!

ERN. Why weren't you in the same place this morning, Rudy. [*Shakes her finger*] I was there, and you weren't there.

RUD. Well—I had an engagement.

ERN. But you had a previous engagement with me.

RUD. I had a positive engagement. There—there were circumstances beyond my control. [*Walking L.*] Got locked up in the station-house all night.

The judge didn't come around till after ten o'clock this morning. I told him he was late. I told him I'd lost an appointment. [*Ernestine suddenly bursts out laughing, and points at Rudolph's boot. He turns and looks himself over, puzzled*]

ERN. Ha, ha, ha, ha, ha! That boot looks so funny—all by itself. Ha, ha, ha, ha!

RUD. You noticed they aren't mates.

ERN. What's become of the other boot, Rudy? I told you to buy a pair of boots.

RUD. Well—I—did buy a pair; but I—I met another gentleman belonging to the same profession as I do. [*Passing R.*] We—we purchased one pair of boots and declared a dividend.

ERN. [*C.*] You gave him the other boot?

RUD. The courtesies of the profession, you know. His left shoe was in a very bad condition. Then we met a boot-black and he needed a job. I always like to encourage honest industry. We got both boots shined up. That cost us five cents apiece, out of your money, Miss Ernestine. Then we met another professional brother; he hadn't any shoes at all. We put our two old ones together and gave 'em to him. So we were all three of us comfortably provided for and perfectly happy; all through you, Miss Ernestine—all through you.

ERN. What did you do with the rest of the money, Rudy?

RUD. The—the rest of the—the money? Well—the fact is—we were all so happy—we all three went into a place—and—and congratulated. [*Sheepishly*]

ERN. "Congratulated?"

RUD. It costs a great deal of money for three men to congratulate each other, Miss Ernestine. When we got through congratulating—there—there wasn't a cent left.

ERN. [*Shaking her head*] Oh, Rudy! [*He stands sheepishly before her. Enter Geoffrey Brown, L.1.E. He looks in cautiously*]

GEOF. Ernestine!

ERN. Geoffrey! [*She runs to him eagerly*]

GEOF. Is your father anywhere near?

ERN. No. [*Looking around*] You got my letter?

GEOF. Letter? No. I was passing, so I jumped over the fence and took my chances. I can run faster than your governor can—and the dog and I are good friends. I wanted another kiss to last me till tomorrow morning. [*Kisses her*]

RUD. You seem to be acquainted with each other.

ERN. John must have left the letter at your house.

GEOF. What did you say in it?

ERN. I've spoken to mother. I'm going to run away with you.

GEOF. You will? We'll run away this very night.

ERN. The sooner, the better! I'm tired of Mr. Lawrence and old Chillblood
—I'm afraid I'll marry him—by mistake.

GEOF. Oh—won't it be fun? [*Delightedly*] I'll telegraph to Aunt Mary at
Perrytown. She'll do anything for me. We'll take the half-past eleven train
tonight. Cousin John will meet us at the station. I'll have a carriage ready at
half-past ten—and I'll wait for you at the veranda. I'll telegraph Cousin John
all about it. He'll have a minister ready—we'll be married as soon as we get
to Aunt Mary's—and—and—that's all. Darling Ernestine! [*The whole of the
last speech is spoken very rapidly. He has both her hands, and they are swinging as he rattles on, Ernestine laughing merrily and chiming in with "Yes"
and with repetition of his words. At the end, he takes her about the waist and
kisses her tenderly. Rudolph who has been watching them with tender interest,
moves towards them. They see him and stand before him somewhat abashed*]

RUD. [*Tenderly, raising his hand*] Bless you, my children—bless you!
[*They drop their heads reverently*]

GEOF. Thank you, sir.

ERN. I—I am sure I—I long for a father's blessing—and I will take yours
for it, Rudy. [*Geoffrey places his arms about her waist and they go out, L.1.E.
Rudolph looks after them a moment, then turns and moves sadly to C. where
he stands with a dreamy look, as if thinking of the past*]

RUD. Her name is Ernestine—[*Ernestine returns L.1.E. She stops, looks
back and kisses her hand; then moves to Rudolph C.*]

ERN. Where did you get your breakfast this morning, Rudy?

RUD. Breakfast? I—I overlooked breakfast entirely this morning. There—
there wasn't anything around to remind me of it. [*Aside*] Except my stomach.
[*Aloud*] The man I spent the night with—he neglected to invite me to breakfast. It—it was a breach of etiquette.

ERN. Oh! Rudy!—you haven't had anything to eat since last night!

RUD. No—not since—since last night. And I don't very often eat at night,
anyway. One doesn't sleep well on a late supper—with oysters and champagne—

ERN. When did you eat yesterday?

RUD. I—I forget the exact time. The fact is—I'm very irregular about my
meals. I know it is a bad habit; my own physician—a sort of family physician
—at the last hospital I was in—said I ought always to take my meals regularly.
But a man gets so engrossed in business, you know—

ERN. Rudy! You haven't had anything to eat since yesterday morning.
Wait right here till I come back. [*She runs up and around the mansion, disappearing R.U.E.*]

Rud.   That little girl has run off to get me something to eat again. How thoughtless a young girl like that is. It never occurred to her that what I really need, just at the present moment, is good advice. She's doing a serious injury to the social fabric, she is. [*Moving to L.C. and sitting*] I'm hungry; and she's encouraging me. [*He holds up his right leg and looks at his boot*] I begin to feel a personal affection for that boot. It was a present from her. I'll keep it to remember her by. [*Takes out a ragged handkerchief, holds it up*] That was a good handkerchief—once. Time destroys all things; the pyramids of Egypt are crumbling away like this handkerchief. [*He puts his foot on his left knee and dusts the boot carefully*] I'll have that boot shined up once a month at least. That'll cost me five cents every time. I'll have to practise rigid economy. [*Rising*] It'll be a heavy tax on my income. But it is a very good thing for a man to have an object in life; something besides himself to provide for and look after. I'll take good care of that boot. [*Looking down at it*] I've got something to live for, now. [*He turns and is walking up C. Stops suddenly, looking off L.3.E. He stands looking off intently. Reenter Ernestine R.U.E. She has a large basket, filled with bread, apples, cakes, grapes, etc. on her arm, and a tumbler of milk in her hand*]

Ern.   Here, Rudy—[*Moving down and placing the basket on chair R.C.*] I've got lots of nice things for you—and here's a tumbler of fresh milk. [*Approaching him. Rudolph still looks off*] Rudy, here's some milk. Rudy! Rudy! [*She lays her hand on his arm. Rudolph looks at her in a dazed way; then off again*] Why—what are you looking at, Rudy? [*Rudolph again looks towards her, and again away, running his finger through his beard and putting his hand to his head as if confused*]

Rud.   Who—who is that lady—and that gentleman? Talking to each other, under the tree?

Ern.   Under the big oak? That lady is Mrs. Whitworth Lawrence. The gentleman is Mr. Lawrence. He has left her and is coming this way. The lady is my mother.

Rud. [*Retiring a step and half staggering*]   Your—your name—is—Ernestine—Lawrence?

Ern.   Oh, no! He isn't my own father. My name is Ernestine Wiegand. [*Walks a little down R.C. as she speaks. Rudolph looks at her in a dazed way; walks down opposite to her; looks at her side-wise, surveying her from head to foot; then walks front, C. He stands there fingering his hair and beard, bewildered. Ernestine goes to chair, R.C., puts down the glass of milk and looks at him. He turns, approaches her, stops, surveys her a moment, turns and walks L. She moves down C. He approaches her; moves his arm as if to embrace her; withdraws it. He places his hand on her head tenderly; again moves*] *as if to embrace her, but withdraws his arm; turns and walks up towards chair, L.C. He looks back at her, and drops sidelong into the chair, turning from her; his head dropped on his breast; his arms thrown up over his head and face; his knees and legs drawn up; a picture of abject misery and intense emotion. Ernestine runs to him and leans over him]* Why, Rudy, Rudy! What is the matter? *[Enter Whitworth Lawrence L.3.E. He pauses as he sees Ernestine and Rudolph; moves down R.C. Sees basket, etc.]*

LAWR.   Ernestine. *[She moves to him]* Go into the house, child. *[Not brusquely but firmly]*

ERN.   Oh! But please, sir—

LAWR.   Run into the house. I will attend to your guest. *[He motions her in. She reluctantly moves to steps; looks back at Rudolph]* He shall have all that you have brought for him. *[He again motions to her. Ernestine disappears in mansion. Lawrence crosses to Rudolph, touches him smartly on the shoulders. Rudolph straightens up suddenly, and glances over his shoulder at Lawrence]* Take what the silly girl has brought out for you—and be off. *[He walks R. Rudolph rises; follows him a step; stops and looks at him]* Well! Take it, I say—and be off. *[Rudolph places his hat on his head, walks L. and sits in chair, erect and firm, folding his arms and looking at Lawrence]* Insolence! What do you mean, sir?

RUD.   Your name is Whitworth Lawrence?

LAWR.   Well?

RUD.   My name is Rudolph Wiegand—Baron von Hollenstein. *[Lawrence looks at him suddenly and sharply, but calmly; a pause]*

LAWR.   Ah! *[Sits R.]* How much money do you want? *[An angry start from Rudolph, but he controls himself]* I am willing to see you comfortable. Indeed, I prefer to do so. I will give you twenty thousand dollars, in cash or its equivalent in bonds—drawing interest and well secured.

RUD.   I have received that from your guests. *[Taking money from his pocket and tossing it towards Lawrence]* You may return it to them.

LAWR.   You refuse my offer?

RUD.   Refuse it? No. I pay no attention to it, whatever.

LAWR.   *[Rising, with a step forward, and a gesture]*   Take your basket, then —and be off—*[Rudolph rises, walks a few steps upstage; turns suddenly]*

RUD.   Robber! *[He attacks Lawrence, grappling with him fiercely. Lawrence easily overcomes him and holds him firmly by the wrists]*

LAWR.   *[Calling]*   John! John, I say! John! *[Then quietly to Rudolph]* Oh, no—I am stronger than you. *[Releases him. Rudolph drops his head]*

RUD.   You are right, you are right. You are stronger than I. *[Aside]* I forgot. I have had nothing to eat since yesterday morning. *[Aloud]* You are stronger than I. [*Enter John from mansion, made up, of course, older than in Act I*]

JOHN.   Called me, sir?

LAWR.   Show this man to the gate. [*Turning away R. John steps to Rudolph C. with a very pompous air and taps him on the shoulder*]

JOHN.   Move h'along—move h'along—[*Rudolph turns quietly and walks up C.; he stops, with his back to the audience and his head dropped. Lawrence looks after him a second; turns and goes into the mansion. John taps Rudolph on the shoulder. Rudolph looks suddenly over his shoulder. John starts back, timidly*] Move h'on, my good fellow, move h'on! The master told me to show you to the gate! [*Rudolph walks up C. slowly, his head dropped. Reenter Rhoda, L.3.E. She stops as she sees Rudolph, he glances at her; then stands with his eyes dropped and his head depressed. She takes her portemonnaie from a pocket, opens it, takes a coin from it, and holds it out to Rudolph. He extends his hand, his whole attitude, that of dejected beggary. She drops the coin into his hand and moves down R. Exits into mansion. Rudolph looks at the coin in his hand a moment; then motions to John, who seems puzzled at Rudolph's motion; advances; hesitates. Rudolph holds out the coin to him. John extends his hand. Rudolph places the coin in it; then draws up with dignity and points L. with an air of command*]

RUD.   Show me to the gate. [*John trips across L.; turns; bows with an obsequious gesture, and precedes him out. Rudolph follows with the dignity of an elegant gentleman*]

ACT III.

SCENE 1: *Drinking den of the ironfounders. Flat in 2. to allow for setting of the second scene beyond, so as to have as short a time as possible for the change, the curtain being dropped. Counter and bar R. Bottles, glasses, etc. appropriate to cheap bar. Rough tables R., R.C., Down L., up L. and up C. Plain chairs, broken and patched up. Doors up C. and L. Roughly marked signs hanging here and there, with names and prices of American drinks. A storm without. Lightning now and then at windows. Night.*

DISCOVERED: *Foundrymen including Owen sitting at various tables, some of them smoking clay pipes, liquor before them. Some playing dominoes. Ironfounder lounging at bar talking with the Barkeeper, general clatter etc., as curtain rises. Enter Overdeck as curtain rises.*

OVER. Hello, fellows! [*Goes to bar*] Ten cents! [*Searching pockets*] I'm a branch of the National Ironfounders Union. The treasury of this particular branch is getting low. [*General laugh*] Ten cents, and I was offered five hundred dollars today fellows. [*Attention*]

OWEN. Five hundred dollars!

OVER. As sure as my name's Bill Overdeck, a curious circumstance happened to me this afternoon. Two foreign-looking gentlemen regularly dressed up fine—they came to my house and asked the missus for me. There was one o' them detective chaps from the police station with 'em. Missus Overdeck was anxious. But I knew I hadn't been doing anything wrong; so I looked 'em all square in the face and asked 'em, in the politest possible manner, what the devil they wanted with me, two such well-dressed cusses as they was. What do you think? They asked me did I remember a little chap named Wiegand, sixteen years ago, in New York when we had a big strike there, and did I know what had become of him. Well, fellows—I did know this little Wiegand in those days mighty well. He and I had many a drink, we did. Out of the same bottle, and worse luck for both of us perhaps. Blessed if them two foreign gentlemen didn't say they'd give me five hundred dollars; five hundred dollars, fellows!—[*General interest and chat*] So I could put 'em in the way o' finding that there little Rudy Wiegand.

OWEN. Rudy! [*General exclamations "Rudy"*]

OVER. His first name was Rudolph. [*Aside*] I didn't think of that before. [*Walks down R.C., as if suddenly thinking*]

OWEN. I wonder where our Rudy is tonight. We boys have got as well acquainted with dancing Rudy as if he'd been in Lawrenceburg four years instead of four days. [*Enter Rudolph L.*] Ah, here he is now. [*General clattering of glasses, etc., cries of "Oh, Rudy," "Hello, Rudy," etc., etc. Rudolph appears wet and shivering. His right foot is now bare and black with mud. He carries the boot protected under his coat. His clothes are covered with mire and he coughs as if he had caught cold by exposure*]

OVER. [*Aside down R.C.*] Rudy!

RUD. Boys. [*Nodding R. and L.*]

OWEN. Where've you been all night! The boys want you to sing and dance for them. [*Clatter of glasses and cries, "Yes, Rudy a dance—a song," "Where've you been?" etc.*]

RUD. I didn't feel like singing tonight, boys.

OWEN. Oh, yes—Rudy—a song! [*Cries "Yes, Rudy," etc., etc. Overdeck who has been standing down R.C. thoughtfully, beckons Rudolph aside*]

OVER. [*Apart*] Would you mind telling me your last name?

RUD. My last name? Rudy.

Over. That's your first name.

Rud. It's both. I dropped the rest. Too many is not good in signing checks.

Owen. Come, Rudy, a song.

Rud. I—I don't feel like singing tonight boys. I've been to bed but I got up.

Owen. To bed, Rudy—[*Laugh*]

Rud. I— I engaged an apartment down in the alley tonight—they got sort of tired of me at the station house. They don't seem to appreciate my society. I engaged an apartment in the alley under that high board fence, you know it sort of leans over and when the wind is in the right direction it's a very comfortable place. [*Laugh*] But the wind wasn't in the right direction tonight. I shut the door and put out the light—figuratively speaking—[*Laugh*] and turned in, but I was restless. I couldn't sleep as well as usual tonight. And when the rain came on, the roof began to leak . . . I wasn't exactly comfortable, so I got up and dressed again.

Owen. Dressed! Ha, ha, ha, ha. [*General laughter*] Put on all your good clothes, Rudy? Ha, ha, ha.

Rud. I—I put on my hat. [*Laughter*] I—I've been wandering around and I—I felt kind o' lonely out in the rain and I—I thought I'd drop in and pay my respects to you boys. [*Applause and laughter*]

Owen. Ha—ha—ha— Good! Well, Rudy? We've all got some more pennies for you tonight, eh boys? [*He tosses down a penny. Cries of "Aye, aye." "Here's the pennies, Rudy!" etc. Most of the men throw down pennies. Rudolph looks at them as they lie around him and stands a moment with a weary, dreary look. He then removes the boot from under his coat, and wipes it carefully with his handkerchief. General laughter. The men pointing each other to the boot*]

Rud. [*Aside, looking intently at the boot*] She gave it to me—the little girl gave it to me. It's all I've got to remember her by, Ernestine! [*He walks to the bar and sets the boot upon it. Returns C., looking back as if anxious for its safety. He proceeds to pick up the pennies*]

Owen. [*Pointing*] There's another Rudy. [*Rudolph glances at him, goes to where he points and picks up the penny. He then returns C., and stands looking at the pennies in his hand*]

Rud. [*Wearily shaking his head*] I—I don't feel like singing tonight, boys.

Owen. Oh, yes, Rudy—a song, and give us a story, too. [*General exclamation, "Story . . . song . . . dance," etc.*] We've paid you—now sing.

Rud. I—I'll try boys, I'll try.

Owen. Drive ahead, Rudy! [*A pathetic recitation, Rudolph then begins to sing a rollicking popular song, trying to give it comic force and gayety, not in a burlesque way, but with a cough and an evident effort to overcome his de-*

pression. He accompanies the song with dancing, but wearily, sadly and with effort, striving to quicken up from time to time, but trying in vain to move with spirit. He stops now and then, almost breaking down; continues, etc.]

RUD. [*At last, giving up*] No use, boys, no use! I can't sing tonight. [*Falling into a chair L. and dropping his head upon the table between his arms*] I can't sing tonight. [*Enter Allen up C.*]

OWEN. Hello, Allen! The chairman of the committee. News! [*Cries of "Chairman," "News"*]

ALLEN. I can say what I have to say in a few words fellows. The general committee has just wound up its meeting. We go on strike tomorrow. [*Cheers, etc.*] The rest of the committee are down at the hall. The sooner you all get there the more you will hear about it. [*General rush for the door and out. Exit Foundrymen, cheering, putting on their coats, etc. Allen locks the door L. He bars the door up C.*] I'm a committee of one for myself, after this; I intend to raise my own wages. Hello. [*Shakes Rudy. Rudy rouses himself from the table and looks at Allen languidly and returns to his position*] All right, Rudy—don't let me disturb you. [*Aside*] Rudy may be of use to me.

OWEN. I say, chum—wasn't that going back on my business interests, driving all my customers off like that?

ALLEN. [*Crossing and leaning on bar*] Old pal.

OWEN. Eh? What's that? Professional lingo, Dick? We're out of that you know; we're respectable now.

ALLEN. I've given respectability a fair show. Honesty doesn't pay. I'm goin' back to the profession.

OWEN. No more o' that for me, old pal. I've quit.

ALLEN. Yes, of course. I got religion and went into honest work. You invested your swag and went to liquor sellin'. That's where I missed it. I'm goin' to return to the profession I was brought up to. This very night.

OWEN. Tonight?

ALLEN. I'm goin' to crack the biggest crib in this part o' the country, old Lawrence's house.

OWEN. Lawrence's. The devil!

ALLEN. Lawrence mansion itself. Go in with me, old pal. Square game, you know—fair divvy.

OWEN. Oh, no, Dick. I'm a respectable citizen now, you know. The boys are a goin' to run me for school inspector next spring. I'll tell you what I will do. Bring your swag down here. I'll take care of it for you.

ALLEN. Terms, pal.

OWEN. Thirty per cent—to an old friend.

ALLEN. Owen, you do the eminently swell gag—you're trying to throw on the lugs. I'll do the work. But it's a damned bad crib to try alone.

OWEN. Yes—it is bad.

ALLEN. John, the footman, is on my side.

OWEN. That helps.

ALLEN. But all he'll do is to leave a pair o' glass doors open—to the veranda —when he turns out the lights.

OWEN. John is only a beginner.

ALLEN. I must have a personal staff. I was thinking—[*He looks across at Rudolph—then at Owen*] What do you think?

OWEN. Rudy?

ALLEN. Mm, to watch the tracks and whistle me down.

OWEN. Rudy hasn't anything to lose and tramps usually get their hand in. They begin on chicken-roosts. Try him.

ALLEN. The State Prison would be a devilish good opening for Rudy—if worst comes to worst.

RUD. [*Gradually arousing himself, as if thinking intently on a subject*] "Take what the silly girl has left you, and be off!" Whitworth Lawrence said he was stronger than I.

ALLEN. [*Watching him*] Whitworth Lawrence!

RUD. The robber! [*Starting up*] If he and I—

ALLEN. A good beginning to a negotiation. Rudy! Take a glass, Rudy.

RUD. Thank you—I will take just a single drop. [*Crossing to bar—fills glass nearly full. Owen checks him. Allen motions to let him go on*]

ALLEN. Charge it to the mutual expense account.

RUD. That's the first square meal I've had since yesterday morning—I—I feel strong, now—strong!

ALLEN. Sit down, Rudy; sit down. [*Rudolph sits at table R.C., Allen sits opposite*] I—I'd like to do you a good turn, tonight. [*Rudolph looks at him in surprise; then half rises and grasps his hand*]

RUD. I should be delighted to have you do it.

ALLEN. I—I'll put you in the way of turning an honest penny, Rudy— Would you like to make a thousand dollars tonight? [*Rudy looks at him. Allen winks. Rudy half rises and grasps his hand*]

RUD. Two thousand . . . Call it millions. When it comes to the imagination—a poor man is inexcusable if he doesn't deal in big figures.

ALLEN. I am talking about hard facts.

RUD. Hard facts? Make it a real one dollar bill and we'll call it square.

ALLEN. A thousand dollars for your share of the work.

RUD. My share?—Work?

ALLEN. Can I depend upon you, Rudy?

RUD. De—depend upon—me?

ALLEN. Whitworth Lawrence. [*Over table*]

RUD. Whitworth Lawrence—[*Moving L. Vacantly*] Stronger than I—"Show this man to the gate."

ALLEN. [*Rising*] You and Whitworth Lawrence are not the warmest of friends, I take it.

RUD. Friends!

ALLEN. [*Quickly*] Whatever there may be between you and Whitworth Lawrence—you may have your revenge tonight, Rudy.

RUD. Re—revenge? [*They go quickly to him. Drink with him*]

ALLEN. [*Leaning over towards him*] Whitworth Lawrence has money—and bonds—in a safe in his house. The house is beyond the reach of the police officers. Can I depend upon you?

RUD. You can depend upon me for doing the right thing every time.

ALLEN. We must crack the crib—

RUD. Crib? I understand. We call it a cradle in German.

ALLEN. We must crack the crib as early as possible, Rudy!—just after the lights are out. We old hands always do that. If people hear a noise, then, they don't mind it. They think it's someone else in the house—and they never interfere with the business before you.

OWEN. Sound principle, old pal—sound principle.

ALLEN. Yes, you know all about it. [*Showing a paper*] A map of the house —drawn by John, the footman. He is with us.

RUD. John, the footman, is with us?

ALLEN. Yes. The safe is in that closet; and the daughter of Whitworth Lawrence—

RUD. [*Suddenly*] The—the daughter of Whitworth Lawrence— Well!

ALLEN. The girl sleeps in that room.

RUD. The daughter—of Whitworth Lawrence—sleeps in that room.

ALLEN. She has diamonds and jewelry. The girl sleeps alone.

RUD. She—sleeps—alone? If Whitworth Lawrence's daughter should—wake up—while you are in her room?

ALLEN. Why—if—if it should come to that—if—if she should wake up—while I am in her room—the—the girl has a small neck, pal. [*Rising and putting his fingers to his throat as he speaks*]

RUD. [*Extending his hand*] I will stick to you like a brother tonight. You can depend upon me. [*Sound of carriage and "Whoa" without, L.*]

ALLEN. [*After a pause*] Enough said, I will. We'll proceed to business. [*He goes L., unlocks door; unbars door up C., waves his hand lightly to Owen. Rudolph passes out C. Allen follows him*]

OWEN. Hell—a carriage! [*Reenter Overdeck door L. bowing in two foreign-appearing gentlemen. Their beards are parted in the middle; one has gold spectacles; the other, single eyeglass; both in dress suits, under open overcoats, which they hold to their throats on account of storm as they enter, but then throw back. Gloves*]

OVER. This way, gentlemen—this way. Two foreign gentlemen. [*Turning and looking around the room*] Where's dancing Rudy?

OWEN. [*Jauntily, wiping glass*] Rudy has a business engagement, tonight. Something in my line, gentlemen? Bourbon sour—hot Scotch—mint julep—flip-flap—corpse reviver—tanglefoot—[*The curtain descends slowly as Owen is rattling off these names, reaching stage before he has finished. The two foreign gentlemen listen with astonishment, the one in spectacles holding his hand to his ear*]

SCENE 2: NOTE: *Orchestral music should begin immediately at fall of curtain on Scene 1, and continue without any intermission whatever, until it rises on Scene 2. The change should be made as rapidly as possible.*
Rich apartment in the Lawrence mansion. A corridor upstage, extending from C. out R., glass doors L.C. extending diagonally down from 4 to 3. They open on veranda. Garden scene without. It may be the same as that of Act II, if suited to night. Doors R.1.E., L.1.E. and up R. Piano R. Table down R.C. Chandelier lighted. Occasional flashes of lightning, during first part of scene, light up view beyond the glass doors. At other times this view is dark, until the appearance of moonlight, as per business directions. The storm without gradually dies away after rise of curtain. The following distinction must be noted: when the moon first comes out brightly on veranda, the chandelier is lit, and the light outside must therefore be vague and dim; when the chandelier jets are turned out, one by one, near the end of act, the light outside becomes full and bright, a gleam being thrown through glass doors across the room.
DISCOVERED: *Ernestine, standing at glass doors L.C., peering out.*

ERN. Oh, what a night! It's awful, running away to get married. I never felt so uncomfortable in my life. [*Clock without*] Ten o'clock. Geoffrey and I are to run away in half an hour. [*A vivid flash. She starts back*] Ugh! It's awful, getting married! I'm almost sorry, now. [*Coming down C.*] I told Geoffrey! [*Enter Lawrence L.1.E.*] No, I'm not. I'm glad.

LAWR. Ernestine—it is your usual bedtime.

ERN. Yes, sir—but—but—I—I don't feel sleepy, this evening, sir.

LAWR. By the way, Ernestine—I have had so much to think of today—I had forgotten it until the present moment; John was to deliver this note for you, to-day, to Geoffrey Brown. [*Taking note from his pocket and extending it towards her*]

ERN. Oh, sir! [*Springing towards him with eager anxiety, to take it. He withdraws his hand suddenly*]

LAWR. You seem particularly anxious! I was about to return it to you unopened. I will read it.

ERN. Oh! [*He deliberately opens the note, she watching him with breathless interest*]

LAWR. [*Reading*] "My own darling Geoffrey"—[*He looks at her sternly*]

ERN. [*Drawing up with spirit*] So he is!

LAWR. [*Reads*] "Mr. Lawrence insists more strongly than ever on my marrying that dried-up old Egyptian mummy that they forgot to bury when they built the Pyramids." [*Looks at her*]

ERN. He is. They did forget him.

LAWR. [*Reading*] "Mother says she would be perfectly willing to have me marry you—and—I will run away with you as soon as I can." [*Looks at her*]

ERN. I will.

LAWR. [*Reading*] "Your own loving little sugarplum."

ERN. I am. [*Spitefully—pouting. Lawrence folds the letter deliberately, and in thought he walks R. and throws open the door R.1.E.*]

LAWR. Go into your room. [*Very firmly, but not roughly. Ernestine marches past him, out R.1.E. and slams the door spitefully. Lawrence locks it and takes the key out, walking away*] I will speak with the girl in the morning. [*Puts the key in his pocket. Looks at his watch*] After ten o'clock. Metcalfe promised to call at eight. [*Merrybone heard whistling without, L. He enters L.1.E. followed by Metcalfe, who passes on to Lawrence R.C.*]

JUDGE. [*L.C.*] Lawrence, old boy—it's all my fault. I had Metcalfe home to dinner with me—the mayor and a few friends. He said he had an engagement with you. I wouldn't let him come till my carriage was ready, and I could come with him. [*Then aside L.C., as Metcalfe joins Lawrence R.C.*] I'd see him further first! "Engagement with Lawrence." [*Putting fingers to the side of his nose*] The young widow!—wanted to be alone with her. [*Mrs. Dashwood heard singing without, up R.C. She enters from R.U. corner*]

MRS. D. Ah—gentlemen! This is a surprise, at this time of the evening. [*The Judge and Metcalfe both hasten to her, up L.C., Metcalfe taking her right hand, and the Judge her left, bowing and smiling. Enter Rhoda L.1.E.*]

Rho. Gentlemen. [*Crossing R. front*]

Judge. [*Looking up*] Mrs. Lawrence.

Met. Madam. [*Both resume their attention to Mrs. Dashwood. Rhoda crosses to Lawrence R.*]

Mrs. D. I suppose we are indebted for this late call to a dinner in the neighborhood—cigars, and champagne, gentlemen? [*Shaking her finger at them*]

Judge. Yes—ha—ha—you are indebted to a small bottle of champagne, madam—about so high. [*Indicating her own height, playfully, with his hand*]

Mrs. D. Ah—judge! [*Curtsying*] I'm afraid you expect me to be sparkling this evening.

Met. It is impossible for you to be more sparkling than usual, madam. [*Aside*] I wonder if she has received my letter.

Judge. [*Aside*] I feel like a bottle of champagne, myself, and I'm going to pop in the course of the evening! [*Aloud*] By the way—there was an interesting episode at my house this evening. It will interest you particularly, Mrs. Dashwood. A poor tramp came into the garden today.

Mrs. D. Ah—singing Rudy!

Rho. [*Aside*] A—a poor tramp? Rudy?

Lawr. The country is infested with tramps.

Met. Two German gentlemen—are in Lawrenceburg—agents of the Johannes von Hollenstein estate, of Berlin.

Lawr. Yes—I know. Well?

Judge. They were among my guests. They brought a letter of introduction to the mayor from the German consul-general in New York. They remarked that they had been making special efforts to discover the nephew of Johannes von Hollenstein, Rudolph Wiegand. [*Rhoda shows emotion. Lawrence notices her. She draws up calmly*] He is the Baron von Hollenstein—if he is alive. The old millionaire left the bulk of his estate to him as the inheritor of his title.

Met. The trouble now is this: there will be interminable legal complications in Germany, unless they can prove that this Rudolph Wiegand is either dead or alive; of course, they don't care a straw which.

Rho. [*Aside*] Dead or alive!

Judge. While we were chatting, one of your own ironfounders, Lawrence, came to the house and insisted on seeing the German agents. We had him in. He had been to their hotel and was quite out of breath. He said that Rudolph Wiegand was one and the same with a tramp in Lawrenceburg, called "Dancing Rudy."

Mrs. D. It is our Rudy! Baron von Hollenstein! [*Aside*] Perhaps I'll marry him some day, instead of either of 'em.

MET. It is a very interesting case. But there will be one great difficulty, from a legal point of view—to establish his identity.

JUDGE. The ironfounder, by the bye, told us that you could identify him, Lawrence—

LAWR. I—I? [*Then deliberately*] I know nothing whatever, about the man. [*Rhoda turns towards him, drawing up and looking him full in the face. He turns towards her, and looks steadily at her*]

RHO. [*Apart*] You—know—nothing, whatever—about—Rudolph Wiegand?

LAWR. [*Firmly*] Nothing—whatever, madam.

RHO. I—I do. [*She turns away from him slowly and crosses to Judge R.C.*] Judge Merrybone—you may say to these gentlemen, who represent the Hollenstein estate, that Mrs. Whitworth Lawrence can identify Rudolph Wiegand.

JUDGE and MET. You, madam?

RHO. Definitely and absolutely; yes. [*Crossing to L.*] I—I have not been feeling well all the evening. I know you will excuse me, if I retire to my room.

JUDGE and MET. Certainly, madam. [*Mrs. Dashwood moves to Rhoda L. Judge Merrybone crosses to Metcalfe up L.C. Lawrence sits at right of table R.*]

MRS. D. Good night, Rhoda. [*Kissing her*]

RHO. [*Holding her hand in her own*] My dreams have been something more than dreams, Nellie, good night. [*Exits L.1.E.*]

MRS. D. [*After a moment, looking after her*] Well—I'm glad he won't be a ghost—any longer. Rhoda doesn't know how to deal with ghosts. She can't keep 'em respectful to her. If I should marry the baron, I'd be his second wife. I won't. [*She turns upstage to glass doors. Judge Merrybone and Metcalfe are talking earnestly in dumb show R.C. She looks over her shoulder*] A-h-e-m. [*They look around at her suddenly. She turns and looks out the door*] The moon is out at last. The conservatory is charming in the moonlight. May I trouble you for my shawl on the sofa—[*Metcalfe and Merrybone start*] Judge Merrybone!

JUDGE. Certainly—delighted. [*He crosses to her with shawl. Metcalfe sits at table. The Judge puts Mrs. Dashwood's shawl over her shoulders, with business, Metcalfe glancing back and showing signs of disgust*]

MRS. D. No—that way—no—yes—that—this way—thank you, judge. Ta—ta—general—ta-ta [*Exit Mrs. Dashwood and Judge through glass doors*]

MET. Well, Lawrence—to business. [*Glances at glass doors anxiously*] I haven't any time to lose.

LAWR. I wish to engage your professional services, General Metcalfe.

MET. I make a specialty of the criminal law. Something in my line?

LAWR. Yes.

MET. Good. I am retained.

LAWR. I will be frank with you.

MET. Of course. Never keep your lawyer in the dark.

LAWR. I have committed a very heavy forgery.

MET. What? [*Starting up with his hands on the table*] Forgery! My dear friend! [*Extending his hand across the table, and shaking Lawrence's hand with warmth*] Dine with me at the club tomorrow evening. We'll talk it over. Private room, we'll make a night of it. How much?

LAWR. Three hundred and eighty thousand dollars.

MET. Good! That's enough to command the respect of the jury.

LAWR. Jury! Never! The matter shall never come before a court.

MET. The amount may be big enough, luckily, to force a compromise. That is our first look-out. If Judge Merrybone doesn't issue an order compelling us to show the books.

LAWR. Can Judge Merrybone issue such an order legally?

MET. Judge Merrybone doesn't care a continental whether a thing is legal or not. It's a devilish bad district to commit a crime in.

LAWR. As I said before, the case shall never come into a court. If, on looking over my papers, you find that it is impossible to prevent discovery—

MET. What then?

LAWR. What the president of the Blackhart Coal Company did today in prison.

MET. Suicide? [*Leaning towards him with his hands on the table*]

LAWR. I shall never see the inside of a prisoner's cell.

MET. Damn it, sir—that would ruin the case! You are my client, sir—if you commit suicide without the consent of your counsel—I'll throw the case up, sir! How many honest business men are there in the directory of your company—any?

LAWR. One.

MET. Who is it?

LAWR. Morgan T. Oxenford.

MET. Wh-e-w. The devil! Morgan T. Oxenford is an honest man. How the deuce did you let such a man as that get in the directory of a great corporation? Oxenford was a guest at our dinner with the judge tonight—and he's spent the last four days, to my certain knowledge, with the agents of the Hollenstein estate—[*Lawrence starts to his feet*] and a lawyer from New York City. [*Lawrence crosses L.*] They are here to inquire into the condition of your company. And if this "Dancing Rudy" turns out to be the Baron von

Hollenstein—your enemy will be on the ground in person! But nothing more can be done tonight. I'll be here at ten tomorrow morning. What shall I order for dinner, at the club? Ah—Mrs. Dashwood! [*Moving up, bowing and smiling, to meet Mrs. Dashwood, who reenters at glass doors, followed by Judge Merrybone. The latter takes her shawl gallantly from her shoulders and crosses to sofa R. with it*]

LAWR. [*Down L.*] My friends—I—if you will excuse me—if Mrs. Dashwood will kindly—

MET. Certainly. Mrs. Dashwood will do the honors of the house.

MRS. D. By all means, Lawrence. I have two protectors.

LAWR. Thank you. Mrs. Lawrence has retired and she did not seem well —I will go to her. [*Moving L. stops*] At ten tomorrow, General Metcalfe?

MET. Eh—[*Looking up from attentions to Mrs. Dashwood*] ten?—tomorrow? Oh, yes, I forgot. Ten, tomorrow morning. [*Immediately resumes his attentions to her*]

LAWR. Tomorrow!—will it ever come? [*Exits L.1E. The Judge walks down R. and sits at R. of table; takes a newspaper, glances at Metcalfe, opens the paper and settles back to read, with it spread out between him and the audience*]

MRS. D. [*Continuing her chat with Metcalfe and shaking her fan at him*] Ah—General Metcalfe!—You understand us poor women so perfectly.

MET. [*Flattered*] Really—I—[*Arranging his necktie with complacent smile*] I assure you, Mrs. Dashwood—I—[*He suddenly catches sight of the Judge and draws up stiffly*]

MRS. D. [*Aside*] He ought to—he's had two wives. [*She walks up and drops into chair C. Metcalfe moves L., sits, with determined manner, glancing at the Judge*] I feel like a soldier's monument—the Goddess of Liberty—with an armed man at each side of her.

MET. [*Aside*] I'll sit out Merrybone, and propose to the young widow, tonight, if it takes me till breakfast time.

JUDGE. [*Turning paper*] Great real-estate case in New York—five columns. [*Settles behind paper*]

MRS. D. Read it to us, judge.

MET. I read it myself this morning.

MRS. D. Ah—something else, then, judge.

JUDGE. [*Turning paper*] The census commissioner's last report.

MRS. D. That will be interesting. How many new spring bonnets were there last year?

JUDGE. [*Looking at paper*] B—B—m—m—nothing about bonnets under the B's. There were six million babies.

MRS. D.   There wouldn't be so many, if there were fewer pretty bonnets.

JUDGE.   Two hundred and ten thousand, five hundred and sixty-one idiots.

MET.   The odd one idiot is a personal acquaintance of mine. [*He and the Judge glance at each other*]

MRS. D.   The majority of them move in the best circles—and they don't wear bonnets.

JUDGE. [*Aside*]   The general is getting irritable. I'll give him a chance. [*Rises*] The light isn't very good in this room, to read by. If you'll excuse me, Mrs. Dashwood—[*Walking up*] I'll go into the library.

MRS. D. [*Pleasantly*]   As you please, judge—but General Metcalfe and I will be lonely. Come back soon.

MET.   As soon as you finish the census report and the real-estate case. [*Mrs. Dashwood extends her hand to the Judge, up C. smiling. He leans forward and kisses it. Metcalfe looks sharply around at the sound, but not before Mrs. Dashwood has jerked away her hand. The Judge suddenly straightens up and raises the paper before him as if reading. Metcalfe rises and crosses R. Mrs. Dashwood walks down and drops upon the piano stool L. The Judge looks over his paper at Metcalfe, who stands turned away grimly. The Judge gives his own face a smart slap with his hand, and looks around as if for the sound, putting his hand to his ear. Metcalfe starts around, at the sound, eyeing him*]

MRS. D.   Did you hear a noise, judge?

JUDGE.   Only the click of a lock somewhere. [*He walks up and out R. through corridor. His whistle is heard after he disappears. Mrs. Dashwood begins playing the same air, and sings, at the piano. Ballad. Metcalfe crosses and stands at her side, upstage, turning the leaves, with smiling attention*]

MET. [*After first stanza—aside*]   I wonder if she did get my letter.

MRS. D. [*After second stanza—during interval music*]   You sent me a letter this afternoon, General Metcalfe.

MET.   Yes—I—I—a letter—yes.

MRS. D.   You have forgotten to turn the page. [*He turns the page hastily, and she goes on at once with the next stanza*]

MET. [*At conclusion of song*]   Lovely, madam—lovely. [*Patting his hands*] You—you—did receive my letter?

MRS. D. [*Rising and crossing R.*]   Yes, general. [*Sitting R.*] You said—

MET.   I said—[*Going to her*] that I hoped for an opportunity to—without danger of interruption—[*Glancing back uneasily at corridor*] to speak with you, madam—when we could be entirely alone—[*Glancing back*] on a subject of—of—[*Glancing back*]

MRS. D.   Another crisis in life.

MET. Of very great interest to myself. That was all I said in my letter, but I will now proceed from that point. A man at my time of life—a man at any time of life—feels the need of a loving companion—a wife! [*Merrybone heard whistling in the other room. Metcalfe draws up, annoyed; walks upstage; looks out at corridor*]

MRS. D. I haven't the slightest idea what you're coming to. No woman ever has at this point. [*Metcalfe returns down R.C.*] The late Senator Dashwood made a similar remark to me, one afternoon, general. It was the very time, by the way, that he proposed to me. The first time.

MET. The first time?

MRS. D. "Senator," said I—"I won't." [*Metcalfe starts angrily*] He proposed to me six times.

MET. I'll be hanged if I propose to you six times, madam! [*Moves L. angrily*]

MRS. D. [*With a merry laugh—merrily*] Don't trouble yourself about the other five, general. I accepted Judge Merrybone in the conservatory, about twenty minutes ago. [*Judge Merrybone reenters up C., stops whistling before he appears. Paper in his hand*]

JUDGE. I say, Metcalfe—there are five hundred and seventy thousand lunatics in the country—and you criminal lawyers are turning out more of 'em every day.

MET. Good night, sir! Good night, madam! [*Exits angrily L.1.E. The Judge, astonished at his manner, follows him to the door, looking after him and whistling. Mrs. Dashwood, R.C., begins dancing daintily in time with him*]

JUDGE. [*Suddenly checking himself and turning*] I beg your pardon for whistling in the presence of a lady—but—[*He sees her dancing and breaks into the whistle with spirit, patting on his knees. She dances merrily a moment. He takes a few steps; joins her, catches her around the waist and turns one or two times with her*]

MRS. D. Ha—ha—ha—ha—judge!—You may kiss me.

JUDGE. [*After kissing her*] Ha—ha!

MRS. D. I just told General Metcalfe you are to be my husband.

JUDGE. You told him! That's why he—ha—ha—ha—ha—ha! I'll run after him. He'll ride home in my carriage, if I don't, and leave me to go on foot. Ha—ha. I'll punch him in the ribs, till they're black and blue. Ha—ha—ha—[*At door L.*] Good night.

MRS. D. Good night. [*He kisses his hand to her and goes out L.1.E. He is heard whistling in the hall. She dances daintily in time with the whistling. It ceases. She runs up to glass doors—opens them—listens. The whistling is heard in the garden, more and more faintly. She keeps one foot moving in time, as she stands on the other and listens at the door*] Ha—ha—ha—ha— Judge Merrybone will make me the best husband and the jolliest one—in America. [*Crosses R.*] The late senator said to me one day—"If you ever should marry another man," said he, "marry an old one—for my sake." "Dashwood," said I, "I will—for my own sake." [*Exits R.3.E. Low music. Enter John L.1.E., a short staff in his hand to turn out the gas. He looks about the room and sees that it is empty; then moves to the chandelier; turns out the lights, then the side brackets. The stage gradually becomes dark and a gleam of moonlight falls across the room through the glass doors. The veranda and view beyond are now, for the first time, fully seen in bright moonlight. John moves to the glass doors; looks out, gives a low signal. It is answered from without. John comes down, glances back, exits L.1.E. A moment's pause. Enter Allen from veranda. Rudolph follows him in. Allen has a dark lantern in his hand. It is closed. Music ceases*]

ALLEN. [*In low tones*] Science, pal—just in the nick of time. No one notices a few sounds now. Keep cool.

RUD. Yes—I keep cool.

ALLEN. This way. [*He moves down L.leaving glass doors open.He throws a quick light on door L.1.E. closing the lantern at once*] You listen at that door. No danger in any other direction. If you hear anything—we can bolt by the veranda. The girl's room is there! [*Pointing*] Keep cool, pal—keep cool.

RUD. I'm cooling. [*Allen steals across to R.1.E. Rudolph follows him. Allen throws a light on the door; tries knob, then crouches and looks into the keyhole*]

ALLEN. The key is out—good. [*He works silently with skeleton keys. Rudolph stands quietly, watching him as he works, with folded arms and a firm look*] This does it. [*He turns the bolt quietly, and rises with his hand on the knob, turning his ear to listen. He sees Rudolph near him; starts up facing him*] What you doing here?

RUD. [*Quietly*] I am learning the business. [*Allen looks fixedly at him, slowly draws a knife from his waistband and takes a step towards him. He raises the knife to Rudolph's breast, and turns the light of the lantern full into his face. Rudolph stands with his hand behind him and looks Allen quietly in the eye, speaking after a pause*] You like my face? You did not give me time to go to a barber's. I owe you an apology. The next time we come out on business, I will put on a dress-suit with a white necktie. [*Allen lowers both hands, closes the lantern and returns his knife, with a smile and a low chuckle*]

ALLEN. You are a cool one. I thought you might be going back on me. You'll succeed in this profession. Go back to that door. [*Turning L. starts, listens*] Hist—pal! [*In a quick whisper*] Somebody moving inside. A hand on the door. Look out for that moonlight. [*He steps back up R.C., crouching in shadow. Enter Ernestine R.1.E. She first puts out her head then steps in. Rudolph moves back C. watching her and still in shadow*]

ERN. Why!—I heard something—something in the lock—and the door is open. I—I wonder if Geoffrey—No!—perhaps he is here. [*She turns to move towards the glass doors. Rudolph steps backwards, as if to avoid her, until he stands in the moonlight. She stops, straightening up with a gasp and a stifled scream. Allen springs forward with a catlike motion and seizes her by the throat. Rudolph springs forward and seizes Allen. The moment Ernestine is free, she screams very loudly and moves to R.L. A quick struggle between Rudolph and Allen. Ernestine screams again. Allen throws off Rudolph, who falls up R. Allen starts to escape by the door. Enter Geoffrey, who strikes Allen. The latter staggers back and around. Geoffrey seizes him under the arms. Enter two police officers by glass doors. They relieve Geoffrey of Allen. One of them handcuffs him. Enter the Sheriff quietly and deliberately by glass doors*]

SHER. Ah, Allen—So soon? They will miss you at the Wednesday evening prayer meetings. [*He motions quietly with his arm and the policemen walk out at glass doors, Allen between them. Enter Lawrence L.1.E. in his shirt and trousers*]

LAWR. What's this—who's here?

RUD. [*Springing up in the gleam of light*] Rudolph Wiegand!

ERN. Rudolph Wiegand?

RUD. I am strong now.

ERN. Father! [*She runs to him. He embraces her*]

RUD. My child.

LAWR. You have arrived in the nick of time, Mr. Sheriff.

SHER. [*Quietly*] So it seems. My men came just in time to be of service. My own arrival at this juncture was accidental.

LAWR. I call upon you to arrest—that man! [*Pointing to Rudolph*] as a common burglar—

ERN. Arrest him—he has just saved my life!

SHER. I come on a more important duty, sir. I am here to arrest yourself, Mr. Lawrence. [*Taking official paper from his pocket and presenting it to Lawrence who recoils*]

ACT IV.

Interval of one year.

SCENE: *Maplegrove Villa. Interior. An air of prettiness and neatness, but with no evidence of wealth and luxury. Large windows reaching to stage, at back, with trailing flowers, and sprays of foliage without. Very simple garden or rural scene at back. Open doors, leading to porch R. Also window, looking on porch. Post and lattice of porch, with flowers, etc. Backing to that of upper window. Doors L.1.E. and up L. Furniture and ornaments showing a woman's taste and care. Piano L.*

DISCOVERED: *Ernestine and Geoffrey. She is sitting quietly sewing, R.C., dressed in white, trimmed delicately with black. He is sitting near her, R., on a low stool, tossing a reel of cotton, as if thinking absently, half turned away from her.*

GEOF. We—we might have been married a whole year, by this time, Ernestine.

ERN. I'm very glad we haven't been.

GEOF. Glad?

ERN. I mean, I'm glad that we didn't run away to get married—and I'm glad that now, when I am married, I shall have the consent of my real, true father.

GEOF. Do you think he will give his consent?

ERN. I shall never marry without it, Geoffrey. It is very different now; besides, I was only a girl when we were going to run away, a year ago. I wasn't quite seventeen years old. Now, I'm nearly eighteen. I'm a woman. We women have such different ideas from young girls.

GEOF. Well! I'm twenty-one now. I'm a man. But I'm sorry we aren't old married people.

ERN. When I am married—

GEOF. When you are married! Why don't you say when we are married.

ERN. You're ruining my spool of white thread. It'll be as black—as black as—

GEOF. As my hands. [*Tossing the reel into her lap and rising petulantly*]

ERN. [*Quietly*] Yes, Geoffrey.

GEOF. I never do anything to please you, now-a-days. [*Walking up to R.C.*] Ever since your father first wrote you from Europe, about—about—

ERN. About the Count von Stollhoffen, of Berlin.

GEOF. Yes, a "count"—with a big title, and a fortune.

ERN. In his last letter—that I received this morning—father says that the Count von Stollhoffen takes a great interest in papa's American daughter.

GEOF. Interest! I suppose your father showed him your photograph.

ERN. The one I had taken when you were with us, last Spring. Do you remember?—I had the violets you bought me in my hair. I sent father a copy of it.

GEOF. I daresay the Count von Stollhoffen will tell your father how much he can afford to settle on you and you'll be sold!—to the highest bidder! I—I'm sure I can't bid very much for you. I—I'm poor.

ERN. [Demurely, sewing] Are you quite sure you cannot offer a higher bid than the Count von Stollhoffen, Geoffrey?

GEOF. [Sadly] I can only offer you my heart.

ERN. Yes. I know. I will send on your offer to father, when I answer his last letter. He can compare it with that of the Count von Stollhoffen. I will accept the offer which he thinks the most valuable.

GEOF. Oh! I—I didn't think you were such a mercenary woman, Ernestine. I—I'm going. [Gets his hat] I say, I'm going.

ERN. [Without looking up] You said, when you came, you could spend the whole afternoon with me.

GEOF. I don't want to be a moment longer in the presence of such a woman as you are. Now that you have become the heiress of a rich German nobleman, you're changed. You're a woman of the world. I'll be a man of the world after this. I'll sit up late at night and I'll drink, and I'll smoke cigars. I'll join a club and I'll tell women I love 'em when I don't. I'll be a man of the world. [Exits angrily by porch R. Ernestine springs up, crosses and looks after him]

ERN. Geoffrey!—Geoffrey! Oh—the stupid! I didn't intend to have another quarrel, today. We had one yesterday—for this week. We were just beginning to have a nice afternoon. [Looking out, enter Metcalfe, R.] Oh, Mr. Metcalfe!

MET. Ernestine, please run and tell your mamma that I wish to see her—on important business.

ERN. Yes, sir. Mamma is in her own room. Sit down, General Metcalfe. [Runs L. Geoffrey appears on porch, looking in through window] That stupid Geoffrey! He wouldn't come back. [Exits L.1.E. Geoffrey enters]

MET. Ah—my young friend—you hurried past me a second ago, in the garden, without condescending to speak to me. Geoffrey! Your father and I were old friends. He left you without means. You are studying law. Let me give you a word of good advice, my boy.

GEOF. Boy!

MET. When you first fell in love with Ernestine Wiegand, she was the legal daughter of Whitworth Lawrence. Whitworth Lawrence shot himself on his way to prison, immediately after his arrest last year. He killed your possible hopes and himself at the same time. As to Mrs. Lawrence—

GEOF. Ernestine's mother and I love each other very much.

MET. Marry her then, my boy—she's a widow. It's all in the family. Do you suppose that she will stand in the way of her own daughter's brilliant prospects in life? No. The girl's father will find some rich and titled suitor for her, in his native land.

GEOF. Yes—heigh-ho—I know he will.

MET. He has an aristocratic family name to look after. Ernestine's son will be the next Baron von Hollenstein. You will not be his father. Confine your attention to the law, my young friend. You will find consolation for your present sorrow in other smiles—the innocent smiles of the burglars, forgers and murderers you will save from justice. The law is a glorious and useful profession. Stick to it. [*Walks up to window at back and looks out*]

GEOF. He is a man of the world. Heigh-ho. [*Turning up*] I suppose he is right. I am sure he is right. The Count von Stollhoffen will be Ernestine's husband, after all. [*Exits sadly, porch R. Reenter Ernestine L.1.E. She has her hat in her hand*]

ERN. [*Running across R.*] Mamma will be down in a moment, General Metcalfe. She is coming now. [*Aside*] I'm sure Geoffrey's gone to sit by the brook—under the old beeches, where we have spent so many happy hours. I always find him there when we've had a quarrel. We'll sit there together and we needn't stop quarreling all the afternoon. Ha—ha—ha. [*Running out R. She is heard calling without*] Geof-frey!

MET. [*Hurrying from window to porch*] My child! Ernestine!

ERN. Geoffrey! [*Without, calling—more distant*]

MET. I have something to say to you.

ERN. Geoffrey! [*Still further away*]

MET. She's away like a deer. [*Enter Rhoda L.1.E. She is in mourning— not deep, but sufficient for courtesy and self-respect, under the circumstances*]

RHO. General Metcalfe.

MET. Madam, I call this morning upon a very interesting errand.

RHO. Interesting? Be seated. [*Sitting L.C.*]

MET. [*Sitting R.C.*] Your former husband, madam—

RHO. My—[*With a slight start*] Well, sir?

MET. The Baron von Hollenstein has returned to America—after arranging the important affairs in his own country which so suddenly claimed his attention. He is now in Lawrenceburg.

Rho. In—Lawrenceburg?

Met. [*Producing a number of legal papers*] He has requested me to call upon you, madam, as his representative.

Rho. I understand. You are here as his legal representative.

Met. His first anxiety, by the way, naturally—concerns his daughter.

Rho. His—daughter? Yes. I knew that a day like this must come. My mind has been made up. I—I long ago came to my final decision. It may break a mother's heart, sir—but I will not rob him of his daughter's love and society in his declining years.

Met. As to that, madam—of course, under this divorce you have an absolute legal control of the child.

Rho. I will not claim it. [*Under more and more emotion and breaking down in tears*] Ernestine told me she was going down by the brook—to the beeches.

Met. Down by the brook?

Rho. It is only a little way. When she returns I will send her to him.

Met. She will probably meet her father. He accompanied me as far as that point and wished me to send her to him, with your consent.

Rho. He—he is so near?

Met. I will now proceed to the special business with which I have been entrusted. This paper is a deed, by which the baron conveys to yourself certain property in this city, acquired through my agency, some months ago— to the value of about sixty thousand dollars. The property is now rented for the sum of six thousand dollars per annum. This paper is an assignment—to you of United States bonds—registered to the amount of fifty thousand dollars—two thousand dollars per annum. This one—[*Rhoda has listened with rising emotion which she has held in check. She now interrupts him, with dignity*]

Rho. You may read no more, General Metcalfe.

Met. Your pardon?

Rho. You may read no more.

Met. I may— Oh—I see. You do not care for the details. Women never do. Total about one hundred and ninety thousand dollars—about fifteen thousand a year.

Rho. I—I recognize the kindness of my—of Baron von Hollenstein—but I cannot accept his generous gift.

Met. You—you cannot accept?

Rho. I cannot accept it.

MET. My dear madam. The baron requested me to convey this matter to you as delicately as possible. I have done so. I merely mentioned the figures. I must beg you to reconsider your resolution.

RHO. Nothing can alter it.

MET. I must urge you to—

RHO. It is useless.

MET. You are absolutely determined?

RHO. I cannot accept the gift.

MET. Madam—you compel me to betray a confidence.

RHO. Betray—a confidence?

MET. When I closed up the estate of the late Whitworth Lawrence—embarrassed by many financial complications—I assured you that a considerable balance remained—besides enough to purchase this little place, Maplegrove Villa, from Mr. Hackleston.

RHO. Well?

MET. There was not only no "balance" from Mr. Lawrence's estate, madam —it did not pay thirty cents on the dollar.

RHO. Then the little fortune I possess—this house—everything I have called my own—it all came through you, from Rudolph Wiegand.

MET. Need I urge you now, madam, to reconsider your resolution? The woman who was once his wife, and who is the mother of his child, should live in a manner worthy of his position and his pride?

RHO. I did not speak of pride before—now I do—I too, have pride. I will leave this house. I will also return the remainder of my little fortune to him.

MET. Madam! I—

RHO. I will go back to that walk of life in which he, fallen from a higher one, first found me. Rudolph and our—our—daughter will live together in the luxury to which his rank—and hers entitles them, in a foreign land. I shall never trouble them. His friends shall never hear from me! But my prayers will be with them both—always. [*Going R.1.E.*]

MET. But my dear Mrs.—

RHO. Your pardon—good afternoon, General Metcalfe. [*Exits L.1.E. Enter Mrs. Merrybone (Dashwood) porch R.*]

MET. [*Looking L.*] Damn it! I've ruined the case.

MRS. M. Ruined another case, general? [*He turns towards her*] I hope I haven't interrupted—

MET. [*Bowing*] Mrs.—Governor—Merrybone.

MRS. M. [*Curtsying*] Senator-elect—Metcalfe.

MET. We haven't met for a year.

Mrs. M. Exactly one year to-night. I'm afraid I have—I—Mrs. Lawrence is a widow.

Met. Madam—I never have anything to do with widows, except on business.

Mrs. M. Oh, you've made a new rule. It is a good one. Don't. I laid down the same rule for my present husband, when we were first married. He says he did so well by not following the rule, once—he doesn't know whether he'll keep it, now, or not. "Merrybone," I always say—"Do exactly as you like; whatever rule you do choose—it'll work both ways."

Met. Ah—exactly—ha—ha—ha—work both ways—[*Aside*] The governor flirts a little. [*Aloud*] Merrybone does smile on a young widow, now and then?

Mrs. M. Mr. Merrybone usually smiles. If he happens to be looking in the direction of a pretty widow, he doesn't make an exception.

Met. [*Aside*] I'll get my revenge on Merrybone. I'd give a thousand dollars to kiss his wife—and two thousand, by Jove!—if he could see me do it. [*Aloud*] The governor isn't with you?

Mrs. M. He's coming. He stopped on the way to see a young clergyman he pardoned out of the penitentiary, and set him up for himself in a new chapel. The governor and I have just run up from the state capitol, for a few weeks. We've been vetoing railroad bills all the year, and we need a rest.

Met. [*Aside*] "The rule will work both ways." I think she is a little jealous of the governor. [*Looks at her smiling. She smiles in return—a little coquettishly. He moves R., she passes him to L. When he is just past her, C., he looks back and speaks, she stopping with her back to him and listening over her shoulder*] I never saw you look so charming as you do today, Mrs. Merrybone.

Mrs. M. Thank you, general. [*Passes on L. Aside*] He calls this business with a widow. I'm not a widow now. I don't come under his new rule. I'm only another man's wife.

Met. You were remarking, my dear Mrs. Merrybone—[*Moving to her L.C. Judge Merrybone appears on porch, stops and watches them through window*] that—you were remarking that the governor does smile on a pretty widow now and then. I—I dare say you—you take your revenge sometimes.

Mrs. M. Frequently.

Judge. [*Aside*] The deuce she does!

Mrs. M. Sometimes when I get thinking of it—at night—

Met. Ah—[*Smiling complacently*] It does prey upon your mind, eh—a little?

Mrs. M. I move my elbow.

JUDGE. [*Aside*] She does, by Jove! She digs me in the ribs with it. I never understood before.

MRS. M. Then he wakes up—and I kiss him.

JUDGE. [*Aside, smiling*] She does!

MET. You might—take a more satisfactory revenge. Heigh-ho-ah, madam, I so often think of the hours I passed in your society, only a year ago—it seems ten years to me.

MRS. M. I often speak of you to the governor.

MET. Indeed. [*Complacently*] You—you frequently speak of me.

MRS. M. When we've been having a quarrel—[*Aside*] and just made it up.

MET. [*Smiling, rubbing his hands and leaning forward*] When you have been having a quarrel—you speak of me to the governor.

MRS. M. "Merrybone," I say, "I'm so glad I didn't marry the other one." [*Metcalfe starts back, she laughs merrily, moving to door L.*] Ta, ta, general, ta, ta. [*The Judge gives his own cheek a smart blow. Metcalfe looks around, the Judge begins whistling, and enters from porch; Metcalfe looks around, then moves up angrily, and faces him R.C. Mrs. M. kisses the Judge and runs out. Metcalfe exits angrily porch R.*]

JUDGE. Ha—ha—ha—ha—ha! [*Whistles. Enter Ernestine, porch R., she looks back beckoning, sees Merrybone*]

ERN. Oh, Judge Merrybone! Governor. [*Going to him*]

JUDGE. My little rosebud; why, you are almost a woman now.

ERN. [*Drawing up*] Yes, sir. [*She looks R. anxiously*] I—I'm very glad to see you, Mr.—Judge—Governor Merrybone—[*Looks R.*] but—

JUDGE. But—

ERN. But I—I—

JUDGE. But you are more particularly anxious to see someone else here—alone. Ha—ha—ha—ha—[*Taps her under the chin*] I'll take a walk in the garden. Ah—these young lovers. I was one, a year ago. Ha—ha—ha—[*Walking R., stops suddenly and looks out seriously*] Heaven bless you, my darling! [*Exits by window up L., glancing back R. as he disappears. Ernestine beckons to R. standing up L.C. Enter Rudolph through porch R. He moves quietly across to her dropping one arm about her waist, raising her chin with his other hand, and looking down into her face*]

RUD. My little pet! I have followed you here—in spite of my own self—as if it were an angel leading me—I could not help coming. I tried to turn back from you, but it was dark behind me; you found me sitting under the same old trees by the brook, where you came to me a year ago. I was hungry then, and you brought me food. I was hungry again, today—hungry for love, my darling! And you brought me food again.

ERN. You will see mother—promise me that, papa.

RUD. Heigh-ho. I am here! Yes, my child—I will. [*Ernestine is going eagerly R.*] Ah—my pet! [*She stops and looks back*] I wish to speak to you, one word. [*She returns to him. He takes her hand in his own*] I am selfish. I was speaking of the happiness that you brought to me. Your own happiness is dearer to me than that. You have nearly all your life before you, my pet. It is a long journey. A young girl does not care to start on that journey alone.

ERN. Alone, papa?—No.

RUD. When I met you under the trees by the brook, there was a young man with you.

ERN. Yes, papa.

RUD. The same young man was with you when we met, at the same place, a year ago.

ERN. Yes, papa.

RUD. I heard the garden gate close—very soon after we entered it, just now —as we were coming up to the walk. [*Geoffrey appears from R. looking in at the window upstage, as if anxious to know how things were going*]

ERN. It—it might have been Geoffrey, papa.

RUD. Yes. [*Aside*] It might have been Geoffrey! [*Sees Geoffrey, the latter not knowing it*] I wrote you about a German young man, Ernestine.

ERN. Yes. [*She does not see Geoffrey. Geoffrey, much interested moves forward R. with signs of jealousy and impatience as the following proceeds*]

RUD. I told you he was very rich.

ERN. Yes.

RUD. He is a count. He is a very great man in Europe. Before I left Germany, he made me a formal proposition for your hand. He will settle a fortune upon you. I will give you a dowry, equal to it. I can speak to your mother about it today. If you marry him, my child, you will become a very great lady. You will have a castle of your own to live in. The Countess von Stollhoffen will be an honored guest in the royal palaces of Europe. Great men and brilliant women will be your friends. Do I not offer you happiness?

ERN. I—I—

RUD. You do hesitate?

ERN. I—I—would rather—marry—Geoffrey, papa!

RUD. Come to my arms, my pet! [*With delight. She runs to him. He embraces her. Geoffrey delighted*] I will answer the Count von Stollhoffen, that my little American girl refuses him! Ah!—you are here, my young friend. [*With a quizzical smile to Geoffrey*] You and I will talk business. What can you settle on my daughter?

GEOF. I—I can only offer her my heart, sir.

RUD. The Count von Stollhoffen did not offer her so large a fortune as that. [*Passes her to him*] My children! I gave you a father's blessing when I was poor and I did not know I was your father. My only hope is this—that you may have so much of love and happiness, in all your life, as I did have, for a little time, when Ernestine was a baby. [*Turning partly away, L., under emotion. Enter Rhoda L.1.E., followed by Mrs. Merrybone. Rhoda stops L. facing Rudolph. They bow to each other in silence. Mrs. Merrybone recognizes the situation and moves up C., looks back*]

MRS. M. The prince in disguise has returned to his own kingdom. [*Merrybone heard whistling in the garden. She starts and listens*] There's my prince. [*She steps upstage daintily in time with the whistling through window and into garden, to L. Ernestine moves back with Geoffrey and R. to porch, as if wishing to leave Rudolph and Rhoda alone*]

ERN. Come and talk with me about the fortune you're going to settle on me, Geoffrey. [*Exit by porch R.*]

RUD. My—Rhoda—my—Mrs. Lawrence.

RHO. Baron—von—Hollenstein.

RUD. I am here—our daughter—Ernestine—I could not help it. I have no right to be here.

RHO. You have every right to be here. This is your own house, sir.

RUD. Mine?

RHO. I have discovered the truth. I—I am glad to express my gratitude to you, in person, for the means which I have enjoyed of living in ease and comfort during the past year. You have offered me another generous gift. General Metcalfe has returned with my answer. I—I have told him to thank you.

RUD. He need not deliver that message.

RHO. And to say to you that while I cannot accept—

RUD. You cannot accept?

RHO. No. I am not willing to live in luxury, now, at the expense of one whom I left, in his poverty—

RUD. Rhoda!

RHO. To wander and suffer alone in the world—while I was sharing the wealth of another. I—I could not accept the gift from him. What I already have, must also be returned.

RUD. You are so proud, Rhoda?

RHO. No—not "proud." I have little enough cause for that, in your presence. I am only just—to you and to myself. I shall become again what I was, before you met me. I will earn my own living—in my own way.

RUD. And our—our daughter—Ernestine?

RHO. I shall not claim the right which the law has given me. Our—our daughter shall be yours.

RUD. You—you refuse to—receive anything—from me—Rhoda?

RHO. I—I must—absolutely; yes.

RUD. And I refuse to receive our daughter from you! [*Rhoda starts*] When you left my home—if it could be called a home—I had brought you and your baby to misery—the little girl shall remain with you, now. She shall toil with you.

RHO. Toil!

RUD. Geoffrey is also poor. He shall work, too. I will not give him or Ernestine wealth, if it is not to be shared with you. I would rather throw it into the sea. Rhoda!—the child is not before its mother in a father's heart. It was you I loved before she came. It was because I loved you so much that I loved our baby!—When she lay in the cradle and smiled upon me, with a smile that you had given her. And all these years—wherever I have wandered, whatever I have suffered, in this last year of luxury as in the rest—I have felt something stronger and deeper in my heart, than even my love for Ernestine! It was the one great love, Rhoda—the strongest, the best, the last in his heart —a man's love for his wife!

RHO. Rudolph! [*Under emotion and turned away from him; dropping her face in her hands*]

RUD. You are proud, Rhoda. You will not accept my gift. You will return to your poverty. Ernestine shall go with you. And I? I can buy with my money—the same thing the world will offer you—and her—without it— misery! [*Walking up. He looks out R. Smiles*] Ernestine and her lover—in the garden—they are walking this way. Rhoda! [*Tenderly reaching his arm towards her*] Come here. [*Rhoda walks up to him. He points out R. She looks out, standing near him*] You see them? Geoffrey is telling our little girl how much he loves her. [*He takes Rhoda's hand, as he speaks, unconsciously*] His arm about her waist. [*His own goes about Rhoda's waist*] They do not— know that you and I can see them, under the trees. Geoffrey is kissing her. [*He draws Rhoda towards him and is on the point of kissing her cheek. He hesitates; draws back; and releases her as if suddenly remembering himself and half embarrassed. Rhoda moves down C., her eyes on the floor*] I did forget the years that have passed since we—I—it seemed to be you and—I—instead of Geoffrey and Ernestine. [*Moving down R.C.*] Rhoda! [*Quietly*]

RHO. Rudolph. [*Her eyes still dropped*]

RUD. Ernestine and Geoffrey will be married.

RHO. As soon as they can be—yes.

RUD. When they do get married, it will not be long before—of course, we cannot tell—nobody knows that—but Ernestine will—there will be another baby.

RHO. I hope so. [*Earnestly, smiling*]

RUD. Yes!—I think so—Ernestine is a good girl. She will call it "Rhoda." [*Ernestine and Geoffrey appear in porch in loving attitude*]

RHO. After me.

RUD. But there are various kinds of babies. If it should be another kind—

RHO. She will call it "Rudolph." [*Ernestine and Geoffrey look through window*]

RUD. Yes. That baby will be the Baron von Hollenstein . . . when we are gone, Rhoda. I—I can see it lying in its cradle, now. Two little white teeth will come. It will pull my hair, and my beard. [*Gradually approaching Rhoda and placing his arm about her*] That little baby will be our grandchild, Rhoda. Our grandchild! [*Gently bringing Rhoda's head to his breast, and patting her cheek, lovingly. Mrs. Merrybone looks in at the window up L.C. The Judge beyond her*]

CURTAIN

KNAVE AND QUEEN

By Sir Charles L. Young, Bart., and Bronson Howard

THIS play was not produced.

TEXT AND SOURCE

The text is based on a photostatic copy of the typescript of the play with corrections in Howard's own handwriting. These corrections are incorporated into the present text without special marking. Corrections in spelling, punctuation, and mechanical form have been made where necessary; otherwise the text stands in its original and complete form. The title-page of the typescript is as follows: Knave and Queen [which is a handwritten revision of the earlier typed title, "Ivers Dean"]/ A/ Comedy [which is a handwritten revision of the earlier typed subtitle, "Drama"]/ in/ Three Acts/ by/ Sir Charles L. Young, Bart.,/ and/ Bronson Howard.

No source of the play has been identified.

CHARACTERS[1]

Paul Daly

Mr. David Chilcote, *a retired merchant*

Capt. Edward Chilcote, *his son*

Mark Fleming, *barrister*

Mr. Whyte Browne

Robert, *a gamekeeper*

A Detective

Magdalen Dorme

Mrs. Chilcote

Kate, *her daughter*

Mary

ACT I: IVERS DEAN. THE KNAVE.

ACT II: THE DRAWING-ROOM OF IVERS DEAN. THE QUEEN.

ACT III: ALSO THE OLD NORMAN RUINS. THE GAME.

[1] In the typescript copy of the play there are the following handwritten notations opposite the indicated characters:

Paul Daly	Fonsberg
Mr. David Chilcote	Comic old man of the hearty style
Capt. Edward Chilcote	Willard
Mark Fleming	Norris
Mr. Whyte Browne	Eccentric fop
A detective	Make up and action without a line
Magdalen Dorme	Rosa Rand
Mrs. Chilcote	Louisa Morse
Kate	Estelle Mortimer [?]
Mary	Josie Batchelden

ACT I.

SCENE: *Ivers Dean, outside the garden. The quaint chimneys of the Dean seen above the foliage, R.U. corner. A low wall or hedge running across stage, with gate up C. A stile, L., at about third entrance. Ruins seen in the distance at back, L.C., perched on a precipice. Their form should be in accordance with the scene of Act III.*

DISCOVERED: *At rise of curtain, Mary enters at gate, C., from garden, with a basket on each arm. She is singing. If she can sing, she'd better sing a full song before going on with the act.*

MARY. Let me see. The left one is for old Mrs. Churchly—and the jellies and things in the right are for the curate's sick wife. I trot around with so many bundles and baskets, I get them mixed up sometimes. Ha, ha, ha! Yesterday I took Miss Magdalen's cast-off gown to that poor widower with one boy baby. Ha, ha, ha! What with a gentleman running in my mistress' head —and a gentleman's gentleman running in mine—we are getting everything so confused at Ivers Dean. [*Sings, and is going over stile L. She starts back*] Who's this? Oh! One of those *tramps*. [*Enter Paul Daly, over stile L. He stops on its top, looks at Mary a moment, steps down. He has the general appearance of a tramp*]

PAUL. I beg your pardon—allow me. [*Offers to assist her over the stile. She tosses her head, avoids him, and steps on the stile, looking back at him contemptuously. She begins to sing and disappears, her voice dying away gradually, Paul looking after her*] My polite attentions have been rejected. If she had been a peeress of the realm, she would have given me her hand and thanked me for helping her over the stile. But she isn't a peeress of the realm. We must make allowances. [*Looks about him*] Snug little place; I wonder what's the best policy to be pursued here. [*Sits on the stile*] Ask for what you can get—or get what you can, without asking. Well, I haven't been in polite society for so long that I may as well do the civil thing for a change. I'll call at the back door; I should think a tale of woe would find them at home. Let me see, ah—yes—I remember; I'm an asthmatic workingman begging my way to London to see my only daughter before she's entirely dead of consumption. [*Enter Mark Fleming, on stile L. He looks about, as if hunting his way. Sees Paul, comes down, pauses R.*] I ask your pardon, sir—but would you kindly let me know how far it is to London?

MARK. Five and forty miles or thereabouts. [*Crosses to R.*]

PAUL. Heaven help me—will my strength last?

MARK. What's the matter?

PAUL. Oh, nothing, thank you kindly, sir—nothing—merely hunger; five and forty miles to tramp and not a penny for a loaf of bread.

MARK. Half a mile further on and you will find a very excellent institution called the Union, where you can stop and get relief.

PAUL. Thank you kindly again, sir, but I'd rather walk on. I'm a very poor man, sir; but even hunger cannot tempt me to part with my self-respect. Honest pride is all that I have left in the world.

MARK. Here's a sixpence.

PAUL. [*Obsequiously taking it*] Thank you, sir. You have saved me the humiliation of begging for charity. [*Exits through gate, C., moving to house R.*]

MARK. [*Laughing*] Now, I wonder what that fellow's definition of the word "begging" is. A queer lot, these tramps. They always interest me. They're such original devils; such a keen perception of the ludicrous. Honest pride—*beautiful!* It seems as though I know that fellow's face, by the way. I've seen it in the dock. A barrister becomes as sharp as a detective in the matter of faces. Where the deuce have I got? I wish I'd taken the dogcart Ned sent down for me. I'm in a labyrinth of prescriptive paths. This looks like Rosamond's Bower—in the middle of the labyrinth. I could swear some beautiful captive was imprisoned here. There's the touch of a woman's hand in every rosebush, a *young* woman, at that. A bed of violets—[*Looking over the wall*] "L-o-v-e." Of course, it's a young woman. I see her hand in that word—and her heart, too. Horticultural spelling. On the bark of that old beech down there, I distinctly saw two names—"Edward" and "Magdalen." This can't be far from Chilcote Hall; I wonder if Ned Chilcote—Pshaw! He's a captain in His Majesty's service. I'm in love myself, but I'm not such a fool as to go cutting my signature on the trees. "Kate Chilcote—Mark Fleming, barrister!" How would that look on the bark of an oak? Here comes fair Rosamond's pretty maid. My curiosity is piqued. [*Reenter Mary by stile, with empty baskets, singing*] Will you kindly tell me whether I am anywhere near Chilcote Hall?

MARY. Straight through the shrubbery—only a few steps, sir.

MARK. Only a few steps! [*Aside*] Suspicious proximity.

MARY. [*Aside*] A friend of young Captain Chilcote, I suppose, coming to visit him?

MARK. [*Aside*] I'll cross-examine the witness. [*Aloud*] And this little cottage is—

MARY. It belongs to my mistress, sir—Miss Dorme.

MARK. Miss Magdalen Dorme?

MARY. Yes, sir.

MARK. [*Aside*] The unerring instinct of a barrister! "Edward—Magdalen." [*Aloud*] An elderly lady.

MARY. Nothing of the kind, sir. There isn't a sweeter young lady than my mistress in the whole country.

MARK. Oh—ah—precisely. I was thinking of an aunt of hers.

MARY. She hasn't any aunt, sir.

MARK. Oh—I'm sorry to hear her aunt is dead.

MARY. She never had any aunt that I know of.

MARK. That pains me still more. It is better to have loved and lost—an aunt—than never to have loved at all. Will you kindly answer me one more question? Have you ever seen a—a Captain Edward Chilcote, of Chilcote Hall?

MARY. Have I— Ha, ha, ha, ha! Have I ever— Ha, ha, ha, ha!—[*Beckons to him archly, he crosses*] I will ask *you* a question. [*Reaching up and speaking in his ear*] Did you ever see your own shadow? Ha, ha, ha, ha! [*Going, looks back*] Ha, ha, ha, ha! [*Mark exchanges winks and nods with her. She sings and goes off through gate C.*]

MARK. Sly dog, Ned is. During my three-months tour abroad he has given me every possible detail about their new home—and how they all moved into it—and not one word about this little dovecot under the eaves, and its occupant. And yet he has sworn to me, by all that is sacred in friendship, he hopes I shall become his brother-in-law. By jove! I have an interest in the family. I'll see what this turtledove looks like. "Edward—Magdalen." Ha, ha, ha! On the old beech— Ha, ha, ha! I'll astonish him by knowing all about it, when we first meet. [*Moving to gate*] Let me see—what excuse shall I give? Impudence befriend me. [*His hand on gate, looks off*] Who's this? A gentleman—eh—oh—it's Whyte Browne. Now how did that mild idiot get so far away from London as this? Perhaps he's a rival of Chilcote—in the affections of fair Rosamond. Ha, ha, ha! [*Enter Whyte Browne, L.1.E.*]

BROWNE. [*Stopping, L., and looking at Mark through his glasses*] Ah—Fleming.

MARK. Ah—Browne.

BROWNE. Returned from the Continent?

MARK. Yes. Money all spent; and you?

BROWNE. I'm looking after my property.

MARK. Your—property? I knew you had a dog, my dear Browne. Did he stray so far from London as this?

BROWNE. You haven't heard of my good luck? Dead uncle. Three intervening heirs. Railroad smashup—quick consumption—typhoid fever. Special providence, you know.

MARK. If Providence keeps on at this rate, the next heir has a remarkably good chance.

BROWNE. Do you see those old ruins over yonder?

MARK. Yes—the remains of a Norman castle apparently—perched on a precipice, and frowning on the peaceful country it once commanded; I was admiring the old castle as I came along.

BROWNE. That's my property.

MARK. Ah. I dare say you have plenty of tenants. I hope the bats pay their rent promptly.

BROWNE. Oh—I've got lots of other tenants, you know. That precipice is two hundred feet high. The precipice is my property, too. I own all the land around here—except this little nook and the Chilcote Hall estate.

MARK. Railroad smashup—quick consumption—typhoid fever—convenient things to have in the family. It's an ill wind that blows nobody any good.

BROWNE. I'm going to get married, too.

MARK. That's another sort of a breeze.

BROWNE. You used to know Miss Kate Chilcote.

MARK. [Quickly] Yes—why? What about Miss Kate Chilcote.

BROWNE. Nothing in particular. She's the woman I'm going to marry.

MARK. The devil you are! [He walks down under excitement. Then upstage, and down again. Browne watches him through his glasses; then turns and looks at the ruins]

BROWNE. My uncle once told me those were the best preserved ruins of their size, in England.

MARK. You are going to marry Kate Chilcote?

BROWNE. Y-e-s. [Mark again moves about, excited. Browne watches him as before, then turns up] My uncle said they were first-class ruins, considering their age; and property like that improves with time, you know. They will be particularly valuable to my great-grandchildren.

MARK. Kate Chilcote has accepted you as her husband?

BROWNE. Y-e-s. [Movement as before] That is—the old ruins—I mean— the old lady—Kate's mother—she and I arranged it between us. I haven't mentioned the subject to the girl, herself. I never met her but twice. She was talking to another fellow both times; and I went off to play billiards.

MARK. Miss Chilcote herself has had nothing to say upon the subject?

BROWNE. N-o. The old ruins—the—the old lady—fixed it up with *me,* you know—and so I let her fix it up with *her,* too. [*Turns*] This is the best view we can get of those ruins.

MARK. You have no affection for Miss Chilcote?

BROWNE. N-o. But I haven't the slightest objection to her, you know. [*Turns*] There's a story to go with those ruins. It belongs to the property.

MARK. I will be frank with you. *I* am interested in Miss Kate Chilcote— and I have every reason to believe that she returns my affection.

BROWNE. Oh!

MARK. [*Approaching him, and speaking sternly*] I tell you this; I will not stand quietly by, and see her heart and mine sacrificed—for the sake of your "property" and her mother's ambition.

BROWNE. That's all right, old boy. I'm in no hurry to get married. There's plenty other old ladies in the world. [*Mark bursts into a fit of laughter, reels across R. and supports himself against a tree*]

MARK. Ha, ha, ha, ha! Here's a rival worthy of my steel! Ha, ha, ha, ha!

BROWNE. You *talk* with the old ruins—I mean—the old lady. I'll not stand in the way; only if she insists on having me for a son-in-law, of course, I'll marry the girl.

MARK. Ha, ha, ha, ha! All right, Browne—ha, ha, ha! I'll talk with the old lady, ha, ha, ha!

BROWNE. My uncle told me a pair of lovers once fell down the precipice from those ruins. Some of the stones gave way. They were both killed. The property was badly damaged.

MARK. Helloa—there's Ned Chilcote, now. Look at him, his eyes fixed upon the ground—his hands thrust deep into his pockets—a perfect stranger would know he was in love.

BROWNE. Y-e-s. He wants to marry the lady that lives here in Ivers Dean —Miss Magdalen Dorme. I can't imagine how he ever happened to *think* of her—*she* hasn't got any mother.

MARK. He'll run against a tree directly. There, he's nearly knocked down a young oak. [*Enter Captain Edward Chilcote, R., rubbing his forehead and straightening out his hat*] Ned, old fellow!

ED. Eh? Oh—Fleming!

MARK. [*Taking his hand*] The oak had the best of it, old boy! Ha, ha, ha! What's all this about? Dreaming?

ED. Oh—nothing—I—I was *thinking.* I'm delighted to see you returned, Mark. Ah—Browne—you will find the ladies back there—they are coming this way.

BROWNE. Y-e-s. [*Going*] Fleming—talk it over with the old lady. Don't mind me.

MARK. Oh, I shan't. [*Exit Browne, R.*] Well, Ned—your groom and dog-cart met me at the station; but it was such a lovely afternoon I preferred to walk. Your man gave me simple directions for finding the short cut across the fields. I found several; but unfortunately none of them took me anywhere in particular. In despair I turned off at right angles and suddenly found myself close to this—what shall I call it—this charming bower.

ED. Heigh-ho— It is indeed a lovely spot.

MARK. Heigh-ho— [*Imitating his sentimental air*] It is indeed! Ha, ha, ha, ha! Ned, I've found you out. I've discovered your fair Rosamond. But as there's no jealous Queen Eleanor in the case, why so much mystery? Ha ha, ha! "Edward-Magdalen"—on the old beech yonder— Ha, ha, ha, ha! A bed of violets. "*L-o-v-e!*" Ha, ha, ha, ha! The maid assured me that you are as familiar an apparition here as a man's own shadow. Come—that's all I know about it—you must tell me the rest, yourself. Trouble in the way? The governor objects?

ED. The governor never objects to anything.

MARK. Mamma, perhaps?

ED. You know my mother's weakness—*family*.

MARK. Ah—I see. The maid said the young lady hadn't any aunt. And Browne just told me she hadn't any mother.

ED. She is an orphan.

MARK. No father, either. That's a bad beginning for a *family*, certainly. She is equally deficient I dare say, in the more remote branches of the ancestral tree. What does that matter to you? If a beautiful woman is ready and willing to do her fair share in providing a man with a posterity, he needn't trouble himself about her ancestry.

ED. My mother is forever telling me that I must make what she is pleased to call a "*good match*."

MARK. None of your common lucifers. She prefers to consign you to the infernal regions of a loveless marriage.

ED. My father would as soon have a fresh attack of the gout as cross her wishes. He says he prefers it, indeed.

MARK. Precisely. The *gout* can be cured.

ED. Who are we—the Chilcotes? Wool—trade—success—money! My father once swept a warehouse. I admire him for his energy. We are rich now. But who are *we*, that I should suffer the horrors of aristocratic affectation? Common people have, at least, one privilege—marrying for love. Throw that privilege away—what do we receive in return? Smiles of contempt from those above us—and from those beneath us—alike! Chilcote Hall! It's name was "Chucksters" before we bought it, three months ago. Mother rechristened it. Bah! If she *must* feed her ambition, let her do it on something besides my heart. [*Crossing*]

MARK. [*With a wise air*] Ah, Ned! I dare say your mother is right after all. A man in love is not a judge of these things; she stands between you and your love, for your own good. Your mother is a wise woman, Ned; she is a wise woman. Here they come. [*Aside, looking out*] That young jackanapes, with his new property, is talking with the old lady. If she stands between me and my love—the infernal old female idiot!—I'll make her my mother-in-law, in spite of her! [*Crosses and pats Ned on the shoulder*] Listen to your mother, Ned; she's a wise woman. [*He walks up, Edward drops into a seat. Enter Mrs. Chilcote and Browne, R. She is talking with Browne and does not see Mark*]

MRS. C. Ha, ha, ha! Ah, Mr. Browne! Ha, ha, ha! If you are as entertaining to the young girls as you are to their mothers—I wonder they give you any peace. You have such a fund of native wit.

BROWNE. Y-e-s. It came with the property, I suppose.

MARK. [*Aside*] Special providence! Like the typhoid fever.

MRS. C. I'm sure you and my darling Kate will be very happy together.

BROWNE. Y-e-s—of course. But *you* must tend to all that sort o'thing. I've got to look after the property, you know.

MARK. [*Coming down*] A-h-e-m.

MRS. C. [*Turning*] Ah— [*Draws up coldly, they bow*] I am glad you have returned to England.

MARK. Thank you. [*Aside*] What an outrageous fib.

MRS. C. [*Aside*] Why *did* Edward ask *him* to visit us, just at this time!

BROWNE. [*Moving to C., between them*] Oh—by the way—Mrs. Chilcote; Mr. Fleming said he wanted to speak to you— [*Fleming springs to him and pulls his coat*] Eh? H'm? He wanted to speak to you about— [*Fleming pulls his coat*] H'm?

MARK. [*Apart*] Leave that to me—damn it! I'll speak to her when I think best.

BROWNE. [*Apart*] All right, old boy. [*To Mrs. Chilcote*] Anything Mr. Fleming says to you—why—don't mind me, you know. [*Walks up. Looks at ruins*]

MRS. C. [*Walking down R.*] What can the man mean by that? [*Enter Mr. Chilcote, followed by Kate, R.*]

MR. C. Ah—my dear—you and Mr. Browne hurried on ahead. Mr. Fleming!

MARK. Mr. Chilcote, Miss Kate.

KATE. Mr. Fleming. [*Moving toward him*]

MRS. C. [*Sharply*] Kate. [*Kate stops, bows to Fleming, who returns it, and then walks to her mother*]

MR. C. I hope you enjoyed yourself on the Continent, Mr. Fleming.

MARK. As much as I possibly could—under the circumstances.

MR. C. Circumstances? [*Glances at Kate, then at Fleming*] Oh—yes—I see. My dear boy—you must never allow circumstances to trouble you. *I* never do.

ED. [*Aside*] No, hang it! He never does. I wish he did.

MR. C. There are so many circumstances in this world. We can't dodge them, you know; and we might as well make the best of them. Weather is a circumstance. Loss of property is a circumstance. A mother is a circumstance. A wife is a circumstance. I never allow circumstances to make me uncomfortable.

MARK. Heigh-ho—a very delightful philosophy.

MR. C. The great secret of happiness is never to allow oneself to be unhappy.

MARK. *Prima facie,* an excellent theory. I trust it works in practice?

MR. C. Perfectly. Thirty years' experience. Try it. Ah—Browne. [*Walks up; Browne has been standing with his back to the audience and looking at the ruins*]

BROWNE. Well today, Mr. Chilcote?

MR. C. Never better, never better.

ED. [*Aside*] The governor never *is* better; always at his best.

MR. C. [*Looking off*] How are the ruins today?

BROWNE. Never better, thank you.

MR. C. Still there, I see.

BROWNE. Y-e-s. That's what I like about ruins. You can always depend on them.

MRS. C. [*Suddenly*] Kate! [*Kate has been talking, L.C., with Mark. She moves to her mother*]

MARK. [*Aside*] Hang the old female ruins—as Browne calls her. She'll be my mother-in-law yet! [*Aloud*] Charming spot—Ivers Dean. It belongs to your estate, I suppose Mr. Chilcote?

MRS. C. It *ought* to but it *doesn't*—heigh-ho.

MARK. Somebody bought it over his head, I presume.

MRS. C. Quite the contrary. It was cut from under his feet.

MR. C. *Is* it any use, my dear, referring to the past! That was only a circumstance, my love—only a circumstance.

Mrs. C. Circumstance, indeed! Ivers Dean belonged to Miss Chilcote, my husband's only sister. Of course she ought to have left it to us. But she was an eccentric creature; she bequeathed it, with a few hundreds a year, to a girl whom her ridiculous philanthropy had rescued from a depth of infamy.

Ed. [*Springing to his feet*] Mother! You have no right to say that.

Mrs. C. Edward!

Mr. C. The Fifth Commandment, my dear boy, the Fifth Commandment.

Mrs. C. From a depth of infamy, I repeat.

Ed. And I repeat, you have no right to say that.

Mrs. C. Oh! Oh! Heigh-ho—to be spoken to like this by one's own son! [*Handkerchief to eyes*]

Mr. C. Never mind, my dear, it's much better than being spoken to like this by anybody else's son. Indulge in a little lively repartee, it will do you good. Say something strong.

Mrs. C. David—you are silly.

Mr. C. By all means, my dear. Say it again.

Mrs. C. You are simply ridiculous.

Mr. C. Go on, my love. It does you good and it doesn't do me any harm.

Mrs. C. You are *too* absurd to notice.

Mr. C. I never allow circumstances to disturb my serenity.

Mrs. C. [*Spitefully*] Oh!—

Mr. C. This is a circumstance.

Mrs. C. [*Angrily*] Mr. Fleming!

Mark. [*Starting from Kate's side*] I beg your pardon.

Mrs. C. I was telling you that Ivers Dean *ought* to belong to us. That it was bequeathed away from us by the abominable artifices of a designing young woman, a female Jesuit—a— [*Enter Magdalen at gate*] Oh, Miss Dorme, we were just talking about you. How are you, my dear? You look rather pale.

Mag. [*Coming through gate*] Thanks, Mrs. Chilcote, I am quite well. [*Crosses to Kate*]

Kate. [*Kissing her*] Dear Magdalen, I haven't seen you for two whole days.

Mag. I have missed you so much.

Mrs. C. [*Aside*] Thinks to creep into my affections through my child. Viper!

Mr. C. Magdalen, my love, our friend, Mr. Fleming.

Mark. I was very nearly trespassing on your grounds, Miss Dorme. Indeed I almost mistook Ivers Dean at first for Chilcote Hall.

Mrs. C. [*Aside*] The idea!

MARK. I should have walked straight into your garden, but a wretched tramp stopped me with the usual tale of woe.

MAG. [*Quietly*] A tramp?

MARK. If nothing worse. The man reminded me strongly of that which a barrister never forgets—his first brief. A murder case. Verdict of manslaughter. Penal servitude for twenty years. There is a strong family likeness among villains. The tramp *reminds* me of the clever rascal.

MAG. Indeed! I saw him, as he hobbled up to the back door; I should judge, however, that he was merely an ordinary beggar. Heigh-ho—it is a dreadful thing to beg. I know it, myself, by experience.

MRS. C. [*Aside*] Mock humility!

MR. C. But troubles like that have their bright side, too. They sharpen the edge of present pleasure. Now, I remember when I swept the warehouse out and put up the shutters—

MRS. C. David!

MR. C. My love?

MRS. C. We will proceed with our walk. [*Crossing L.*]

MR. C. Plenty of time for that, my dear. We're going nowhere in particular and it doesn't make the slightest difference when we get there. As I was saying—when I look back to the time that I used to sweep out the—

MRS. C. [*L.*] David!

MR. C. My love! [*She takes his arm and walks him L. He continuing, trying to look back*] When I used to sweep out—

MRS. C. Mr. Chilcote! You chose the honorable career of a merchant, in your early days. That is sufficient. We are all aware of the fact.

MR. C. Yes, but my dear— [*She hurries him out L. She suddenly reappears*]

MRS. C. Kate! [*Kate starts from conversation with Mark, R., and is crossing to her mother*]

MR. C. [*Reappearing*] I swept out the warehouse every—

MRS. C. Mr. Chilcote! [*Hurries out with him*]

MR. C. [*Heard without*] Every day for two years, my dear—and I put up the shutters every— [*His voice dies away in the distance, as if muffled by Mrs. Chilcote's hand*]

MARK. [*Moving quickly to Kate, L.C.*] Kate!

KATE. Mark!

MARK. I don't think your respected mother will miss you for a few moments. She has more imperative duties before her. [*He gives her his arm. They walk down L. She sits, near him*]

ED. [*Moving to Magdalen*] Magdalen! [*They move to R., half upstage and sit. Browne walks down to near Kate and Mark. He stands a moment, as if expecting to enter into conversation. They continue absorbed in each other. Browne walks across to Magdalen and Edward, R. They are also devoted to each other, without noticing him. He walks C., and looks at each couple alternately*]

BROWNE. One—two—three—four—five. I'm the *odd* one. Figures never lie. Fleming is wasting his time. He ought to be talking with the old lady. I'll go and look at the property. [*Exits L. In the following scene, each couple is absorbed in conversation, without noticing the other. Each couple converses in appropriate dumb show when not speaking aloud. There must be no break in this business. Rehearse following scene very carefully!*]

ED. [*To Magdalen*] Magdalen—Magdalen! I can bear this suspense no longer.

KATE. [*To Mark*] Do have patience.

MARK. But this confounded Whyte Browne—

ED. Tell me all you feel, Magdalen.

MARK. [*To Kate*] Tell him he's a donkey, at once—and have done with it.

MAG. [*To Edward*] I dare not tell you all that is in my thoughts, Edward!

MARK. Why shouldn't you? He *is* a donkey—ten to one he'll agree with you. You and I *must* be man and wife, Kate!

ED. Misery for both!

KATE. Mother is so determined on this marriage.

MAG. Your mother is determined this marriage shall *not* take place.

ED. Of course, I respect my mother, Magdalen—

MARK. [*Aside*] Hang the old ruins! [*To Kate*] If your respected mother continues to insist—

ED. I promise you, Magdalen, I shall find means of overcoming her objections— [*Earnestly*] or else!— [*Magdalen checks him*]

MARK. If worse comes to worst—we must let the old lady—ah—your respected mother—slide.

KATE. Oh, Mark!

MARK. I beg your pardon—that's a *legal* phrase; Blackstone—two-thirteen —case of Bardell versus Pickwick—old law Latin.

ED. Let me have *some* hope. Tell me, once—with your own lips—do you love me, Magdalen? [*Magdalen turns away*]

KATE. [*Aside*] If it was only proper! I wish I could tell him how much I love him.

MAG. [*Shaking her head*] Your mother is right. There is a social barrier between us.

ED. We will *defy* society!

KATE. I—I— [*Crying*] I'm going to live an old maid, Mark.

MAG. A woman who does that makes herself miserable for life. [*Mark goes on earnestly with Kate as if making ardent love*]

ED. [*Vehemently, but in subdued voice*] Magdalen, I *love* you! How madly! My long—my almost silent devotion—is the proof. I can bear this no longer. You *must* speak the word. [*She rises*] Leave obstacles to me— I will surmount them. I have waited long enough for this. Speak *now*—or bid me leave you, forever. I demand it as my right. Magdalen!

MAG. [*Turning to him*] Edward! [*He clasps her in his arms. Kate suddenly starts up, with a little scream as Mark is about to put his arm about her*]

KATE. Oh!

MARK. Kate! [*She turns suddenly to him. He catches her in his arms*]

ED. Angel!

MRS. C. [*Without, calling*] K-a-t-e!

MARK. The—devil! [*Mark drops Kate, who staggers and catches herself. Mark walks up L. Looks at ruins. Edward up and down R. Enter Mrs. Chilcote, C. She stops, L.C., looking at the others in turn, and drawing up indignantly*]

MRS. C. Kate! [*Points L.*] Go to your father! [*Kate goes out, L., demurely. Mrs. Chilcote stands in a majestic attitude*]

MARK. [*Aside. Looking at Mrs. Chilcote*] Melrose Abbey looks majestic; I'd like to see her in the moonlight.

MRS. C. Edward!

ED. Mr. Fleming and I will proceed to Chilcote Hall, mother. [*He moves to Magdalen, apart*] I will return to you, Magdalen. [*Magdalen passes him; turns; they bow. She passes up R.C. Edward about to go. Mark moves down to him and taps him on the shoulder*]

MARK. Respect your mother's advice, Edward. She is a wise woman.

ED. [*Aside*] Magdalen has given me new life. [*Exits R.*]

MARK. Miss Dorme. [*They bow*] Mrs. Chilcote. [*They bow profoundly, she very haughty. He turns away, looks back at her. Aside*] Old Kenilworth! She'll be my mother-in-law yet. [*Exits R. Mrs. Chilcote about to go. Magdalen moves forward a few steps with dignity, making a slight sound, to attract attention. Mrs. Chilcote partly turns, inclines her head haughtily and sails out L.*]

MAG. He loves me! He loves me! Could he have spoken to me as he has spoken if he knew the history of the woman to whom he blindly offers his devotion? Would he not rather hate me if I told him all? No, his nature is too noble. Had I the choice into what ranks of society I should be born? If I have been an outcast and a vagabond, does not the verdict of infinite justice acquit me of all guilt? What are the poor street arabs, that they should be branded at their melancholy christening with the felon's mark? Are they not as human as the rest? Miss Chilcote took me from a workhouse, God bless her! She made me what the world calls a lady. The knowledge of Edward's love almost makes me mad. Why should I not accept it? The story of my earlier years is buried in the past. [*Paul appears at the gate*] So it shall never cast a gloom about him. My future unclouded life shall make his happy. [*Moving toward house*]

PAUL. I beg your pardon, ma'am.

MAG. [*Starting*] What do you want here?

PAUL. Merely, ma'am, that I am nearly starving, and your servants would not listen to my tale of woe. Starving, ma'am. I want a crust of bread.

MAG. A crust of bread. Oh, you shall have it at once. [*Advances to gate. Paul's eyes are fixed on her, he does not move*] Let me pass and I will get for you what you want.

PAUL. I want something besides a crust of bread, I want—*recognition!*— [*She starts back*] Magdalen Dorme! Why, don't you know me, Maggie?

MAG. Paul Daly!

PAUL. [*Coming through gate*] You recognize me.

MAG. Paul Daly, here!

PAUL. By a piece of that old good luck of mine which you used to admire so much—Paul Daly, *here!*

MAG. I never thought to see *you* again. I believed—

PAUL. That I was consigned to a living tomb. You thought that a sentence of penal servitude for twenty years would crush me down and kill me.

MAG. An escaped felon!

PAUL. And a very hungry one. Now, Maggie, darling—

MAG. Silence! Choose your language better.

PAUL. Beggars can't afford to be choosers. The words were once familiar enough.

MAG. *What* do you want?

PAUL. Want? Something to eat at present. The servant pointed you out as the owner of this house. I've been watching and waiting, till your grand friends went away—to introduce myself. Get me something to eat at once. [*Magdalen passes up and out at the gate*] The owner of this property! So the servant said. How has Magdalen managed that, I wonder. She was always a clever girl. But she was troubled with that inconvenient thing which the preachers call a "conscience." It was always a mystery to me where she picked up such a *clean* conscience in the *filthy* streets of London. Hang the girl! I was in love with ner. But she put on airs, as if she had as good a right to be virtuous as a duchess with fifty thousand a year. I'm in love with her yet! And she is even more beautiful in her fashionable dress than she was in her rags. The prison walls do not shut out dreams. I have dreamed of her, wandering about the streets—an outcast as of old. Bah! The world calls her above me, now. We shall see; I can look up as well as down! How did Magdalen get all this? *I* can't imagine any other method than a forged will. But *her* notions are so different from mine. She has obtained it by *fair* means. Ah—well—heigh-ho—I don't find fault with her for being honest—though that raises her higher above me than her wealth and her fine clothes. *Is she out of my reach?* [*Reenter Magdalen, with basket*]

MAG. There—satisfy your hunger. [*Paul takes basket, sits R.C., eats. He sees a silver fork, puts it in his pocket. Throws the case knife away, and uses a clasp knife from his own pocket*]

PAUL. [*Eating*] I suppose you have forgotten what hunger is. It is astonishing how soon a full stomach forgets such trifles. How did you manage to get all this?

MAG. The lady to whom this house belonged found me in London, four years ago. She rescued me from want. She gave me more than wealth—an education. We came to love each other dearly. She left me independent.

PAUL. Ah—m'm—a female philanthropist. Wine! Port wine! Old vintage. You're a real lady bountiful, Magdalen, my dear— Isn't it easy to be good—when you are rich? What an honorable, high-minded man I should be in the country, with a few spare thousands a year. With my experience, what a splendid judge I should make.

MAG. You have been in penal servitude nearly five years—

PAUL. Four years and eight months by the prison clock.

MAG. Has not the just reward of crime taught you to reflect—has it not softened your heart?

PAUL. Soften my heart! Go to Dartmoor! Gaze across the prison walls and see what softening influence in the wide, misty, miserable, space that lies beyond.

MAG. Paul, for the sake of the past, for the sake of the time when we were children together—for the sake of the rough boyish affection which you showed me then, I am willing to do all in my power, as I myself have been rescued, now to rescue you.

PAUL. Now, that's what I call quite sister-like. What's your income? It'll cost something to rescue me, you know. [*Looks about him*] Pretty little house —garden—lawn—conservatory—rare exotics—a brougham, perhaps—say a thousand pounds a year, what's to be my share of all this?

MAG. *Your—share?* Nothing whatever.

PAUL. But you said you were going to *rescue* me! Philanthropy, like every other luxury, costs money.

MAG. Paul Daly! Let us understand each other. You think to trade upon your knowledge of my past. I will not *buy* your silence. Come, vagabond and felon—go round the village—go to Chilcote Hall—go to the great houses in the neighborhood, where I am received as a guest, and say of me what you please! Which of us will suffer most from notoriety?

PAUL. As clear a head as ever, Maggie; the game is in your hands— [*Aside*] at present. My turn will come. [*Aloud*] Rescue me in your own way, and as economically as you choose.

MAG. I will give you fifty pounds on one condition, leave England. Go to America—or Australia. Write to me. I will then endeavor to give you the chance of starting afresh and earning a competence by honest work.

PAUL. Fifty pounds—that's a very small amount to be rescued on. Suppose we call it a hundred.

MAG. Very well—a hundred. Wait at the Duke's Head Inn, in the village. I will obtain the money, and send it to you by the servant, whom you just met. She knows you by sight.

PAUL. Why not wait here?

MAG. Because *I prefer not!* What guarantee have I that you will keep your word?

PAUL. My *personal security*— if I hang about England, I'm likely to love my "personal security."

MAG. Well—go.

PAUL. No tender farewell at parting?

MAG. Go.

PAUL. [*Going L. Turns fiercely upon her*] And if I should return with your money, and hurl it at your feet! If I claim something dearer to me than all the wealth in your possession? You are more beautiful than ever, Magdalen Dorme! [*She recoils from him in horror; then draws up with scorn and points L.*]

MAG. Go! My servant will wait upon you with the money. [*Paul shrinks from her and goes over stile L.*] He loves me, still! The same fierce passion that burned in his eyes when they last rested on me. Perhaps his love is more fitting for *me*—than that of Edward Chilcote. [*Drops her head into her hand and walks down L. Reenter Edward R.*]

ED. [*Moving toward her*] Magdalen!

MAG. [*Turning on him suddenly*] Leave me!

ED. Leave—you!

MAG. [*Rapidly*] You have known me as a poor girl—the recipient of your good aunt's charity. I will tell you all. She took me from the *workhouse*. You start! There is more. I was an outcast girl upon the streets of London—*pure* —Heaven knows! But a companion of the men and women who fill our prisons. *They* may claim me, *any* time, for their *comrade*. Leave me—Edward Chilcote—leave me!

ED. Magdalen! [*Turning to her eagerly, as if to embrace her. She repulses him*]

MAG. You *still* love me. You will *still* make me your wife?

ED. A thousand times—yes!—Magdalen.

MAG. Come to me again, Edward—in half a year from now.

ED. Half a year!

MAG. Promise me not to look at me—except by accident—never to speak to me again—not even to write—within all that time. Seek *other* women— more fitting companions for such as you. Come to me again at the end of that time—if you like! [*Walking up to gate*] You will find me here—alone. [*At gate, opening it*]

ED. Magdalen!

MAG. Nay—I insist. As you love me, Edward—do not ask me to do that, in haste, which might make both of us wretched for life. *I* can wait. *You* must wait, too. [*Exits into garden. Edward turns sadly R.C.*]

ED. Six months! Heigh-ho—eternity! [*Paul Daly reappears over stile. He approaches. Edward glances sharply at him. He extends his hand. Edward drops a coin into his hand, and walks sadly out R.*]

PAUL. [*Looking after him*] Bless your kind heart, sir! I will *save* you from this unfortunate marriage. [*Sharply*] *I,* too, shall be here at the end of half a year!

ACT II.

SCENE: *Drawing-room at Ivers Dean. Evidence of a woman's taste. A clock, R. A cabinet, L. Double window up C. Opening to veranda, door, L.2.E. Door, R.2.E. It will be well, if convenient, to have a distant view of the ruins seen through windows.*

DISCOVERED: *Magdalen, reading an old letter.*

MAG. [*Reading*] "My darling Magdalen: You drove me from you this afternoon, without one loving word of farewell. Six months! Be it so. But I *must* write this to you. It seems an eternity to me. I have noted the very moments. It was half past three that we parted. I will obey you to the letter—

six months to the moment—cost me what suffering it may. I appreciate the delicacy which prompts you to enact the sacrifice. Trust me. I shall return at the expiration of the time. I shall not lose a single moment. Lovingly and sadly—your eviled lover—Edward." [*She folds the letter and places it in her bosom*] The six months have passed! All of it but—let me see—[*Looking at clock*] forty minutes; ten minutes before three. He will obey me to the letter, he said—and he will not lose a minute. Heigh-ho—that letter was written six months ago. Edward Chilcote has been in scenes of gayety since then, with merry tourist parties—among the Alps—at Venice—Florence—Rome and Madrid. Beautiful eyes have looked into his; women of culture and blue blood have courted him for his wealth. Heigh-ho— *I* have lingered on alone—one image in my heart and none other in my eyes. He has kept his word to the letter. Once, only, in all that time has a ray of light come to me. [*She walks to cabinet, L., and takes a worn letter from it*] Ha, ha, ha, ha! Poor, dear, stupid Whytie Browne! I love him as if he were my brother. I have worn out his good sweet letter, reading it over and over again. [*Reads*] "My dear Miss Dorme: Pardon me for the liberty I take in writing to you—" Pardon him!—how many times I have *blessed* him for it! "The Alps are awfully high. We've seen lots of ruins. But I like the ruins on my property as well as any of them—" Ha, ha, ha! "Kate and I like each other better and better the longer we travel together. I write to Fleming for her every day or two. The old ruins—" The word "ruins" scratched out. "The old lady still insists that Kate and I shall get married. We are trying to get her out of the notion. But the old lady is so persistent—I'm almost afraid we'll have to marry each other, and leave Fleming out in the cold—" Ha, ha, ha, ha! "Edward Chilcote is the stupidest member of the party—[*She kisses the letter*] He doesn't talk with anybody. None of the young ladies we meet can get him interested at all—[*Kisses letter*] I saw him sitting by himself on a rock, this morning, scratching on a stone with a knife. When he walked away I went to the place. He had scratched your name on the rock. [*She kisses the letter repeatedly*] I thought this might interest you. That's the reason I wrote." The darling fellow! I'll throw my arms about his neck, and kiss him, when we meet—if I'm not on my guard. Heigh-ho. This letter was written *four* months ago; what may not have happened within that time? The family returned yesterday morning. He has made no sign yet. Ah—well—it is not time. He is obeying me to the letter. [*She goes up and sits at window, looking out*] The dear old ruins—that Whytie Browne is so fond of. Heigh-ho— How many hours have I spent on the crumbling parapet—during the past six months—trying to read, and wondering if Edward would come back to me. Heigh-ho, I dreamed myself a maiden of the days of chivalry, looking over the hills, and watching for her knight. [*Enter Mary, L.*]

MARY. [*Aside*] There she is! She's always there—looking up at them ruins—except when she climbs the hill and is sitting on the big tower. I'm glad Mr. Edward has come home. I've been awful afraid she'd come tumbling down the precipice some day; and people might say it was on purpose. [*Aloud*] Miss Magdalen.

MAG. [*Rising*] Mary— [*Comes down*]

MARY. I've just been over to Chilcote Hall, Miss Magdalen.

MAG. Yes. [*Eagerly*]

MARY. I went to see Miss Kate's waiting-maid. Miss Kate was not well yesterday.

MAG. Kate! Yes, I knew there was some good cause—or she would have come to see me before this. Kate—yes—and—and—

MARY. Mr. Edward—

MAG. Well!—

MARY. Mr. Edward's gentleman walked back with me, Miss Magdalen.

MAG. Yes—go on.

MARY. He said he saw such lots of pretty waiting-maids travelling on the Continent. [*Magdalen turns away impatiently*] But there wasn't one of them he liked as well as me, Miss Magdalen. He remembered me all this time; I was afraid he might forget me.

MAG. [*Aside*] Another woman's heart has been beating, at Ivers Dean. [*Aloud*] I am glad you are so happy, Mary.

MARY. He says they had an awful time with Mr. Edward, ma'am.

MAG. An—an—awful time—with Mr. Edward?

MARY. Mr. Edward has been as cross as a bear for the whole six months.

MAG. Oh—cross!

MARY. Cross as a bear with a sore head—ma'am. Them's his exact words.

MAG. [*Aside, joyously*] He has been thinking of me!

MARY. He came near kicking William downstairs, ma'am, whenever anything went wrong.

MAG. I'm *so* glad!

MARY. But William says it was very uncomfortable, ma'am, and Mr. Edward kept saying "damn it."

MAG. Dear Edward! *He* has been as miserable as *I* have been. [*Joyously*]

MARY. They were in Naples, and Mrs. Chilcote wanted to go on for three months longer. She was determined to go to Egypt. Mr. Edward said the party might go to Jericho if they wanted to, *he* was coming home; and he took the train—and they telegraphed him to wait at Florence. They all came back with him, Miss Magdalen—and Mr. Edward gave William half a crown nearly every time he looked at him, all the way home. [*Magdalen takes letter from her bosom and kisses it repeatedly*] William said his master told him he would come over here at exactly half past three.

MAG. "Six months to the moment."

MARY. He said his master wouldn't send a note—but he gave William a crown and told him, if *you* happened to hear of it—by accident—he'd give him another crown. I thought I'd help William earn the other crown, Miss Magdalen.

MAG. And here is a crown for *you*, Mary. [*Giving her money*]

MARY. Thank you, miss. I wish Mr. Edward would come back from a six months' tour every day in the year—for *your* sake—Miss Magdalen. [*Exits L.3.E.*]

MAG. [*Reading letter*] "Trust me. I shall return at the expiration of the time. I shall not lose a moment." [*Looks at clock*] How slowly the hands do move! [*Chilcote appears on veranda, at window, C., smiling at Magdalen through the glass*] Mr. Chilcote! Edward's father! [*Runs up and opens lattice*]

MR. C. Glad to see you, my dear. May I come in?

MAG. Certainly. I am delighted to see you back.

MR. C. [*Entering, stepping over sill*] Thank you, my dear. [*Magdalen gives him both hands*] Is that all you've got for me, Maggie—after six months? [*She raises her face. He kisses her*] That's better. That's a very pleasant circumstance.

MAG. You are quite well, Mr. Chilcote?

MR. C. Never better, my dear—never better.

MAG. And your daughter, Kate?

MR. C. Never better, my dear—never—no, Kate isn't quite as well as usual. Fatigued with her journey. Her mother kept her in all day yesterday, and made her stay in bed until after one o'clock today. She was just finishing breakfast when I left the Hall.

MAG. And—and—Mrs. Chilcote—is well?

MR. C. Never better, my dear—never—no. She has another attack of her neuralgia. If it keeps on, I shall go up to London and live at the club. I always do.

MAG. Captain—Edward Chilcote—is—well?

MR. C. Never better, my dear—never—no—not exactly—that is—yes. I never knew him better in my life than since we reached Boulogne on the way home. His mother has had an awful time with that boy, for the last six months. If anything ever made the slightest difference to me, I should say that he was the most uncomfortable travelling companion that could be found in all England. He seemed *determined* not to enjoy anything. He said the cathedral at Cologne was a humbug—a humbug, my dear! The cathedral at Cologne!—a humbug! He turned up his nose at Mount Blanc—his nose, my dear—at the *Alps*! He shrugged his shoulders at the Coliseum in Rome! He spoke in the most disrespectful terms of the Last Judgment—by Michael Angelo; and the language he used to the Venus di Medici was absolutely insulting. His mother wanted to go to Egypt and see the Pyramids—the family tombs of the Pharaohs—as she called 'em. Edward said he didn't care for old families, anyway. He lost his appetite, too. The *only hearty meal* I saw him eat was in the steamer on the Channel—coming back to England.

MAG.   On the Channel? [*Aside*] How he loves me!

MR. C.   He, he, he! I can't imagine what so suddenly transformed my son into a young bear cub. The boy has been a continual source of amusement to *me*. But his mother took it differently.

MAG. [*Aside, nodding her head*]   She is still my enemy.

MR. C.   By the way, Magdalen—I came in to have a chat with you—something—about you—and—Mrs. Chilcote. Sit down, Magdalen, dear. It's a very peculiar matter. [*Magdalen sits*] If anything ever disturbed me, I might feel a little uncomfortable—but I *don't*—only I thought that you ought to know something about it. I will tell you everything, my dear. Mrs. Chilcote is *not your friend*.

MAG.   I am quite aware of that.

MR. C.   Mrs. Chilcote found a letter waiting for her when we arrived at Chilcote Hall, yesterday morning. She became very much excited and immediately sent a dispatch to London. A strange gentleman came up posthaste on the evening train—a military-looking man.

MAG.   A strange gentleman.

MR. C.   He had a lot of legal-looking documents with him. Mrs. Chilcote and he talked together for an hour or more; and she spent half the night trying to tell me what it was all about. I fell asleep. I woke up two or three times and she was still explaining it to me. Somehow I lost the thread of the thing—but she was talking about Ivers Dean—and my late sister, Elizabeth—and a—a—forged will.

MAG. [*Starting to her feet*]   A forged will!

MR. C.   One time when I was awake, she said Ivers Dean belonged by rights to *us*—and not to you—she had papers in her possession, she said—and then there was something about you and more about the—the forged will—and—then I fell asleep again. That's all I know about it. [*Magdalen turns and walks upstage. Kate passes window, stops; raps on the glass; kisses her hand and disappears. Mr. Chilcote, rising*] There's Kate, now. I'm convinced it's all about Edward, my dear. There wouldn't be any trouble about Ivers Dean, if you and Edward— [*Kate runs in L.2.E.*]

KATE. Magdalen!

MAG. Kate! I'm so glad to see you again. [*Kate kisses her delightedly several times and rapidly*]

KATE. You dear, darling girl! All this time, and you would not even write to me! Nor let me write to you—it was cruel! Mother insisted on keeping me in the house—but I've escaped from the cage at last. So papa got the start on me. Ha, ha, ha! A surreptitious *tête-à-tête*! Ah—I've caught you— [*Shaking her finger at Mr. Chilcote*] having a flirtation with Magdalen—all by yourself. Ha, ha, ha! What would mama say? Ha, ha, ha! But you must go now, papa, dear. Magdalen and I have so many, many things to talk about. [*Proceeds to throw off her wraps, up R.*]

MAG. [*Down L.C.*] Mr. Chilcote—I thank you very much for this call. You are a kind, good friend. But do not trouble yourself.

MR. C. Oh—I shan't. I never do. Only, Magdalen, my dear—I have made it a rule for the last thirty years—never to oppose Mrs. Chilcote in anything. It's an excellent rule. Follow that rule yourself, my love. It always works well. [*Exits L.2.E.*]

KATE. Magdalen! [*She runs to her and kisses her again*] I've got such lots of things to tell you—but we can't say a word just now—till I tell you something else. I'm doing something very naughty. I was so afraid papa wouldn't go.

MAG. Why—what *can* it be, Kate?

KATE. It's awful—but I haven't seen him for nearly six months, you know.

MAG. Seen *him*? There is no man here.

KATE. Not *yet*. The train from London doesn't arrive till a quarter before three. There hasn't been time, yet, to get here from the station.

MAG. Station—train?

KATE. Whyte Browne telegraphed to *him* last night that we were all in Chilcote Hall again. *He* telegraphed to Whyte Browne this morning. This is the way it read: "Two-forty-five train. Ivers Dean. Mark Fleming."

MAG. Oh, I see. Ha, ha, ha! The rogue! Ha, ha, ha! He is prompt.

KATE. Such cool impudence!

MAG. Ivers Dean! As if it were his own house.

KATE. As if I would meet him here, *of course*!

MAG. Ha, ha, ha! He was not far wrong in that, Kate. But Mr. Whyte Browne—he seems to be engineering your love affairs, Kate.

KATE. The darling fellow—I love him dearly! I love him as if he were my second brother. He has corresponded with Mark regularly—ever since we've been gone. Mark wrote about nothing but me. Whytie handed me Mark's letters without ever reading them himself. Ha, ha, ha, ha! He said they didn't interest him.

MAG. Ha, ha, ha, ha!

KATE. Mother took Mr. Browne with the party because he was engaged to me, you know. Ha, ha, ha, ha!

MAG. Ha, ha, ha, ha!

KATE. You ought to see Whytie and mother together. Ha, ha, ha! He seems to think it all depends on *her*. It has never entered his head that either of *us* has any choice in the matter. Ha, ha, ha! He argues with her by the hour, sometimes, in his mild way, to convince her that it will be better for both of us not to marry each other. Mother always comes out ahead. Then Whytie comes to me and asks in a dejected way—"What do you think we'd better do about it, Kate?" Ha, ha, ha, ha! "The old lady is *determined* we shall marry each other—and she gets the best of me every time." Ha, ha, ha, ha!

MAG. Ha, ha, ha, ha!

KATE. [*Starting*] Footsteps on the snow! [*Looks at clock*] It is time! [*Runs up to window, suddenly draws back*] Mother!

MAG. Mrs. Chilcote!

KATE. And Whytie Browne. She *always* takes him with her. Mother does not know I have left Chilcote Hall. Your bedroom! [*She runs out at door R.2.E. Mrs. Chilcote and Browne pass window, but without looking in*]

MAG. A forged will! She opens her new campaign at once. She comes to confront me with the charge. As for Edward's love for me and mine for him —I could say nothing—I could do nothing. I am glad she has chosen another field of battle. A forged will! I did not dream she was so bitter an enemy as that. She will find I have nerve enough, now—and the will, too—to meet her in open conflict. [*Exits at door R.2.E. Enter Mary, L., followed by Mrs. Chilcote and Whyte Browne*]

MRS. C. Say to Miss Dorme that Mrs. Chilcote wishes to see her.

MARY. [*With a toss of the head*] Yes, ma'am. [*Exits R.2.E.*]

MRS. C. The very servant is impertinent. [*Sits down L.*]

BROWNE. I beg your pardon, Mrs. Chilcote—but I suppose you have no particular use for me here. Won't you let me go and look at the property?

MRS. C. On the contrary—I *have* use for *you*.

BROWNE. Oh— [*Walks up R.C.*]

MRS. C. [*Aside*] I may need a witness. [*Reenter Mary R.2.E.*]

MARY. [*Pertly*] Miss Dorme wishes me to ask you to be seated. She will wait upon you—at her leisure. [*Exits with an air, L.*]

MRS. C. [*Aside*] Oh, her leisure, indeed! These airs will change. If she had the least idea of the object of my errand, she would hasten out of her room, and throw herself at my feet. Her "leisure" would be of very short duration. [*Reenter Mary, L.2.E. followed by Mark Fleming, who is speaking as he enters*]

MARK. Say to Miss Dorme that Mr. Fleming—[*Sees Mrs. Chilcote and Browne; stops up L.C.*] Ah—Mrs. Chilcote—I'm delighted—[*Aside*] Oh, Lord! [*Aloud*] Browne.

BROWNE. Fleming.

MARK. [*To Mary, confused*] Say to Miss Fleming—I mean, Miss Chilcote —I would say, Miss Browne—say to Miss *Dorme*—that I have called—on— business. [*Exit Mary R.2.E.*]

MRS. C. [*Aside*] Business! What can be his "business" here? [*Aloud*] I am glad to see you so near Chilcote Hall so *soon* after our arrival home, Mr. Fleming.

MARK. Thank you.

MRS. C. [*Aside*] A remarkable coincidence. I wish he were in Kamschatska.

MARK. [*Aside*] I wish I was in the Fejee Islands, just at this moment. [*Crossing down R.*] Happy thought! I'd *eat* her. Boiled mother-in-law. It makes my mouth water. [*Reenter Mary, R.2.E.*]

MARY. *She* sent word—that *she* will see you—as soon as *she* possibly can. [*Exits L.2.E.*]

MARK. [*Aside*] Confound that girl's emphasis! If *she* hasn't let the cat out of the bag—*she* [*indicating Mrs. Chilcote*] isn't as sharp an old cat as I thought *she* was.

MRS. C. [*Aside*] *She* sent *me* a very different message. [*Browne walks down R., near Fleming*]

BROWNE. Fleming, my boy.

MARK. Browne! [*Turning to him and taking his hand warmly. Apart*] How shall I ever thank you for all your friendly offices? I owe you a debt of gratitude.

BROWNE. Don't mention it, my dear fellow. It was a pleasure. Name your first boy after me. If I'm his father, I'll name him after you. Speak to our respected mother-in-law. You'd better do it at once. I've said all I can on the subject. But the old lady corners me in the argument, every time. *I* have no desire to marry Miss Kate, you know—but I can't prove the point. You speak to her, Fleming.

MARK. I will. [*Browne walks up C., to window*] I might as well have it out now as any time.

BROWNE. [*Looking out of window, back to audience*] The ruins don't look much older than they did six months ago.

MARK. [*Aside*] I'll have a shy at old Melrose Abbey at once. [*Moving to C.*] Mrs. Chilcote—

MRS. C. [*Glancing up at him, then away*] Mr. Fleming.

MARK. I would like to speak to you in all seriousness and with the most profound respect—concerning the hopes which I have entertained in regard to your daughter, Miss Kate Chilcote. I have six hundred pounds a year, fixed income—besides a growing legal practice. I—

MRS. C. [*Rising*] Mr. Fleming—allow me to inform you, once for all, that I do not care to converse on that subject. The hand of my daughter is already engaged to Mr. Whyte Browne.

BROWNE. [*Turning down R.*] Oh, but you mustn't mind me, you know.

MARK. [*Apart to Browne*] Argue it out with her. Logic, my boy. Show her she's wrong. [*Walks up C.*]

MRS. C. Mr. Whyte Browne, you are my daughter's affianced husband.

BROWNE. Yes; but don't you see—Kate doesn't want to marry me.

MARK. [*Aside, up C.*] Major proposition.

BROWNE. And I don't want to marry Kate.

MARK. [*Aside*] Minor proposition.

BROWNE. We wouldn't be comfortable together, you know.

MARK. [*Aside*] Conclusion—a perfect syllogism.

MRS. C. Mr. Browne—you and my daughter Kate *shall* be married. [*Browne turns towards Mark with a motion of the hands and shrug of the shoulders, as if he were saying, "No use, you see"*]

MARK. [*Aside*] Floored. Woman rises as usual—heavenly being!—superior to earthly logic. [*Browne walks up across to L.C. Mrs. Chilcote crosses, R. front. Mark joins Browne*] Logic won't work, old fellow! *Assert yourself—assert yourself!* I'll back you up. Be a man!

BROWNE. [*Drawing up*] I will. [*He steps forward, L.C., Mark stepping back of him, L. Mark pats him on the shoulder*] Mrs. Chilcote— [*She turns full toward him. He flinches. Mark pats him. He draws up*] I wish to say—distinctly—that I don't want to marry your daughter—and—I— [*Wavers, Mark pats him*] I won't.

MRS. C. *Mister*—Browne! [*Browne wavers, Mark pats him as before. He draws up*]

BROWNE. I'll be *damned* if I will! [*He staggers back, supported by Mark*]

MRS. C. [*Thunderstruck*] Oh!—oh!— [*She throws out her arms and stag-*

gers. Browne sees her yielding, draws up and struts down L., then moves up and down L., triumphantly. Mark hurries across and supports Mrs. Chilcote]

BROWNE. Fleming—talk to the old lady. I'll go and look at the property. [*Exits L.*]

MRS. C. *Mister* Fleming—my *dear* Mr. Fleming—support me.

MARK. A-h! [*Supporting her*] Mother!— [*She starts up; looks at him sharply. She then drops her head and arm on his shoulder; he puts his arm about her waist and they walk up the stage, R.C. She starts from him suddenly, seeing Kate's wrap and bonnet. She picks them up. He moves down, across L.*]

MRS. C. Kate—Kate, herself—*here!* [*Reenter Magdalen, L.2.E. She moves in with dignity, stops R., and looks at Mrs. Chilcote*] My daughter, Kate Chilcote, is in *this* house!

MAG. She *is*, madam. That will do, Mary.

MARY. Oh, what a row! [*To Mark*] I told you *she* was here, sir. [*Exits L.2.E. Mark walks down to extreme L. Nervous*]

MAG. [*Turning and speaking through door, R.*] Kate, my dear—your mother wishes to see you. [*Kate walks in demurely and sheepishly, her eyes dropped, and moving down to extreme R. Mrs. Chilcote steps half downstage, C. She looks from one to the other. Both look guilty and uncomfortable*]

MARK. [*Aside*] I wonder what's going to happen next.

MRS. C. Catharine!—

KATE. [*Timidly*] Mama.

MRS. C. You will return to Chilcote Hall, at once.

KATE. Yes, mama. [*She runs across toward door, L.*]

MRS. C. Catharine!

KATE. Mama.

MRS. C. Here are your wraps—and your bonnet.

KATE. Yes, mama. [*She runs to her mother; hastily throws the things on, thoroughly frightened, and starts for door again*]

MRS. C. Catharine!

KATE. Mama.

MRS. C. Take Mr. Fleming's arm. [*Kate and Mark both astonished. Kate looks at her mother, then at Mark, then at her mother again. She moves timidly down to Mark; edges her hand through his arm, finally taking an almost affectionate position, and looking back at her mother*]

KATE. *Yes*—mama!

MARK. [*Throwing across his left hand so that it rests on hers*] Yes, mama.

MRS. C. Mr. Fleming will spend the night at Chilcote Hall. He will return, hereafter, and make us a long visit.

KATE. [*With a long breath*] Yes, mama. [*They walk up to door, L.*] Good-by, Magdalen.

MAG. Good-by.

KATE. [*To Mark*] Tell me all about it, Mark—quick! I'm dying to know. [*He shows her out L.*]

MARK. [*To Magdalen*] I can settle the—the—"business"—on which I called, Miss Dorme—with Miss Chilcote. [*Exits L.2.E.*]

MRS. C. [*Aside*] I suspected as much.

MAG. Now, madam—perhaps you will kindly honor me with the cause of your own visit to Ivers Dean. I am at leisure.

MRS. C. Indeed. I will trespass but a few minutes upon your valuable time. I merely wished to say to you, that I have no desire to treat you with unbecoming harshness.

MAG. I am glad you have reconsidered the subject.

MRS. C. You have been fully exposed.

MAG. [*Quietly*] Exposed?

MRS. C. But I will not take advantage of my knowledge, to bring you to personal punishment, unless you compel me to do so.

MAG. [*Calmly*] Punishment?

MRS. C. If you will quietly relinquish your claim on Ivers Dean, and the accompanying estate, to its proper owner, the heir-at-law of Elizabeth Chilcote, my husband, I will take no legal action to convict you of the *forging* of a *will*—by which you gained possession of that property. [*A pause. Magdalen unmoved. Aside*] She is utterly unconcerned. The brazen confidence of a hardened young criminal!

MAG. Have you finished, madam?

MRS. C. For the present—yes. You may send your answer to Chilcote Hall. [*Magdalen walks across quietly to door, L. Turns to Mrs. Chilcote*]

MAG. Whatever may be the future ownership of Ivers Dean, madam, you will please remember that *I* am in possession, *now.* [*She throws the door open*] Await my answer at Chilcote Hall. On your dying bed—I trust you will die at an advanced old age, madam—on your dying bed, ask your attendants if "*my answer*" has arrived. [*Mrs. Chilcote sails out with dignity*] The new campaign is open. I am in my castle! [*Mrs. Chilcote passes window; stops, looking in. She draws up angrily and disappears, R.*] Is it possible— [*Walking down C.*] that Mrs. Chilcote has—she wishes to blacken my name to her son—has she come so far as that? Has she suborned some villain to— no—I cannot believe it. She is only, after all, an overambitious and a somewhat unscrupulous mother. Is it not more likely—a military-looking man! I have no enemy in the world, who— [*Pauses*] Yes—I have—*one!* [*Enter Mary, L.*]

MARY. A gentleman wishes to see you, Miss Magdalen. [*Giving her a card*]

MAG. [*Reading card*] "Pierre Frederic Delevaine." Show the gentleman in. [*Exit Mary. R.C., reading card*] "Pierre—Frederic—Delevaine." [*Reenter Mary, followed by Paul Daly. He is handsomely dressed, with mustache, military air and bronzed face. He pauses, L., Magdalen bows slightly and motions him down L. He bows and moves down*] Mary—you may take the basket over to Widow Churchly's. It has been ready two hours.

MARY. [*To Magdalen, glancing at Paul*] I beg your pardon, Miss Magdalen—but Kittie is out, too; and if I go, there'll be no one in the house but Jane the cook; she's blind in one eye and deaf in both ears.

MAG. Tell Jane she may run down to the village—and visit blind Margery, for an hour or two.

MARY. Then there'll be no one in the house. Just as you please, Miss Magdalen—just as *you* please. [*Exits L.*]

MAG. Be seated, Mr.— [*Looks at card*] Mr.—Paul Daly.

PAUL. Thank you. [*Sits L.*] I'm glad the detectives haven't as sharp eyes as you have, Maggie.

MAG. [*After sitting R.*] We will make this call as short a one as possible.

PAUL. My dear Magdalen—

MAG. Pardon me; I will give you an opportunity to speak presently. Let us each say what there is to say without interruption. We shall economize time in that manner.

PAUL. [*Aside*] Cool as ever. She'll get the start of me, yet.

MAG. You promised to leave England forever. You have broken faith with me. But let your mind rest easy upon that subject. I am not in the least disappointed. I expected it. You are a thief, a burglar, and a murderer. Of course—you are a liar, also. [*Paul springs up angrily, Magdalen retains her seat and motions to him quietly*] Be seated, Mr. Daly. [*Paul resumes his seat*]

PAUL. [*Aside*] Magnificent courage that woman has! How I love her for it! I'll stake everything—but I shall win her!

MAG. You arrived at Chilcote Hall yesterday evening, in answer to a telegram from Mrs. Chilcote?

PAUL. [*After a quick glance*] Go on.

MAG. Mrs. Chilcote found a letter from you, on her return, informing her that you had documents in your possession going to prove that Ivers Dean came into my possession by a forged will.

PAUL. [*Aside*] She has seen the letter already. [*Aloud*] Proceed.

MAG. You have been working this case up for the past six months. You knew that the witnesses to the will were both dead. The hundred pounds I sent you enabled you to accomplish some new and profitable villainy. You then hired some keen, but disreputable, attorney to work up a case for you.

PAUL. You've been wandering about in the form of a spirit, Maggie—looking over my shoulder.

MAG. It puzzles me—somewhat—why you should attempt to deprive me of that very property, without which I can be of no use to you.

PAUL. [*Earnestly*] You cannot guess the reason, Magdalen Dorme?

MAG. Yes; you love me. [*He starts to his feet, clasping his hands*] And you wish to get me into your power. Be seated, Mr. Daly. You are interrupting me. [*He resumes his seat*] I cannot even *pity* the unrequited love which seeks to ruin and degrade its object. When we met again, Paul Daly, six months ago, I was your friend. I am now your enemy. I shall be, however, an open-handed enemy. I shall denounce Mr. Pierre Frederic Delevaine to the police as Paul Daly, the escaped convict, as soon as I possibly can, after you leave this house. You will consult your own interests by leaving the vicinity of Ivers Dean and Chilcote Hall as rapidly as possible.

PAUL. I admire your pluck, Maggie. Not one woman in fifty thousand, in a lonely house like this, and all her servants gone, would dare say such a thing as that to a desperate man like me. I admire your keen wit, too. You have traced this little conspiracy of mine as accurately as if you were an entire corps of detectives and a prosecuting barrister. But you are wrong, for once. Pierre Frederic Delevaine is *not* Paul Daly. Paul Daly is dead.

MAG. Dead?

PAUL. Dead and buried. I attended his funeral. I read an obituary notice of him, in the police reports. It was not very complimentary! But I dropped a friendly tear on the poor fellow's bier. Following the name of the escaped convict Paul Daly, in the prison records, there is inserted this memorandum —"Killed in a brawl at the Three Ships Tavern, White Chapel." I had the curiosity to read the entry myself. There is so much red tape in these official matters, it will take more than the assertion of one young lady—herself accused of forgery—to establish an identity between a living gentleman, with plenty of money, and a dead convict. You have been frank with me. I am frank with you.

MAG. Have you anything further to say, sir?

PAUL. Yes. But I will be brief. My primary object in this matter of a forged will is to separate you from Mr. Edward Chilcote—and to bring you, so far as possible, as you have yourself suggested, within my own power.

MAG. Yes. [*Calmly*]

PAUL. As to the Ivers Dean estate, there is a tolerably good chance, with the evidence I have secured—

MAG. By bribery.

PAUL. Of course—how otherwise?—a tolerably good chance of depriving you of the estate. But that will depend on my continuance in the scheme. There is a certainty, I think of securing the other object. However strong evidence it may require in a court of law to prove an honest will a forgery, enough suspicion can be thrown on it to prevent a marriage between the woman accused of such a crime and the son of the heir-at-law.

MAG. Proceed.

PAUL. I come here this afternoon—to make a compromise. The terms I propose are expressed in two words—our marriage. [*Magdalen starts, shrinking*] I think I will make you a good husband, Magdalen. We will live here quietly together in Ivers Dean; you will find me the most domestic husband in the world. I have seen enough of "life," as people call it. I am anxious to settle down—a dressing gown, slippers, and a loving wife. We will raise a family and become eminently respectable— Who knows?—some future Delevaine may yet become a peer of the realm. *Consider* the subject, Magdalen. Weigh it carefully in your mind. And remember—don't confuse Pierre Frederic Delevaine with a man you once knew named Paul Daly. Paul Daly is dead.

MAG. [*Rising*] Paul Daly shall *rise* from the tomb! [*Paul starts to his feet and looks at her fiercely, but half shrinking*] Trick the officers of justice as you may—his death—the funeral—the record—they shall all be nothing. Paul Daly shall have his resurrection in *this* world!—only to be buried again within the walls of Dartmoor prison.

PAUL. [*Fiercely*] Magdalen Dorme!— [*He rushes to her and seizes her by the wrists*] If Paul Daly rises from his tomb—remember this— [*Hissing in her ear*] He was a *murderer!* Beware of him! [*She looks him full in the eye*]

MAG. I am alone in the house. There is no one else within hearing. Do your worst, Paul Daly! [*She looks steadily at him. He releases her wrists, and shrinks from her gaze, moving down L.C.*] Coward! [*He turns toward her savagely*] Coward as well as *villain!*

PAUL. [*Aside. Turning away L.*] The spirit of a lioness!

MAG. [*Bursting into a laugh*] Ha, ha, ha, ha!—I flattered myself I was playing the leading female rôle in a tragedy. I am only the heroine of a farce. Ha, ha, ha, ha, ha!— [*Walking R.*]

PAUL. She is laughing at me!

MAG. Ha, ha, ha, ha! I will see if my maid has returned. I shall tell her to call a police officer. In the meantime—play out your own character in the farce. Jump out of the window, while I am away. Ha, ha, ha, ha!— [*Crosses*

L. He crosses R. front. She stops at door and looks back at him] Ha, ha, ha, ha!— [*Exits L.2.E.*]

PAUL. She has almost persuaded me that I *am* Paul Daly. If I *am*—the sooner I disappear from this, the better. She is right. This *is* a farce. It may yet become a tragedy. In the meantime, however, I will follow her advice. [*He goes up to window, throws open the sash and starts back; moves down*] Edward Chilcote! Coming this way. The farce is becoming more and more comical. [*He opens the door, R. Starts as he looks in*] Her bedroom! Ha, ha, ha! This will be particularly farcical! [*Exits into the room, closing the door*]

MAG. [*Without, as she opens door*] If there is no policeman at hand, Mary —the errand boy at the inn will do. It is not a *serious* case. Ha, ha, ha, ha! [*She enters laughing; looks around*] He has adopted my suggestion. "Reenter heroine." Ha, ha, ha!— [*Then seriously*] This farce will have another act. What scene will the curtain next rise on? [*Looks at clock*] Nearly half past three. Edward! [*She feels of her hair*] I must rearrange my toilet. [*She moves to door, R., and has her hand upon the knob. The door is partly open. She stops and listens as if to a sound from the window*] Footsteps! [*Edward appears suddenly at window, with an eager manner, looking in*]

ED. Magdalen! [*Magdalen turns; her hand still on knob and leaning back against the door, as if supporting herself, and looking up eagerly but half coyly at him*]

MAG. Edward! [*He steps in eagerly; stops and points at the clock*]

ED. Six months to the moment, Magdalen! I have obeyed you. [*He extends both arms. She runs up to him joyously. He embraces her*] My own dear Magdalen! It has been an *age* of *misery* to me. [*The door of Magdalen's room opens and Paul appears*]

PAUL. Maggie, my darling, I— [*He shrinks back R., as if surprised and confused. Edward steps L.C., thunderstruck. Magdalen glances at Paul; then drops her head, standing C.*]

TABLEAU

ACT III.

SCENE: *The ruins of an old castle. At back of stage is a wide archway in a very crumbling condition. At the left upper corner is an old tower, extending beyond wing. A door opens from tower above, leading by a step down to a platform on a level with top of the arch. This platform is formed by an angle in the masonry. A crumbling parapet runs along the back of the platform. Loose fragments of stone lying upon it. The platform may be supported by a buttress extending toward front. On the right of the archway is seen a distant view, showing that the ruins stand on a high precipice, overlooking the surrounding country. It will enhance the effect, where this can be done, to have Ivers Dean seen nestling among the trees in the central distance, showing the same architectural forms as seen in Act I. A larger building on the left is Chilcote Hall.*

DISCOVERED: *Magdalen on the platform, leaning idly against the tower and looking off, an open book in her hand hanging at her side. Music as curtain rises, and continuing a moment. Enter Whyte Browne, accompanied by a Gamekeeper, R.1.E. When Browne speaks, Magdalen looks around, then sits reading the book.*

BROWNE. The lunch is all ready, in the shooting box, Robert?

GAME. It'll be all ready, sir, before the party arrives.

BROWNE. The party will be on the property in a few minutes, now. You're ready to feed the pheasants for us?

GAME. All ready, sir. There hasn't been a more likely lot of young pheasants on the property for many a long year. [*Walks R.*] Your uncle couldn't hunt much during the last few years of his life—he had the gout; so there ain't a many foxes.

BROWNE. Y-e-s. The gout *is* bad for hunting. But I dare say Uncle John could hunt quite as well *with* the gout as I can *without.*

GAME. Better, Master Whyte. Ha, ha, ha! Better, sir. Ha, ha, ha! I don't want to say anything disrespectful, Master Whyte, but if your Uncle John had had both arms in a sling and his two feet done up in cotton—he—he wouldn't have missed that rabbit that you let go the other day—the one that ran between your legs, you know. Ha, ha, ha!

BROWNE. Y-e-s. But I was looking at the dog, you know. He looked so funny, standing there with his nose sticking straight out before him.

GAME. [*Aside*] Ha, ha, ha, ha! I wonder if he expected the dog's nose to be sticking out *behind* him. Ha, ha, ha, ha!

BROWNE. And his tail stuck straight out in the opposite direction.

GAME. Ha, ha, ha, ha! Did you expect his nose and his tail to point in the *same* direction, Master Whyte? Ha, ha, ha, ha!

BROWNE. N-o; but that was one thing that confused me. You told me the dog was a pointer, but you didn't tell me which end he pointed with.

GAME. Ha, ha, ha, ha!

BROWNE. [*Seeing Magdalen*] Ah—Miss Dorme.

MAG. Mr. Browne.

BROWNE. I'm glad to see you are on the property, Miss Dorme.

MAG. Thank you. I have been a frequent trespasser, as your keeper will testify, during the past few months. He and I have become quite familiar friends. I have even dropped in at the shooting box, now and then; but this is my *favorite* spot. I am under obligation to you for many a pleasant afternoon, here by myself. Some of my time would have hung wearily enough without your charming ruins, Mr. Browne.

BROWNE. The obligation is on my side. You're an ornament to the property, you know. The *old* ruins look so nice with a *young* woman on them. Such a contrast, you know.

MAG. Thank you, Mr. Browne.

BROWNE. But how did you manage to get up there? *I* tried to climb up once but I fell back and tore my clothes. You couldn't have crossed on the old arch?

MAG. Oh, no. The arch is hardly strong enough, now, to sustain its *own* weight. You have not discovered it, yet? There is a winding stairway in this old tower.

BROWNE. Yes, I dare say, but—

MAG. I have discovered its entrance—among a heap of débris. It is overgrown with briars—down among the rocks yonder, only a few steps.

BROWNE. Oh—I remember, now. Edward Chilcote told me that you and he found an entrance to the tower, wandering around here all by yourselves, you know, nearly a year ago—before he went to the Continent.

MAG. [*Rising*] I will come down to you.

BROWNE. I won't trouble you to do that. I'll find the way.

MAG. I will come down. [*Exits into tower*]

BROWNE. [*Coming downstage*] Rather odd! The old stairway is on my property. I must put it in the inventory. [*To Gamekeeper*] Have you seen anything more of the strange gentleman—that has been spending so much time about the property?

GAME. Yes, your honor, he was up at the box this morning, before seven o'clock. I don't know where he sleeps, but he gets up very early in the morning for a gentleman—though he doesn't seem to have anything in particular to do after he gets up.

BROWNE. Encourage him, Robert. I'm anxious to get a look at him, myself. Encourage him to remain on the property.

GAME. I will, sir. He plays me a good game of cards, and is a rather jolly companion. I'll encourage him, sir. I'll look after the lunch, your honor. [*Exits L.*]

BROWNE. I wonder if it *is* that military-looking fellow, that appeared so mysteriously at Chilcote Hall on the night of our return, and disappeared as suddenly next day. [*Enter Magdalen, L.U.E.*]

MAG. Mr. Browne. [*Coming down and giving him her hand*]

BROWNE. I wanted to speak to you, Miss Magdalen, about two things— though I'm not quite certain the two things aren't *one* thing, you know. Mr. Edward Chilcote and that military-looking chap—

MAG. Mr. Edward Chilcote and Captain Delevaine! One thing, Mr. Browne?

BROWNE. Why, no—not exactly one thing—only somehow they seem to have something to do with each other; and you—

MAG. I? How do either of those—gentlemen—interest *me*, Mr. Browne?

BROWNE. Not at all—not in the least. Only this Captain Delevaine, as he calls himself—I think he's—on the property.

MAG. [*Interested*] On—on the—property?

BROWNE. Y-e-s. So I judge from what my gamekeeper says about a new visitor to the shooting box.

MAG. [*Aside*] I was certain he was not far from Ivers Dean. He knows we are on his track; but he has an object to gain. Paul Daly will risk much, rather than fail in that object.

BROWNE. What I particularly wanted to speak to you about was the other thing—Mr. Edward Chilcote?

MAG. Well?

BROWNE. He's been in such an awful state since the day after we returned home about two weeks ago. He said he might come up here with me today, but I begged him not to—I was afraid he would toss himself over the precipice, or something. Kate told me that you wouldn't see him. He's been threatening to shoot Captain Delevaine if he ever crossed his path again, and he's raving because he can't see you, and the old ruins—his respected mother, I mean—she helps on the row. She *always* helps on a row. I'm going to accept the old lady's urgent invitation to find quarters somewhere else, if this sort o' thing keeps on. The only comfortable person in the house is old Mr. Chilcote. He says it's nothing but a circumstance, anyway. Everybody else is so deuced uncomfortable—I thought, perhaps—you know—I—I fixed things up with Mr. Fleming and Miss Kate—I thought I might fix things up with Mr. Edward and you, you know.

MAG. My dear Mr. Browne, I know you wish to act as a friend; but you will forgive me— [*Putting her hand in his*] if I ask you never to refer to the subject again?

BROWNE. Certainly. It's not my affair, at all. I'm not engaged to you or Edward as I was to Kate, you know. Here comes the party.

MAG. The party?

BROWNE. They're going to look at the property. [*Enter Kate, followed by Mark, L. Kate runs up to Magdalen and kisses her. Mark and Browne talk, up R.*]

KATE. Oh, I've caught you now; you cannot escape. You wicked, wicked thing! To keep us all out of the house. I can't imagine what could have happened, but poor Edward has been frantic. You've been a naughty, cruel girl. But I've caught you now—and I'm going to keep you awhile. [*Kisses her, puts her arm about her waist and they walk up L.*]

MARK. [*To Browne, up R.*] Your gamekeeper describes him as a—

BROWNE. The exact description of the fellow that arrived from London the day after we got home. He had a long talk with our future mother-in-law.

MARK. [*Moving down*] Miss Dorme.

KATE. [*With Magdalen, up L.*] You can't have her. I've got too much to say to her. She hasn't let me get a sight of her for nearly two weeks.

MARK. I wish to see you on business, Miss Dorme. [*Magdalen walks down L.*]

KATE. Business? I am jealous. Mr. Fleming has never had any "business" with *me*. *I* shall flirt with *you*, Whytie, dear. [*Joining Browne, up R.C.*]

BROWNE. Y-e-s. We'll have one of our desperate flirtations.

MARK. [*To Magdalen*] I have reason to believe that the object of our search is in this vicinity.

MAG. So I understand.

MARK. I called at Ivers Dean on the way from the station, this morning. Mary said you were up here; I hoped to meet you. I have fully succeeded, at last, in arousing the interest of the authorities. The officers at Dartmoor already had been suspicious that Paul Daly was not dead—in spite of the funeral and the record. A detective came from London with me today. He is now at the Duke's Head Inn—disguised as a clergyman.

MAG. Bad as Paul Daly is, I dread sending him back to the horrors of a living tomb.

MARK. This is now my affair, not yours. You have placed it in my hands. *I* have no womanly compunctions. [*Moving R.*]

MRS. C. [*Without, L., calling*] *Will* you come, Mr. Chilcote? Or *must* I send for a pair of horses [*Enters L.1.E.*] to drag you up hill? [*She stops C. Seeing Magdalen, who passes her, moving upstage, with a haughty bow, Mrs. Chilcote moves down L., without recognizing her*]

BROWNE. Here's our mother-in-law. Now, there'll be a row on the property.

MARK. [*R.*] Browne, my boy. [*Browne moves down to him R. Kate joins Magdalen up R.C. They walk off together, up R. Mrs. Chilcote stands rigidly L., looking off. Mark, apart to Browne*] Will you do me a favor, old fellow? [*Taking a card from his pocket*]

BROWNE. Certainly. [*Fleming writes*] Do you know, I'm a trifle anxious, Fleming. Our mother-in-law is getting up steam, fast. There'll be an explosion on the property.

MARK. Ask your gamekeeper to ride down to the Duke's Head Inn, at once. Tell him to ask for the *Reverend Mr. Samuel Robertson,* and give him that card, in person.

BROWNE. The *Reverend Mr. Samuel Robertson*—certainly. Are you and Kate going to be married on the property?

MARK. Not today. Unfortunately *this* reverend gentleman has not a license for making people happy—rather the other way. [*Browne crosses L., stops near Mrs. Chilcote. He raises his hat. She sails by him, up C., with a slight inclination of the head*]

BROWNE. Old Melrose Abbey will knock down some of the other ruins before she gets through. Fleming, keep an eye on our mother-in-law. [*Exits L.1 E.*]

MRS. C. [*Suddenly*] Oh! oh! [*Looks around, upstage, then off R.*] Kate has gone off with that wretch. Kate! [*Calls*]

MARK. I beg your pardon, madam—

MRS. C. Sir? [*Walking down R.*] Kate!

MARK. Your pardon, Mrs. Chilcote—but I can convince you, I think, that it is for your interest to treat Miss Magdalen Dorme with the most profound respect.

MRS. C. Indeed! Profound respect! Indeed! [*Enter Mr. Chilcote, L.4.E. He comes down, across L., puffing and blowing*]

MR. C. Well—whew—I—I must say—whew—if anything—whew—ever disturbed me—I—should—whew—but there's one gratifi—whew—cation—I —I'm up here now, and—it's—whew—downhill all the way back. Whew— it is only a circumstance, after all. I—I'm—whew—perfectly—comfortable.

MARK. [*C.*] I was just suggesting to your wife, Mr. Chilcote, that it might be to her interest to treat Miss Dorme with respect.

MR. C. Exactly—whew—what *I* suggested to her. Whew. She's been telling all the neighbors—within—whew—twenty miles—that Miss Dorme is—a —whew—forger.

MRS. C. And why not, sir?

Mr. C. If you—whew—can't *prove* it, she could get ten thousand pounds damages out of us.

Mark. [*Emphatically*] At least!

Mr. C. [*Starting*] Lord bless me! Do you really think it would be as bad as that?

Mark. More likely fifteen thousand pounds.

Mrs. C. *Mr.* Fleming! But we have the *proofs* in our *possession*.

Mark. I am a barrister, madam. What you call the "proofs" are not worth the paper they are written upon, to protect you from a libel suit.

Mr. C. [*Anxiously*] But surely, Magdalen will not—

Mark. The man who brought you those papers has disappeared. The police are now on his track, as an escaped convict. So much for your "proofs."

Mrs. C. But Magdalen will not—

Mark. On the contrary, she *has*.

Mr. C. Has—what?

Mrs. C. What—Mr. Fleming—what?

Mark. Begun proceedings in a libel suit for twenty thousand pounds damages.

Mrs. C. Oh, the *viper!* [*Walking up*]

Mr. C. [*Walking up*] You see what that infernal tongue of yours has brought upon us, madam.

Mark. I happened to meet her solicitor in London before I came down this morning. He had heard that I was engaged to Miss Kate—a member of the family—and he asked me, in a bantering sort of a way, what I thought we should do about it.

Mrs. C. Twenty thousand pounds!

Mr. C. Twenty thousand!

Mark. The nominal figure. Of course, they won't get that; fifteen thousand, probably; ten thousand, certainly.

Mr. and Mrs. C. *Certainly?*

Mark. Not the shadow of a doubt.

Mr. C. Now, madam, I hope you're satisfied—*you old lunatic!*

Mrs. C. Ah! [*Moves to him*] David!

Mr. C. Matilda! [*They fall on each other's neck*]

Mark. I had no authority, of course, but I hinted at a compromise. You might turn over Chilcote Hall to Miss Dorme in exchange for Ivers Dean [*Mrs. Chilcote starts*], with a few thousand pounds to boot. I think we could arrange it.

Mrs. C. Chilcote Hall—Ivers Dean!

Mr. C. A few thousand pounds to boot!

MARK. Ivers Dean would be a trifle small for your family, but you might build an addition.

MR. C. Build an addition!

MRS. C. What *is* to be done, Mr. Fleming?

MARK. Done? An apology from Mrs. Chilcote to Miss Dorme, might knock down the damages a few thousand—perhaps stave off the suit altogether.

MR. C. Make it, my dear, at once—make it.

MRS. C. I will, David, I will. [*Going*] *Dear* Magdalen! [*Exits R.1.E.*]

MR. C. [*Walking up and down L., excitedly*] Fifteen thousand pounds— Chilcote Hall—Ivers Dean—a few thousands to boot—build an addition! I'll swear the woman into an insane asylum! Go around destroying my property with her tongue, that I've been making thirty years with my hands! The old female lunatic! I'll put her in a straight-jacket!

MARK. [*Patting him on the shoulder, down L.*] My dear Mr. Chilcote, it's only a circumstance.

MR. C. *Damn* circumstances! [*Turns up L.*]

MARK. Ha, ha, ha, ha, ha, ha, ha! [*Laughing heartily and walking R.*]

MR. C. [*Up L., turning*] So, sir! *You* can laugh! [*Mark beckons to him. He approaches him. Mark beckons again. Mr. Chilcote moves down to him, wonderingly. Mark punches him in the ribs. Mr. Chilcote recoils and looks at him. Mark punches him again. Mr. Chilcote recoils*]

MARK. [*Confidentially*] I was speaking in a prophetic way.

MR. C. A—a—a prophetic way?

MARK. I was only letting Mrs. Chilcote know what probably *would* happen—if she kept on in her present course.

MR. C. But the—the libel—suit?

MARK. [*Snapping his finger*] Fudge!

MR. C. Miss Dorme's attorney? He met you in London this morning!

MARK. She hasn't any attorney.

MR. C. The—the—Ivers Dean—Chilcote—

MARK. A barrister's li-cense.

MR. C. Kee—ee—ee—ee— Ha, ha, ha, ha! [*Embraces Mark, dances upstage and back, laughing*] I'm glad you did it—I'm glad you did it! Ha, ha, ha, ha! [*Looks off R.*] I'm glad you did it—she's kissing Magdalen— Ha, ha, ha! I'm glad you did it! I feel so happy, I could almost kiss the old lady myself. Ha, ha, ha, ha! [*Going, turns back*] Mark, my boy, you are a younger man than I am—take my advice; follow my example—I've made it a practice for thirty years. *Never let circumstances disturb your equanimity. I* never do. [*Exits R.1.E. with a smile of profound content*]

MARK. Ha, ha, ha, ha, ha! [*Looking R.*] The old lady is making a perfect love feast of it. She has no idea of changing residences with Miss Dorme and building an addition. Ha, ha, ha, ha! I flatter myself I can construct a falsehood with a ready grace that does honor to my profession. I was *born* a barrister. Ha, ha, ha! [*Looks out, up L.*] Edward Chilcote! I understand Magdalen has declined to see him since their first meeting after his return. He has called again at Ivers Dean. Mary, the maid, told him she was at the ruins. He is seeking her. I wonder what can have happened at that meeting between them. She has made me her confidential adviser in the case of Captain Delevaine—né Paul Daly—but she utterly refuses to put the case of Mr. Edward Chilcote in my hands. [*Walking down L. Enter Edward L.4.E.*]

ED. Fleming.

MARK. Chilcote.

ED. You here?

MARK. I am, but ˙don't be disappointed; Miss Magdalen Dorme is also here.

ED. Ah! Indeed!

MARK. As her maid undoubtedly informed˙you. That accounts for your own presence.

ED. [*Sighs*] You are right.

MARK. As usual. [*Looks R., and motions Edward back*] Magdalen and Kate are coming this way. [*Edward retires up R. Magdalen and Kate walk in R.1.E., arm in arm*]

KATE. I am so glad mama has apologized to you, Magdalen, and promised to take it all back among the neighbors.

MAG. I, too, am glad; though I cannot imagine what good angel could have brought her to change her mind so suddenly. [*Kate looks across at Mark, then at Magdalen, then at Mark again. She crosses to Mark, L., and puts her arm through his, looking up into his face*]

KATE. [*To Mark*] I strongly suspect that *this* is the "good angel."

MARK. We two angels will wander off together, and leave these two mortals [*Kate looks over her shoulder and sees Edward, up R.*] to entertain each other. We will illustrate a famous expression in the romance of religion—the "love of the angels." [*They nod to Magdalen. Exit L.1.E. Magdalen walks across L.*]

ED. [*Moving down R.C.*] Magdalen.

MAG. [*Starting, then with dignity*] Mr. Chilcote.

ED. A faithful lover can at least ask justice, Magdalen. The woman he loves *might* give him more. He can *demand* that much as his right.

MAG. Have I denied you "justice"?

ED. Yes. I have not so much as asked an explanation. My faith in you is too strong, Magdalen, my love too pure—I have not insulted you by asking anything.

MAG. [*Tearfully*] True—true, Edward; you were too noble—too generous for that.

ED. And you? After the first shock of surprise—as that man stood before us—I turned to you lovingly. You ordered me from your presence as if *I* had committed a crime against *your* honor. Your door has been closed to me since that day. No charge from me. I believe it to have been some scoundrel's trick. Yet I am banished from your presence without a word.

MAG. Do you know what a woman's pride is, Edward Chilcote? I will tell you. It is something so sensitive, she cannot look into the eyes of the man who loves her, if there be anything between them reflecting on her honor—that demands an "explanation."

ED. I have asked for none.

MAG. No. If you had!—I could have looked boldly in your face, and refused to answer you—with the air of an empress. But you did not. As you turned your face so lovingly to me, all trust and confidence, at the moment when you might have suspected everything, I thought of that sudden start—the flitting expression of doubt—I knew the seeds of suspicion had been planted in your heart, in spite of your honest manliness and your deep affection. Answer me truly, Edward! Since that fatal moment, have you not started from your reveries, to find jealous thoughts—suspicions long suppressed—struggling for a mastery in your mind? Have you not fought against them—have they not returned again and again, when your faithful love has been off its guard? Is there not something there, which ought *not* to be there, if the woman you are dreaming of should become your wife?

ED. Magdalen, I— [*With a wave of the hand*] I—

MAG. You confess it with a gesture. What "explanation" can a woman like me give which shall kill all the small suspicions that may spring up hereafter? My woman's pride tells me there is none. There was too much for you to take on trust already, Edward. My humble origin—my early life—my former companions—I can never be your wife. [*Walking up L.*]

ED. Magdalen! [*Approaching her. She turns with a gesture, checking him*]

MAG. I will be just to you, Edward. Within a few days, perhaps—weeks at the utmost—I will tell you all about the man who has thrust himself between us. Come to me as a friend—*only* as a friend—and I will speak frankly with you. A woman can "explain" such things to a "friend" but not to her future husband. [*She approaches him, extending her hand*] Come to me as a friend, Edward—the door of Ivers Dean will not be closed to you.

ED. [*Sighs, reluctantly taking her hand*] As a friend. [*She drops his hand and walks up L.*] Magdalen. [*She pauses and looks back at him*] I am an intruder here. Do not leave your favorite place. I will return to Chilcote Hall.

MAG. Thank you, Edward. I *do* prefer to remain here. Ivers Dean has lost its attractions for me. [*Exits L.4.E.*]

ED. [*Moving up and looking after her*] Seeking the old hidden stairway that she and I discovered during our rambles here last summer. Ah, those happy hours! [*Starts eagerly, stops*] No, I will not follow her. I will leave it to the future. [*Enter Paul Daly, R.1.E.*]

PAUL. [*Looking back*] I'm in a hornet's nest. They are all here. [*He faces Edward, who suddenly turns upon him*] The devil! The enemy's right wing. Maneuvers, Captain Delavaine, strategic maneuvers.

ED. Pardon me, sir. Though we have met before, at Ivers Dean, and I saw you once at Chilcote Hall, I have never had the honor of an introduction. But I wish to ask you a question.

PAUL. Certainly, by all means, I delight in answering questions. [*Aside*] It gives one such a fine opportunity to lie. [*Aloud*] You are curious to know, perhaps, how I happen to be here. I am immensely fond of field sports—most military men are. I've rented a little box down here, with right of shooting. Pheasants just coming in. I've been so much engaged I have found it quite impossible to pay my respects at Chilcote Hall again. I have just been making my apologies to your respected mother. [*Magdalen issues from the tower above, stepping down to the platform. She starts on seeing Paul, and watches the speakers*]

ED. The question I wished to ask is this: Can you give me any valid reason why I should not seize you by the throat and hurl you over that precipice? [*Paul glances at him in surprise*]

PAUL. Several. I prefer the long way round.

ED. That reason does not interest *me*.

PAUL. You would be hung. That *does* interest *you*.

ED. I have less objection to being hung, perhaps, than you imagine. I am willing to *defy* the laws and take the risk, though I will do so in another direction. I am a captain in Her Majesty's service; *you* are a scoundrel. For the chance of taking your life, however, I will waive all distinctions of etiquette. You have a military air, though hardly the air of a gentleman. I will assume that you are my equal. [*Hands him a card*]

PAUL. Thank you. You do me honor.

ED. I do! And I am doing myself a disgrace. I am fully aware of the fact. You, I imagine, are a desperate man. So am I—for the time being. The laws are fitted to our case, precisely. The survivor runs a fair chance of following his unsuccessful opponent to the next world. Let me hear from you. [*Edward is walking L. Sees Magdalen; starts; glances back at Paul and goes out L.*]

PAUL. I'll be in luck—as things look—if he doesn't "hear of me" through the police reports. Curse that woman! She has set the detectives on me—in the teeth of all my threats. She knows I am near Ivers Dean, too, and could *murder* her, in that lonely spot, at any hour of the night. Magnificent courage. She flinches at nothing. Magdalen Dorme, I love you!

MAG. Paul Daly! [*He starts, turns, springs forward and looks up at her*] I will give you one more chance of escape. I cannot bear the thought of consigning a fellow being to the miseries of a convict prison. Fly! A detective arrived from London this morning. He has learned of your whereabouts—he has been sent for—he is now, perhaps, within calling distance—I will have mercy on you—fly!

PAUL. Magdalen Dorme! I *ask* no mercy. [*He springs rapidly up the pile of masonry on the right of the arch, and is about to cross. Magdalen screams and motions him back. He hesitates*]

MAG. Oh! It will not bear your weight—you will be hurled over the precipice. [*He springs across recklessly. A huge stone falls, but the arch remains intact. Paul seizes Magdalen's wrist fiercely. She shrinks from him, powerless*]

PAUL. Magdalen Dorme! I love you. You rejected, long ago, my impure love—I have offered to be your lawful husband. *Fraud* and *threats* and *trickery* have failed to make you mine in *life—force* shall make you mine in *death*. The officers of the law shall find us *both—at the foot of the precipice*. [*A struggle. Magdalen screams. Mark runs in hurriedly, L.2.E. He bounds across, and runs up the masonry on the right of arch. Kate follows Mark and stops R., looking up. Paul, seeing Mark, releases Magdalen, lifts a huge stone with both hands, and hurls it upon the arch, which breaks, leaving a wide gap. Fleming on one side, Paul on the other, staring at each other. Magdalen crouches half fainting L. Edward emerges from the tower, quietly, and stands just back of Paul, looking at him. Paul turns suddenly as if to seize Magdalen again. Edward seizes him by the throat. Paul draws a knife. A very brief struggle. Edward secures the knife and holds Paul, crouching, at his side with a firm grasp*]

ED. Fraud, threats, and *trickery*! *You* have given me the explanation which *she* refused. [*The Detective, dressed as a clergyman, walks in quietly at L.2.E. He stops and looks up calmly at the situation. Edward releases Paul*

and turns toward Magdalen] Magdalen! [*Embracing her. Mark walks down
to Kate, R.*]

PAUL. [*Addressing the Detective*] Jack Harkason! You very reverend
devil! You've got me again—haven't you, Jack?—and you attended my funeral, too—I saw you there. [*The Detective quietly walks up, his back to
audience. He puts his hand to the pocket in the tail of his coat, draws out a
pair of handcuffs, and tosses them up to Paul, who catches them, and continues*] Thank you. I'll do the gentlemanly thing. [*He fastens them on his
own wrists*] You've always been kind to me, in your way—tell them you captured me, Jack. It'll be a feather in your cap. Give my compliments to the
keeper of Dartmoor prison—and tell him to alter the date in the record of my
death—but nothing more. Paul Daly— [*Stepping suddenly upon the parapet*]
is dead! [*He throws up his manacled hands and plunges backward from the
parapet. A scream from Kate and Magdalen. Edward springs forward as if to
catch him; then recoils from the edge, and supports Magdalen. Mark supports Kate. The Detective walks calmly to the arch and looks over. Browne
walks in quietly L.2.E. He stops abruptly and looks at the broken arch a
moment*]

BROWNE.   What the deuce—oh, hang it!— Look at the property.

CURTAIN

[*If the curtain is called up, Browne can add—"I knew our mother-in-law
would explode!"*]

ONE OF OUR GIRLS

ONE OF OUR GIRLS

FIRST produced at the Lyceum Theatre, New York, November 10, 1885, with the following cast of characters:

DR. GIRODET	LOUIS JAMES
M. FONBLANQUE	GEORGE F. DEVERE
CAPT. JOHN GREGORY (*Fifth Lancers*)	E. H. SOTHERN
COMTE FLORIAN DE CREBILLON	F. F. MACKAY
HENRI SAINT-HILAIRE	VINCENT STERNROYD
LE DUC DE FOUCHÉ-FONBLANQUE	
ANDRE	F. WILLIAMS
MME. FONBLANQUE	IDA VERNON
JULIE	ENID LESLIE
MISS KATE SHIPLEY	HELEN DAUVRAY
PIERRE	WILLIAM PAYSON

The above production ran for two hundred nights, terminating May 22, 1886.

Reopened December 7, 1886, with the following cast:

DR. GIRODET	J. E. WHITING
M. FONBLANQUE	GEORGE F. DEVERE
CAPT. JOHN GREGORY (*Fifth Lancers*)	E. H. SOTHERN
COMTE FLORIAN DE CREBILLON	J. G. SAVILLE
HENRI SAINTE-HILAIRE	FRANK RODNEY
LE DUC DE FOUCHÉ-FONBLANQUE	J. W. PIGOTT
MME. FONBLANQUE	IDA VERNON
JULIE	ENID LESLIE
MISS KATE SHIPLEY	HELEN DAUVRAY

The above production apparently closed by December 20, 1886.

The present edition is taken verbatim from the privately-printed edition bearing the following title-page: One of Our Girls/ A Comedy in Four Acts/ by/ Bronson Howard/ Copyright by Bronson Howard.

A few typographical errors in the above edition have been corrected in the present text.

It may be noted that the scene (in Act III) in which Kate risks her reputation in order to protect Julie in Henri's apartment is similar to a scene in Sardou's *Les Pattes de Mouche* (Scène IX, Acte deuxième). But Howard stated that *One of Our Girls* was entirely original.[1] There is no reason to doubt Howard's word in the matter; it is possible, of course, his memory may have been faulty on this point.

[1] See *In Memoriam*, p. 28.

CHARACTERS

Dr. Girodet

M. Fonblanque

Capt. John Gregory (Fifth Lancers)

Comte Florian de Crebillon

Henri Saint-Hilaire

Le Duc de Fouché-Fonblanque

Andre

Pierre

Mme. Fonblanque

Julie

Miss Kate Shipley

Solicitor

Paris: the château Fonblanque, and an apartment in the rue de Rivoli.

Act I: French ideas and American ideas.
AN INTERVAL OF SIX MONTHS.

Act II: An international kiss.

Act III, Scene I: The French result of a French marriage.
Scene 2: An American girl and an English officer in a French situation.

Act IV: A scientific experiment.

ACT I.

Scene: *Apartment in the Château Fonblanque, in the suburbs of Paris. Richly furnished and upholstered. Large double doors up C. Doors up R., up L. and R.1.E. Mantelpiece and fire down L. Large table, C., half upstage. Armchairs, L.C. and R. Small table, R. High-backed chair up R.C. Small chairs, R.C. and up C. When the double doors at back are thrown open, a richly furnished drawing-room is seen.*

Discovered: *M. Fonblanque, sitting down, L.C., in thought.*

Fonb. Our little daughter, Julie, is to sign her marriage contract this morning! It seems only yesterday that she was first brought to me in her nurse's arms. [*Enter Dr. Girodet, up R., looking at a document in his hand*] You have finished with the solicitor, François?

Doct. Yes. The marriage contract is quite correct, if it satisfies you. Thank Heaven! I have had nothing to do with the document, except to save you the trouble of reading it over with the lawyers.

Fonb. I am under great obligations to you, cousin. These business affairs always annoy me.

Doct. And the marriage of a young girl is a strictly "business" affair. The solicitor says that the Count de Crebillon has insisted, to the last, that you told him Julie's dowry was to be six hundred and fifty thousand francs.

Fonb. The count assured me that the offer of his hand to my daughter was based on that amount.

Doct. He threw in his heart for nothing. [*Aside*] It's all it's worth!

Fonb. I didn't care to insist on the difference between us; it was only fifty thousand francs.

Doct. It would be a pity for a stern father to blast an ardent lover's affection for so small an amount. [*Gives Fonblanque the paper and turns away, R.*] I suppose it has become my duty, at last, Phillippe—my formal and painful duty—to congratulate you on Julie's approaching marriage.

Fonb. Your "painful" duty! You have persisted in opposing this union from the first. The Count de Crebillon's title is one of the oldest and most honorable in France.

Doct. His title? Yes. But the count himself!

Fonb. His ancestors—

Doct. His character! When a family improves as it grows older, it commands my most profound respect. So does a cheese. But in the case before us, if we test the cheese, I would say, the family—

Fonb. The Crebillons of the fourteenth century figure most conspicuously in the pages of Froissart's chronicles.

Doct. The Crebillons of the nineteenth century figure most conspicuously in the columns of the sporting press. The present count is a roué; a notorious duellist; and, without the dowry he is about to gain with your daughter, he would soon add the honorable degree of "Bankrupt" to that of "Gambler." His first wife was a disgrace to his title; but even she did less to dishonor it than he, himself, has done.

Fonb. The count has his peccadilloes, I admit. As to his first marriage, he appreciates the error very deeply; but, luckily, there were no children. The real question at issue is that of uniting two streams of noble blood. On all questions of that kind, my dear François, your ideas are always—I may call them revolutionary; and, really, I object to them.

Doct. I dare say you object to the revolution of the earth around the sun—because it wasn't mentioned in Froissart, and you have grave doubts of the social respectability of the planetary system. The more recently discovered planets are mere parvenus.

Fonb. The Count de Crebillon's personal character is a mere incident in the progress of a noble family.

Doct. And poor little Julie? She, too, is a mere incident.

Fonb. Julie is delighted at the idea of becoming a married woman.

Doct. I can quite understand that. She longs to be free from the restraints to which every young girl is condemned—in France, at least—from infancy to matrimony. She can see little or nothing of the world, and she dreams of pleasures in store for her beyond her prison bars. Marriage, to a young French girl, means all that freedom does to a convict. Of course, Julie is happy at the idea of becoming a married woman. But does that fact relieve you, cousin, of all responsibility for the character of the man whom you have chosen for her husband?

Fonb. In marrying the count, Julie merely fulfills her social duty, in the position to which she was born. Our own family dates back many centuries—

Doct. Yes. The original ape, from which the rest of the human race descended, was a pet monkey in the Fonblanque family. Phillippe, you are trying to unite two great French families by a young girl's hand. Mark my words—her heart will be crushed between them! [*Enter Mme. Fonblanque, up R.*]

MME. F. I have just left our dear little Julie. She's the brightest and merriest bride-elect that ever signed a marriage contract. Her governess can do nothing with her; and her dressing-maid can hardly keep her still long enough to arrange her hair. [*Sitting, R.*] Haven't you heard her laughing?

DOCT. [*Up C.*] I hope I shall hear her laugh in the future.

FONB. By the bye, my dear—[*Showing a note*] I received a letter from Henri Saint-Hilaire.

MME. F. [*Up C.*] From Henri!

FONB. He reached Paris, from South America yesterday. I dare say he will be out here today.

MME. F. How very strange! Julie told me that she dreamed of Henri last night. I have been thinking of him, myself, continually of late.

DOCT. I have always hoped that Henri Saint-Hilaire would be something more to Julie than her old playfellow. For my own part, I heartily wish that he were in the place of the Count de Crebillon, today.

FONB. You are talking nonsense, François. I—I—love Henri, myself, very dearly.

MME. F. And I also; very dearly!

FONB. We always have—both of us. Henri was an excellent student, too; and he has already distinguished himself in his humble profession. But he is a mere scientific man.

MME. F. We cannot forget our own blue blood, François.

FONB. Henri has no family whatever.

DOCT. No family! Etienne Geoffrey Saint-Hilaire! The discoverer of truths in science that have advanced the human race! Isidore Saint-Hilaire! Mere scientific men! Their names and their works have carried the glory of France beyond the reach of her armies. The Crebillons and the Fonblanques, mentioned by Froissart, were only preparing the way for such men as they! That is the family of Henri Saint-Hilaire! [*Enter Pierre, up L.*]

PIERRE. M. le duc de Fouché-Fonblanque.

DOCT. Here's more Froissart. Damn Froissart! [*Enter the Duc de Fouché-Fonblanque, up L. Exit Pierre*]

DUC. Mathilde! Phillippe!

FONB. and MME. F. Victorien!

DUC. François! [*To Doctor, bowing*] My dear cousin.

DOCT. [*Bowing*] On my mother's side.

DUC. I am quite aware that you are related to the Fonblanque family, on your mother's side, doctor, but why do you mention the fact so particularly whenever *I* address you as my cousin?

DOCT. Out of respect for my father's memory.

Duc. Oh! That has something to do with science, I suppose. I never do know what you are talking about, doctor. [*Turns down*] I lost another hundred thousand at the races, yesterday, Phillippe. That makes nearly a million francs since January. I haven't been so lucky this year as I was last; I lost only *half* a million francs last year. Someone always tells me which horse is going to win, and I always bet on that horse; and then one of the other horses comes in first. Speaking of my losses, by the bye, some of my creditors are getting anxious. When did you say you expected Mme. Fonblanque's rich American niece from New York?

Fonb. We may hear of her arrival at any moment, now.

Duc. I thought you said about this time. You wrote to her father, informing him that I would marry the girl as soon after her arrival in France as possible. Did you say anything about the dowry I should expect?

Fonb. I asked him to communicate with me on that subject.

Mme. F. We have received a photograph of Kate.

Duc. Oh! Her name is Kate.

Mme. F. Here it is, duc.

Duc. Thank you; I'll look at it, presently. What do you think we ought to put the dowry at, Cousin Phillippe? We must remember, of course, that Mr. Shipley is a—not exactly a common tradesman, I believe—but an ordinary business man; and only an American business man at that.

Fonb. He is a banker and capitalist.

Doct. [*Up R.C.*] You mustn't sell your title too cheaply, duc.

Duc. Pardon me, doctor, but I don't like that word *sell*. A nobleman is *not* a common tradesman. As to this little American girl, herself, I must remember that she will come to me without education, or the manners of a lady. Of course, I know that she is your niece, Mathilde; but, as your sister ran away from France with an American husband, twenty years ago—

Mme. F. Ah, duc! it was a source of untold grief to us. Our families were never reconciled—until—

Doct. Until Mr. Shipley had made a large fortune.

Mme. F. Until we felt that further persistence in our family pride would be unchristian. When my sister returned to visit us, seven years ago, I wished to detain her daughter in France. If they had allowed me to do so, the girl would have been a refined and well-bred lady, now. As it is, you cannot expect the elegance of manner and the accomplishments, which have been beyond her reach, in a partially civilized country.

Duc. Of course not. I shall be obliged to introduce her to the ladies of my family; it will be a great trial to them.

Mme. F. It will, indeed.

Duc. I think the dowry should be at least twice as large as I should expect if I were conferring my hand and title on a lady of our own nationality.

Mme. F. Quite double the amount. [*Enter Pierre, up L.*]

Pierre. A letter, monsieur.

Fonb. [*Taking it*] From New York. [*Exit Pierre, up L.*] This is Mr. Shipley's answer.

Duc. Ah! [*Sits, C.*]

Fonb. [*Reading*] "New York, March 21st, 1885. My dear Fonblanque: Kate will sail on the Ville de Paris to-morrow." This letter must have come by the same steamer; she is in France, now! [*Reads*] "My bankers in Paris are Messrs. Drexel, Brown & Co. I have instructed them to accept Kate's checks to the amount of five thousand dollars. When she needs more, she will advise me by cable." Accept Kate's checks? A girl of nineteen doesn't know what the word "check" means!

Mme. F. I'm sure Julie hasn't the slightest notion.

Doct. I have been informed that American girls *do* understand the expression. An American patient of mine, in Paris, once told me that both his daughters used the word check frequently, in conversation with himself.

Duc. What does Mr. Shipley say about my approaching marriage with his daughter.

Fonb. [*Reading*] "I remain, in haste, yours, etc., Robert G. Shipley."

Duc. Is that all there is in the letter?

Fonb. [*Reading*] "Over." [*Turns page*] A postscript!

Duc. A—a postscript!

Fonb. [*Reading*] "You spoke in one of your letters about some duke that wants to marry my daughter."

Duc. Some—duke?

Fonb. "If his morals are good, I haven't any objection to him. He and Kitty may settle it between them. What business is the duke in?" [*The Duc starts to his feet. The Doctor shows suppressed laughter*]

Duc. Business!—I!—in business!

Doct. Send him your business card, duke! [*Taking a card from table and continuing, as if reading from it*] "Le Duc de Fouché-Fonblanque, speculator in thoroughbred horses—imported from England; and in wealthy young girls —imported from America."

Duc. "Kitty" and I—can "settle the matter"—between us? What has the girl, herself, to say about it? Mr. Shipley hasn't any objection to me!

Doct. If your morals are good.

Duc. In the name of all that's incomprehensible, what have a gentleman's morals to do with his marrying another man's daughter?

Doct. Nothing whatever—in France.

Fonb. [*Rising*] Captain Gregory! [*Enter Captain John Gregory, up R.*] Good morning.

Capt. Good morning, M. Fonblanque! Madame! Duc! Dr. Girodet!

Duc. and Doct. Captain!

Mme. F. I trust you have slept well—your first night at the Château Fonblanque.

Capt. Thank you, yes. Beautiful suburbs, Paris. I took a charming stroll this morning, about ten miles—all by myself. I'm enjoying my visit immensely. [*Enter Pierre, up L., with a card on salver. Fonblanque takes it*]

Fonb. Our niece, my dear! [*Reading*] "Miss Kate Shipley, Park Avenue, New York." I will meet her. [*Exits up L., followed by Pierre*]

Duc. The Indian princess has arrived.

Mme. F. A young American girl, captain.

Capt. Ah! I never met any Americans, myself. [*Moving to mantel, L.*] Major Radclift, of our regiment, got acquainted with a number of Americans, once. *They* were girls. He told me they were rather nice. Most girls are rather nice! [*Enter Kate, up L., followed by Fonblanque. She stops, up L.C., glancing about, quickly, then dropping her eyes. She looks up and advances a few steps towards Mme. Fonblanque, who has risen. Kate stops, as if noticing her cool dignity of manner, and waits for her to speak*]

Mme. F. My niece!

Kate. Aunt! [*She goes to her with a quick step, but stops suddenly, before her, again checked by her manner. Mme. Fonblanque kisses her forehead*]

Mme. F. We are glad to see you in France again, Kate.

Kate. I—I thank you. [*Choking*] Forgive me, madame, but—[*Touching her eyes*] when I first saw you, it—it seemed as if my own mother were standing before me. On the night she died, four years ago, she drew me to her breast, and kissed me; and she said that I must take that kiss—to her sister, in France.

Mme. F. My child! [*With some feeling, though still with calm dignity, taking Kate's hand. Kate kisses her*]

Fonb. Let me introduce you to our friends, Kate. This is Dr. Girodet, a relative.

Doct. You and I will be very good friends, my dear.

Kate. [*Heartily*] I am *sure* we shall be, doctor.

Fonb. Captain Gregory, of the British Army; our niece.

Capt. Miss Shipley! [*Bowing*]

Kate. [*Bowing*] Captain!

Capt. [*Aside*] *She's* rather nice!

FONB. Our cousin, the Duc de Fouché-Fonblanque. [*The Duc advances up L.C., bowing*]

KATE. Duc! [*With a bow*] I'm very glad to meet you, Captain Gregory. [*Crossing to him, in front of Duc. The Duc rises from his bow, looking astonished, and turning to Doctor*]

CAPT. Thank you. I trust you had a pleasant voyage, Miss Shipley.

KATE. Charming!

FONB. It was a long distance for a young girl to come, alone, with no one but your governess in charge of you. [*Sitting, R.C.*]

KATE. My—governess—uncle? I'm nineteen years old.

MME. F. The same age as Julie.

KATE. Has Julie a governess?

MME. F. All young girls in France have, until they are married.

KATE. I am my own governess; and papa's, too. Every American girl is. Papa needed a governess badly, poor darling, after he lost dear mamma, until *I* was old enough to look after him. I keep house for him, aunt, and manage all the servants. If a girl doesn't learn how to govern herself before she's married, I don't see how she can govern her husband and the rest of her household afterwards. [*Sitting, L.C.*]

DUC. [*Aside*] Govern—her—husband!

KATE. I arrived in Paris on Tuesday evening, and should have come out here at once, only I had so many purchases to make. I bought two new trunks, and I filled them both. I wanted to see my bankers, too.

DUC. [*Aside*] Her bankers!

MME. F. [*Aside*] A young girl of nineteen with a banker!

KATE. Papa gave me some New York Central shares for my last birthday present, and, just before I sailed, he wanted to sell them for me. But they were only ninety-nine cents, and the secretary of the company is superintendent of our Sunday school. The clergyman told me that he whispered to him, on the previous Sunday, while he was changing his gown in the vestry, just before the sermon, that New York Central shares were sure to go up. So I told papa not to sell mine. My bankers in Paris told me, yesterday, that they were a hundred and ten! Dear papa! I never could get him to go to church, but he'll go regularly after this!

FONB. You say you have no governess; but surely you were not alone on the voyage.

KATE. Oh, no! A family—old friends of ours—came on the same steamer; a father and mother and their two sons. I was never alone; one of the young gentlemen was always with me.

MME. F. [*Aside*] One of the gentlemen!

KATE. The party came as far as Rouen, also, on the train from Havre. I came the rest of the way alone.

FONB. All the way from Rouen to Paris! It was very unsafe, my dear girl!

MME. F. And highly imprudent!

KATE. I have traveled hundreds of miles alone, in America; why not here? But I confess my first experience was an extremely disagreeable one. A gentleman sat opposite to me, when we left Rouen. That is, I mistook him for a gentleman at first, because I heard his servant address him as a "Count" before the train started.

DUC. You were alone in the compartment with a—a count!

KATE. All alone, duc!—with a French count—in a French train—on a French railway—in France. To tell the truth, the count made himself exceedingly disagreeable to me the first five miles.

DOCT. My child!

MME. F. What did you do?

KATE. I looked him straight in the eye, for the *next* five miles; and he changed his compartment at the first station.

CAPT. [*Aside*] If I were charging a redoubt, I shouldn't like to meet an American girl on top of it.

FONB. You must never expose yourself to such a risk again, Kate.

KATE. I never shall. If I ever again see a nobleman in a railway train, I'll get into another compartment. But Cousin Julie! I'm longing to see her again.

FONB. You have come just in time to witness the signing of her marriage contract.

KATE. What's that, uncle?

FONB. Have they no such ceremony in America!

KATE. The only marriage contract I ever heard of is where a gentleman asks a young lady to be his wife, and she says "no" and changes it to "yes" before he has time to drop her hand; then they kiss each other. That's the American ceremony. But we never have any witnesses to the contract!

MME. F. Allow me to remark, my niece, that a gentleman in France is never permitted to be alone with a young lady, even after they are engaged to be married, much less to kiss her!

KATE. It's different in America. I've never been engaged myself, but a lot of other girls I know have been. When two young people, there, are making love, other people get to the furthest room in the house, and shut all the doors between. If anyone looks into the parlor, he dodges back as if he'd just thought of an engagement somewhere else. Two lovers in America are put in quarantine. They might as well be on a desert island together—but they never seem to be lonely!

MME. F. Do gentlemen in your country make love to young ladies in person, then?

KATE. They'd all die old bachelors if they didn't. You are in the Fifth Lancers, Captain Gregory?

CAPT. Yes.

KATE. I met Major Radclift, of your regiment, in Paris, yesterday.

CAPT. Oh!

KATE. He said you were visiting here.

CAPT. Ah!

KATE. He told me you were the bravest officer in the regiment.

CAPT. Yes. I mean—exactly—that is—of course—I would say—I—I beg your pardon—[*Moving up*] but I haven't had my regular exercise this morning; I'll take a few turns in the garden. [*Aside*] Damn Major Radclift! [*Exits up L.*]

DOCT. Captain Gregory never beat a retreat like that in the face of an enemy. [*Enter Pierre, up L.*]

PIERRE. M. le Comte de Crebillon has arrived, M. Fonblanque.

FONB. [*Rising. To Duc*] Will you join us, duc?

DUC. With pleasure. [*Exit Fonblanque, up L., followed by Pierre*] Au revoir, Miss Kate!

KATE. Au revoir! By the bye, duc, my father received a letter from uncle just before I left New York.

DUC. Yes?

KATE. About a matter of business.

DUC. [*Aside*] Business! [*Aloud*] I requested M. Fonblanque to address your father.

KATE. I am papa's agent. But I'll not detain you, now. We will settle the —business—at some future time.

DUC. Yes. [*Aside, going*] I've proposed to an American girl! I'll leave it to my lawyer. I could never manage it myself. [*Exits, up L.*]

DOCT. [*Aside, sitting at table, up C.*] I suspect the duc's creditors will have to wait awhile for that dowry. [*Mme. Fonblanque rises, R. Kate rises, L.*]

MME. F. The apartments prepared for you, Kate, are at your service.

KATE. Thank you, aunt; but I left all my trunks at the hotel, to follow me.

MME. F. [*Aside*] All her trunks!

DOCT. [*Aside*] Opening skirmish of the campaign—a French aunt and an American niece. [*A book or paper before him*]

MME. F. Did I understand you to say that you were alone in the streets of Paris, yesterday and the day before?

KATE. Yes, aunt.

MME. F. Surely, there was a maid, at least, with you.

KATE. I never had a maid. It's bad enough to look after the other servants.

MME. F. Permit me to say that no young lady, in Paris, is expected to be seen on the streets without a suitable companion.

KATE. If a girl can't be trusted alone at nineteen, aunt, she can't be at ninety. I spent all yesterday afternoon at the Louvre gallery.

MME. F. The Louvre! No young girl should visit a public gallery without a governess, or other older companion. They all contain many pictures which are highly improper for a young girl.

KATE. I hadn't any governess to point out the improper pictures, so I looked at the others. My friends came on from Rouen, and joined me again, yesterday noon. One of the young gentlemen took me to a concert in the evening.

MME. F. I am positively shocked! You—you went out—in the evening—with a gentleman!

KATE. Yes, aunt.

MME. F. Let me say to you, once for all, that nothing whatever of that kind must ever occur again, while you are under my roof.

KATE. Surely, aunt, when a young lady is entrusted to a gentleman's care, he is her natural protector until she returns to her home.

MME. F. I dare say you have invented a new kind of young man in America.

KATE. There must be *some* gentlemen, here, that can be trusted like that. What kind of young men do girls *marry* in France—nice girls, I mean—like Julie and me?

MME. F. I will converse with you further, my niece, when we are at leisure, on the customs to which young girls are expected to conform in countries more civilized than America.

KATE. Thank you, aunt. I will try to do everything I can to please you, while I am a visitor at your house. If I find it impossible to do so, without sacrificing my own self-respect, I shall cease, of course, to be a visitor. [*They both bow with great dignity. Mme. Fonblanque moves up L.*]

DOCT. [*Aside*] End of the first encounter. There'll be plenty more! [*Rising*]

MME. F. You will assist M. Fonblanque and myself in receiving our guests, François?

DOCT. I will follow you, madame. [*Exit Mme. Fonblanque, up L. Julie runs in, gaily, up R.*]

JULIE. Uncle François! [*Throws her arms around the neck of the Doctor, who receives her in his arms*] I'm going to be a married woman, uncle! Just think of it! [*Laughing*] A married woman!

DOCT. My pet! I hope you will always come to me with a smile like that on your face. [*Kisses her and turns to go. He turns again, throws her a kiss, smiling, and goes out, up L. Julie throws a kiss after him, then turns down C. She stops abruptly, and looks at Kate*]

JULIE. Why! It isn't—Oh!

KATE. [*Extending her arms*]   Julie!

JULIE. Kate! [*The two girls are clasped in each other's arms*] I've been wishing so much you could be here, today. Let me look at you! Take off your hat! [*Taking her hat*] There! [*Drawing back and looking at her*] I'd have known you anywhere; and yet—you have changed, too; you—you seem like a woman, now.

KATE. And you seem to me the same sweet, innocent girl of twelve that I remember you—seven years ago.

JULIE. Yes; and I am very tired of being a sweet, innocent girl. Aren't you? But I am to be married, in a few weeks, and—oh! I can be your chaperon!

KATE. [*Laughing*]   My chaperon!

JULIE. You won't be obliged to have your governess with you all the time. Have you a nice governess? I have. She never tells mamma anything I do. Ha, ha, ha! I ran away from governess, in Paris, last week, and I was all alone on the streets for nearly two hours! I was almost run over, once; but it was such fun! Ha, ha, ha! I went into the Champs Élysées all by myself! Governess found me, at last, in front of one of the marionette shows; she was awfully frightened, but she never said a word about it to mamma. If your governess isn't a nice one, you shall have mine, as soon as I'm married.

KATE. Thank you, my dear; I'm perfectly satisfied with my own governess; when I do anything wrong, she never calls anyone's attention to it. But now you must tell me, darling—[*Putting her arm around her waist, and walking to and fro*] all about your marriage. You must be very happy.

JULIE. Yes; I am. My trousseau will be lovely!

KATE. Is the gentleman light or dark?

JULIE. He has dark hair and eyes, I believe, but I barely noticed him when he called. [*Kate stops, L.C., drops her arms from Julie's waist, and falls back, step by step, staring at her*] Mamma didn't tell me, till just before he came, that he was to be my husband; and it seemed so strange, you know. I hardly raised my eyes; and the room was rather dark, too. My wedding dress is to be white brocaded satin, with a long train—it will be the first train I ever had —with sprays of orange blossoms running—

KATE. You are going to marry a man you have never seen but once—and you didn't look at him, then—and the room was dark!

JULIE. The count was obliged to leave Paris that afternoon.

KATE. Oh! He's a count.

JULIE. Yes. A gentleman usually calls at least twice before the contract is signed, but he wrote to father and apologized. He couldn't get back until this morning.

KATE. Didn't he ever propose to *you?*

JULIE. The count proposed to father for my hand, of course.

KATE. Why didn't you tell him to *marry* your father?

JULIE. Ha, ha, ha, ha! It's quite immaterial to me which of us he marries.

KATE. You do not love him, Julie! You cannot, of course.

JULIE. Love him? No; I'm only going to marry him!

KATE. Oh! That's all!

JULIE. Married! I can go where I please, and see what I please. I can meet anyone I like—and there must be a lot of nice, wicked things in the world that an innocent young girl doesn't know anything about. I'm to be a married woman!

KATE. Ah! I see. A canary to be suddenly released from its cage! We American birds are bred in the open air, Julie; we're a little wild, perhaps, but we choose our own mates; and we settle down very comfortably in our nests, with them, afterwards. Do girls really marry men, in France, before they have listened to words of tenderness and affection from their lips? It doesn't seem—forgive me, Julie—but it doesn't seem modest and womanly to me for a girl to become a man's wife before she has heard such words— before they have even kissed each other.

JULIE. Kissed each other! Oh! That would be very wrong—before marriage.

KATE. If a girl doesn't love a man so much she can't help kissing him, she oughtn't to marry him at all. But you and I can't make each other understand these things. We have been brought up so far apart, and in such different countries. We'll talk about old times, when we were children together; we understood each other perfectly, then. Is the old garden just as it used to be? And—oh!—where is the big boy, now, that used to play with us? He was three or four years older than we were; the one that was visiting here.

JULIE. Henri Saint-Hilaire?

KATE. Yes; that was his name.

JULIE. Henry went away from France soon afterwards; but he came back for a few months about two years ago, and he visited here, again. Do you remember the old well, Kate, down in the furthest and darkest corner of the garden?

KATE. Yes, indeed, I do, and the story about it. If a girl sees a gentleman's face beside her own, when she looks down into the water, on a moonlight night—that gentleman will be her husband. We girls used to climb up and look over the curb, but, ha, ha, ha, ha! We always omitted a very important part of the ceremony; we didn't take the gentleman with us.

JULIE. I did see a face beside mine, one evening, about two years ago. It was during Henri's last visit; the very night before he went away again. Ha, ha, ha! It was such a lark! I ran around one side of the château, and Henri ran around the other side. Governess saw us coming back, but she never said anything about it.

KATE. The story of the old well won't turn out true in this case, Julie!

JULIE. [*With a shade of momentary sadness*] Of course not. It *couldn't* turn out true. Henri doesn't belong to an old French family, as I do. [*Then brightening and looking around, laughingly, her fingers to her lips*] H—s—h! I'll tell you a secret. Henri kissed me at the old well! Ha, ha, ha!

KATE. You said, just now, that it was wrong, in France, to allow a gentleman to kiss you, before you are married to him.

JULIE. But I'm not going to marry Henri.

KATE. Oh!

JULIE. Besides, there was nobody looking, and *that* isn't wrong, in any country! Ha, ha, ha, ha! Henri gave me his picture, set around with diamonds, which he had gathered for me, himself, in Brazil! Here it is; you shall see how he looked two years ago. [*Takes miniature from her dress, suspended by a ribbon to her neck*]

KATE. You are wearing that picture, on your breast—today? Today, Julie?

JULIE. I've worn it there ever since Henri gave it to me. I shall tell him so when he comes back to Paris. He'll be very glad to learn I've always remembered him. What fun we used to have together. Ha, ha, ha! [*Laughing and kissing the picture*] This looks exactly as he did then.

KATE. I hope Henri Saint-Hilaire will never return to Paris.

JULIE. Oh, yes; he's on his way home, now.

KATE. Julie! [*Earnestly, laying her hand on her arm*] You must never see him.

JULIE. Why! Ha, ha, ha, ha! What queer notions you American girls do have about everything! [*Moving R., upstage*] When I'm a married woman, Henri and I can see each other as often as we like.

KATE. Julie! Julie! [*Enter Fonblanque, up L.*]

FONB. Ah, Julie, you are here. [*Enter the Count de Crebillon, up L. Kate moves down R. Fonblanque crosses to Julie, upstage, L. The Count moves down L. He and Kate see each other. She starts and looks him, firmly, in the eye. He looks at her, steadily, a moment, then turns away*]

COUNT. [*Aside*] The little American Gorgon that stared me out of countenance, the other day!

FONB. Julie, my darling, your mother and I must soon give you up—to one who will care for your happiness hereafter, as we have done till now. Count! [*Leading Julie across*] We are giving you, today, the treasure of our house and of our hearts.

KATE. Her husband!

COUNT. I trust that I shall be worthy of such a gift. [*Taking Julie's hand, leaning over it, gracefully, and kissing it. Julie stands before him, with downcast eyes*]

KATE. Uncle!

FONB. Kate! Pardon me! The Count de Crebillon! Our niece!

KATE. I wish to speak with you, uncle, on a subject which concerns Julie's happiness—for life.

FONB. Your mother has gone to your room, Julie. The count and I will join you both in the drawing-room. [*Julie moves up, across R. Looks back*]

JULIE. My happiness—for life! Everybody has something to do with that, except myself. [*Exits, up R.*]

KATE. Alone, if you please, count! [*The Count inclines his head and passes up L. He turns and bows, deeply, to Kate, who now bows low, in return. Exit Count, up L.*] My dear uncle, I told you that a stranger, on the way from Rouen, made himself offensive to me, by his attention. I did not tell you all. I could not, then. The man insulted me! He was the Count de Crebillon!

FONB. Indeed! A most unfortunate coincidence. The count will be glad, of course, to apologize, both to you and me, for the mistake he made.

KATE. Apologize—for—his—mistake!

FONB. I trust it will be a lesson to you. The mistake was a natural one. A respectable young girl, in France, is not expected to place herself in such a compromising position. You must be more careful in the future. As to the count, himself, believe me, he will treat you, hereafter, with the most profound respect. [*Exits, up L.*]

KATE. A lesson—to *me*! Such a man as that is considered a proper husband for a young girl—and Julie will sign her marriage contract with the picture of another in her bosom! This is France! My mother's country! But you left it, mother, with the husband your own heart had chosen. Julie! My poor Julie! What must be the end? [*Enter Pierre, followed by Henri Saint-Hilaire, up L.*]

HENRI. I'll not go into the drawing-room, Pierre. I'll wait here till they are at liberty. [*Coming down L.C. Exit Pierre, up R. Henri sees Kate*] I beg your pardon.

KATE. M. Henri Saint-Hilaire! I recognized you at once.

HENRI. Is it not the little American girl, that—

KATE. Yes, monsieur. I am the same little American girl—[*Extending her hand, frankly*] that you knew at Château Fonblanque, seven years ago.

HENRI. [*Taking her hand*] I'm very glad to see you here again. I often think of you, when I am thinking of Julie. I have not seen *her* for two years. She is in the drawing-room with the others, I suppose.

KATE. [*Looking down*] Yes! She is there, with the rest. [*Then raising her head, looking straight into his eyes, speaking slowly and distinctly*] Our little playmate is going to sign her marriage contract, this morning.

HENRI. Ah! [*With a gasp, starting back*] Her marriage contract!

KATE. Oh! I feared it *might* be a blow to you, Henri; but you ought to know the truth at once.

HENRI. Julie—to be married to another! It is for this that I have struggled —for this that I have been dreaming of her, in a foreign land—for an end like this. Another's wife! Julie! Julie! [*Enter Pierre, up R., with large ink-stand and pens. He is followed by an elderly gentleman, the Solicitor, with the contract in his hand. Pierre places the inkstand, etc., on the table. The Solicitor lays the contract on table and opens it*]

SOLIC. [*To Pierre*] The contract is quite ready. [*Pierre throws open the double doors at back. Guests are seen: Ladies and gentlemen in groups. Among them are the Captain, the Duc and Dr. Girodet; also M. and Mme. Fonblanque, Julie and the Count. The Solicitor offers the pen, bowing to the Count, who moves down. A general movement down through the double doors, the guests forming a background of the picture. The Count takes the pen, turns and bows to Julie; then signs the contract. He then extends the pen to Julie, who moves down and takes it. She sees Henri*]

JULIE. Oh! Henri! [*She drops the pen and rushes down, laughing, brightly, and extending her hands*] You've come back already. [*Henri takes her hand, eagerly*] I'm very, very glad to see you again.

HENRI. Julie!

COUNT. Shall we finish the signing of the marriage contract, mademoiselle? [*With the pen in his hand*]

JULIE. Eh? Oh, yes, of course! I forgot! Ha, ha, ha, ha! [*She runs across, takes the pen and is signing the contract as the curtain descends. Henri is looking steadily at Julie. The Count is looking at Henri; Kate from Julie to Henri*]

ACT II.

SCENE: *The Château Fonblanque. Another apartment, opening upon garden. Perforated windows at back, similar doors up L., and window down L., all looking to garden, in which ornamental lanterns hang among the trees. The right upper corner of the apartment opens by arches to large room beyond. Door, R.I. Upright piano down L. Chair and small table, L.C. Ottomans, R.C. and L.C. Small escritoire, R. of C., with chair. A lamp, lighted, on escritoire is the only light of this apartment. Moonlight over the garden and streaming through the window and door, L., while the effect of a dim light in the room is to be secured by the painting, the lamp, etc. The actual light on the stage should be almost full; apartment beyond brilliantly lighted.*
DISCOVERED: *Kate, sitting at escritoire. She is arranging paper, etc., as the curtain rises.*

KATE. [*Writing*] "My own darling papa: I've just spent three mortal hours at the dinner table, and there's a grand reception to follow, at eleven. The gentlemen are still at their cigars. I have run away from the ladies to write you a letter in time for tomorrow's mail. I was trying on all my lovely new dresses this afternoon, so I hadn't time to write before. There were sixteen people at dinner—m—m—m—[*Continuing, as if giving words or lines as she writes*] m—m. Awfully full dress. Ambassadors in court costumes, officials in all their decorations, and military officers in their full uniforms—m—m—m—m. The young English officer I told you about—the one that was visiting here when I first came—he has come back from England again, and is now living in Paris. He is here tonight, and he sat next to me at dinner." [*Speaks*] He told me that he couldn't stay away from France. It's very curious—I didn't tell him so—but, after he returned to London, I found it all I could do to keep away from England. [*Writes*] "I am dressed in pistache ottoman silk and velvet to match, and"—[*Speaks*] Father won't understand a word of that. [*Writes*] "It cost seven hundred dollars." [*Speaks*] He'll understand that. I know they're all awfully shocked at my costume tonight, especially by the diamonds. A young girl in France isn't allowed to wear diamonds at all; but give any American girl a pair of solitaire earrings, and look at her ears the next time you meet her—no matter where. They regard me here as a wild, young Indian princess, anyway. I might as well dress like one and enjoy myself. They ought to be glad I have anything on, except a string of beads around my waist. For the last five months, since Julie was married to the count, and I've been the only unmarried girl in the house, aunt has been holding her breath all the time to see what I'd do next; an American girl, in Paris, is always doing something next, and its always the very last thing the people here expect a girl to do. They think a young woman ought to be so fresh and "innocent," as they call it. Well! I tried as hard as I could to please aunt, at first. I haven't any objection to being innocent for a few months, but, somehow, I can't understand French innocence; and they can't understand my sort of innocence. So now I'm just my own American self; and that's all I intend to be. I'll surprise 'em with a war whoop one of these days. [*Writes*] "Papa, dear, they can't make me out, here, at all. I'm shocking everybody awfully, and I'm getting worse and worse every day. Poor, dear aunt reminds me of a very dignified elderly hen with one chicken to look after, and that chicken a duck. My languages come in very nicely with the foreign swells here. I've been talking German with a grand duke, tonight, and Italian to a prince; but, whatever language I talk in, I seem to shock people, all the same." [*Speaks*] I verily believe they're astonished to hear me talk any human language. I'll learn Choctaw before I come again, and confine myself to it; that's the only way an American girl can keep from shocking people in Europe. As to my other accomplishments—ha, ha, ha! When I played one of Beethoven's sonatas in B flat, the other day, that fat marchioness nearly choked with astonishment; and I ended it off so suddenly with "Yankee Doodle" that she nearly tipped over backwards on the little Spanish count. If she had, there'd 'a been one less foreign ambassador at dinner today. Ha, ha, ha! For the life of me, I couldn't help telling him, when he complimented me on my playing a classical selection, that I picked it all up in Europe during the last six months, and that New York ladies never played on anything at home but a tom-tom; and they went about barefooted, except on Sunday, and then they went to church in moccasins, embroidered with beads. [*Writes*] "The worst of it is, papa, they believe everything one says about America, and I can't help telling them awful fibs. I'd die if I didn't." [*Speaks*] I believe that nice, old, French field-marshal half suspected I wasn't telling him the exact truth, tonight, when he got his wig twisted over his left ear, and I tried to make it pleasant for him by saying that nearly all American gentlemen over thirty years old wore wigs, because they usually scalped each other before that age. I've often heard father talk about his best friend being scalped right in Wall Street. It would have been all right if I'd stopped there, for it didn't surprise him a bit; it seemed to be exactly what he expected Americans to do to each other. To save my life, I couldn't help going on till I thought of something that would surprise him. When I told him that an American kept his eye on the top of his enemy's head every time he met him with his hat off, and as soon as his hair began to grow thin he scalped him at once before it was too late, the old gentleman did have a puzzled expression, then. [*Writes*] "If any-one ever tells them the truth about some things I've told 'em here, there'll be war between France and America." Ha, ha, ha, ha, ha! [*Leaning back and laughing very heartily. Speaks*] If I were in the drawing-room, now, with aunt and the other French ladies all looking on me as a young female bar-barian, I—I'd be dancing a war dance among 'em! I know I should! Ha, ha, ha, ha! [*Springing to her feet and dancing in a dainty, half imitation of an Indian war dance, laughing, gaily, as she does it, and giving herself up to the spirit of mischief*] Ha, ha, ha, ha! I can imagine the fat marchioness staring at me through her glasses, and poor, dear aunt, resigned to her fate, as a dowager duchess at her elbow remarks: "A native American custom, I sup-pose." Ha, ha, ha, ha! [*Enter Captain Gregory, from apartment up R., in full Lancer's uniform, evening dress. He stops and looks at her through his single glass. She sees him and stops dancing, suddenly*] Oh! Ha, ha, ha, ha! You shall dance, too, captain. [*Runs across to piano and plays "Yankee Doodle," with great spirit and full, rattling accompaniment; stops suddenly and looks over her shoulder*] You're not dancing. Perhaps you prefer a different air. [*Plays "God Save the Queen," singing the last few words of the stanza*] Is that more to your fancy?

CAPT. I think those two airs go particularly well together. I hope they al-ways will go together, and I never wished so so much, as—as since I found myself a visitor at the same house, six months ago, with an American girl, Miss Kate, in a foreign country.

KATE. When you left us, captain, it seemed as though I was further from my own country than ever; and when you came back to live in Paris, the Atlantic Ocean didn't seem half as wide. The only time I ever feel quite at home here is when I see your English face, and when I hear you speak our language, even if you don't speak it exactly as I do.

CAPT. I learned French in Paris, but I never had a chance to acquire the correct English accent in New York.

KATE. [*Rising and crossing, R.*] I shall be delighted to teach you how to speak your own language, captain. [*Aside*] And I'll teach him what to say to me in it, too, if I can.

CAPT. [*Crossing, L.*] I could take lessons from a dear little nose like her's all day.

KATE. Do I ever shock you, captain, as I do the rest of them here?

CAPT. Frequently. [*She turns, abruptly, drawing up*] I like to be shocked.

KATE. Oh!

CAPT. Shock me again! It's delightful!

KATE. I'm just finishing a letter to father. [*Sitting at escritoire, R.C.*]

CAPT. I'll stroll into the garden.

KATE. Don't go, please. I'll be ready to shock you again in a moment. I've only to send my love, and sign my name, and put in the postscript.

CAPT. [*Aside*] Her love!

KATE. [*Writing*] "He has just come in, and he looks so nice in his uniform." [*Looks over her shoulder at him*]

CAPT. [*Aside*] I've been trying to tell that girl I love her for the last three weeks, only they never gave me a chance to be alone with her; and now I *am* alone with her, I don't know how to begin.

KATE. [*Writing*] "I love him more and more." Oh! stupid!

CAPT. Eh?

KATE. [*Altering a word*] "I love you more and more—[*Writing*] dear papa."

CAPT. She was thinking of some other fellow. Whoever he is, he can't be stupider than I am. How do fellows talk to girls when they're really in love with them?

KATE. [*Writing*] "A dozen warm kisses." [*Kisses her hand to him, behind his back*]

CAPT. Miss Kate! [*Turning; she turns back, just in time to avoid being caught*]

KATE. [*Writing*] "For you, papa."

CAPT. I beg your pardon.

KATE. "Your loving daughter, Kate." [*Folds letter, etc.*] You were about to say, captain—[*Rising*]

CAPT. I was—I was merely going to—to—from the very first moment I saw you, Miss Kate—

KATE. One moment, please. [*Returns to escritoire; opens letter and writes*] "Postscript. I feel that something very serious is going to happen tonight, papa." Go on, captain.

CAPT. When I returned to London, I found I couldn't—I—well—I came back to Paris and took apartments, so that I could be near to—to—and—then I—then I met you again, you know. [*Aside*] I wonder what father said to mother when he proposed.

KATE. [*Writing*] "I shall have something very important to tell you in my next letter!"

CAPT. [*Aside*] If a fellow could overhear his father, he'd know the right thing to say, himself, when his own turn came, because a fellow's father succeeded—of course!

KATE. Did you ever see the old well, captain, down at the foot of the garden, hidden away among bushes and creepers, where only the moonlight can reach it?

CAPT. I stumbled on it one morning when I was visiting here. Queer old place.

KATE. I think I'll stroll down to it now. [*Crossing, L.; stops at door, in the moonlight. Aside*] I wonder if I shall see his face there, beside mine. [*Aloud*] I'm not a bit afraid of going alone, captain. You—you needn't follow me. [*Exits into garden, L. The Captain looks after her a moment, then moves up to door*]

CAPT. It looks awfully dark out there, beyond the lights, for a girl, alone— [*Enter Julie, from apartment, up R.*]

JULIE. Strolling into the garden, captain?

CAPT. I was going to light another cigar. [*Exits to garden*]

JULIE. [*Looking out after him*] Kate is there, too! She has disappeared beyond the rose bush. They are going to the well, together—as—as— Heigh-ho! As Henri Saint-Hilaire and I did, once. It is years—it seems so many years! —since that night. [*Coming down; takes the miniature from her breast*] How little I knew that Henri's face, looking up at me from the water, was engraved so deeply in my heart. I was only a careless young girl, then. I hardly knew I had a heart. Kate can choose for herself. [*At casement, down L., looking out, the moonlight falling on her*] She will carry her husband's picture in her breast. We women in France are not allowed to do that. Ah! [*She gives a short, quick scream, springing back a few steps*] A face staring at me—a woman's face! [*She moves, cautiously, towards the window again, peering out. Henri Saint-Hilaire enters, R. front, from apartment. He stops, R., looking at her*] It is gone. She was not one of the servants. [*Turning*] Henri!

HENRI. I have been looking for you—to say good-by.

JULIE. You are going early.

HENRI. I leave France tomorrow.

JULIE. What do you mean, Henri?

HENRI. I shall return to South America, to continue the studies in which I was engaged before I hurried home, a few months ago.

JULIE. This is a sudden resolution.

HENRI. No; I made the resolution long ago—but I— Heigh-ho! I have not acted upon it.

JULIE. Will you—be gone—long—Henri?

Henri. If I ever return—

Julie. Ever!

Henri. It will be many years from now. I shall always think of you as one of my dearest friends, as the little playmate of my boyhood, and it will be pleasant to feel that you are thinking of me in the same way.

Julie. You—you are going away—perhaps—forever!

Henri. Yes. I must go. Good-by. [*Extends his hand. She extends hers, but withdraws it as it touches his, turning away*]

Julie. Tomorrow! And you will leave me alone! Alone?

Henri. I leave you with your friends; with your parents and—[*Hesitates*]

Julie. And—my—husband. I am never so utterly alone as when I am with *him*.

Henri. Julie!

Julie. Terribly alone! I must lead the life of solitude now to which I have been condemned by my marriage. I was ignorant of the world—almost ignorant of right and wrong—they call it "innocence"—and I was given to him! I did not think of love. He did not expect it from me, nor care for it. I was perfectly contented with that, at first, but I am bound to a man who would despise a woman's heart if she could give it to him; a man so cold, and cynical, and heartless, that I shrink from him almost with terror, whenever he is in my presence. [*Sinking upon ottoman, L.C.*] A woman cannot live and not love, Henri. You have been near me, too. [*Hides face in hands*]

Henri. We—we ought not to have been near each other.

Julie. Do not despise me, Henri! Do not despise me!

Henri. I am despising myself for having been here, to profit by your misery. He is your husband, Julie, and I have no place between you. When I came back to France and found you promised to another, there was but one manly and honorable course before me. I was a coward, and I did not take that course. I should have returned at once to my work, but I remained in Paris. I have allowed myself to be a constant visitor here, as in the old times, when we were children. I—I—have determined to be a coward no longer. I shall leave France tomorrow. Good-by. [*Extending his hand*]

Julie. Good-by. [*Slowly reaching out her hand, back of her, without turning. He takes it, presses it to his own, drops it by her side and moves back, still looking at her*] Alone with him!

Henri. I am, indeed, leaving her alone. She shrinks from her husband in terror, now! What has the future in store for her? I shall only live on and suffer, for the memory of my love. But she, tender, and gentle, and weak, is bound to one who will crush her young life out—slowly but surely! Julie! [*Impulsively moving towards her*] I *pity* you, with my whole heart! [*Drop-*

ping to his knees at the side of the ottoman, and seizing her hand] I pity you, my poor girl, I pity you.

JULIE. Henri. [*He is pressing her hand to his lips. Enter the Count, from apartment, up R., with cigar. He stops, up R.C., and looks at them*]

HENRI. I shall suffer, too, Julie; I shall suffer, too. Fate has been cruel to us both.

COUNT. M. Saint-Hilaire! [*Henri starts to his feet, stepping back, L., and facing the Count. Julie rises and moves to R.C.*]

HENRI. Count de Crebillon!

COUNT. [*To Julie, at her side*] Go into the drawing-room at once, and join the other ladies. [*She retires, step by step, R., under fear and emotion*]

JULIE. They will meet! Henri will be killed! [*Then, with a sudden thought*] Uncle François! I will speak to him. He will prevent it. [*Exits, R., by apartment*]

HENRI. Count! Believe me, your wife is spotless. I had just bade her farewell, intending to leave France tomorrow, forever. My own feelings overcame me at the last moment. She is not responsible for those feelings. I need hardly add, however, that I am responsible.

COUNT. You have arranged to leave France, tomorrow? We will settle the matter before morning, if you like.

HENRI. The sooner the better.

COUNT. We need not disturb the company. We can arrange the affair quietly between ourselves during the evening. Au revoir, monsieur.

HENRI. Au revoir, count. [*The Count strikes a match and is re-lighting his cigar as he goes out to garden, up L. Enter the Doctor, up R., from apartment. He watches the Count going, then turns to Henri*]

DOCT. Henri! Was it for this that I watched over you in childhood and youth, as if I were your father? I saw, with tender interest, your growth in knowledge; I have seen you adding new honor to the name which your grandfather made illustrious in science. Have you learned nothing better from kindly nature than to crush a beautiful flower—like Julie?

HENRI. Oh! Doctor Girodet. I should not have been here tonight. I should have fled from temptation many months ago. I have tried to do so over and over again, but the struggle was too great for me. Oh! If you only knew how I have struggled. I have loved Julie from my boyhood, when she was a little thing that came to my arms as innocently as a bird might rest in my hand. When I saw her again, after a long absence, a girl of seventeen, it was with a man's heart, and with all its passion, that I loved her, then! I dreamed of returning and claiming her from her parents. Oh! My friend! My father! You can never know the agony I suffered when I found Julie promised irrevocably to another! [*Dropping into chair at table, L.C., his face in his hands*] She was lost to me, forever!

DOCT. Yes, Henri! She was lost to you. Whatever you suffered, you should not have forgotten that Julie is bound in honor and truth to another.

HENRI. To such another—[*Looking up, suddenly, with clenched fist*] I could have borne it as a man should bear the worst, if Julie had been given, in her trusting innocence, to one who might have made her forget that I existed—in the gentle love of a wife and mother. I could have borne even that in my own solitude, for I should have known, at least, that she was not unhappy. But a gambler and a profligate! Notorious in every resort of aristocratic vice in Paris! The very money he has gained with her in payment for his title and his family he is spending among men and women as vicious as himself. He will make Julie more and more wretched as years go on. My blood boils like melted iron when I think of it. [*Starting to his feet*] But I can kill him, now—I can kill him!

DOCT. You have arranged for a meeting?

HENRI. Yes!

DOCT. If the count should not meet you?

HENRI. He *will!*

DOCT. If he should drop the matter?

HENRI. He cannot!

DOCT. I shall try to effect a settlement, Henri. [*Henri stands and looks at him*] For the sake of Julie's good name.

HENRI. Her name!

DOCT. If you do not hear from the count before—say, noon, tomorrow—will you promise me to carry out the good resolution which you have so often broken—to leave France, at once?

HENRI. You will tell the count that I shall wait till noon tomorrow to hear from him?

DOCT. Trust me, Henri. I shall be as careful of your honor as you could be yourself.

HENRI. I know you will. I—I give you the promise.

DOCT. Try to forget your sorrows in your profession, Henri. Be a hermit, hereafter, in the modern Religion of Science.

HENRI. My dear, old friend. [*With a warm grasp of the hand. He moves R., pauses at door. Aside*] The count *will* meet me! [*Exits, up R., through apartment*]

DOCT. If I can prevent this duel, it will be the first time the Count de Crebillon has ever hesitated to meet a man who has once aroused his passion or offended his honor. It is a curious fact in human nature that men who do most to sully their own honor are always the most sensitive when other people trifle with it. [*A long and piercing, but distant, scream from a woman without, up L. The Doctor starts, listens and goes to door, up L., where he looks out. He shrugs his shoulders, turning away. Kate runs in from garden, in alarm*]

KATE. Oh! Doctor! [*Going to him*] Did you hear that scream?

DOCT. Yes. It was startling at first, but I once heard a similar scream in the garden.

KATE. What was it?

DOCT. The footman was kissing one of the maids. [*Kate draws back*] If he'd been murdering her, she couldn't have thrown more agony into her voice. When a woman screams, she screams. The girl didn't seem a bit grateful when I rescued her.

KATE. Captain Gregory has run back to see what it was.

DOCT. He was in the garden, with you?

KATE. Yes. [*Looking down*]

DOCT. I didn't hear *you* scream. I hope the captain won't meet one of the maids. Some of them are very pretty.

KATE. But, doctor, I can't help feeling there was something more in that cry than you imagine. A few moments ago, as I was picking out the path among the trees, I saw a woman peering into the house.

DOCT. Indeed?

KATE. She was not dressed like a servant, so far as I could tell in the shadow of the tree under which she was standing. A ray of moonlight fell across her face. Our eyes met for a second, and she suddenly disappeared. When I heard that scream, just now, doctor, the picture of that woman's face seemed as clear in my mind as when she was looking into my eyes.

DOCT. What was the face like?

KATE. It was pale and thin; a hard, cold face, yet it must have been beautiful once.

DOCT. Was the figure of that woman—

KATE. Tall and slender. [*Enter the Count, from garden, up L.*]

DOCT. Ah! Count! You were in the garden—you heard the voice just now?

COUNT. Yes. I presume it was merely some poor wretch in charge of the police—[*Walking down L.*] in the street beyond.

KATE. Do you think that was it, doctor.

DOCT. I dare say.

KATE. Poor creature! I pity her. [*Going up; then, suddenly, aside*] I must get Pierre to run out and post my letter to father, and I'll put in another postscript. I'll ask papa for his consent. I'm quite sure, now, the captain will propose to me before the next steamer. [*Exits, up R., through apartments*]

Doct. Count, you have arranged for a meeting with Henri.

Count. Yes; tonight. Will you accompany us, doctor. I shan't give you much trouble with the boy. I'll only wound him slightly—in the arm or the wrist.

Doct. If you and Henri Saint-Hilaire meet, you will not separate until one of you has received a fatal wound.

Count. Indeed! It is a serious passion with him, then? If the young man insists, of course, we must carry it through in his own way. [*Then, with sinister significance*] Do you think there is any doubt as to *which* of us will be wounded fatally?

Doct. Not the slightest doubt. You are one of the coolest, most experienced and most formidable duellists in France; he is a young student of science, whose only knowledge of the weapons you will use is such as every young Frenchman acquires in the ordinary course of his education. But there is enough blood upon your soul, already, count. [*The Count starts, nervously, looking at the Doctor, then walking upstage. He turns up C., glances out, L., quickly and nervously, walks down L., touching his forehead with his handkerchief*]

Count. What do you mean?

Doct. Two men have fallen victims to your unerring skill in the duelling field.

Count. Oh! [*With relief*] I am in no humor tonight to talk of these subjects.

Doct. M. Saint-Hilaire will wait to hear from you until noon tomorrow. He has given me his promise that if he does not hear from you by that time he will leave France, at once.

Count. Very well. Settle it as you like. I will not challenge him. [*Exits, R.1.E. The Doctor looks after him a moment, then walks up L. He looks out to garden; glances back at the door, R.1.E.*]

Doct. "Merely a poor wretch, in charge of the police." The voice did not seem as distant as that, to me. The first Countess de Crebillon committed suicide in the gardens at Monaco, three years ago. She was an adventuress, and a fugitive from justice at that time. I never saw her, myself, but she was tall and slender and said to be very beautiful. [*Looks out a moment in thought, then glances at the door, R.1.E.*] The night air will be refreshing. [*Exits to garden. Enter the Duc, R., from apartment*]

Duc. I wonder where Miss Kate is? I've been trying to arrange the matter of our marriage for the last six months. My creditors are getting anxious. I don't understand this American way of conducting matrimonial affairs. Our own way is much simpler. One arranges it all with the girl's parents, and that's the end of it. [*Enter Kate, up R., from apartment. She runs across, upstage, looking out, L.*]

KATE. The captain hasn't returned yet. I begin to think he did meet one of the pretty housemaids. [*Turns down; stops, suddenly, seeing the Duc, who is down R.*]

DUC. Miss Kate!

KATE. Duc!

DUC. I received another letter from your father this afternoon. I've been looking for you in the drawing room.

KATE. Sit down.

DUC. Here! Alone?

KATE. Yes! Alone! I won't hurt you. [*Sits, L.C.*] I'm not afraid of being alone with a gentleman, and my father isn't afraid of having me. [*Aside*] If my reputation can't stand that, I'm perfectly willing to lose it, and the first French woman that finds it is welcome to it. I dare say she'll need it. [*Aloud*] Sit down.

DUC. Certainly! [*Sitting, R.C.*] Whenever I say anything to you about our marriage, Miss Kate, you refer me to your father; and when I write to him he seems to forget it for about a month each time, and then he refers me back to you. If we were all on the same side of the ocean we could get on faster.

KATE. When you first fell in love with me, duc, we were three thousand miles apart. I appreciate the compliment very highly. Of course, your interest in me increased very rapidly as the steamer on which I left New York approached the coast of Europe, at the rate of eighteen miles an hour.

DUC. I—I don't quite follow you, Miss Kate.

KATE. Concerning my dowry—

DUC. Ah—yes!

KATE. Now, you do follow me. What do you think your title, including yourself, is worth, cash! Will two million francs do? Father will pay you that amount.

DUC. Two million francs! [*Rising*]

KATE. On the day you and I are married.

DUC. My solicitor will draw up the contract at once.

KATE. Oh! No! [*Rising*] We cannot possibly sign the contract yet, duc. Being an American lady, I must insist on following the customs of my own country. Before a marriage contract can be duly ratified in America, there must be certain preliminary formalities, which propriety there demands. The gentleman is expected to make love to the lady, and to win her heart.

Duc. I'm sure I shall be delighted to pay the most devoted attention to you, Miss Kate. I will make love to you with pleasure. [*Approaching her and attempting to press her hand. She withdraws it*]

Kate. Not personally, duc! You misunderstand me. A lady and gentleman, in America, always make love to each other through their lawyers!

Duc. Their—lawyers? Oh!

Kate. If you will kindly send me the name and address of your solicitor, I will also engage one, and they will enter into negotiations on the subject; when I am duly advised by my own lawyer that you have won my heart, I will sign the marriage contract, but not till then, duc. [*Walks up*]

Duc. [*Aside, down R.*] What a very remarkable country! There are so many queer things in America. Half the gentlemen in the smoking-room had something extraordinary to tell about America, and they all said Miss Kate told them so.

Kate. [*Looking out. Aside*] The captain is coming up the path. [*Aloud*] I don't think it is best for us to be alone, together, any longer, duc.

Duc. No. I will retire. [*Rising; then aside, going*] I wonder how long it takes a lawyer to win a lady's heart? [*Exits, R.*]

Kate. Captain Gregory won't need a solicitor! [*Looking out; then turns downstage*] He was just going to ask me to be his wife, as we leaned over the curb of the old well, together—his eyes were looking straight up into mine, from the water—when I ran away from him. The word "yes" was so close to my lips, if I hadn't run away, I'd have answered him before he'd asked me the question. And I had just let him catch me again, under the old oak with mistletoe on it, when we were interrupted. I'll let him finish the question, now. Ha, ha, ha! A woman in love is like a girl playing kiss-in-the-ring; she runs away until she's afraid she won't be caught; then she stops. [*Dropping on ottoman, R.C.*] I've stopped. [*Folding her hands, demurely, as if waiting. Enter the Captain, up L., from garden. He looks at Kate, then takes a book from the table, L.C., looks at her again, sits on ottoman, L.C., opens the book. She looks at him*] I hope he hasn't stopped playing kiss-in-the-ring. [*Aloud*] What book are you looking at, captain?

Capt. [*Reading title*] "The Code of Social Etiquette in France, by Mme. la Countesse de Bassonbille."

Kate. Aunt gave that to me to study. She thought I needed it—badly.

Capt. Someone has been marking it. [*Reads*] "If you desire to wed a young girl"—

Kate. Oh! That is such a curious passage. I marked that double, you see.

CAPT. Oh! It was you!

KATE. Eh! [*Then dropping her head*] Yes, I did it. [*Aside*] All the parts marked are about how people get married.

CAPT. [*Aside*] I never took up a girl's book that everything like that wasn't marked in it. Perhaps this will tell a fellow how the French fellows manage it, when they're in love. It may help me. [*Glances at her, then reads aloud*] "If you desire to wed a young girl—[*Glances at her again*] you must get a mutual friend to make the first advance, or you may get the clergyman, or the family lawyer."

KATE. Ha, ha, ha, ha!

CAPT. An officer in Her Majesty's service might as well ask the clergyman or a family lawyer to charge a battery for him. But the French way isn't so bad, after all. Miss Kate—[*Rising*] I—I wish I had someone—a lawyer or a clergyman, or something—[*Approaching her*] to—to say—exactly what I want to say to you. I'm only a soldier, you know.

KATE. Did you ever read Longfellow's poem, "Miles Standish"? The hero and heroine were alone, together, as you and I are, and she said to him—the hero's name is John—

CAPT. The same as mine—

KATE. So it is.

CAPT. What did she say to him?

KATE. "Why don't you speak for yourself, John!"

CAPT. Eh? Speak for myself?

KATE. That's what the girl in the poem said.

CAPT. Oh! What did that John answer?

KATE. Oh! Well—he ran away without saying a word.

CAPT. Oh! Did he? [*Walks away, L., thinking*]

KATE. But, captain, he came back again—

CAPT. [*Returning to her, quickly*] And he told her he loved her—I'm sure he did! I love you, Miss Kate, with my whole heart. [*She starts to her feet, turns towards him with her eyes dropped, then extends both hands, frankly*]

KATE. And I love you—[*He seizes her hands, eagerly*] too earnestly and too sincerely to disguise it. I know that you are brave, and good, and true. I am very, very glad you love me.

CAPT. I tried my best not to love you, because I have nothing to offer you but a—a sword, and a heart, and a pair of spurs, and a uniform, with me in it. But I couldn't help loving you! May I write to your father? This very night?

KATE. I have written to him. [*He stares at her*] I put in another postscript.

CAPT. Oh!

KATE. I knew you were going to propose to me, six weeks ago.

CAPT. I wish I'd known it as soon as you did. We'd have saved a lot of time. I must join the regiment sooner than I expected. I—I—I wish we could get married before I go. I'm sorry your father is so far away.

KATE. I'll send him a cable. [*Runs to escritoire. Writes*] "To Robert G. Shipley, Park Avenue, New York. I am going to get married."

CAPT. I hope he'll give his consent.

KATE. Oh! A mere formality like papa's consent can come by mail—[*Still writing*] after we are married. I'm only telling him the facts now. [*Writes*] "I love him very, very, very much." [*Speaks*] Three "verys"—at forty cents a word; they're worth it! [*Enter Mme. Fonblanque, up R. She stops, up C. Kate writes*] "Please send me your blessing and enough money for my trousseau."

MME. F. [*R.*] Alone! With a gentleman!

KATE. There! [*Rising and going to him, L.C.*] If you'll take that to Brown, Drexel & Shipley, the bankers, tomorrow morning, they'll send it for me.

CAPT. I—I would like to give you—just one honest, English kiss.

KATE. You may—and I will kiss you, because I love you, John! [*They kiss. Mme. Fonblanque gives a short, sharp, bark-like scream, drawing up, stiffly. The lovers start and shrink back a little, left of C.*]

MME. F. I am utterly astonished, my niece! I am petrified!

KATE. Captain Gregory has asked me to be his wife.

MME. F. And you have allowed him to kiss you. Worse than that, you have kissed him!

KATE. We love each other.

MME. F. Shocking!

KATE. Why, aunt, dear, a kiss is the only seal that nature has given us for a marriage contract. Kiss me again, Jack! [*He kisses her. Mme. Fonblanque drops into a chair, with a little scream*]

ACT III.

SCENE 1: *The Château Fonblanque. Another apartment. Corner of the room, up C. Large opening to a hall, up L.C. Bay window, up R.C. Sunlight on foliage beyond window, with a few rays falling inside. Doors, R.1E. and L.1E. Ottoman, up C. Armchair, R.C. Ornamental table, L.C., with chair.* DISCOVERED: *Julie, standing up C., her head resting, wearily, against the casement of the bay window.*

JULIE. The very spots of sunshine on the grass seem like shadows this morning. I am growing blind—blind to everything that used to make life beautiful and bright. Life! What is life, to cling to? What is life, now, that I should fear to lose it? I dreamed, last night, that I was sleeping, and Henri was planting flowers in the earth above me; I was sleeping so quietly and peacefully. [*She reaches up and picks a small branch of leaves falling through the casement from a vine*] He and I planted this vine together. [*Walking down*] I used to scold the gardener if he ever touched it. One day, I overheard the old man say that he feared his little mistress would water that vine with her tears some day. I didn't know what he meant then, but I do, now—I know, now! [*In chair, L.C., dropping her head onto her arms on the table, and sobbing. Enter the Count, R.1.E. He stops, R., looking at her*]

COUNT. In tears, madame? [*Julie looks up at him, brushes her eyes, quickly, and rises*]

JULIE. You have returned to the château earlier this morning than usual, monsieur.

COUNT. You were weeping because I did not return still sooner. [*Crossing to her*] You pay me a very high compliment; the more so as I spend so many of my nights away; and I frequently do not return at all the next day. But, now I think of it a second time, it is just possible that your tears have not been flowing for *me*. Pardon me. [*He takes her wrist in his left hand, quietly, and is about to take the branch of leaves in his other hand. She struggles, very slightly. He presses her wrist, firmly, looking at her; then takes the leaves from her fingers, turning away. She starts, as if to take them again, but restrains herself*] It is late for the dew to be lingering on the leaves, and yet there are drops upon these. I fear I was flattering myself; perhaps your tears were falling for another. Pray, do not check them on my account, madame. We, all of us, have sad memories; but we should feel sadder still to lose them. Their roots must be moistened with our tears, now and then. But the autumn is at hand, and every leaf must soon fall—[*Picking the leaves off and dropping them to the floor*] one after another. Memories, too, must fall away, one by one, from our lives. [*Turns, R.*] I am sorry that I disturbed your thoughts at such a sacred moment. I came to offer you an apology. I so far forgot myself, last evening, as to interrupt you and M. Henri Saint-Hilaire in one of those emergencies when every considerate husband is expected to be elsewhere. But even the most scrupulous of husbands will make a mistake, now and then, unless he is given fair notice that his presence is undesirable. I trust you will forgive my indiscretion. There was no intentional breach of etiquette, on my part, I assure you.

JULIE. I beg of you, monsieur, to say whatever you have to say to me at once.

COUNT. I will detain you only a moment. At the earnest solicitation of Dr. Girodet, after the incident last evening, I consented to—to give the young man his life.

JULIE. Dr. Girodet sent me word that the matter had been settled—amicably.

COUNT. I claim no merit for my magnanimity, however. M. Saint-Hilaire is to leave France today.

JULIE. Yes.

COUNT. And I haven't the slightest objection to have a man passionately devoted to my wife—if he is five thousand miles away. Perhaps it would be unreasonable to object to my wife's devotion to him—even to a former lover —at such a distance. But I have one thing to say to you, madame. I have never dreamed, for a moment, that I was the happy possessor of your affections. And, if I remember correctly, I have never spoken to you of love.

JULIE. Never.

COUNT. Pardon my frankness if I say that I have no interest in that subject. Whatever my faults may be—and I do not profess to be perfect—I am not a hypocrite.

JULIE. You have never deceived me, in that respect.

COUNT. But I *have* an interest, madame—a very serious interest—in my honor as a husband—before the world. That is in your keeping. I shall protect the name I bear—at all hazards. Whatever blots there may be on our family escutcheon, that of cowardice has never been there. Do not forget that you, also, bear my name. [*Exits, up L.*]

JULIE. His honor as a husband! His name! I never should have borne it! Father! Mother! You have given me a greater burden than my poor weak nature can bear. Oh, that my dream last night were true. I long to be asleep —asleep. Why should I not be? [*She sees the leaves on the floor, picks them up, quickly and nervously; goes to door*] Henri leaves me today—forever! [*Exits, R.1.E. Enter Mme. Fonblanque, up L., in elegant morning wrapper*]

MME. F. I have not recovered, yet, from the shock which I received last night. If I had seen Julie, herself, kissing a gentleman, I should have been less bewildered. Julie, at least, is a married woman, and has the privilege of deciding upon her own course in matters of that nature. For an unmarried girl to be guilty of such an action is unpardonable! [*Down L.C. Enter Fonblanque, up L., in morning wrapper*]

FONB. Good morning, Mathilde. [*Kisses her hand*]

MME. F. Good morning, my husband.

FONB. I trust you have slept well, after the dinner and the reception last evening.

MME. F.   I have been somewhat troubled in my sleep.

FONB.   I am very sorry. I have passed a restless night, myself. [*Moving R.*] I can't get it out of my head that we forgot to invite some very important personage, in high position, to our reception. It has been quite like a nightmare to me. I feel certain that some calamity has occurred, or is about to do so. And among my letters, this morning, I find a note from the prefect of police.

MME. F.   What can the prefect have to say to you?

FONB.   He requests me to meet him, in a private room at the prefecture, at one o'clock today.

MME. F.   What can it mean?

FONB.   I have been asking myself the same question ever since I opened the note. It is couched in the most courteous terms possible, of course, to one of my social position. But it is so particularly polite. I was quite startled when I read it. If I had committed a murder, the authorities couldn't have treated me with more respectful consideration. It seems that Dr. Girodet had something to do with the matter; his name is mentioned by the prefect.

MME. F.   Possibly that may explain his very sudden disappearance last evening. I saw nothing of him after about eleven o'clock. But I supposed a professional engagement had called him away.

FONB.   You, also, have been troubled in your sleep, Mathilde?

MME. F.   About our American niece, Phillippe. I have just sent Pierre to say to her that I wish to see her here. A calamity did occur at the Château Fonblanque last night.

FONB.   You alarm me!

MME. F.   I don't wonder you had a nightmare.

FONB.   Relieve my suspense!

MME. F.   I saw Kate Shipley kissing Captain Gregory!

FONB.   I cannot believe it!

MME. F.   With my own eyes!

FONB.   A young girl cannot possibly kiss a gentleman—in France.

MME. F.   She learned how to do it in another country. What is worse, Phillippe, she told me, to my very face, and in his presence, that she *loved* Captain Gregory.

FONB.   Mathilde! [*Dropping into chair, R.C.*]

MME. F.   What is still worse, she's going to marry him!

FONB.   And discard a duke! I can believe anything of the girl after that. Poor Victorien! Our cousin had set his heart upon her fortune—I would say— upon Kate.

MME. F.   I had looked forward to their marriage with so much pleasure.

Fonb. I hoped to have given the child my blessing, in the absence of her father. How much is it that the duke owes us, now?

Mme. F. Three hundred thousand francs. [*Enter Kate, R.1 E., dressed for the carriage. She is adjusting one glove, the other in her hand. Mme. Fonblanque sits, L.C.*]

Kate. Aunt, dear, good morning; uncle! I was dressing to go out when Pierre brought me your message, or I should have come down at once. I am going to make a call, in Paris. Julie has kindly lent me her carriage this morning. What did you wish to say to me, aunt?

Mme. F. I wish to speak with you, seriously, about the very remarkable incident which came under my personal observation last evening.

Kate. Remarkable, aunt? A gentleman, whom I love very dearly, proposed to me; I accepted him, and afterwards I kissed him. That is the regular order in which we American girls do those things. The next time I see Captain Gregory I shall do it again. Here, I believe, the lady waits until she is married before she kisses the man she loves, or any other gentleman.

Fonb. You have so far forgotten your duty to us, your present guardians, as to—to choose a husband for yourself?

Kate. Yes, uncle. I have chosen for myself; and I much prefer to kiss the man I love, before marriage, to kissing one I do not love, afterwards. *We* are very particular about what is proper in a woman. We do not think that even a marriage ceremony, without love, can make a kiss modest or womanly. I have something serious to say to you, aunt. Do you remember, on the day I first arrived, I said that, if I ever found it impossible to please you, without sacrificing my own self-respect, I should cease to be a visitor at your house? I feel, aunt—and uncle—I am very sorry to say it—but that has come! I have followed the dictates of my own heart; you take a view of what I have done which neither my father nor I can accept; and my self-respect compels me to leave the Château Fonblanque.

Mme. F. I will not say, then, what I had intended, when I sent for you— that it is no longer desirable for you to remain here.

Kate. Thank you, aunt, for not saying it. I was about to call on the friends from New York, the family I crossed the ocean with; they have returned to Paris. I know they will be glad to have me with them, at their hotel. I will go there, tomorrow, with your permission.

Fonb. But what may your father—

Kate. Oh! Anything I do will suit papa; it always does. Aunt, dear, forgive me for all the trouble I have been to you. I tried, very hard at first, to act as if I wasn't an American girl, for your sake. But I am, aunt, and I couldn't help being one—if—if all the armies in Europe surrounded me, with their bayonets pointed at the prettiest bonnet I have. Ha, ha, ha, ha! Sometimes I've been a very wicked girl, too; but I couldn't help that, either. That wasn't because I'm an American girl, aunt. It was just because I'm a girl. No girl can help that—I don't care where she was born; only girls in different countries have different ways of being wicked. We American girls have discovered some new ways; that's all.

MME. F. You have acted very wrongly, indeed.

KATE. Our first trouble of all, aunt, was about a dressing-maid.

MME. F. You refused to have one.

KATE. I felt that she would be in the way, especially when I was dressing.

MME. F. She should have accompanied you whenever you walked out, and you would not allow her to do so.

KATE. I found that I didn't care to be responsible for her morals.

MME. F. Julie's governess took charge of you, at my own request, after Julie was married. Madame Rabeau informed me, in less than a week, that *you* had taken charge of *her*.

KATE. I was compelled to, aunt; I saw that she needed careful watching. Besides, I used to give her lessons in the studies you asked her to teach me. But still—as I said before—I *have* been very wicked. I've told more fibs since I've been in Paris than half a dozen girls ought to tell in the same length of time. I don't tell fibs, at all, in New York, now. But, somehow, when one of us American girls comes to Europe—well, if people *will* believe everything one says about things at home, how can any girl that likes fun help telling fibs? Please say to Field Marshal Corlette, uncle, that he needn't be afraid of going to America for fear of losing all his wigs.

FONB. Wigs?

KATE. I'm afraid he got an idea from me that it's dangerous to wear hair at all in the United States. It isn't dangerous, uncle, except when its natural. And I told the Archduke Contagowskoff that I never saw a dinner party with more than one course until I came to Europe. That isn't true, uncle; we often have two courses, and once I was at a dinner where they had three. The Prince de Molzrieaux remarked to me, last night, that he hoped some day to go to America and shoot buffaloes. I told him there were plenty in Central Park. That *is* true. There are two buffaloes in the park; and they *are* plenty. But the prince may have received a wrong impression. The Spanish ambassador is a widower, and he doesn't intend to remain so, I believe; he told me he had heard that American gentlemen had an enormous amount of money. I said I didn't know anything about that, but when a New York girl wanted some pin money, she telegraphed to her father, and he sent it up in a wagon. Later in the evening he asked me for my father's address. Tell him for me, uncle, before he has time to write that I—I was—exaggerating—a little. Papa never sent me anything but a handcart full in all my life. And I told the Marchioness de—the fat marchioness, aunt—but I haven't time, now, to tell about all the wicked fibs I've told 'em.

FONB. You need not take that trouble. Hereafter, whatever information our friends may have received about America—

KATE. Tell them it isn't true, uncle; and you may say I did it. I'm *very* sorry, indeed, but my health would have broken down if I hadn't done it! [*Enter Pierre, R.1.E., a letter in his hand*]

PIERRE. [*To Kate*] A note for you, ma'm'selle, from Madame la Countess.

KATE. [*Taking note*] For me, Pierre?

PIERRE. Madame asked me to give it to you as she was leaving the château, a moment ago. [*Walks up L.*]

MME. F. Did the countess say where she was going, Pierre?

PIERRE. She did not, madame.

KATE. She has taken her carriage, of course.

PIERRE. No ma'm'selle. The carriage is still waiting at the door for yourself. [*Exits, up L.*]

KATE. A note from Julie, for me. [*Opening it*] You will pardon me?

MME. F. and FONB. Certainly. [*Kate glances at the note, starts slightly, catches her breath, but recovers herself, as if not to arouse their attention*]

KATE. Julie merely wishes me to make a purchase for her in the Boulevard des Italien.

FONB. [*Rising*] I will write to your father and tell him how sorry Madame Fonblanque and I both are that your visit has come to a conclusion.

KATE. Thank you, uncle, dear.

FONB. [*Aside*] I really shall miss the girl very much. I like her. [*Exits up L. Mme. Fonblanque crosses, R. front, turns*]

MME. F. We shall both be deeply grieved, my niece.

KATE. I shall be as sorry to leave you, aunt, as you will be to have me leave. [*Exit Mme. Fonblanque, R.1.E. Kate returns, suddenly, to the letter in her hand; reads it*] "My darling, darling Kate; I can bear the misery no longer. You are stronger and better than I am, but you—and you only—can understand me. Tell father and mother—oh—tell them nothing! My room will be empty. That will be enough for them to know. Julie." She has fled— to the man she loves! The carriage is at the door. I will follow her! [*Turning quickly, to go up. Enter the Count, up L. Kate stops, suddenly*] Count!

COUNT. Mademoiselle, you are in haste.

KATE. [*Passing him*] Yes, monsieur, I have an engagement. [*Moving up, as he walks down. She stops, C., as he crosses, R., and sees the miniature in*

his hand dangling by the ribbon. She speaks, aside] He has Julie's miniature
of Henri in his hand.

COUNT.   You are looking at this trinket. I just picked it up on the grand
staircase. It is a portrait of M. Saint-Hilaire. He may as well take it to South
America with him. I will return it to him, in person, with my compliments.

KATE. [*Aside*]   Ah! He will find Julie there.

COUNT. [*Looking at his watch*]   A quarter to twelve; there is only just
time.

KATE.   Pardon me, count, but—that is my picture.

COUNT.   Yours!

KATE.   I have been looking for it everywhere.

COUNT.   A gentleman does not give his portrait, framed in gold and set in
diamonds, to a mere friend.

KATE.   I am very glad you have found it.

COUNT.   M. Saint-Hilaire is fortunate. And Captain Gregory? Madame
Fonblanque informed me, last evening, that you had chosen him as a husband; I congratulate the captain, especially on the fact that his rival is going
away before your marriage. Husbands are not always so fortunate. Permit me.
[*Offering the locket*]

KATE. [*Taking it*]   Thank you.

COUNT.   When M. Saint-Hilaire is gone—you will marry Captain Gregory,
of course; but your heart will be unoccupied. If I could hope—

KATE.   You addressed me in a tone like that once before, count!

COUNT.   I did; on the occasion of our first meeting—in the train, near
Rouen. But we were total strangers, then. We are not strangers, now. On the
contrary—I know you perfectly.

KATE. [*Aside*]   Oh! if there was someone near to resent his insolence!
[*Aloud*] You say you know me, count; know this—I hate you! [*Exits, up L.*]

COUNT.   Ha, ha, ha, ha! That woman *would* be worth fighting for. I've
never quite forgiven the girl for playing the prude with me so successfully,
when we first met. She compelled me to apologize to my respected father-in-
law, on her account; and she has been laughing in her sleeve at me all the
time; carrying on her intrigue under my very eyes. M. Saint-Hilaire is general in his attentions. My own wife is merely one among other ladies in the
circle of his fancy. I mistook a boy's passing fancy for the serious passion of
a man. Dr. Girodet was wrong. The young Lothario would have been quite
contented with a slight wound in his arm. I might arrange a meeting with
him, yet. No, I'll keep my word with the doctor. Besides, it's Captain Gregory's turn now. [*Walking, L., laughing, lightly*] I'll not interrupt Miss Kate
and M. Saint-Hilaire. [*Stops suddenly, with a change of expression*] Or was

the girl lying to me? [*Rings bell, sharply*] *Was* it she who dropped that miniature on the grand staircase? [*Enter Pierre, up L.*] I wish to speak with the countess.

PIERRE. Madame la Countess left the château a few moments ago, monsieur.

COUNT. Order the carriage at once.

PIERRE. The carriage is out with—

COUNT. The coupé, then! Tell the groom I am in haste.

PIERRE. Yes, monsieur. [*Exits up L.C. The Count moves to door, R.1.E.*]

COUNT. M. Saint-Hilaire leaves France today. I will bid him good-by! [*Exits R.1.E.*]

SCENE 2: *Apartments in the Rue de Rivoli. Large window at back, showing Paris beyond. Daytime. Doors at R.C. and L.C., set at an angle of about 45 degrees, half facing the audience. The door at R.C., well upstage; that at L.C., about 3d entrance. The furniture and ornaments of the room are such as are suitable to a rich, young, French gentleman and scientist who has gathered many objects of curiosity and scientific interest in foreign lands. Table up C.; chair near table. A long, low ottoman or lounge, R. An ottoman, down L. Duelling rapiers crossed above window, at back, with wire masks, pads, gloves, etc.*

DISCOVERED: *Andre, on stepladder at back, getting down the masks, pads, rapiers, etc., from over the window.*

ANDRE. This is the suddenest move my young master has made yet. At one o'clock this morning, M. Henri wakes me up and says: "Andre! Have everything ready to leave Paris this afternoon for South America." It never does take us long to start for a place a few thousand miles off. When we left Brazil, seven months ago, M. Henri said: "Andre! We will start for Paris in two hours." Two hours! And fifteen boxes of curiosities and scientific rubbish, besides our portmanteaus! Thank Heaven! We're going to leave all the scientific rubbish behind this time. But wherever master is, he'll need his fencing tools, of course. A pair of rapiers in a gentleman's room serve to defend his honor by implication, so to speak. [*During the above he has got the various articles from the wall and descended, placing the ladder near door, and the masks, gloves, etc., and one of the rapiers on the table, C. He now stands down C., with one of the rapiers in his hand*] His honor! I'm very glad I haven't any honor to defend. Susanne divides her kisses about equally between the barber and me. All right; she has enough kisses for us both, and some to spare for the baker. But when a *lady* divides her kisses like that, two of the gentlemen fight about it, and she kisses the third gentleman while they're doing it. That's honor. Ha! [*Striking a position, suddenly, L.C., fencing vigorously, with an imaginary foe, his back to door, R. Enter Henri, R. He stops, looking at Andre, who continues fencing, stepping back step by step. Henri pats him on the shoulder*] Pardon, monsieur! I was imagining myself a gentleman.

HENRI.   Is everything ready?

ANDRE.   Everything; except the rapiers. [*Laying the one in his hand on the table, across the other*] You told me to get them down, but not to pack them up until you gave me further orders.

HENRI.   No! There has been no caller, nor a letter, while I've been out?

ANDRE.   Your friend, the English officer, was here, monsieur.

HENRI.   Captain Gregory?

ANDRE.   He said M. le Docteur Girodet had told him you were going to-day, and he asked me what train you would leave by, as he would like to meet you at the station; but I could not tell him.

HENRI.   Go to Captain Gregory's apartments, Andre, in the Rue Scribe, and say that I shall be here until two, at least. I am sorry I was out when he called.

ANDRE.   Yes, monsieur. [*Going; takes ladder over his shoulder*] What orders shall I leave with the janitor?

HENRI.   Tell him to send me any note or letter at once.

ANDRE.   And visitors?

HENRI.   He may let them come up. Hurry back.

ANDRE.   Yes, monsieur. [*Going, R. Henri takes up one of the rapiers, at the table*] I'll run around and kiss Susanne good-by. The baker is never there at this hour. [*Exits R., with stepladder*]

HENRI.   Not a word from the Count de Crebillon, yet. Dr. Girodet has succeeded. I cannot thank him for his good offices. I might have saved her, or the count delivered *me,* from a future that both of us dread to meet. [*Puts down the rapier and looks at his watch*] Twelve o'clock. There is no hope, now; and I can only keep my promise, and my resolution, broken so often, to leave France. [*Dropping upon ottoman, down L.*] How vividly I remember the day I left Paris, two years ago. [*Looks up over his shoulder at the door, R.*] Come in! [*Listens*] I was mistaken. When I bade her farewell, that day, there seemed to be a look in her eyes which said, "Come back to me, Henri." I dared not say anything of my hopes, then, for fear that they would vanish, as daydreams do, when we speak of them to others. [*A timid knock at the door, R. Henri rises*] Come in! [*Moving forward a step. The door slowly opens and Julie enters. Henri stops, L.C., looking at her. She enters, timidly, her hand on the side of the door, her eyes dropped. She moves down R.C., her eyes still fixed on the floor, and with faltering steps. She at last glances up at him and moves quickly to the ottoman, falling upon it on her face*]

JULIE. Don't think that I'm a bad, wicked woman, Henri, but I shall die if you leave me with him. I couldn't help coming to you; I couldn't help it.

HENRI. Julie! [*He springs forward, crossing to her; leans over her; hesitates a moment, eager to seize her in his arms, but holding himself back by a strong effort of the will; then forces his hands behind him and moves back a few steps*] You—you have fled from your home—to me!

JULIE. What will you think of me—what *must* you think of me?

HENRI. I think—that they have driven you to despair.

JULIE. I have chosen between this and death.

HENRI. I am too near despair myself, Julie, to save you.

JULIE. I have taken my choice between a life which I could endure no longer—and your contempt.

HENRI. My—contempt!

JULIE. You can never love me now as you used to.

HENRI. I would not lose, for all the world, Julie, the respect for you which has always been a part of my love. I have worshiped at a shrine, and I would not dare to violate its sanctity now.

JULIE. Oh, Henri! Why have they robbed me of a love like yours? [*Rising*] I will not rob myself of such a love. I said that I had chosen between your contempt and death. I did not choose rightly.

HENRI. [*Standing*] What do you mean?

JULIE. Since we parted, last night, my thoughts have wavered a thousand times. When I left home, today, I did not know where I was going. It was only from a last, sudden, desperate thought that I came to you. When I knocked at your door, the world became darker than it had ever been before. I seemed to be extinguishing the only light that had been left to me. But you do still love me? [*Turning to him*]

HENRI. [*Seizing her hand*] Never so much as I do now. [*She kisses his hands, passionately, then suddenly tears herself away from him and starts up towards door*] What will you do? [*He springs after her and detains her*]

JULIE. [*Turning and looking at him*] I will take your love with me, Henri, to another world.

HENRI. Julie! [*Enter Kate, up R. She steps in, suddenly. The glove held in her hand in previous scene is now gone*]

KATE. M. Saint-Hilaire—[*Julie walks down L. Henri steps R.*] I came here to save my cousin from herself—and from you, monsieur. [*Moves down to Julie*] Julie—my darling! [*Julie turns and buries her face in Kate's bosom*] Come with me, dear! You must return to your home. Whatever you suffer there, you will find more misery still in leaving it. The carriage is at the door. Come, darling! [*A knock, firm and decided, at the door, R. Kate and Julie start. Henri turns, quickly, goes to door and places his hand on the knob*]

HENRI. [*In a low voice*] In that room for one moment—[*Pointing to door, L.*] until I can dispose of my visitor.

KATE. Yes. Julie, come!

JULIE. No! [*Drawing up; then, half aside*] I would sacrifice everything—life itself—for his love—but—[*Aloud*] I do not care for the world, now. Let them come in, whoever it may be. [*The knock repeated*]

KATE. [*Glancing R., then in her ear*] It *may* be the count!

JULIE. I will meet him. [*Then, with a sudden thought*] But Henri's life! Ah! [*She hurries out at door, L. Kate pulls it shut, secures the knob, carefully; she then turns to Henri, quietly*]

KATE. There, monsieur. It's all right, now. Your visitor may come in.

HENRI. [*Advancing towards her*] But you, Miss Kate!

KATE. I?

HENRI. Your own reputation!

KATE. Oh! thank you. I forgot *I* had one to lose, too. [*Going*] I'm not accustomed to these French situations. [*Exits at door, L. Henri moves to door and throws it open. He starts, slightly, and steps back*]

HENRI. Count de Crebillon! [*Inclining his head*] Enter, monsieur. [*Moves down, across to L.C. Enter the Count. He stands a moment at door, looking at Henri, then turns to close it. He stoops down and picks up Kate's glove from threshold, without*] A personal call from you is an unexpected honor, count.

COUNT. I can quite believe that my visit was unexpected, M. Saint-Hilaire. [*Glances at table*] I see you have weapons at hand; not with any hostile intent, I trust.

HENRI. I did expect to use them. I suppose that I should have seen your own representative before this time.

COUNT. You did not meet Dr. Girodet again, last evening? [*Walking down, R.*]

HENRI. He was called away, suddenly, I believe.

COUNT. You must have wondered that you did not hear from me. I assured the doctor that I would pass over the little incident that led to a misunderstanding between us. I have apologized to the countess already. Permit me to apologize to you, also.

HENRI. I am not in the humor for jesting with anyone, much less with you, and upon such a subject.

COUNT. [*Looking up, sharply, at him*] You will find, M. Saint-Hilaire that I can be in earnest, also—in deadly earnest; I have found a lady's glove upon your threshold.

HENRI. Well, monsieur?

COUNT. And the carriage of the Countess de Crebillon is waiting upon the street below—at your door! I will drag my wife from your room, monsieur!

HENRI. Pardon me, count—[*Moving to before door, L.*] but you shall not enter my private apartment.

COUNT. With your permission or without it, I will enter that room.

HENRI. Without it, then, monsieur. [*They face each other a moment, with set teeth. The Count then moves, quietly, up to the table, takes one of the rapiers and moves down R., facing Henri. Henri steps to the table, takes the other rapier, and moves back to the door, facing the Count*]

COUNT. Stand aside, monsieur!

HENRI. You shall not enter! [*The Count lunges forward, fiercely. Two or three quick passes. A scream is heard within the room*]

COUNT. Aha, monsieur! [*He attacks Henri with great vigor and angry determination. A knock at door, R. The combat continues. The knock repeated. Enter Captain Gregory*]

CAPT. Fencing, gentlemen? [*They stop, suddenly, dropping the points of their weapons*]

COUNT. [*Walking down L.*] Monsieur Saint-Hilaire and I are practicing, captain.

CAPT. Without your masks, or the pads and gloves. It's dangerous sport. Glad I found you in at last, Henri. Thanks for sending round for me. I'm sorry you're going. [*Henri staggers*] I say, old fellow! [*Springing forward and supporting him. Henri drops the rapier. The Captain places him in a chair near table*] You are wounded!

HENRI. A little thrust in the side. Only the point; a mistake. The count and I—were—so interested—we both forgot ourselves for a moment.

CAPT. [*Feeling Henri's side and putting his handkerchief to it*] You Frenchmen find as much amusement in this sort o' thing, I dare say, as we Englishmen do in punching each other's heads.

COUNT. I will get something for your wound, monsieur, and you will need water. I can find it in this room, I suppose? [*Moving to door, L.C.*]

HENRI. Ah! [*Trying to spring up*]

CAPT. [*Restraining him*] Hold on, old boy! The wound will be a serious one, if you go on in this way.

COUNT. You must avoid excitement, monsieur. [*Exits at door, L.C.*]

HENRI. Coward! [*With a quick struggle, releasing himself from the Captain. He snatches up the rapier and springs toward the door. The Captain seizes him and forces him by main strength back into the chair, holding him firmly as he proceeds*]

CAPT. I think I understand the situation; it's all in dead earnest, I see. But there shan't be murder on your soul, Henri, so long as I'm a stronger man than you are; and I'm likely to be for some time to come. [*The Captain stands with his back to R., as he holds Henri. The Count reappears, L.C., coming in backwards and bowing*]

COUNT. Mademoiselle! [*Enter Kate, L.C.*] I ask a thousand pardons!

KATE. Captain Gregory—here! [*The Captain turns and sees Kate; falls back a few steps, R.*]

CAPT. Kate!

COUNT. M. Saint-Hilaire! I ask your forgiveness, also, for my intrusion at such a moment. [*Putting rapier on table. Aside*] The little American devil— [*Walking down R.*] was telling me the truth after all.

KATE. [*Aside*] What must he think of *me!* But I must play the part to the end—for Julie's sake. [*Moving a step forward, L.C. Henri rises and stands before the door, L.C. The Count stands down R., tapping one hand with the glove*]

COUNT. Ha, ha, ha! A pretty little glove!

KATE. I must have dropped it—after I left the carriage. May I trouble you for it?

COUNT. I am almost tempted to keep it. I envy you, monsieur; or perhaps I ought to envy Captain Gregory. The hand to which this glove belongs has been promised to him in marriage. He will be obliged to share its caresses with other men. [*An angry start from the Captain, up R.C., but he restrains himself*] But, all the same, it is a very pretty hand.

KATE. [*Aside*] I must still endure his insolence.

COUNT. If you can so far overcome your English prejudice against duelling, captain, as to defend your honor against M. Saint-Hilaire, I shall be very glad to act as your second.

CAPT. The relation which I bear to the lady's hand, count, is my own affair, not yours.

COUNT. By all means; I would not intrude for the world. One serious word to you, mademoiselle; you will please not borrow the Countess de Crebillon's carriage, with the family crest on its panels, the next time you have a disreputable intrigue with a gentleman. Whatever ideas of propriety may happen to prevail among the ladies of America—

CAPT. [*Stepping forward*] Permit me to return Miss Shipley her glove, count.

COUNT. Certainly, captain! [*Handing him the glove, with a bow. The Captain draws back his arm and strikes him violently in the face with it*]

CAPT. I have succeeded in overcoming my English prejudice against duelling, monsieur.

COUNT. I am quite at your service, at any time, after you have met M. Saint-Hilaire. He has a prior claim upon your honor. Of course, I cannot meet you, as a gentleman, until you have settled that claim.

CAPT. M. Saint-Hilaire is wounded.

COUNT. Ah! I forgot! Whenever you please, captain.

CAPT. I have orders by telegraph to be in London tomorrow morning.

COUNT. Very well; at once.

CAPT. Thank you. [*He turns to Kate, with the glove*]

KATE. Not—not for me—you must not fight—for me!

CAPT. May I take this with me?

KATE. [*Eagerly*] You still value it?

CAPT. May I take it?

KATE. Yes. [*The Captain turns up R.*] But you must not risk your life for me!

CAPT. We have no time to lose, count. [*Exits up R.C. The Count follows him up; turns at door*]

COUNT. I go with one of your lovers, mademoiselle, and I leave you alone with the other. I am sorry that I am not a third.

KATE. Ah! [*With a burst of anger*] I have had enough insults from you, count, and from your race. [*Moving towards him*] I have a protector, now. With all my heart, I hope he will *kill* you!

COUNT. We shall see! [*Exits R. Kate staggers with sudden weakness, supporting herself by chair, R.C.*]

KATE. What will be the end! [*Then, with a sudden thought*] Henri! [*Henri springs toward her from door, L.C., placing the rapier on table and putting up his arms to support her*] Not me—not me—I can take care of myself. Julie! She fainted when she heard your swords: I left her on the balcony. [*Henri starts towards door, L.C. He stops, bringing one hand to his breast and wavers, on his feet. Kate continues, not seeing him, and looking away R.*] He still loves me; but, if he fall, his last thought of me will be—what? John! [*Henri falls backwards, towards the audience, at full length. She turns*] Henri! Henri! [*She falls to her knees at his side, her hands on his heart*]

ACT IV.

SCENE: *The Château Fonblanque. Same scene as that of Act I. The double doors open, showing drawing-room at back, and the furniture rearranged. The large table up R., with small chair at the left. Armchair at right of table. Armchair up L., near mantel. The other pieces of Act I, to taste. Enter the Duc de Fouché-Fonblanque, through drawing-room, his hat in his hand.*

DUC.   Phillippe is out. Extraordinary circumstance! He has taken his nap at this hour, regularly, for the last twenty years. I wonder if he, also, is one of the parties to the duel. His name wasn't mentioned at the club, though nearly everybody else's was. [*Enter Mme. Fonblanque, R.1.E., in elegant wrapper*] Ah! Mathilde!

MME. F.   Victorien!

DUC.   Sorry to disturb you at this hour; Pierre said you were dressing for the evening; but—do you know anything about the affair this afternoon?

MME. F.   What "affair"?

DUC.   Ah! You haven't heard of it at all, yet? There are all sorts of rumors at the club. Somebody has been fighting a duel with somebody else.

MME. F.   Indeed!

DUC.   Whether anybody killed anybody or not, nobody can find out, but everybody says somebody was killed. The police arrived on the spot just in time to see the carriages drive off, in accordance with their regular instructions. I called at the count's private apartments, in the city, on the way here, but all I could get out of the janitor was, the physician had left instructions that he wasn't to be disturbed.

MME. F.   The count was concerned in it?

DUC.   A gentleman at the club was looking out of the window, and he saw Dr. Girodet going rapidly by in a carriage, and the count lay back on the seat with his face very pale.

MME. F.   Really, duc, I trust that nothing serious has happened to my dear son-in-law, the count. You have aroused my curiosity.

DUC.   So it has mine. Captain Gregory's name has also been mentioned in connection with the affair, but that is evidently an error. A member of the club told me that one of the other members had been told by another gentleman that he had just seen the captain walking, quietly, on the Boulevard. He asked him to join him in a drive to the Bois, but he thanked him, kindly, and said he wished to finish his cigar. M. Saint-Hilaire was one of the principals in the duel.

MME. F. Henri! [*Very earnestly*]

Duc. Dr. Poncilett was called to attend him. One always gets the latest news at the club, but it sometimes requires deep thought to understand it. It's very difficult to put this and that together. The count was wounded with a broadsword. M. Saint-Hilaire was shot. They were fighting each other. I have it all on the highest possible authority.

MME. F. I hope Henri's life is not in danger!

Duc. Let me offer you my sympathy. I have heard that Henri's father and you were deeply in love with each other, before you were married.

MME. F. Considerations of family made our union impossible. But— H-s-h—[*Looking around*] M. Fonblanque knows nothing of the circumstance.

Duc. Trust me implicitly, Mathilde. The same individual can hardly expect to monopolize a woman's hand and her fortunes, and also her affections. I'm sure my cousin Phillippe is too well-bred to be so unreasonable. [*Enter Fonblanque, up R.*]

FONB. Ah, Cousin Victorien!

Duc. Phillippe, have you heard anything about—

FONB. It has come to you already, then?

Duc. I was just telling Mathilde—

FONB. I dare say everyone at the club is talking about it. The simple truth is this; it is a mere ordinary case of suicide.

Duc. and MME. F. Suicide!

MME. F. Henri Saint-Hilaire!

Duc. The count!

FONB. They have nothing to do with the matter. The prefect of police—

Duc. I understood the police didn't interfere.

FONB. On the contrary, they have the entire matter in charge, and they have managed it with the utmost discretion.

Duc. The duel!

FONB. I received a notice from the prefect this morning.

MME. F. Oh, yes; what was it, Phillippe?

Duc. It occurred this afternoon.

FONB. It occurred last night.

Duc. I—I wonder if we are talking about the same thing.

FONB. The prefect was extremely polite to me, and he assured me he was conducting the investigation as a mere matter of routine formality. There are half a dozen similar cases in Paris every day. In the present instance, the woman—

Duc. Ah! We hadn't got to the woman, in the club, yet, but we were all looking for her.

FONB. A total stranger took the liberty of committing suicide in the gardens of the Château Fonblanque last evening.

MME. F. In our own grounds?

FONB. The fact was discovered by Dr. Girodet, about half past ten. He communicated with the police at once. The prefect is a personal friend of his, and he was considerate enough to conduct the affair without disturbing us or our guests, Mathilde. It was extremely kind on his part. It would have been very embarrassing, indeed. It annoys me exceedingly as it is.

MME. F. Do they know who it was?

FONB. There was nothing whatever to identify the person, and the prefect trusts that I shall hear nothing more of the unfortunate incident. I am sorry it has got to the club, cousin.

DUC. It hasn't. I was speaking of another matter entirely.

MME. F. Victorien was saying that our son-in-law, the count—

FONB. Oh! by the bye, I rode to the Bois after I left the prefect. The Marquis de Polignac leaned over from his carriage and remarked that he hoped the news he had just heard was not true—that the Count de Crebillon had been seriously wounded in a duel. You can imagine my feelings as a father. After a turn or two more in the Bois, I told the coachman to drive home, at once.

DUC. I believe the count is seriously wounded.

FONB. I wish you would learn something definite about it. I'll go and take my afternoon nap; it is two hours after my usual time. If anything of special interest transpires, Mathilde, you may have the servant wake me. [*Exits yawning, R.1.E.*]

MME. F. M. Fonblanque and I are both very anxious about the count.

DUC. I'll drive down to the club again.

MME. F. Do, Victorien. I'll finish my dressing, now. [*Going*] Au revoir, cousin.

DUC. Au revoir. [*Exit Mme. Fonblanque, R.1.E.*] I feel anxious about the count, too. I bought a little mare from him yesterday morning, and yesterday evening he offered to lay me three to one against her the first time I raced her. I'd like to get a few points about her. I hope he isn't seriously wounded. It's very queer, but I never do buy a horse from a man that he doesn't offer me the odds against it. [*Going up L. Enter Kate, through drawing-room, L. She moves in rapidly, coming down R.C., without seeing the Duc, who stops, up L.C.*]

KATE. The servants here have heard nothing. Five hours of agony and suspense since he left to meet the most dangerous duellist in Paris! I could not stay longer with Julie. Perhaps uncle or aunt have—[*Going, R.*]

Duc. Miss Kate.

Kate. Oh! Can you tell me, duc? Has any news come of—

Duc. The duel?

Kate. Yes! Captain Gregory!

Duc. The captain is severely—

Kate. Wounded!

Duc. No! I've got everything mixed up this afternoon; everybody says at the club that somebody—

Kate. O—h!

Duc. I was going back to learn something more definite.

Kate. Yes—go—by all means—at once!

Duc. I'll return presently, with the exact facts. [*Exits up L.*]

Kate. What torture! I can learn nothing. The captain has not returned to his apartments. I felt like a mad woman in the street, and everything going on as if his life were not at stake. I have nowhere to turn. [*Dropping into the chair, up L. Enter Captain Gregory, with Pierre, in drawing-room*]

Capt. On second thoughts, Pierre—

Kate. Ah!

Capt. I'll not disturb M. Fonblanque—[*Walking down R.C.*] if he is taking his afternoon nap.

Kate. Alive—and safe!

Capt. I will leave a note. I merely dropped in to pay my respects before leaving for London tonight, and to see Miss Shipley.

Kate. To see me!

Capt. Has she returned to the château?

Pierre. Ma'm'selle is here, monsieur.

Capt. Oh! I beg your pardon.

Kate. Captain—Gregory!

Capt. Will you excuse me one moment, Miss Shipley? I wish to leave a note with Pierre for M. Fonblanque.

Kate. Oh—certainly! [*He sits at table, R.C.*] A note! and I am absolutely dying to know what's happened.

Capt. [*Writing*] "My dear M. Fonblanque: Being compelled to return to London this evening, I dropped in to say good-by to Madame Fonblanque and yourself, and to apologize for shooting your son-in-law. With warm regards to you both, I remain—" It's lucky for me I do remain. The count is a good shot.

Kate. [*Aside*] I'm choking! [*Aloud*] Captain!

Capt. One moment. [*Addresses it*] Pierre, you may give this to M. Fonblanque, with my card—[*Rising*] but don't disturb him. [*Exit Pierre, up R.,
with note*] Yes?

Kate. And you are unhurt, thank Heaven! But I hope you haven't killed
him.

Capt. I really can't say.

Kate. He—fell?

Capt. Yes.

Kate. He may be dying—now!

Capt. Possibly. But I'm under the impression he isn't.

Kate. You fought with swords!

Capt. No.

Kate. Pistols!

Capt. Yes.

Kate. You met in the field, your seconds gave the word, you fired!

Capt. Yes.

Kate. The count was wounded—go on.

Capt. That's all.

Kate. Oh! You Englishman! You'd let a woman die gasping for knowledge. Do tell me something about it!

Capt. You've told me.

Kate. You have heard nothing since?

Capt. No.

Kate. Oh! John! To think that you may have killed a man.

Capt. I'm sorry to say that I may have killed a number of men, while I
was fighting for my country, when I didn't see half as much good to be gained
by it, though the members of the British Cabinet did.

Kate. Captain Gregory, you have risked your life, today, to defend me
from an insult, because I was a woman; but you found me in a—in a most
compromising position. I cannot explain to you why I was there; but I need
not say—that—you are—free—from your obligations to me.

Capt. Oh!

Kate. Of course—our—our engagement is at an end.

Capt. Ah!

Kate. After what has happened, there can be—no further relations—between us, of any kind.

Capt. M—m.

Kate. [*Aside*] He might show some interest in the subject, even if he does
despise me.

Capt. You were in the private apartment of another gentleman.

KATE. Yes, I was; and that ought to excite some kind of emotion in *any* girl's lover, even if he *is* an Englishman!

CAPT. You were there—with the Countess de Crebillon.

KATE. You know the truth?

CAPT. I know it now.

KATE. How?

CAPT. You've just told me.

KATE. Oh!

CAPT. I *guessed* it was the countess. I've been long enough in France for that, and I thought you wanted the count out of the way at that particular moment. But I knew one thing absolutely—whoever it was, *you* were not there alone.

KATE. Why did you know that? [*Advancing*]

CAPT. [*Approaching her, looking full into her eyes and speaking very earnestly*] Because my confidence in you is as strong as my love!

KATE. Ah! [*Clasping her hands, joyously*] You fought the count because you believed in me?

CAPT. I'm too good an Englishman to risk my life for a woman that isn't worth fighting for!

KATE. Jack! [*Resting her head on his breast*]

CAPT. You remarked just now that our engagement was at an end.

KATE. Never! 'Till I'm your wife! [*Fondling him, with his head between her hands, looking into his face. She suddenly gives a little cry and leads him down by the left ear, which is tipped with black court-plaster*] You are wounded!

CAPT. I forgot to mention that. The count's bullet took the tip of my ear off.

KATE. You were so near to death as that? My own pet British Lion! [*Embracing him, then resting her head on his shoulder. He takes the glove from a pocket*]

CAPT. I've brought this back to you. [*Holding it up*]

KATE. You may keep it now, John.

CAPT. Until the hand that fits it is mine!

KATE. My knight!

CAPT. When I looked at that on the way to the field, I felt somehow, that the count was in danger.

KATE. The count! [*Drawing back*] Oh, Jack! Jack! I hope you haven't killed him.

CAPT. I hope so, too. [*Enter the Doctor, in drawing-room, L.*]

KATE. Dr. Girodet! [*The Captain glances up and walks, L., to mantel*] Now we shall know the worst. I dare not ask him! [*Walking up L.C. Enter Fonblanque, up R.*]

FONB. Ah! captain, you are still here. The servant has just given me your note and card.

CAPT. I asked him not to disturb you. [*Enter Mme. Fonblanque, R.1.E., now in afternoon dress*]

MME. F. Captain!

CAPT. Madame!

FONB. Mathilde, I have just discovered that we omitted to send an invitation, for last evening, to the Austrian ambassador.

MME. F. Is it possible! [*Very anxiously*] How very, very unfortunate!

FONB. It has quite broken up my afternoon nap. I couldn't sleep at all. It was you, by the bye, captain, who had a duel with our son-in-law this afternoon. [*Sitting, R.C.*]

MME. F. The captain! [*Pleasantly*] Then you can tell us something about it. [*Sitting, R.*] Do you happen to know the result?

CAPT. The count has been under Dr. Girodet's care. [*The Doctor advances, C.*]

FONB. François, I trust you can relieve the very painful tension which suspense has produced in the minds of Madame Fonblanque and myself.

DOCT. When we left you on the field, captain, we drove as rapidly as possible to the count's apartments in Paris. After reaching there, he fell into a restless slumber. When he awoke, I was standing at his bedside. I told him that he had only a few minutes to live.

KATE. Oh! [*Sinking into the chair up L.C.*]

DOCT. The count turned pale, and he trembled like a frightened girl. The frequently-tested courage of the duellist failed him at that moment. Gamblers are always superstitious, and men who are most ready to risk their lives in the field of honor shrink with absolute horror when the Angel of Death hovers over them in the stillness and loneliness of the sick room. These facts in human nature quite agree with a theory of mine in the study of psychological phenomena in their relations to the functions of physical life. I once had a prolonged discussion with Professor—

KATE. But—doctor!

DOCT. Pardon me. This is a digression, and you, of course, cannot share the interest in the subject which I feel as a scientific man. The count came more and more under the influence of some secret terror that convulsed his frame. At last he told me to open a small drawer in a cabinet. I did so, and I found a picture there, of a woman. He whispered in my ear that I would find a face like that in the deserted well of the Château Fonblanque. I answered him that I had already seen it there. While our friends were entering the château, last evening, by the carved mahogany doors, the body of a dead woman, an unbidden guest, passed silently out through the little gate in the garden wall. The first Countess de Crebillon had confronted her husband.

MME. F. The first countess!

DOCT. She might have confronted a tiger, in the jungles of India, with less danger. The count has never allowed trifles to stand in the way of his own good fortune. Your daughter, cousin, has never been the Countess de Crebillon.

MME. F. Julie!

FONB. My daughter!

DOCT. The count did not know until that moment that his wife was still living. They were separated when the official mistake at Monaco occurred, three years ago. It had become her interest to disappear from the world, and she took advantage of the mistake, until her husband's second marriage and his renewed wealth made it to her interest to return to life.

KATE. Oh! John! John! [*Sobbing, in her chair*]

DOCT. What is it, my dear?

KATE. The count! A human being's death is upon my—my husband's soul.

DOCT. Not at all! The count will be perfectly well in a week! [*Kate, Mme. Fonblanque and M. Fonblanque start to their feet, the Captain starts around, all looking at the Doctor*]

KATE. You said he had only a few moments to live!

DOCT. I told *him* so; and I am under great obligations to you, captain, for giving me an opportunity to act as an amateur detective. Your bullet went just near enough a vital part for my purpose. But it was quite harmless, I assure you. It is in my waistcoat pocket at the present moment. The count's written confession is in another pocket.

KATE. My Jack! [*Moving down to Captain, R.*] You haven't killed a man, after all.

DOCT. From a scientific point of view, the experiment was an interesting one. It illustrates this fact: The unusual activity of the nerve centers in the brain, popularly known as "conscience," can be excited artificially. In other words, there is no actual physical necessity for men to wait till they are dying before repenting of their sins. I shall prepare a report of the case for the Academy of Science. How is your ear, captain?

CAPT. Very well, I thank you—what there is left of it.

FONB. Mathilde, my dear, we must speak to Julie.

MME. F. She left the château this morning, Phillippe, and she has not returned yet.

KATE. Julie is at the bedside of the man she loves, uncle; and she can remain there, innocently, now. M. Saint-Hilaire has been very severely wounded.

FONB. Henri is wounded, too?

MME. F. Henri!

FONB. I—I trust he will recover.

KATE. The physician says that he may, with careful nursing; and Julie will give him that.

DOCT. Let us hope that he will recover, cousin. Let us hope that you have not robbed a brave young lad of his life, and your own daughter of her happiness, for the sake of the Fonblanque family. [*Returns up R.C.*]

MME. F. [*Aside*] He was your son, Isidore!

FONB. [*Aside*] Pauline, you were Henri's mother! [*They turn, slowly, catch each other's eyes, and draw up. Both sit. Enter the Duc, up L., quickly*]

DUC. We've got all the facts at the club, now. Captain Gregory is dead! [*General attention. The Duc sees the Captain, puts up his glasses, and stares at him*] I had it on the highest possible authority!

KATE. It isn't his ghost, duc. [*Turning to the Captain and putting her hand in his*]

CAPT. If it is—[*Dropping his arm about her waist*] it isn't so bad being a ghost.

DUC. I beg your pardon, Miss Kate—but—

KATE. Oh! Ha, ha, ha, ha! I forgot all about the—the business affair—between us, duc. Captain Gregory has been his own solicitor.

DUC. I really don't understand you.

DOCT. I hope your creditors will wait, duc, until a Frenchman *can* understand an American girl.

KATE. I will write to papa. He will find a place for you, if *I* ask him, in one of the railway companies he owns.

DUC. A place—for a duke—in a railway company!

KATE. I dare say you can marry in New York. A few of our girls, a very few, but still a few, are quite willing to pay the debts of European noblemen.

DUC. Telegraph your father, please; perhaps he knows a girl like that. [*Turns up L.C. Enter Pierre, up L.*]

PIERRE. A telegram—for Miss Shipley.

KATE. Oh! [*Taking it. Exit Pierre*] A cable dispatch, from papa—[*Opening it*] in answer to the one you sent for me last night. [*Reading*] "From

Robert J. Shipley. Fifty-five words. Get married at once, and bring him to New York." Certainly; of course!

Capt. Oh! Very well; settle it between you.

Kate. "Who is—he?" O-h! Ha, ha, ha, ha! I forgot to tell him your name. But papa has perfect confidence in my judgment. I've given my attention to matters of this kind. Papa hasn't. [*Reads*] "Would run over to wedding, but there is a corner in Pennsylvania Central."

Capt. What's a corner?

Kate. I'll explain all those things to you after we're married. [*Reads*] "Have cabled twenty thousand dollars to bankers in Paris." For my trousseau! [*Reads*] "And placed two hundred thousand dollars government bonds to your credit here." My wedding present! Dear papa! That's a part of the corner.

Duc. Corners are nice.

Kate. Some folks think so, and some don't. I can't make out this word. [*Reads*] "B—l." [*The Captain crosses to her, C.*] Oh, yes; my father's blessing!

Capt. [*Looking over her shoulder*] So it is! [*Reads*] "Blessing. Prepaid."

Doct. Very liberally prepaid.

Duc. I hope some New York father will bless me.

Capt. *You* shall be my blessing!

Kate. I hope so, Jack! My mother has given me her blessing, too, for I— I am sure it was she that chose you for—my husband.

CURTAIN

BIBLIOGRAPHY OF PLAYS

Note: Unless otherwise specified, New York is understood to be the place of production.

1. FANTINE. *A Drama.*
   First produced in Detroit, 1864.

2. SARATOGA; Or, PISTOLS FOR SEVEN. *A Comedy in Five Acts.*
   First produced at Fifth Avenue Theatre, December 21, 1870.
   Produced as *Brighton* at Court Theatre, London, May 25, 1874.
   Produced as *Seine Erste Und Einzige Liebe* in Germany.
   Printed about 1870.

3. DIAMONDS. *A Comedy in Five Acts.*
   First produced at Fifth Avenue Theatre, September 3, 1872.

4. LILIAN'S LAST LOVE. *A Play in Five Acts.*
   First produced at Hooley's Theatre, Chicago, September 4, 1873.
   Original version of *The Banker's Daughter* (q.v.).

5. MOORCROFT; Or, THE DOUBLE WEDDING. *A Comedy in Four Acts.*
   First produced at Fifth Avenue Theatre, October 17, 1874.

6. ONLY A TRAMP.
   Unproduced. Written about 1877.
   Original version of *Baron Rudolph* (q.v.).

7. HURRICANES. *A Comic Drama in Three Acts.*
   First produced at Hooley's Theatre, Chicago, May 27, 1878.
   Produced as *Truth* at Criterion Theatre, London, February 8, 1879.
   Copyright, 1873.

8. OLD LOVE LETTERS. *A Comedy in One Act.*
   First produced at Park Theatre, August 31, 1878, as a curtain raiser to
   Hurricanes.
   Privately printed; copyright, 1897, by Bronson Howard. Copyright, 1906, by Bronson Howard (In Renewal).

9. THE BANKER'S DAUGHTER. *A Drama in Five Acts.*
   First produced as *Lilian's Last Love* (q.v.).
   First produced under present title at Union Square Theatre, September 30, 1878.

Produced as *The Old Love and the New* at the Court Theatre, London, December 15, 1879.

Privately printed; copyright, 1878.

10. WIVES. *A Comedy in Five Acts.* Adapted from Molière's *L'École Des Maris* and *L'École Des Femmes.*

First produced at Daly's Theatre, October 18, 1879.

11. THE OLD LOVE AND THE NEW.

Later version of *The Banker's Daughter* (q.v.).

Produced at the Court Theatre, London, December 15, 1879.

12. BARON RUDOLPH. *A Drama in Four Acts.*

Later version of *Only a Tramp.*

First produced in England at the Royal Theatre, Hull, August 1, 1881.

First produced in New York at the Grand Opera House, September 12, 1881.

13. FUN IN A GREEN ROOM. *A Comedy in Three Acts.*

First produced at Booth's Theatre, April 10, 1882.

14. KNAVE AND QUEEN. *A Comedy in Four Acts.* Original title, *Ivers Dean.*

Written in collaboration with Sir Charles L. Young, Bart.

Unproduced; unpublished. Probably written about 1882.

15. YOUNG MRS. WINTHROP. *A Play in Four Acts.*

First produced at Marylebone Theatre, London, September 21, 1882.

First produced in New York at Madison Square Theatre, October 9, 1882.

Printed about 1899.

16. ONE OF OUR GIRLS. *A Comedy in Four Acts.*

First produced at Lyceum Theatre, November 10, 1885.

Privately printed; copyright, 1897.

17. MET BY CHANCE. *A Romance in Four Acts.*

First produced at Lyceum Theatre, January 11, 1887.

18. THE HENRIETTA. *A Comedy in Four Acts.*

First produced at Union Square Theatre, September 26, 1887.

Produced as *The New Henrietta* at the Knickerbocker Theatre, December 22, 1913; revision by Winchell Smith and Victor Mapes.

Privately printed, 1901.

Reprinted in A. G. Halline's *American Plays,* 1935.

19. RAILWAY KING (or, THE RAILROAD KING).

Unfinished. Manuscript of synopsis and some roughly-sketched dialogue.

Probably written 1888-1892.

20. SHENANDOAH. *A Military Comedy in Four Acts.*
    First produced at Boston Museum, November 19, 1888.
    Produced at Star Theatre, September 9, 1889.
    Privately printed, 1897.
    Reprinted in A. H. Quinn's *Representative American Plays,* 1917 (revised edition, 1930); also in M. J. Moses's *Representative Plays by American Dramatists,* Vol. III, 1921.

21. ARISTOCRACY. *A Comedy in Four Acts.*
    First produced at Palmer's Theatre, November 14, 1892.
    Privately printed; copyright, 1898.

22. THE TITLE. *A Comedy in Four Acts.*
    Unproduced; unpublished; incomplete. Manuscript dated 1895.

23. PETER STUYVESANT. *A Comedy in Four Acts.* Written in collaboration with Brander Matthews.
    First produced at Providence, R.I., September 25, 1899.
    Produced at Wallack's Theatre, October 2, 1899.

24. LADYSMITH. *A Military Comedy in Four Acts.*
    Unproduced; unpublished. Written 1900 or after.

25. KATE. *A Comedy in Four Acts.*
    Unproduced.
    Published in novel-drama form, 1906.

26. (Unnamed play). *A Comedy in Three Acts.*
    Early stage of composition only. Manuscript describes characters and gives synopsis of incidents.
    No date.

BIBLIOGRAPHY OF HOWARD'S OTHER WRITINGS

1. "The Autobiography of a Play." Appeared first as a lecture delivered at Harvard in 1886. Printed in *In Memoriam,* 1910. Printed as a separate volume, *The Autobiography of a Play,* Dramatic Museum of Columbia University, New York, 1914. (Discusses the revision of *Lilian's Last Love* into *The Banker's Daughter,* and the revision of the latter into *The Old Love and the New.*)

2. "Our Schools for the Stage," *The Century Magazine,* o.s., Vol. LXI, pp. 28-37 (November 1900). (Defends the theatre as a vocation and discusses the "art of acting.")

3. "Theatrical Premières," *Sunday Magazine,* January 28, 1906. (States that the personal rights of the actor are protected more in America than in England. Defends the commercial attitude of the New York manager.)

4. "The American Drama," *Sunday Magazine,* October 7, 1906. Reprinted in Montrose J. Moses's *Representative Plays by American Dramatists.* (Traces the growth from 1890 of an American "school" of dramatists and dramatic criticism; indicates influence of Ibsen; stresses importance of heeding public taste.)

5. "Trash on the Stage and the Lost Dramatists of America," an address delivered before the Lambs Club of New York; printed in the *In Memoriam* volume. (Admits that most of American drama is inferior, but defends the few plays that are of lasting value. States that the financial success of the "trashy" plays is necessary to keep the theatres open. Contends that the significant American dramas will have to come from the professional dramatists, not from the literary men.)

GENERAL BIBLIOGRAPHY

Anonymous. "The Plays of Bronson Howard," *Century Magazine,* Vol. III, pp. 465-6 (January 1883). (Hails Howard's success, especially in face of difficult conditions; points out originality in material, skill in construction, the use of humor and wholesome dialogue.)

Anonymous. "Mr. Bronson Howard Illustrates and Defines," *Harper's Weekly,* Supplement, February 2, 1889.

Anonymous. "The Works of Bronson Howard," *Bookman,* Vol. X, p. 195 (November 1899). (Paragraph account of his plays and method of composition; speaks of *The Henrietta* as the best, which grew out of an actual case, according to this article.)

Archer, William. *English Dramatists of To-day.* London: 1882, pp. 209-19. (Commendatory account of Howard.)

Briscoe, Johnson. "The Pioneer American Dramatist," *Green Book,* Vol. XI, pp. 749-56 (May 1914).

Brown, T. A. *A History of the New York Stage from the First Performance in 1732 to 1901.* 3 vols. New York: 1903.

Clapp, J. B., and Edgett, E. F. *Plays of the Present.* Dunlap Society Publications. New York: 1902. (Theatrical notices of *Aristocracy, The Henrietta, Saratoga,* and *Shenandoah.*)

Clark, Barrett H. *The British and American Drama of To-day.* New York: 1915, pp. 219-27. (Authoritative account of Howard.)

Clark, Barrett H. *A Study of the Modern Drama.* New York: 1925; 1928. (Authoritative data pertaining to Howard.)

Edgett, E. F. See Clapp, J. B., above.

Ford, James L. "The Banker's Daughter," *Munsey's Magazine,* Vol. XXXIV, pp. 199-202 (November 1905). (Favorable review of this play; sketch of Howard's career.)

Frohman, Daniel, and Marcosson, I. *Charles Frohman: Manager and Man.* New York: 1916. Chap. VI.

Halline, Allan G. *American Plays.* New York: 1935. (Reprints *The Henrietta* and contains a critical introduction to Howard in general.)

Halline, Allan G. *Main Currents of Thought in American Drama.* Thesis. University of Wisconsin: 1936. (Expands material in introduction in *American Plays.*)

Hamilton, Clayton. "Bronson Howard," *The Bookman,* Vol. XXVIII, pp. 55-6 (Sept. 1908). (States that though Howard had an effective talent, he was not a genius and did not have a well-articulated philosophy of life; however, claims for him an important place in history of American drama.)

In Memoriam, Bronson Howard. Addresses Delivered at the Memorial Meeting, October 18, 1908, at the Lyceum Theatre. New York: 1910. (Contains important material. Among the contents are: "An Appreciation," by Brander Matthews; "A Brief Biography," by Harry P. Mawson; "Among His Books," by John Ernest Warren; "The Autobiography of a Play," by Howard; "Trash on the Stage and the Lost Dramatists of America," by Howard. Includes a bibliography of plays, but it is not accurate.)

Mabie, Hamilton Wright. "American Plays Old and New," *Outlook,* Vol. CII, pp. 945-55 (December 28, 1912). (Discusses Howard's idea of business as the American theme; "business is, in fact, the one thing from which art has the least to fear"; surveys contemporary dramatists.)

Mapes, Victor, and Smith, Winchell. *The New Henrietta.* New York: 1913. (Revision of *The Henrietta.*)

Marcosson, I. See Frohman, Daniel, above.

Matthews, Brander. "An Appreciation," in *In Memoriam;* also in *North American Review,* Vol. CLXXXVIII, pp. 504-13 (October 1908). (Thoughtful survey of Howard's work.)

Matthews, Brander. "Bronson Howard," in *Gateways to Literature.* New York: 1912.

Matthews, Brander. *These Many Years.* New York: 1917. (Scattered commentary relative to Howard.)

Montgomery, G. E. "Bronson Howard," *The Theatre,* Vol. I, pp. 469-70 (August 2, 1886).

Morris, Clara. *Life on the Stage*. New York: 1901. (Chapter on *Saratoga*.)

Moses, Montrose J. *Representative Plays by American Dramatists, 1856-1911*. New York: 1921. (Reprints *Shenandoah*. Discusses Howard's Americanism, his theories of drama, the artisan character of his work, the genesis of *Shenandoah*.)

Moses, Montrose J. *The American Dramatist*. Boston: 1925.

Quinn, Arthur Hobson. *A History of the American Drama from the Civil War to the Present Day*. New York: 1927, Chap. I, pp. 39-65. Single volume edition, New York: 1936. (Excellent survey of Howard's work.)

Quinn, Arthur Hobson. *Representative American Plays*. New York: 1930. (Reprints *Shenandoah* with introduction.)

Thomas, Augustus. "Introduction" to *The Autobiography of a Play*. See Bibliography of Howard's other writings.

Towse, J. Rankin. "Bronson Howard," *Book Buyer*, Vol. XVI, pp. 113-17 (March 1898). (Emphasizes Howard's growth in dramatic powers. Some inaccurate biographical data.)

Winter, William. *The Life of David Belasco*. 2 vols. New York: 1918. (Errs in saying that one act of *The Banker's Daughter* was written by A. R. Cazauran; only one scene was.)

America's Lost Plays